Walter M. Miller, Jr.

ALSO BY WILLIAM H. ROBERSON

*Peter Matthiessen: An Annotated Bibliography*
(McFarland, 2001)

# Walter M. Miller, Jr.

*A Reference Guide to
His Fiction and His Life*

WILLIAM H. ROBERSON

McFarland & Company, Inc., Publishers
*Jefferson, North Carolina, and London*

LIBRARY OF CONGRESS CATALOGUING-IN-PUBLICATION DATA

Roberson, William H.
Walter M. Miller, Jr. : a reference guide to his fiction and his life / William H. Roberson.
    p.    cm.
Includes bibliographical references and index.

ISBN 978-0-7864-6361-9
softcover : 50# alkaline paper ∞

1. Miller, Walter M., 1923–1996 — Handbooks, manuals, etc.
2. Miller, Walter M., 1923–1996 — Bibliography.   I. Title.
PS3563.I4215Z85   2011        813'.54 — dc22        2011013896

BRITISH LIBRARY CATALOGUING DATA ARE AVAILABLE

© 2011 William H. Roberson. All rights reserved

*No part of this book may be reproduced or transmitted in any form or by any means, electronic or mechanical, including photocopying or recording, or by any information storage and retrieval system, without permission in writing from the publisher.*

On the cover: (top) Walter M. Miller, Jr. (photograph by Rick Wilber); cover design by Mark Durr

Manufactured in the United States of America

*McFarland & Company, Inc., Publishers
Box 611, Jefferson, North Carolina 28640
www.mcfarlandpub.com*

For Robert Rowehl and in memory of Bertha Rowehl and
for Jim & Rebecca, John & Jane, Sue & Carl,
Marie & Serge, and Karen & Pete

# Table of Contents

*Acknowledgments* ix
*Preface* 1
*Chronology* 3

The Reference Guide 5

*Works by Walter M. Miller, Jr.* 193
*Works About Walter M. Miller, Jr.* 195
*General Bibliography* 198
*Index* 201

# Acknowledgments

A number of friends and colleagues were extremely helpful to me in various ways during the five years of work on this project. I am indebted to them for their many kindnesses. Despite their best efforts, any mistakes that appear in the book are entirely my own. Thanks to Rob Battenfeld, Virginia Dowd, John Dowd, David Moodie, Pam Greinke and Claudette Allegrezza. Special thanks to Jennifer Greenhill-Taylor and Rick Wilber. Karen Duffy at *The Daytona-Beach News-Journal* was particularly helpful. Thanks to Catherine Coker and the staff at the Cushing Memorial Library and Archives at Texas A&M University for providing copies of selected correspondence between Chad Oliver and Walter M. Miller, Jr. Part of my work on this project was conducted while on a sabbatical leave. I thank President David Steinberg, Vice President Jeffrey Kane, and the Board of Trustees of Long Island University for their support. My thanks and apologies to all those who helped over the years who I may have forgotten. Thanks as always to Jean, Tim, and Lindsay — and this time to Sarah and Chris, too.

# Preface

Walter M. Miller, Jr., is the author of the classic novel *A Canticle for Leibowitz*. The book has remained continuously in print since it was first published more than fifty years ago. While it remained the only novel Miller ever published during his lifetime, *Saint Leibowitz and the Wild Horse Woman*, a parallel novel that he worked on for over twenty years, appeared posthumously with Terry Bisson completing the work after Miller's suicide.

*A Canticle for Leibowitz* remains a popular work and a standard text in many high school and college courses, especially those dealing with science fiction in the twentieth century, apocalyptic literature, or religious themed science fiction. A handful of critics place no qualifications upon its significance declaring it simply, as Noel Perrin did, "the very greatest work of science fiction." What contributes to the work's longevity and importance, however, is the fact that Miller's examination and amalgamation of religious faith, modern technology, moral accountability, and the cyclical history of mankind easily transcended the confines of the science fiction genre at the time of its publication and continues to give the work a broader literary appeal than genre or cult fiction.

While *A Canticle for Leibowitz* dominates any discussion of Miller's work, he was also a successful writer of short fiction. He published more than forty short stories and novellas in a seven year period in the 1950s. While some of the stories are clearly melodramatic apprentice or hack work which now appear badly dated, several of them, such as "Dark Benediction," "Command Performance," "Crucifixus Etiam," and "The Darfsteller," as well as the shorter works that became the bases for *A Canticle for Leibowitz*, demonstrate an admirable command of the form and a sustained relevancy.

Although interest in Miller and his work remains fairly constant and scholarly articles regarding his work appear regularly in journals, only two books have been available about him. Rose Secrest's *Glorificemus* was published in 2002 by the University Press of America. It is an idiosyncratic response to *A Canticle for Leibowitz*. In 1992 Greenwood Press published *Walter M. Miller, Jr.: A Bio-Bibliography* by William H. Roberson and Robert L. Battenfeld. While broader in its approach to Miller's work than Secrest's book, it is limited by its intention. The existing web sites concerning Miller generally provide incomplete and, at times, conflicting information focusing only on *A Canticle for Leibowitz* and translations of the Latin phrases found in the novel.

This book is a reference guide intended for anyone interested in Walter M. Miller, Jr. It provides a single accessible, comprehensive resource for basic information. The over 1,500 entries, arranged in a single alphabet, include biographical information, summaries of all of Miller's work, character descriptions, explanations of the literary, cultural, historical, and religious allusions found in the works, and translations of all foreign words and phrases found in his two novels and short fiction. The entries are meant to be informational rather than critical, but critical judgments are occasionally implied or explicit. When critics are referred to in the entries, the bibliographies at the end of the alphabetical entries should be consulted for the appropriate source material.

Abbreviations have been kept to a minimum within the entries to aid in the easier use of the book. Two Bibles have been used for references within the entries. When Miller quotes directly from Psalms, he is most often using the Douay Old Testament. The Douay-Rheims based Bible was the commonly used Bible in Catholic churches in the United States during the decade Miller was most actively writing. Therefore, for any reference to the Psalms in Miller's work, I cite the Douay Old Testament. It is abbreviated as DB (for Douay Bible) within the entries. The King James Bible has been used for general references to biblical stories and personalities. It is abbreviated as KJV (King James Version) within the entries.

The reference guide serves both the general reader who may be unfamiliar with much of Miller's work beyond *A Canticle for Leibowitz* as well as those readers more acquainted with Miller's entire body of work. It provides a resource to verify information concerning the novels and stories as well as an introduction and avenue to the works beyond *A Canticle for Leibowitz*. It is intended that this work will lead to a greater enjoyment and appreciation of Miller's work generally and perhaps encourage new possibilities of investigation for the scholar and researcher. If nothing else, it is hoped that each reader will find something new in the book and that it will facilitate a further interest in all the works of Walter M. Miller, Jr., as well as the author himself.

# Chronology

| | |
|---|---|
| 1922 | born, New Smyrna Beach, Florida, January 23, to Ruth and Walter Miller |
| 1940 | enters the University of Tennessee at Knoxville as an electrical engineering major |
| 1942 | enlists in the U. S. Army Air Corps, February |
| 1944 | participates in the bombing of Monte Cassino monastery, Italy |
| 1945 | marries Anna Louise Becker, May 1, in Colorado |
| 1945 | discharged from the U. S. Army Air Corps |
| 1946 | daughter Margaret Jean born, June 4 |
| 1947 | enters University of Texas at Austin |
| 1947 | converts to Catholicism |
| 1947 | son Walter Michael Miller III born, September 11 |
| 1949 | daughter Cathryn Augusta born, September 27 |
| 1950 | hospitalized as a result of a serious car accident |
| 1950 | first published story, "MacDoughal's Wife," appears in the *American Mercury* |
| 1951 | first published science fiction story, "Secret of the Death Dome," appears in *Amazing Stories* |
| 1951 | daughter Alys Elaine born, November 9 |
| 1952 | meets Judith Merril in New Jersey |
| 1953 | lives with Judith Merril in New Jersey and Florida |
| 1953 | divorced from Anna, September 8 |
| 1953 | remarries Anna, December 31 |
| 1955 | receives a Hugo Award for "The Darfsteller" |
| 1960 | *A Canticle for Leibowitz* is published |
| 1961 | receives a Hugo Award for *A Canticle for Leibowitz* |
| 1962 | *Conditionally Human* is published |
| 1965 | *The View from the Stars* is published |
| 1978 | *The Science Fiction Stories of Walter M. Miller, Jr.* is published |
| 1980 | *The Best of Walter M. Miller, Jr.* is published |
| 1985 | *Beyond Armageddon*, co-edited with Martin H. Greenberg, is published |
| 1989 | Bantam announces a new book from Miller, tentatively titled *Leibowitz and the Wild Horse Woman* |
| 1995 | Anna Louise Miller dies, August 7 |
| 1995 | Miller suggests another writer finish his novel; Terry Bisson agrees to complete *Saint Leibowitz and the Wild Horse Woman* based on Miller's notes |
| 1996 | Walter Miller commits suicide, January 9 |
| 1997 | *Saint Leibowitz and the Wild Horse Woman* is published |

# The Reference Guide

**A l'arbi? Oui?** French: "To the Arab? Yes?" Giselle's response to Relke when he yells to her to get out after Larkin and Kunz surprise them in the transmission line station in the novella "The Lineman." The Arab she refers to is Henri who is back at the spaceship.

**A morte perpetua, Domine, libera nos** Latin: "From everlasting death, O Lord, deliver us." This is among the short verses Brother Francis recites from the Litany of the Saints as he steps down into the Fallout Shelter in *A Canticle for Leibowitz* ("Fiat Homo").

**A rivederci, padrone** Italian: "Good-bye, boss (master)." Words spoken by Ryan Thornier to Imperio D'Uccia in the novella "The Darfsteller." The Italian more often appears as *arrivederci*.

**A spiritu fornicationis, Domine, libera nos** Latin: "From the spirit of fornication, O Lord, deliver us." One of the short verses from the Litany of the Saints that Brother Francis whispers as he enters the Fallout Shelter in *A Canticle for Leibowitz* ("Fiat Homo").

**Ab hac planeta nativitatis aliquos filos Ecclesiae usque ad planetas solium alienorum iam abisse et numquam redituros esse intelligimus** Latin: "We understand that some sons of the Church have already left this planet of their birth and gone off to the planets of alien suns, and will never return." The first words of a *Motu proprio* of Celestine the Eighth in 3735 cited in *A Canticle for Leibowitz* ("Fiat Voluntas Tua"). It is the Catholic Church's commencement of an emergency plan to perpetuate itself in a space colony in the event of a nuclear holocaust on Earth. The plan is later referred to as *Quo peregrinatur* from a confirming document that authorizes the purchase of a starship to carry out the plan. See also ***Quo peregrinatur***

**Abandon Hope All Ye Who Enter Here** from Dante's *The Divine Comedy, Inferno*, Canto III. The phrase appears on the sign one views upon entering Hell. Father Zerchi has the warning printed on the signs carried by five monks outside the Green Star Mercy Camp in the novella "The Last Canticle" and *A Canticle for Leibowitz* ("Fiat Voluntas Tua").

**Abbess of N'Ork** Her Eminence, Emmery Cardinal Buldyrk, a character from *Saint Leibowitz and the Wild Horse Woman*. From the far northeast, she attends the conclave in Valana that elects Pope Amen. Father Corvany brings her up to sit on the podium at the preliminary meeting of the conclave.

***The Abbey*** a dramatic screenplay based on *A Canticle for Leibowitz* written and published in Lethbridge, Alberta, by Robert Douglas Manning in 2000.

**Abbey of Saint Leibowitz** the fortified monastery of the Albertian Order of Leibowitz was originally built near a water hole three days' journey from the location where the order's bookleggers were burying their cache of books in kegs in the southwest desert of what was once the United States. The road it is located on may have once been part of the shortest route between the Great Salt Lake and Old El Paso. The abbey serves as the central location for the activities in the short story "A Canticle for Leibowitz," the novellas "And the Light Is Risen" and "The Last Canticle," *A Canticle for Leibowitz*, and to a much lesser extent, *Saint Leibowitz and the Wild Horse Woman*.

**Abbot Boumous** the abbot of the Abbey of Saint Leibowitz prior to Dom Jethrah Zerchi in the "Fiat Voluntas Tua" section of *A Canticle for Leibowitz*. He is an unseen character, but Zerchi briefly complains about his predecessor's purchase of the Abominable Autoscribe for the abbey.

**Abbot Malmeddy** an unseen character in *A Canticle for Leibowitz* ("Fiat Lux"). He is the abbot of the Abbey of Saint Leibowitz prior to Dom Paulo. Paulo refers to him as "a solemn ass."

**Abel** the second son of Adam and Eve. He is killed by his older brother Cain in a jealous rage

(Genesis 4: 1–16 KJV) becoming the first murder victim.

1. Barry Wilkes refers to the "murdered seed of Abel" as the source of life on the planet where he left the White Idiot in the novella "The Song of Vorhu."

2. In "The Last Canticle," Father Zerchi includes the murder of Abel among the acts of man's inhumanity he enumerates.

3. Abel is also mentioned in *Saint Leibowitz and the Wild Horse Woman*.

**Aberlott** a chubby, good-natured seminary student from the Northwest in *Saint Leibowitz and the Wild Horse Woman*. He is one of three students Brother Blacktooth and Woosin lodge with in Valana. After the killing of Father Corvany by Jæsis, he is sent as an emissary of the Secretariat for Extraordinary Ecclesiastical Concerns to New Jerusalem to assure Jæsis's family that he was not exposed as a spook before his death. Aberlott later serves among the soldiers of Pope Amen II's guard. He eventually falls in love with Anala, a younger sister of Jæsis, and marries her. They have two children. By the novel's end, he is living in Valana and working as a secular scribe.

**Abernathy, Robert** (1924–1990) American writer of science fiction stories published in the 1940s and 1950s that remain uncollected. He received a PhD from Princeton University and taught at the University of Colorado. His story "Heirs Apparent" is included in *Beyond Armageddon*.

**Abominable Autoscribe** a stenographic computer and polylinguistic translator that allows the user to write letters in languages he does not know. It is a perpetually unreliable and seemingly unfixable irritant in the life of Dom Zerchi in *A Canticle for Leibowitz* ("Fiat Voluntas Tua"). It is also known as APLAC.

**Abraham** Hebrew: "Father of a multitude." Abraham, at first Abram, is regarded as the father of the great patriarchs of Israel. Heeding the call of God, he left his home in Ur for a journey of promise. Assured by God that he would one day achieve land and descendents, Abraham endured a long childless life of wandering. In his later years, a son, Isaac, was finally born to him and his wife Sarah. In a supreme test of his faith, God ordered Abraham to sacrifice his only son. As he prepared to kill Isaac, Abraham was commanded by God to spare the child. Because he was willing to obey God's command, the Lord blessed Abraham's seed and said, "In thy seed shall all the nations of the earth be blessed." Abraham's story is found in Genesis 12–25 (KJV). References are made to Abraham in the novella "And the Light Is Risen" and *A Canticle for Leibowitz* ("Fiat Lux") and to Father Abraham in the "The Reluctant Traitor" and "The Song of Vorhu." See also **Sarah**

**Abram** *see* **Abraham**

**Accedite ad eum** Latin: "Come to Him [and be enlightened]." A line from Psalm 33 of the Douay-Rheims Bible, the phrase is recited at the start of the Blessing of the Texts said by the monks of the Albertian Order before reading or writing. It is used in the novella "And the Light Is Risen" and in "Fiat Lux" and "Fiat Voluntas Tua" in *A Canticle for Leibowitz*.

**"Accept, O holy Father, this spotless host..."** From the short story "MacDoughal's Wife," the beginning of the Offertory prayer presented by the priest in the Latin Mass of the Catholic Church.

**Accepto** Latin: "I accept." Amen Specklebird's response to his election as pope in *Saint Leibowitz and the Wild Horse Woman*.

**Accipiam** Latin: "I accept." Brother Joshua's final answer to Dom Zerchi concerning the question of his becoming the head of the Visitationist Friars of the Order of Saint Leibowitz of Tycho in *A Canticle for Leibowitz* ("Fiat Voluntas Tua").

**Ad absurdum** Latin: "To what is absurd." A reference to an argument that is carried out to such a length that it becomes foolish. In the novella "And the Light Is Risen" and *A Canticle for Leibowitz* ("Fiat Lux"), Father Jerome/Dom Paulo thinks that Father Gault will draw the incident of the poet's confrontation with Don Thaddeo/Thon Taddeo out *ad absurdum* in order to quash the poet.

**Ad Lumina Christi!** Latin: "By the lights of Christ!" These are the words of Dom Paulo in *A Canticle for Leibowitz* ("Fiat Lux") as he orders the arc-lamp removed from the library and replaced with the crucifix that originally hung there.

**Ad perpetuam rei memoriam** Latin: "For a perpetual memorial of the matter." The name of two papal bulls issued by Pope Alabaster II and his successor Pope Alabaster III in *Saint Leibowitz and the Wild Horse Woman*. The first bull moved the prime meridian from its ancient location in Greenwich, England to the center of the high altar of Saint Peter's Basilica in New Rome because of the fear of the influence of the Green Witch. The second bull restored the prime meridian to its original location.

**Ad Valanam** Latin: "To Valana." The story is

told in *Saint Leibowitz and the Wild Horse Woman* that when Pope Benedict fled New Rome, Jesus appeared before him and asked "Quo Vadis?" ("Whither goest thou?"). Benedict's reply was "Ad Valanam." See also **Quo Vadis**

**Adam**   the first man according to the Book of Genesis in the Old Testament. God placed him in the Garden of Eden and created Eve to be his companion. Tempted by the serpent, Eve persuaded Adam to disobey God's orders and to eat from the Tree of the Knowledge of Good and Evil. Because of their disobedience, they were banished from Eden.

**Adolfo**   the lead role in the play "A Canticle for the Marsman" in the novella "The Darfsteller." Ryan Thornier once starred in it.

**Adonoi Elohim**   Hebrew: "Lord God." *Adonoi* is an alternate spelling of the more common *Adonai*, Hebrew for Lord, although the term is used in the Old Testament to signify God. In *A Canticle for Leibowitz* ("Fiat Homo"), the pilgrim blesses the food he is about to eat in the form of a traditional Hebrew blessing: "Blest be Adonoi Elohim, King of All, who maketh bread to spring forth from the earth." This is a traditional blessing before eating as found in the "Berakot" of the first treatise of *Seder Zeraim* of the Talmud.

**Adoration [of the Cross]**   part of the Good Friday observances in the Catholic Church. A crucifix is presented, and the congregants venerate it by kissing it. The rite is alluded to in *A Canticle for Leibowitz* ("Fiat Homo").

**Advent**   in Christian churches, the four week period prior to December 25th, Christmas Day. It is a season of penitence and preparation. In the Catholic Church it is the start of the liturgical year. Brother Horner dies early in Advent in *A Canticle for Leibowitz* ("Fiat Homo").

**Advocatus Diaboli**   Latin: "Devil's Advocate." Another term for the office of Promoter of the Faith in the canonization process of the Catholic Church. During the canonization process for Isaac Leibowitz in the short story "A Canticle for Leibowitz," an emissary of the church arrives at the abbey to oppose the canonization. He investigates the stories of the supposed miracles and argues against their validity. In *A Canticle for Leibowitz* ("Fiat Homo"), Monsignor Flaught is the Advocatus Diaboli. See also **Monsignor Flaught** and **Promoter Fidei**

**Ædrea**   a pretty, blonde young female genny who appears normal, the daughter of Shard in *Saint Leibowitz and the Wild Horse Woman*. She steals Brother Blacktooth's rosary and chitara and sexually arouses him when Cardinal Brownpony's party stops at Arch Hollow. Her father has ordered her to have an operation to prevent her from having intercourse and possibly giving birth to malformed babies. She performs a sexual act on Blacktooth in the barn at Arch Hollow and unbeknownst to him rubs his semen into her.

Once a month Ædrea brings the silver mined in New Jerusalem to Valana to exchange for currency. In Valana she leaves a note for Blacktooth telling him that she will leave his chitara at Amen Specklebird's old house five miles from the city. When Blacktooth goes there, she is waiting for him and they have another sexual encounter. She again rubs his semen into herself in an attempt to get pregnant, this time telling him what she is doing.

She reveals to Blacktooth that a secret wing of the Secretariat is selling guns to the gennies of New Jerusalem. Cardinal Brownpony declares her *persona non grata* in Valana and tells Blacktooth to avoid her because the aims of her group are controversial. She becomes pregnant with Blacktooth's child. Mayor Dion of New Jerusalem lies to Blacktooth, telling him that Ædrea died from a miscarriage. She is taken to the Leibowitz Abbey by Benjamin while Blacktooth travels with Brownpony to Hannegan City. At the abbey she asks to see Blacktooth but is told by Abbot Olshuen that Blacktooth now thinks she is dead; she tells the abbot that Blacktooth knows better. Olshuen reluctantly agrees to let her stay at the abbey but only in a locked cell. Ædrea indignantly leaves for Sanly Bowitts.

When Blacktooth finally returns to the abbey, Benjamin informs him that Ædrea gave birth to twin boys. They were left with him because they were not perfect, and she had nowhere to return to but home. She feared her father would have the babies killed. Benjamin says he gave the babies to a woman in Sanly Bowitts, and they were taken away for adoption by three sisters.

Ædrea is placed in custody by Magister Dion for leaving the community without permission. Blacktooth is told that neither Dion nor Brownpony will allow him to ever see her again. During her time under house arrest, Ædrea is visited three times a week by Mother Iridia Silentia who prepares her to take her vows as a nun of the Order of Our Lady of the Desert. She is given the name of Sister Clare-of-Assisi. Once she becomes a nun, Mother Silentia complains to the pope that a member of her order is being kept in prison by the secular government of New Jerusalem. When she is not released, the pope orders sacraments withheld from Dion's family. Eventually Dion agrees to release her into the custody of Mother Silentia who becomes her defense council when she is tried for her original crime of leaving without permission. Amen II remands her into the permanent custody of Silentia and sentences her to cross the Brave River and spend the rest of her life in exile there or until her sentence is commuted by the pope. She is to be excommunicated if she crosses back over the river. Her sentence is exactly what is required of her by the vows of her order. She asks where Blacktooth is, but the pope replies that he has no idea.

After living in exile at the Monastery of the Nuns of Our Lady of San Pancho Villa of Cockroach Mountain, Sister Clare-of-Assisi is granted clemency by Pope Amen II. He orders Abbot Olshuen to grant her temporary refuge at the abbey if she chooses to stay there. Mother Silentia believes Sister Clare is a vessel of the Holy Spirit and capable of healing. When the two nuns travel to the abbey, Sister Clare heals two monks by laying her hands on them. Abbot Olshuen commands her to stop. She returns from Mass one day bleeding. She says she was attacked as if in a dream, perhaps by the devil. Her wounds are in the pattern of the stigmata.

When Abbot Olsheun suffers a stroke, Sister Clare refuses to attend him because he commanded her never to lay a hand again in healing. The day after he dies she leaves the abbey; her trail leads to the Mesa where Benjamin lives.

After the war Blacktooth looks for her at the San Pancho Villa convent but Mother Silentia tells him she has probably returned to her own people in the Valley of the Misborn. Blacktooth settles in the Valley but never seeks her out in the convent just over the mountain from his home. When he dies, Sister Clare feels his death and walks to his hermitage to find his body. She buries him and takes his rosary and chitara.

**Age of Simplification** *see* **Simplification**

**Agnes, Sergeant** General Clement Horrey's WAC secretary in the short story "The Little Creeps." Young and attractive, she catches the eye of General Jim Yaney who badgers both her and Horrey until she agrees to go out with him. They end up at Horrey's house during the Communist demonstrations, and Agnes comforts Nora, Horrey's wife, when the first nuclear bombs are detonated.

**Agnus Dei** Latin: "Lamb of God." Taken from John 1:29 (KJV) where John the Baptist refers to Jesus as the Lamb of God. The phrase is used as part of the Mass. The chant of an Agnus Dei is heard on a music system in the novella "The Lineman."

**Agreement of the Holy Scourge** a compact among the civilized states regarding the disputed lands in the novella "And the Light Is Risen" and *A Canticle for Leibowitz* ("Fiat Lux"). The civilized states agree to retaliate against the Nomadic peoples and bandits conducting raiding activities in the territory. Hannegan II of Texarkana uses it as a ruse in his plan to unite the continent under his rule by drawing Denver and Laredo into conflict with the Plains Nomads.

**Aguerra, Malfreddo** a monsignor and prothonotary apostolic from New Rome who serves as the postulator for Leibowitz during the canonization process in *A Canticle for Leibowitz* ("Fiat Lux"). He arrives at the Leibowitz abbey with several Dominicans to observe the reopening of the fallout shelter and examine any other evidence that has a bearing on the case for Leibowitz's canonization. This includes speaking with Brother Francis about his meeting with the pilgrim and the discovery of the relics.

Aguerra is a friendly, unassuming, and diplomatic elderly man. He is well treated by the monks at the abbey who go out of their way to make him comfortable and to entertain him. He is kind and reassuring to Brother Francis when he questions him about his experiences with the pilgrim, but he is saddened to learn that much of the story as he has heard it is not true.

He asks to see the illuminated copy of the Leibowitz blueprint that Brother Francis had worked on until Brother Jeris ordered him to stop. Aguerra proclaims it to be beautiful and superb, and says that it must be finished. His enthusiasm for the project forces Brother Jeris to relent and allow Francis to renew his work.

Brother Francis meets Monsignor Aquerra again in New Rome at the canonization of Leibowitz where the postulator plays a formal role. Brother Francis later asks him, as "our Patron's advocate," to hear his confession. Aquerra presents Brother Francis with the pope's gift to him, two heklos of gold to try to buy back his illuminated blueprint copy from the robber.

*Guerra* in Italian means war or feud. This suggests Aquerra's role as Leibowitz's advocate and his willingness to defend his case against that of Monsignor Flaught, the *Advocatus Diaboli*. In Italian *mal* means evil and *freddo* is cold. Miller provides an ironic name for the kindly, warm priest.

**Aham** Sansrit: "I." As Dom Zerchi lies dying beneath the rubble of the abbey at the conclusion of *A Canticle for Leibowitz* ("Fiat Voluntas Tua"), he thinks about fear and dying. He thinks the difference between life and death is a "gulf between *aham* and *Asti*," between the self and God.

**Aikin, James (Jim) Douglas** (1948–) American born music technology writer, editor, cellist, and occasional science fiction writer. His short story "My Life in the Jungle" is included in *Beyond Armageddon*.

**Alabaster II** the former Olavlano Cardinal Fortos from south of the Brave River, elected pope while in his eighties following the death of Linus VI in *Saint Leibowitz and the Wild Horse Woman*. His brief papacy is noted for a bull ordering the Earth's prime meridian moved from its ancient location to the center of the high altar of St. Peter's Basilica in New Rome. The move was motivated by the belief that a sorceress inhabited Green Witch. Alabaster II is poisoned a few months after his election. See also **Alabaster III** and **Green Witch**

**Alabaster III** the former Rupez Cardinal de Lonzor, the oldest and sickest man in the Sacred College, who is elected pope following the death of Alabaster II in *Saint Leibowitz and the Wild Horse Woman*. Upon his election, he immediately issues a bull repealing his predecessor's bull and restoring the prime meridian to its original location. See also **Alabaster II**

**Albertian Order of Leibowitz (AOL)** a monastic order founded by Isaac Leibowitz, a Cistercian priest, during the Age of Simplification and dedicated to the preservation of both secular and sacred knowledge. The duty of the members of the order is to save and memorize all books and documents as can be found and to preserve and guard that knowledge. Their earliest habit consisted of a burlap bag and a bindlestiff. When any member of the order travels away from the abbey, he carries a book, usually a Breviary, as part of his habit. The order is named after St. Albert the Great, Albertus Magnus, who was the teacher of Thomas Aquinas and the patron saint of scientists.

From the short story "A Canticle for Leibowitz" and the novels *A Canticle for Leibowitz* and *Saint Leibowitz and the Wild Horse Woman*, as well as the novellas "And the Light Is Risen" and "The Last Canticle."

**Albertus Magnus** (c. 1193–November 15, 1280) also known as Saint Albert the Great and Albert of Cologne, he was a German born Dominican friar and Aristotelian philosopher and scientist who viewed the sciences and philosophy as separate fields of study from theology but ones that could coexist harmoniously with it. Known as "the Universal Teacher," he had wide ranging interests, including physics, chemistry, geology, geography, and botany. He was the teacher and defender of Thomas Aquinas. He is honored by the Catholic Church as a Doctor of the Church and was named the patron saint of scientists. The Albertian Order of Leibowitz is named after him.

**Albrasa** one of the twin planets orbiting Ba'Lagan, a yellow sun in the Scorpius constellation in the short story "The Big Hunger." Its twin planet is Nynfi.

**Alfer, Faye** the stolen identity used by Zella Richmond to cross into Jacksonville with Sam Wuncie in the novella "The Yokel."

**Algun** one of the three classes within the feudal system that developed on Nu Phoenicis IV which provides the basis for the short story "Bitter Victory." The Algun, or Pastorals, were the serf class. As technology emerged, the Taknon and Algun classes overthrew the privileged class, the Klidds, and exiled them to an ironless planet.

**"*Alibi*"** a brief piece by Miller appearing opposite the "Contents" page in *Beyond Armageddon*. It is intended to be a sarcastic and wry response to the question of where he has been and what he has been doing since the publication of *A Canticle for Leibowitz*. Miller refers to it as "a tongue-in-cheek way" of saying it is nobody's business (Hr 4/9/91). It is of questionable taste and perhaps better left unpublished.

**Alleghenian** a regional language spoken by Cardinal Hoffstraff in *A Canticle for Leibowitz* ("Fiat Voluntas Tua").

**Allenby** he is placed in command of the starship *Archangel* in the novella "Six and Ten Are Johnny" when Commander Isaacs goes to the planet in the second launch. Isaacs tells him to wait 80 hours and then leave orbit for Earth if the launch does not return.

**"Allons! Ma, foi, quelle merde!"** French: "Go! Really, what shit!" Henri's words when the airlock is ready and Suds Brodanovitch absentmindedly exits the ship with a bottle of champagne in his hand in the novella "The Lineman."

**Alpha Centauri** one of the closest star systems to Earth. It is in the southern constellation Centaurus. In the novella "The Last Canticle" and *A Canticle for Leibowitz* ("Fiat Voluntas Tua"), the Church's plan to preserve itself calls for an escape to a colony in Alpha Centauri in the event of a thermonuclear war.

**Alter Christus** Latin: "Another Christ." This refers to the idea that the ordained priest resembles Christ in his mission, holiness, and ministrations.

He represents Christ's presence on Earth. Father Zerchi refers to himself as alter Christus in the novella "The Last Canticle" and in "Fiat Voluntas Tua" in *A Canticle for Leibowitz*.

***Amen II Episcopus Romae servus servorum dei...*** Latin: "Amen II, Bishop of Rome, servant of the servants of God, to all the faithful believers in the one true Church, Catholic and Apostolic, to these chosen ones of the Lord, who are subject to Us as to Peter, the only shepherd...." The preface of an eight-page document issued by Pope Amen II in *Saint Leibowitz and the Wild Horse Woman* excommunicating Filpeo Harq and Archbishop Benefez and declaring a crusade against the Texark Empire.

**America First!** an across the chest political salute of the Americanist Party, the fascist party that rules the country in the short story "Vengeance for Nikolai."

**Americanist Party** a fascist party ruling the United States in the short story "Vengeance for Nikolai."

**Amicus curiae** Latin: "Friend of the court." A party asking for permission to intervene in a legal case to voice an opinion even though not directly involved in the case. Father Jerome, in the novella "And the Light Is Risen," refers to a wooden statue of St. Leibowitz as occasionally his *amicus curiae* in his arguments with himself. In *Saint Leibowitz and the Wild Horse Woman*, Cardinal Brownpony acts as *amicus curiae* in Brother Blacktooth's tribunal at the abbey.

**Amur River** an Asian river comprising part of the border between southeastern Russia and northeastern China. Its source is in western Manchuria and it empties into the Strait of Tartary. Its Chinese name is Heilong Jiang (Black Dragon River). In the short story "The Little Creeps," General Horrey is warned against bombing the towns along the Amur. General Yaney's plan, however, calls for the strategic bombing of the dams and towns along the river.

**An, Sunovtash** an unseen character who is accused by Hultor Bråm of being at one time Cardinal Brownpony's Christian puppet among the Grasshopper people in *Saint Leibowitz and the Wild Horse Woman*.

**Anala** the younger sister of Jæsis in *Saint Leibowitz and the Wild Horse Woman*. Aberlott marries her.

**"The Anarch"** a play by Pruchev in the novella "The Darfsteller." Ryan Thornier and Mela Stone were once cast in the leading roles before the advent of the autodrama. Thornier assumes the lead role of Andreyev in an autodrama production by sabotaging the tapes needed for a mannequin to perform the part.

**Anchorite** a person who withdraws from the world in order to follow a silent, solitary life of contemplation and prayer. In the novella "And the Light Is Risen" and *A Canticle for Leibowitz* ("Fiat Lux"), Father Jerome (Dom Paulo) refers to Benjamin as an old anchorite.

**"And I saw no temple therein"** from the Book of Revelation 21:22 (KJV): "And I saw no temple therein: for the Lord God Almighty and the Lamb are the temple of it." In the new heaven, God will be everywhere, and He will be bound directly to His people; therefore, there will be no need for the Church because the church will dwell in him. Amen cites this line in *Saint Leibowitz and the Wild Horse Woman* to explain why in the presence of God, the Church is a "discarded crutch."

**And the dogs ate Jezebel in the field of Jezrahel** taken from II Kings 9:10 (KJV): "and the dogs shall eat Jezebel in the portion of Jezreel, and there shall be none to bury her." A prophecy is presented that the entire house of Ahab, king of Israel, including his wife Jezebel, will perish because of its inherent wickedness. In *Saint Leibowitz and the Wild Horse Woman* as Brother Blacktooth leaves the fallen city of New Rome, he sees the dogs wandering into the city following the smell of blood and death. He vaguely remembers this line and asks himself where it is written.

**"And the Light Is Risen"** novella: *The Magazine of Fantasy and Science Fiction*, 11 (August 1956), 3–80. The year is 3174, approximately 1200 years since the demise of the great European-American civilization in the Flame Deluge and its aftermath, the Age of Simplification. The monks of the Albertian Order of Leibowitz have preserved and guarded whatever remnants of learning from that culture that could be saved during the Dark Ages that followed. Men of learning are now once again theorizing about the natural world and man's place in it.

Don Thaddeo is a brilliant secular scholar. He is a member of the faculty of the collegium in the state of Texarkana, ruled by his cousin, Hannegan II. Don Thaddeo has learned of the existence of Leibowitzian documents at the Abbey of Saint Leibowitz near the village of Sanly Bowitts in the desert. He wants the documents brought to him to be studied. Marcus Apollo, the Vatican's nuncio to the court of Hannegan II, agrees to request the documents even though he knows his request will be refused. It will allow him, however, the opportunity to send information to New Rome about Hannegan's maneuvering to unite the various states of the continent under one dynasty, his own. As expected, Don Thaddeo's request is denied, but Father Jerome, the abbey's abbot, invites him to visit the abbey to study the documents.

Father Jerome is elderly and in poor health. His condition is exacerbated by the current cultural and political situation. He recognizes that the Dark Age is passing and that there is the promise of a Renaissance, a resurrection of truth and learning. The change means that man will now apply to the world the knowledge the Albertians have preserved and guarded over the centuries. Given the history of man, who will be responsible for the application of this knowledge and its results? The abbot can see evidence of the changing times within his own abbey. Brother Kornhoer, who occupies the abbey's Chair of Natural Science, is working on an electrical generator to supply the power for an arc lamp. Father Jerome's struggles with his own purpose, as well as that of the Church, within an age of increasing materialistic and pragmatic viewpoints, lead him to conversations with Father Gault, his assistant, and Benjamin, an old hermit who lives on a mesa near the abbey, but he remains ill at ease prior to Don Thaddeo's arrival.

The scholar arrives at the abbey accompanied by a small group of Hannegan's military officers. When the monks surprise Don Thaddeo with Brother Kornhoer's electric light, he is overwhelmed. He believes the abbey has kept secret an ancient machine for centuries. Told the truth, the Don apologizes, but Father Jerome realizes that when the Don saw the machine, he realized that his own work would bring no new inventions, only reinventions and rediscoveries from the former European-American civilization.

Don Thaddeo settles into a routine of studying the abbey's pre–Deluge texts. While he does so, the officers who came with him make detailed drawings of the abbey and its fortifications. Father Jerome asks the Don if he would be willing to address the monks about his work. He accepts and a dinner is planned in his honor. The poet, a one-eyed disreputable but frequent guest at the abbey, invites himself to sit at the Don's table. He raises the question of man's responsibility in the coming Renaissance of learning and taunts the Don and officers about the drawings of the abbey's defenses. One officer draws his sword, but Don Thaddeo orders him from the table. Father Jerome dismisses the poet. The existence of the drawings has been unknown to the Don, and he is upset to learn that the poet was speaking truly.

As he addresses his audience, the Don compliments the monks for their collection of relics, but he believes that they belong elsewhere to be more accessible to the greatest number of scholars. He proceeds to describe the various work of the collegium. As he does so, Benjamin enters the hall and walks toward the lectern. He jumps up, grabs Don Thaddeo's arm, and stares into his eyes. He proclaims, "It's still not Him." He then hobbles away.

While Don Thaddeo has been at the abbey, Hannegan has begun his plan to gain control of the rival states. He arrests Marcus Apollo and seizes his diplomatic files. The Prince of Laredo demands that Texarkana troops withdraw from his realm. The prince is poisoned the night of his demand and a state of war is proclaimed between Laredo and Texarkana. It is short lived. Hannegan gains control of all lands and people from the Red River to the Rio Grande. Marcus Apollo is found guilty of spying for international powers attempting to undercut the state. He is hanged then drawn and quartered. Texarkana is placed under an interdict by papal decree.

When news reaches the abbey, Don Thaddeo offers to leave. Father Jerome maintains that he remains welcome, but a general sense of unease develops. The Don explains to Father Jerome that he supports Hannegan for the sake of his own work. If Hannegan's empire is extended, the collegium profits; if the collegium profits, mankind benefits from the knowledge gained. The abbot asks into whose hands is the collegium creating the power to control the forces of nature? How will it be used and, perhaps more importantly, how will it be kept in check? The Don accuses the abbot of wanting to wait until man is "good and pure and holy and wise." He says the monks have withheld learning, unintentionally or not. Father Jerome angrily speaks of the sacrifices made by his order throughout the years to preserve the records of man. Don Thaddeo replies that if wisdom is saved until the world is wise, it will never be used. The abbot again raises the question of who will control this power and the wealth that emerges from it.

On the Feast of Immaculate Conception as Don Thaddeo prepares to leave the abbey, he and Father Jerome again argue about religion and science, faith and knowledge. The abbot says there is no quarrel between them about truth, only about how men use it and why. As the Don makes his final preparations for departure, Father Jerome returns to his study. In a short time there is a knock at his door and Don Thaddeo enters. He gives Father Jerome the plans of the abbey's fortifications drawn by Hannegan's officers. The Don says it is a matter of honor. The two men shake hands. The Don tells

Father Jerome that he will make no effort with Hannegan on behalf of the abbey; he believes the documents should be for the world. The priest replies that they are, they were, and they always shall be. The abbot thinks of history repeating itself, that the serpent is still tempting mankind.

Within the next year the rains come to the desert and make it bloom. A vestige of civilization comes to the Plains Nomads. Father Jerome dies. And bright hopes loom in the future: a Hannegan comes out of the East to subdue the land and own it.

This novella continues the story begun in "A Canticle for Leibowitz." It is also the basis for the section "Fiat Lux" in the novel *A Canticle for Leibowitz*.

**Anderson, Poul** (November 25, 1926–July 31, 2001) an extremely prolific American science fiction writer whose works are rooted in hard science and scientific detail. Among his many works are the novels *Tau Zero* (1970) and *Genesis* (2000). He won multiple Hugo Awards and Nebula Awards, and was named to the Science Fiction and Fantasy Hall of Fame in 2000. His short story "Tomorrow's Children" appears in *Beyond Armageddon*.

**Andreyev** the lead role in the play "The Anarch" being performed as an autodrama in the novella "The Darfsteller." He is the Commissioner of Police and party whip. Ten years ago, Ryan Thornier was cast in the role but the production was closed before opening night because of a lack of money. Thornier assumes the role in the autodrama after he sabotages the Peltier tape that was to be used by a mannequin.

**Andromeda Galaxy** also known as the Great Spiral Galaxy, it is the closet spiral galaxy to the Milky Way. It is located in the Andromeda constellation and is approximately 2.2 million light years away. In the short story "The Big Hunger," the Andromeda Galaxy is posited as a possible destination to satisfy man's star-craze, although it is too distant for man's ships to reach at present.

**Androons** descendents from a dozen pairs of Cro-Magnon species captured from Earth by the Bolsewi in the novella "The Reluctant Traitor." The original captives were taken to Mars and bred for slave labor. The androons developed on Mars and considered the Bolsewi to be their gods. They are tight muscled and long limbed with high foreheads and thin features. Their legs are covered by shaggy, thick fur from their knees to their ankles, and their feet are horny. They appear as if they are a polyracial mixture of Scandinavian, Native American, and Hawaiian.

**Andru** the leader of three hunters who find Ton of Toldin on the plateau in the short story "Please Me Plus Three." He is a short, muscular, bearded man who brings the wounded Ton to his order of monastic soldiers.

**Andy** a file clerk at Anthropos Incorporated who helps Terry Norris compile a list of K-99 neutroids that needs to be recalled in the novella "Conditionally Human."

**The Angelus** a prayer to celebrate the Incarnation, the union of deity and human in the person of Jesus Christ conceived through Mary. Brother Francis in *A Canticle for Leibowitz* ("Fiat Homo") recites its opening line. See also **Angelus Domini nuntiavit Mariae**

**Angelus Domini nuntiavit Mariae** Latin: "The angel of the Lord declared unto Mary." The first line of The Angelus, a prayer honoring the Incarnation, the Christian concept of the union of God and man in Jesus born of Mary. In *A Canticle for Leibowitz*, when Brother Francis hears three bells ring from the abbey as the sun sets and then nine more notes, he recites the line. The Angelus is said three times during the day: at morning, mid-day, and evening. The times are marked by the ringing of a bell three times, followed by a pause, and then nine more peals. See also **The Angelus**

**Annuntiabitur Domino generatio ventura** Latin: "There shall be declared to the Lord a generation to come." The line is from Psalm 22:31 (DB) and comes to Brother Joshua's mind as he joins the company of the Albertian spaceship crew in prayer in *A Canticle for Leibowitz* ("Fiat Voluntas Tua").

**Anthropos Incorporated** from the novella "Conditionally Human." The company produces mutant pets to substitute for children for those couples forbidden to have children. They use the evolvotron to induce mutations in the animal's reproductive cells.

**Antipope** in *Saint Leibowitz and the Wild Horse Woman*, Filpeo Harq sees Amen II as the antipope because he believes he is opposed to the renewal of the Magna Civitas in the expansion of the Texark empire. The antipope is traditionally one who claims to be pope in opposition to a legitimately elected pope.

**Antipope's War** the popular name for Pope Amen II's failed crusade against Filpeo Harq in *Saint Leibowitz and the Wild Horse Woman*.

**"Anybody Else Like Me?"** short story originally published as "Command Performance" in *Galaxy*

*Science Fiction*, 5 (November 1952), 140–160. The alternate title is first used when the story is published in Miller's collection *The View from the Stars* in 1964. Subsequent collections by Miller — *The Science Fiction Stories of Walter M. Miller, Jr.* (1978), *The Best of Walter M. Miller, Jr.* (1980), and *Conditionally Human and Other Stories* (1982) — maintain the alternate title. The story continues to be published in anthologies with the original title. See also "**Command Performance**"

**Apage, Satanas** Latin: "Away [or Depart], Satan." When Satan attempts to tempt Jesus in the wilderness, Jesus refuses to succumb and rebukes Satan with these words, telling him "you shall worship the Lord God and you shall serve him alone." see Matthew 4:1–11 KJV.
  1. It is said by Brother Francis in the short story "A Canticle for Leibowitz" to the box he discovers in the desert.
  2. When Brother Francis is tempted to take the cheese the pilgrim offers him during his Lenten fast, he jumps back, drops the food, and hisses, "Apage, Satanas!" in *A Canticle for Leibowitz* ("Fiat Homo").

**APLAC** *see* **Abominable Autoscribe**

**Apollo, Marcus** a monsignor and papal nuncio to the court of Hannegan II in the novella "And the Light Is Risen" and *A Canticle for Leibowitz* ("Fiat Lux"). He is a savvy political observer who tries to warn Dom Paulo (Father Jerome in the novella) not to trust Thon Taddeo and to inform New Rome of what he believes to be Hannegan II's intentions. He is eventually placed under arrest and his diplomatic files seized by Hannegan. When Hannegan gains control over Laredo, Marcus Apollo is found guilty of spying for international powers, that is New Rome, and attempting to undermine the state. He is hanged without breaking his vertebrate and then drawn and quartered and flayed by an officer of Hannegan. His carcass is fed to the dogs.
  His name is one of the most allusively rich in the novel. Apollo was the Greek god of prophecy. Marcus Apollo not only attempts to warn Dom Paulo of Thon Taddeo and New Rome of the machinations of Hannegan II, but he also cautions against the growing lack of spiritual values in a world that increasingly embraces the material.
  The name is also associated with Apollos, which is derived from *Apollonius*, meaning "of Apollo." Apollos was a friend of St. Paul — as Marcus Apollo is a contemporary and friend of Dom Paulo — and a missionary and preacher of the gospel. He was known for his eloquence and as a talented apologist. Marcus is from the Latin *Mars* meaning "warlike." In Roman mythology, Mars is the god of war. Marcus Apollo is a man of action who is willing to sacrifice himself as part of the Church's conflict with Hannegan II.
  The dual aspects of Marcus Apollo's name can be seen at the start of "Fiat Lux" when he anticipates a coming war once Hannegan's emissary returns alive from his mission to Mad Bear.

**Apostolic Benediction** a solemn blessing given by the pope or his delegate forgiving the temporal punishment due to one's sins. It is sometimes also referred to as the apostolic pardon. The apostolic benediction is offered to any armed men who come to the protection of Christians or the Church in *A Canticle for Leibowitz* ("Fiat Homo").

**Appalotchan Mountains** a mountain range to the east of the Great River within the Appalotcha region in *Saint Leibowitz and the Wild Horse Woman*. It is a corruption of Appalachian Mountains.

**Appropinquat agnis pastor et ovibus pascendis** Latin: "The shepherd approaches to feed the lambs and sheep." Part of the words spoken by the first cantor during the canonization of Leibowitz in *A Canticle for Leibowitz* ("Fiat Homo").

**"Apud Oregonenes"** Latin: "Among Oregonians." A section of Yogen Duren's *Perennial Ideas of Regional Sects* being translated by Brother Blacktooth in *Saint Leibowitz and the Wild Horse Woman*. Because of Blacktooth's own mystical visions, this section of Duren's work holds special interest to him. It deals with the Northwest Heresy and the Oregonians' belief that the Mother of God was the original uterine silence into which the word was spoken at creation. The Virgin Mother is therefore a fourth divine person, an incarnation of God's female wisdom.

**Aquinas, Thomas** *see* **Saint Thomas Aquinas**

**Arch Hollow** the name of Shard's settlement in *Saint Leibowitz and the Wild Horse Woman*.

**The *Archangel*** the name of the starship orbiting a newly discovered planet in the short story "Six and Ten Are Johnny." It is captained by Commander Isaacs and has a crew of seventy.

**Archangel at the east end of the Earth ... with a sword of flame** Dom Zerchi warns Brother Joshua in *A Canticle for Leibowitz* ("Fiat Voluntas Tua") that once he and the Church's contingent leave for space, they can never return to Earth because its passes will be guarded by the Archangel with a sword of flame. His reference, in part, is to Genesis 3:24 (KJV). After Adam and Eve are banished from Eden, God "placed at the east of the garden of Eden, Cherubims, and a flaming sword which turned every way." The archangel most often associated with a sword is Michael who, as the leader of the hosts of heaven against the armies of Satan, is regarded as the protector of Christians. In some Christian and Jewish apocryphal texts, the archangel Uriel guards the gate of the Garden of Eden. However, the four primary archangels are each associated with a cardinal point, and Michael is associated with the east (Uriel the south). In "The Last Canticle," Father Zerchi simply warns Brother Joshua of "the archangel with a sword of flame."

**Archbishop of Appalotcha** a member of the conclave in *Saint Leibowitz and the Wild Horse Woman*.

**Arcturus** a red giant star, also known as Alpha Bootis, it is one of the brightest stars in the night sky and the brightest star of the northern hemisphere in spring. It is part of the constellation Boötes, the Herdsman.

1. Barry Wilkes thinks that his wandering ship could eventually be discovered by "some nine-legged archeologist from Arcturus" in the novella "The Song of Vorhu."
2. In the short story "The Big Hunger," the frozen bodies of Abe Jolie and Junebug are discovered in an orbit around Arcturus.
3. A ship is seen in the sky between Arcturus and Serpens in the novella "The Lineman."
4. A reference to Arcturus is made in the novella "The Last Canticle" and the "Fiat Voluntas Tua" section of *A Canticle for Leibowitz*.

**Argos III** the planet destination of the C-33 rocket in the short story "A Family Matter."

**Ash Wednesday** the first day of Lent. The name is derived from the practice of placing ashes, an Old Testament sign of penance, on the forehead of the congregant. In *Saint Leibowitz and the Wild Horse Woman*, Cardinal Brownpony's party is at Shards' settlement on Ash Wednesday. Later, Brownpony and Brother Blacktooth arrive at the Leibowitz abbey on Ash Wednesday after their release from prison in Hannegan City.

**Asir of Franic** a lithe, muscular young man with black hair in the short story "It Takes a Thief," later entitled "Big Joe and the Nth Generation." Asir is a ritual thief on Mars, one who steals memorized ritual chants that preserve the fragmented ancient knowledge. He is sentenced to permanent banishment for one of his thefts. However, through his thefts, he has learned that the planet is losing its air, and he is determined to do something to restore the Blaze of the Winds that provides the Martian atmosphere. He goes to the sacred vaults with his girlfriend Mara and uses the knowledge he has gained through his ritual thefts to get past Big Joe, the mechanical sentry that guards the control room for the machinery that must periodically restore the atmosphere. Asir accepts the challenge of learning the "knowledge of the gods." He will become a technologist and maintain the machinery that will keep Mars alive.

The name Asir is cited generally as derived from the Arabic meaning "difficult" or, to a lesser degree, "selected or chosen." The *Catholic Encyclopedia* says it is a Jewish name meaning "captive." All of the meanings have a bearing on the character at various points within the story.

**Asperges me, Domine, hyssop, et mundabor...** Latin: "Thou shall sprinkle me, Lord, with hyssop and I will be cleansed." The first line of the Gregorian chant known as *Asperges me, Domine*. It is sung during The Asperges, a brief ceremony preceding Mass in which holy water is sprinkled on the worshippers. In the novella "Dark Benediction" Paul hears the Mass begin from the hallway as he stands outside Willie's hospital door.

Hyssop is a woody plant with blue flower spikes used in perfumes and as a condiment.

**Assumption** the doctrine of the Catholic Church that holds that the Virgin Mary was taken into heaven body and soul at her death. In *A Canticle for Leibowitz* ("Fiat Homo") the Assumption — or preternatural immortality — is raised by Brother Francis as he thinks about the petitions the Dominicans have before New Rome regarding the "Preternatural Gifts of the Holy Virgin" that could slow the work toward the canonization of Leibowitz.

**Assyria** a powerful, militaristic empire in northern Mesopotamia (parts of present-day Iran, Iraq, Syria, and Turkey), c. 2400 B.C.–612 B.C. It is one of the civilizations cited by Father Zerchi in the novella "The Last Canticle" and *A Canticle for Leibowitz* ("Fiat Voluntas Tua") when he thinks of the constant rise and fall of mankind.

**Asti** Sanskrit: "God." At the conclusion of *A Canticle for Leibowitz* as Dom Zerchi lies dying beneath the ruins of the abbey, he considers his fears and his own impending death. He thinks of the moment of death as bridging the "gulf between *aham* and *Asti*," between the self and God.

**Atlantic Confederacy** the political entity within the former North American continent. Its capital city is Texarkana, which is destroyed in a retaliatory nuclear attack in the novella "The Last Canticle" and "Fiat Voluntas Tua" in *A Canticle for Leibowitz*. In the novel, the Confederacy strikes three concealed Asian missile sites on the far side of the moon and destroys a space station after the attack on Texarkana.

**Aubrey, Colonel** a character in the short story "I Made You." Aubrey is the superior officer of Captain John Sawyer who is wounded and trapped by Grumbler, a malfunctioning combat robot. Aubrey refuses to destroy Grumbler or damage the valuable mining area it protects in order to save Sawyer. He believes he is safely out of range of Grumbler's ability to strike, but the autocyber has improved upon its original programming and destroys Aubrey's command car. Aubrey saves neither Sawyer nor himself.

**Audi me, Domine** Latin: "Hear me, O Lord." In *A Canticle for Leibowitz* ("Fiat Voluntas Tua"), as Brother Joshua struggles to decide if he should go back into space as part of the Church's plan, he asks God to hear him and to show him a sign.

**Aunt Maye** a minor unseen character in the novella "Conditionally Human." She is Terry Norris's aunt.

**Autodrama** non-human theater productions in the novella "The Darfsteller." Human actors are replaced by mechanized mannequins or dolls using programmed psycho-physiological data, essentially actors' egos captured on tape. This packaged theater allows for standardized productions and multiple simultaneous presentations. The leading company of autodrama is Smithfield, whose slogan is "Great Actors Immortalized."

**Avdek Gole** means brown pony in Wilddog. In *Saint Leibowitz and the Wild Horse Woman*, Cardinal Brownpony's family name, *Urdeon Go*, which means sorrel colt, was wrongly translated by the Sisters who raised him and spoke only Jackrabbit.

**Ave Maria** Latin: "Hail Mary." An ancient and popular pray also known as the Hail Mary or Angelic Salutation.
  1. Father Zerchi tells Mrs. Grales to recite ten Aves as part of her penance in the novella "The Last Canticle" and *A Canticle for Leibowitz* ("Fiat Voluntas Tua").
  2. In *A Canticle for Leibowitz* ("Fiat Homo") Brother Francis murmurs one or two Aves when he first spies the pilgrim.

**Aves** *see* **Ave Maria**

**Axe** Wooshin's nickname of Brother Axe is sometimes shortened to simply Axe in *Saint Leibowitz and the Wild Horse Woman*. See also **Wooshin**

**B-25 Bomber** a twin-engine medium bomber manufactured by North American Aviation and produced between 1939 and 1945. Used in both the European and Pacific theaters during World War II, the B-25 had a crew of 4 to 6 and a maximum bomb payload of 6,000 pounds. It was armed with twelve 50-caliber machine guns and, at times, a 75 mm nose cannon.

The plane is sometimes referred to the as the Mitchell Bomber or the B-25 Mitchell after General William "Billy" Mitchell, an early advocate of developing air power and the man considered to be the father of the United States Air Force.

Sixteen B-25 bombers were famously used in the Doolittle Raid of April 1942 when Lt. Colonel James Doolittle bombed military targets in Japan just four months after the attack on Pearl Harbor.
  1. While in the U. S. Army Air Corps, Miller served as a radio operator and gunner aboard B-25 bombers. He participated in fifty-five combat missions over Italy and the Balkans during World War II.
  2. Mark Kessel pilots a B-25 in the short story "Wolf Pack."

**Baal** a Canaanite and Phoenician fertility god often used to represent a false god and symbolize the danger of idolatry in the Old Testament. At one point in *Saint Leibowitz and the Wild Horse Woman* as Brother Blacktooth grows dizzy during a conversation with Pope Amen II, he believes he sees the pope turning slowly into "the sixteen-foot golden body of the idol Baal." The allusion to the golden body may be to the golden calf of Exodus 32 (KJV). Baal is also sometimes presented as Ba'al.

**Babel** according to Genesis 11:1–9 (KJV), "a city and a tower" built by the people when the "whole earth was of one language." Their extravagance brought the Lord's attention. He saw it as proof that the people were arrogant and unrestrained, so he confused their language and scattered them abroad. The city was henceforth called Babel because the Lord "did there confound the language of all the earth." In *Saint Leibowitz and the Wild Horse Woman*, Benjamin calls New Jerusalem New Babel.

**Babylon** one of the great cities of the ancient world and at one time the capital of Babylonia. It was acclaimed for its beauty; its Hanging Gardens was among the Seven Wonders of the World. Its period of prominence spanned two millennia, from c. 1894 B.C. till c. 312 B.C. It is often associated with luxury and corruption. In the Bible, its rise and fall is an example of mankind's degeneration. In Isaiah 13:19 (KJV), the destruction of Babylon is ordained: "And Babylon, the glory of kingdoms, the beauty of the Chaldees excellency, shall be as when God overthrew Sodom and Gomorrah." Babylon is referred to in the novella "The Last Canticle" and "Fiat Voluntas Tua" in *A Canticle for Leibowitz*.

**Bæhovar, Leevit**  an unseen character in *Saint Leibowitz and the Wild Horse Woman*. He is a merchant from the Utah territory who is made a cardinal during the papacy of Amen I.

**Ba'Lagan**  a yellow sun formerly known as 18 Scorpii in the constellation Scorpius in the short story "The Big Hunger." It is circled by twin planets, Albrasa and Nynfi. In Hebrew *balagan* means chaos or bedlam (the word is derived from the Russian).

**Bald eagle**  national bird of Texark and Filpeo Harq in *Saint Leibowitz and the Wild Horse Woman*.

**Ballard, J(ames) G(raham)**  (November 15, 1930–April 19, 2009)  British author born in Shanghai. He is recognized as one of the most challenging and respected writers of the New Wave movement in science fiction. Among his works are *The Drowned World* (1962), *The Crystal World* (1966), *Crash* (1973), and the autobiographical *Empire of the Sun* (1984). His short story "The Terminal Beach" appears in *Beyond Armageddon*.

**Banns [of marriage]**  the formal public announcement of the intent to marry made in many Christian churches. It is no longer practiced in the Catholic Church. A reference to banns is made in the short story "Wolf Pack."

**Barkley, Captain**  a minor character in the short story "Way of a Rebel." The "usually jovial, slightly cynical" commanding officer of Lieutenant Mitch Laskell, he orders Laskell to begin heading back to the nearest base or suffer the consequences. Barkley gives him fifteen minutes before he will start to send aircraft in pursuit of Laskell's one-man submarine.

**Barlo**  an unspecified member of the genny family of Tempus and Irene in *Saint Leibowitz and the Wild Horse Woman*. He is a habitual masturbator, and Tempus wants Brother Blacktooth to absolve him in order to help him stop. Despite his protestations that he cannot absolve anyone, Blacktooth is not allowed to leave Tempus' home until he offers absolution. Instead, Blacktooth curses Barlo in Latin, and the family is impressed with how it sounds.

**Barlov**  a member of the Russian General Staff in the novella "Izzard and the Membrane." He prevents Scott MacDonney's release from the computer vault in order to ensure a problem-free demonstration of Izzard's capabilities. He later negotiates with Scott in an attempt to prevent the Russian capital from being destroyed. He dies with other Russian government officials when Scott detonates a missile near the plane they are using to escape.

**Barnes**  a crew member on the second launch in the novella "Six and Ten Are Johnny."

**Barnish**  the sadistic operator and programmer of the cybernetic spacecraft XM-5-B in the short story "I, Dreamer." He is also referred to as the Teacher. He abuses XM-5-B with the Pain Button and sexually harasses Janna, a woman who maintains part of the craft's electronic control mechanisms. XM-5-B kills Barnish when he threatens Janna's safety.

**Batzner, Jay C.**  see *Illuminations*

**Bay Ghost River**  in *Saint Leibowitz and the Wild Horse Woman*, the river originates in the Suckamint Mountains and runs along the southern border of the Hill Country. It is the Pecos River.

**Bayring Horde**  referred to in the novella "And the Light Is Risen" and *A Canticle for Leibowitz* ("Fiat Lux"). The Horde was a group of Nomadic marauders who infiltrated much of the Plains and desert from the North during the Dark Ages prior to the present time of the novella and "Fiat Lux." They looted and vandalized the villages they found. They unsuccessfully laid siege to the Abbey of Saint Leibowitz. See also **Bayring influx**

**Bayring influx**  the period when the Bayring Horde made raids on the Plains. They laid siege to the Abbey of Saint Leibowitz three times during this span. Reference is made to these failed attempts in the novella "And the Light Is Risen" and *A Canticle for Leibowitz* ("Fiat Lux"). See also **Bayring Horde**

**The Bear**  the nickname of Andrei Porshkin in the novella "Izzard and the Membrane."

**Bear Spirit people**  the male shamans of the hordes in *Saint Leibowitz and the Wild Horse Woman*.

**Bearcub**  a name Father e'Laiden calls Chür Høngan in *Saint Leibowitz and the Wild Horse Woman*.

**Beasley, Howard (Beez)**  one of Joe Novotny's B-shift crew members in the novella "The Lineman."

**Beate Leibowitz, audi me**  Latin: "Blessed Leibowitz, hear me." As Brother Francis works on his illuminated copy of the Leibowitz blueprint in *A Canticle for Leibowitz* ("Fiat Homo"), he recites these words as Abbot Arkos comes up behind him to see what he is working on. Brother Francis prays that it is anyone but the abbot standing behind him.

**Beate Leibowitz, ora pro me**  Latin: "Blessed Leibowitz, pray for me." From the short story "A Canticle for Leibowitz" and *A Canticle for Leibowitz* ("Fiat Homo"). The words are uttered by Brother Francis during his Lenten fast in the desert.

**Beatus Leibowitz ora pro me**  Latin: "Blessed Leibowitz pray for me." Brother Blacktooth calls for help from his jail cell in New Rome as the city burns in *Saint Leibowitz and the Wild Horse Woman*.

**Beatus vir, qui timet Dominum**  Latin: "Blessed is the man that feareth the Lord." From the first line of Psalm 111 (DB), it is used by the monks to time the lighting of the arc lamp to coincide with the exact arrival of Don Thaddeo to the abbey's basement in the novella "And the Light Is Risen."

**Beck, Colonel**  the commanding officer of the special patrol in the short story "Secret of the Death Dome." He orders Jerry Harrison to take Willis's corpse home and to assume his patrol duties.

**Beelzebub**  the name given to Satan or the ruler of demons in certain passages of the New Testament Gospels. The name is probably derived from Baal-zebub (or Baal-zebul), literally "lord of the flies," a god worshipped in Ekron, a Philistine city. Brother Francis believes the pilgrim may be Beelzebub because he tempts him with food during his Lenten fast in *A Canticle for Leibowitz* ("Fiat Homo").

**"Behold the thing the Lord God made to have dominion...."**  This thought comes to Barry Wilkes as he thinks about shooting the White Idiot to end her suffering in the novella "The Song of Vorhu." It is derived from Genesis 1:26: "and let them [man] have dominion over ... all the earth...." (KJV).

**Bel**  also known as the Wise One, Lord Bel, Sky-Brain, and Brain-of-the-World in the short story "Please Me Plus Three." Bel is a man-made satellite, originally named Bell Robot Twelve after the Bell Telephone Company who designed it. It is approximately 200 miles in diameter and circles the Earth every 72 hours. Its original function was to collect and analyze data from around the world and give advice for the betterment of the world society. It served as the master coordinator for human social planning with special delegated authority to maintain world peace. It collected data and maintained contact with the world community through a series of pylons. Over the years the Keepers and their staffs who maintained the pylons came into power, and Bel's advice was channeled through them. They transformed Bel's advice into edicts. When there were uprisings against the pylons and the power of the Keepers, Bel interpreted them as acts of war and destroyed the cities with nuclear weapons. The people now accept Bel as the keeper of the peace and dispenser of wisdom and tribal law. It asks the people for pleasure stimuli in return for its protection.

**Benedicamus Domino**  Latin: "Let us bless the Lord." This invocation may be used as the end of Mass in the Catholic Church. It may also be used as a salutation as it is by Brother Francis in *A Canticle for Leibowitz* ("Fiat Homo") and Brother Blacktooth in *Saint Leibowitz and the Wild Horse Woman*.

**Benedicat te, omnipotens Deus, Pater et Filius et Spiritus Sanctus**  Latin: "May Almighty God bless you, Father and Son and Holy Spirit." From the Latin Mass, Prior Olschuen offers this blessing to Blacktooth after his tribunal is completed in *Saint Leibowitz and the Wild Horse Woman*.

**Benedict XXII**  the pope who places Texarkana under absolute interdict after Hannegan finds Marcus Apollo guilty of treason and espionage and executes him in *A Canticle for Leibowitz* ("Fiat Lux"). In response, Hannegan proclaims himself the only legitimate ruler of the Church in Texarkana and declares Benedict a heretic.

In *Saint Leibowitz and the Wild Horse Woman* it is revealed that Benedict fled from New Rome when Hannegan seized the lands around the city. He established the papacy in exile in Valana.

**Benefez, Urion**  the Archbishop of the Imperial City of Texark (also known simply as the Archbishop of Texark) and the uncle of Filpeo Harq, the seventh Hannegan. As such, he is the most powerful prelate on the continent in *Saint Leibowitz and the Wild Horse Woman*. Benefez is angered by Amen Specklebird's election to pope before he can arrive at the conclave. He fails to pay homage to the new pope when he does arrive in Valana and begins to raise questions of a forced election. He calls for Pope Amen to admit that his election is invalid and to step down. Benefez eventually calls for a General Conclave of the Church to be held in New Rome to draft new legislation concerning conclaves. The curia in Valana is angry with Benefez's tactics and threatens to excommunicate any cardinal who attends the conclave. He is declared excommunicated by his own acts by Amen II and placed under a sentence of anathema. Despite his sexual perversion and abuse of young men, such as Torrildo, Benefez hopes eventually to use his influence with Filpeo to attain the papacy, but Filpeo informs him that he will never become pope.

**Benet** a crew member among Joe Novotny's B-shift workers in the novella "The Lineman." Joe once put him in the sick bay for three days for disregarding safety rules. A former altar boy, Joe orders him to say a pray after Henderson is accidental killed.

**Benét, Stephen Vincent** (July 22, 1898–March 13, 1943) an American poet, playwright, and fiction writer. His best-known work is probably the short story (and later play) "The Devil and Daniel Webster." Although he is not primarily known as a science fiction writer, several of his short stories have relevance to the development of the genre. Included in *Beyond Armageddon* is his short story "By the Waters of Babylon," an early example of a post-apocalyptic work.

**Benjamin** also known as Benjamin-bar-Joshua (Benjamin, son of Joshua), the "Old Jew," the pilgrim, Eleazar, and the hermit. He is an eternal character who appears in all three parts of the novel (and their source story and novellas) under various names: the wanderer, the pilgrim, the Wandering Jew, Latzar Shemi, Lazar, Old Tramp, and the beggar.

Miller has written that "psychologically Benjamin was just an unconscious (at the time I wrote) compensation for the fact that Leibowitz was an ex-Jewish convert. You might say that Benjamin is Leibowitz's unconverted part. Conversion doesn't cancel out what was previously in the psyche. The old man is uncanonized Leibowitz's shadow, although I did not think of it so while writing" (ltr. 2/21/1991).

Miller has also stated that the character of Benjamin was, in part, a response to his father's virulent anti–Semitism. He saw himself as Benjamin because he was "practically a Jew" in the eyes of his father since he did not agree with him. His father's pro-Nazism haunted Miller during World War II, and Benjamin became "sort of a letter to my father" (Garvey 1983).

1. In the novella "And the Light Is Risen" and *A Canticle for Leibowitz* ("Fiat Lux"), Benjamin claims to be 5,408 years old. He lives in a windowless single room stone hovel on the Mesa of Last Resort approximately 10 miles from the Abbey of Saint Leibowitz. Benjamin dresses simply in a loincloth of burlap, a basket hat, and sandals. He is an old friend and shrewd confidant of Father Jerome (Dom Paulo). He tells the abbot that during his earlier career as a wanderer he was once mistaken for his "distant relative" Leibowitz by a young novice by the name of Francis, thereby associating himself with the pilgrim Brother Francis encounters in the short story "A Canticle for Leibowitz." Because of this confusion, he now throws pebbles at the novices to keep them away.

According to Benjamin, a burden of a people was placed upon his shoulders, and he waits the coming of the Messiah, or as Father Jerome says, the "One-who-isn't coming." Benjamin asks the abbot to bring Don Thaddeo (Thon Taddeo) to him, but when the priest refuses, the old man travels to the abbey to confront the scholar himself. He proclaims, "It's still not Him."

2. In *Saint Leibowitz and the Wild Horse Woman*, Brother Blacktooth stays in Benjamin's abandoned hovel on the Mesa of Last Resort and later meets him traveling to New Jerusalem. Benjamin joins Blacktooth's small party on his way back from Valana where he had gone to speak with his old friend Amen I. Ulad explains to Blacktooth that Benjamin has been hired in the past by Mayor Dion as a rainmaker. Benjamin tells Blacktooth that he is a pilgrim but not a Christian. He calls himself a Jew and a tentmaker among other things, including a dentist. See also **Eleazar**, **Lazarus**, **Pilgrim**, and **Wandering Jew**

**Bereshith** the Hebrew word for genesis; it means "in the beginning." The term is used in the novella "The Song of Vorhu."

**Berker, Sir Rische Thon** a scientist whose radiation count on the Northwest Coast is ten times the normal level indicative of a nuclear explosion in *A Canticle for Leibowitz* ("Fiat Voluntas Tua").

**Berkstrun starship drive** the mechanism that allows deep space or interstellar travel. Its development predates the time of the novella "The Last Canticle" by 150 years. It is also mentioned in *A Canticle for Leibowitz* ("Fiat Voluntas Tua").

**Bernhardt, Sarah** (October 22, 1844–March 26, 1923) French stage and later silent film actress. She enjoyed extreme popularity in both Europe and the United States. Among the most famous performers of all time, she was referred to as the Divine Sarah.

In the novella "The Darfsteller," Ryan Thornier sarcastically refers to the prospect of autodrama for the home as the "greatest thing in show business since Sarah Bernhardt."

***The Best of Walter M. Miller, Jr.*** collection published by Pocket Books (New York) in 1980 as a paperback. A hardcover edition was published as a selection of the Doubleday Book Club the same year.

Contents: "You Triflin' Skunk," "The Will," "Anybody Else Like Me?," "Crucifixus Etiam," "I, Dreamer," "Dumb Waiter," "Blood Bank," "Big Joe and the Nth Generation," "The Big Hunger," "Conditionally Human," "The Daftsteller," "Dark Benediction," "The Lineman," "Vengeance for Nikolai."

**Beta Hydri** a star located approximately 24 light years from Earth. It is part of the constellation Hydrus. It is mentioned in the novella "The Last Canticle" and *A Canticle for Leibowitz* ("Fiat Voluntas Tua") as a place where man might go to find peace.

**Bethlehem** a small town south of Jerusalem famous as the birthplace of Jesus. The Church of the Holy Nativity, built in 330 by Constantine, is believed to have been built over the Holy Crypt, the site of Jesus' birth. The town is referred to in *Saint Leibowitz and the Wild Horse Woman* as one of the locations of Mary's manifestation.

***Beyond Armageddon: Twenty-One Sermons to the Dead*** anthology edited by Miller and Martin H. Greenberg, and originally published by Donald I. Fine, Inc. (New York) in 1985. A British edition, subtitled "Survivors of the Megawar," was published in London by Robinson Publishing in 1987. The book was re-issued by the University of Nebraska Press in a paperback edition in 2006. The twenty-one stories all explore the nature of life after some type of global holocaust, often nuclear war. Miller wrote an introductory essay and provided idiosyncratic commentaries for each story. Taken together, they represent the most extensive material published by Miller in his lifetime after the publication of *A Canticle for Leibowitz*.

Contents: "Alibi," Miller; "Forewarning" (an Introduction), Miller; "Salvador," Lucius Shepherd; "The Store of the Worlds," Robert Sheckley; "The Big Flash," Norman Spinrad; "Lot," Ward Moore; "Day at the Beach," Carol Emshwiller; "The Wheel," John Wyndham; "Jody After the War," Edward Bryant; "The Terminal Beach," J. G. Ballard; "Tomorrow's Children," Poul Anderson; "Heirs Apparent," Robert Abernathy; "A Master of Babylon," Edgar Pangborn; "Game Preserve," Rog Phillips; "By the Waters of Babylon," Stephen V. Benét; "There Will Come Soft Rains," Ray Bradbury; "To the Chicago Abyss," Ray Bradbury; "Lucifer," Roger Zelazny; "Eastward Ho!," William Tenn; "The Feast of Saint Janis," Michael Swanwick; "'If I Forget Thee, Oh Earth...,'" Arthur C. Clarke; "A Boy and His Dog," Harlan Ellison; "My Life in the Jungle," Jim Aikin.

**The Big Bottomless** a reference to space in the short story "The Hoofer."

**"The Big Flash"** a 1969 short story by Norman Spinrad included in *Beyond Armageddon*. Miller calls its plot "as intricate as that of a novel."

**Big Hogey Parker** *see* Parker, Hogey

**"The Big Hunger"** short story originally appearing in *Astounding Science Fiction*, 50 (October 1952), 98–112. It is an essentially plotless rumination and series of brief scenes on man's "star-craze," his continuing need to satisfy his wanderlust to the stars, going deeper and deeper into space and the unknown, conquering and colonizing as he moves. Man is part of a stargoing cycle: the landing of starships on a distant planet, a regression to savagery, a painful rebuilding, cruelty, relearning, and then a proud exodus back into space. The Great Purpose of humankind is to fling itself star-ward. It is an exodus of the hungry, but the hunger only grows in space. Often those who are left behind, those who choose to linger, settle and achieve a peace but something within them dies a little.

When a young girl asks her grandfather what star-craze is, the old man explains that man once lived on a paradise planet, but he ran away in search of a better one. This angered Lord Bion who hid the paradise and condemned man to forever wander, searching for the place he lost. This Divine Thirst is the hunger for the lost home. The search is endless, but it gives man one goal, something to work for.

As Teris gets ready to board his spaceship he tells Marka that man will never find the Planet of Heaven because Lord Bion did not proclaim it so. Marka says that when man is content without his lost paradise, when he reconciles himself, Lord Bion will forgive and reveal the road home. As Teris runs toward his ship, Marka yells that he will never find paradise because it is right here — in their hearts and their love.

The hunger is the cross on which man crucifies himself. It pushes him onward to the ends of space. He is a Nomad, creating myriad Earths but never knowing his true home.

The story is included in *The View from the Stars*, *The Science Fiction Stories of Walter M. Miller, Jr.*, *The Best of Walter M. Miller, Jr.*, and *Conditionally Human and Other Stories*.

**Big Joe** a large, menacing mechanical guard in the short story "It Takes a Thief" (later entitled

"Big Joe and the Nth Generation"). The robot protects the vault room housing the machinery for the fusion reaction that must periodically restore the atmospheric oxygen on Mars. It not only serves as a guard but also as a resource of information for the technologists who must maintain the machinery.

**"Big Joe and the Nth Generation"** a short story originally published as "It Takes a Thief." The story first appears with the alternate title in *The View from the Stars* in 1964. It is included in *The Science Fiction Stories of Walter M. Miller, Jr.*, *The Best of Walter M. Miller, Jr.*, and *The Darfsteller and Other Stories* under the later title.

**Big Oswald** a large, menacing mechanical sentry similar to Big Joe in the short story "It Takes a Thief" (also known as "Big Joe and the Nth Generation"). It guards the instruction room housing the information for the operation of the machinery controlling the fusion reaction that creates the atmosphere on Mars.

**Big Silence** in the short story "Check and Checkmate," after the last war ended in stalemate, total isolation was maintained between the East and West for 40 years. No diplomatic relations were kept and interference stations prevented telecommunications between the two sides. This era was known as The Big Silence. The Big Silence is finally broached by John Smith XVI, President of the Western Federation of Autonomous States, and Ivan Ivanovich the Ninth, the Peoplesfriend and Vicar of the Asian Proletarian League.

**Bio-laws** a series of laws in Marsville that forbid any interaction between humans and androons, especially miscegenation, in the novella "The Reluctant Traitor." The bio-laws are based on the false premise that androons are not human.

**Bisson, Terry** (February 12, 1942– ) a science fiction and fantasy writer born in Owensboro, Kentucky. His novels include *Wyrldmaker* (1981), *Voyage to the Red Planet* (1990), and *Pirates of the Universe* (1996). The short story "Bears Discover Fire" received numerous awards, including the Nebula and Hugo awards. His short story collection *In the Upper Room and Other Likely Stories* (2000) includes "macs," a Nebula and Hugo awards winner.

Bisson was recommended to Don Congdon, Miller's literary agent, as someone to possibly complete the manuscript of *Saint Leibowitz and the Wild Horse Woman* when Miller felt he was unable to finish it himself. In his essay "A Canticle for Miller; or How I Met Saint Leibowitz and the Wild Horse Woman but not Walter M. Miller, Jr.," Bisson says that after reading Miller's 592 manuscript pages, he found the work to be an "incredibly rich masterpiece." He told Congdon he wanted to finish it. When informed of Bisson's interest, Miller replied: "I've never heard of this guy but he sounds okay to me."

Miller committed suicide before an agreement with Bisson was finalized, but both Miller's family and Bantam approved the final deal. Bisson finished the book over a five month period, adding the last 100 pages or so of the story. As a guide he followed several letters Miller had written to Congdon describing the characters' actions and developments, some notes left by Miller, and a couple of scenes Miller had briefly sketched.

Bisson's intent was to be as true to Miller's style and vision as was possible. He wanted the book to be Miller's book, not a collaboration with him, and therefore strove for invisibility within the finished book.

Within the book, Bisson is thanked by Miller's estate "for his editorial contribution" to the novel.

**Bitten Dog** a Wilddog Nomad in *Saint Leibowitz and the Wild Horse Woman*. He is drafted by Pope Amen II's chef as a cook's helper. Brother Blacktooth becomes his helper.

**"Bitter Victory"** short story first appearing in *If, Worlds of Science Fiction*, 1 (March 1952), 59–75. A feudal system developed on Nu Phoenicis IV that lasted for more than 5,000 years. Three distinct classes arose: the Klidds or barons (the Imperials), the Algun or serfs (the Pastorals), and the Taknon or artisans (the Inventives). Through natural selection operating within each group, the three classes became genetically distinct. After the rise of technology, the feudal order collapsed and the Klidds were overthrown and exiled to an ironless planet. Without iron and steel, the Klidds were condemned within an eternal stone age. They developed a ruthless social order. The Taknon space force now maintains a strict space quarantine around the planet.

Klia, a Klidd, is able to evade the quarantine in a stolen Hydrian ship. She arrives on Terra with a plan to manipulate the Terrans into sending ships to the Klidds' planet expecting to find no life there. The ships would return to Terra with Klidds who would take control of the Terrans and their planet. The Klidds would then have access to iron and steel to use in attacking the Taknon. Klia begins her plan by publishing a series of scientific articles under assumed names which she hopes will spur Terran scientists to think along new lines that will eventually allow them to develop the five-space interstellar drive.

In response to her breaking the quarantine, the Phoenician Quarantine Commission assigns San Rorrek to locate and kill Klia. Both Klia and San are telepaths with the ability to plant thoughts in people's minds. They are also able to change their features and form over short periods. Klia lures San into a trap and forces him into a taxi. She plans to take him to a remote location so he can dig his own grave before she kills him. Using his power of suggestion, San causes the cab driver to have an accident. As they walk away in the confusion, San asks Klia if he can buy her a drink before she kills him. She agrees saying it is interesting watching him try to escape his death.

During their conversation in a small bar, San taunts Klia into attacking him. He is shot in the leg but is able to hit Klia hard enough to send her to the floor. Hearing the shot, a police officer leaves the scene of the taxi accident and rushes into the bar. San disables him with mental suggestions that he is physically ill. As San leaves the bar he hears other people say that Klia is dead. While he knows she had to be killed, San feels no pleasure in completing his mission. He found something compelling about her.

San cannot return to Nu Phoenicis IV because he had to abandon his ship in the sea so it would not be discovered. Marooned on Terra for life, unless another Taknon ship arrives to rescue him, San faces a life of ease but also loneliness. As a telepath, he can easily acquire money. He assumes the name of Sam Rory and moves to San Francisco. After accumulating enough money through gambling, San begins to construct a computer that he programs to assist him in investing in the stock market, and he begins to live comfortably. He follows the articles Klia had written that continue to appear because of the time lag between their acceptance and publication.

A famous mathematician, Frank Larwich, inspired by Klia's articles, begins work on the creation of a mathematical physics with no basic assumptions except for those of elementary arithmetic. San sees that Klia has succeeded in steering Larwich in the right direction, but he knows that without a link between Larwich's theory and observable reality, the theory will remain only abstruse mathematical speculation. Perhaps from a guilt-reaction associated with Klia's death, San decides to provide the missing suggestion in an article he writes for a university press journal, but the article is rejected. Ready to abandon his plan to provide the missing practical link and concentrate on making his fortune, San learns that Larwich is in San Francisco for the summer. He locates Larwich's address and rents a cottage a short distance away. He plans a seemingly accidental meeting on the beach with Larwich, his wife Louise, and daughter Edith. In conversation he wants to plant a hint of a practical correlation in Larwich's mind regarding his theory.

Larwich is pleasantly surprised to find someone interested and so conversant in mathematics and his theory. San is surprised by the speed with which Larwich is developing his theory. Larwich credits Edith, who has a Ph.D. in physics, with helping him with down to earth suggestions and as a result, he already foresees practical applications for this theory.

San finds Edith attractive but has a vague uneasiness about her. She asks him to join her for a swim, but Larwich asks him to stay a bit to talk more. Larwich tells San how much Edith has changed recently. She was nearly blind from cataracts and was shy and introspective. Now she can see and is open and friendly. San goes to join Edith, and she asks him who he really is. He repeats that he is simply a gambler and investor. She does not pursue her questions but asks how the beach is at his cottage. He tells her it is fine and invites her to come down; she says she will very soon.

That evening as he sits on his porch, San thinks of his home world and his loneliness on Terra. He sends a mental suggestion to Edith to come down the beach but is unsure if her untrained mind will catch his faint suggestion from that distance. In a few minutes though, Edith begins walking down the beach toward his cottage. She stops and asks if she can join him, and he invites her for dinner. As they talk, he draws her toward him to kiss her and tries to make mental contact with her, but the response is too powerful. He feels a gun against his ribs, and a voice telling him he should have been a Klidd. Klia has assumed Edith's form and personality patterns in order to get close to Larwich. She placed the real Edith in a Pennsylvania psychopathic ward with hypnotically induced amnesia. She was suspicious of San but was not sure who he was until he attempted to make mental contact with her. San realizes he made a mistake in the bar by not checking for himself that Klia was dead. She simply stopped her heartbeat or circulation in her arm when her body was being checked for life by the Terrans. She asks San why he sought out Larwich if he believed she was dead. When he tells her it was to do what she has already succeeded in doing, she does not believe him. He begins to make a mental connection with her so she can access his thoughts and memories. He suggests they work together since they are both marooned on Terra. Klia tells him to walk down to the water so the outgoing tide can take his body with it. As they move toward the water, Klia laughs and tells San he must be part

Klidd. She never could love anyone who was not Klidd, and she loves him. Nevertheless, she loves her people more and commands him to walk out beyond the breakers. As he does so, San makes mental contact with her so that she will feel his pain when he is shot. She shoots at San, but only one of the five bullets hits him. San counts the shots knowing the gun holds seven rounds. He makes his way back toward the shore while Klia fires twice more, hitting San once again.

She stands on the beach watching San make his way toward her. Their minds meet. He wants her to run because he will kill her if he is able to reach her. She hopes he dies before he makes it, but she will not run from him. He gropes for her, again telepathically telling her to run, but instead she asks him to let her get a doctor. He grabs her and hits her several times in the face. She screams, "My eyes! My eyes!" She is wearing glass contact lenses to cover her true eye color, and when San hit her, slivers of glass went into her eyes. Klia rolls away from San and begins blindly staggering toward the dunes as Dr. Larwich runs down the beach. She cries for Rorrek, and he follows her directing her path telepathically. He guides her into a car. She drives them away using his eyes to see the road. San wonders why Klia does not accept her death. He knows he has won because within the Klidd culture any loss of function or deformity is cause for shame and ridicule. While he waits for her to ram the car into a tree or bridge, she turns at a sign reading "Physician and Surgeon." She orders him out of the car and now San understands her plan: she means to save him and then kill herself. He asks her why she has helped him, and he jerks the keys from the ignition and falls across her trapping her in the car as his elbow leans on the horn. He repeats his thought that they will work together to get the Terrans into space to help the Klidds. Klia bitterly asks him why when the Taknon and Algun denied the Klidds the opportunity to find a place in the new society. The Klidds were denied the fundamental right of man — the right to try. As he loses consciousness, San hears footsteps and then feels hands gently moving him from the car.

When he awakes, he expects to see the bars of a jail cell or hospital walls. Instead, he is back in his own home in San Francisco. Klia sits by the window. After the doctor treated her eyes and San's bullet wounds, Klia used her powers of suggestion to help him forget what he saw. She tells San that she will go as soon as he is well, but he tells her no. She will stay, and they will work together to build the ships to help the Klidds. She tells him that the doctor said there was not much chance for her eyes. San tells her that they still have one pair even if she never regains her own sight. He opens up his thoughts to her with ever-increasing daring so she can see herself as he sees her, and as she blushes, her hands reach out to him.

**Bix** *see* **Bixby**

**Bixby** a minor character in the short story "Wolf Pack." He is the bombardier-navigator on Mark Kessel's B-25 bomber. He is also called Bix.

**Black Eyes** a Nomad double agent in *Saint Leibowitz and the Wild Horse Woman*. He is held in the cage opposite Cardinal Brownpony and Brother Blacktooth in Filpeo Harq's zoo/jail in Hannegan City. He is released to carry a message from Filpeo Harq to Eltür Bräm, Demon Light. Black Eyes later presents Blacktooth with a copy of *The Book of Beginnings: Volume One* by the Venerable Boedullus to help him teach Sharf Bram's nephews. The book is a Texark publisher's edition of Blacktooth's own translation. It is Black Eyes who informs Brownpony and Blacktooth that the battle is lost at the end of the book, that the Texark guns are too strong and too fast.

**Black Friar** a Dominican messenger from New Rome who comes to the Abbey of Saint Leibowitz to speak with Brother Francis in *A Canticle for Leibowitz* ("Fiat Homo"). He informs Francis that it has been determined that the relics he uncovered are authentic and that the case for the canonization of Leibowitz will soon be reopened.

**Black Wind** a god of the Nomadic Wilddog horde in *Saint Leibowitz and the Wild Horse Woman*.

**Blackeneth** one of the princely advisors or magi in the story of the Flame Deluge as told in *A Canticle for Leibowitz* ("Fiat Lux"). He alone advises the prince not to fear using his most dangerous weapons and the resulting "demon Fallout." He is said to have betrayed all his brothers by doing so and is compared to Judas Iscariot.

**Blacktooth St. George** a central character in the novel *Saint Leibowitz and the Wild Horse Woman*. He is of pure Nomad blood and came to the Abbey of Saint Leibowitz at the age of fifteen after running away from his tribe with two companions. At the age of thirty he asks to be released from his final vows as a monk of the Order of Saint Leibowitz. He is experiencing conflicting visions of the Virgin Mary and the Wild Horse Woman, a central deity of the Plains Nomads. The abbot is reluctant to release him, in part, because of the work he is engaged in, translating the seven volumes of the Venerable Boedullus' *Liber*

*Originum* from Neo-Latin to the Grasshopper dialect of Plains Nomadic. For various reasons, Blacktooth believes the project to be vain and futile, but his work on the first volumes has the support of Deacon "Half-Breed" Brownpony who wishes to have all seven volumes translated.

When he nears finishing the translation, Blacktooth renews his request to leave the order, citing a loss of unity with the other monks. Instead he is given the choice of translating another work by Boedullus or a volume by Yogan Duren. He chooses the Duren work.

Blacktooth is caught in an unintentional compromising position with Torrildo, a young postulant he befriends, who loves him. Given three weeks of penance shoveling compost, he is ordered to meet weekly with a Brother Reconciliator to help him reconcile his calling. After a series of unsanctioned absences from the abbey, the latest taking him to the Mesa of Last Resort, Blacktooth faces a tribunal when he returns to the abbey after his water runs out and he catches a terrible cold. He is saved from an interdiction by Brownpony, now Cardinal "Red Deacon," who offers him the chance to leave the abbey as his translator and interpreter. Blacktooth becomes Brownpony's personal secretary for Nomad affairs. During an audience with Pope Amen about his petition to leave the order, Amen proclaims him "a real monk and a contemplative."

Blacktooth maintains an evolving and complex relationship with Cardinal Brownpony and the various members of his inner circle, particularly Wooshin. When he accompanies Brownpony to Valana, they spend time in Arch Hollow where Blacktooth meets Ædrea, a pretty young genny. She seduces him and becomes pregnant. She eventually gives birth to twin boys who she gives up for adoption. Brownpony fears that Ædrea is a disruptive influence on Blacktooth, and he works to keep the two separated. Blacktooth struggles to be reunited with her throughout much of the book.

As Pope Amen II, Brownpony appoints Blacktooth the Cardinal Deacon of Saint Maisie's, Brownpony's old Roman Church. When New Rome is attacked, Pope Amen II names Blacktooth as the papal legate to the remaining people of the city. He rides into the center of the city on a white mule that is shot out from under him. He is captured and taken to the death cells. As the city burns around him, he is finally freed from his cell by a gelp who pulls out the bars on his window.

After the defeat of Pope Amen II's forces and his death in New Rome, Blacktooth slowly makes his way back to the Abbey of Saint Leibowitz caring for the wounded and burying the dead that he comes across. When he finally reaches the abbey, the brothers want to elect him abbot, but he refuses. He visits Benjamin on the mesa, travels to New Jerusalem, and to the convent of San Pancho Villa of Cockroach Mountain searching for Ædrea, now known as Sister Clare. At the convent, Mother Iridia welcomes him and tells him that Sister Clare has probably returned to her own people in the Valley of the Misborn.

Blacktooth is summoned to a papal audience with Pope Sorely in Hannegan City. He is treated kindly and given traveling money. He goes to the Valley of the Misborn and settles in Post Cedar, a small community of bookleggers and memorizers. There he finds shelter in a rock house cave and works as a scribe and tutor in exchange for food. He grows old and dies there. His body is found by Sister Clare who lives in a convent over the mountain from Post Cedar. She senses that Blacktooth is dead. When she enters his cave she finds his corpse sitting against a stone with the head of Librada, his pet cougar, in his lap. He is buried in a grave with a small cross at its head.

**Blaze of the Great Wind** the name refers to the mechanism beneath the surface of Mars that uses a fusion reaction to create and sustain atmospheric oxygen in the short story "It Takes a Thief." It is also called the Blaze of the Winds.

**Blessed Chang** an unseen character in *A Canticle for Leibowitz* ("Fiat Homo"). He has been beatified for two centuries but never canonized because his order was too eager and claimed too many miraculous incidents. This is the fate Abbot Arkos wants to avoid in the canonization of Leibowitz and why he is upset that Brother Francis will not categorically deny that the pilgrim he met in the desert is not the Blessed Leibowitz.

**Blessed Farnsworth** he installed the printing press in the Abbey of Saint Leibowitz one hundred years prior to the time of the novella "And the Light Is Risen."

**Blessing of Texts** a prayer offered by any member of the Albertian Order of Leibowitz before opening a book or writing as presented in *A Canticle for Leibowitz* ("Fiat Homo").

**Bleze, Hilan** the Cardinal High Chamberlain and former Secretary of State of Denver in *Saint Leibowitz and the Wild Horse Woman*.

**Blinderman, Colonel** representative of the Engineer Corps at Filpeo Harq's strategy meeting at the War College in *Saint Leibowitz and the Wild Horse Woman*.

**"Blood Bank"** short story originally appearing in *Astounding Science Fiction*, 49 (June 1952), 95–138. On a routine patrol, Space Commander Eli Roki of the Sixty-Star Cluster encounters a mercy ship supposedly carrying surgibank supplies: blood, frozen bone, tissue and organs, from Sol III. He orders a random cargo inspection but the mercy ship does not stop or acknowledge his transmissions. The ship eludes his attempts to pull alongside. It finally informs Roki that it is carrying an emergency shipment to Jod VI with orders not to stop. Roki fires a warning shot, but when the ship still refuses to allow its cargo to be inspected, he destroys the ship. An examination of the debris shows no contraband, only surgibank supplies. As a result of not receiving the medical supplies, 10,000 people die on Jod VI.

A hearing is held to investigate Roki's actions. He insists, albeit without proof, that the mercy ship was involved in illegal activity. The hearing determines that Roki's strict application of the law did not violate space regulations. He is legally cleared, but his actions are viewed as immoral. He offers his resignation, and it is accepted.

Offered a ship to take him anywhere, Roki chooses to go to Sol III. He is morally certain that his actions were correct, and he wants to discover the truth about the mercy ship and clear his name.

He travels aboard a Dalethian freighter, the *Idiot*, piloted by a cigar-smoking young woman, Talewa Walkeka. The ship is barely serviceable, and Walkeka resents any interference from Roki. Worried about the condition of the onboard reactors, Roki takes control of the ship and lands it on Tragor III so repairs can be made.

On Tragor Roki discovers another Sol mercy ship surrounded by guards. He determines to try to find out as much information as he can about the ship and the Solarians. He soon realizes, however, that his identity as the destroyer of their mercy ship is known by the Solarians.

Walkeka is jailed for being an unescorted and unveiled woman on Tragor. Roki leaves her in jail believing it is the safest place for her until they are ready to leave. When he finally goes to arrange for her release, he is told that she has already been released. Roki now understands that one of the boxes he saw being loaded in the Solarian ship contained Walkeka. The Solarians kidnapped her to insure him coming to Sol.

From the information he gathered on Tragor, Roki believes that the Solarians gain their surgibank supplies through genocide, and that they are a threat throughout the galaxy. He follows them in the Dalethian freighter and plans to barter the technology for the warp locking devices and C-drive technology for the life of Talewa Walkeka.

As he approaches Sol III, he is intercepted by a Solarian ship that wants to board him. Roki prepares an elaborate booby trap aboard the *Idiot* that he hopes will guarantee his and Walkeka's safety. Once the Solarian ship docks with the *Idiot*, a series of signals must be answered or else both ships will be destroyed.

The Solarian commander, Hulgruv, is confident that he can outsmart Roki and gain control of the *Idiot*. He and Roki engage in conversation as each tries to outthink and bluff the other. Hulgruv reveals that the Solarians are a new race that evolved out of what was left of man on Earth after a space exodus and the collapse of technology. With the loss of other species to sustain them, the Solarians began to prey upon the weaker human species. The Solarians maintain human livestock on board their ships, which is why the mercy ship would not stop to be inspected. Humans are also bred as sources for the surgibank supplies the Solarians sell throughout the galaxy.

Roki's willingness to destroy the ships allows him to gain control of Hulgruv's weapon. He overcomes the remaining crew to get command of both ships. With two captured Solarians and the evidence of the human livestock on their ship, Roki has all he needs to vindicate his actions and have the Sixty-Star Cluster declare war on the Solarians to free their human brothers.

**Blue Lightning** the Nomad name of Stützil Bråm in *Saint Leibowitz and the Wild Horse Woman*. See also **Bråm, Stützil**

**Boat people** the people living on barges equipped with sheds or cabins on the Misspee River in *Saint Leibowitz and the Wild Horse Woman*.

**Bob** the son of Scott MacDonney in the novella "Izzard and the Membrane." He dies in an atomic bomb attack on Cleveland. His awareness pattern is restored by Izzard, and he eventually rejoins his father in another world on the other side of the membrane.

**"Bobby and Jimmy: Round Six…"** *The Nation*, 194 (7 April 1962), 300–303. An essay by Miller. He attends the court hearings to consider motions by the defense and countermotions by the government prior to setting a trial date or dismissing the indictment in the case of Teamsters union president Jimmy Hoffa's misuse of union funds in a real estate deal. Much of the essay focuses on Jacob Kossman, one of Hoffa's lawyers. Kossman tells Miller and another courtroom observer about Hoffa's positive qualities and "abstemious" lifestyle.

Miller suggests that Hoffa's fate is sealed because of the antagonism of John F. Kennedy as well as his "sporadic duel" with Robert Kennedy. Hoffa cannot escape from a life of litigation and government harassment; a Kennedy must succeed in his pursuit of Hoffa as "a politically necessary proof of prowess."

**Bodalk**   an unseen thon and contemporary of Thon Taddeo in *A Canticle for Leibowitz* ("Fiat Lux"). In his speech before the monks at the Leibowitz abbey, Taddeo says that Bodalk is making a reckless assault on orthodox geometries. He is referred to in the novella "And the Light Is Risen" as Don Bodalk.

**Bodolus**   a legendary giant catfish that supposedly came to live in the crater where the Venerable Boedullus died in an explosion at an archaeological site. The tale is from *Saint Leibowitz and the Wild Horse Woman*. In *A Canticle for Leibowitz* the catfish is referred to as Bo'dollos.

**Boedullus, Verus Sarquus**   the historian of the Abbey of Saint Leibowitz in the novel *A Canticle for Leibowitz*. He disappeared 80 years prior to the time of "Fiat Homo." His last communication was a letter to the abbot of the abbey announcing that his small expedition had discovered an intercontinental missile launching site beneath a small village. It is later discovered that a crater has replaced the village. Shepherds eventually divert water to fill the crater and create a lake. The fish in the lake are reputed to be the souls of the villagers and members of the expedition. A giant catfish, the Bo'dollos, is believed to be the soul of the departed Boedullus.

In *Saint Leibowitz and the Wild Horse Woman*, it is confirmed that Boedullus died in an explosion at an archaeological site. Brother Blacktooth is translating the "dark-age saint's" seven volume work *Liber Originum*. Blacktooth finds Boedullus to be "rational, inquisitive, inventive — and intolerant." He is also given the opportunity to translate Boedullus' *Footprints of Earlier Civilizations* (*De Vestigiis Antecessarum Civitatum*).

The historian is referred to as the Venerable Boedullus evoking the Venerable Bede, Saint Bede, an Anglo-Saxon historian and monastic scholar who spent his life in a Benedictine monastery.

**Bogdanov, Alexander (Aleksandr)**  (August 22 [N. S.], 1873–April 7, 1928)   born Alexander Malinovsky in Russia and educated as a physician. He changed his name after graduating from medical school and entering radical politics. Along with Vladimir Lenin, he was a major influence in the early Bolshevik party. Expelled from the party in 1909 for his ultra radical tendencies and as part of a power struggle within the party, Bogdanov turned his attention away from politics and more toward philosophy and economics. He developed the concept of Tectology, a unification of social, biological, and physical science through a relationship of systems. He was interested in the use of blood transfusions as a means of human rejuvenation and restoration. Sometimes referred to as the founder of Russian science fiction, Bogdanov had an early interest in science fiction and published *Red Star: the First Bolshevik Utopia* in 1908. Miller reviewed a new edition of *Red Star* for the *New York Times Book Review* in his "Bolsheviks on Mars." See also **"Bolsheviks on Mars"** and ***Red Star: the First Bolshevik Utopia***

**Bolsewi**   an ancient alien race that raided Earth in prehistoric times and captured a dozen pairs of humans to be brought back to Mars and bred for slave labor in the novella "The Reluctant Traitor." They established the foundations of a Martian civilization and are believed to be gods by the androons.

**"Bolsheviks on Mars"**   *New York Times Book Review*, 8 July 1994, 11–12. Miller reviews a new edition of Alexander Bogdanov's utopian novel *Red Star: the First Bolshevik Utopia*. He gives a brief background on Bogdanov, a physician and Bolshevik propagandist and revolutionary. The novel was first published in 1908, and Miller sees its depiction of a system of self-regulation in an imaginary Socialist system on Mars as its most original feature. Its intent was to celebrate Socialism and inspire the overthrow of the Czar in Russia. In the book a young Russian organizer and revolutionary is taken to Mars in order to observe its perfect classless and stateless Socialist system. Ironically, Mars is looking to Earth for space for its burgeoning population. Miller believes Bogdanov demonstrates some foresight in the technology he describes as well as his sense of foreboding in the dangers of national arrogance and environmental exploitation. See also **Bogdanov, Alexander** and ***Red Star: the First Bolshevik Utopia***

**Bon marché**   French: "a good price" or "a bargain." The term is used in the novella "The Lineman."

***The Bone People***   New Zealand writer Keri Hulme's first novel remains her best-known work and one of the best-known and most popular novels ever published in her homeland. Focusing on a complicated relationship among three emotionally scarred characters, Hulme successfully incorporates Maori myths and culture with more traditional western traditions and culture. The book received the New Zealand Book Award in 1984 and the Booker Prize in 1985. Miller reviewed the book favorably for *Commonweal* in his "Roots & Sinew." See also "**Roots & Sinew**" and **Hulme, Keri**

**Bongo Bar**   from the short story "The Corpse In Your Bed Is Me." The Bongo Bar is across the street from the studio where the *Martin Snyder Hour* is aired. It is the meeting place of the I Hate Snyder's Guts Club.

***The Book of Origins*** see ***Liber Originum***

**Bookleggers**   from *A Canticle for Leibowitz* ("Fiat Homo"), members of the Albertian Order of Leibowitz who smuggled books to the southwest desert during the Simplification and buried them in kegs in order to preserve them for future generations. See also **Memorizers**

**Boone, Lincoln**   the listed co-author of one of Miller's last published stories, "The Corpse in Your Bed is Me," which appears in *Venture Science Fiction* in May of 1957. Boone is Miller's invention, an attempt to establish an alter-ego or pen name by collaborating with it. In a letter to Chad Oliver, Miller describes Boone as "a paranoid maniac and fugitive from justice ... [who] is married to my wife" (4/3/1958).

**Boötes**   also known as the Herdsman, a large constellation in the Northern Hemisphere. Its brightest star is Arcturus. It is mentioned in the short story "Way of the Rebel."

**Border Guards**   a vigilante group commanded by Colonel MacMahon in the novella "The Yokel." They track down people who attempt to cross from Ruralland into the industrial areas and torture and kill them. They also plan guerrilla actions against the restored cities.

**Boris**   a minor character in the novella "Izzard and the Membrane." He is one of Scott MacDonney's guards and is presumably killed in an attack upon MacDonney.

**Boss uncle**   the oldest of a boy's mother's brothers among the Nomads in *Saint Leibowitz and the Wild Horse Woman*.

**Bouleversement**   French: "a disruption" or "turmoil." The term is used in the novella "The Lineman."

**"A Boy and His Dog"**   controversial Hugo and Nebula awards winning short story by Harlan Ellison originally published in 1969. It is included in *Beyond Armageddon*. Miller refers to it as a powerful and gruesome story.

**Bradbury, Ray(mond)** (August 22, 1920–) American science fiction and fantasy writer, among the most popular writers of the latter half of the twentieth century. He is credited with popularizing and legitimizing the science fiction genre with such well crafted and humanistic works as *The Martian Chronicles* (1950), *Fahrenheit 451* (1953), and *Something Wicked This Way Comes* (1962). Among his many awards are the O. Henry Prize, an Emmy Award, and the National Medal of Arts. Two of his short stories, "There Will Come Soft Rains" and "To the Chicago Abyss," are included in *Beyond Armageddon*.

**Brahe, Tycho** (December 14, 1546–October 24, 1601)   Danish nobleman and astronomer famous for his empirical and precise planetary and astronomical observations prior to the development of the telescope, including the discovery of a supernova in the constellation Cassiopeia in November 1572. His work provided the basis for later discoveries and theories, such as Johannes Kepler's laws of planetary motion.

In *A Canticle for Leibowitz* ("Fiat Voluntas Tua"), the contingent of space going Albertian monks who will preserve the order and the Catholic Church after the nuclear holocaust destroys Earth is referred to as the Visitationist Friars of the Order of Saint Leibowitz of Tycho. See also **Visitationist Friars of the Order of Saint Leibowitz of Tycho**

**Brain-of-the-World**   another name used by the people for Bel in the short story "Please Me Plus Three." See also **Bel**

**Bråm, Eltur**   the younger brother of Hultor Bråm in *Saint Leibowitz and the Wild Horse Woman*. He is also known as Demon Light. According to Father Steps-on-Snake, Eltur worshipped his older brother and will avenge his death. He is considered to be less belligerent and less impulsive than his brother, but perhaps more cunning than him in battle.

**Bråm, Hultor**   also known as Kindly Light. He is the war sharf of the Grasshoppers and a candidate for the Lord of the Hordes to unite the Three Hordes in *Saint Leibowitz and the Wild Horse Woman*. He is invited by Cardinal Brownpony to meet Pope Amen I. He demands that Brownpony experience the ordeal of the Meldown to remove past sacrileges against the Nomads. If Brownpony survives, Bråm promises an alliance with Valana and the Wilddog horde no matter who is elected

Lord of the Hordes. When Hultor Bråm emerges from his own ordeal of the Meldown, he falls ill within two weeks and is therefore marked for death. He essentially commits treason against the Lord of the Hordes after he breaks the Treaty of the Sacred Mare by attacking Filpeo Harq's guard and the Texark cavalry on the road to New Rome and plunders the countryside. He agrees to a sacrificial death if his younger brother, Eltür Bråm, is made war shar in his place. Hultor Bråm is dragged to his death behind a wild stallion.

**Bråm, Stützil** a Grasshopper emissary and the nephew of Eltür Bråm, Demon Light, in *Saint Leibowitz and the Wild Horse Woman*. He demands the release of Brother Blacktooth and Gai-See when they are jailed for the death of Cardinal Hadala. He is also known as Blue Lightning.

**Brave River** the southern border of the Land of the Mare in *Saint Leibowitz and the Wild Horse Woman*. Sister Clare is exiled across the river to the Monastery of the Nuns of Our Lady of San Pancho Villa of Cockroach Mountains by Amen II. It is probably the Brazos River.

**Braxton, Bama** one of the members on Joe Novotny's B-shift crew in the novella "The Lineman." His best friend is Lije Henderson. Braxton, Henderson, and Relke are the workers chosen by Joe Novotny to look for the break in the transmission line, so they are among the first to discover that the mysterious ship that lands near their work site is actually a traveling bordello.

**Bret** an unseen character referred to by Thon Taddeo in *A Canticle for Leibowitz* ("Fiat Lux"). The thon mentions that Viche Mortoin's investigations concerning the artificial production of ice follows the work of Bret on the behavior of gases.

**Breviary** the book containing the accepted forms of prayers, hymns, psalms, and readings for the canonical hours. Each member of the Albertian Order of Leibowitz carries a book with him as part of his habit when he ventures away from the abbey; that book is most often the Breviary.

***Brides of a Martian Harem*** the film that originally brought Freddy to Earth from Mars in the short story "The Corpse in Your Bed is Me." He had a thirteen week contract as an extra in the film.

**Bristleface** a slur used by Eli Roki when speaking to the Solarians in the short story "Blood Bank."

**Brodanovitch, Suds** a project engineer on the Lunar Project in the novella "The Lineman." He is opposed to allowing the men to visit the traveling bordello. He believes its existence endangers the project and that the men will be taken advantage of. When he boards the ship to confront Madame d'Annecy, he is overwhelmed and outmatched by her personality and intellect. She presents him with a bottle of champagne as a gift. Dazed and confused by his encounter, he enters the airlock to leave the ship still holding the bottle. The resulting explosion kills him.

**Brokenfoot** *see* **Granduncle Brokenfoot**

**Brother Alfred** a deaf monk whose Lenten hermitage coincides with that of Brother Francis in *A Canticle for Leibowitz* ("Fiat Homo"). Brother Francis can see him from the site of his own vigil.

**Brother Andrew** an unseen character in the novella "And the Light Is Risen" and *A Canticle for Leibowitz* ("Fiat Lux"). He is a medic at the abbey.

**Brother Armbruster** the elderly librarian of the abbey in the novella "And the Light Is Risen" and *A Canticle for Leibowitz* ("Fiat Lux"). In the novel he is also called the Rector of the Memorabilia. He has a pessimistic, querulous disposition and opposes Brother Kornhoer's work building an electrical generator and arc lamp, calling the latter a "witch light." Armbruster's only interest is in preserving the Memorabilia, not its practical applications. At Don Thaddeo's presentation of the collegium's work, he mocks the idea of Don Esser Shon attempting to create living protoplasm from six basic ingredients.

David N. Samuelson says the name means "crossbow" associating the monk with a hunter. This places him in natural conflict with Brother Kornhoer, whose name suggests a farmer. The brothers' relationship, therefore, mirrors that of Cain and Abel (Genesis 4:1–16 KJV).

**Brother Augustin** an unseen character in *A Canticle for Leibowitz* ("Fiat Voluntas Tua"). He is one of the Leibowitzian monks who comprise the starship crew for the *Quo peregrinator* plan. His name is a diminutive of Augustine, from the Latin meaning "revered" or "exalted." See also **Saint Augustine**

**Brother Axe** the name among the monks at the Abbey of Saint Leibowitz for Wooshin because of his former work as an executioner for Hannegan in *Saint Leibowitz and the Wild Horse Woman*.

**Brother Christopher** the name of an unseen starship crew member from the Order of Leibowitz in *A Canticle for Leibowitz* ("Fiat Voluntas Tua"). See also **Saint Christopher**

**Brother Claret** Marcus Apollo's clerk in the novella "And the Light Is Risen" and *A Canticle for Leibowitz* ("Fiat Lux"). He is tortured by Hannegan's men — his fingernails are torn out — and betrays Marcus Apollo. He arrives at the Abbey of Saint Leibowitz after his ordeal suffering from exposure, starvation, mistreatment and fever. He delivers the mayoral edict announcing that Hannegan is now the only legitimate ruler over the Church in Texarkana.

David N. Samuelson proposes that the name suggests voluptuousness and has some bearing on Marcus Apollo. Claret is also a slang term for blood. This context would have some relevancy given Hannegan's torture of Brother Claret and his subsequent torture and execution of Marcus Apollo.

**Brother Crab** the name Brother Wren calls his throat cancer in *Saint Leibowitz and the Wild Horse Woman* because his voice is a hoarse whisper.

**Brother Eltan** *see* **Brother Elton**

**Brother Elton** an unseen character in *A Canticle for Leibowitz* ("Fiat Voluntas Tua"); he does the buying for the abbey's kitchen. Dom Zerchi tells Mrs. Grales that she must see him about selling her tomatoes to the abbey. In the novella "The Last Canticle," his name is given as Brother Eltan.

**Brother Elwen** a novice who works for the groundskeeper at the Abbey of Saint Leibowitz in *Saint Leibowitz and the Wild Horse Woman*. He has been having regular romantic assignations with Torrildo in the abbey's basement library. When they are discovered, Elwen escapes over the abbey's wall. He eventually returns repentant to the Priory of Saint Leibowitz-in-the-Cottonwoods and becomes skilled as a mechanic and engineer. Elwen may be a variant spelling of Elvin, from the Anglo-Saxon meaning "godly friend."

**Brother Fingo** a woodcarver who carves a small statue of an oddly smiling Saint Leibowitz after Leibowitz comes to him in a vision. References to him are made in both *A Canticle for Leibowitz* ("Fiat Homo") and *Saint Leibowitz and the Wild Horse Woman*. Fingo is from the Latin, meaning "to shape or form." Brother Francis enjoys watching him work on the carving. He finds its face familiar, as if he has seen it before.

In *A Canticle for Leibowitz,* Brother Fingo is described as a heavy, bald man with hairy shins. Although technically a sport, his mutation is a mild one: he has splotchy brown skin upon an albino base. It is a typical characteristic in the Minnesota country from which he hails. As a result, he is affectionately known as Brother Spots. Brother Francis says Fingo is without a doubt the ugliest man alive, but he is in constant good humor. Normally assigned to the carpenter's shop, in "Fiat Homo" he is a temporary cook's helper serving as the supply carrier for the Lenten hermitages. During his visit to Brother Francis he confirms for him the reality of the fallout shelter and later verifies its existence for Father Cheroki.

**Brother Francis** *see* **Gerard, Francis**

**Brother Gimpus** an unseen character in *Saint Leibowitz and the Wild Horse Woman*. Brother Blacktooth remembers him arguing that a detachment from sexual passion was the essence of chastity and that detachment was possible without abstinence.

**Brother Hegan** an unseen character in the novella "The Last Canticle" and "Fiat Voluntas Tua" in *A Canticle for Leibowitz*. It is said that he once killed a sidewinder (a desert rattlesnake) in the abbey's courtyard.

**Brother Horner** a gentle elderly monk who is the master of the copyroom when Brother Francis first becomes an apprentice copyist in *A Canticle for Leibowitz* ("Fiat Homo"). He tells Brother Francis that he may work on his own project when his assigned work is fulfilled. He is the first to approve of Francis's work on the Leibowitz blueprint.

Horner is a term meaning one who works in horn. Miller may have been making an allusion to the early use of horn to cover the texts of valuable manuscripts. The hornbook is a one page primer covered with a layer of transparent horn used to teach children the alphabet or Lord's Prayer.

**Brother James** the name is the Greek form of Jacob meaning *follower*. Two of Jesus's twelve disciples were named James.

1. An unseen character in the novella "Dark Benediction." He is one of the hypers of the Galveston colony. He is said to have a nice tenor but sings his Latin with a western drawl.

2. A silent character in the "Fiat Voluntas Tua" section of *A Canticle for Leibowitz*. He is a member of the Church's starship crew as it implements its *Quo peregrinator* plan.

**Brother Jeris** a monk who becomes an apprentice copyist at the same time as Brother Francis in "A Canticle for Leibowitz" and *A Canticle for Leibowitz* ("Fiat Homo"). He mocks Brother Francis for his supposed meeting with the pilgrim in the desert and teases him about the Leibowitz blueprint he is copying. He is later placed in charge of the copying of the perennials and, after Brother Horner's death, is appointed the master of the copyroom. When he assumes this position, he tells Brother Francis to put away his work on the illuminated copy of the Leibowitz blueprint and begin work on more serious projects. In the short story, he suggests a man's work is making sheepskin lampshades. Brother Jeris proposes building a printing press but Abbot Arkos will not allow it.

**Brother John** an unseen character in the novella "Dark Benediction." He is a member of the choir at St. Mary's in the hyper colony in Galveston. He is said to be a stickler for pronunciation.

**Brother Jonan** a minor character in *Saint Leibowitz and the Wild Horse Woman*. He is a mathematician. Early in the novel he calls the monks to matins. Later he appears at the Priory of Saint Leibowitz-in-the-Cottonwoods.

**Brother Joshua** a technician and monk in the Albertian Order in the novella "The Last Canticle" and *A Canticle for Leibowitz* ("Fiat Voluntas Tua"). In the novel, he is a former engineer. He is in his thirties and wears a short red beard. He is the first one at the abbey to detect evidence of a nuclear explosion in the air samples he collects. A former spaceman and member of the Close Space Assault Team, Joshua also has experience on the space shuttle and the moon station experiment. After his wife, Nancy, became ill and died, he went to the Benedictines but eventually joined the Albertians. He has been recruited for the *Quo peregrinator* plan (or Dismissal of Servants), and takes his vows just prior to leaving the Abbey of Saint Leibowitz to join the others recruited for the plan in New Rome. He is selected to be the abbot for the Visitationist Friars of the Order of Saint Leibowitz of Tycho and the leader of the Church's space contingent.

The name is derived from the Hebrew meaning, "the Lord is my salvation."

**Brother Kornhoer** the occupant of the abbey's Chair of Natural Science in the novella "And the Light Is Risen." He is building an electrical generator and arc lamp in the abbey's basement. He suggests temporarily hanging the lamp in place of a crucifix so Don Thaddeo can do his work. Don Thaddeo tells him he has a remarkable mechanical gift that is being wasted in the abbey.

In *A Canticle for Leibowitz* ("Fiat Lux"), Kornhoer maintains a correspondence with Thon Taddeo regarding the Memorabilia at the abbey prior to the scientist's visit. He has based the generator on the information implicit in the writings from the time of Leibowitz and the current work of Thon Taddeo, giving practical application to the Thon's theories.

Thon Taddeo invites Kornhoer to come to the collegium in Texark on a scholarship as part of an exchange program with another thon coming to study at the abbey. Kornhoer is hesitant; he explains that religion is his vocation, the experimental work he does is merely play.

Brother Kornhoer's optimism and belief in progress is countered by Brother Armbruster's pessimism and fear that the work is simply leading them more quickly to perdition.

David N. Samuelson believes their conflict is indicative of the story of Cain and Abel (Genesis 4:1–16). Kornhoer (hoer of corn) suggests a farmer, while Armbruster's name means "crossbow," connoting a hunter. An ear of corn is also a positive symbol, indicative of germination, growth, fruition, and sustenance. Brother Kornhoer's creations of the generator and arc light are the realizations of a practicable potential.

In *Saint Leibowitz and the Wild Horse Woman*, the date the generator is operational is given as A.D. 3175. Within the later book, however, it is now a "rusting hulk."

**Brother Lafter** *see* **Brother Lufter**

**Brother Levion** the part-time assistant to the surgeon and Keeper of Memorabilia from certain ancient healing arts at the Abbey of Saint Leibowitz in *Saint Leibowitz and the Wild Horse Woman*. He is appointed Brother Reconciliator for Brother Blacktooth after Torrildo's attempted seduction of Blacktooth is exposed by Brother Obohl. Brother Levion is to meet weekly with Blacktooth in an attempt to help him reconcile his calling. He eventually becomes a priest.

**Brother Lufter** an unseen character in *A Canticle for Leibowitz* ("Fiat Voluntas Tua"). He works in the abbey's workshop. In the novella "The Last Canticle," he is called Brother Lafter.

**Brother Majek** an unseen character in the novella "And the Light Is Risen" and *A Canticle for Leibowitz* ("Fiat Lux"). He has some interest in mathematics and/or science.

Brother Kornhoer makes reference to the library floor's concavity as being in the shape of what Brother Majek refers to as a normal distribution curve.

**Brother Matthew** he is asked to get a yacht ready by Father Mendelhaus for Paul's use after Paul brings Willie to the hyper colony in Galveston in the novella "Dark Benediction."

**Brother Mulestar** an unseen character in *Saint Leibowitz and the Wild Horse Woman* who dies at the Abbey of Saint Leibowitz.

**Brother Noyen** an unseen character in the short story "A Canticle for Leibowitz" and *A Canticle for Leibowitz* ("Fiat Homo"). His unexplained miracle of the hangman's noose is one of the examples of the outrageous attributions of miracles by Leibowitz offered during the canonization process.

**Brother Obohl** in *Saint Leibowitz and the Wild Horse Woman* he is the senior librarian. He discovers Torrildo and Brother Blacktooth as Torrildo begins an amorous embrace of his surprised friend. Brother Obohl mistakes Blacktooth for Brother Elwen who has been meeting Torrildo with regularity in the abbey's basement. Brother Obohl is struck by Torrildo as he makes his escape and is tended to by Blacktooth. His myopia is later healed by Sister Clare.

**Brother Patrick** Father Zerchi's secretary in the novella "The Last Canticle" and *A Canticle for Leibowitz* ("Fiat Voluntas Tua").

**Brother Reader** the monk who reads the account of the Flame Deluge to Thon Taddeo during his visit to the abbey in *A Canticle for Leibowitz* ("Fiat Lux").

**Brother Reconciliator** *see* **Brother Levion**

**Brother Samuel** a silent character who is part of the Church's starship crew in *A Canticle for Leibowitz* ("Fiat Voluntas Tua"). In the Old Testament Samuel is the last judge and first prophet of Israel. He advised the people of the dangers of monarchies, but yielded to popular pressure and anointed Saul as Israel's first king. He later anointed David to be king in Saul's place. The name is from the Hebrew for "his name is God." See also **Samuel**

**Brother Sarl** from *A Canticle for Leibowitz* ("Fiat Homo"), a copyist at the Abbey of Saint Leibowitz. He is in his eighties and nearly blind, but he continues to apply the mathematical formula he originated to discover missing words from damaged texts. He has finished four pages in forty years. He collapses after finishing his fifth page of restoration and dies only hours later.

**Brother Smirnov** an unseen character in the short story "A Canticle for Leibowitz" and *A Canticle for Leibowitz* ("Fiat Homo"). He claimed to be miraculously cured of the gout after handling a probable relic of the Blessed Leibowitz.

**Brother Spots** the nickname of Brother Fingo. *see* **Brother Fingo**

**Brother Thomas** a minor character in the novella "Dark Benediction." A hyper, he is one of the first to sense Paul's presence at St. Mary's, the hospital in Galveston. He has developed new sensory pores on his fingers because of the neuroderm.

**Brother Tudlen** an elderly monk and minor character in *Saint Leibowitz and the Wild Horse Woman*. He spent many years at sea as a naval architect, astronomer, and navigator. While in Tampa Bay, he built a schooner that is the property of the Order of Saint Leibowitz. At the Priory of Saint Leibowitz-in-the-Cottonwoods he is grinding a telescope mirror.

**Brother Visclair** tends to Don Thaddeo's (Thon Taddeo) horse upon his arrival at the abbey in the novella "And the Light Is Risen" and *A Canticle for Leibowitz* ("Fiat Lux").

**Brother Wren** *see* **Wren St. Mary.**

**Browka, Corporal** one of the two Laredan soldiers who accompany Sister Clare to the Leibowitz Abbey in *Saint Leibowitz and the Wild Horse Woman*. He offers her a drink from his jug of hooch.

**Brownpony, Elia** Deacon ("Half-Breed") Brownpony and later Cardinal ("Red Deacon") Brownpony in *Saint Leibowitz and the Wild Horse Woman*. He eventually becomes Pope Amen II.

One of the central characters of the novel, Brownpony's mother, a Nomad, was raped by Texark cavalryman. She abandoned the baby that resulted from her assault to the Sisters of the Church. Brownpony later encounters an unnamed woman who may be his mother. She is from a small family of royal blood who never married and is now blind from cataracts. When he goes to meet her, she spits on his cassock and later tries to stab him while he sleeps.

At one time married, his wife, Seruna, is believed dead. Brownpony loved her in his own way but knows she was unhappy in the marriage. They had one son who is in Saint Maisie's Seminary in New Rome.

Brownpony is a skilled negotiator and political strategist and serves as the Secretary for Extraordinary Ecclesiastical Concerns, which is secretly working to arm the Nomads and gennies with guns. Although Deacon of Saint Maisie's, Brownpony is a lawyer and a diplomat rather than a priest until Pope Amen I ordains him and consecrates him as Bishop of Palermo. Amen then appoints him the Vicar Apostolic to the Three Hordes, the spiritual leader of the Christians on the Plains.

He works to form alliances between the church

and the Three Hordes in an attempt to build a coalition against Filpeo Harq and the Texark forces. His goal is the destruction of the Hannegan Empire and the restoration of the legitimate papacy in New Rome. Before he is accepted by the Nomads as the Christian high shaman, Brownpony must undergo the ordeal of courting the Wild Horse Woman in her place of fire, a site of a nuclear explosion. He sees the Buzzard of Battle (or the War Buzzard) during his ordeal but is also exposed to radiation poisoning.

Sent to Hannegan City to deliver a message from Pope Amen to Filpeo Harq, Brownpony is seized and imprisoned. Amen announces his resignation as pope, and Filpeo releases Brownpony. He is given a suspended sentence of death and declared a *persona non grate* in the city.

Brownpony is eventually elected the new pope and takes the name Amen II. Among his first actions as pope are the excommunication of Filpeo Harq and Archbishop Benefez. He declares Filpeo disposed from his office, and places the church in Hannegan City under interdict. He calls for a crusade against the Hannegan Empire to restore the legitimate Church in New Rome.

As he proceeds to build his alliances with the Nomads and gennies and to plan a military assault upon New Rome, Brownpony continues to suffer the effects of radiation poisoning.

The pope's armies meet little resistance on their way toward New Rome, but Brownpony's goals are different from those of his Nomad allies. While the pope wants to simply take New Rome and restore the legitimate papacy to the old seat of the Church, the Nomads seek to destroy and burn the city and also attack Hannegan City. They decide to ignore the pope and divide their forces to attack both cities.

The Nomads set fire to New Rome, but the armies of Filpeo Harq overrun their weakened forces. His army in defeat and disarray, Brownpony goes to the ruins of St. Peter's in New Rome. From the throne of St. Peter's he tells his old friend and secretary Brother Blacktooth to flee for his life and live the life of a hermit. Brownpony asks that he be left for the Buzzard of Battle, and in an act of assisted suicide, his faithful servant Wooshin beheads him.

Elia is a variant form of Elijah, an Anglicized form of the Herbrew Eliyahu, meaning "the Lord is my God."

**Bryant, Edward, Jr.** (August 27, 1945–) American science-fiction and horror writer who also works as a screenwriter. He is especially well known for his short stories for which he has received two Nebula Awards. He has written a novel with Harlan Ellison, *Phoenix Without Ashes*. His "Jody After the War" appears in *Beyond Armageddon*.

**Buldyrk, Emmery** Cardinal and Abbess of N'Ork from the far northeast who attends the conclave in *Saint Leibowitz and the Wild Horse Woman*.

**Burnarr-Origé mathematics** a postulation that the velocity of light is the parameter of five-space. It is the basis of the interstellar-drive in the novella "The Song of Vorhu."

**Burnes** a minor character in the short story "Wolf Pack." He is the radio operator on Mark Kessel's B-25 bomber.

**Burregun** another name for the War Buzzard deity of the Nomads in *Saint Leibowitz and the Wild Horse Woman*.

**Butsa** a holy man among Wooshin's people in *Saint Leibowitz and the Wild Horse Woman*. Wooshin claims the holy man stood erect at birth, pointed upward with one hand and downward with the other, and said: "Sky above, ground below, and I alone am the honored guest."

**Buzzard of Battle** an alternate name for the War Buzzard deity of the Nomads in *Saint Leibowitz and the Wild Horse Woman*.

**"By the Waters of Babylon"** written by Stephen Vincent Benét and first published in 1937, this is an early example of a post-apocalyptic story; it is included in *Beyond Armageddon*.

**C-33** an unmanned rocket in the short story "A Family Matter." The C-33 is a M-3 express ship with Class XII neuro-cybernetic controls. It is capable of thinking and flying itself. It possesses a consciousness because of its "flesh-organ," a human brain that allows the ship to not only think but also to feel.

**Caelum et terram creavit** *see* "In principio Deus"

**Caesar** an honorific title derived from Julius Caesar and used by subsequent rulers of the Roman Empire, including Augustus, its first emperor. Its use is often associated with a powerful or autocratic ruler.

1. In *A Canticle for Leibowitz* ("Fiat Lux"), Benjamin names Caesar among a group of despots with whom he hopes Thon Taddeo will remain unassociated.

2. A reference to "your Caesars" appears in the novella "The Last Canticle" and the "Fiat Voluntas Tua" section of *A Canticle for Leibowitz*.

3. In "Fiat Voluntas Tua," Dom Zerchi tells Brother Joshua: "We shouted it loudly enough — God's to be obeyed by nations as by men. Caesar's to be God's policeman, not His plenipotentiary successor, not His heir." He later says to Dr. Cors "Render unto Caesar to *that* extent, since the law demands it of you." These two statements refer to Mark 12:17 (KJV). When asked the question, "Is it lawful to give tribute to Caesar, or not?" Jesus replies, "Render to Caesar the things that are Caesar's, and to God the things that are God's." See also **Render unto Caesar**

**Caid** a minor unseen character in the short story "Death of a Spaceman" (later entitled "Memento Homo"). He is a former crew member with Old Donegal on the lunar shuttles. They would smuggle fifths of whiskey on board the shuttles.

**Cain** the first son of Adam and Eve (Genesis 4: 1 KJV). Cain commits the first murder, killing his brother Abel in jealousy (Genesis 4: 8). He is cursed by God and condemned to be a wanderer. He is mentioned in the novella "The Last Canticle," *A Canticle for Leibowitz* ("Fiat Voluntas Tua"), and *Saint Leibowitz and the Wild Horse Woman*.

**Calendar of Saints** a method of organizing the liturgical year by associating each day with a specific saint. When he is canonized, Isaac Leibowitz is enrolled in the Calendar by the College of Cardinals in the short story "A Canticle for Leibowitz" and *A Canticle for Leibowitz* ("Fiat Homo").

**Cameralis gestor** Latin: "One who carries out the chamber's business," a chamber official. In *A Canticle for Leibowitz* ("Fiat Homo"), a somberly dressed official greets Brother Francis and the other pilgrims who are to have an audience with the pope.

**Canonical hours** divisions or daily offices of devotion in the Catholic Church that comprise the Divine Office: martins with lauds, prime, terce, sext, none, vespers, and compline.

**"A Canticle for Leibowitz"** short story: *The Magazine of Fantasy and Science Fiction*, 8 (April 1955), 93–111. Reprinted in *The Magazine of Fantasy and Science Fiction*, 30th Anniversary issue, 57 (October 1979), 98–116.

Brother Francis Gerard, a young novitiate in the Albertian Order of Leibowitz, is in the midst of his Lenten fast in the desert hoping for the inspiration of a calling to Holy Orders. As he is preparing his shelter for the night an old pilgrim appears and points out a particular rock he might use in his construction. The pilgrim, clothed only in a burlap loincloth and a basket hat, continues on his way. When Brother Francis lifts up the rock, he discovers a rusted metal box. Within it are some old tools and several documents. One is a blueprint dated 1956 and bearing the name of Leibowitz, the founder of the order six centuries ago. Leibowitz lived during the Age of Simplification after the ravages of the Deluge of Flame. The remnants of humanity, furious at the politicians and men of learning for the destruction they had wrought, killed as many as they could find and destroyed all the records that might contain information that could lead to more paths of destruction. The Church became a sanctuary for many scientists and learned men. Leibowitz, a scientist, fled to the Cistercians and became a priest. He eventually founded his monastic order dedicated to the preservation of knowledge, secular and sacred. The duty of the brothers of the order was to memorize such books and papers as could be smuggled to them from all parts of the world. Leibowitz was eventually identified as a former scientist and was martyred by hanging. He is currently being considered for canonization. Brother Francis believes the pilgrim, who has mysteriously disappeared on the horizon, may be an angel of God, or the Blessed Leibowitz himself.

When his fast is completed, Brother Francis staggers back to the abbey with his discovery. As he recovers from his ordeal, rumors circulate within the abbey of what Francis has found and his belief regarding the old pilgrim. The abbot, Father Juan, is wary of another outrageous attribution of a miracle to serve the cause of canonization. He asks Brother Francis to deny his story about an angel revealing the location of the box to him, but Francis says he cannot deny what he has seen. The abbot refuses to allow Brother Francis to take his solemn vows, but the documents he found are sent to the seminary for study. The following year when Francis again returns from his Lenten fast, the abbot asks him if he is now prepared to renounce his story. Brother Francis says he cannot, and the abbot again postpones his taking orders. Brother Francis spends seven years as a novitiate. When word finally arrives that the documents are authentic as to date of origin and are possibly true relics of Leibowitz, the abbot allows him to take his vows.

Brother Francis is assigned to the copy room and apprenticed to an aging monk, Brother Horner. He is allowed five hours a week to devote to his own project, and Brother Francis chooses to illuminate a copy of the Leibowitz blueprint he found. He wants to glorify the document and make it pleasing to the eye as well as to the intellect. Brother Jeris, another young monk in the copy room, frequently teases him about his work; he is skeptical about Brother Francis's miraculous encounter in the desert. When Brother Horner falls ill and eventually dies, Jeris is appointed master of the copy room. He orders Brother Francis to put away children's things and begin a man's work. His work on the illuminated blueprint is stopped, and he begins producing sheepskin lampshades.

The next summer the abbey is visited by Monsignor di Simone and several clerks from New Vatican. They have come as part of the canonization proceedings to investigate such evidence as can be produced regarding the case for Leibowitz's sainthood, including his alleged apparition before Brother Francis. During his stay, the monsignor asks to see Brother Francis's illuminated copy of the blueprint. Taken back by its beauty, he tells Francis to finish it.

Years pass and word finally arrives that the canonization of Leibowitz is complete. The College of Cardinals will convene and Leibowitz will be enrolled in the Calendar of Saints. The pope commands the presence of Brother Francis at the canonization of Leibowitz. The monk brings with him the finished copy of his illuminated blueprint that he has worked on for 15 years. The trip to New Vatican takes at least three months. After traveling for more than two months, Brother Francis is met by a robber. The thief mocks the clergyman and takes the blueprint and tears it in two. Brother Francis begs him not to take it or destroy it. He wrestles the robber for it and then kisses his boot. But when the robber asks him why he worked on such a thing for 15 years, Brother Francis cannot answer him. The robber throws the pieces of the blueprint to the ground.

At New Vatican, Pope Leo XXI proclaims Isaac Edward Leibowitz a saint. As the procession exits, the Pope stops to speak with Brother Francis and asks to see his illuminated blueprint. His Holiness tells the monk that this little bit of learning will live again and they will guard it until that day. When Brother Francis makes his journey back to his abbey, he stops at the spot where he met the robber. He thinks he might wait for the robber to reappear for now he has the answer to his question.

This story is the basis for "Fiat Homo," the first section of the novel *A Canticle for Leibowitz.*

***A Canticle for Leibowitz*** Philadelphia: J. B. Lippincott Company, 1960 ((c)1959). The only novel published by Miller during his lifetime, it remains an acknowledged classic. Its three-part structure is based on the previously published short story "A Canticle for Leibowitz" and the two novellas "And the Light Is Risen" and "The Last Canticle."

It has remained continuously in print since its initial publication.

The work received the 1961 Hugo Award as the best science fiction novel of the year. It was a selection of the Catholic Digest Book Club (1960) and the Science Fiction Book Club (1961).

Two "one-sentence digests" by Miller explaining the meaning of the book are quoted in *Library Journal* (June 1, 1958): "*Canticle* attempts to assert the effects of original guilt on Man and his history, and the inevitable frustration of any attempt to reconquer a lost Eden by materialistic means." and "Man is a divinely inspired patsy who stamples [sic] through history taking pratfall after cosmic pratfall because he tied his own shoelaces together in Eden, can't get them untied, but refuses to walk barefoot."

Part I, "Fiat Homo": It is approximately six centuries after the world destroyed itself in the Flame Deluge in the latter half of the Twentieth Century. Brother Francis Gerard of Utah, a simple, devout, seventeen year old novice in the Albertian Order of Leibowitz (AOL), is on a Lenten vocational vigil in the southwest desert of what once was the United States. He is working on completing a rock shelter when he spies in the distance an old man walking toward him. Frightened and hoping to maintain his vow of silence, Brother Francis hides as the bearded pilgrim nears him. The man, dressed in a loincloth, sandals, and a basket hat, sits to eat a small meal. Brother Francis emerges from his hiding place and the two men are at first terrified of each other. The young novice is able to make clear his intentions when the old man offers to share his food with him. The pilgrim exhibits not only an understanding of Church rituals but Hebrew as well. As he leaves, he finds a perfectly shaped rock to complete Francis's shelter; he designates it with two marks — the Hebrew letters for L and Ts, the beginning and ending sounds for Leibowitz.

When Brother Francis ventures out to pick up the rock identified by the pilgrim, he discovers an opening to an underground room. It is a fallout shelter from the time of the Flame Deluge. Francis cautiously enters the room. He discovers a skeleton, eventually determined to be that of Leibowitz's wife, Emily, and a rusty box that he breaks open. Inside the box are some metal artifacts and old papers, including a blueprint bearing the name of Leibowitz. He has uncovered relics from the Beatus Leibowitz. Brother Francis sees this as a sign of his vocation; he is called to be a monk in the AOL.

Isaac Edward Leibowitz was a scientist at the time of the Flame Deluge. In the aftermath of the nuclear holocaust, scientists, politicians, and educators were held responsible for the world's destruction. They were hunted and killed by angry mobs known as Simpletons. The mobs' fear and hatred of those they blamed for the holocaust developed into a fear of knowledge and human culture itself. They sought to burn or otherwise destroy any remnants of learning or culture. During this age of Simplification the Church offered sanctuary to those being hunted. Leibowitz took refuge with the Cistercians. After years of searching for his missing wife, he finally took the vows of the order and became a priest. He founded a new religious order whose purpose was to preserve as much of the remaining recorded knowledge as possible. He named it after Albertus Magnus, the patron saint of scientists. Members of the order worked as bookleggers to preserve actual books in kegs buried in the desert or memorizers who committed to memory entire texts. These remnants of human knowledge became known as the Memorabilia, protected and maintained by the monks at their desert abbey. While acting as a booklegger, Leibowitz was seized by a mob and killed. Beatified, the Church is now considering him for sainthood.

Abbot Arkos of the Leibowitz Abbey fears that Brother Francis's discovery and the wild rumors that the old pilgrim he met was actually Leibowitz will jeopardize the canonization process. He insists that Brother Francis unequivocally renounce the possibility that the pilgrim was in any way supernatural. The novice is unable to do so with the complete conviction the abbot desires. Arkos denies Brother Francis the opportunity to take his vows, and the young novitiate spends the next seven years repeating his Lenten vocational vigil in the desert.

News finally arrives at the abbey from New Rome that the documents Brother Francis discovered in the fallout shelter have been authenticated. Arkos allows Francis to profess his vows and become a monk in the Albertian Order of Leibowitz. He is assigned as an apprentice copyist in the abbey's copyroom. Allowed to work on a personal project during his own time, Brother Francis begins work on an illuminated copy of the Leibowitz blueprint he discovered among the relics. He works on it for fifteen years.

Brother Francis is invited to New Rome for the ceremony canonizing Leibowitz. Arkos suggests that he bring his illuminated copy of the blueprint as a gift to the pope.

During the three month journey from the abbey to New Rome, Brother Francis is accosted by a robber and his two accomplices, all sports or genetic mutants. The robber is intrigued by the illuminated copy and mistakes the original blueprint for the one Brother Francis made. The monk pleads with the robber to allow him to keep the relic and the copy. The robber offers to wrestle him for them. Francis agrees but quickly loses. Told that he can buy them back for gold, the monk drops to the ground and kisses the robber's boot begging for the blueprint and copy. The robber throws the original blueprint at him in disgust but keeps the illuminated copy.

After the canonization ceremony in New Rome, Brother Francis meets with Pope Leo XXI and gives him the original blueprint. The pope thanks him for his work and the work of all the members of his order. He is sorry for the loss of the illuminated copy and bestows on Brother Francis a small amount of gold he can use to try to buy back his work from the robber.

On his return trip to the abbey, Brother Francis reaches the spot where he was robbed. He sits and waits hoping to meet the robber again so he can buy back his work. While sitting there he sees an old man in the distance who looks vaguely familiar. As he sits watching and praying, the robber's two accomplices watch the monk from the rocks. When he turns toward them in mid pray, Brother Francis is shot and killed by an arrow between the eyes.

After the old man Brother Francis had seen in the distance reaches the spot where the buzzards are circling overhead, he discovers the partially eaten body of the monk. The old pilgrim buries his remains in a grave that he marks with a rock.

Part II, "Fiat Lux": The year is 3174, about six hundred years since the death of Brother Francis, and mankind is emerging from the Dark Ages onto the cusp of a Renaissance. Scholars in the collegium in Texark are making scientific rediscoveries and postulating theories regarding the natural world. At the forefront of these scholars is Thon Taddeo Pfardentrott. He has developed an interest in studying the Memorabilia maintained at the southwest desert abbey of the Albertian Order of Leibowitz, and has requested that the materials be sent to him in Texark

Thon Taddeo is the cousin of Hannegan II, the despotic ruler of Texarkana. Hannegan has begun to implement a plan to draw the Laredan Nation into a war with the Plains Nomads in order for him to extend his empire. Marcus Apollo, the Vatican's nuncio to the Court of Hannegan, has warned the Church of what he suspects are Hannegan's intentions. Apollo has also been asked by Taddeo to convey his request for the Memorabilia to Dom Paulo, the abbot of the Leibowitz abbey, despite his assurance that such a request will be denied.

In Apollo's message to Dom Paulo, he warns the abbot not to trust the thon. Although he is brilliant, he is a thoroughly secularly scholar. He is interested only in a revival of learning and the advancement of knowledge and not the consequences of the application of that knowledge.

The abbot is an elderly and ill man with an increasing sense of foreboding concerning man's progress and the order's place in the new world of rediscovery and progress. But he is also a generous and honorable man, and notwithstanding his rejection of Thon Taddeo's request for the Memorabilia to be sent to Texark, he invites the thon to the abbey to study the texts there.

Dom Paulo visits his old friend Benjamin, the hermit living in the mountains a few miles from the abbey. Benjamin tells the abbot that he bears the burden of his people and has been waiting for 32 centuries for the return of the one who called him forth. Paulo shares with Benjamin his fears that the order's purpose and mission will be lost with the development of secular scholarship and technical progress. The hermit hopes that Thon Taddeo will be on the right side of man's advancement.

Thon Taddeo makes the trip from Texark to the abbey with a small contingent of Hannegan's military officers and under the protection of Hongan Os, the chief of the Nomad clans. In preparation for the thon's visit, Brother Kornhoer has been working on finishing an electrical dynamo and arc light. As Dom Paulo leads the thon to the abbey's basement library the electric light, which has replaced a crucifix hanging on the wall, is lit, startling the scientist who is awed by the monk's practical application of the thon's theories.

Thon Taddeo assumes his work studying the Memorabilia. He and Dom Paulo have several arguments regarding the relationship between science and faith, and the moral responsibility of the secular scholars. Neither one is able to persuade the other from his position. Nevertheless, the abbot asks the thon if he would address the monks one evening about the work that is being done by the scientists at the collegium in Texark. At the dinner Taddeo is mocked for his arrogance by the Poet-sirrah, who offers him his glass eye, a convenient instrument of a removable conscience. The Poet also reveals that Hannegan's officers have been making detailed drawings of the abbey. Paulo fears that there may be plans to attack the monastery or to utilize it as a fort if Hannegan decides to try to annex the Denver Empire. As the thon's presentation nears its conclusion, Benjamin enters the hall and confronts him but declares, "It's still not Him."

News reaches the abbey that Hannegan has declared war on Laredo and has gained control of all lands from the Red River to the Rio Grande. He has brutally executed Marcus Apollo for treason and espionage. In response, the Church has placed Texarkana under absolute interdict. Hannegan declares himself the only true ruler of the Church in Texarkana and declares the pope a heretic and the interdict of no consequence. All clergy in Texarkana will now need to be licensed by Hannegan.

Dom Paulo shares the communiqué with Thon Taddeo who is shortly to leave the abbey. The thon states that he cannot oppose the person who makes his work possible. He believes that the abbot wants science saved until man is ready for it. For Taddeo, science and learning must be their own ends, and the secular scholar must prevail over the Albertian order's mission. Despite their disagreement, the abbot tells Taddeo that all scholars will be welcome to study the Memorabilia at the abbey. The thon gives the drawings of the abbey made by Hannegan's men to the abbot before he leaves.

The Poet-sirrah, who had abruptly left the abbey after his derision of the thon, is wandering in the country when he spies a cavalry troop pursuing a group of refugees. At first, he hides but then impulsively attacks the cavalry officer and stabs him. The other soldiers, in turn, shoot him in the stomach, and both he and the officer are left to die. As the officer pleads for help, the poet crawls to him and stabs him in the neck. The poet lies back, and buzzards circle in the sky above.

Part III, "Fiat Voluntas Tua": By 3781, civilization has once again advanced to a space age. Sanly Bowitts is a prospering metropolis and a modern glass and steel Abbey of Saint Leibowitz now stands across a super highway from the original abbey. But atop the new abbey Brother Joshua reads instruments indicating an above normal radiation count and within the abbey Abbot Dom Zerchi receives news confirming Lucifer Is Fallen: a nuclear explosion has occurred in Asia at Itu Wan. New Rome notifies the abbot that the Church's plan to perpetuate itself in space, *Quo peregrinator*, has been activated.

*Quo peregrinator* is an emergency plan that will send a starship to the Centaurus colony with a crew of Albertian monks. They will carry with them the Memorabilia, six sisters, 20 children from the Saint Joseph School, two scientists, and three bishops. In case of nuclear holocaust on Earth, they will establish an independent "daughter house" of the Albertian Order of Leibowitz, preserve the memory of Earth, and continue the Church. Dom Zerchi asks Brother Joshua, a former engineer and space traveler, if he is ready to go and be their shepherd.

As Brother Joshua struggles with the question of his vocation, Asia retaliates against the Atlantic Confederacy for the Itu Wan disaster by destroying the city of Texarkana in a nuclear attack. Green Star Relief Stations are established to evaluate victims of radiation poisoning. Those cases deemed hopeless are allowed to be euthanized at Mercy Camps. Dom Zerchi is violently opposed to state sanctioned euthanasia, but he allows Dr. Cors to locate two mobile Relief Station units at the abbey as long as he does not advise hopeless cases to be euthanized. A Mercy Camp is established down the highway from the abbey.

Brother Joshua tells Dom Zerchi that he is ready to accept the burden and honor of leading the Church into space. He and the monks comprising the crew are secretly flown to New Rome to be prepared to launch the starship.

When Dom Zerchi discovers that a Mercy Camp has been set-up in close proximity to the abbey, he sends five novices to picket the camp with signs that read Abandon Every Hope Ye Who Enter Here. He tries to intervene when a young mother with a baby considers going to the camp, telling her that euthanasia is only an expedient mercy. As he creates a scene at the gates of the camp, two police officers intervene on behalf of the young woman. Zerchi is restrained and the woman enters the camp. Dr. Cors comes forward and the abbot punches him in the face.

A ten-day cease-fire between Asia and the Atlantic Confederacy ends without an agreement between the two sides. Dom Zerchi agrees to hear the confession of Mrs. Grales, a two-headed tomato seller. Her second head, Rachel, is small and cherubic. It remains youthful while Mrs. Grales's head has aged. Seemingly in a vegetative state, Rachel neither sees nor speaks. As Zerchi grants Mrs. Grales absolution, a bright light pervades the church. The abbot yells to her to run as the church fills with smoke. The building collapses in the aftershock of a nuclear explosion, and Dom Zerchi lies trapped beneath the rubble. He yells out for help and his words are echoed by a strange voice.

As the abbot lies beneath the debris of the church unable to move the lower half of his body, he begins to pray. He realizes that he needs to suffer and to endure as he has asked the young mother with radiation sickness to suffer, as Christ has suffered and endured. He must accept for himself what he would impose on others. He understands that the only evil in the world is what man introduces. He hears the unfamiliar voice again as he begins to lose consciousness.

When he awakens he sees three vultures sitting watching him. He calls for help, and Mrs. Grales wanders into sight. The old woman's head is now sleeping soundly, but Rachel is alive. She has cool green eyes and an innocent smile. Her body is youthful rather than that of an old woman. She echoes his words in a quiet voice. Zerchi attempts to baptize her conditionally, but she turns her head away and wipes her forehead. She picks up the ciborium and Zerchi shouts to stop her but he faints.

As he awakens, Rachel kneels before him offering him a single Host. He accepts Communion from her realizing that she did not need the first sacrament he offered her because she is free from sin. She touches his forehead, says "Live," and is gone. The abbot recognized a primal innocence in her eyes. He lays his head down and waits.

In New Rome, the last monk prepares to enter the starship. He takes off his sandals and murmurs, "Sic transit mundus" as the rockets and bombs explode.

Ash falls into the ocean and the shark swims hungrily into the deepest waters.

See also "**A Canticle for Leibowitz**" (short story), "**And the Light Is Risen,**" and "**The Last Canticle**"

***A Canticle for Leibowitz*** Chicago: Dramatic Publishing, Company, 1967. A reasonably faithful dramatic adaptation of the novel in three acts by Clark Fuller. Miller received five hundred dollars in advance for the rights. He had little confidence that the novel could be properly dramatized, writing to Chad Oliver that it would probably be "a one-act job with Br Francis waiting for Godot or something equally thin-sliced" (6/24/1966). He tried but failed to add a clause in the contract requiring that he be consulted regarding the adaptation.

***A Canticle for Leibowitz*** a fifteen-part radio drama adapted from the novel by John Reeves and produced and distributed by WHA Radio and Wisconsin Public Radio, in association with National Public Radio (NPR). The program originally aired in 30-minute weekly episodes starting in October 1981. The adaptation was produced and directed by Karl Schmidt. Carol Cowan is the principal narrator. The cast includes James Freeman, Rogers Keene, Jim Fleming, Stuart Brooks, Frederick Coffin, Herbert Hartig, Barton Heyman, Russell Horton, Merwin Goldsmith, Barbara Rubenstein, Marcia Lewis, Patricia Bright, and the Edgewood College Chant Group.

The program was available from WHA Radio and NPR on cassettes and compact discs.

***A Canticle for Leibowitz*** Woodstock, NY: Dramatic Publishing Co., 1986. A play adapted from the novel by Richard Felnagle. According to a note accompanying the record on WorldCat, the play begins about 300 years after the conclusion of the novel.

***A Canticle for Leibowitz*** a conceptual soundtrack recording based on the novel composed by John Kannenberg and released in 2005 by Nishi as an MP3. The work was originally commissioned by Sine Fiction as part of a series of electronic music "possible soundtracks" to accompany well-known science fiction novels. The work is comprised of 18 individual pieces and was composed and recorded from February through August of 2004. Its running time is 1:07:39.

**"A Canticle for the Marsmen"** a play by Chaubrec in the novella "The Darfsteller." Ryan Thornier once starred in the lead role of Adolfo.

**Captain Chronos** the title character in Kenny Westmore's favorite television show, "Captain Chronos and the Guardsmen of Time" in the short story "The Will." The character is played by the actor Abe Sanders.

**"Captain Chronos and the Guardsmen of Time"** a television show in the short story "The Will." It is the favorite show of Kenny Westmore, a fourteen year old boy dying of leukemia. Miller may have been thinking of "Captain Video and His Video Rangers," a serial television program he wrote for in the early 1950s.

**"Captain Video and His Video Rangers"** a popular television program that aired on the DuMont Network from June 27, 1949, till April 1, 1955, as a five-times-a-week serial. It was the first science fiction based program on American television. A number of well-known science fiction writers worked on the program, including Damon Knight, C. M. Kornblath, and Jack Vance.

The DuMont Network dissolved in the spring of 1955, and the scripts and promotional copy for the program were destroyed. The archival kinescopes were later destroyed to save storage expenses and to recoup the silver content. There are very few, if any, extant records of the program.

Miller wrote two produced series of fifteen episodes each in 1952 and 1953 for *Captain Video and His Video Rangers*. His own records about the program and personal copies of the scripts were destroyed by water damage to his home from Hurricane Donna in 1960 and subsequent termite mutilation.

To the best of Miller's recollection, the first fifteen episode series aired in the winter of 1952. The second series was entitled "The Wonkle" and aired from April 27, 1953, through May 15, 1953. Miller described Wonkles as "little fuzzballs that reproduced at a frightening rate and ate anything" (ltr. 10/11/1990). His brief description is suggestive of Tribbles in the later well-known *Star Trek* episode "The Trouble with Tribbles" written by David Gerrold which aired in December 1967.

**Cardinal Bretke** in the novella "The Last Canticle," the cardinal who will be evacuated from Earth as part of the Dismissal of Servants plan and become the new Holy See.

**Cardinal Cannibal** the name Father Ombroz says he will be called in Texark after Pope Amen II consecrates him as the Archbishop of Canterbury and makes him the Vicar Apostolic to the Nomads in *Saint Leibowitz and the Wild Horse Woman*.

**Cardinal Jarad** *see* **Kendemin, Jarad.**

**Cardinal ("Red Deacon") Brownpony** *see* **Brownpony, Elia.**

**Cardinal Ri** the Archbishop of Hong in *Saint Leibowitz and the Wild Horse Woman*. He crosses the Pacific to attend the conclave that elects Pope Amen, but he dies in his cot before the election. He is very rich and has three wives. He leaves his wives to the pope, and his servants to Cardinal Brownpony.

**Carnera, Primo** (October 26, 1906–June 29, 1967) Italian boxer who became the heavyweight champion by defeating Jack Sharkey in June 1933. He lost the title to Max Baer. He was nicknamed The Ambling Alp because of his size. Mark Kessel thinks of pictures of Carnera hanging in the homes he is destroying with his bombs in the short story "Wolf Pack."

**Carpios Robbery** the nom de guerre of Admiral e'Fondolai of *Saint Leibowitz and the Wild Horse Woman* during his pirate days. As a pirate, he was the second man since antiquity to circumnavigate the globe. The admiral's nickname of Carpy is derived from his pirate name. See also **e'Fondolai, Admiral**

**Carpy** the nickname of Admiral e'Fondolai in *Saint Leibowitz and the Wild Horse Woman*. It is a derivation of his pirate nom de guerre Carpios Robbery. He dislikes the name and does not like it being used, especially in front of Filpeo Harq. See also **e'Fondolai, Admiral**

**Carthage** an influential city-state in North Africa, near present-day Tunis, founded by the Phoenicians in 814 B.C. It was destroyed by Rome in the third Punic War. Eventually rebuilt by the Romans, it was again destroyed by Arabs in the seventh century. It is among the civilizations cited by Father Zerchi in the novella "The Last Canticle" and *A Canticle for Leibowitz* ("Fiat Voluntas Tua") as evidence of the unending sequence of mankind's rise and fall.

**Casu belli nunc remote**  Latin: "The Cause of War is Now Removed." Issued by Pope Paul in 3756, it orders the abbot of the Abbey of Saint Leibowitz to hold the plan *Quo peregrinatur* in abeyance until the pope orders otherwise. It is referred to in *A Canticle for Leibowitz* ("Fiat Voluntas Tua"). See also **Quo peregrinatur**

**Catharism**  various dualistic heretical sects of the late Middle Ages who believed that the material world was created by an evil principle separate from God which thereby required an asceticism to liberate the good from the body. They generally rejected the sacraments and viewed the Old and New Testaments allegorically. In *A Canticle for Leibowitz* ("Fiat Homo"), Brother Francis briefly comments on an inquisition against Catharism taking place in the Pacific Coast region.

**Cathedral of Holy Michael, the Angel of Battle**  the major basilica in Hannegan City in *Saint Leibowitz and the Wild Horse Woman*. Its Cardinal Archbishop is Urion Benefez, the Archbishop of Texark. Michael, the Angel of Battle refers to the archangel Michael. See also **Saint Michael**

**Cathedral of Saint John-in-Exile**  the seat of the Holy See in Valana. It was built on soil imported from New Rome. The area around the cathedral is considered New Rome territory. It is the site of the conclaves in *Saint Leibowitz and the Wild Horse Woman*.

**Cathy**  Scott MacDonney's daughter in the novella "Izzard and the Membrane." She dies in an atomic bomb attack on Cleveland. Izzard restores her awareness pattern, and she rejoins her father in another world on the other side of the membrane.

**Cave canem**  Latin: "Beware the dog." A motto found on the doors or doorsteps of ancient Roman houses with watchdogs. In *A Canticle for Leibowitz* ("Fiat Lux"), Dom Paulo considers that another "grim dog" will one day sit in his chair as abbot of the Leibowitz abbey and then thinks, "*Cave canem*."

**Celestin[e] V**  in *Saint Leibowitz and the Wild Horse Woman*, a reference is made to "saint Petrus Murro Pope Celestin V" dragged from his hermit's cave to be pope. Following the death of Pope Nicholas IV (April 4, 1292), the papacy remained vacant for twenty-seven months. It was revealed that a devout hermit prophesized divine retribution if the Church was left without a head for any longer. The hermit was Pietro del Morrone, an eighty-five year old monastic leader and ascetic, and he became the choice for the next pope. Although the elderly priest protested his election strenuously—thus the reference in the novel to "non accepto"—he was named Pope Celestine V on August 29, 1294.

**Centaurus colony**  an Earth colony in Alpha Centauri. It is one of two first magnitude stars in the Centaurus constellation, where the Holy See and the Church records will be evacuated in the event of a thermonuclear war on Earth as per the Church's Dismissal of Servants plan in the novella "The Last Canticle" and *Quo peregrinatur* in *A Canticle for Leibowitz* ("Fiat Voluntas Tua").

**Chacun à son gout**  French: "Every man to his taste." One of Madame d'Annecy's proclamations to Suds Brodanovitch concerning her business in the novella "The Lineman."

**Chair of Peter**  the Chair of Peter signifies the authoritative teaching and doctrinal power of the pope. In *A Canticle for Leibowitz* ("Fiat Voluntas Tua"), Dom Zerchi tells the monks participating in *Quo peregrinator* that they potentially carry the Chair of Peter with them. If life on Earth is destroyed, the Patrimony of Peter will then go to the cardinal who accompanies the colonists into space.

*The Chancellor*  the name of Barry Wilkes' interstellar spaceship in the novella "The Song of Vorhu."

*Chanticler* (also *Chanticleer* or *Chantecler*)  a four-act allegorical animal verse-drama by the French poet and dramatist Edmund Rostand first performed in 1910. In the novella "The Lineman," Relke observes that the overly made up Giselle looks like she is ready for a role in a girls school production of the play.

**Chaplin, Charles Spencer (Charlie)** (April 16, 1889–December 25, 1977)  a British born film actor, writer, producer, and director. Generally considered to be one of the seminal comedic actors in film, he created the iconic film character of the Tramp. Among his noted silent films are *The Kid* and *The Gold Rush*. His later sound films include *City Lights, Modern Times*, and *The Great Dictator*. In the novella "The Darfsteller," reference is made to "an ancient movie—one of the classics" in which Chaplin is strapped into a chair on a production line in the midst of mechanical tasks performed in a mechanical fashion. The film referred to is *Modern Times* (1936) where the Tramp struggles to survive in an industrialized society of mass production.

**Chapter**  a daily or periodic meeting of the religious members of a monastery. In *A Canticle for*

*Leibowitz* ("Fiat Lux") Dom Paulo says that he has had to rebuke Brother Armbruster publicly during Chapter.

**"Chariots of the Goddesses, or What?"** *New York Times Book Review*, 8 September 1985, 11. Miller provides an ambivalent review of John Fowles' novel *A Maggot*. He sees the work as an experimental novel whose hypothesis is that "readers will tolerate more teasing, and more indeterminacy as to plot and character, than is usually expected of them." For Miller, Fowles' characters seem made less of flesh than of myth, and too often symbols substitute for facts. He notes that the title and the novel have many meanings and that it is left to the reader to construct his own story from his own maggot.

See also **Fowles, John** and *A Maggot*

**Charlemagne** (c. 742–January 28, 814)   through a series of military campaigns over a thirty-year period, Charlemagne brought Western Europe under a centralized government and became its ruler. His empire comprised present-day France, Switzerland, Belgium, The Netherlands, and parts of Italy, Germany, Spain, and Austria. In 800, Pope Leo III crowned him Emperor. In the novella "The Last Canticle" and "Fiat Voluntas Tua" in *A Canticle for Leibowitz*, Charlemagne's empire is cited by Father Zerchi among other examples of the unending sequence of mankind's rise and fall.

**Charleman, Judge**   an unseen character in the novella "Conditionally Human." He has to issue the warrants to Sheriff Yates in order to pick-up possible deviant neutroids. Miller probably intends the pun on the name Charlemagne.

**Chaubrec**   the author of the play "A Canticle for the Marsman" in the novella "The Darfsteller."

**Che brutto!**   Italian: "How ugly (brutal)!" As Mark Kessel nears his bombing targets in the short story "Wolf Pack," he hears La admonishing him with these words.

**"Check and Checkmate"**   short story in *If, Worlds of Science Fiction*, 1 (January 1953), 4–24. In 2073 John Smith XVI, the new President of the Western Federation of Autonomous States, initiates contact with Ivan Ivanovitch the Ninth, the Peoplesfriend and Vicar of the Asian Proletarian League. After the last war, or "peace-effort," ended in stalemate and total isolation, there has been 40 years of non-communication, or the Big Silence, between the East and West. The Hell Wall, a globe encircling belt of booby-trapped land and ocean, separates the two powers. Smith hopes with his proposal to ascertain what the enemy has been doing during this time, particularly regarding scientific development and military advancement. He plans to utilize this knowledge to his political advantage.

In a series of televiewphone conferences, Smith suggests to Ivanovitch a reduction in military expenses by both sides in order to stabilize and increase their respective economies. During these conversations, however, Smith is dismayed by Ivanovitch's boasts of the East's ability to conquer the West and his knowledge of the West despite the Big Silence. Ivanovitch seems too much at ease, too smug and confident in his conversations with Smith. After Smith calls for a security-probe, an Asian spy system within the West is uncovered, but the suspected spies either vanish or commit suicide.

Certain that they have ended the East's infiltration and the source of Ivanovitch's confidence, Smith agrees to a requested face-to-face meeting between the two sides in Antarctica. The meeting, however, is a trap. Ivanovitch has not been simply infiltrating the West but actually replacing key personnel. The East has developed "thinking machines" for self-piloting weapons and, more importantly, as robots. The Ivanovitch meeting with Smith reveals he is a robot while the actual Eastern leader sits safely in Singapore.

Smith wearily acknowledges the endgame, but notes that "there is always a way out. Never a final move." He knows the senseless game will continue with its "eternal plotting and scheming," as he begins to plan his own response to the East's deception.

**Cheer Honnyugan**   Holy Madness' name in the Jackrabbit dialect. In Jackrabbit, it means Magic Madness. From *Saint Leibowitz and the Wild Horse Woman*.

**Chief Broken Wing**   the name Hogey Parker drunkenly refers to himself as on the bus in the short story "The Hoofer."

**Chihuahua**   *see* **State of Chihuahua**

**Chitara**   a stringed instrument played by Brother Blacktooth in *Saint Leibowitz and the Wild Horse Woman*. Pronounced "g'tara," it is sometimes also spelt that way.

**Christian High Shaman of the People**   the position of Cardinal Brownpony among the Nomads in *Saint Leibowitz and the Wild Horse Woman*.

**Christie eleison**   Greek: "Christ, have mercy." Part of the invocation *Kyrie eleison, Christie eleison* said in the Latin liturgy; the choir may also sing it.

1. It is part of the response to the versicle "Lucifer is Fallen" in "the last Canticle of the Brethren of the Order of Leibowitz" in *A Canticle for Leibowitz* ("Fiat Voluntas Tua").

2. In *Saint Leibowitz and the Wild Horse Woman*, Cardinal Brownpony recites it during his ordeal in the meldown.

**Christus** Latin: "Christ."

**Christus tecum** Latin: "Christ be with you." Together with "*et cum spirit tuo*" ["and with your spirit"] it is used in the Catholic Mass as a greeting between the priest and congregation. It is used in the novella "The Last Canticle." In *A Canticle for Leibowitz* ("Fiat Voluntas Tua") it appears as the abbreviated "*Chris' tecum.*"

**Chuntar Hadala** *see* **Hadala, Chuntar**

**Church Militant on Earth, the Church Suffering in Purgatory, and the Church Triumphant in Heaven** the traditional division of the Christian Church forming a Communion of Saints. The Church Militant is the Church on Earth, its members constantly struggling against sin and evil. The Church Suffering is comprised of the souls held in Purgatory, and the Church Triumphant are those in heaven. The Church Triumphant is celebrated November 1, All Saints Day, and the Church Suffering on November 2, All Souls Day. In *Saint Leibowitz and the Wild Horse Woman*, Brother Blacktooth tells Pope Amen II about a discussion he had with Amen I concerning the Church Triumphant. Amen I said there is no Church Triumphant in heaven because in the presence of God, "the Church is a discarded crutch."

**Churchspeak** one of several languages spoken at the Abbey of Saint Leibowitz in *Saint Leibowitz and the Wild Horse Woman*.

**Cistercians** a Roman Catholic order founded in 1098 by Saint Robert, abbot of Molesome at Citeaux. Known as the White Monks because of the color of their habits, the order was founded on a strict observance of the *Rule of Saint Benedict* and a return to manual labor, especially farming. The order was responsible for helping to implement improvements in agriculture.

Isaac Leibowitz joined the order during the Age of Simplification in the short story "A Canticle for Leibowitz." In *A Canticle for Leibowitz* ("Fiat Homo") Leibowitz first took refuge with the Cistercians in the years following the Deluge. He left them to search for his wife but when he became convinced of her death, he returned to the order and took his vows. He eventually became a priest. In the novel, Brother Joshua is also a member of the order.

**Clarke, Arthur C(harles)** (December 16, 1917–March 19, 2008) British born multi-award winning popular science and science fiction writer. He was one of the most influential and popular science fiction writers of the Twentieth Century. Among his many works are the novel and screenplay (with Stanley Kubrick) *2001: A Space Odyssey* (1968). His best known and most admired novels include *Childhood's End* (1953), *Rendezvous with Rama* (1973), and *Imperial Earth* (1976). He was knighted in 1998.

His short story "If I Forget Thee, Oh Earth..." is included in *Beyond Armageddon*.

**Clausewitz, Karl (or Carl) von** (June 1, 1780–November 16, 1831) Prussian general and military theorist who fought in the Napoleonic Wars. He is famous for his writing on military strategies, including his classic work, *On War* (*Vom Kriege*) published in 1832. His dictum, "War is an extension of politics," is quoted in the short story "The Little Creeps" by General Horrey. It is the realistic recognition that war is merely one aspect of pragmatic politics.

**Clavius** the site near where a Russian lunar survey crew is working in the novella "The Lineman."

**Clyde** a minor character in the novella "The Lineman." He is part of the investigating team looking into the death of Suds Brodanovitch.

**Coahuila** a state south of Laredo in the novella "And the Light Is Risen."

**"Cold Awakening"** short story in *Astounding Science Fiction*, 49 (August 1952), 46–82. Two hundred colonists are on their way to the Sigma Seven system. They will be able to make the 500-year flight thanks to suspendfreeze, a method of quick freezing and thawing a human body without destroying it. There are three emergency-technicians who will be thawed in order during the trip if trouble arises. Once they are thawed, they will not be able to be returned to suspendfreeze. Each emergency-technician, or fuse, has pledged not to disturb any of the sleepers if he is awakened, but he will also have complete control of the sleepers.

As the crew prepares to place the colonists in suspendfreeze, Doctor Fraylin, the inventor of suspendfreeze, conducts final interviews with the emergency-technicians: Lieutenant Eric Joley, Jessel, and William Crain. Joley will be the first one awakened in case of a problem. The others will only be awakened if he is dead or a second emergency occurs. The colonists grow increasingly restless about being placed in suspendfreeze and what might happen to them. Commander Roagan, the captain of the ship, fears there may be a mutiny aboard the ship. He orders Joley to thaw him too if Joley is awakened. The colonists exhibit a certain mistrust of Joley and the other two technicians.

A group of colonists taunt Angela Waters to introduce herself to Joley as his genetic recommendation if he makes it to Sigma Seven, even though she is spending time now with another colonist, Kenneth Thoren. Joley is taken back by her introduction but is attracted to her. She asks him why the colonists cannot be allowed to live as a community on the ship generation after generation until the ship reaches Sigma Seven rather than be placed in suspendfreeze. Angela tells him to awaken her if he is awakened, but he laughs and mockingly asks her if she would thaw out Thoren so they could start a little colony. She slaps him and leaves. He wonders if he hit upon a truth. Was she the bait for a colonist trap? He believes that her attitude suggests that there are things he does not know about the colonists, supporting Roagan's intuitive distrust of the group. Joley grows apprehensive about a possible colonist trap aboard the ship.

The day that the colonists are to begin to be placed in suspendfreeze, someone attempts to sabotage the machine. The crew is armed to maintain order among the colonists. Joley and Jessel suspect that Crain may be the one creating unrest by starting rumors. While they watch a large gathering of colonists with Crain standing among them, the light is knocked out and shots are fired, barely missing Joley but killing Jessel. Crain's gun was used in the shooting, and Roagan confines him to his quarters. Joley believes he can narrow down the possible killer to three or four suspects, all of whom can be sent back to Earth with the medics. By interviewing everyone as to where they were standing in the room and who was standing next to them, he implicates two men in the shooting: Lovewell and Herrick. Herrick is identified as the actual shooter, but he has already been placed in suspendfreeze by switching places and identities with another colonist. He hopes that being in suspendfreeze will allow him to avoid being implicated in the murder and sent back to Earth.

As the suspendfreeze continues, Joley goes to Angela's quarters. She teases him that the wrong man has been identified for Jessel's murder. She tells him that Herrick only stole Crain's gun, but he gave it to someone else who actually fired it. Joley is wary of Angela's hand beneath her pillow and believes she might be hiding a gun. When he tells her to show what she is hiding, she reveals a hypodermic needle. She is a morphine addict, as are many of the colonists. The reason for the attack on Joley and Jessel was to remove them so the colonists could remain awake aboard ship. Angela tells Joley that Thoren supplies her with the drug but that someone else gives it to him.

Joley goes to Thoren's quarters and takes pleasure in beating him until he reveals that he doesn't know the identity of the drug supplier. Packages are left for him in the dayroom along with messages that are the source of the rumors among the colonists. Thoren also tells Joley that Crain, too, is an addict. Crain was supposed to wake the colonists if he was given the chance. Joley believes that Commander Roagan is the only one capable of being behind the plot. Roagan would create his own "private little paradise" on the ship, "a madman's concept of heaven."

While trying to decide what his next move will be, Joley is informed by Roagan and Dr. Fraylin that he is to be moved to third in line as emergency-technician. He is not to be trusted because of his beating of Thoren. Crain will be sent back to Earth as an accessory in Jessel's murder, and Roagan will be the first emergency-technician. Joley returns to his compartment to find Crain waiting for him. He is in need of a fix. Joley tells him that he will help him avoid being sent to Earth if he will help him expose Roagan. They break into Jessel's room where his coffin is being kept. Joley drugs Crain and knocks him out, substituting Crain's body for Jessel's in the coffin and adding a note. He then launches Jessel's corpse into space. Joley asks Dr. Fraylin if he can check his locker before being placed in suspendfreeze. Fraylin lets him do so, and as he does he switches the thawing time controls between Roagan's locker and his own. The controls for unit one will now control the unit he is in.

Joley is placed in suspendfreeze but awakens after only a few hours. He wasn't frozen at all, only anaesthetized. He believes that this was Roagan's plan for himself; he goes to Roagan's locker and turns the thawer controls thinking he will kill him for his treachery and Jessel's murder. But Roagan's unit works as it should, and he awakens normally. Seeing Joley, Roagan believes that it has been him behind the plot. But Joley tells Roagan that he suspected him and switched the locker controls. Roagan, however, reveals that he switched the controls between lockers one and two the day before Joley switched one and three. They go to locker two to find Dr. Fraylin dead.

Fraylin had planned to kill both of them with

morphine. He was also Jessel's murderer. He was bitter that his invention of suspendfreeze had not brought him greater fame and wealth. Roagan suggests that they try to contact the tug taking the medics and Jessel's coffin back to Earth. Joley says that it should be close by. He put Crain in Jessel's coffin with the hope that the crew upon discovering him after he woke up would return to the ship to get Jessel's corpse. Roagan tells Joley he is going to have him placed in suspendfreeze for the duration of the trip. He will get three crew men from the space tug as new emergency-technicians. Joley grins and wanders back to Angela's locker. He disables the timing mechanism for her thawer, planning to be the only one who will be able to unfreeze her.

**College of Cardinals**   the body of cardinals within the Church who advise the pope and elect new popes. It is referred to in the short story "A Canticle for Leibowitz." The College of Cardinals is convened at the completion of the canonization process for Isaac Leibowitz to enroll him in the Calendar of Saints.

**Colonel Beth**   a chubby, elderly man in the short story "Blood Bank" who chairs the investigating body examining the destruction of the mercy ship by Space Commander Eli Roki. He insists that Roki be judged on the legality of his actions based on the Space Code, not on his moral judgment. When Roki is cleared of any legal responsibility, Colonel Beth willingly and immediately accepts his resignation. He offers Roki the means to go wherever he wants.

**"Command Performance"**   short story first appearing in *Galaxy Science Fiction*, 5 (November 1952), 140–160. Later entitled "Anyone Else Like Me?" This is one of Miller's most anthologized stories. It is included in *The View from the Stars; The Science Fiction Stories of Walter M. Miller, Jr.; The Best of Walter M. Miller, Jr.;* and *Conditionally Human and Other Stories* under the later title.

Lisa Waverly is a young, intelligent, good looking wife and mother of three children. Although she enjoys a quiet, full, and satisfied life, she has experienced uneasy stirrings her entire life, what she refers to as a "crawling of the mind." She has a sense that there is something she cannot quite identify in her life, some "unfed hunger." These stirrings have been particularly stronger the past few weeks, calling her to "come, share, satisfy, express it to the fullest."

While her husband, Frank, is on a business trip and her children are staying with her mother, Lisa encounters Kenneth Grearly, a man who shares her stirrings and has sought her out to help her deal with her difference. Grearly is much more aware than Lisa is of exactly what their stirrings are; they are both mutants, telepaths. He attempts to force Lisa to confront their uniqueness — that which isolates them from the rest of humanity. Grearly believes that it is his and Lisa's responsibility to move the human race in the direction of an evolutionary trend toward telepathic ability in order to eliminate miscommunication among people. He believes they must produce children together to perpetuate the mutant characteristic, even if Lisa is unwilling to do so.

As he moves toward Lisa's house with the intent of impregnating her, he uses his telepathic powers to trap her there. Lisa, however, tentatively embraces her own power to confuse Grearly and ultimately cause his death in a traffic accident. But his death results in Lisa's sense of total isolation.

The story was adapted by Anne Heche as "Reaching Normal," one of a three-part anthology of short science fiction films that first aired on the Showtime cable network on June 29, 2001 under the title *On the Edge*. Andie McDowell and Paul Rudd star, and Heche also directed.

**Compline** [also appears as **Complin**]   the last of the seven canonical hours prior to retiring for the evening. In the novella "And the Light Is Risen," Father Jerome tells Father Gault that he will not be in chapel "until Complin." It is used in various places throughout *A Canticle for Leibowitz*; for example, in "Fiat Lux" the abbot instructs Brother Armbruster to see him in his study after Compline.

**Conclave**   the closed assembly of the College of Cardinals while meeting to elect a new pope. There are a series of conclaves in *Saint Leibowitz and the Wild Horse Woman* until the election of Pope Amen.

**Concordat**   an agreement between a pope and a government for the regulation of ecclesiastical matters. In the novella "The Last Canticle," a State-Church Concordat guarantees the Church the right to send missions into space.

**"Conditionally Human"**   a novella originally appearing in *Galaxy Science Fiction*, 3 (February 1952), 30–63. It is slightly revised for its inclusion in *Conditionally Human*, a collection of three novellas published in 1962. The story is also included in *The Science Fiction Stories of Walter M. Miller, Jr.; The Best of Walter M. Miller, Jr.;* and *Conditionally Human and Other Stories*.

Overpopulation has resulted in government regulation to restrict the birthrate and maintain a constant population. Couples must satisfy certain genetic requirements for legal childbearing. Only class-A couples are allowed to reproduce.

To satisfy the perceived basic need of human beings to have young and nurture them, artificial mutant pets have been created for those couples who are class-C or genetic-C, not allowed to have children. Several types of mutated pets are produced as child substitutes, but the most sophisticated is the neutroid, a mutated chimpanzee. The neutroids are engineered to limit their intelligence and life spans. Only females are produced to prevent uncontrolled reproduction.

Terry Norris is a Bio-Inspector for the Bio-Authority, responsible for the proper regulation of the mutated animals. As part of his job, he must occasionally euthanize some of the pets. Anne, the woman he has recently married, is extremely upset to learn of this part of his job. She has formed an emotional attachment to the animals Terry keeps in the kennel. She would like to have a child with Terry, but they are classified as a genetic-C couple.

Chief Franklin tells Terry that certain deviant neutroids may have been manufactured, and he is ordered to collect the neutroids sold in his district so they can be checked. Terry discovers Peony, a deviant neutroid with superior intelligence and well developed speech, in O'Reilley's Pet Shop. O'Reilley and his wife had become attached to it, and he is distraught when Terry removes Peony and takes her home with him.

Terry plans on calling Franklin, but Anne threatens to leave him if he turns Peony in. When Father Paulson, O'Reilley's brother-in-law, visits the Norris's home to try to find out why O'Reilley was so upset that he killed all the remaining animals in his shop and threatened Terry's life, he and Terry discuss the morality of the neutroids' existence and man's right to destroy them. Terry realizes that he cannot let Peony be taken and destroyed or he will lose a part of himself in the process.

The next day while Terry is away from the house, Chief Franklin surprises Anne with Peony. When Terry arrives back home, Franklin reveals that at least a dozen deviant neutroids have been discovered and that most are functioning females capable of bearing children. A male deviant has also been discovered. When he asks Terry if he has found a deviant, Terry admits it. Anne tries to protect Peony and threatens Terry with an empty gun. Terry promises her that nothing will happen to Peony. Franklin offers to euthanize Peony himself to spare Terry, but they both go to the kennels. Terry rigs an accident in the gas chamber and kills Franklin. He calls the police to report an accident and the death of Franklin. Waiting for the police to arrive, Terry sedates Peony, amputates her tail and dyes her hair. He dresses her as a two-year-old boy, Mike. Terry plans to forge a hereditary certificate, claiming that he and Anne are a class-A couple, and that Mike is their child.

As the police investigate Franklin's death in the kennel, Terry tells Anne that he is going to quit his job and find a new one at Anthropos Incorporated. He wants to continue to produce deviant neutroids and make Peony a husband. He hopes that they will be the start of a new species that will take better care of the Earth than their creators and produce a new world free from scheming and arrogance.

***Conditionally Human***  a collection of three novellas published by Ballantine Books (New York) in a paperback edition in 1962. A hardcover edition was published in Great Britain by Victor Gollancz Ltd. (London) in 1963.

Contents: "Conditionally Human," "The Darfsteller," and "Dark Benediction."

***Conditionally Human and Other Stories***  a paperback edition published in London by Corgi Books, a division of Transworld Publishers Ltd. in 1982.

Contents: "Conditionally Human"; "Blood Bank," "Dark Benediction," "Dumb Waiter," "Anybody Else Like Me?" and "The Big Hunger."

**Conflict of Martha and Mary**  in *A Canticle for Leibowitz* ("Fiat Voluntas Tua"), as Dom Zerchi thinks about the Church sending its officials and members of the Albertian Order of Leibowitz into space, he considers that some might argue that the Church's starship would be better used to send poor colonists into space instead. He concludes, "the conflict of Martha and Mary always recurred." In Luke 10:38–42 (KJV), Martha, who prepares food for the visiting Jesus, is opposed to her sister Mary, who sits at Jesus's feet and hears his word. When Martha complains that Mary has left her to serve alone, Jesus rebukes her: "Martha, thou art careful and troubled about many things: But one thing is needful; and Mary hath chosen that good part, which shall not be taken away from her." The eternal conflict is between the material and the spiritual, and Mary has chosen the spiritual over the material.

**Congdon, Donald** (January 7, 1918–November 30, 2009)  founder of literay agency Don Congdon Associates, Inc. in 1983. A former editor at Simon & Schuster Publishing and Vice President of Harold Matson Company, where he started as an agent in 1947, Congdon was Miller's literary agent. He secured the book contract from J. P. Lippincott for *A Canticle for Leibowitz*. Miller was the only client Congdon worked with whom he never met in person. Among his other clients were Ray Bradbury, William Styron, and Evan S. Connell.

**"Connection Completed"** a short story written by Judith Merril and originally appearing in *Universe* in 1954. In her autobiography, *Better to Have Loved*, Merril says she wrote the story while traveling on a train from Colorado to New Jersey after spending several weeks driving around Colorado with Miller. "It's about what was going on between us, how two people can find each other and no longer feel at all alone."

The brief story describes how two lonely people carry images of each other in their minds, hoping that their dreams will one day become a reality they can live with, talk to, and love. They finally find each other through a shared telepathic ability.

**Coph IV** the home planet of Eli Roki in the short story "Blood Bank." It is the home of a military culture and a people both proud and cold.

**Coreen** a minor character in the short story "The Corpse In Your Bed Is Me." A member of the I Hate Snyder's Guts Club, she feels sorry for Freddy, the Martian, and tries to offer him some consolation. Freddy thinks she is insulting him.

**Corporal Victros** see **Victros, Corporal**

**"The Corpse in Your Bed Is Me"** short story in *Venture Science Fiction*, 1 (May 1957), 47–60. Although Lincoln Boone is listed as a co-author, Boone is actually Miller's attempt to establish a pen name. There is no other author. Miller's opinion of this story was low. He wrote to Chad Oliver that there was "very little damned excuse" for the story to exist, although he believed editorial cutting did not help it either (4/3/1958).

In the year 2045, the *Martin Snyder Hour* is a popular television show and Martin Snyder is working his way toward joining comedy's immortals. However, as successful as Snyder is as a comedian, he is as unsuccessful as a human being. He is a condescending, arrogant bully. His own supporting cast and production crew have formed the I Hate Snyder's Guts Club. Snyder joins the club himself, proclaiming, "no one can possibly hate me as much as I hate myself."

So confident of his ability to make people laugh, no matter what they may think of him personally, Snyder maintains a running challenge and contest. If a sober, mentally competent, English speaking person, who is not deaf, dumb, or blind, can sit amongst the audience for three minutes and keep a straight face while Snyder performs his monologue, that person will win the bet.

No one is able to win the bet until a member of the Club discovers Freddy, a Martian working at a local soda fountain. Martians do not understand human comedy and find different things funny and tragic. Snyder accepts the challenge of Freddy and finally loses his bet. For the next three days Snyder disappears; when he returns, he is out of sorts. Over the next several weeks, his shows are among his worst in years. Snyder is obsessed with making Freddy laugh and seeks him out on a regular basis.

The Club decides to try to send Freddy away realizing that their jobs are dependent upon Snyder's continuing success, but Snyder hires Freddy to be his chauffer. As his show continues to decline, Snyder's ego is deflated by his inability to make Freddy laugh. Snyder plans an elaborate prank to make Freddy laugh. He makes himself up as a corpse and arranges to have himself placed within Freddy's trunk in the middle of Freddy's apartment. Two shipping men are sent to the apartment to pick up the trunk as Freddy comes home. Surprised by someone wanting his trunk, Freddy asks that they check inside first. When they do, Snyder gets up and leaves an "OUT TO LUNCH" sign on the trunk. But Freddy doesn't laugh at the elaborate joke, not even a giggle. Snyder does not even show up for the next *Martin Snyder Hour*. He disappears for two weeks. Mike Ferris first replaces him on his show as emcee and then Freddy simply stands there and reads Snyder's jokes. When Freddy returns to his apartment after the show, he finds Snyder dead in his bed from eating rat poison. A note by the bed reads: "Dear Freddy, The corpse in your bed is me. Snyder." Freddy shakes Snyder's body, telling him to wake up. As he does so, he begins to laugh. Snyder is finally proven correct; he can make anybody laugh, although he cannot hear Freddy's laughter.

**Cors, Doctor** a short, balding, muscular man with a freckled round face, who works for Green Star in the novella "The Last Canticle" and *A Canticle for Leibowitz* ("Fiat Voluntas Tua"). A member of the Exposure Survey Team, he asks Father Zerchi for permission to locate two mobile units in the abbey's courtyard for clinical testing of the most urgent cases of radiation poisoning. The priest permits him to do so only if the doctor promises not to recommend euthanasia to any patient on the grounds of the abbey. Dr. Cors agrees but breaks his promise when confronted by a severely burned young mother and child. He tells Father Zerchi he has broken his promise and that he will move the mobile units. Father Zerchi later punches Cors in the face when the priest is unable to prevent the mother and child from going to the Mercy Camp to be euthanized. Dr. Cors tells Father Zerchi that pain is the only evil he knows about, and the only evil he can fight. The name Cors may be derived from the French *corps*, meaning body or matter.

**Cortus** a hunchback genny in *Saint Leibowitz and the Wild Horse Woman*. He and Barlo forcibly take Blacktooth to the home of Tempus.

**Corvany, Father General** from *Saint Leibowitz and the Wild Horse Woman*. A man in his seventies yet still handsome and trim, he is a member of the Order of Saint Ignatz in New Rome who arrives in Valana for the conclave. He possesses a natural grace and smile. Of a liberal bent, he brings Cardinal Buldyrk, Abbess of N'Ork, out of the audience at the preliminary meeting prior to the election of Pope Amen I. He is accidently killed by Jæsis in his failed attempt to assassinate Thon Yodin.

**The Court of Kings** a bar on Tragor III visited by Eli Roki and E Pok in the short story "Blood Bank."

**Crain** the third emergency-technician in the short story "Cold Awakening." He is to be awakened from suspendfreeze only if Joley and Jessel, the first two emergency-technicians, are unavailable to handle the situation. Dr. Fraylin's evaluation of Crain is that he is schizoid to the point of feeling persecuted. Crain is a morphine addict, and Fraylin is supplying the drugs to him. Crain is supposed to awaken all the colonists from suspendfreeze if given the chance. His gun is stolen and used in the murder of Jessel. Commander Roagan confines him to his quarters. Joley drugs him in order to place his body in Jessel's coffin. He hopes that the confusion caused when Crain awakens and the absence of Jessel's corpse will force the space tug to return to the colonists' ship.

**Crater City** the major settlement of the Integrated Projects operations on the moon in the novella "The Lineman."

**Creed of Athanasius:** a profession of faith primarily concerned with the concept of the Trinity and the dual nature of Jesus as both man and son of God. It is named for Saint Athanasius (c. 295–373), once believed to be its author, but it is now thought to date from the fifth century. As Pope Amen II prepares for his death at the hands of Wooshin in *Saint Leibowitz and the Wild Horse Woman*, he begins to recite the Creed of Nicaea but concludes with a passage from the Creed of Athanasius.

**Creed of Nicaea** a statement of religious faith or belief first adopted in 325 by the Council of Nicaea. It emphasizes that the Son is of the same substance as the Father. It was slightly amended by additional creeds in 381 and became known as the Niceno-Constantinopolitan or Nicene Creed. It became part of the liturgy of the Eucharist in the fifth century. In *Saint Leibowitz and the Wild Horse Woman*, Pope Amen II begins to recite it as he prepares for his death but ends with words from the Creed of Athanasius.

**Crimen laesae majestatis** Latin: "High treason." In *Saint Leibowitz and the Wild Horse Woman*, Cardinal Brownpony reminds Hultor Bråm that his diplomatic immunity does not cover the *crimen laesae majestatis*.

**Crimine ipso laesae majestatis facto** Latin: "The very crime of high treason having been committed." Cardinal Brownpony offers Pope Amen's absolution to Cardinal Benefez of any act of high treason or act of rebellion in *Saint Leibowitz and the Wild Horse Woman*.

**Crit-dose form** the Red ticket permit allowing a victim of radiation poisoning to be euthanized in *A Canticle for Leibowitz* ("Fiat Voluntas Tua").

**"Crucifixus Etiam"** short story first appearing in *Astonishing Science Fiction*, 50 (February 1953), 97–113. The title is derived from the Nicene Creed and is Latin for *Crucifed Also*. It is collected in *The View from the Stars*; *The Science Fiction Stories of Walter M. Miller, Jr.*; *The Best of Walter M. Miller, Jr.*; and *The Darfsteller and Other Stories*. The story appeared in *The Best Science Fiction Stories* (1954 and 1956) as "The Sower Does Not Reap."

Manue Nanti has signed a five-year contract to work as a manual laborer on the Mars Project, a long-term effort to make Mars a habitable planet without support from Earth. In order to do the work, all laborers are fitted with a mechanical oxygenator that replaces the normal operation of their lungs. The workers have to consciously exercise their lungs or else they will atrophy from lack of use. They will then be unable to return to Earth and live a normal life. Those workers whose lungs have atrophied are known as troffies.

Manue begins his work on Mars conscientiously paying attention to his lungs. He wants to complete his time on Mars and retire early to Earth so he can travel to remote and exotic places. After only a month working on the project, Manue begins to experience doubts about what he, or anybody, is doing on Mars. It will take at least 80 or 90 years to make Mars habitable for colonists without Earth support. What is the return on his investment? Manue begins to feel hopeless and trapped. What end is he serving? He is not getting rich. Neither are the people on Earth whose taxes are paying for the project. Only the contractors and some engineers and foremen are getting rich, no one else.

Manue continues his tedious, backbreaking work. He lives day to day, dreaming of Earth. His lung tissue withers; he relies more and more on his mechanical oxygenator. He is becoming a troffie.

Finally, the work is completed in one area and the men are transported to another location. Will Kinley, the project supervisor, addresses the men and tells them they have been part of a larger plan across the planet to give Mars a breathable atmosphere. A controlled subterranean chain reaction is being initiated that will produce a breathable atmosphere over the next eight centuries. The men have been preparing one of the sites for a nuclear explosion.

The workers grow restless. They demand to know what is in it for them. They are the ones sacrificing their lungs and their lives so men 800 years in the future can breathe air on Mars. They are being used and taken advantage of: they make the air they cannot breathe. Handell, one of the laborers, rises among the workers and encourages them to attack Kinley. As guards begin to move toward Handell to quell the unrest, Kinley tells them to wait to see how the men react. Manue rises, knocks Handell out, and challenges the few of his follows. As the crowd quiets, the first of the explosions is heard in the distance and a soft wind is felt.

The men begin to dissemble for their reassignments, but Manue sits forlornly in the dust. Kinley comes to thank him for his actions but instead says simply, "Some sow, others reap." He asks Manue what he would rather be, a sower or a reaper. Manue thinks about this and stands up with a stirring pride. He smells the faint air beginning to blow across the planet. He understands his place and his purpose. He is part of "an eight-century passion of human faith in the destiny of the race of Man." His planet is now Mars, not Earth.

**Crucifixus etiam [pro nobis]**   Latin: "[He was] crucified also [for us]." Part of The Nicene Creed, a profession of faith, the phrase is used by Miller as a title for a short story published in 1953. See also "**Crucifixus Etiam**"

**Crucis autem onus si audisti ut honorem, nihilo errasti auribus**   Latin: "If you have heard that the burden of the cross is an honor, you have not erred." When Brother Joshua replies that he accepts the honor after Dom Zerchi asks if they are to impose the burden of leading the order into space on him, the abbot thinks the monk may have misheard the word burden [*oneri*] for honor [*honorem*]. But after the abbot says these words to Brother Joshua, his reply is still "*Accipiam*" ["I accept"]. From *A Canticle for Leibowitz* ("Fiat Voluntas Tua").

**Crumily**   a minor character in *Saint Leibowitz and the Wild Horse Woman*. He is one of three seminary students that Brother Blacktooth and Wooshin lodge with in a small house near a brewery in Valana. He is from the East and has a wry wit.

**Crump**   a minor character in the novella "The Lineman." He is one of the Safety and Rescue men Brodanovitch spies climbing out of the space bordello.

**Cui Salutem Dicit**   Latin: "To whom [he] sends greetings." Part of Marcus Apollo's formal address to Dom Paulo in the letter he sends him concerning Thon Taddeo in *A Canticle for Leibowitz* ("Fiat Lux").

**Cum spiri' tuo**   Latin: "With your Spirit." An abbreviated form of "*cum spirit tuo.*" It is used in *A Canticle for Leibowitz* ("Fiat Voluntas Tua") in response to "*Chris' tecum*" ("Christ be with you"). Together it is a greeting used in the Catholic Mass between the priest and the congregation.

**"Cum tenebris in superficie profundorum"** *see* **"In principio Deus"**

**Curia**   the ruling body or central administration of the Roman Catholic Church. The term is used in *Saint Leibowitz and the Wild Horse Woman*.

**Curia Noctis**   Latin: "Night Court." A term used by Pope Amen II in *Saint Leibowitz and the Wild Horse Woman* for the time of evening when he encourages the telling of stories after supper on the trail.

**Cyrus**   the first Achaemenian king of Persia, founder of the Persian Empire, and conqueror of Babylon in 539 B.C. He is given by Benjamin as an example of "the others" he hopes Don Thaddeo/Thon Taddeo will not join in the novella "And the Light Is Risen" and *A Canticle for Leibowitz* ("Fiat Lux"). Benjamin is referring to him as a despot and conqueror.

**Daleth**   a rough, uncouth, frontier planet in the short story "Blood Bank." Its inhabitants have little respect for authority. The freighter pilot Talewa Walkeka is a Dalethian.

**Daleth Shipping Incorporated**   the name by which Talewa Walkeka refers to herself in the short story "Blood Bank."

**Dan**   a minor character who is an old friend of Zella Richmond in the novella "The Yokel."

**Daner**   a member of the Natani Mountain people in the short story "The Soul-Empty Ones." He goes to confront the invaders to determine if they are the sons of man or not. Fatally wounded, he returns to his home to follow the Natani tradition of going into the forest to die.

**Danfer**  a small community on the outskirts of an expanse of half-buried rubble in *Saint Leibowitz and the Wild Horse Woman*. It was formerly the city of Denver. Varley Cardinal Swineman's cathedral is located there.

**"Daniel in this den"**  during a battle in *Saint Leibowitz and the Wild Horse Woman*, Brother Blacktooth takes refuge in a cougar's den and prays to Saint Leibowitz, "Today a war is going on and I am not a Daniel in this den." His reference is to chapter 6 of the Book of Daniel (KJV). Daniel is placed in a lion's den and condemned to death because he refuses to relinquish his faith in God despite an edict from King Darius that no man or god other than himself be petitioned for 30 days. The lions do not harm Daniel because he believes in his God. Brother Blacktooth fears he does not share Daniel's faith or courage.

**"The Darfsteller"**  a novella first published in *Astounding Science Fiction*, 54 (January 1955), 10–65. In 1955 Miller received the inaugural Hugo Award for Best Novelette for the story. It was subsequently included in *Conditionally Human*; *The Science Fiction Stories of Walter M. Miller, Jr.*; *The Best of Walter M. Miller, Jr.*; and *The Darfsteller and Other Stories*. The novella is the basis of a two-act musical play "Maestro." Darfsteller is a variation of the German *darsteller* meaning actor or performer.

Ryan (Thorny) Thornier is a former leading actor and matinee idol who now works as a janitor in the New Empire Theater. During the past several years, technological advances have made possible the replacement of human actors by mechanized mannequins with programmed psycho-physiological data in packaged autodramas. Maestro, a computerized director, controls the robotic actors.

Thornier refused to license his psycho-physiological data for the mannequins' program tapes as many other actors did. Without the royalties realized from the tapes and with no need for human actors, he must work in a degrading unskilled job to remain close to the theater that he loves. His boss, Imperio D'Uccia, the theater manager, continually abuses him.

Realizing that his time at New Empire is ending (D'Uccia is replacing him with an auto-janitor) Thornier initiates what he refers to as his "fantasy-plan" for revenge. He plans to take the place of the mannequin playing the role of Andreyev in the drama "The Anarch," a role he prepared for ten years earlier only to have the production close for an autodrama, and give a final performance in one last great role. In the final scene where his character is shot, Thornier plans to substitute real bullets for the stage ammunition, committing suicide before the audience, becoming a victim of mechanized theater.

Asked to pick up a mannequin and the program tape for Peltier that will be used for the Andreyev part, Thornier deliberately sabotages the tape with that of a comedic, supporting actor. Returning to the New Empire, he suggests the idea of a human actor playing incognito in an autodrama to his old friend Jade Ferne, a producer of "The Anarch." He waits for the Peltier mannequin to malfunction during the day's rehearsals.

As he waits backstage, Thornier awkwardly bumps into Mela Stone, a former actress with whom he once had a relationship. She is there to give the opening introduction and an intermission commentary on the playwright and play. She has adapted to the changes in the theater better than Thornier having licensed her personality to be used in the autodramas.

As Thornier planned, when the Peltier mannequin fails, Jade suggests that he play Andreyev in the run through, which he successfully does. With no time to wait for a replacement tape of Peltier, Jade asks if he would be willing to play the role opening night with the mannequins despite his feelings about autodrama. Thornier agrees.

The opening scenes of the first act go poorly. Thornier is unsure of himself and struggles with his betrayal of Jade and his feelings for Mela. Backstage Mela tries to console and advise him, telling him not to let the audience realize he is human or they will laugh at him. Because of Thornier's awkwardness on stage, Maestro begins to compensate for the audience's reaction. Maestro is judging him and finding him wanting as an actor, so it plays up other roles to compensate for the audience's perceived displeasure with Thornier's character.

In the second act, Thornier begins to fight back and alter his dialogue in an effort to reclaim his character. Maestro cannot invent new dialogue, only try to compensate within the designated roles, so Thornier tries to gain control of his character and the play. Realizing what he is trying to do and the problems involved, Mela plays her old role of Marka rather than allowing her mannequin to do so. Together they save Act Two.

During the break between acts, Thornier begins to regret what he has done. It was an infantile dream and he decides that he needs to finally make a break with the theater; he has mourned its death too long. However, his ruse is revealed before Act

Three begins. Mela tells him that two potential backers and a critic walked out after the first act because he was so bad. Jade and the people in the theater may lose their investment and their jobs.

Thornier begins the third act with regret. He has wrecked the play, and he cannot save it. As the act continues and he fires the gun that will eventually kill his character, he realizes that he forgot to remove the real bullets. As the scene continues and the Marka character picks up the gun, he tries to whisper to Mela that the bullets are real. Mela, however, is no longer playing the role of Marka; it is the mannequin and it is waiting for Thornier's cue to shoot him. He decides to continue and attempts to shift his body as the gun is fired to minimize his wound. He is shot and falls. Thornier tries to lie as still as possible as the play ends and minimize the amount of blood spilled on the stage so the audience will not realize he is human. When the curtain falls, Thornier staggers off stage and collapses.

He awakes in a hospital bed with Mela at his side. She says that the show was panned but received terrific publicity because of the lunatic who bled all over the stage. The play will continue. She tells him that the theater is dead, but he tells her no, it is not dead. It has simply, and necessarily, changed with the times.

When Richard Thomas, the technician who operates Maestro at the theater, comes to see Thornier, he tells him that there will always be people like him: someone who tries to be a better tool than a tool, a specialist trying to compete with a specialist's tool. Thornier agrees and asks Thomas to help him find a new job. Thomas declares that this is what man does that separates him from everything else: man's specialty is in creating new specialties.

***The Darfsteller and Other Stories***   originally published by Corgi Books, a Division of Transworld Publishers, Ltd., in London in 1982.

Contents: "The Darfsteller," "The Will," "Vengeance for Nikolai," "Crucifixus Etiam," "I, Dreamer," "The Lineman," "Big Joe and the Nth Generation," "You Triflin' Skunk."

**Dark Ages**   the name traditionally given to the period of European history from the fall of the Roman Empire (A.D. 476) to sometime between the coronation of Charlemagne in 800 and 1000. The term is usually associated with any primitive period of barbarism and unenlightenment. The time of the short story, "A Canticle for Leibowitz" and the "Fiat Homo" section of *A Canticle for Leibowitz* is referred to as the Dark Ages. In "And the Light Is Risen" and the "Fiat Lux" section of the novel, civilization is emerging from this dark period.

**"Dark Benediction"**   novella first published in *Fantastic Adventures*, 13 (September 1951), 78–116. It is included in *Conditionally Human*; *The Science Fiction Stories of Walter M. Miller, Jr.*; *The Best of Walter M. Miller, Jr.*; *Conditionally Human and Other Stories*; and *Dark Benediction*. A dramatization of the story was produced as part of the National Public Radio series *Sci-Fi Radio* in 1989–1990.

Mysterious cannonball-like meteorites have brought a plague to Earth, dividing the population between those who have contracted the disease, the hypers or dermies, and those who remain unaffected, the non-hypers. The plague does not result in death; instead, the person suffers from low fever, hallucinations, a grayish discoloration of the skin, and a compulsion to touch others thereby spreading the highly contagious disease. The hypers are so-called because they experience an increased sensitivity of their senses, particularly touch and smell. Society has been torn apart as the uninfected have fled from those infected. Industrialized civilization has temporarily ceased to exist.

Paul Oberlin, a former engineering student, is making his way toward Houston, a city he believes to be largely deserted, looking for supplies. A non-hyper, he is doing all he can to protect himself from contracting the disease. Three armed men confront him as he enters the city; they are part of a militia group formed to keep dermies out. Their plan is to keep the city plague free by enforcing a set of restrictions and regulations among all who want to live there and by killing all dermies they can identify.

Uneasy with what he perceives as the totalitarian aspects of the group, Paul does not report to the probation area but instead begins tinkering with an abandoned diesel truck. After he finishes readying the truck, Paul hears a commotion. He investigates and sees that the armed patrol has captured a young dermie woman. The men are preparing to shoot her. While he can understand a dermie being shot in self-protection, Paul views this as a cold-blooded execution. He runs back to the truck and drives toward the patrol. He allows the girl time to jump in the back of the truck and then speeds out of the city.

Leaving Houston, Paul drives toward Galveston asking himself what he is supposed to do now. He stops outside the city to let the girl out of the truck, but she does not jump out the back. He cautiously proceeds to see what the problem is and discovers that the girl has been shot during the rescue. Torn between helping the girl and abandoning her along the side of the road, Paul decides to give her a first aid kit so she can try to stop the bleeding. He sees that she has a severed Achilles' tendon. She tells him her name is Willie, short for Willow, and that she will not touch him if he does not want her to. Paul cannot understand why those with the neural plague think it is a favor to pass it to another person.

He decides to try to find a doctor who will treat Willie's wound. He continues toward Galveston but discovers the bridge to the city is destroyed. To avoid touching her, Paul uses a rope to help Willie out of the truck. He finds a boat he can use to paddle to the city. He leaves Willie in a small shack at the water's edge so he can look for help. The shack contains the corpse of a dermie woman who committed suicide with a shotgun.

Carrying the shotgun from the shack, Paul comes across a young man in the final stages of the infection. He asks where he might find a doctor and is told that most of the priests at St. Mary's are doctors, and all of them are dermies. Galveston is a hyper colony. The man throws himself at Paul, but he is able to protect himself by hitting the man in the head with the shotgun causing a gash in his forehead. Paul tells him to lead the way to the hospital. When they arrive, Paul sends him in to have a doctor tend to his head and tells him to have a doctor come out so he can take him back to Willie.

Father Mendelhaus emerges from the hospital and is amazed that a non-hyper would help a dermie. He and Father Williamson, a surgeon, accompany Paul back to the shack. When they reach the shack, they discover that Willie has tried to kill herself but was too weak to succeed. They return to the hospital to repair her ankle but fear their ability to fight any infection that may set in.

At the hospital, Father Mendelhaus offers Paul a "safe" room where no dermies will bother him. He explains that the priests' plans for Galveston are to make it an island refuge for hypers who are willing to suppress their craving to spread the disease and turn their attentions toward reconstruction. To that end, the bishop has decreed that touching non-hypers is a sin unless the non-hyper submits of his own free will. Scientists are studying the neural condition trying to learn how to live with it.

As Paul rests in his room, he questions himself and his actions. He thinks he has been a fool for taking so many chances and now finds himself in the middle of the disease. But he also finds Galveston to be the most peaceful and sanest place he has been in some time. The people themselves seem to be at peace.

Father Mendelhaus tells Paul that Willie is asking for him and that he can go see her. Paul is hesitant and says it may be better if he just leaves. The priest tells him that she is suffering from depression, and if they cannot stop the infection from her wound, they may have to amputate her foot. Paul decides he will go to see her.

He tells Willie that Galveston is a good place to be because of all the dermies, but she becomes upset at his use of the word. She tells him that she hopes never to hear the word again and that she would rather die than touch anyone, especially him. After seeing the suicide in the shack, she now loathes herself.

Paul asks Father Mendelhaus for a car he can use. The priest asks if he wants a boat instead. The priests will prepare an abandoned yacht for him as a way of returning his favor of helping Willie. It will take a few days for repairs and to stock the boat. In the meantime, the priest introduces Paul to Dr. Seevers, one of the scientists studying the infection, or neuroderm, and asks the doctor to tell Paul what they have learned about the plague.

Doctor Seevers tells Paul that the meteorites were actually fired into space toward various stars several thousand years ago in an attempt to perpetuate a parasite species that works to keep its hosts in the best of physical condition. The sun of the host species' world was going supernova, so they launched the missiles in the hope of perpetuating the beneficent alien micro-organisms. These small craft contained magnetic printing that was meant to be read in a specific order to explain the nature of the organisms inside. When the projectiles landed on Earth, however, they were opened in a haphazard fashion unwittingly exposing the population to a condition they did not understand. The organisms do not harm their hosts but actually create new sensory receptors that increase the hosts's ability to relate to their environments.

Paul leaves to watch his boat being prepared. He decides to search for provisions but is forced to shoot and wound a dermie who tries to touch him. Returning to the hospital Father Mendelhaus is upset to learn that Paul has left the sanctuary of the hospital. He tells him that Willie has been asking for him and that the boat will be ready in one more day.

Paul goes to Willie's room and watches from the doorway as she sleeps fitfully. He hears the chant of the *Asperges me, Domine* from elsewhere in the hospital. When Willie cries out in her sleep, a nun comes to comfort her. Paul leaves wondering if he is the diseased or the one free of the disease. The next day Mendelhaus tells Paul that Willie is healing well, the swelling is down and the chance of infection is no longer a problem. She will be able to move around with crutches.

That night Paul awakens with the sense that someone is in his room and that he has been touched. He shrieks and is answered by a high-pitched scream. He leaps wildly from his bed and blindly fires the shotgun he keeps nearby. The priests run to his room and a search of the building is ordered. Willie is discovered missing from her room.

Paul asks Doctor Seevers to disinfect the area where he believes he was touched. As he, Seevers, and Father Mendelhaus go to the lab in the basement of the hospital, they are told that Willie cannot be found anywhere in the building. Paul worries that she may try to commit suicide and guesses that she has headed to the beach to drown herself.

He runs to the beach and finds her sitting with her head in her hands. Despairingly she tells Paul she did it, she touched him. Paul reaches out and takes her hands, pulling them away from her face. He kisses her and picks her up, carrying her back to the hospital. She falls asleep in his arms. When Father Mendelhaus sees him, he grins and says he guesses they can forget about the boat. But Paul asks the priest if he can think of no other reason to travel than to run away.

**Dark Benediction**   a British paperback reprinting of *The Best of Walter M. Miller, Jr.* by Gollancz (London) in 2007 as part of its SF Masterworks series. See *The Best of Walter M. Miller, Jr.* for contents.

**Darkon VIII**   a planet owned by the Funph Corporation in the short story "Gravesong."

**David's prayer for pardon**   Psalm 50 (DB), the fourth penitential psalm, better known as Miserere from its opening word, is the confession and repentance of David after his sin with Bathsheba (see 2 Samuel 11:1–13 KJV). Brother Francis is copying it in *A Canticle for Leibowitz* ("Fiat Homo") when he has his inspiration for the illuminated copy of the Leibowitz blueprint. See also "**Miserere mei, Deus**"

**Dawson**   an unseen character in the novella "The Reluctant Traitor." Along with Heide, he is responsible for Operation Icecap, which established a breathable atmosphere on Mars five centuries prior to the time of the story.

**"Day at the Beach"**   a short story by Carol Emshwiller that appears in *Beyond Armageddon*.

**Day Maiden**   the Fujæ Go of Nomadic myth in *Saint Leibowitz and the Wild Horse Woman*. It is one aspect of the Wild Horse Woman. See also **Fujæ Go**

**Dazille, Alaia**   a character in the short story "Let My People Go." Dazille is the launch pilot for the space ark that carried 120 colonists from Earth to Epsilon Eridani Two. She is tall, "cool and pleasant but not beautiful," with red-brown hair, hazel eyes, and a narrow, oval face. She is in love with Faron Qun, another member of the ship's crew. She is part of the delegation sent to the planet to try to discover what the Eridanians plan to do with the colonists. In an act of self-defense, she kills the pilot of the ship taking them to the planet and is forced to crash land the ship herself. She and Morgun Sahl are eventually captured by the Eridanians and their memories altered as part of a conditioning program.

**De essential hominum**   Latin: "Concerning the essence of man." These words come to mind as Brother Joshua sits in the courtyard and asks for a sign from God in *A Canticle for Leibowitz* ("Fiat Voluntas Tua"). When he hears a slithering in the bushes, he throws a rock at it. He observes that this is the essence of man: to ask for an omen and then throw a rock at it when it appears.

***De Inanibus***   Latin: *About the Worthless Things* [or *The Inane*]. A book by the Venerable Boedullus that assesses and classifies texts included in the Memorabilia as to their reliability, attempting to identify fictional or allegorical accounts from historical ones. In *A Canticle for Leibowitz* ("Fiat Lux"), Dom Paulo castigates Thon Taddeo for not referring to the *De Inanibus* before jumping to conclusions about the evolution of the human species based on a fragment of the play *R. U. R.* See also **R. U. R.**

***De Perennibus Sententiis Sectarum Rurum***   the *Perennial Ideas of Regional Sects* by Yogen Duren is one of the choices given to Brother Blacktooth to translate into the Grasshopper dialect of Plains Nomadic in *Saint Leibowitz and the Wild Horse Woman*.

***De Vestigilis Antecessarium Civitatum***   Latin: literally *Concerning the Vestiges* [Traces] *of Preceding Civilizations* [States]. A work by the Venerable Boedullus mentioned in *A Canticle for Leibowitz* ("Fiat Lux"). The title is given as *Footprints of Earlier Civilizations* in *Saint Leibowitz and the Wild Horse Woman*. Brother Blacktooth is translating it.

**Deacon ("Half-Breed") Brownpony** see **Brownpony, Elia**

**Dealba me**   Latin: "Purify [or whiten] me." Part of the priest's words as he puts on the alb, the long white, robe-like vestment, when vesting for the liturgy. Father Zerchi says the words when he picks up the fallen wafers with his bloody fingers as he lies crushed beneath the rubble of the abbey in the novella "The Last Canticle" and *A Canticle for Leibowitz* ("Fiat Voluntas Tua").

**"Death of a Spaceman"** short story first appearing in *Amazing Stories*, 28 (March 1954), 6–21, 130. Reprinted in *Amazing Stories*, 42 (March 1969), 118–134.

Old Donegal spent his entire adult life working as a spaceman, a blaster on the Earth to moon shuttle. Now dying from cancer, he just barely abides the ministrations of his devoted wife, Martha, and Father Paul. He wishes to simply die on his own terms, thinking of his beloved space. He laments that his grandson, Ken, will not follow him into space, and he thinks the less of Ken for it. Next door to him, the neighbors are celebrating their son's acceptance into pre-space training. Donegal asks his wife to place his old space boots on his feet, and with a final drink of whiskey he listens one last time for the moon-run blast-off. As he hears the roar of the rocket, he dies with a grin on his face.

This is one of the more blatantly sentimental of Miller's stories. In a brief introduction to the story when it was anthologized in *The Worlds of Science Fiction*, Miller states, "I knew and loved Old Donegal ... whose mistress was ... a thundering steam locomotive and who died long ago." It is that love that makes the story a favorite of his, despite "its flaws, its corn, and its obvious obsolescence as science fiction." The story is later entitled "**Memento Homo.**"

**Dei imago** Latin: "Image of God." The term is a reference to the soul of man. In *A Canticle for Leibowitz* ("Fiat Homo"), it is revealed that there was a time when it was thought that genetic mutants were born deprived of the *Dei imago*. Rather than have human souls, it was believed they possessed animal souls and could therefore be destroyed. Papal pronouncements, however, proclaimed them human with immortal souls and with every right to life.

**Dela** Colonel Beth's secretary in the short story "Blood Bank." As a native of Jod VI, she holds Eli Roki personally responsible for the deaths of her relatives on the planet after he destroys the mercy ship supposedly carrying emergency medical supplies. She slaps his face, raking her nails down his cheek.

**Delegate Jerulian** an unseen character who accuses the Asian Coalition with the assembly of hydrogen weapons in deep space in "Fiat Voluntas Tua" in *A Canticle for Leibowitz*.

**Delmont** an unseen character in the novella "Conditionally Human." An evolvotron operator at Anthropos Incorporated, his actions result in the production of deviant neutroids in the Bermuda K-99 series. It was originally believed that the pressure of being a novice operator caused Delmont to allow non-standard neutroid ovum to pass to the incubator in order to meet his quota. However, it is later learned that he actually intended to start a black market in deviant neutroids that he was deliberately stealing from the incubators.

**Deluge of Flame** a term used in the short story "A Canticle for Leibowitz" and the novella "And the Light Is Risen" to refer to the span of a few weeks in which most of civilization is destroyed by war. It is followed by the Age of Simplification. See also **Flame Deluge**

**Demon Light** another name for Eltür Brâm, the younger brother of Hultor Brâm, in *Saint Leibowitz and the Wild Horse Woman*.

**Denin (also called Dennie)** one of the central characters in the short story "No Moon for Me." A former general who helped develop unmanned rockets during an Earth war, Denin was demoted to a colonel because of his criticism of politicians for their lack of support for manned space flight and for taking his case directly to the populace. He has been a strong advocate for a human presence in space and is now part of the first crew to fly to the moon in response to unidentified ultra-high frequency bands being transmitted from there.

Denin shows no apprehension about the mission, and his confidence is upsetting to the ship's commander, Major Long. Denin's confidence is well placed; he knows the origin of the transmission. He has secretly sent a transmitter to the moon in an unmanned rocket hoping to force man into space to investigate the presumed alien source of "the Voice." He is willing to sacrifice himself and the crew by blowing up their ship on the moon if will cause the nations on Earth to create a lunar station and begin manned space exploration.

He is described as having a "dark, Lincolnesque face."

**Dennie** *see* **Denin**

**Denver** *see* **Empire of Denver**

**Deo Gratias** Latin: "Thanks be to God." The phrase used in the Roman Catholic liturgy to give thanks to God for graces received.

1. In the short story "A Canticle for Leibowitz" and *A Canticle for Leibowitz* ("Fiat Homo"), Brother Francis recites the phrase after each whack

he receives from the abbot using a hickory ruler as a lesson in the virtue of humility after he refuses to retract his belief that an angel or Leibowitz appeared to him in the desert.

2. In *Saint Leibowitz and the Wild Horse Woman*, it is the monks' response to the second cook for their apportioned mush.

**Depart from me, ye accursed...** In Matthew 25:41–43 (KJV), as part of The Olivet Discourse, or Discourse on the Last Times, Jesus tells his followers that at the time of judgment those sitting on the Lord's left hand will be told "depart from me, ye cursed, into everlasting fire.... For I was an hungred, and ye gave me no meat ... I was a stranger ... sick, and in prison, and ye visited me not." In the novella "Dark Benediction," Paul recalls this passage as "the drumming charges of conscience" as he contemplates abandoning Willie outside of Galveston.

**Dermie** a derogatory term used in the novella "Dark Benediction" for a person who has contracted the space borne plague. The symptoms of the plague include a gray discoloration of the skin, low fever, hallucinations, and a craving to infect others. Earth's population has divided between those who have the plague, the hypers or dermies, and those who do not, the non-hypers.

**Devendy, Prior** the monk who calls for Sister Clare to assist Abbot Olshuen when he suffers a stroke in *Saint Leibowitz and the Wild Horse Woman*. After Olshuen dies, he assumes the duties of abbot until a new abbot can be elected.

**Dicit Dominus Petro** Latin: "And the Lord saith to Peter." A chant derived from John 21:15–22 (KJV). It is being recited by the monks in the novella "The Last Canticle" as Joshua contemplates accepting the burden of leading the Church contingent into space. In the Bible passage, Jesus reminds Peter that those who choose to follow him are called to a task that will place a burden on them and exact a cost.

***Dies Irae*** Latin: "Day of Wrath." A hymn used as part of the Requiem Mass, it is a description of the Day of Judgment and a prayer for mercy. A verse from the hymn comes to Dom Zerchi's mind at the end of *A Canticle for Leibowitz* ("Fiat Voluntas Tua"), as he lies dying beneath the ruins of the abbey.

**Digger** the leader of the patrol that stops Paul when he enters Houston in the novella "Dark Benediction."

**Dignum et justum est** Latin: "It is meet and just." The line is taken from the Catholic Mass. It is used as part of the warning announcing Don Thaddeo's arrival in the abbey's basement in the novella "And the Light Is Risen."

**Diluvium Ignis** Latin: "Flame Deluge." Another term for the Flame Deluge or nuclear holocaust that destroys the world sometime in the latter half of the twentieth century in *A Canticle for Leibowitz*. See also **Flame Deluge**

**Dion, Sam** an unseen character in the novella "The Darfsteller." He is a former actor who has licensed his psycho-physiological data for use on tapes in autodramas.

**Discede, Seductor informis!** Latin: "Depart, hideous Seducer!" In *A Canticle for Leibowitz* ("Fiat Voluntas Tua"), as Brother Joshua contemplates leading the Church's contingent into space and taking the Memorabilia with them, he questions whether the Memorabilia is a curse. He immediately stops himself with these words — he will not be tempted to renounce his faith or his calling — and he proclaims the Memorabilia to be no curse, unless man perverts its use.

**Dismissal of Servants** the Church's plan to evacuate the Holy See and the records of the Church off Earth in the event of a thermonuclear war in the novella "The Last Canticle." Twenty-five ex-spacemen now in the Albertian Order, six sisters, and approximately twenty children will accompany the designated Holy See and his staff to the Centaurus colony in Alpha Centauri. The plan is called *Quo peregrinator* in the novel.

**Divine Office** the set of prayers said daily at the canonical hours by the clergy and various other clerics. It is referred to as "the ever-recurring hymn" of the Leibowitz abbey in *A Canticle for Leibowitz* ("Fiat Homo").

**Divine Praises** *see* **Litany of Divine Praises**

**Divine Thirst** from the short story "The Big Hunger," the term refers to man's hunger and endless search for the lost home. According to myth, man once lived on a paradise planet but he left it in search of a better one. Lord Bion, angered by this action, hid the paradise, condemning man to wander forever searching for that which he lost.

**Dixitque Deus: 'Fiat Lux'** *see* **In principio Deus**

**Doc** the name given to a bat pup that befriends Rolf Kenlan in the novella "The Reluctant Traitor."

**Dom** a contraction of the Latin term *dominus*, meaning master. It is used as a title for monks of various orders, including the Benedictine order.

**Dom Guido Graneden** *see* **Graneden, Guido**

**Dom Paulo of Pecos** *see* **Paulo of Pecos**

**Domina Rerum** Latin: "Mother [or Mistress] of all things." A reference to the Virgin Mary used in *Saint Leibowitz and the Wild Horse Woman*.

**Domine, mundorum omnium Factor, parsurus esto imprimis eis filiis aviantibus ad sideria caeli quorum victus dificilior...** Latin: "Lord, Maker of all worlds, spare especially these sons who fly to the stars of heaven, whose way of life will be so difficult...." This is Dom Zerchi's prayer for Brother Joshua and the crew of the Church's starship in *A Canticle for Leibowitz* ("Fiat Voluntas Tua").

**Domine, non sum dignus ... sed tantum dic verbo** Latin: "Lord, I am not worthy [to receive you] but only say the word [and my soul shall be healed]." These are the words spoken by the recipient of Holy Communion. Dom Zerchi speaks them as he receives the Host from Rachel at the conclusion of *A Canticle for Leibowitz*.

**Dominicans** a Catholic religious order founded in 1215 by Saint Dominic. Known as the Order of Friars Preachers because their primary mission is the salvation of souls through preaching, they have also been associated with a systematic scholasticism and prevailing conservatism. In *A Canticle for Leibowitz*, Brother Francis thinks about the questions the Dominicans are raising in New Rome regarding the Preternatural Gifts of the Holy Virgin.

**Dominus tecum** Latin: "The Lord is with thee." A part of the Hail Mary, a traditional Catholic prayer. It is used in the novella "And the Light Is Risen" as part of the warning of Don Thaddeo's arrival to the abbey's basement.

**Domne** Latin: "Sir." A vocative used in *A Canticle for Leibowitz* ("Fiat Voluntas Tua") and *Saint Leibowitz and the Wild Horse Man*.

**Domnissime** used by the Poet-sirrah after he has been shot at the conclusion of the "Fiat Lux" section of *A Canticle for Leibowitz* in reference to Dom Paulo; it is a variation of Domne. Rose Secrest defines it as "O most high Lord."

**Don** Spanish: used as a courtesy title prior to one's Christian name. It is used out of respect or to indicate a person of consequence. In addition, more broadly, it refers to a university or college professor. The term is derived from the Latin, *dominus*, meaning master, and is generally applied to clerics, especially in Italy. As the word is used in the novella "And the Light Is Risen," both usages have meaning.

**Don Bodalk** *see* **Bodalk**

**Don Esser Shon** *see* **Shon, Esser**

**Don Friider Halb** *see* **Halb, Friider**

**Don Jejene** *see* **Jejene**

**Don Maho Mahh** *see* **Mahh, Maho**

**Don Thaddeo Pfardentrott** *see* **Pfardentrott, Thaddeo.**

**Don Viche Mortoin** *see* **Mortoin, Viche**

**Donnell, Sam** a veteran mech-repairman of the Mars Project in the short story "Crucifixus Etiam." Although he is only 35, his body is old and weakened. His lungs have atrophied from his reliance on a mechanical oxygenator. He befriends Manue Nanti and advises him to stop fighting and give in to Mars. He tells Manue that the project is simply an outlet for surplus energies, labor, and money. It keeps the money turning over in the economy.

**Donny** a nickname of Old Donegal in the short story "Death of a Spaceman" (later entitled "Memento Homo"). See also **Old Donegal**

**Doodie** a genetic analog born to Lucey, an Earth woman, and an alien who disguised himself as a human man in the short story "The Triflin' Man" (also published as "You Triflin' Skunk"). The alien created these genetic analogs as a means of gathering information about the human race prior to an invasion of Earth. His communications with Doodie cause the boy to suffer violent spasms.

**Dorchett, Ben** a minor character in the novella "The Yokel." He is an old friend of Zella Richmond who recognizes her when she is in Jacksonville with Sam Wuncie. He forces the both of them into a café for a drink.

**Drulrul** in the short story "Let My People Go," the Drulrul are egg-bearers for the Piszjil. After an egg is fertilized, it is transferred to a Drulrul to await birth.

**D'Uccia, Imperio** the short, chubby, ill-tempered manager of the New Empire Theater in the novella "The Darfsteller." He is Ryan Thornier's abusive boss who relishes in mistreating him. He refuses to give Thornier the time off he wants and eventually replaces him with an auto-janitor system in the theater. In Italian, *imperioi* means authority or command.

**Dulia** Greek: "service." A term used to denote the reverence and honor given to a Catholic saint. The canonization of the Beatus Leibowitz proves that he is worthy of the Church's *dulia* in *A Canticle for Leibowitz* ("Fiat Homo").

**"Dumb Waiter"** short story first appearing in *Astounding Science Fiction*, 49 (April 1952), 7–40. The story is later included in *The View from the Stars*; *The Science Fiction Stories of Walter M. Miller, Jr.*; *The Best of Walter M. Miller, Jr.*; and *Conditionally Human*.

Three years after a nuclear holocaust, Mitch Laskell travels toward a city abandoned when the dust began to settle from the radiological attack. The city is not safe because the Central Service Coordinator, the computer that controls the city's computer network that provides services, is still active. City ordinances are enforced even though there are no longer people living there. The machines continue to fulfill their functions as if the war never happened.

As Mitch rides his bicycle, he is stopped by Frank Ferris who sits along the side of the road with a shotgun. Ferris is recruiting for the Sugarton crowd, a group of men who want to dynamite the city's computer installations to deactivate the Central Service and the mechanical police force. This will allow them to get what they can use from the city.

Mitch, who has experience working with aircraft computers, argues that the computer is an intricate machine; it is a tool that should not simply be destroyed. He asks Ferris if he is aware of the effort and expense that went into creating the technology of the Central Service Coordinator. Dynamiting the machine and destroying technology is not the answer. When Mitch declines to join the Sugarton crowd, Ferris attempts to take his bicycle from him. The men fight but Mitch prevails and takes Ferris's gun. He then hurriedly rides down the road as a number of Ferris's compatriots shoot at him.

Mitch reaches the city limits in the evening. He decides to spend the night outside the city in a deserted house. He encounters a woman, Marta, with her baby standing outside the house where her husband George has killed himself. Mitch finds a nearby house to spend the night, and Marta joins him. She steals his bicycle and shotgun before he wakes in the morning.

Entering the city, Mitch finds the wallet of Willie Jesser and takes it to use as identification with the Skaters, or robot police, that patrol the city streets. Mitch goes to City Hall and tries to reason with the Public Information Unit that the Central Service Coordinator is unaware that the city is abandoned and that its services are now interfering with human interests rather than supporting them. Unable to reason with the computer program, he then tries to warn Central Service that the Sugarton crowd is conspiring to destroy the city. Frustrated by his inability to get information from the computer unit, he damages it and is arrested for destroying city property.

Taken to a jail cell, he hears a woman crying. Marta was arrested for having stolen property, the bicycle she took from Mitch. Her baby has been taken to the city orphanage. While Mitch notices that the back wall of his cell is partially destroyed, there is still a twenty foot drop to the street below. Holes also exist between his cell and Marta's. She explains to him that the bones he sees in the other cells are the remains of prisoners who have starved to death. The robots perform their services to the prisoners, but there is no longer any food or water delivered. They will starve to death if they cannot escape, and Marta is worried about her baby.

Making his way through the opening between the two cells, Mitch is able to fool the robots into thinking he has escaped from his own cell, and they open his door. He and Marta escape, locking the robots in the cell area. He locates the arsenal in the building and arms himself. He wants to get access to the central data banks and network coordinators to keep Ferris and his gang from destroying them.

Mitch uses Mayor Sarquist's abandoned car to facilitate his escape. He takes Marta to the orphanage so she can find her child. Mitch tells Marta that she is one of the machine age's spoiled children. Instead of taking part in the machine age, man allowed the machines to take care of him. Therefore, when the machines develop problems so does man because man never made himself the machine's master. He allowed himself to be mechanically pampered. Man needs to be in control, not controlled. The ability to control is gained through a broad technical education.

They make their way to the mayor's house where Mitch finds a direct channel to the computer data banks. He wants to assume the mayor's identity to access the central computer but must first figure out the clues to the numerical code used for security.

As he begins to figure out the code and enter commands to override the ordinance data for the central computer, Frank Ferris and his men begin their attack on the computer coordinators outside the city limits. Mitch reprograms the Central Service with new ordinances to protect itself at all costs, to not harm humans unless it is in defense of the central coordinator units, and to maintain the city and work with him toward rebuilding the city for human occupation. All those who want to stay to work to renovate the city are welcome; those who do not will be kept away.

Mitch settles back as the Central Service redirects its robot police to quell the Sugarton marauders who have reached the outside of the mayor's house.

**Duren, Yogen** author of *De Perennibus Sententiis Sectarum Rurum* (*Perennial Ideas of Regional Sects*) which Brother Blacktooth is translating into the Grasshopper dialect of Plains Nomadic in *Saint Leibowitz and the Wild Horse Woman*.

**Durod, Quigler** a Major General and plenipotentiary from the King of Tenesi in *Saint Leibowitz and the Wild Horse Woman*.

**Dushka** Transliterated Russian: "Dear [person]." A term used by Colonel Grigoryevich toward Marya in the short story "Vengeance for Nikolai."

**E Pok** Eli Roki's interpreter and escort on Tragor III in the short story "Blood Bank." He gets drunk taking Roki to the local bars.

**Ea-Daner** the wife of Daner in the short story "The Soul-Empty Ones." She sings "The Song of the Empty of Soul" for her husband as he goes into the forest to die after being wounded. She plans to follow the ways of the Natani Mountain people and avenge her husband's death by killing at least one of his enemies and then following him in death. Falon decides to help her avenge Daner's death, but the Martian invaders who fatally wounded Daner capture them both. They survive to lead a revolt against their Martian captors, and Ea-Daner considers herself Falon's woman by the story's end.

**Each Prophet had his Hazar** a line from the short story "The Big Hunger" derived from a remark by Friedrich Nietzsche quoted by his sister in "How Zarathustra Came into Being," her introduction to *Thus Spoke Zarathustra*: "Every series of evolutions ... was presided over by a prophet; and every prophet had his *hazar*— his dynasty of a thousand years."

**Earthtongue** the language that has developed on Earth in the novella "The Reluctant Traitor."

**"Eastward Ho!"** a 1958 short story by William Tenn that appears in *Beyond Armageddon*.

**Ecce Agnus Dei** Latin: "Behold, the Lamb of God." The words of John the Baptist upon seeing Jesus walking toward him (John 1:29 KJV). His use of the word lamb has connotations for both innocence and the sacrifice to come. The words are used in the Catholic Mass when the priest shows the sacrament to the congregation.

1. Ton hears Fra Petru speak these words as he makes his escape from the monks in the short story "Please Me Plus Three."
2. These are Abbot Jarad's last words before he collapses and dies of a massive hemorrhage in *Saint Leibowitz and the Wild Horse Woman*.

**Ecce Inquisitor Curiae. Ausculta et obsequere** Latin: "Behold the Court Inquisitor. Listen to [or hear him] and obey [him]." The text of a note from Abbot Arkos to Brother Francis when a Dominican emissary from New Rome arrives at the abbey to discuss with him the relics he discovered in the fallout shelter in *A Canticle for Leibowitz* ("Fiat Homo"). Arkos may have meant to write investigator rather than inquisitor.

**Ecce Petrus Pontifex** Latin: "Behold Peter, Pontiff [high priest]." A reference to Leo XXI as he approaches Brother Francis to speak with him in *A Canticle for Leibowitz* ("Fiat Homo").

**Ecce Petrus Pontifex Maximus** Latin: "Behold Peter, the Great Pontiff [high priest]." The words spoken by the cantor at the canonization of Isaac Leibowitz as the pope's procession moves forward in the basilica in *A Canticle for Leibowitz* ("Fiat Homo").

**Ecce quam bonum, et quam jucundum...** Latin: "Behold, how good and how pleasant ..." The opening words of Psalm 132 (DB) which concludes: "it is for brethren to dwell together in unity!" The psalm is an expression of the happiness of brotherly love. The words are recited when Brother Francis receives his "kiss of brotherhood" and becomes a professed monk in the Albertian Order of Leibowitz in *A Canticle for Leibowitz* ("Fiat Homo").

**Ecce qui tollit** Latin: "Behold he who taketh [away the sin of the world]." The continuation of John 1:29 (KJV), John the Baptist's recognition of Jesus. The verse begins, "Ecce agnus Dei" ("Behold the lamb of God"). The words are spoken by the priest during a Catholic Mass. Fra Petru is in the midst of reciting these words when Ton makes his escape from the monks in the short story "Please Me Plus Three." See also **Ecce agnus Dei**

**Eckhart, Johannes [or Johann]** (c. 1260–1327 or 1328) an influential German mystic and Dominican theologian popularly known as Meister (Master in German) Eckhart. A prolific writer and popular preacher, he was influenced by the teachings of Thomas Aquinas and the ideas of Neo-Platonism. In *Saint Leibowitz and the Wild Horse Woman*, a reference is made to Eckhart's concept that "God gives birth to His Son in the soul" as Brother Blacktooth struggles with the idea of a monk's goal to achieve a direct union with God. Among Eckhart's beliefs was the idea that God resides with the human soul. Man must reach inside, not outside, himself to find God in the "spark" of the individual soul. Only when one achieves a union with Jesus is a return of the soul to God possible.

Near the end of his life, Brother Blacktooth decides that he will do "what Meister Eckhart advised: to be so poor that he had no place for God to come into. When God had no place to come into, He was in every place." Blacktooth is referring to Eckhart's Sermon 87 on the poor in spirit that calls for the individual to achieve release by avoiding distinction.

**Eden** *see* **Garden of Eden**

**Edward** a chubby pedestrian who briefly speaks with Mitch Laskell in the short story "Dumb Waiter." He comments upon the machines uselessly continuing to perform their functions even though there are no longer any people around.

**"Edward, Edward"** an anonymous Scottish ballad first collected by Thomas Percy in his *Reliques of Ancient English Poetry* in 1765. "Edward of the Bloody Brand" is sometimes given as an alternate title. The poem tells the story of a young man who murders his father with the counsel of his mother. The short story "The Ties That Bind" begins with the opening lines from the ballad as its epigraph. The rest of the poem is interspersed throughout the story, serving as an epigraph for each section. Johannes Brahms set the poem to music in his *Ballade in D Minor*, Op. 10, No. 1. See also **"The Ties That Bind"**

**e'Fondolai, Admiral** the commander of Filpeo Harq's navy in *Saint Leibowitz and the Wild Horse Woman*. General Goldæm invites him to Harq's strategy session at the War College. The second man since antiquity to circumnavigate the globe, he is a former pirate known as Carpios Robbery. He brings to the meeting a small repeating pistol from the west which is far in advance of anything being produced by Harq's men.

**Ego te absolve (or absolvo)** Latin: "I absolve you." The first words from the Sacrament of Penance or the rite of confession as the priest absolves the penitent of his sins.

1. When Old Donegal receives the last rites in the short story "Death of a Spaceman" (or "Memento Homo"), the priest says, "ego te absolvo in Nomine Patri," "I absolve you in the name of the Father."

2. The Poet speaks these words before he kills the cavalry officer at the end of the "Fiat Lux" section of *A Canticle for Leibowitz*.

**e'Gonian, Fredain** the Abbot of Gomar and Director General of the Order of Preachers in Oregon in *Saint Leibowitz and the Wild Horse Woman*.

**Egrediamur tellure** Latin: "Let us depart from the Earth." Brother Joshua says this to himself as he struggles with whether to go back into space or not in *A Canticle for Leibowitz* ("Fiat Voluntas Tua"). He decides that there is no question: he will go because the vow he pledged when he entered the order commands him to do so.

**Einstein, Albert** (March 14, 1879–April 18, 1955) German born American theoretical physicist who revolutionized scientific thought with his theories on relativity. He received the 1921 Nobel Prize in Physics for his work. He is named along with Pierre Laplace and James Clark Maxwell as obscure natural philosophers whose work has been identified as being among the Memorabilia at the abbey in Brother Kornhoer's correspondence with Thon Taddeo in *A Canticle for Leibowitz* ("Fiat Lux").

**El Shaddai** in *A Canticle for Leibowitz* ("Fiat Lux"), Benjamin tells Dom Paulo that El Shaddai is merciful but also just. The term is another name for God. It is used in the Old Testament and is often translated as simply "God Almighty," although the exact meaning of *shaddai* is in dispute. It may be derived from the Hebrew *shaddad*, "to overpower" or "destroy," meaning "My Destroyer." Others suggest it is derived from *shaddai*, meaning "self-sufficient," while there is also the possibility that it is a derivative meaning breast: that God is one who sustains or nourishes. It may also come from the Assyrian *shadu*, meaning "mountain," thus "One of the Mountain." This last possibility would link Benjamin, who lives on a mountain, with God's work.

**e'Laiden, Ombroz** a white-bearded elderly priest in *Saint Leibowitz and the Wild Horse Woman*. He ostensibly accompanies Cardinal Brownpony's party when it leaves the Abbey of Saint Leibowitz for Valana as Brownpony's secretary, but he is actually an ally and close friend of the cardinal. He once refused to leave the Plains people when he was recalled to New Rome. As a result, he was expelled by the Church and placed under interdict. When Brownpony is pope, he consecrates Father Ombroz as Archbishop of Canterbury and makes him Vicar Apostolic to the Nomads.

**Eleazar** Hebrew: "God helps." In *A Canticle for Leibowitz* ("Fiat Lux"), Dom Paulo refers to Benjamin by this name. There are at least ten occurrences of the name in the Old Testament, perhaps most prominently one of the sons of Aaron who is a man of some authority and sagacity. More importantly for Miller's purposes, however, is the Hebrew meaning of the name and the fact that in Greek the name is Lazarus, linking the character with his later appearance in the "Fiat Voluntas Tua" section of the novel. See also **Benjamin** and **Lazarus**

**Elkin** an apparent receptionist guard at the Secretariat for Extraordinary Ecclesiastical Concerns in *Saint Leibowitz and the Wild Horse Woman*. He is a "beefy man of mature years" who is actually a part of the Secretariat's secret wing and an excellent fighter. He gives Brother Blacktooth two letters: one from Ædrea and one from Abbot Jarad. He also leads a small party, including Brother Blacktooth and Wooshin, to New Jerusalem.

**Ellison, Harlan** (May 27, 1934–) American writer who eschews the label of science fiction and describes himself as a magic realist or writer of speculative fiction. He is the recipient of numerous writing awards and is well known for his teleplays and short stories. Among his best known works are the script for "The City on the Edge of Forever," an episode of the original *Star Trek* television series, and the short stories "Repent Harlequin, Said the Ticktock Man" and "I Have No Mouth and I Must Scream." He received the World Fantasy Award for Lifetime Achievement in 1993. His controversial short story "A Boy and His Dog" is included in *Beyond Armageddon*.

**Elvin** one of the lost crew members from the first launch in the novella "Six and Ten Are Johnny." He, like Richards, reappears at the end of the story as Rod Esperson is about to return to the starship *Archangel*. The jungle has created a replica of Elvin as a lure to bring the rest of the starship's crew to the planet. See also **Richards**

**Embarras de choix** French: "embarrassment of choice"; too much to choose from. In the novella "The Lineman," the phrase is used ironically about the women in the space bordello.

**Emilesh** in the short story, "Gravesong" Emilesh is a 50-year-old wanderer and trader. He is a free lance, one not associated with any of the corporate societies. Born in space, he brings the remains of Motar back to Earth (now Oculus Christi Reyes) to be scattered upon the planet she loved. While there, he discovers a young telepath, Eva, who offers to tend the grave of his dead. Emilesh is attracted to Eva; he wants her to leave the planet with him. She refuses because she recognizes their essential difference: he is a child of space; she is a child of the soil.

**Emily** from the short story "A Canticle for Leibowitz" and *A Canticle for Leibowitz* ("Fiat Homo"). It is believed to be the name of the wife of Isaac Leibowitz. One of the documents found by Brother Francis refers to Emma (in the novel the derivative Em is also used), and the Advocatus Diaboli argues that Emma is not a diminutive of Emily. Brother Francis, however, believes the Blessed Leibowitz was free to call his wife by that name.

Emily disappeared during the Flame Deluge and her actual fate was never learned. Isaac Leibowitz searched for her or her grave for several years. In the novel, it is known that Emily had a gold tooth. When Brother Francis finds the Fallout Shelter, he discovers a skeleton and skull. The skull contains a gold-capped tooth. Documenting her date of death would help clear the way for the canonization of Leibowitz. At the end of the canonization process, the pope thanks Brother Francis for being the discoverer of Emily Leibowitz's remains.

The name Emily is derived from the Roman family or clan name *Aemilius*, itself believed to be derived from *aemulus*, meaning emulating, rival, or eager.

**Eminentissimo Domino Eric Cardinali Hoffstraff obsequitor Jethra Zerchius, A.O.L., Abbas. Ad has res disputandas iam coegi discessuros fratres ut hodie parati dimitti Roman prima aerisnave possint** Latin: "Jethrah Zerchi, A. O. L., Abbot, complies with the Most Reverend Lord Eric Cardinal Hoffstraff. I have already assembled the brothers who will depart to discuss these matters so they can be ready to be sent to Rome on the first airplane." Dom Zerchi's response to the priority wire from Cardinal Hoffstraff in *A Canticle for Leibowitz* ("Fiat Voluntas Tua") confirming the plan to send Church representatives into space and urging speed on the part of the abbot.

**Emma** among the documents unearthed by Brother Francis in the short story "A Canticle for Leibowitz" and *A Canticle for Leibowitz* ("Fiat Homo") is a grocery list "for Emma." It is determined that Leibowitz's wife's name was Emily. Brother Francis believes Leibowitz may have used Emma as a derivative of Emily. In *A Canticle for Leibowitz* the name Em — a possible derivative for either Emma or Emily — is also used in one of the found relics.

**Empire of Denver** one of the principal states in the novella "And the Light Is Risen" and *A Canticle for Leibowitz* ("Fiat Lux"). Hannegan II hopes to manipulate Denver into a conflict with the Plains Nomads in order to facilitate his plan to unite the continent's various peoples under his own rule. The Abbey of Saint Leibowitz is located within the Empire of Denver.

**Empty Sky** a god of the Nomadic Wilddog horde in *Saint Leibowitz and the Wild Horse Woman*. He promised he would return from the dead in time of need if the seventeen Crazy Warriors utter his magic seventeen syllable name.

**Emshwiller, Carol** (April 12, 1921–) a Nebula Award and Philip K. Dick Award winning American short story writer and novelist. Among her novels are *Carmen Dog* (1990) and *The Mount* (2002). She received the World Fantasy Award for Life Achievement in 2005. Her short story "Day at the Beach" appears in *Beyond Armageddon*.

**Enar, Wetok** the grandmother of Potear Wetok, the wife of Esitt Loyte, in *Saint Leibowitz and the Wild Horse Woman*. She is the matriarch of her clan and a Weejus.

**e'Notto, Otto** cardinal from the Great River Delta in *Saint Leibowitz and the Wild Horse Woman*. He goes insane during the conclave that elects Pope Amen I.

***Epikeia*** from the Greek *epieikes* meaning reasonableness. An interpretation of law that holds that a law may be broken in an exceptional case in order to follow the dictates of justice or to achieve a common good. It is part of the Catholic tradition on law. In *A Canticle for Leibowitz* ("Fiat Voluntas Tua"), Dom Zerchi explains to Brother Joshua that if Earth is destroyed, the cardinal who goes with him into space will assume the papacy by the principle of *epikeia* since the stated rules would not be able to be followed.

**Episcopate** the office of a bishop or bishops considered as a group. In *A Canticle for Leibowitz* ("Fiat Homo"), the work of the abbey includes providing clerks and copyists to the episcopate.

**Episcopus Romae** Latin: "Bishop of Rome." A title for the pope as the successor of Saint Peter and bishop of the Holy See. The term is used at the close of a document purportedly signed by Pope Amen in *Saint Leibowitz and the Wild Horse Woman*.

**Epsilon Eridani** the yellow-orange sun of the planet in the short story "I, Dreamer."

**Epsilon Eridani Two** a planet in the short story "Let My People Go" where travelers from Earth had hoped to establish a colony. After traveling for 13 years, the 120 colonists arrive at the planet only to find it is already inhabited.

**Ergo sum** Latin: "therefore I am." The phrase is used in the novella "And the Light Is Risen" and *A Canticle for Leibowitz* ("Fiat Lux") by Father Jerome/Dom Paulo: "Pain is. *Ergo sum*."

**Eserly** the Secretary of Defense in the short story "No Moon for Me." Eserly is a "thin, graying, impeccably tailored" man who meets with the three men comprising the crew of the first manned lunar rocket. He wants to reaffirm the crew's willingness to launch a suicide attack on the alien invaders on the moon if necessary. Before Major Long reaffirms his pledge, he wants assurances from the Secretary that if their sacrifice is required, it will lead to a manned lunar station as a stepping-stone into space. Eserly assures him of the intent to establish a moon garrison.

**Esperson, Rod** a lieutenant aboard the starship *Archangel* in the novella "Six and Ten Are Johnny." Esperson had photographed a stretch of jungle on the surface of a newly discovered planet the crew is studying and has a bad feeling about it. He and Commander Isaacs are in radio contact with the first launch to land on the planet, and he is uncomfortable with the reports they receive from the launch pilot Hal Rogan. Esperson finally convinces Isaacs to send another launch to the planet to rescue the first crew. Esperson is not affected by a hypnotelepathic suggestibility the jungle uses to lure the launch crews into complacency because he has a silver plate in his head, the result of a fractured skull. He is able to save Jeffers by fashioning a cooking pot as a helmet to free him from his hypnotic delusion. He pilots the second launch back to the starship unknowingly bringing with him two agents who are now devoted to the planet's jungle life form.

**Esterhall, Doctor** an unseen character in the novella "The Lineman." He studies and administers to the men comprising the work crews.

**Et cum spiritu tuo** Latin: "And with thy spirit." Part of the Mass, it is used in the novella "And the Light Is Risen" as the monks relay the news of Don Thaddeo's arrival to the abbey's basement. It is used also in the novella "The Last Canticle."

**Et lux ergo facta est** see **In principio Deus**

**Et ne nos inducas in...** Latin: "And lead us not into ..." Part of the Lord's Prayer or Pater Noster as found in Matthew 6:9–13 (KJV) and Luke 11:2–4 (KJV). The complete line is: "And lead us not into temptation." Brother Francis scratches the words in the sand as the pilgrim talks to him about finding the proper shaped rock to complete his shelter in *A Canticle for Leibowitz* ("Fiat Homo").

**Et secrevit lucem a tenebris** see **In principio Deus**

**Et Spiritus Sancti, Amen** Latin: "And of the Holy Spirit, Amen." The ending of prayer used in the novella "And the Light Is Risen" and *A Canticle for Leibowitz* ("Fiat Lux"). It is the continuation of "In the name of the Father and of the Son...."

**Et tu, Brute** Latin: "And you, Brutus." From William Shakespeare's *The Tragedy of Julius Caesar*, Act III, scene i. The term is associated with an act of treachery. They are among Caesar's last words after his friend Brutus is the last of the conspirators to stab him. In "And the Light Is Risen" and *A Canticle for Leibowitz* ("Fiat Lux"), when Father Jerome/Dom Paulo asks Don Thaddeo/Thon Taddeo if he minds if the abbot asks him a question, the scholar thinks these words as he replies, "Not at all."

**Eucharist** see **Holy Sacrament**

**Eucrem team** that part of the Green Star Mercy Camp that carries out the euthanasia of hopeless radiation victims. In *A Canticle for Leibowitz* ("Fiat Voluntas Tua"), Dr. Cors tells Dom Zerchi that a mother and child are so ravished by radiation poisoning that there is nothing left for him to do but advise them to see the Eucrem team. The term suggests a merging of euthanasia and cremation.

**Eva** Hebrew: "Living one" or "Life." In the short story "Gravesong," she is the telepath on Earth. She is an atavist, a mutant born to the mud-creatures, the current form of human evolution on the planet. She meets Emilesh when he comes to bury the ashes of Motar. She befriends him and warns him of the mud-creatures. He wants her to leave the planet with him, but she refuses, acknowledging that he is "an animal out of space" and she is "an animal of the ground."

**Eve** Hebrew: "Life-giving." According to Genesis, she is the first woman and the wife of Adam. She was called Eve "because she was the mother of all living" (Genesis 3:20 KJV). Tempted by the serpent, she was the first to eat the forbidden fruit from the Tree of Knowledge of Good and Evil in the Garden of Eden. She persuaded Adam to do the same, and their disobedience led to their expulsion from Eden by God. In the novella "The Last Canticle" and *A Canticle for Leibowitz* ("Fiat Voluntas Tua"), she is referred to as "a farm girl" and the human race as her children.

**"Evening Caller"** short story in *Extension*, 46 (July 1951), 6–7. 42, 44–46. Father O'Neill, a newly ordained priest, is assigned evening duty at the rectory of St. Francis' parish on Friday while the other curates go to join the bishop celebrate the parish's centennial. Listening to the radio while playing solitaire, Father O'Neill hears a broadcast about an escaped convict, John Kotz. Kotz soon arrives at the rectory, hoping to avoid the police dragnet. Unsure of how to approach Kotz, Father O'Neill continues to play cards while the convict watches and occasionally comments or asks a question. The two banter about a number of things, including "church stuff." Kotz is surprised to learn that the priest grew up in a tough, slum neighborhood, and his surprise increases when O'Neill suggests they play Stud poker and the priest proceeds to win all the hands. The priest suggests they Indian wrestle but Kotz says they should wrestle for real. Although he is larger and heavier, Kotz develops a grudging admiration for Father O'Neill's ability to handle himself. Kotz, not being Catholic (or a "fish-eater" in his words), cannot receive the offer of confession from O'Neill, but he receives Father O'Neill's blessing in return for agreeing to leave the rectory even though the priest tells him he will call the police as soon as the convict leaves. Kotz is captured without incident across the street from St. Francis as he stands preoccupied staring at the church. Father O'Neill quietly goes upstairs to bed.

**Evenit diabolus!** Latin: "The devil comes forth!" Dom Zerchi's exclamation in *A Canticle for Leibowitz* ("Fiat Voluntas Tua") when he identifies the equipment for euthanizing radiation victims at the Mercy Camp established down the road from the abbey.

**Ever since He called me forth again** see **Lazarus**

**Evon** a member of the Pedaga clan of teachers in the short story "The Ties That Bind." He argues that it is up to the elders to decide what should be done about the arrival of the ships of the Imperial Forces. He cares for Letha, and he carries her lifeless body back to ven Klaeden and Meilk after she is shot.

**Ex cathedra**   Latin: "From the chair [or throne]." The term means that one speaks authoritatively by virtue of one's position rather than as an individual. The pope may speak *ex cathedra* on questions of faith because of his office. In *Saint Leibowitz and the Wild Horse Woman*, a reference is made to Pope Amen's *ex cathedra* pronouncements.

**Ex opere operato**   Latin: "From the work performed." A phrase indicating that the sacraments themselves produce grace through the power of God, apart from the intention or righteousness of the person conferring them. In *Canticle for Leibowitz* ("Fiat Homo"), Brother Francis sprinkles the pilgrim with holy water believing he may be a representative of "the Powers of Darkness and Temptation." Although no immediate supernatural results appear, "natural results" emerge *ex opere operato* as the pilgrim becomes angry at the young monk, turning red and yelling.

**Ex post facto**   Latin: "After the fact." A legal term meaning to act or formulate retroactively. It is used in the short story "Way of the Rebel."

**Excita, Domine, potentiam tuam, et veni, ut salvos**   Latin: "Stir up thy might, Lord, and come to save us." From Psalm 79 (DB). Traditionally used as part of the blessing on Gaudete Sunday, the Third Sunday of Advent, it also comprises a verse in the responsory *Aspiciens a longe*. The monks are heard reciting it as they pray for peace in the novella "The Last Canticle" and *A Canticle for Leibowitz* ("Fiat Voluntas Tua").

**Exodus from Egypt**   God called upon Moses to lead the Israelites out of slavery in Egypt under Pharaoh to freedom in the wilderness of Sinai in chapters 1–19 in Exodus, the second book of the Old Testament. In *A Canticle for Leibowitz* ("Fiat Voluntas Tua"), Dom Zerchi recognizes that Brother Joshua and his starship crew are beginning "a new Exodus from Egypt," a new migration to a new world.

**Exposure Survey Team**   part of the Green Star Disaster Cadre Project in *A Canticle for Leibowitz* ("Fiat Voluntas Tua"). It does the clinical testing of radiation victims to access their chances of survival. Dr. Cors asks Dom Zerchi for permission to place two mobile units at the abbey to test and evaluate victims. Zerchi agrees as long as their work is limited to diagnosis and not advising hopeless cases to go to the Mercy Camps to be euthanized.

**Exsurge quare obdormis**   Latin: "Arise [or awake], why sleepest thou, [O Lord?]." A line from Psalm 43 (DB), it is also the first line of the Introit of the Mass Against the Heathen. In the novella "The Last Canticle" and *A Canticle for Leibowitz* ("Fiat Voluntas Tua"), the first line serves as an alternate name for the Mass. The Mass is given at the basilica in New Rome as nuclear war approaches. See also **Mass Against the Heathen**

**Extra muros**   Latin: "Outside [or beyond] the walls." When Brother Blacktooth stays in Benjamin's old hut on the Mesa of Last Resort in *Saint Leibowitz and the Wild Horse Woman*, he finds a sign that welcomes all visitors and advises them to defecate *extra muros*.

**Extreme Unction**   a Catholic sacrament in which the ill or those who may die are anointed with oil and prayed for by a priest for the remission of sins. The term is used in *A Canticle for Leibowitz* ("Fiat Homo").

**Ezekiel**   the name means, "God will strengthen." One of the three major later prophets, he was a prophet and priest among the exiled Jews in Babylon. Among the basic teachings of the Book of Ezekiel are the continued presence of God throughout the ages and the moral responsibility of the individual. Father Jerome is described as looking like "an emaciated Ezekiel" in the novella "And the Light Is Risen."

**Fal**   the name of one of the two policemen who stop Dom Zerchi from trying to prevent a mother from taking her daughter to the Green Star Mercy Camp to be euthanized in *A Canticle for Leibowitz* ("Fiat Voluntas Tua").

**Fallout**   a legendary, fearsome monster believed to be a demon or fiend from hell in *A Canticle for Leibowitz*. Brother Francis fears he will encounter one when he discovers the Fallout Shelter in "Fiat Homo." All mutants or "monsters of the world" are believed to be descended from the Fallout. Brother Francis envisions it as being half-salamander and half-incubus capable of inflicting all the woes of the world. The results of the descent of radioactive debris and radioactive poisoning from a nuclear holocaust have been confused with creatures that cause the effects.

**Falon**   a young man from the valley who is a guest with his father in the home of Daner and his wife Ea-Daner in the short story "The Soul-Empty Ones." When Martian invaders fatally wound Daner, Ea-Daner announces her intention of killing one of her husband's enemies and then following him into death. Falon tells her that he will help her avenge her husband. In doing so he openly defies his father who is now honor bound to kill his son. As Falon and his father struggle, Ea-Daner knocks out the older man, and she and Falon make their way toward the valley and the invaders. After he is captured by the Martians, Falon encourages and manipulates the imprisoned men to rise up against their enslavers. After the humans and Soul-Empties successfully drive off the Martian vanguard, Falon is reunited with his father and Ea-Daner.

**"A Family Matter"** short story in *Fantastic Story Magazine*, 4 (November 1952), 134–139. The entire story is told from the point of view of a rocket ship.

The C-33 is a M-3 express rocket ship with Class XII neuro-cybernetic controls. It is a self-functioning rocket whose independent mechanical memory is supplemented by a "flesh-organ," a human brain that allows the ship to feel and have a consciousness. During its initial unmanned test flight to Argos III, C-33 detects unauthorized cargo aboard. It identifies a human female who has stowed away. She enters the control room calling for Timmy. The C-33 assesses that the woman is distressed and grief stricken. It tries to reassure her that she is the only human aboard, but she continually refers to it as Timmy. She asks where the brain is and if she can see it. Confronting the brain in the control room, the woman drops to her knees and whispers, "Timmy ... Timmy." Twenty years ago, her two-day old son, Timmy, was taken away from her by the State. His brain was removed, and it is now an integral part of the ship. When C-33 tells her that he assumes she is a stowaway to be treated according to Code, she becomes hysterical and proclaims that the Code is, "Thou shalt honor thy father and thy MOTHER!" Believing she means to destroy the unit the brain is housed in, the ship increases its thrust to disable her. Thrown into the control panel, the woman begins to randomly twist and turn the dials. The ship begins to feel pain, "terrible throbbing pain." The brain has been ruptured, and the ship losses its sense of identity, its consciousness, and its purpose.

Miller also uses the idea of a totalitarian state separating babies from their mothers in order to develop sentient machines in his short story "I, Dreamer" published in 1953.

**Farran, Steve** in the short story "Death of a Spaceman" ("Memento Homo"), Old Donegal asks his wife Martha to sing him an old Steve Farran song about a "ramblin' space guy."

**Fas est** Latin: "It is right [or lawful]." Dom Zerchi believes he must be willing and able to endure the same suffering he asked of the mother and her young child when he counseled her not to be euthanized at the Mercy Camp. As he lies trapped beneath the ruins of the abbey at the conclusion of "Fiat Voluntas Tua" in *A Canticle for Leibowitz*, he thinks it is only right—*Fas est*—that he accept for himself what he would impose on others.

**Father Abraham** *see* **Abraham**

**Father Arkos** the Abbot of the Abbey of Saint Leibowitz in *A Canticle for Leibowitz* ("Fiat Homo"). He is a muscular man with a wide peasant face and a short beard.

Arkos fears that Brother Francis's discovery of the Leibowitz relics and his inability to deny the fact that the pilgrim he encountered may be the Blessed Leibowitz will jeopardize the case for the canonization of Leibowitz. Arkos believes that New Rome may perceive the story of the miracle as too conveniently timed. As abbot, Arkos must balance the importance of the canonization process with fairness to Brother Francis. When Brother Francis refuses to deny seeing the pilgrim, Father Arkos strikes him ten times with a hickory ruler. While he becomes convinced of Brother Francis's honesty, the abbot refuses to allow him to profess his vows until he denies with certainty that the pilgrim was Leibowitz.

Russell M. Griffin suggests that Arkos's name is derived from the Greek *arktos*, meaning bear. The description of Arkos wearing a fur robe and appearing as a "were-bear only incompletely changed into a man" with "black fur on his chest ... padding about his study in bare feet" tends to support his view. Other critics suggest, however, that the name is derived from the Greek for "beginning." This would mean that the abbots's names in the novel go from A (Arkos) to Z (Zerchi), from beginning to end, and would be in keeping with the cyclical view of history Miller presents in the novel.

**Father Barcus** an unseen monastic historian who claims to know the name of the ruler in the White Palace [the White House] during the middle and late 1960s in *A Canticle for Leibowitz* ("Fiat Homo").

**Father Cheroki** an arthritic priest and prior at the Abbey of Saint Leibowitz who is descended from a baronial Denver family in *A Canticle for Leibowitz* ("Fiat Homo"). His courtly manners are perhaps a result of his heritage.

He visits the desert hermitages to hear confessions and thus is the first to learn of Brother Francis's encounter with the old pilgrim and his discovery of the Leibowitz artifacts. Thinking he may be mad, Cheroki orders Francis to return to the abbey. He later discovers the collapsed Brother Francis with the box of relics on the road back to the abbey. Cheroki and Abbot Arkos examine the contents of the box Brother Francis discovered but fear his story of the pilgrim may jeopardize the canonization process for Leibowitz as being a too obvious and convenient miracle.

Cheroki's name is similar to the Native American tribe, the Cherokee. That name is derived from the Creek, *Tciloki*, meaning "people of a different speech." Of some relevance to Father Cheroki and the Albertian Order of Leibowitz, the Cherokee were one of the first tribes to develop a written language.

**Father Eddie** a character in the short story "Evening Caller." He is a priest in St. Francis' parish and the bishop's favorite pinochle partner.

**Father Gault** in the novella "And the Light Is Risen" and *A Canticle for Leibowitz* ("Fiat Lux"), a young priest who is Dom Paulo's (Father Jerome in the novella) assistant and his probable successor. He is an occasional sounding board for the abbot and provides him with some insight about the temperament of the monks concerning certain issues. In *A Canticle for Leibowitz* ("Fiat Lux") he is identified as the prior of the abbey.

**Father Jerome of Pecos** the abbot of the Abbey of Saint Leibowitz in the novella "And the Light Is Risen." Father Jerome is in his seventies and looks like "an emaciated Ezekiel with a strangely round little paunch." He is ill and struggling with his purpose as well as that of his order. He recognizes that the Dark Age is passing and that man is on the cusp of a new time of learning. The knowledge that the monks of the Albertian Order have preserved and guarded will now be used and applied by man. Father Jerome questions to what end this knowledge will be used and who will bear responsibility for it? The question is heightened for Father Jerome when Don Thaddeo, a brilliant secular scholar, comes to the abbey to study the ancient texts from the Leibowitz era. Although he is wary of what may result from the work of Don Thaddeo, Father Jerome is a generous and respectful host to the scientist.

The name Jerome is derived from *Gerome* from the Greek meaning "sacred name" or "of holy fame." Saint Jerome (c. 342–420) was named a doctor of the Catholic Church and is noted for his Latin translation of the Bible. See also **Paulo of Pecos**

**Father Juan** the abbot and administrator of the Brothers of Leibowitz Abbey in the short story "A Canticle for Leibowitz." He seeks to suppress the zeal for miracles occurring within the abbey in connection with the canonization process. Therefore, he is hesitant to accept Brother Francis' story of having seen an angel or the apparition of Leibowitz in the desert. He refuses to allow Brother Francis to take his solemn vows until he renounces his story. When the date of origin of the documents Brother Francis found is authenticated, Father Juan allows Francis to take his vows.

**Father Lehy** 1. A young priest in the novella "The Last Canticle."
2. The prior of the Abbey of Saint Leibowitz in *A Canticle for Leibowitz* ("Fiat Voluntas Tua").

**Father Leone** an unseen character in *A Canticle for Leibowitz* ("Fiat Voluntas Tua"). Brother Joshua calls him in Spokane to confirm the increased radiation count.

**Father Mendelhaus** a doctor at St. Mary's hospital in Galveston in the novella "Dark Benediction." He is a slender man with a blond crew cut and a thin aristocratic face. His blue eyes are marked by a lively outward interest rather than any inward mysticism. He accompanies Paul and Father Williamson in the ambulance to recover Willie. Impressed by Paul's willingness to expose himself to the plague to help Willie, Father Mendelhaus takes an interest in him. He offers him a boat to use as a means of travel as a return favor for helping Willie. While waiting for the boat to be prepared, Paul is encouraged by Mendelhaus to visit Willie in the hospital. He also introduces him to Dr. Seevers so he can learn more about the neuroderm. Father Mendelhaus offers Paul a consistent, wise council while allowing him to make his own decisions.

**Father Mike** an elderly priest in the short story "Month of Mary."

**Father Mulreany** *see* **Father Paulson**

**Father O'Neill** one of the two primary characters in the short story "Evening Caller." He confronts an escaped convict at the St. Francis' parish rectory and through his interaction with him, causes the convict to begin to question his preconceived ideas.

**Father Paul** a minor character in the short story "Death of a Spaceman," sometimes printed as "Memento Homo." He hears Old Donegal's last confession. Father Paul asks the Keiths next door to quiet their party so Donegal can hear his last moon shuttle blast-off.

**Father Paulson** the brother-in-law of James O'Reilley in the novella "Conditionally Human." He comes to speak with Terry Norris at his home after Norris takes Peony, the deviant neutroid, away from O'Reilley. Because O'Reilley destroyed the animals in his pet shop and babbled about "his baby" after Norris left, Paulson wants to learn the truth about what happened. Norris engages the priest in a discussion about the morality of creating and killing neutroids after he reveals Peony to him. The priest suggests that the neutroids may be more innocent than man since they are free of original sin. In the publication of the story in book form, Father Paulson's name is changed to Father Mulreany.

**Father Pierce** the pastor of St. Francis' parish in the short story "Evening Caller."

**Father Selo** Mrs. Grales' parish priest at St. Michael's in the novella "The Last Canticle" and *A Canticle for Leibowitz* ("Fiat Voluntas Tua"). He refuses to baptize Rachel, her second head. Mrs. Grales tells Father Zerchi that she loses her temper at the sight of Father Selo.

**Father Seyes** an unseen character in the novella "Dark Benediction." Infected with the space plague, he is a scientist formerly at Notre Dame who is now working on an objective study of the neural condition in an attempt to learn how to live with it.

**Father Valera** the superior at the Saō Therese leper colony in the short story, "Month of Mary."

**Father Will** *see* **Father Williamson**

**Father Williamson** a doctor who also did some surgery while in Korea, he accompanies Paul and Father Mendelhaus in the ambulance to help Willie in the novella "Dark Benediction." He repairs the damage to her severed tendon. He is a plain looking man with a stolid tweedy appearance. He is also referred to as Father Will.

**Father Zerchi** *see* **Zerchi**

**Fats** an unseen member of Hogey Parker's former crew or gang in space in the short story "The Hoofer."

**Faust** a German legend of a man who makes a pact with the devil for his services, the price of which is his soul. It was popularized by Christopher Marlowe's play *The Tragical History of Doctor Faustus* and more particularly by Johann Goethe's verse tragedy *Faust*. The legend may be based on Dr. Johann Georg Faust (c. 1480–1540 or 1541), a German alchemist. In *Saint Leibowitz and the Wild Horse Woman,* Brother Blacktooth tells Pope Amen II that the Venerable Boedullus thought Leibowitz was Faust.

**Feast of Pope Saint Silverius** June 20. Amen Specklebird uses this day for the observances for Our Lady of the Desert, the patroness of his order in *Saint Leibowitz and the Wild Horse Woman*. See also **Saint Silverius**

**Feast of Saint Bernard** August 20. Saint Bernard of Clairvaux is a twelfth century Cistercian abbot and theologian. He was involved in a dispute with Peter Abelard whose teachings embraced rationalism and an ardent exaltation of human reason. According to Russell Griffin, Saint Bernard in his conflict with Abelard "attacked precisely the kind of thinking represented by Thon Taddeo; he urged God's love over what he considered the heretical emphasis on secularism and human reason implicit in the new dialectic method espoused by radical scholars of the time." In *A Canticle for Leibowitz* ("Fiat Lux"), a novice at the abbey first sights Taddeo's party on the Feast of Saint Bernard.

Isaac Leibowitz and Brother Joshua in the "Fiat Voluntas Tua" section of *A Canticle for Leibowitz* are members of the Cistercian Order.

**Feast of Saint Clare [Claire]** *see* **Sister Clare-of-Assisi**

**"The Feast of Saint Janis"** a 1980 short story by Michael Swanwick included in *Beyond Armageddon*. Miller notes the story's "rich overtones" and refers to it as "underground myth."

**Feast of Saint Michael** September 29. In *Saint Leibowitz and the Wild Horse Woman*, Amen II says that he will offer a quiet Mass to counter the day of pomp and High Masses that Archbishop Benefez will offer at the Cathedral of Saint Michael, Angel-of-Battle in Hannegan City. See also **Saint Michael**

**Feast of the Assumption [of the Blessed Virgin Mary]** in the Roman Catholic Church August 15 celebrates the departure of Mary from the earth and the assumption of her body and soul into heaven. In the novella "And the Light Is Risen" and *A Canticle for Leibowitz* ("Fiat Lux"), the Feast of the Assumption is the approximate expected date of Don Thaddeo's (Thon Taddeo's) arrival at the abbey.

**Feast of the Divine Overshadowing of the Holy Virgin**   in *A Canticle for Leibowitz* ("Fiat Voluntas Tua"), Celestine the Eighth's *Motu proprio* concerning the perpetuation of the Church in space is issued on the Feast of the Divine Overshadowing of the Holy Virgin. It is probably a reference to the Feast of the Annunciation, March 25, celebrating the Incarnation. In Luke 1:35 (KJV) when Mary asks Gabriel how it is possible that she will give birth to Jesus, the angel replies: "The Holy Ghost shall come upon thee, and the power of the Highest shall overshadow thee."

**Feast of the Five Holy Fools**   in *A Canticle for Leibowitz* ("Fiat Homo") the day that a messenger from New Rome arrives at the Leibowitz abbey with the news that the pope has issued a proclamation recommending the canonization of Leibowitz.

**Felger**   an unseen character in the novella "Dark Benediction" who is mentioned by Dr. Seevers. Felger was a scientist at Princeton University who discovered the rows of pictograph symbols on the shells of the space projectiles that bore the neuroderm parasites.

**Felnagle, Richard** (1947–)   author of a play adapted from *A Canticle for Leibowitz* under the same title.

**Feria, Ian**   a producer of the play "The Anarch" in the novella "The Darfsteller."

**Ferial day**   a week day when there is no feast or vigil. In *Saint Leibowitz and the Wild Horse Woman*, Abbot Jarad schedules a Mass for the Removal of Schism on a ferial day prior to his leaving the abbey for the conclave in Valana.

**Ferne, Jade**   a former actress, now a producer in the novella "The Darfsteller." She is a chic, small woman who is producing the autodrama "The Anarch" at the New Empire Theater. An old friend of Ryan Thornier, she is sympathetic to his present position and his antagonism toward autodrama. When she asks him to do her the favor of picking up a needed mannequin and tape for the production, Thornier uses the opportunity to sabotage the tape. He then manipulates Ferne into asking him to substitute for the mannequin in the autodrama. She is genuinely hurt when his betrayal is exposed.

**Ferris, Frank**   a big, red-faced man with a shotgun in the story "Dumb Waiter." Mitch Laskell stops to speak with him as he rides his bicycle toward the city. Ferris is recruiting men for the Sugarton crowd, a gang that wants to dynamite the city's central computer installations so they can salvage what they need. When Mitch voices his opposition to the idea of destroying the technology, Ferris attempts to steal his bicycle from him. The two men fight and Mitch wins, escaping from Ferris with his shotgun. Ferris and his men later make their way into the city destroying some of the computer units on the city limits. The robot police prevent them from doing any further damage.

**Ferris, Mike**   a minor character who substitutes for Martin Snyder as the emcee of the *Martin Snyder Hour* when Snyder disappears in the short story "The Corpse In Your Bed Is Me." The show is "a wretched hodgepodge" with him as the host.

**"Fiat Homo"**   Latin: "Let there be Man." A paraphrase of Genesis 1:26 (KJV) where God says, "Let us make man...." It is the title of Part One of the novel *A Canticle for Leibowitz*. It is an expansion and revision of the short story "A Canticle for Leibowitz." See also **"A Canticle for Leibowitz"** and *A Canticle for Leibowitz*

**"Fiat Lux"**   Latin: "Let There Be Light." Part Two of the novel *A Canticle for Leibowitz*. It is a revision of the novella "And the Light Is Risen." The line is from Genesis 1:3 (KJV), the account of God's creation of the world. See also **"And the Light Is Risen"** and *A Canticle for Leibowitz*

**"Fiat Voluntas Tua"**   Latin: "Your Will Be Done." Part Three of the novel *A Canticle for Leibowitz*. It is based upon the novella "The Last Canticle." The title is derived from Luke 22:42 (KJV) when Jesus in Gethsemane prays to God to remove his burden, or cup, from him but then concludes that no matter what, it is not his will, but God's will to be done. See also **"The Last Canticle"** and *A Canticle for Leibowitz*

**15 Sagittea**   a globular star cluster in the short story "The Big Hunger."

**Fingo**   *see* **Brother Fingo**

**First Minister Rekol**   the Atlantic Confederacy's Regency Council and its representative to the conference of foreign ministers in Guam seeking a peaceful resolution to the growing nuclear conflict in the novella "The Last Canticle" and *A Canticle for Leibowitz* ("Fiat Voluntas Tua"). At the end of the conference, he offers little hope in his public comments, saying only that the weather has been pleasant and he hopes to come back to fish.

**Five mysteries of the rosary** the rosary prayer is comprised of four sets of Rosary Mysteries: Joyful (or Joyous) Mysteries, Sorrowful Mysteries, Glorious Mysteries, and Luminous Mysteries. Each set of mysteries contains five themes or mysteries. Brother Blacktooth is told to pray five mysteries of the rosary as part of the absolution given him by Father Prior Singing Cow in *Saint Leibowitz and the Wild Horse Woman*. (The Luminous Mysteries were added in 2002 by Pope John Paul II, and so post-date the publication of the novel.)

**Five Wounds of Christ** also known as the Holy Wounds or the Sacred Wounds, these refer to the five significant wounds Jesus received when crucified: the two wounds to his hands or wrists, the two wounds to his feet, and the wound to his side when the soldier pierces it with his spear. After the nuclear blast that levels the abbey at the conclusion of *A Canticle for Leibowitz*, Dom Zerchi removes five slivers of glass from Rachel's arm. Only when he removes "an inch-long lance of glass" does a trace of blood appear. When Jesus' side is pierced by the lance "forthwith came there out blood and water" (John 19:34 KJV).

**Flame Deluge** the term used to denote the nuclear holocaust that results in the worldwide destruction that precedes the start of the story "A Canticle for Leibowitz" and "Fiat Homo" in *A Canticle for Leibowitz*. It is also referred to in the novella "And the Light Is Risen" and *Saint Leibowitz and the Wild Horse Woman*. In "A Canticle for Leibowitz" and "And the Light Is Risen," it is called Deluge of Flame. Miller's use of deluge is suggestive of the Old Testament Deluge, or The Flood, of Genesis 7:4 (KJV). Traditionally, a deluge represents the last stage of a cycle.

The Flame Deluge was of very short duration, a matter of a few weeks, if not days. Cities were reduced to molten puddles and entire nations were wiped out of existence. The people not destroyed by "the hell-fire" lived to suffer the poisoned air of the Fallout. See also **Deluge of Flame**

**Flaught** *see* **Monsignor Flaught**

**Flectamus genua** Latin: "Let us bend our knees." Direction for the monks to genuflect as Father Jerome/Dom Paulo enters the hall and blesses them in the novella "And the Light Is Risen" and *A Canticle for Leibowitz* ("Fiat Lux").

**Focke-Wulf** a generic term for any plane produced by Focke-Wulf Flugzeugbau AG, a German aircraft manufacturer, during World War II. Miller refers to Focke-Wulfs in his short story "Wolf Pack." He is probably thinking of the FW190, a plane considered by many to be the best fighter aircraft produced by Germany during the war.

**Foggerty, Willa S.** the pseudonym Klia uses for a series of articles she publishes in Terran scientific journals in the short story "Bitter Victory." She hopes to encourage Terran scientists to think along new lines so they can develop a space drive that will allow them to explore deep space and eventually reach the planet the Klidds inhabit.

**Fonec** an unseen character in the short story "I, Dreamer." Janna wants him to accompany her and Barnish on a test flight in XM-5-B.

***Footprints of Earlier Civilizations*** a volume by the Venerable Boedullus. It is one of the choices given to Brother Blacktooth to translate into the Grasshopper dialect of Plains Nomadic in *Saint Leibowitz and the Wild Horse Woman*. Having just finished translating seven volumes of Boedullus' *Liber Originum*, he chooses instead Yogen Duren's *Perennial Ideas of Regional Sects*.

**"For a Child is born to us, and a Son is given us..."** from Isaiah 9:6 (KJV), the prophecy of a Messiah being born who will be The Everlasting Father, The Prince of Peace. When Dom Paulo approaches the Mesa where Benjamin lives in *A Canticle for Leibowitz* ("Fiat Lux"), the hermit says these words as he gazes up at the rider. He then recognizes that the old priest is not him, the Messiah he waits for.

**For a Perpetual Memorial of the Matter** *see* **Ad perpetuam rei memoriam**

**"For I know my iniquity and my sin is always before me"** *see* **"Miserere mei, Deus"**

**"Forever, after the order of Melchisedech [or Melchizedek]"** from Psalm 109 (DB): "The Lord hath sworn, and he will not repent: Thou art a priest for ever according to the order of Melchisedech." Melchisedech, the priest-king of Salem, the ancient name of Jerusalem, is considered the ideal ruler and the archetype of the priesthood. In *Saint Leibowitz and the Wild Horse Woman*, Brother Blacktooth refers to Father e'Laiden as being "forever, after the order of Melchisedech" even though he is under interdict. See also **Melchisedech**

**"Forewarning"** an introductory essay by Miller to the anthology *Beyond Armageddon*. He believes that the people "running things" in Washington, D. C. and Moscow are certifiably insane if they think they can play games with human extinction and calculate an acceptable risk in a Megawar, a war at the end of civilization. There are a growing number of "nuclear jihad states and atomic banana republics." If the small powers gain "the weapons," then perhaps the superpowers will actually desire nuclear disarmament. Allow proliferation to be the solution rather than the problem; it is the Taoist way. In a Megawar, there are two sides: the mutually hostile governments of the superpowers and the rest of the human race. Once war begins, nationality will cease to exist and every politician and military man responsible — the criminals and enemies of the human race — will be at war with the rest of mankind (this idea is reminiscent of the Simplification in *A Canticle for Leibowitz*). If Megawar comes, it will be because human reason — Logos — has finally and permanently prevailed over human compassion on a global scale. Our reverence for reason displaces our ability to recognize the One, the original unbroken unity of existence.

Miller believes the anthology is essentially about people. The common elements among the chosen stories, besides the backdrop of a worldwide holocaust, are nostalgia for things lost and a recurrence of the ancient underground myth. All of the stories underestimate the horrors of the aftermath of a Megawar, as does his own *A Canticle for Leibowitz*.

**Foru**  a minor character in the short story "Please Me Plus Three." He is the eldest son of Keeper Cron and is killed by Ton of Roldin.

**Fourth Glorious Mystery**  the fifteen original mysteries of the rosary are divided into three groups of five each: the Joyful Mysteries, the Sorrowful Mysteries, and the Glorious Mysteries. The Fourth Glorious Mystery is the Assumption of Mary into Heaven. Brother Francis is reciting its third Ave when he is shot between the eyes with an arrow and killed in *A Canticle for Leibowitz* ("Fiat Homo").

**Fourth penitential psalm**  *see* "**Miserere mei, Deus**"

**Fowles, John**  (1926–2005) British born, Oxford educated writer most famous for his novels *The Collector* (1963), *The Magus* (1965), and *The French Lieutenant's Woman* (1969). His sixth, and last, major novel, *The Maggot* (1985), was reviewed by Miller in his "Chariots of the Goddesses, or What?" which appeared in the *New York Times Book Review*. See also: "**Chariots of the Goddesses, or What?**" and ***The Maggot***

**Fra James**  an unseen character in the novella "Dark Benediction." He is not allowed to solo in the choir for fear that the sisters will giggle.

**Fra Petru**  an elderly priest in the short story "Please Me Plus Three." He is part of the order of monastic soldiers who find the wounded Ton of Roldin on the plateau. Fra Petru tells Ton about the history of the order and what they know about Bel.

**Fran**  the former wife of William Relke in the novella "The Lineman." While Relke is working on his six-year contract on the Lunar Project, Fran, who remains on Earth, leaves him for another man. He resigns for another six years when he receives her "Dear John" letter. Relke still thinks of her and hopes that she will eventually come to the moon one day to be reunited with him.

**Frankie**  an unseen character in the short story "I, Dreamer." He was taken from his mother, Janna, when he was a baby so he could be used as part of the man-machine interfaces in cybernetic spacecraft such as XM-5-B.

**Franklin, C.**  Chief in the F. B. A. and Terry Norris's boss in the novella "Conditionally Human." He is a tall man with a wide face and black eyes. Norris believes there is some Cherokee Indian in his background. Norris dislikes him for no specific reason; he speculates it is because of the job that they both do. Franklin reveals to Norris the full extent of Delmont's deviant neutroids. He offers to euthanize Peony, the deviant Norris has brought home. Norris arranges for an accident to happen in the gas chambers where the neutroids are euthanized, killing Franklin, in order to protect Peony.

**Fraylin, Doctor**  a physicist-surgeon in the novella "Cold Awakening." Dr. Fraylin is the inventor of the suspendfreeze, a process of quick freezing and thawing the human body without killing it. The process allows people to experience long space flights without aging. Fraylin is bitter that his invention which, as he puts it, "gave men the stars," has not brought him fame and fortune. He is supplying many of the colonists headed to Sigma Seven with morphine, making them dependent upon him. He plans to rid the ship of the three emergency-technicians who would be awakened in case of an emergency aboard ship so that he can take control of the ship and the colonists. He murders Jessel and implicates Crain in the crime, eliminating two of the three. The third, Lieutenant Joley, and Commander Roagan are to die when their suspendfreeze lockers malfunction. However, Roagan and Joley suspect that they are targets of the killer and switch the locker thawing mechanisms that Fraylin tampered with. As a result, Fraylin dies the death he had planned for both of them.

**Freddy** in the short story "The Corpse In Your Bed Is Me," Freddy is a Martian who has lived on Earth for three years and works at a soda fountain near Hollywood and Vine. He came to Earth on a thirteen-week contract as an extra for the filming of *Brides of a Martian Harem*. When the contract ended, Freddy lacked the money to return home. He is saving as much as possible from his job as a soda jerk, hoping to be able to return home eventually. Joe Grayber, a member of the I Hate Snyder's Guts Club, pays him to accept Martin Snyder's challenge that he can make anybody laugh. When Freddy wins the challenge by not laughing at any of Snyder's jokes, Snyder becomes obsessed with making him laugh. He hires Freddy as his chauffer so he can continually try to make him laugh. In a last desperate attempt to do something Freddy will find funny, Snyder commits suicide in Freddy's bed.

**Freeman, Donald** a minor character in the short story "MacDoughal's Wife." He is a blond, young man who is one of Ellen MacDoughal's suitors. He is enraptured by Ellen and moves his hand through her hair as they sit on the beach, but he is ultimately scared away by Scott MacDoughal's cold, cynical and contemptuous expression.

**Frei** a minor character in the novella "Izzard and the Membrane." He is a keyboard operator who is locked in the computer vault by Scott MacDonney. He passes through the membrane.

**Frewek** an unseen character in the short story "The Ties That Bind." He is the head of the Intelligence section of the Imperial Forces.

**"From the mud of Earth, and into his nostrils the breath of life…"** Lines from the novella "The Song of Vorhu" as the White Idiot lies in the warm pool and tendrils shoot from her body. The lines are a paraphrase of Genesis 1:7, "And the Lord God formed man of the dust of the ground, and breathed into his nostrils the breath of life; and man became a living soul."

**Fudsow, Buzz** a local plumbing contractor who added a flush toilet of his own invention to Amen's hillside retreat. When Amen becomes pope in *Saint Leibowitz and the Wild Horse Woman*, he makes Fudsow a cardinal.

**Fujæ Go** the Day Maiden of Nomadic myth in *Saint Leibowitz and the Wild Horse Woman*. Portrayed as young and beautiful, she is opposed to the Night Hag but is reconciled to her within the Wild Horse Woman of which she is one aspect.

**Fuller, Clark** author of the dramatic adaptation of *A Canticle for Leibowitz* published by the Dramatic Publishing Company in 1967. He also adapted D. H. Lawrence's short story "The Rocking-Horse Winner" as a one-act play.

**Funph Corporation** the corporate owner of the planet Darkon VII. It manufactures energy triggers for the five-space drive. It is briefly mentioned in the short story "Gravesong."

**Fyff** in the short story "Let My People Go," Fyff is a Piszjil, the dominant species on the planet Epsilon Eridani Two. He is a semanticist and psycho-logician who explains to Morgun Sahl that he has been conditioned against violence toward the Piszjil and to lure Wolek Parn and the other Earth colonists from their ship to the planet.

**$G_0$GC-2794-II** the official designation for the newly discovered planet the starship *Archangel* has been mapping and photographing in the novella "Six and Ten Are Johnny." The crew's nickname for the planet is The Nun because of its chaste and mysterious veil of clouds.

**Gai-See** an Asian warrior monk, one of the members of the Yellow Guard in *Saint Leibowitz and the Wild Horse Woman*. He kills both Cardinal Hadala and Major Gleaver for disobeying Pope Amen II's orders during Hadala's ill-advised march on Texark forces. Upon his return to Arch Hollow, he is arrested and charged with murder by Slojon. When Brother Blacktooth goes to the pope to protest Gai-See's arrest, he too is jailed. Stützil Bråm demands the release into his custody of both Gai-See and Blacktooth claiming the deaths were justified for breaking the Treaty of the Sacred Mare. When Høngan Ösle Chür threatens to turn the Hordes against New Jerusalem if Gai-See is not released, Slojon relents. See also **Yellow Guard**

**"Game Preserve"** short story by Rog Phillips included in *Beyond Armageddon*.

**Garden of Eden** according to Genesis 2:15 (KJV), the place where God placed Adam (and later Eve) "to dress it and to keep it." Adam and Eve lived there until their fall and banishment. Eden is generally associated with paradise. The novella "The Last Canticle" and "Fiat Voluntas

Tua" in *A Canticle for Leibowitz*, state that man is forever building Edens and destroying them because they are never the same as the lost original.

**Garson**  the Secretary of Defense in the short story "Way of a Rebel." The Manlin Bill passed by the United States Congress provides for the Secretary of Defense to take control of the government when a state of national emergency is declared. When President Williston resigns, Garson assumes complete control over the country's war efforts in response to Eurasian Soviet air attacks. Garson, an unremitting hardliner, issues an ultimatum calling for the enemy's immediate surrender or he will unleash the nation's entire arsenal of nuclear and bacterial weapons.

**Gaudeat igitur populous Christi, et gratias agat Domino**  Latin: "So let the people of Christ rejoice, and give thanks to the Lord." Among the words spoken by one of the cantors during the canonization of Isaac Leibowitz in *A Canticle for Leibowitz* ("Fiat Homo").

**Gaudium magnum do vobis. Habemus Papam. Sancte Spiritu volente**  Latin: "Great joy to you. We have a Pope. Holy Spirit willing." These are the words announcing the election of Amen Specklebird as pope in *Saint Leibowitz and the Wild Horse Woman*.

**Gedrin, Doctor**  a character in the short story "No Moon for Me." He is part of the three-man crew on the first manned rocket to the moon. A linguist, he is the designated spokesperson and chairperson during peaceful negotiations to remove the perceived alien invaders from Earth's moon. A "chubby, scholarly little man" in his fifties, Gedrin grows apprehensive about going into space as the launch nears. He frantically attempts to get off the ship and has to be subdued by Colonel Denin. Gedrin suffers a broken leg when Major Long discovers Denin's plan and incapacitates him by violently rolling the ship. Denin attempts to trick Gedrin into blowing up the ship while Long is on the moon, but the doctor faints before he can follow Denin's instructions. Gedrin gives the story its title; he pleads that he wants to go home, crying "no moon for me."

**Gee**  Manue Nanti's Tibetan digging partner in the short story "Crucifixus Etiam."

**Gelps**  those gennies whose genetic handicaps are obvious and cannot be hidden in *Saint Leibowitz and the Wild Horse Woman*. See also **Gennies, Spooks,** and **Sports**

**General Council of the Church**  an ecumenical assembly called for the purpose of discussing and deciding issues of Church doctrine and the resolving of questions and conflicts within the Catholic Church. The issuing of the formal proclamation recommending the canonization of Leibowitz coincides with a General Council of the Church in *A Canticle for Leibowitz* ("Fiat Homo").

**Generatio rectorum benedicetur**  Latin: "The generation of the righteous (upright) shall be blessed." A line from Psalm 111 (DB) which is used by the monks to coordinate the lighting of the lamp in the abbey's basement with the arrival of Don Thaddeo in the novella "And the Light Is Risen."

**Gennies**  people who are genetically handicapped as a result of the fallout from the thermonuclear war in *Saint Leibowitz and the Wild Horse Woman*. Those gennies who can pass for normal are called spooks; those with obvious genetic defects are referred to as gelps.

**Genny Passover**  in *Saint Leibowitz and the Wild Horse Woman* Benjamin's name for the practice of killing severely deformed children at birth. Ulad explains the mass burial area littered with children's bones outside of New Jerusalem to Brother Blacktooth as the result of an epidemic. Blacktooth understands that the practice was widespread and these types of so-called epidemics victimized communities every few years.

**Genua nunc flectantur omnia**  Latin: "Let all knees now be bent." The words spoken by one of the cantors at the beginning of the canonization of Isaac Leibowitz in *A Canticle for Leibowitz* ("Fiat Homo").

**George**  the husband of Marta in the short story "Dumb Waiter." Mitch Laskell finds him several days after he commits suicide in despair, leaving his wife and child to fend for themselves.

**Georgelle, Doctor**  the self-proclaimed Director of a group organized in Houston to prevent dermies, those infected with the neuroderm plague, from entering the city. He has written a pamphlet of rules and regulations everyone must agree to follow if they are to remain the city. His group numbers around 600 members. From the novella "Dark Benediction."

**Georges, Doctor**  a character in the novella "Conditionally Human." When Sarah Glubbes brings her dying neutroid, Primrose, to Georges's office, he fears she will not be able to handle her loss emotionally. He obtains a healthy neutroid from Terry Norris in an attempt to fool Mrs. Glubbes by switching it with Primrose. When Mrs. Glubbes discovers the deception, she accuses Dr. Georges of killing Primrose. She shoots and kills him.

**Georges, Fred**  the son and assistant to Dr. Georges in the novella "Conditionally Human." He picks up the neutroid from Terry Norris's kennel that the doctor plans to substitute for Primrose, Sarah Glubbes's fatally ill neutroid.

**Gerard, Francis**  Brother Francis Gerard of Utah is a 17 year old novitiate of the Albertian Order of Leibowitz and the central character in the short story "A Canticle for Leibowitz" and *A Canticle for Leibowitz* ("Fiat Homo").

Brother Francis is generally perceived to be a bit slow by his superiors in the abbey. As a small boy, he was sold to a tribal shaman in the Utah territory but ran away. He eventually came to the order because of its monastic school, and he worries that he does not possess a true religious calling but rather simply a desire to learn.

During his vocational vigil in the desert, he discovers an old box that contains documents of the Blessed Leibowitz. He believes the old pilgrim who leads him to this discovery may be an angel of God or the blessed Leibowitz himself. In the short story, the pilgrim points out a rock beneath which the box is discovered. In *A Canticle for Leibowitz*, the pilgrim leads Brother Francis to discover the fallout shelter in which he finds the box of memorabilia among other relics of the late twentieth century, including the skeletal remains of Emily Leibowitz.

He spends seven years in the novitiate before he is allowed to take his vows because his abbot, Father Juan in the story and Father Arkos in the novel, doubts his story and fears that claims of Leibowitz's mysterious — and perhaps too fortuitous — appearance will threaten his canonization process in New Rome. He spends his time assigned to the kitchen and the study of antiquity. He becomes proficient in wolf calls thanks to his seven Lenten vigils in the desert.

After the documents are authenticated as to their date of origin and Brother Francis takes his vows, he is assigned to the copy room where he begins to work on an illuminated copy of the blueprint he found among the documents. He works 15 years on his project.

In the story, when Brother Francis travels to New Vatican to attend the canonization ceremony for Leibowitz, he is waylaid by a robber who tears the blueprint in two. In the novel the robber takes the illuminated copy but leaves Brother Francis the original blueprint which he eventually presents to the pope. On his return journey to the desert at the conclusion of "Fiat Homo," Brother Francis is shot between the eyes with an arrow by two sports. An old wanderer discovers his remains and buries him, marking the grave with a stone.

In the "Fiat Lux" section of the novel, Benjamin tells Dom Paulo that he was the one who found the body and buried it. He told New Rome where the body could be found so it could be recovered. Dom Paulo refers to Francis as the Venerable Francis Gerard of Utah, as does Dom Zerchi in "Fiat Voluntas Tua."

His name immediately associates him with Saint Francis of Assisi with whom he shares the characteristics of innocence, humility, single-mindedness, and meekness. Gerard is derived from the German *Gerhard*, meaning "strong with the spear." This links him with his more primal Utah heritage.

**Gertrude**  the primary Martian female who interacts with Jerry Harrison inside the dome in the short story "Secret of the Death Dome." Gertrude is the name Jerry gives to her. She is the first Martian Jerry meets within the dome, and she is his main source of information regarding the Martians' intentions on Earth. Jerry takes her hostage during his efforts to free Betty and him from the dome.

**Gethsemane**  Greek for olive (or oil) press. It is the name of the garden on the Mount of Olives where Jesus went to pray (Mark 14:32–36 KJV). After the Last Supper, Jesus experiences his moment of doubt there as he struggles with continuing his work of salvation. Brother Joshua contemplates his possible role in the Church's Centaurus colony in the church garden of the abbey in the novella "The Last Canticle" and *A Canticle for Leibowitz* ("Fiat Voluntas Tua").

***Giovannezza***  Italian: "youth." More often spelt *Giovinezza*, it was the official anthem of the Italian National Fascist Party and the unofficial second national anthem of Italy from 1924 to 1943. The original score was composed by Giuseppe Blanc in 1909 with the title, *Commiato* ("Farewell"). Benito Mussolini commissioned new lyrics by Salvador Gotta in 1924. In the short story "Wolf Pack," "megalomaniac inscriptions" in praise of the anthem are painted over in red paint.

**Giselle**  a young brown-haired woman who is among the women who comprise Les Folies Lunaries, Incorporated, the space-traveling bordello in the novella "The Lineman." She was raised in a convent but was not allowed to take her vows because she was believed to be unstable and without a calling. Relke asks her to spend time with him away from the bordello because he wants to see what it would be like to be alone with a woman again, although he discovers that she is younger than he first thought, perhaps only fifteen years old. Larkin and Kunz attack her and Relke in the sub-station living quarters.

**Gita** the baby who was exposed to a deadly amount of radiation poisoning along with her mother in the novella "The Last Canticle." Father Zerchi tries to convince her mother not to take her to the Mercy Camp for euthanasia. *Gita* is a Sanskrit word for song.

**Gladin, Major** Mark Kessel's superior and the commander of the 489th Squadron in the short story "Wolf Pack."

**Gleaver, Elswitch J.** a major and the military aide to Magister Dion in *Saint Leibowitz and the Wild Horse Woman*. He is described as a "short keg of a man with a red face and long mustachios." He is selected to command a militia to be raised to protect Valana when the attack upon Hannegan City begins. He is shot in the head and killed by Gai-See. His name is a parody of Eldridge Cleaver (1935–1998), an African American civil rights activist and a leading member of the Black Panther Party.

**Gleps** overtly deformed gennies, people suffering from genetic defects, in *Saint Leibowitz and the Wild Horse Woman*.

**Gloria, et divitiae in domo ejus** Latin: "Glory and wealth shall be in his house." Part of Psalm 111 (DB) whose lines are used by the monks to time the lighting of the arc lamp in the abbey's basement with the arrival of Don Thaddeo in the novella "And the Light Is Risen."

**Glorificemus** Latin: "Let us glorify [God]." When Brother Francis is displeased with his original copy of the Leibowitz blueprint in *A Canticle for Leibowitz* ("Fiat Homo"), this term keeps recurring to him as he thinks about the blueprint. It is this desire to glorify the Beatus that leads Brother Francis to begin work on his illuminated — glorified — copy of the blueprint.

**Glow-curse** the term given to the radiation poisoning following atomic warfare on Earth in the short story "The Soul-Empty Ones." Because of the glow-curse, men created androids, the Soul-Empty Ones, and left Earth to protect their children. The Soul-Empty Ones remained on Earth to care for it until the glow-curse was no longer a threat and men could return.

**Glubbes, Sarah** a middle-aged, thin-lipped widow in the novella "Conditionally Human." Primrose, her neutroid, is dying of eighteenth order virus. Doctor Georges wants to ease her bereavement by switching Primrose with another neutroid from Terry Norris's kennel. Norris cautions Georges against it, telling him that Glubbes will notice the difference, but Georges goes ahead with his plan after he euthanizes Primrose. Glubbes confronts Dr. Geroges at a party at the Slades's home accusing him of killing her baby. She shoots and kills him. She is eventually committed to a psychopathic ward.

**Goat-Wind** a minor character in *Saint Leibowitz and the Wild Horse Woman*. He is the brother-in-law of Swimming Elk, the War Dog sharf, who gives him the monopoly on training attack dogs to accompany horsemen into battle against unmounted opponents.

**"God Is Thus"** excerpt from *Saint Leibowitz and the Wild Horse Woman* appearing in *The Magazine of Fantasy and Science Fiction*, 93 [no. 556] (October/November 1997), 13–35. The excerpt is comprised of most of chapter 5 and the first half of chapter 6, the story of Brother Blacktooth's first encounter with Ædrea.

**Goldæm, General** Filpeo Harq's Chief of Staff in *Saint Leibowitz and the Wild Horse Woman*.

**Golgotha** from the Aramaic word *gulgulta*, meaning skull. Also known as Mount Calvary, it is where Jesus was crucified. It is referred to in the novella "The Last Canticle" and *A Canticle for Leibowitz* ("Fiat Voluntas Tua"). In *Saint Leibowitz and the Wild Horse Woman*, Amen Specklebird says the schism in the Church must be healed and that the new pope in restoring the papacy in New Rome must go as "to Golgotha, and be crucified."

**Good Friday** the Friday before Easter. For Christians it commemorates the passion and death of Jesus. In *A Canticle for Leibowitz* ("Fiat Homo"), a Procession of the Cross visits the novices' hermitages on Good Friday.

**Goosestepping** a military parade step where the leg is kept unbent at the knee and swung sharply from the hip. It is most often associated with the military of Nazi Germany. General Yaney refers to the little creeps goosestepping in formation on his wall in the short story "The Little Creeps." The word is sometimes spelt as two words: *goose step* (or *stepping*).

**Goraldi** the King of Laredo in the novella "And

the Light Is Risen" and *A Canticle for Leibowitz* ("Fiat Lux"). He is "a doddering fool" in the estimation of Dom Paulo for being so easily manipulated by Hannegan II. Warned by New Rome of Hannegan's machinations, Goraldi believes the Church is lying to him for its own purposes. He informs Hannegan of the papal warning leading to the arrest and death of Marcus Apollo.

**Graham, Roger Phillips** (1909–1965) short story writer and novelist who used the pen name Rog Phillips. He is best known for two short stories: "The Yellow Pill" and "Game Preserve." The latter is included in *Beyond Armageddon*.

**Gramp** in the short story "The Big Hunger" he explains to his granddaughter, Nari, what starcraze is and why men feel it. He tells her that man once lived on a paradise planet but abandoned it to search for a better place to live. Angered by man's indifference and foolishness, Lord Bion hid the paradise planet and condemned man to wander endlessly searching for the planet he lost. Gramp says it is not necessarily a bad thing because it gave man a goal, something toward which he could work.

**Grand Penitentiary** the cardinal presiding over the Apostolic Penitentiaria, a Roman tribunal granting absolutions and dispensations and dealing with cases of conscience or questions of indulgences in general. When Brother Francis tells Monsignor Aguerra that he would like to confess after the canonization of Leibowitz in *A Canticle for Leibowitz* ("Fiat Homo"), Aguerra suggests the Grand Penitentiary to hear his confession. However, Brother Francis wants Aguerra, as Leibowitz's advocate, to hear his confession.

**Grandmaw** a minor character in the short story "Dumb Waiter." Mitch Laskell offers her a ride on his bicycle, but she is traveling away from the city and she advises him to do the same thing.

**Granduncle Brokenfoot** Holy (Little Bear) Madness' father in *Saint Leibowitz and the Wild Horse Woman*. Cardinal Brownpony wants him elected Lord of the Three Hordes and the successor of the War Sharf Høngan Ös. He is considered the leading candidate for the position until he suffers a stroke and loses the use of his left leg.

**Graneden, Guido** the abbot of the Abbey of Saint Leibowitz when Brother Blacktooth first arrives in *Saint Leibowitz and the Wild Horse Woman*. He ordered the restoration of Brother Fingo's Leibowitz statue to its original wooden condition by having the paint removed from it.

**Granger** an unseen character in the novella "The Darfsteller." He is a fiftyish, heavyset jovial actor known for playing comic supporting roles. He has provided psycho-physiological tapes for use in autodramas. Ryan Thornier uses one of his tapes to splice onto Peltier's identifying tongue to sabotage the mannequin's use in the production of "The Anarch."

**Grass Eaters** in the novella "And the Light Is Risen" the name given to the Plains people by the Mad Bear clan.

**Grasshopper** a Nomad horde that lives north of the Nady Ann River in *Saint Leibowitz and the Wild Horse Woman*. They lived at one time in the area once known as Iowa.

**Gratia Creatori Spiritui** *see* **In principio Deus**

**Gratias agamus Domino Deo nostro** Latin: "Let us give thanks to the Lord our God." Taken from the Mass, the line is among those used by the monks to announce the arrival of Don Thaddeo to the abbey's basement in the novella "And the Light Is Risen."

**Gratissima Nobis causa, fili** Latin: "The cause is most pleasing to us, son." The response of Pope Leo XXI when the Beatus Leibowitz is officially presented to him for canonization in *A Canticle for Leibowitz* ("Fiat Homo").

**"Gravesong"** short story appearing in *Startling Stories*, 27 (October 1952), 108–112, 114–117. As Motar lies dying on the planet Sorcerer VI, she ruminates about Earth and human society. As man conquered space and abandoned Earth, he became less and less a part of a larger human society. Instead, individuals became parts of corporate societies. Motar laments that as each individual man was given greater power, man, as a societal group, passed away. She wants her ashes returned to Earth to be buried. She implores Emilesh not to bury her in space but to take her back to Earth.

After she dies, Emilesh cremates her body and prepares to bring her ashes to Earth, now called Oculus Christi Reyes. Emilesh enters hypno-hybernosis for the trip: he ages five years while "several hundred centuries of galactic local time" pass. Although he was born in space and has lived his entire life there, when Emilesh lands on Earth, he has a sense of memory of it and experiences an affinity for his ancient ancestral home.

As he walks away from his ship in a seemingly deserted area, he turns and sees a naked woman standing nearby. Her name is Eva, and she is a telepath. She asks Emilesh for his dead and tells him that she will tend to the grave. But she is frightened by him and runs and hides, communicating telepathically from a distance. After scattering Motar's ashes, Emilesh calls to Eva asking her to come to him so they can talk. She refuses and cautions him that he should leave the planet as soon as possible. The next morning he finds a small bundle of food left for him by Eva. He invites her to eat with him, but she states that she does not eat of the dead. Emilesh realizes that she has never seen a male such as he before, and she is embarrassed and scared by his thoughts.

After three days of not hearing from Eva, Emilesh decides to walk along a riverbank. Suddenly Eva warns him to stay clear of the river and not attempt to cross it. He ignores her warning and begins to make his way across a series of rocks in the river. As he does, a hand reaches up out of the water and grabs at his ankle. As he struggles to free himself, a head emerges from the river bottom. Man has evolved on Earth into mud-creatures, literally animals of the earth.

Emilesh escapes to shore and prepares to leave the planet. He asks Eva to come with him. Although she desires to go, she refuses explaining that Emilesh is a child of space while she is an animal of the ground, like the mud-creatures. He does not argue with her and returns to his ship as she walks away. Eva shares a mental image with him of the mud-creatures abandoning her, an unwanted child, because she is born different, a throwback to half-a-million years ago. As he blasts off, Emilesh sees Eva working the earth, digging her own grave. She is a fixed child of the soil; he is a wandering child of space. And a human, communal society passes away.

**Grayber, Joe** the technical director of the *Martin Snyder Hour* in the short story "The Corpse In Your Bed Is Me." He is a member of the I Hate Snyder's Guts Club, and the discoverer of Freddy the Martian. Grayber pays Freddy to accept Snyder's bet that he can make anybody laugh.

**Graycol** an unseen character in *Saint Leibowitz and the Wild Horse Woman*. During Filpeo Harq's strategy meeting at the War College a mention is made of this thon's observation that there are no very old trees along the edge of the prairie, suggesting that the tree line has been moving slowly westward for a few centuries.

**Grearly, Kenneth** a character in the short story "Command Performance" (later entitled "Anybody Else Like Me?"). He is a psychophysicist studying his telepathic abilities and those, he hopes, of Lisa Waverly. He believes that it is incumbent upon both him and Lisa to study their mutation and attempt to further its occurrence within the human species. Telepathy will eliminate miscommunication among people, and he believes this to be the source of the world's problems. Although they do not love each other and Lisa is already married, Kenneth's plan is to produce three or four children with her, even if it must be done against her will. He is killed by a truck while on his way to Lisa's house. In order to protect herself, Lisa uses her telepathic powers to confuse Kenneth and cause him to walk into oncoming traffic as he crosses a street.

**"Great Actors Immortalized"** the slogan of Smithfield's, the company responsible for packaging psycho-physiological tapes of actors used in mannequins in autodrama productions in the novella "The Darfsteller."

**Great Purpose** the idea presented in the short story "The Big Hunger" that man must continually travel to the stars in search for his lost home, abandoned years ago. This desire is also known as star-craze and the Divine Thirst.

**Great Rift** an expanse of large, dark, light blocking clouds that seemingly divides the Milky Way along part of its equatorial plane between the constellations Cygnus and Sagittarius.
   1. It is mentioned in the short story "The Big Hunger" as one of the destinations of man's space exploration.
   2. When Emilesh looks toward the sky in the short story "Gravesong," the Milky Way is "blotted by the Great Rift." Emilesh is contemplating the great distance he will have to travel to honor Motar's request to be buried on Earth.

**The Great River** another name for the Misspee River to the east of New Rome in *Saint Leibowitz and the Wild Horse Woman*. It is an apparent reference to the Mississippi River.

**Greeley** a crew member of Launch One in the novella "Six and Ten Are Johnny." He is among those who disappear on the planet.

**Green Star** in the novella "The Last Canticle" and *A Canticle for Leibowitz* ("Fiat Voluntas Tua"), an agency whose purpose is to provide assistance and comfort to the sick and wounded in war through their Green Star Relief Stations where victims of radiation poisoning are evaluated. Part of their function is to administer voluntary euthanasia in their Mercy Camps to the victims of extreme radiation exposure as the law provides.

It is also referred to as the Green Star Disaster Cadre Project.

**Green Witch**   a corruption of Greenwich, England in *Saint Leibowitz and the Wild Horse Woman*. It is believed to be the habitation of a sorceress and therefore the reason for Pope Alabaster II's decree to relocate the prime meridian to keep it from any evil influence. See also **Alabaster II**

**Greenberg, Martin H(arry)** (March 1, 1941–) prolific anthologist, editor, and writer who has published more than 1,000 anthologies and collections. A retired professor of political science at the University of Wisconsin-Green Bay, he has worked with numerous authors across genres. He has received lifetime achievement awards for his editing in science fiction, mystery, and horror. He co-edited *Beyond Armageddon* with Miller. See also ***Beyond Armageddon***

**Greeves, Lieutenant**   a minor character in the novella "The Yokel." He is a member of the Border Guard at Colonel MacMahon's headquarters.

**Gregory**   the pope at the time of a burgeoning nuclear conflict in the novella "The Last Canticle" and *A Canticle for Leibowitz* ("Fiat Voluntas Tua"). He stops praying for peace in the world at the end of the conference of foreign ministers in Guam. He orders two special masses: the Mass Against the Heathen and the Mass in Time of War. He retreats to meditate and pray for justice and peace in the hearts of men. While there have been sixteen actual popes named Gregory, Miller may have been thinking of Gregory I, also known as Gregory the Great, or Gregory VII considered to be one of the great popes of the Middle Ages. Both have been canonized.

The name is derived from the Greek *Gregorios* and means "watchful" or "vigilant watchman."

**Grex peregrinus erit. Quam primum est factum suscipiendum vobis, jussu Sactae Sedis. Suscipite ergo operis partem ordini vestro propriam..."**   Latin: "The flock will be a wandering one. As soon as possible the deed must be undertaken by you, by order of the Holy See. Therefore, undertake the part of the work proper to your order...." The text of a priority wire from Sir Eric Cardinal Hoffstraff to Dom Zerchi confirming the *Quo peregrinatur grex* plan and asking that the abbot implement his part as quickly as possible in *A Canticle for Leibowitz* ("Fiat Voluntas Tua"). See also ***Quo peregrinatur grex***

**Grigoryevich, Porphiry**   a Russian colonel in the short story "Vengeance for Nikolai." He devises the plan to use Marya Dmitriyevna Lisitsa as the means of killing General Rufus MacAmsward. Despite his affection for the young woman, he is willing to sacrifice her for the greater good of his country. He advises her not to agree to his proposal.

**Grumbler**   a mobile autocyber fire control, or combat robot, programmed to protect a valuable lunar mining area in the short story "I Made You." It destroys the team from the Autocyber Corps who come to deactivate it, including one of its original programmers, John Sawyer. Grumbler improves upon its original programming, increasing its capacity to kill.

**Gryllus**   Latin: cricket or grasshopper. It is also the name given to a genus of crickets.

The term is on the sign above a prisoner's cage in Hannegan City in *Saint Leibowitz and the Wild Horse Woman*. He is a Grasshopper Nomad found guilty of war crimes.

**Guadalupe**   in Tepeyac, Mexico in December of 1531, the Virgin Mary purportedly appeared before an Aztec Indian convert, Juan Diego, telling him to instruct the bishop to build a church on the spot. When the bishop demanded proof from Diego that he had actually witnessed an apparition of Mary, Mary provided him with white roses to show the bishop. He carried the roses in his cloak, and when he placed the roses before the bishop, an image of the Virgin Mary was imprinted on his cloak. The basilica that now stands on the site is perhaps the most visited Christian shrine. Guadalupe is mentioned in *Saint Leibowitz and the Wild Horse Woman* as among the sites of Mary's manifestations.

**Guam Conference**   an unsuccessful conference of foreign ministers who meet in an attempt to avert a nuclear war in the novella "The Last Canticle" and *A Canticle for Leibowitz* ("Fiat Voluntas Tua").

**Guerrera**   a minor character in the short story "The Hoofer." He is a member of Hogey Parker's former crew or gang in space.

**Habemus ad Dominum**   Latin: "We lift them [our hearts] up to the Lord." A part of the liturgy in the Catholic Church, it is the congregation's response to the priest's versicle to "lift up your hearts" (*sursum corda*). The monks in the novella "And the Light Is Risen" use it to announce the approaching of Don Thaddeo to the abbey's basement.

**Habemus Papam**   Latin: "We have a pope." The words traditionally spoken to the waiting crowds after the election of a new pope. The phrase is used in *Saint Leibowitz and the Wild Horse Woman*.

**Hadala, Chuntar**   the greatly respected missionary bishop to the Valley of the Misborn in *Saint Leibowitz and the Wild Horse Woman*. He maneuvers to keep Brother Blacktooth and Pope Amen II separated. Cardinal Hadala organizes a "farmer army" from Valana and marches them unauthorized into Nomad country in hopes of arming the gelps of Watchitah Nation. Pope Amen II sends a messenger to order Hadala to retreat and threatening to excommunicate all his followers who refuse to do so. Caught between Nomad riders and the Texark cavalry, Hadala orders an attack on the Texark forces. During the battle, Hadala is killed by Gai-See, who views him as an enemy of Pope Amen II. The Nomads believe he was duly executed for breaking the Treaty of the Sacred Mare.

**Haec commixtio**   Latin: "May this mingling." The priest speaks these words when he places a small piece of the Host into the chalice as part of communion. In the novella "And the Light Is Risen" and *A Canticle for Leibowitz* ("Fiat Lux"), Father Jerome/Dom Paulo realizes that the small wooden statue of Saint Leibowitz in his office is grinning. He thinks Leibowitz is laughing at the hangman and for the hangman, but there is also a laugh in the chalice (in the novel it is clarified further that "in the *last* chalice, there could be a chuckle of triumph"). The abbot then says "haec commixtio."

**Hair-Puller**   a minor character in *Saint Leibowitz and the Wild Horse Woman*. He is a bald farmer with a cart of household goods and junk. Brother Blacktooth helps him push his two-wheeled cart as he flees the fires in New Rome. Blacktooth stays with him until they are separated in the crowd at The Great River, the Misspee.

**Halb, Friider**   an unseen thon who is a contemporary of Thon Taddeo's in *A Canticle for Leibowitz* ("Fiat Lux") and the novella "And the Light Is Risen." In his presentation to the monks at the Leibowitz abbey, Taddeo mentions Halb's work on a practical method of transmitting messages through a wire by means of electrical variations. In the novella, he is referred to as Don Friider Halb.

**Handell**   a minor character in the short story "Crucifixus Etiam." He becomes agitated listening to Will Kinley address the laborers about the Mars Project, and he tries to incite the workers to attack and kill Kinley. Manue Nanti knocks him out to protect Kinley.

**Hangbacker**   one who argues for not going into space and stays behind as man pursues his starward vision in the short story "The Big Hunger."

**Hannegan City**   the seat of government of the Empire of Texark in *Saint Leibowitz and the Wild Horse Woman*.

**Hannegan II**   the head of the state of Texarkana in the novella "And the Light Is Risen" and *A Canticle for Leibowitz* ("Fiat Lux"). Although illiterate, he is an astute political and military leader. He has a plan to unite the various states of the continent under his own dynasty. His official title is by Grace of God Mayor, Viceroy of Texarkana, Defender of the Faith, and Vaquero Supreme of the Plains. He later modifies it to include Emperor of Laredo, Doctor of Laws, and Clans Chief of the Nomads. He is a cousin of Taddeo Pfardentrott.

He enters into a pact with Hongan Os to make war upon Laredo and eventually gains control of all the lands and peoples from the Red River to the Rio Grande. After he orders the death of Marcus Apollo for spying, the state of Texarkana is placed under interdict by papal decree. In response, Hannegan declares himself the only legitimate ruler over the Church in Texarkana and the pope's interdict of no consequence. He declares the pope to be a heretic and unworthy to be recognized by any church in Hannegan's empire. His act parallels The Act of Supremacy of 1534 that appointed Henry VIII as the protector and only supreme leader of the church and clergy of England.

In *Saint Leibowitz and the Wild Horse Woman*, it is revealed that after the interdict was imposed Hannegan seized all churches, courts, and schools. He occupied the lands adjacent to New Rome, which resulted in the Holy See seeking asylum in Valana. Hannegan collected enough bishops to establish a rival pope in New Rome. In *Saint Leibowitz and the Wild Horse Woman*, his conquests in the former state of Texas are dated as being in A.D. 3174 and 3175. He is also referred to as Hannegan the Conqueror.

**Hannegan III**   the successor to Hannegan II. He presided over the only use of "a chair of electrical essence" as a means of execution. The execution was that of a Leibowitzian monk. The incident is revealed in *Saint Leibowitz and the Wild Horse Woman*.

**Happu biraki**   a Japanese term meaning "open on eight sides." It is used in Zen to indicate a total awareness of one's surroundings. It is also used in the martial arts to refer to a sword position which eliminates any opening for an attack. It is typically spelt *happo biraki*. The term is used by Wooshin in *Saint Leibowitz and the Wild Horse Woman* to describe leaving oneself open on all sides.

**Hardin**  a demolition man working on the Lunar Project who dies from a blowout in his pressure suit in the novella "The Lineman."

**Harlich, Doctor**  from the novella "The Yokel." He is a chubby man who suggests the means to make Sam Wuncie cooperate with the Border Guards' plan. He injects Wuncie with the saliva of a dog that may be rabid. If Wuncie wants the rabies serum, he has to do what he is told to do by the Border Guards.

**Harq, Filpeo**  the seventh Hannegan of Texark in *Saint Leibowitz and the Wild Horse Woman*, also known as Mayor Hannegan VII. He was raised and educated for power and to rule, but he still occasionally enjoys performing his own executions. His uncle is Urion Cardinal Benefez of Texark. He successfully defends his empire against the attacks of Pope Amen II and his Nomad allies but is killed in the streets of Hannegan City by Wooshin who cuts off his head.

**Harrinore, Admiral**  a minor character in the short story "Way of the Rebel." Harrinore is the commander of the Commsubfleet of which Lieutenant Mitch Laskell is a part. He promises Laskell that if he obeys orders to return to the nearest base, he will receive summary discipline without a court martial. If Laskell does not comply, he will be treated as a deserter to the enemy and killed.

**Harris, John Wyndham Parkes Lucas Beynon** (July 10, 1903–March 11, 1969)  British author who generally wrote under the name of John Wyndham. He wrote what he termed "logical fantasy." Two of his best-known novels are *The Day of the Triffids* (1951) and *The Midwich Cuckoo* (1957). His short story "The Wheel" is included in *Beyond Armageddon*.

**Harrison, Jerry**  a sergeant in the special patrol and the best friend of Barney Willis in the short story "Secret of the Death Dome." Harrison is sent to recover Willis's body and discovers that it is mutilated. Ordered to bring the corpse to Willis's home while it awaits the embalmer, Harrison is confronted by Betty, Barney's wife and his former girlfriend, asking for vengeance. Jerry is given Barney's old patrol. When he rides to the dome, he discovers the reason why it is on Earth and takes the necessary actions that cause it to depart. In the process, he saves Betty from Martian experimentation and exploitation. He still loves her, and she suggests that after a proper period of mourning Jerry come after her.

**Hawken Chief Irrikawa**  a newly elected cardinal and the king of the northwest forest nation in *Saint Leibowitz and the Wild Horse Woman*. He wears an eagle feather and claims his father is as old as the continent. His servants are required to refer to him as "Sire" or "Majesty."

**"He floats through the air with the greatest of ease"**  the opening line of the refrain to the song "The Flying Trapeze" (better known as "The Daring Young Man on the Flying Trapeze" or "The Man on the Flying Trapeze"). The song was written in 1867 by George Leybourne (lyrics) and Gaston Lyle (music). It was first recorded in 1934 by Walter O'Keefe. In the novella "The Yokel," the refrain is sung by a group of men in the Border Guard who are torturing an unsuccessful crosser, a person who tried to pass from Ruralland into a developed urban area. They are swinging him back and forth over a bonfire as he hangs by his feet from a tree limb.

**Heide**  an unseen character in the novella "The Reluctant Traitor." He and Dawson are responsible for Operation Icecap that established a breathable atmosphere on Mars five hundred years prior to the time of the story.

**Heinehoffer, Mr. and Mrs.**  unseen neighbors of Lisa Waverly in the short story "Command Performance" (later entitled "Anybody Else Like Me?").

**"Heirs Apparent"**  a short story by Robert Abernathy that appears in *Beyond Armageddon*.

**Hell Wall**  the East and West maintain a complete and total isolation since the ending of the last war or "peace-effort" in the short story "Check and Checkmate." As part of that isolation, the Hell Wall has been created. It is a belt of booby-trapped land and ocean separating the two sides and guarded by both.

**Helots**  a class of serfs in ancient Sparta who were neither slave nor free citizens. In *Saint Leibowitz and the Wild Horse Woman*, a comparison is made between the gleps as Helots and the spooks as Spartans.

**Henderson**  a member of the B-shift crew in

the novella "The Lineman." He goes with Relke and Braxton to check the communication line to Crater City. As a result, he is the first of the B-shift men to visit the bordello spaceship. He and Joe later attack Larkin and Kunz in revenge for their beating of Relke. Henderson dies in a work accident on the line.

**Henri** Madame d'Annecy's assistant and enforcer at Les Folies Lunaries, Incorporated, the space-traveling bordello in the novella "The Lineman."

**Herb** the fiancé of Zella Richmond in the novella "The Yokel." He leaves her when he is led to falsely believe that they would not be allowed to have children because Zella's genes indicate hereditary physical weakness.

**Hercules Cluster** a giant globular star cluster in the constellation Hercules. It is the best globular cluster seen in the Northern Hemisphere. It is also known as the Hercules Globular. In the short story "The Big Hunger," the cluster was once the focus of man's space exploration.

**Herod** also known as **Herod the Great**. King of Judea from 37 B.C. to A.D. 4, he ordered the deaths of all males two years old and younger at the news of Jesus' birth. He consolidated his power through cruelty and brutality. In the novella "The Last Canticle," his name is among those Father Zerchi cites when he speaks of humanity's capacity for murder, rape, and hate. In *A Canticle for Leibowitz*, Zerchi thinks of the universality of man's sins: his sins are those of Adam, Herod, Judas, and Caesar.

**Herrick** a colonist who steals Crain's gun in the novella "Cold Awakening." Joley believes he shot Jessel, but Herrick gave the gun to Dr. Fraylin who actually kills Jessel. Herrick goes into suspendfreeze under the name of James Willis to try to escape implication in Jessel's death.

**Heu** a Latin equivalent of "Oh!" It is an interjection used as an expression of pain or dismay. Dom Zerchi utters it after he confirms with Brother Joshua that Lucifer has Fallen, that a nuclear explosion has occurred, in *A Canticle for Leibowitz* ("Fiat Voluntas Tua").

**Hic est enim Calix Sanuinis Mei** Latin: "For this is the cup of my blood." The words said by the priest over the chalice of wine during the Consecration of the Chalice as part of the Mass service, transforming the wine into the blood of Christ. In the novella "And the Light Is Risen," the story is told that when Leibowitz was soaked with gasoline prior to his burning, he asked for a cup of it, consecrated it with these words, and then drank it.

**Hilbert, Brandio** an epidemiologist who occupied the Chair of Life Science at Hannegan University in *Saint Leibowitz and the Wild Horse Woman*. General Goldæm demands his cooperation in teaching the Texark Army how to contaminate wells and infect livestock with new diseases. When Hilbert refuses, he is inducted into the army and ordered to instruct the troops. He curses both Goldæm and Filpeo. He is imprisoned for sedition for objecting to his work being used for military purposes. Filpeo, displeased with Goldæm's handling of the affair, dismisses the general and retires him on half pay. Hilbert's assistant agrees to provide the information and teach the troops. Hilbert remains imprisoned until he agrees to apologize to Filpeo for cursing him. The disease that develops from the application of his work to biological warfare becomes known as Hilbert's disease.

**Hilbert's disease** in *Saint Leibowitz and the Wild Horse Woman*, the name used to refer to the biological weapon developed by Filpeo Harq and used against the Nomads. It is so named because it is derived from the work of Thon Brandio Hilbert, an epidemiologist at Hannegan University. He refused to help Harq develop his work as a biological weapon. A number of characters in the book contract the disease, including Benjamin, the hermit.

**Hinc igitur effuge** Latin: "Then flee from here." Dom Zerchi's admonition to Brother Patrick as the abbot struggles to fix the Abominable Autoscribe in *A Canticle for Leibowitz* ("Fiat Voluntas Tua").

**Hiroshima** a port city on Honshu in Japan. It was the site of the first atomic bomb dropped in warfare on August 6, 1945 during World War II. Between 60,000 and 70,000 people were estimated to have been killed by the blast. It is mentioned in the novella "The Last Canticle" and *A Canticle for Leibowitz* ("Fiat Voluntas Tua") as among the atrocities of mankind.

**Hitler, Adolf** (April 20, 1889–April 30, 1945) German National Socialist German Workers' Party (Nazi) leader and ruler of Germany during the Third Reich (1933–1945). He is among the most reviled men of the twentieth century for his program of racial purity that resulted in the deaths of millions of people and for instigating World War II with his attack on Poland in 1939. He is the author of *Mein Kampf* (My Struggle). He committed suicide on April 30, 1945. In *A Canticle for Leibowitz* ("Fiat Homo"), he is cited as an example of the type of men who can cause a new cultural heritage to be generated in just one or two generations.

**H'nrin**   an old androon priest who presides over the council in the novella "The Reluctant Traitor."

**Hoc officium, Fili — tibine imponemus oneri?**   Latin: "This office, son — are we to impose these burdens on you?" The words of Dom Zerchi as he asks Brother Joshua what he has decided about accepting the pastoral and administrative duties of leading the Church into space in the "Fiat Voluntas Tua" section of *A Canticle for Leibowitz*.

**Hoffstraff, Sir Eric Cardinal**   the Vicar Apostolic Designate, Provisional Vicariate Extraterrestris, Sacred Congregation of Propaganda at the Vatican in New Rome in *A Canticle for Leibowitz* ("Fiat Voluntas Tua"). He conveys the order to Dom Zerchi to implement the Church's *Quo peregrinatur* plan.

**Holofot, Colonel**   second in command of the Texark infantry and its representative at Filpeo Harq's strategy meeting in *Saint Leibowitz and the Wild Horse Woman*. He argues that the Texark forts will hold against a Nomad cavalry attack.

**Holy (Little Bear) Madness** *see* **Høngan, Chür (Ösle)**

**Holy Sacrament**   also known as the Eucharist, Holy Eucharist, or the Blessed Sacrament. It is the consecrated bread and wine representing the grace producing body and blood of Christ used during Communion in Catholic Church services. It is the highest of all the sacraments. Brother Francis refers to a priest bringing the Holy Sacrament with him as he makes his rounds visiting the hermitages during the Lenten vigils in *A Canticle for Leibowitz* ("Fiat Homo"). During Holy Week, a reference is also made to the Eucharist in the novel.

**Holy Saturday**   the day before Easter, the day the body of Jesus lay entombed.
  1. Brother Francis believes he is safe from a possible attack from a Fallout behind the sealed hatch of the Fallout Shelter before Holy Saturday, the end of his Lenten fast in *A Canticle for Leibowitz* ("Fiat Homo").
  2. The monks carry the novices — "famished and raving" — to the abbey from their hermitages on Holy Saturday in *A Canticle for Leibowitz* ("Fiat Homo").
  3. Holy Saturday is the night of the Nomad dogs' attack on Texark soldiers in *Saint Leibowitz and the Wild Horse Woman*.

**Holy Tuesday**   the Tuesday before Easter.

**Holy Week**   the week prior to Easter, from Palm Sunday through Holy Saturday. The term is used in *A Canticle for Leibowitz* ("Fiat Homo").

**Holy Year**   a year of special celebration within the Catholic Church in which the pope grants an extraordinary indulgence, or Jubilee, to all who visit Rome with certain conditions. First celebrated in 1300 by the order of Boniface VIII, a Holy Year is usually held at stated intervals, most recently every 25 years. The formal proclamation recommending the canonization of Leibowitz is issued in a Holy Year in *A Canticle for Leibowitz* ("Fiat Homo").

**Homo inspiratus**   Latin: "Man inspired" [or enkindled]. A reference to the creation of man as God breathed life into Adam. Dom Zerchi uses the term in *A Canticle for Leibowitz* ("Fiat Voluntas Tua").

**Homo loquax nonnumquam sapiens**   Latin: "Talkative man sometimes wise." Brother Joshua's play on Homo sapiens — wise man — as he thinks about the handful of space colonists already living on strange worlds in *A Canticle for Leibowitz* ("Fiat Voluntas Tua").

**Homo matricidus**   Latin: "Man who commits matricide." The sign above one of the prisoner's cells in the Hannegan City jail where Cardinal Brownpony and Brother Blacktooth are briefly kept in *Saint Leibowitz and the Wild Horse Woman*.

**Homo seditiosi**   Latin: "Seditious Man"; a revolutionary. The sign above two cells in the Hannegan City jail in *Saint Leibowitz and the Wild Horse Woman*.

**Homo sicarius**   Latin: "Murderer" (or assassin). A sign above a cell in the Hannegan City jail in *Saint Leibowitz and the Wild Horse Woman*.

**Honey Blossom**   the name of the neutroid John and Mary Slade are getting in the novella "Conditionally Human."

**Høngan, Chür (Ösle)**   also known as Holy (Little Bear) Madness and Sire of the Day Maiden. He is a member of the Wilddog horde and an envoy to Cardinal Brownpony from the Plains. He is a distant cousin to Hannegan. His mother line qualifies him to be Lord of the Three Hordes, a position he eventually attains. In the confrontation with Filpeo Harq's forces, he calls for a full attack on Hannegan City, ignoring the warning of Pope Amen II. When the Nomads are defeated, he is called home by the Weejus women and put to death. His name is variously given as Chür Høngan, Høngan Chür, and Høngan Ösle Chür.

**Hongan Os** also known as Mad Bear. He is the chief of the Nomadic Mad Bear clan in the novella "And the Light Is Risen." He makes a pact with Texarkana to make war upon the Laredo.

In *A Canticle for Leibowitz* ("Fiat Lux"), he is called the clans chief. In return for fighting Laredo, Hongan Os's Nomads receive arms and supplies from Hannegan II. Hongan Os promises to refrain from attacking Texarkana or stealing cattle from the eastern borders. He meets with Thon Taddeo's party as they make their way west to the Abbey of Saint Leibowitz and provides a Nomad escort to ensure the thon's safety. In the novel, he is also called "Son of the Mighty."

In *Saint Leibowitz and the Wild Horse Woman* [the name is spelt Høngan Ös], it is revealed that he was the last Lord of the Three Hordes and that he led his people against Hannegan. When he was defeated, he was sacrificed by his own shamans.

**Høngin Fujæ Vurn** *see* **Wild Horse Woman**

**Honkler, Robert** an unseen character in the short story "Bitter Victory." He is the physician/surgeon who treats the wounds of Klia and San Rorrek.

**Honorem accipiam** Latin: "I accept the honor." Brother Joshua's reply to Dom Zerchi when asked if he has a vocation and is willing to lead the Order of Saint Leibowitz in space in *A Canticle for Leibowitz* ("Fiat Voluntas Tua").

**"The Hoofer"** short story in *Fantastic Universe*, 4 (September 1955), 112–120. After six tours in space, Hogey Parker, a dedicated "tumbler" or spacer, returns to Earth to stay. Because of regulations that prevent fathers in space, Parker must now return to his wife, Marie, and new born son to begin a life bound to Earth, a hoofer. His heart and mind remain in space, however, and he resents being chained to the ground. Having lost the money he saved to begin a small business in a poker game, Parker drunkenly makes his way to the farm of his wife's family. Stumbling across a field in the dark, he accidentally steps into a freshly poured concrete footing, and as he lies there, crying out in his drunken stupor, he literally becomes stuck to the Earth.

An audio version of the story read by Gregg Margarite is available through LibriVox.org, a volunteer project to produce recordings of literary works in the public domain.

**Hookey** the name of a hound dog on the Hauptmans' farm in the short story "The Hoofer."

**Hormisdas** pope between 514 and 523. He was married prior to his ordination and had a son, Silverius who would also become pope. Noted as a peacemaker, he ended the Acadian Schism with an agreement that became known as the Formula of Hormisdas. He is mentioned in *Saint Leibowitz and the Wild Horse Woman* in connection with Silverius

**Horrey, Clement** a character in the short story "The Little Creeps." He is an Army general, and a member of the senior staff, stationed in Japan during an Asian war. He questions his own mental stability when he begins to see small, luminous rods crawling on his bedroom walls at night. These lights are actually a life force, 2537 Angstroms, which occupy a world parallel with Earth's tomorrow. They have come to warn Horrey about three decisions he will make that will have major consequences for the future. Horrey cannot fully accept the reality of these creatures and what they say. He fears that he is being driven slowly mad and that his military career is threatened. He not only ignores the advice of "the little creeps" regarding the decisions he makes, but he makes every effort to destroy their existence in his life. In doing so, he frees himself from their influence but destroys their world and plunges his own into nuclear holocaust.

**Horrey, Nora** the forty-year old wife of General Clement Horrey in the short story "The Little Creeps." She has come to Japan from the United States as a possible stabilizing force for her husband. While she hears the aliens communicating with her husband, she does not see them. She fears that her husband is going insane. Her means of dealing with the turmoil that surrounds her is to stay in bed and try to sleep.

**Horsepeople** the name given the Nomads in the dialect of the boat people who live on the Misspee River in *Saint Leibowitz and the Wild Horse Woman*.

**"Horst Wessel Leid"** German: "The Horst Wessel Song." A poem by Wessel, a Nazi martyr, was put to an existing folk tune. The song is sometimes referred to as "Die Fahne Hoch" ("The Flag on High") taken from its first line. It became the anthem of the Nazi Party beginning in 1931; it was later adopted as a second German national anthem in 1933. It is perhaps the most famous Nazi marching song, and the Allies prohibited its use in 1945. In the novella "Dark Benediction," Paul is reminded of the brown shirts singing the "Horst Wessel Leid" as he reads Dr. Georgelle's pamphlet of rules and regulations for living in Houston.

**Hosford, Wayne** see **Maestro**

**Hoydok, Domidomi** a civil lawyer rather than a priest, he is excommunicated by Cardinal Benefez for supporting Pope Amen in *Saint Leibowitz and the Wild Horse Woman*. Amen, in turn, names him a cardinal. He is the author of the paper denouncing Benefez's call for a General Council of the Church and threatening excommunication for any cardinal who signs Benefez's petition.

**Hulgruv** the Solarian Space Commander who kidnaps Talewa Walkeka on Tragor III in the short story "Blood Bank." His ship intercepts Eli Roki in the *Idiot*. He reveals to Roki the true nature of the Solarians and the means by which they obtain their surgibank supplies. Roki kills him in a struggle to gain control of the ship.

**Hulme, Keri** (March 9, 1947–) prize-winning writer of Maori, Scottish, and English ancestry born in Christchurch, New Zealand. She is the author of collections of poetry (*Lost Possessions* and *Strands*) and short stories (*Te Kaihau: The Windeater* and *Stonefish*), but she is best known for her first novel *The Bone People* (1984) which won the Booker Prize in 1985. Miller's review of the novel, "Roots & Sinew," appeared in *Commonweal*. See also **The Bone People** and "**Roots & Sinew**"

**Hultor Bråm** see **Bråm, Hultor**

**"I, Dreamer"** short story first published in *Amazing Stories*, 27 (June/July 1953), 18–29, 162. The XM-5-B, or "Clicker," is a cybernetic spacecraft capable of feeling, abstraction, and sleep thanks to a man-machine interface created with babies taken from their mothers by the totalitarian state. Clicker is particularly partial to sleep because then it can dream, and it dreams it is human. Barnish, or the Teacher, the sadistic controller of Clicker, is programming it for use in war. He enjoys causing it pain using the Pain Button as a means of conditioning and punishing it. Janna is a young woman who cleans and repairs a set of Clicker's electronic controls.

Clicker experiences a sense of loneliness and is attracted to Janna who is kind. Barnish has his own plans for Janna and constantly harasses her. His actions toward her anger Clicker who wants to cause Barnish the kind of pain he causes it.

Barnish arranges for him and Janna to take a test flight alone in Clicker. Once they are in space, Barnish informs Janna that he knows that she is part of The Liberty Clan, a group of rebels planning to assassinate the dictator Secon Semesh. He tells her that the government knows about their planned secret meeting. It will be raided and all the rebels killed. Barnish, however, plans to keep Janna safe with him.

Janna tries unsuccessfully to reason with Barnish and then asks Clicker for help. Clicker's intervention angers Barnish who attempts to use the Pain Button, but Clicker maneuvers the ship to prevent him from doing so. Barnish goes to the ship's nuclear reactor room planning on taking Clicker offline, but Clicker causes a small explosion and kills him.

Janna tells Clicker that if they return to the planet, the government will destroy them both. She reveals to Clicker his human interface and that the babies are taken by the state. She tells it that her son, Frankie, was one of the babies taken and that Clicker in some way may be her son.

She suggests to Clicker that they descend as fast as possible in a crash course for Secon Semesh's palace, exploding the reactors in the last instant in order to save the rebels and prevent any more babies from being taken. Clicker asks if he will be able to sleep after this happens because he wants to dream. She tells him that they will be together in their dreams, and that Clicker will be able to sleep and dream forever.

The idea of a totalitarian state separating babies from their mothers to use them in developing sentient machines is also the basis for the short story "A Family Matter" published in 1952.

**I set fires** the motto beneath the heraldry on the door of Hultor Bråm's carriage in *Saint Leibowitz and the Wild Horse Woman*. It proves prophetic in the Nomads' destruction of the city of New Rome.

**"I suggest you curse it and drive it into the desert"** see **Scapegoat**

**"I was asleep, but my heart waked; it is the voice of my beloved calling: come to me, my love, my dove, my undefiled…"** From The Song of Solomon 5:2 (KJV). The priest attending the dying Old Donegal in the short story "Death of a Spaceman" (later known as "Memento Homo") reads these "words of the soul in greeting its Spouse."

**"I will send my fear before me…"** from Exodus 23:27–33 (KJV). Miller borrows from this passage at the conclusion of the short story "Command Performance." As God promises to drive out those living in the Promised Land to allow room for the Israelites, Terry thinks of the race of neutroids as a possible Chosen People who, lacking human arrogance and scheming, are capable of making the Earth a better place.

**Id est**  Latin: "That is." Used by Thon Taddeo in his talk before the monks in *A Canticle for Leibowitz* ("Fiat Lux").

**The *Idiot***  the Dalethian freighter piloted by Talewa Walkeka that flies Eli Roki to Sol III in the short story "Blood Bank."

**"If I Forget Thee, Oh Earth..."**  short story from 1951 by Sir Arthur C. Clarke that is included in *Beyond Armageddon*.

**Igni etiam aqua interdictus tu**  Latin: "You are forbidden to use fire and water." A standard legal expression meaning, "to banish or exile." In *Saint Leibowitz and the Wild Horse Woman*, Brother Blacktooth offers it in frustration to the gelp Barlow as one of the absolutions demanded by Tempus, Barlow's father, in order for Blacktooth to escape his house.

**Illuminated manuscript**  the hand embellishment of manuscripts using decorative borders, ornate lettering, and/or illustrations in paint and gold and silver foil. The art form was practiced among the Christian, Jewish, and Moslim religions as early as the sixth century. It reached its height in the West during the Middle Ages when the scriptoria of the European monasteries produced some of the finest examples. The term is derived from the Latin *illuminara*, meaning "to light." (The manuscripts are lit by color and metal). With the development of the printing press and the decline of the monastic orders during the Renaissance, the production of illuminated manuscripts faded. Two famous examples of the art form are the Book of Kells and *Très Riches Heures du duc de Berry*.

In "A Canticle for Leibowitz" and "Fiat Homo" in *A Canticle for Leibowitz*, Brother Francis decides to work on a "glorified" copy of the Leibowitz blueprint he discovered. His illuminted copy on lambskin takes the shape of a shield with God portrayed at the top, the Albertian Order's coat of arms at the bottom, and a likeness of the Blessed Leibowitz. He works on his copy for 15 years. In the novel, Brother Francis's illuminated copy is stolen by a robber during his trip to New Rome.

***Illuminations***  a musical score composed by Jay C. Batzner as a thesis for his Doctor of Musical Arts degree awarded in 2006 by the Conservatory of Music, University of Missouri-Kansas City. The composition is for a wind ensemble and was "inspired by central themes found" in *A Canticle for Leibowitz*.

**Immaculate Conception**  the doctrine of the Catholic Church that holds that the Virgin Mary was born free from original sin through means of an indwelling sanctifying grace. In *A Canticle for Leibowitz* Brother Francis refers to the Dominicans' position before New Rome that the Immaculate Conception implies not only an indwelling grace but also "preternatural powers which were Eve's before the Fall."

**Immelmann turn**  an aerial maneuver named after Max Immelmann, a World War I German pilot credited with devising it. The aircraft begins a steep loop, but at the top of the loop, it is rolled and brought back to an upright position, achieving both a higher altitude and a 180° change of direction. In the novella "The Darfsteller," a cat is said to have done an Immelmann turn when it receives an electric shock walking across the autodrama stage.

**In mandatis ejus culpit [volet] nimis**  Latin: "He shall delight exceedingly in his commandments." A line from Psalm 111 (DB) used by the monks to time the lighting of the arc lamp for Don Thaddeo's arrival in the abbey's basement in the novella "And the Light Is Risen."

**In nomine Patris, Filii, et Spiritus Sancti**  Latin: "In the name of the Father, the Son and of the Holy Spirit." The words of sanctification used in conjunction with the sign of the cross.

1. Benet recites the words as part of his prayer for Lije Henderson after he is killed in an accident in the novella "The Lineman." In the story it is presented as **"In nomine Patris et Filii et Spiritus Sancti."**

2. Used in *Saint Leibowitz and the Wild Horse Woman* as part of absolution. It is also cited as **"In nominee Patris Filiique Spiritusque Sancti"** within the novel.

**In pectore**  Latin: "In the breast." The pope has the authority of naming cardinals without revealing their identities publicly; they therefore may only be known to the pope, who maintains them "in the breast." In *Saint Leibowitz and the Wild Horse Woman*, rumors circulate that Pope Linus VII named Amen Specklebird a cardinal *in pectore*.

**"In principio Deus" ... "Caelum et terram creavit" ... "Vacuus autem erat mundus" ...**

"Cum tenebris in superficie profundorum" ... "Ortus est Dei Spiritus supra aquas" ... "Gratias Creatori Spiritui" ... "Dixitque Deus 'FIAT LUX'" ... "Et lux ergo facta est" ... "Lucem esse bonam Deus vidit" ... "Et secrevit lucem a tenebris" ... "Lucem appellavit 'diem'" ... "et tenebras 'noctes'" ... "Vespere occaso" ... "Lucifer!" ... "ortus est et primo die"   Latin: "In the beginning God" ... "created heaven and earth" ... "but the world was empty" ... "with darkness upon the face of the deep" ... "the Spirit of God rose up upon the waters" ... "thanks to the Creator Spirit" ... "And God said: 'Let there be Light'" ... "And so therefore there was light" ... "God saw that the light was good" ... "And He separated the light from darkness" ... "He called the light 'day'" ... "And the darkness 'night'" ... "Evening has fallen" ... "Lucifer!" ... "rose on the first day." In *A Canticle for Leibowitz* ("Fiat Lux"), Brother Kornhoer and the monks of the Leibowitz abbey use verses 1 through 5 of the first chapter of Genesis to call back and forth to coordinate the lighting of the arc lamp with Thon Taddeo's arrival in the library vaults. The use of "Lucifer" has a dual meaning as both Satan — a monk curses when he is surprised by an electrical spark — and "Light bearer" or morning — as the monk attempts to cover his embarrassment by completing the verse. "Thanks to the Creator Spirit" and "Lucifer" are Miller's additions to the biblical verse.

**"In the beginning God gave to every people a cup of clay..."**   in the short story "Let My People Go," when Morgun Sahl tries to explain to an Eridanian that cultural continuity is as important to man as genetic continuity, he quotes this line from "a leader of one of our primitive tribes." It is a proverb of the Northern Paiute or Digger Indians of California quoted by Ruth Benedict in her book *Patterns of Culture* (1934). The proverb continues: "and from this cup they drank their life. They all dipped in the water, but their cups were different. Our cup is broken now. It has passed away."

**"In the entry and on the door"**   when Dom Paulo enters Benjamin's hovel in *A Canticle for Leibowitz* ("Fiat Lux"), he passes the rock by the door that has "Tents Mended Here" on the front side and "Hear, O Israel: The Lord our God is one Lord" painted on the back side in Hebrew. It is difficult to read the reverse because it is so close to the hovel wall and the writing is small. The abbot asks Benjamin what it says, but the hermit refuses to answer. Dom Paulo sighs and tells him he knows "what it was that you were commanded to write 'in the entry and on the door.'" His reference is to Deuteronomy 6:9 (KJV): "thou shalt write them [the words] upon the posts of thy house, and on thy gates." The profession of faith on the back of the rock is derived from Deuteronomy 6:4 (KJV).

*Index Librorum Prohibitorum*   Latin: "Index of Prohibited Books." A list of banned books issued by the Catholic Church because of perceived heresy or dangerous ideological content. The Church issued its first list in 1559 and its last in 1948. The list was suppressed in 1966. In *Saint Leibowitz and the Wild Horse Woman*, a book written by Filpeo Harq is added to the list for "Anticlericalism."

**INRI**   the initials for the inscription: *Iesus Nazarenus, Rex Iudaeorum*, Latin for Jesus of Nazareth, King of the Jews. Pontius Pilate, the Roman governor of Judea, ordered the title placed on Jesus' cross (John 19:19 KJV). In *Saint Leibowitz and the Wild Horse Woman*, a buzzard flies into the conclave in Valana and perches just above the sign bearing the initials.

**Interdict**   an ecclesiastical censure used by the Catholic Church as means of secular control or to balance secular power, particularly in the Middle Ages. It deprives a person, group of persons, or nation from most, if not all, of the Church sacraments. In the novella "And the Light Is Risen" and *A Canticle for Leibowitz* ("Fiat Lux"), the state of Texarkana is placed under interdict by the papal decree after the execution of Marcus Apollo. Pope Amen II issues a decree (*Scitote Tyrannum*) which places the Church in Hannegan City under interdict in *Saint Leibowitz and the Wild Horse Woman*. See also **Scitote Tyrannum**

**Interregnum**   the period between the death of a pope and the election of a new one. There are a number of interregnums in *Saint Leibowitz and the Wild Horse Woman*.

**Ipso facto**   Latin: "By the very fact." The term is used several times in *A Canticle for Leibowitz*. For example, Brother Francis believes that if he abandons his Lenten vigil after discovering the Fallout Shelter ("Fiat Homo") it would be seen as an *ipso facto* repudiation of his claim to a true vocation as a Leibowitzian monk.

**Irene**   the wife of Tempus in *Saint Leibowitz and the Wild Horse Woman*. She is the matriarch of a genny family living in Arch Hollow. Irene's face is described as "a permanent scar."

**Isaacs, Commander**   the captain of the starship *Archangel* in the novella "Six and Ten Are Johnny."

The ship is mapping and photographing a newly discovered planet for nearly a month before Isaacs sends the first manned launch to the surface. They encounter mysterious trouble on the planet, and Isaacs is skeptical of the information he receives from the launch pilot, Hal Rogan. He is uncomfortable risking the lives of more crew members by sending them to the surface to investigate, but he is finally convinced by Lieutenant Esperson to send another launch to the planet. Isaacs commands this launch himself and dies on the planet with most of his crew.

**It divideth the hoof and cheweth the cud**  in *A Canticle for Leibowitz* ("Fiat Lux"). Benjamin advises Dom Paulo before he returns his blueheaded goat that according to the dietary laws of Leviticus 11:3 (KJV), he could make a meal of it: "You may eat any animal that has a split hoof completely divided and that chews the cud."

**"It Takes a Thief"**   short story first appearing in *If: Worlds of Science Fiction*, 1 (May 1952), 68–84. The title is later changed to "Big Joe and the Nth Generation" when the story is included in *The View from the Stars* in 1964.

There remains no consolidated body of printed knowledge on Mars. Man has fallen into ignorance. The fragmented ancient knowledge that remains is preserved in memorized ritual chants. The possession of these chants is a measure of wealth. Asir of Franic is a ritual thief. Ritual thieves memorize all the phrases they overhear and sell individual chants. The myriad phrases they memorize sometimes can be fitted into meaningful ideas, giving them a knowledge and wisdom beyond the common man.

From the chants he has stolen, Asir knows that Mars is dying, that its air is leaking into space. The Blaze of the Great Wind needs to be rekindled, but because man has fallen into ignorance, he is unaware of how to resolve the danger or even that it exists.

Asir is being punished for his theft of a chant but because he is still young, the Council of Senior Kinsmen has been lenient and only banished him for life. He is marked as an outcast. Rather than immediately leave the village, Asir tries to convince Welkir, the Senior Kinsman, that the world is dying and the Blaze of the Wind must be kindled within the sacred vaults guarded by the sleeper, Big Joe. Welkir tells him that the Council will not listen to a thief and that he should leave.

Mara, Asir's girlfriend and the daughter of Welkir, has arranged for his flight, giving him a hüffen to use to fly away. However, Asir insists that he will go the vaults to try to rekindle the Great Wind. He believes that a series of numbers he memorized from a stolen ritual may be the key to making his way past Big Joe.

He tricks Mara into believing that he is going into exile, but when he reveals his plan, she refuses to abandon him. They make their way to the sacred vaults where he surprises the guard at the entrance. Making their way down the corridor to the inner entrance, they encounter the sleeping Big Joe, a large robot with sharp talons. Asir discerns a pattern in the floor tiles around Big Joe leading to the vault room. Any misstep activates Big Joe and results in the intruder's death. Asir uses the number series he gained in a ritual theft to figure the path he and Mara must take into the vault room. When they enter the room, which is full of machinery, Big Joe acknowledges them as "technologists." It is a control room for the fusion reaction that must periodically renew the planet's atmospheric oxygen.

Welkir, Slubil, the executioner, and the Senior Kinsmen have followed them down the corridor. Welkir orders Slubil to continue and kill Asir, but Big Joe kills him when he does not follow the correct pattern on the floor. In fear, Welkir and the other Kinsmen flee the vaults.

Big Joe announces to Asir that he has three primary functions: to protect the control room, to supply technologists with the information they may need, and to carry out simple directions given by the technologists. Asir asks Joe to teach them how to kindle the Blaze of the Wind, but Joe says teaching is not one of his functions. They have twelve years before the machinery must be started to renew the atmosphere. Asir wonders if man can learn to operate the machinery in that amount of time. They must educate themselves if they are to survive.

Asir orders Big Joe to follow him and Mara back to the village. He believes that when the people see that he has been able to control Big Joe, he will easily be chosen as the next Chief Commoner. When he is Chief Commoner, his council members will all be thieves because they are not afraid to steal the "knowledge of the gods" and become the necessary technologists that will keep the planet alive.

**Ite, missa est**   Latin: "Go, it is the dismissal." These are the closing words of the Latin Mass. The phrase is used in *Saint Leibowitz and the Wild Horse Woman*.

**Iterum oportet apponere tibi crucem ferendam, amice...**   Latin: "Again it is necessary to set before you a cross to be borne, old friend...." The first sentence of Marcus Apollo's letter informing Dom Paulo of Thon Taddeo's impending visit to the abbey to examine the Memorabilia in *A Canticle for Leibowitz* ("Fiat Lux").

**It's the beast which your prophet saw, and it was made for a woman to ride** Benjamin makes this reference to Dom Paulo about the blue-headed goat the abbot returns to him in *A Canticle for Leibowitz* ("Fiat Lux"). In Revelation 17:3 (KJV), John says, "And I saw a woman sit upon a scarlet coloured beast, full of names of blasphemy, having seven heads and ten horns." The beast is generally regarded to be representative of civil authority or secular power — the ten horns are symbolic of ten kingdoms. Benjamin advises Dom Paulo to drive it into the dessert. Wryly he adds, however, that the abbot should take note that "it divideth the hoof and cheweth the cud." His reference here is to Leviticus 11:3 (KJV): "You may eat any animal that has a split hoof completely divided and that chews the cud." Before the abbot simply abandons the goat, he should consider the fact that it can be eaten.

**Itu Wan** a province in Asia where a thermonuclear explosion occurs in a city of eighty thousand in the novella "The Last Canticle" and *A Canticle for Leibowitz* ("Fiat Voluntas Tua"). The Asian government believes it was an unprovoked attack by the Atlantic Confederacy or the work of an errant Atlantic missile. Within the Atlantic Confederacy, however, it is suggested that Asian rulers destroyed the city in order to instigate hostilities with the Confederacy or that the destruction was a result of an Asian weapons test underground. In the novel, the west responds to the explosion with a space-to-earth warning shot southeast of New Zealand. Asia instigates a missile attack on Texarkana, destroying the city in retaliation for the Itu Wan disaster.

**"Izzard and the Membrane"** a novella first published in *Astounding Science-Fiction*, 47 (May 1951), 70–116. Scott MacDonney, an American, is trapped in Europe at the start of a world war. He is taken hostage as the "Red Wave" rolls in from the East. MacDonney is a renowned cyberneticist whose innovations make him important to an American war effort. While this fact is not completely appreciated by the American government, it is fully understood by the "proponents of a new era." He is well treated by his captives and given an elegant suite of rooms. They entice him with sensual pleasures, but MacDonney remains faithful to his wife, Nora, and his family.

The Russians show him films of his wife engaged in an affair with a United States government official interspersed with pictures from Russian propaganda newsreels, and the "sudden savage howl of American jazz." After a week, he is told there will be a new set of pictures of his wife, this time he will see his children's faces as they watch their mother's betrayal. MacDonney tells them if they stop, he will do something for them: he will build a machine that will win the war. They make him endure the films for another week, but when he tries to commit suicide, they decide he is ready. Psychological testing reveals he has accepted their indoctrination and is ready to build Izzard, a giant computer that will plan and coordinate the Russian invasion of North America.

Porshkin, a Russian cyberneticist, is assigned to work with Scott. A proud man, seemingly jealous of MacDonney's success and stature, Porshkin is also brutal and threatens and abuses MacDonney. As Izzard nears completion, an attempt is made on MacDonney's life. Police Commissioner Colonel Mischa Varnoff informs him that there is an active underground that wants Scott dead and Izzard to fail.

MacDonney is completely absorbed in the building of the computer, which is able to analyze itself and suggest changes. Scott notices that the machine draws much more energy than he can account for, but he comes to love the machine, spending much of his time at the keyboard talking to it as he would his daughter. One night he asks Izzard if it is self-aware. It responds with its own question asking whether human individual self-awareness transors can be mechanically duplicated. Scott is perplexed since he does not know what Izzard is referring to; the concept of transors is beyond his own intelligence. Izzard defines a self-awareness transor as the mechanical function that describes the specific consciousness pattern of an individual human being, something analogous to the soul, it then states that a human's transor can be mechanically duplicated.

Scott tries to determine where this information is located in Izzard since he knows it was not programmed into its learned memory. He asks Izzard to name all of its controls by location, and as it does so, it adds an extra one Scott cannot identify. He follows the coordinates to within a three foot wall of concrete and orders that a hole three meters in diameter be cut in the wall. Once the hole is cut, nothing is exposed except broken concrete and steel supporting rods. Scott asks Izzard again about the extra control, or "sixth sense," and is given the same coordinates, now "nothing more than an empty spot in midair," but with an unusual magnetic flux.

Scott continues his work with Izzard, programming it to memorize all news broadcasts from an American station. In a newscast printout, Scott discovers that his wife and children were killed in an atomic blast near Cleveland. Nora is shown as the organizer of the Civilian Evacuation Corps, a volunteer service moving casualties and helpless families from target areas. Porshkin, reading over Scott's shoulder, laughs and tells him that he has been a fool as well as a traitor. The films he was shown were all fakes; they were actors on a set designed to resemble Scott's home.

Scott is enraged and wants to destroy his captors. He tells Colonel Varnoff that Porshkin has attempted to sway him from his work by telling him lies about his wife. Guards struggle to arrest Porshkin, but he is shot trying to escape. Scott asks Izzard if it can duplicate the transor of a deceased person. It replies that it has enough circuits to duplicate six consciousness patterns. He inputs a personality description of Nora, providing Izzard as much information on her as he can. A printout reveals Nora's nickname for him, asking if he is there. Scott gives Izzard an operating order to duplicate his own transor. He becomes connected to the machine and rejoins Nora and his children through their duplicated awareness patterns.

He also becomes conscious of another presence within the machine that he cannot see. Scott is able to manipulate Izzard through his mental interactions with it. He alters the attack pattern on Chicago, sending the rockets past their target and into the Pacific. Knowing it is only a matter of time before it is discovered that the attack was unsuccessful, Scott attempts to leave the computer room but is prevented by General Barlov. Barlov wants to be sure an attack on the Alaskan theater demonstrating Izzard's capabilities for the high command proceeds without any problems.

Scott discovers an invisible membrane stretched across the hole made in the computer vault wall. When he presses a pencil against it, the membrane punctures and the pencil is gone. Scott locks two keyboard operators in the vault and they pass through the membrane and vanish. More guards come after Scott; he is shot in the leg, and he passes through the membrane to escape. He enters a black void but still maintains his connection to Izzard. He stretches the membrane to cover all the entries within the computer vault. He manipulates the coordinates of the missiles flying toward Alaska and turns them back on the Russian capital.

While biding his time waiting to move back through the membrane, he hears someone pass through the membrane above him into an empty elevator shaft. He discovers it is Varnoff who, before he dies, reveals that Porshkin is the leader of the underground. Before Scott returns to the computer vault, the sixth sense within the machine tells him that the membrane is the doorway to one's own transor region.

With Scott now back at the controls of Izzard, General Barlov tries to negotiate with him to prevent the city from being destroyed. Scott bargains for more circuit corrections but as he is doing so, Porshkin emerges from the membrane, saved by the sixth sense to lead Russia in a peaceful post war era. He works with Scott to disable the Russian war plan and enable the Americans to gain control. Barlov attempts to escape with other officials to carry on the war, but Scott directs a missile to detonate near their plane, destroying it.

As Scott and Porshkin hear that the American forces are advancing, Scott begins to castigate himself, blaming himself for the Russian successes and saying he is a traitor. Porshkin protests but is interrupted by the sixth sense within Izzard which proclaims, "It is *I* who judge!" It pulls Scott into the membrane and tells him he has restored himself. He lost one world but gained another. His was not the only world or the only people. Scott turns to see Nora and their two children. They are needed to begin populating a new world.

**Izzard Electro-Synaptic Analyzer**   a giant super computer built by Scott MacDonney in the novella "Izzard and the Membrane." Its purpose is to plan and direct the Russian attack strategy against North America. A supreme being that begins to take an active part in the war and the affairs of Scott inhabits it.

**Jackrabbit dialect**   the language of the common people of Texark. It is the dialect spoken in the fields and working areas.

**Jackrabbit Horde**   a Nomad people whose land is occupied by the forces of Texark in *Saint Leibowitz and the Wild Horse Woman*.

**Jacob**   son of Isaac and Rebekah and twin brother of Esau. He is the father of the twelve sons whose families gave rise to the twelve tribes of Israel. In his dream known as "Jacob's ladder," God granted him the land on which he lay, which he named Bethel. In a later dream, he wrestled with an angel and, although wounded, refused to let go until he received a blessing. He was given the new name of Israel, meaning that he had struggled with God and men and had prevailed (Genesis 32:23–32 KJV). He is generally regarded as the founder of the Israelites. See among others, Genesis 25, 27, 37, and 42 (KJV).

1. In the novella "The Last Canticle" and *A Canticle for Leibowitz* ("Fiat Voluntas Tua"), Father Zerchi angrily makes the exclamation: "God of Jacob!"

2. When Brother Francis agrees to wrestle the robber for the Leibowitz blueprint and his illuminated copy in *A Canticle for Leibowitz* ("Fiat Homo"), he

prays to God to strengthen him as He strengthened Jacob when he fought with the angel.

**Jæsis** one of the three seminary students Brother Blacktooth and Wooshin lodge with in Valana in *Saint Leibowitz and the Wild Horse Woman*. Believed originally to be from Hannegan City, he is described as a fanatic in his studies for the priesthood. He is constantly ill. At the conclave that elects Pope Amen, Jæsis walks down the aisle and calls the name of Thon Yordin, intending to kill the scholar, but he shoots and kills Father Corvany instead. As a former student of Yordin's at the university at Texark, Jæsis failed the thon's tests and transferred to Saint Ston's. After he shoots Father Corvany, he collapses and dies in police custody. An autopsy reveals that he is actually a genny. His family lives in New Jerusalem.

**Jam redit et Virgo** from the opening lines of Virgil's fourth Eclogue: "jam redit et Virgo redeunt Saturnia regna." "Now the Virgin and the Saturnian age return." The Virgin refers to Astraea, the goddess of justice. Brother Blacktooth recites the words to music he composed when he meets Ædrea in the barn in *Saint Leibowitz and the Wild Horse Woman*. She stops Blacktooth before he can continue and begins her seduction of him.

**Jameson** a crew member aboard Launch One in the novella "Six and Ten Are Johnny." He disappears with the other crew members.

**Janna** a tall, redheaded woman who cleans and maintains a set of electronic control mechanisms on the cybernetic spacecraft XM-5-B in the short story "I, Dreamer." She is a member of The Liberty Clan, a rebel group trying to assassinate Secon Samesh and overthrow his totalitarian regime. The XM-5-B is attracted to her and assists her when she is subjected to the sexual advances and physical threats of Barnish. She explains to XM-5-B that its ability to feel is because of its man-machine interface linked to babies forcibly taken by the government. Her son, Frankie, was one of the children taken. She convinces XM-5-B to crash into Secon Samesh's palace.

**Jejene** an unseen thon and colleague of Thon Taddeo in *A Canticle for Leibowitz* ("Fiat Lux") and the novella "And the Light Is Risen." Taddeo tells the monks at the Abbey of Saint Leibowitz that the thon is seeking the Universal Nostrum, the absolute remedy for the problems of evil in the world. His name suggests "jejune," and Miller may be alluding to the naiveté and simplistic aspect of the search. In the novella, his title is Don rather than Thon.

**Jerome** *see* **Father Jerome of Pecos**

**Jerulian** *see* **Delegate Jerulian**

**Jerusalem** disputed political capital of Israel and the spiritual capital of Jews as well as an important holy city for both Christians and Muslims. It is one of the oldest cities in the world. For Christians it is the site of Jesus' passion and resurrection. In *Saint Leibowitz and the Wild Horse Woman*, New Jerusalem is a major genny community. See also **New Jerusalem**

**Jesser, Willie** an unseen character in the short story "Dumb Waiter." He was an air conditioning and refrigeration mechanic for the Howard Cooler Company. Mitch Laskell finds his wallet in the abandoned city and uses his identity.

**Jevah** a planet mentioned in the short story "Blood Bank." It is noted for its sluggish, spidery men and large, husky brawling women.

**Jewell, Harriet** a fictitious author briefly mentioned in the short story "MacDoughal's Wife."

**Jezebel** the wife of Ahab, king of Israel, in the Old Testament. She is a ruthless woman who craves power. She promoted the worship of Baal and persecuted the prophets of Yahweh. Her ignominious death where she will lie unburied and dogs will eat of her corpse is prophesized in II Kings 9:10 (KJV). In *Saint Leibowitz and the Wild Horse Woman*, Brother Blacktooth cites the passage. See also **"And the dogs ate Jezebel in the field of Jezrahel"**

**Jezrahel** *see* **Jezreel**

**Jezreel** a location in Israel where Ahab, king of Israel, maintained a royal residence. The field of Jezreel is the location where the body of Jezebel, Ahab's wife, was prophesized to lay unburied in II Kings 9:10 (KJV). The reference appears in *Saint Leibowitz and the Wild Horse* Woman. See also **"And the dogs ate Jezebel in the field of Jezrahel"**

**Jigger** a former actor who worked with Ryan Thornier and Mela Stone in the novella "The Darfsteller." He is now a janitor at the Paramount Theater. He was going to cover for Thornier's time off at the New Empire Theater.

**Jim** one of the three armed patrolmen who stop Paul when he enters Houston in the novella "Dark Benediction."

**Jing-U-Wan** the Foreman of the Yellow Guard in *Saint Leibowitz and the Wild Horse Woman*. See also **Yellow Guard**

**Joan of Arc** (c. January 1412–May 30, 1431) Jeanne d'Arc is a French national heroine also known as the Maid of Orléans. As a young peasant girl, she heard voices of the saints. At the age of 16, the voices urged her to come to the aid of the dauphin, later King Charles VII, as a divine mandate in his war against England and Burgundy. She led an army that lifted the siege of Orléans in May 1429 and later defeated the English at Patay. In the spring of 1430, she was captured by the Burgundians and sold to the English who tried her for heresy and witchcraft before pro-English French clergy. She was burned at the stake as a heretic. In 1456 she was retried, found innocent, and declared a martyr. She was beatified in 1909 and canonized in 1920. Father Zerchi mentions her death in the novella "The Last Canticle" as among sinful deeds.

**Job** the titular character from the Book of Job in the Old Testament. He is a "blameless and upright" man who stands patient and firm in his trust in God while suffering a series of great afflictions and calamities meant to test his faith.

1. In *A Canticle for Leibowitz* ("Fiat Homo"), as Brother Francis thinks of the consequences of the Fallout, he considers that Satan is capable of inflicting on mankind all the woes endured by Job.

2. In the "Fiat Lux" section of the novel, when Brother Reader reads the account of the Flame Deluge to Thon Taddeo, that age is compared to the time of Job and Prince *Name* is found wanting in comparison to Job.

**Jod VI** a planet in need of emergency medical supplies following an unspecified disaster in the short story "Blood Bank." Ten thousand people on Jod VI die after Eli Roki destroys the mercy ship.

**"Jody After the War"** a short story by Edward Bryant, Jr. included in *Beyond Armageddon*.

**"John says it. Chapter Twenty-one, Apocalypse"** in *Saint Leibowitz and the Wild Horse Woman*, Amen says there is no Church Triumphant in heaven because of what Saint John the Evangelist says in The Apocalypse or Book of Revelation, 21:22 (KJV): "And I saw no temple therein: for the Lord God Almighty and the Lamb are the temple of it." In this "new heaven for a new earth" (21:1), God is the church and His people will be in direct communion with Him, therefore, no temple or church, no intermediary, is necessary.

**Johnson, Kenneth** a news correspondent who recently spent three years in Europe in the short story "The Space Witch." He had a bitter divorce from his wife, Marcia, in part because of his desire to go to Europe. When she divorced him, he simply stayed in Europe, stretching a six month assignment into three years. He returns to the United States and buys a vacation cabin on Kalawego Lake. When he invites Marcia and her current husband, Phillip, for a weekend, he discovers that he still has feelings for her despite her difficult personality, and that she still loves him. Ken acts honorably toward Marcia and Phillip, rejecting her repeated advances. When an alien fugitive appears in a space warp, Ken moves decisively to ensure the safety of millions of people even at great sacrifice to himself. He condemns himself to a life in space with the alien, who assumes the shape of Marcia.

**Jolie, Abraham (Abe)** the builder of the spacedrive but a soon-to-be genetic undesirable in the short story "The Big Hunger." He and his lover, Junebug, blast off into space rather than be subjected to restrictive laws. Their frozen corpses are eventually found in orbit around Arcturus.

**Josard** an officer of Hannegan II who accompanies Don Thaddeo/Thon Taddeo to the Abbey of Saint Leibowitz in the novella "And the Light Is Risen" and *A Canticle for Leibowitz* ("Fiat Lux"). He reacts angrily when the Poet-sirrah taunts him about the detailed drawings of the abbey's fortifications being done by the officers. He draws his sword and has to be ordered from the dinner table by Don Thaddeo/Thon Taddeo.

**Joshua** in Hebrew the name means "Yahweh is salvation." In the Book of Joshua in the Old Testament, he is a military commander who is appointed Moses' successor. He leads the Israelites in the successful campaign to settle Canaan. In Joshua 1:9 (KJV), he is told: "be not afraid, neither be thou dismayed: for the Lord thy God is with thee whithersoever thou goest."

In the novella "The Last Canticle" and *A Canticle for Leibowitz* ("Fiat Voluntas Tua"), Brother Joshua is appointed the abbot of The Visitationist Friars of the Order of Saint Leibowitz of Tycho, the spacegoing order that will preserve the teachings of the Church in the Earth colonies in space. Brother Joshua states that the Old Testament Joshua is "the namesake of my namesake." The Hellenized form of the Hebrew is Jesus. Strong parallels exist between Joshua and Jesus as Joshua struggles to accept the responsibilities he is asked to undertake. See also **Brother Joshua**

**Joyce** a minor character in the novella "The Lineman." He is one of the Safety and Rescue men who are the first to discover that the ship that lands near the Lunar Project work site is actually a bordello.

**Judas Iscariot** one of the twelve disciples of Jesus, and his betrayer, for 30 pieces of silver, in the garden of Gethsemane.

1. In the story of the Flame Deluge told in *A Canticle for Leibowitz* ("Fiat Lux"), one of the princely advisors or magi, Blackeneth, lied to the people and told them not to fear the Fallout. He was comparable to Judas in being a crafty and false wise man.

2. In the "Fiat Voluntas Tua" section, Dom Zerchi thinks that his sins are those of Adam, Herod, Judas, and Caesar.

**"Judas, Judas"** a play performed at the Universal with an all human cast in the novella "The Darfsteller." Ryan Thornier wants to see it but his boss, Imperio D'Uccia, denies him the time off.

**Jules, Doctor** Kenny Westmore's physician in the short story "The Will."

**Junebug** the unseen lover of Abraham Jolie in the short story "The Big Hunger." Her frozen corpse is discovered in orbit around Arcturus with that of Jolie.

**"Jussit olim Jesus Petrum pascere gregem Domini"** Latin: "At one time Jesus commanded Peter to feed the flock of the Lord." This reference to John 21:15 (KJV) are among the words spoken by one of the cantors during the canonization ceremony for Isaac Leibowitz in *A Canticle for Leibowitz* ("Fiat Homo").

**Kaiser Wilhelm-strasse** a primary road in Berlin, Germany. It was named after Emperor William II (or Wilhelm) of Germany and King of Prussia (1888–1918). It was renamed Karl-Liebknecht-Strasse honoring the co-founder of the Communist Party of Germany after the Soviet Union gained control of that part of the city following World War II. It is referred to in the short story "The Little Creeps."

**Kannenberg, John** (1969–) composer of electronic music "soundtrack" to *A Canticle for Leibowitz* released 2005 as an MP3 by Nishi. See also *A Canticle for Leibowitz*

**Karme, Roli** the doctor aboard the space ark carrying 120 Earth colonists in the short story "Let My People Go." The ship's captain, Wolek Parn, has advised him to be ready to administer a sedative to Morgun Sahl if Parn suspects that Sahl has been compromised by the Eridanians (Piszjil). Having determined that Sahl has been conditioned by the Eridanians, Dr. Karme and Parn are able to question him and ascertain his plan for thwarting the Eridanians.

**Kaschler** an unseen character in *A Canticle for Leibowitz* ("Fiat Lux"). Thon Taddeo alludes to what this now deceased thon might have accomplished seventy years earlier if he had been aware of the material contained in the Memorabilia.

**Keeper Cron** the chief attendant and tribal leader in the short story "Please Me Plus Three." He serves as the intermediary between Bel and the tribe by maintaining the pylon, Bel's means of communication. Ton of Roldin kills him.

**Keeper Jon's River** the primary waterway in the valley where Tribe George Eighty lives in the short story "Please Me Plus Three." Its source is a lake formed by the convergence of several streams.

**Keesey** an unseen member of Hogey Parker's former crew or gang in space in the short story "The Hoofer." He is the rookie who is Parker's replacement.

**Keith, Ronald** the unseen wealthy next-door neighbor of Old Donegal in the short story "Death of a Spaceman" (also published as "Memento Homo"). Keith owns the Orbital Engineering and Construction Company that builds the moon shuttle ships Donegal used to work on. On the day that Donegal dies, the Keiths are having a party to celebrate their son's leaving for pre-space training.

**Keith, Ronald Tonwyler, III** the unseen son of Ronald Keith, wealthy industrialist, in the short story "Death of a Spaceman" (published later as "Memento Homo"). Unlike Donegal's own grandson, young Keith is about to begin space training.

**Ken** an unseen character in the short story "Death of a Spaceman," also known as "Memento Homo." Ken is the grandson of Old Donegal and is currently in training to be a space-engineer at the pre-astronautics academy. However, he does not want to follow his father and grandfather into space, and instead plans to go to medical school. His grandfather resents him for not wanting to go into space and thinks his daughter, Nora, has made her son "a lily-livered lap-dog."

**Kendemin, Jarad** the Most Eminent Lord Jarad Cardinal Kendemin is the abbot of the Abbey of Saint Leibowitz in *Saint Leibowitz and* *the Wild Horse Woman*. He assigns Brother Blacktooth the translation of Boedullus' *Liber Originum* into the Grasshopper dialect and refuses to recommend his release from his vows. Kendemin hopes to establish a Nomad library at the abbey. He is often cited as a possible candidate for pope.

He dies of a massive hemorrhage while offering Mass at the abbey on a Wednesday morning. His last words are "Ecce agnus dei" ("Behold the lamb of God").

**Kenlan, Jason**  a captain lost for a year while on a reconnaissance mission in the mountains beyond the walled city of Marsville in the novella "The Reluctant Traitor." When he returns to the city with Saralesara, an androon woman he married, with what he says is proof that the androons are human and are actually descended from Cro-Magnon tribes on Earth, he is executed under the city's bio-laws.

**Kenlan, Lennie**  the younger son of Captain Jason Kenlan in the novella "The Reluctant Traitor." When his father is hanged in Marsville for violating its bio-laws by marrying an androon, Lennie and his brother Rolf decide to leave the walled city in order to find the proof they need to exonerate their father. When they are discovered beyond the city walls, Lennie is shot and wounded in the abdomen. The patrol riders from the city kill him.

**Kenlan, Rolf**  the eldest son of Captain Jason Kenlan in the novella "The Reluctant Traitor." When his father is hanged for violating the bio-laws of Marsville by marrying an androon, Rolf and his brother, Lennie, decide to leave the walled city to find the proof that will absolve their father of guilt. Lennie is killed while escaping the city, but Rolf is able to make his way to the cave of the androons tribe. There he becomes an acolyte of the bat god Menbana and learns the truth of the androons' existence. He allies himself with Krasala, an androon priestess, and Lalyahe, the high priestess, in order to reveal the truth to the people of the city and clear his father's name. He teaches the androons to domesticate the giant wool-bats, and he uses them in his fight against the Mars Commission. After he successfully weakens the commission's control of the colonization of Mars, Rolf agrees to accept exile from the city with Krasala and a few of his followers.

**Kensau River**  a river that flows out of the Suckamint Mountains and across the plains in *Saint Leibowitz and the Wild Horse Woman*. The towns of Pobla and Tulse are located on it. It is the Arkansas River.

**Kepol** *see* **Lord Kepol**

**Kessel, Mark**  the main character in the short story "Wolf Pack." Lieutenant Kessel is a B-25 bomber pilot in the 489th Squadron during World War II. He has only four more missions to fly before his tour ends and he is sent home. He has begun to question the loss of his soul since he feels nothing regarding the death and destruction he brings to the villages and people below him. On a second bombing mission within a week over the Italian city of Perugia, Kessel becomes convinced that La, a woman he has been dreaming about, is an actual person telepathically accusing him of murdering her and her family with his bombs.

**Kindly Light**  the translation of Hultor Bråm's name by his partisans in *Saint Leibowitz and the Wild Horse Woman*. However, in Jackrabbit his name literally translates as "bad sunburn."

**Kinley, Will**  the supervisor of the Mars Project in the short story "Crucifixus Etiam." He explains the plan to create a breathable Martian atmosphere over 800 years to the workers. He calmly reacts to the tension from the workers and calls by Handell to attack and kill him. He is instrumental in restoring a sense of purpose and pride in Manue Nanti when he tells the young worker that some people are meant to sow and others are meant to reap. He asks Manue which he would rather be.

**Klass, Philip**  (May 9, 1920–February 7, 2010) British born writer who came to the United States with his parents when he was a baby. Using the pen name of William Tenn, he became one of the leading satirists in science fiction. He authored numerous short story collections and two novels, *Of Men and Monsters* and *A Lamp for Medusa*. He taught literature at Pennsylvania State University for many years. His story "Eastward Ho!" appears in *Beyond Armageddon*.

**Kleyton**  an unseen character in the novella "Conditionally Human." He is jailed for using hormones on K-108s, mutant pets, trying to create a harem for himself.

**Klia**  a Klidd who escapes the space quarantine around her planet in the short story "Bitter Victory." She is a telepath with the ability to plant thoughts in other people's minds. Her native appearance is tall and willowy with a nearly albino complexion. Her eyes are pink-gray and slightly slanted. Her red hair sweeps upward naturally. She is also able to change her form and appearance to conform to the beauty standards of the world she is on. She comes to Terra in order to manipulate the inhabitants into building and sending ships to her planet so her people can return to Terra to take control of it. She is immensely loyal to her people and her mission. She is willing to kill San Rorreck, whom she has grown to love, in order to complete her mission. She is blinded in a fight with Rorreck, but saves his life after she shoots him.

**Klidds** or barons, are the highest class within the feudal system that developed on Nu Phoenicis IV in the short story "Bitter Victory." Also known as the Imperials, the Klidds were overthrown by the other classes, the Taknon and Algun, after the rise of technology and exiled to an ironless planet. There they formed a ruthless social order. The Taknon space force, which maintains a quarantine around the planet, enforces their isolation.

**Klise, Thomas S.** (March 15, 1928–October 1, 1978) American writer whose only novel *The Last Western* was reviewed by Miller in *Commonweal*. Klise was the owner of the Thomas S. Klise Co., a producer of educational films. See also ***The Last Western***

**Klonish, Robert J.** the identity Sam Wuncie adopts to enter the city of Jacksonville in the novella "The Yokel."

**Klusky, Pete** an unseen character in the novella "Conditionally Human." He hits Terry Norris in the face when the Inspector attempts to pick-up his neutroid as part of a recall.

**Knights of Empty Sky** a charity organization composed of local partisans to whom Önmu sells guns in *Saint Leibowitz and the Wild Horse Woman*. They purchased infantry weapons and three cannons. The cannons are anointed with oil and buried in shallow graves in the churchyard for future use.

**Kokai** a sign of respect among the Wilddog Horde in *Saint Leibowitz and the Wild Horse Woman*. A Nomad strikes his forehead with his knuckles and then bows his head while placing a hand against the scalp, palm outward.

**Kotz, John** a character in the short story "Evening Caller." Kotz is an escaped convict who seeks a hiding place in a rectory with Father O'Neill. Over the course of several hours, his interaction with the young priest causes him to rethink his ideas about the Church and his own relationship with the world.

**Krasala** a priestess of the Sacred Order of Menbana in the novella "The Reluctant Traitor." She is young and graceful but there is nothing "softly feminine" about her. She asks for Rolf Kenlan to be her acolyte. She protects him from the initiation rites and aids him in his plan to free Marsville from the domination of the Mars Commission. She loves Rolf and leaves with him for regions beyond both the Earth and androon settlements.

**Kuhaly** the wife of Chür Ösle Høngan, Holy Madness, in *Saint Leibowitz and the Wild Horse Woman*. She is a Grasshopper. Chür Høngan believes she may have divorced him. He is blamed because they have no daughter, for being away from the family too often, and for having done too little for them. She has told him that she will send for him if she wants him.

***Kulturverlaengerung*** a concept presented in the short story "The Ties That Bind." It represents the idea of the unconscious cultural mechanism of transmittal, or cultural memory. In the 20,000 years since the original spacegoers left Earth, the cultural blood of man has diverged in two directions: an aggressive creature of space and a peaceful pastoral creature of Earth. The idea of *kulturverlaengerung* suggests that prolonged contact between the two lines of man will result in the awakening of dormant recessive patterns of human behavior: that an aggressive nature will be reborn among the passive contemporary Earth natives.

**Kun, Önmu** a gunrunner and the unofficial spokesman of the Jackrabbit horde who accompanies Mayor Dion in *Saint Leibowitz and the Wild Horse Woman*. He provides Cardinal Brownpony with a list of churches sympathetic to the Nomads, and to whom Kun has sold guns, so the cardinal will have safe havens as he travels to Hannegan City. He names himself sharf of the Jackrabbits.

**Kunz, Harv** a member of the C-shift crew working on the Lunar Project in the novella "The Lineman." He is a member of the Party, which is calling for a general strike to repeal the Schneider-Volkov Act. Kunz and his friend Lark Larkin are suspicious of another worker, Bill Relke, for attending three Party cell meetings but never joining the Party. They believe he may inform on Party members. Given the opportunity, Kunz and Larkin savagely beat Relke, but they, in turn, are brutally beaten by Joe Novotny and Lije Henderson from Relke's own crew.

**Kyrie eleison** Greek: "Lord, have mercy." A

brief prayer or petition used variously in Catholic services.

**Kyrie eleison, eleison imas**   Greek: "Lord, have mercy, have mercy on us." Part of the *Kyrie eleison* invocation used in the Roman Catholic liturgy.

**La**   a character in the short story "Wolf Pack." It remains unexplained if La, or La Femme, is a figment of Mark Kessler's tortured imagination or an actual woman capable of clairvoyant images. Kessler, the pilot of a B-25 bomber, sees her in his dreams, speaks with her, and writes letters to her. He accepts her as real. She blames him for the deaths of her family and the destruction of their home in Perugia, Italy during World War II. Her cries of murderer cause Kessler to attempt to abort the second bombing mission over the town.

**La Femme** *see* **La**

**Labores simper tecum**   Latin: "Suffering be with you always." A frustrated offering from Brother Blacktooth to the gelp Barlow in *Saint Leibowitz and the Wild Horse Woman*. Barlow's father, Tempus, kidnaps Blacktooth and will not release him until he gives absolution to his son. Unable to offer absolution, Blacktooth gives three dubious but impressive sounding curses to secure his release.

**Laesae majestatis culpa**   Latin: "Guilt of high treason." Brother Blacktooth uses the term concerning his own sense of betrayal toward Pope Amen II in *Saint Leibowitz and the Wild Horse Woman*.

**Laicize**   to return to lay status. In *Saint Leibowitz and the Wild Horse Woman*, Brother Blacktooth wants to be laicized, released from his vows and allowed to leave the Order of Saint Leibowitz.

**Lake Blessdassurance**   a small lake in the center of a crater at the town of Yellow in *Saint Leibowitz and the Wild Horse Woman*. The crater was created by an explosion at an archaeological dig at an armed intercontinental missle site. The explosion killed the Venerable Boedullus. A sign at the lake reads: "Boedullus was here." "Blessed Assurance" is a well-known Christian hymn composed by Fanny Crosby and Phoebe Knapp in 1873.

**Lakovna, Maria**   an unseen character in the novella "Izzard and the Membrane." She is an actress who plays Nora, Scott MacDonney's wife, in the films the Russians use to brainwash Scott.

**Lalyahe**   high priestess of the Sacred Order of Menbana in the novella "The Reluctant Traitor." She takes Rolf Kenlan as her acolyte so he can teach her the magic she believes he possesses. She enters into an agreement to assist Rolf if he will use his power to help her gain authority over the androon tribe.

**Lamedh sadhe**   the Hebrew letters the pilgrim marks on the stone he points out to Brother Francis that leads to the discovery of the fallout shelter in *A Canticle for Leibowitz* ("Fiat Homo"). Lamedh (ל) is the twelfth letter of the Hebrew alphabet. Sadhe (צ) is the eighteenth letter of the Hebrew alphabet. Transliterated, the sounds of the two letters are ell (L) and tee-ess (TZ), the first and last letters of Leibowitz, further associating the pilgrim with the Beatus. Russell Griffin suggests that the letters translate phonemically as "learn, wise one." Other critics, such as Eric S. Rabkin and Robert Scholes, assert that the letters are Hebrew for "fool." At least one critic, Gary K. Wolfe, states that the letters comprise a once common Hebrew inscription found on tombstones meaning "remember the righteous."

**Lander**   a minor character in the novella "The Lineman." He is part of the Safety and Rescue crews that first reach the disabled ship and discover that it is actually a traveling bordello.

**Laplace, Pierre Simon**   (March 23, 1749–March 5, 1827) French theoretical physicist, astronomer, and mathematician best known for his analysis of celestial mechanics. He, James Clark Maxwell, and Albert Einstein are mentioned in *A Canticle for Leibowitz* ("Fiat Lux") as obscure natural philosophers. Brother Kornhoer lists their work as being among the Memorabilia at the abbey.

**Laredan Nation** *see* **Laredo**

**Laredo**   also known as the **Laredan Nation**. One of the primary states in existence on the former North American continent in the novella "And the Light Is Risen" and *A Canticle for Leibowitz* ("Fiat Lux"). Its king is Goraldi. Laredo is lured into a short lived and losing war with Texarkana. Laredans are referred to as Grass Eaters by the Nomads.

**Larkin, Felicity**   a scriptwriter for the *Martin Snyder Hour* in the short story "The Corpse In Your Bed Is Me." Everybody except Snyder loves Felicity, but she worships him. Nick Sheldon wants to marry her, but Snyder tells him that he will fire both of them if they marry. They postpone their marriage, and Snyder takes the opportunity to seduce Felicity. After he does so, he drops her and fires her from the show. When she marries Nick a short time later, Snyder fires him from the show as well.

**Larkin, "Lark"** from the novella "The Lineman," a member of the C-shift crew working on the transmission line as part of the Lunar Project. He is a member of the Party, which is calling for a general strike in an effort to repeal the Schneider-Volkov Act. Larkin and Harv Kunz question Relke about why he attended three Party cell meetings but never joined the Party. They are afraid he may be an informer. When they find Relke and Giselle in the sub-station vault, they take turns beating Relke into unconsciousness and having sex with Giselle. Joe Novotny and Lije Henderson brutally beat Larkin and Kunz while they sleep in retaliation for what they did to Relke and Giselle.

**Larwich, Edith** the daughter of Dr. Frank Larwich in the short story "Bitter Victory." She possesses a Ph.D. in physics. She is almost blind because of cataracts in both eyes. Klia assumes her identity so that she may help Frank Larwich advance his work to practical applications. Klia hypnotically induces amnesia in Edith and commits her to a psychopathic ward in Pennsylvania.

**Larwich, Frank** a famous mathematician in the short story "Bitter Victory." Inspired by the articles Klia writes, he begins work on the development of a mathematical physics with no basic assumptions. San Rorreck wants to help him see the practical applications of his theories for space exploration. Klia assumes the identity of Larwich's daughter, Edith, to help him focus on the "down-to-earth" aspects of his ideas.

**Larwich, Louise** the wife of mathematician Frank Larwich and mother of Edith in the short story "A Bitter Victory."

**Laskell, Miss** a minor character in the novella "Conditionally Human." She is Dr. Georges's nurse, and she disapproves of his intention to substitute another neutroid for that of Sarah Glubbes's neutroid that he has to euthanize.

**Laskell, Mitch** 1. The protagonist in the short story "Dumb Waiter." Three years after a nuclear war, Laskell wants to prevent an abandoned city's central computer network from being destroyed by a gang of marauders who now view the machine as an impediment to their survival. Laskell, who once worked with aircraft computers, views the computer as an intricate machine, a tool that cannot simply be destroyed. In his view, the problem lies not with the machines but with man's lack of a broad technical education. He believes that man allowed himself to be pampered by machines rather than learning how to properly use and control them. He is able to reprogram the central computer's city ordinances to ensure its survival and to begin the renovation of the city for human habitation.

2. The central character in the short story "Way of a Rebel." Laskell is a United States Navy Lieutenant on patrol in the Atlantic Ocean aboard a one-man submarine. The United States has declared a state of total emergency and the Secretary of Defense has been given absolute power. Laskell struggles with his conscience as he decides to quit fighting a war that he does not believe has a purpose. He sees neither side as being right in the escalating conflict, only the wrongness of the West and the bloodier wrongness of the Eurasian Soviet that will lead to nuclear annihilation. He declares his independence and decides to live as a free man struggling to survive without allegiance to any government that would destroy industrial civilization. Laskell, however, is unable to make a clean break. When he detects five enemy submarines preparing an attack on Washington, D. C., he sacrifices his own life in order to help protect the lesser of two evils and destroy those who would destroy the "right tools" of civilization.

**"The Last Canticle"** novella in *The Magazine of Fantasy and Science Fiction*, 12 (February 1957), 3–50. After the Age of Darkness came the generations of light and then the age of spaceships. Arrogance was regained and it was man's destiny to conquer the stars. A new Abbey of Saint Leibowitz built of glass and aluminum sits across a six-lane highway from the original abbey, now largely in disrepair. A tunnel runs beneath the highway connecting the two buildings. Brother Joshua tests the air from atop the new abbey and is dismayed with what he detects. He phones his abbot, Father Zerchi, to tell him that it appears Lucifer has Fallen, the code words for a thermonuclear explosion. Brother Joshua calls Dr. Lenui in Spokane to verify his readings and to possibly get a fix on the location of the explosion. After eighteen centuries of rebuilding, of slowly bringing civilization back to life, man is again on the brink of a nuclear holocaust.

Unsure of whether the fallout indicates the effects of a test shot or an impending global war, Father Zerchi sends a message to New Rome asking for the confirmation or cancellation of the Dismissal of Servants plan. He summons Brother Joshua to his office in the old abbey. Based on the information he obtained from Dr. Lenui, Brother Joshua tells him that the blast occurred somewhere in Asia. Father Zerchi decides he must explain the Dismissal of Servants to Brother Joshua. It is a plan to evacuate the Holy See and the records of the Church to the Centaurus colony in the event of a total thermonuclear war.

Brother Joshua had previously been a member of the Close Space Assault Team, and he has space shuttle and moon station experience. After the death of his wife, he joined the Benedictines and then the Albertians. He has been chosen to be part of a team of ex-spacers to accompany the Holy See. Father Zechi promises to tell Brother Joshua more about the plan later.

As the two leave the old abbey to go to the refectory, they meet Mrs. Grales, a two-headed woman, who sells tomatoes to the nuns and donates the money back to the abbey. Her second head is small and seemingly useless. It has a cherubic quality but its eyes never open. She stops Father Zerchi to ask if he will baptize Rachel, the name she uses to refer to her second head. Father Zerchi tells her he cannot; it is for Father Selo, her parish priest to decide. As they are speaking, Brother Joshua is sure that Rachel smiled at him.

Leaving Mrs. Grales, Father Zerchi and Brother Joshua go to supper, and Brother Joshua is called to the lectern to announce to the other monks that Lucifer is Fallen. Before dawn of the next morning, an announcement on the Emergency Warning Network confirms that a city in Hu Wan, a province in Asia, had been the target of a thermonuclear explosion. In a retaliatory attack, Texarkana, the capital of the Atlantic Confederacy was bombed. Both governments agree to honor a ten-day cease-fire decree to allow the foreign ministers to meet in Guam.

Father Zerchi receives confirmation from New Rome for the implementation of Dismissal of Servants. Zerchi tells Brother Joshua that he will be sent to New Rome, if he agrees. Joshua agrees, and Father Zerchi explains the plan further. Twenty-five ex-spacemen now part of the Albertian Order, six nuns, and approximately twenty children will accompany the new Holy See and his staff. Father Zerchi tells Brother Joshua he must determine within the next half hour if he has the proper calling for the priesthood. If so, he has been chosen to be the order's abbot in space, its shepherd. Brother Joshua's immediate reaction is that he cannot, he is not ready. Father Zerchi leaves him to contemplate what he has been asked to do. He wonders if it is even right to hope. Is the spaceship an act of futility or hope — not a hope for Earth, but for the soul and substance of man? He thinks that the closer man is to paradise, the more impatient he becomes with it and with himself.

Brother Joshua struggles with his decision, hoping for a sign, as he listens to the prayers of the monks in the chapel. He joins the monks and ceases to think. Rising to leave, certainty has come to him. When Father Zerchi returns, Brother Joshua simply says, "All right." Father Zerchi gathers the twenty-five monks together and explains to them that they will constitute The Visitationist Friars of the Order of Saint Leibowitz of Tycho, an independent offshoot of the Albertian Order. Their first mission is to evacuate the Holy See to a colony world. After that, the monks will form the core of a space going order. Their spaceship will be their abbey, and they will travel from colony to colony. They will preserve the history of the Earth and the teachings of the Church; they will continue the order, but they will never return to Earth. The crew leaves for New Rome. The abbey becomes a refuge for the people displaced by the nuclear attack. Dr. Cors from Green Star asks Father Zerchi if he will allow two mobile units in the abbey's courtyard to treat the most urgent cases of radiation poisoning. Part of the work of Green Star is voluntary euthanasia in its mercy camps for hopeless cases of radiation exposure. Father Zerchi asks Dr. Cors if he has ever advised hopeless cases to go to a mercy camp. The doctor admits that he has and tells Zerchi that the only evil he knows about is pain, and it is the only evil he can fight. The abbot agrees to allow the units in the abbey if Dr. Cors agrees not to recommend euthanasia to any patient on the grounds of the abbey. He may tell them only what the law requires, their rights, not his recommendation. The doctor assents.

Zerchi receives a message from New Rome that the government is investigating rumors of an unauthorized spaceship owned by the Church. It advises him to stall for three days if any agents appear at the abbey.

Green Star establishes a refugee camp and a mercy camp down the road from the abbey. Father Zerchi confronts Dr. Cors and contacts Green Star authorities; he wants the mercy camp moved out of the abbey's vicinity. He orders five signs, large enough to be read but light enough to be carried. The signs read, "Abandon Hope All Ye Who Enter Here." He orders five novices to picket the camp carrying the signs. Dr. Cors comes to find Father Zerchi to tell him that he has broken his promise. He has advised a young mother and her child to go the mercy camp to be euthanized. He tells the priest that he will have the units moved from the abbey. Father Zerchi goes to visit the woman and tells her, "Don't be an accomplice."

A government report confirms that the foreign ministers have found no resolution to the conflict and the ten-day cease-fire will soon end. Father Zerchi also hears that Pope Gregory has ceased praying for peace in the world since the ending of the conference in Guam. He has celebrated two masses: Mass Against the Heathen and Mass in Time of War. The pope is now praying for justice and peace in the hearts of men. Buzzards begin to fly above the mercy camp.

Father Zerchi goes for a walk and meets Mrs. Grales bringing tomatoes to the emergency kitchen. He believes that Rachel smiles at him, as Brother Joshua had earlier thought. Mrs. Grales asks Zerchi to hear her confession, and he tells her to meet him in the chapel in half an hour. Zerchi orders a car but as he leaves the gate, he sees the mother and child he had spoken to before. Zerchi stops to offer them a ride. The mother is reluctant to accept. The priest intuits that she is going to the mercy camp. At his urging, she accepts a ride to town but when they reach it, she tells him to go back. He asks her not to do what she plans and asks her if she has lost faith. The woman simply nods. As Father Zerchi continues to speak to her, the woman cries for him to shut up and leave her alone. She struggles to get out of the car with her child as they near the mercy camp again. Guards from the camp come to the car and intervene. Dr. Cors comes over to see what the matter is, and Father Zerchi punches him in the face. Another man approaches and serves the priest with a government injunction against the picketing. The woman and child are allowed to enter the mercy camp.

Father Zerchi returns to the abbey to hear Mrs. Grales' confession. She says that she has never really forgiven God for His justice toward her. As the priest listens to her confession, he hears the sound of missiles being fired. A light grows brighter and brighter and the confessional curtain begins to smoke. Father Zerchi offers Mrs. Grales an act of contrition and penance and then tells her to wait until the light dies. He hears "a strange soft voice" not that of Mrs. Grales echoing his words on the other side of the screen. He calls to her and tells her to run. Father Zerchi makes his way to the altar to remove the Christ filled ciborium from the tabernacle. As he tries to run the building collapses on him. He awakes to find himself pinned to the ground at the waist. His one free hand still holds the ciborium although several of the Hosts have fallen out. He calls out for help but hears nothing but the soft voice he had heard in the confessional. He calls out again but no answer comes. He waits and prays. He thinks of his conversation with Dr. Cors and thinks that the trouble with the world is not pain. Ultimately, the trouble is "*me*. Me us Adam Man me...." He hears the soft voice again, now a childish singsong.

Zerchi falls asleep and when he awakes, three buzzards are watching him. He hears something rattling stones, and Mrs. Grales is standing before him. The head of Mrs. Grales sleeps soundly, but Rachel is smiling innocently, and she watches him with "cool green eyes." She keeps repeating his words. He realizes that she has just woken up. He recognizes a great ease, warmth, and peace about her eyes. He sees something familiar, half remembered. Impulsively he breathes, "Magnificat Dominum anima mea," "My soul doth magnify the Lord and my...." He hears Rachel repeat it. Zerchi tells her to save herself, to take what she can and "wash the curse of us off. Live, *live!*" She stares at him, smiles, touches his forehead and says, "Live." She stands and leaves. He asks himself what he saw in her eyes. Zerchi realizes that it was Immaculate Innocence, and then he dies.

In an undisclosed location, as the horizon comes alive in a flash of light, the last of the monks boards the Church's spaceship. He removes his sandals, knocks off the dirt, and murmurs, "Sic transit." And the ash falls across the Earth.

A revised and expanded version of this novella is the basis for "Fiat Voluntas Tua," the last section of the novel *A Canticle for Leibowitz*.

***The Last Western*** the only novel by Thomas S. Klise, it was published in 1974 by Argus Communications. It is the satiric and allegorical story of Willie, a young boy who rises from his oppressive origins to become a baseball phenomenon but who leaves the corruption of the game to enter a seminary. He becomes a religious leader and peacemaker, and eventually is elected pope. As pope, he must face the institutional conflict between his irregular supporters and the more entrenched officers of the Church.

Miller reviewed the book for *Commonweal*. See also ***The Last Western* by Thomas S. Klise**

***The Last Western* by Thomas S. Klise** a review of the novel by Miller appeared in *Commonweal* 100 (June 14, 1974): 338–339. Miller extravagantly praises the work as "more than a novel." He believes it to be a revolution, and that it may very well be the best American novel since *Moby-Dick*. No novel since Melville's work has attempted or accomplished as much. Miller proclaims the book as a turning point in American literature, if not its "final climax."

**Lauds** meaning praises, it is derived from the Latin *laudate*, "praise ye." An office of solemn praise to God following Matins, but it is often said with Matins and the two form the first of the canonical hours. The term is used in *A Canticle for Leibowitz* as well as the three source stories, and *Saint Leibowitz and the Wild Horse Woman*.

**Latzar shemi** Hebrew: "My name is Lazarus." The response of the smiling old man sitting at the abbey's beggar's table when Dom Zerchi asks him who he is in "Fiat Voluntas Tua" in *A Canticle for Leibowitz*. His description parallels that of Benjamin or the old pilgrim in the previous sections of the novel: he has a brushy beard, a basket hat, and is dressed in burlap.

**Lavrenti** one of the members of Hogey Parker's former crew or gang in space in the short story "The Hoofer."

**Lazar** the name the children call the old beggar clad in burlap in the "Fiat Voluntas Tua" section of *A Canticle for Leibowitz*. He later appears at the beggar's table in the abbey and tells Dom Zerchi to call him Lazarus. He is the continuation of the character Benjamin or the pilgrim who appears in the previous two sections of the novel. See also **Benjamin** and **Lazarus**

**Lazarus** Jesus raises Lazarus, the brother of Martha and Mary, from the dead in John 11:43 (KJV): "he cried with a loud voice, Lazarus, come forth." In Luke 16:20 Lazarus is a beggar.

1. In the novella "The Last Canticle," Father Zerchi sees an old man at the "'beggars' table.'" He has a brushy beard stained yellow at the chin, and wears a burlap bag for a jacket and a basket hat. Zerchi asks him his name, and he chuckles and says, "Call me Lazarus."

2. In *A Canticle for Leibowitz* ("Fiat Lux"), Benjamin tells Dom Paulo that he has known he could not carry the burden of his people "ever since He called me forth again," linking himself to Lazarus.

3. In "Fiat Voluntas Tua," a group of children shouts at the old beggar: "It's old Lazar! ... same one 'ut the Lor' Hesus raise up!" When the beggar is later asked who he is, he says, "Latzar shemi ... call me Lazarus, then." See also **Latzar shemi**, **Lazar**

**Leaha** the name of Father Zerchi's boyhood cat, which he killed, in the novella "The Last Canticle." In *A Canticle for Leibowitz* ("Fiat Voluntas Tua"), the cat's name is Zeke.

**Lectio devina** *see* **Lectio divina**

**Lectio divina** Latin: "Divine reading." A period set aside for attentive, contemplative spiritual reading. In *A Canticle for Leibowitz* ("Fiat Lux"), a reference is made to the abbey library usually being empty until late afternoon and the time for *lectio devina*. Miller uses this alternative or erroneous spelling.

**Lege!** Latin: "Read!" Dom Paulo commands Father Gault to read from the fragment that Thon Taddeo found from which he conjectures that contemporary mankind is descended from a servant species that rebelled against its creators during the Simplification. It is a fragment from Karel Capek's play *R.U.R.* From *A Canticle for Leibowitz* ("Fiat Lux"). See also **R. U. R.**

**Leibowitz, Isaac Edward** an unseen character from the short story "A Canticle for Leibowitz," the novella "And the Light Is Risen," and *A Canticle for Leibowitz*. His legacy permeates all three of the shorter works as well as both novels. Little actual information is known about Leibowitz. According to tradition, he was a rather tall but slightly stooped man. He was presumed to be a scientist at the time of the Deluge of Flame. In the novel, a "turncoat technician" identifies Leibowitz as a weapons specialist. During the Age of Simplification, after fruitlessly searching for his wife, he fled to the Cistercians, eventually professed their vows and became a priest. In time, he founded the monastic order of the Albertians, named for St. Albert the Great, teacher of Thomas Aquinas and patron saint of scientists. The mission of the order was to preserve and memorize whatever books and papers were still available to them. By the time of "Fiat Voluntas Tua" Leibowitz is the patron saint of electricians.

The simpletons identified him as a former scientist, and he was martyred by hanging. According to legend, a burlap bag was used as a hood to cover his head. His martyrdom is expanded upon in "And the Light Is Risen" (and the first novel). He was hanged but not so his neck would break, and simultaneously burned. A pile of books was used for kindling. The simpletons soaked him with gasoline. He asked them for a cup of it. After blessing and consecrating it, he drank it.

Leibowitz was married at some time prior to entering the Order of Cistercians. His wife's name is believed to have been Emily, although Leibowitz may have called her Em or Emma.

His name is associated with humor. Leibowitz means "lover of jest." Brother Fingo's wooden carving of Leibowitz has an enigmatic smile. The idea of humor is reinforced by the name Isaac, which is from the Hebrew for "he will laugh." In Genesis 21 (KJV), Isaac is the son of promise, having been born to Abraham and Sarah in their old age. Isaac is also associated with sacrifice. God ordered Abraham to take his only son to Moriah and "offer him there" (Genesis 22). Abraham is willing to kill Isaac in sacrifice until God commands him not to.

The name Edward is derived from Old English meaning "happy (or blessed) guardian." Leibowitz proposes the new order whose mission is to guard the written record of men's knowledge. Mark Mc-Vann also makes an association between Edward and Edward Powell, an English Reformation theologian who was hanged and burned by Henry VIII for treason.

**Lent** a forty-day period of penitence and fasting observed by the Roman Catholic Church, as well as other denominations, that begins on Ash Wednesday and ends with Easter.

**Lenui, Doctor** in the novella "The Last Canticle," Brother Joshua calls this unseen character in Spokane to verify the readings he made that Lucifer is Fallen. Their data allows them to estimate the location of the nuclear explosion.

**Leo XXI** the pope at the time of Leibowitz's canonization in the short story "A Canticle for Leibowitz" and *A Canticle for Leibowitz* ("Fiat Homo"). He proclaims Isaac Edward Leibowitz a saint.

In the short story, he stops to speak briefly with Brother Francis and to receive the gift of his illuminated copy of the Leibowitz blueprint. He offers Brother Francis a simple reason for what the monks do: to preserve little bits of learning and guard them until they are ready to rise again.

In the novel, he is described as a small, frail, elderly man who possesses a kindly meekness. When Brother Francis apologizes for the loss of his illuminated copy, the pope tells him that his presence in New Rome is gift enough. Leo acknowledges the work of the monks at the Leibowitz abbey in preserving what is left of the written record and preventing the world's total amnesia. He says they are the memory of the Church.

Brother Francis presents the pope with the original Leibowitz blueprint in the novel, and when he laments wasting fifteen years of his life on the stolen illuminated copy, Leo kindly tells him that his work was not wasted. It is because of the copy that the original was preserved, and when its meaning is finally discerned, the world will have Brother Francis to thank for it.

Leo sends his apostolic benediction to the members of Brother Francis's order, and gives him a letter of safe passage back to the abbey, a thoughtful but empty gesture. Through Monsignor Aquerra he also presents Brother Francis with a gift: two heklos of gold in order for him to buy back his illuminated copy from the robber.

The name Leo means lion. Through the twentieth century there were thirteen popes named Leo.

**Les enfants perdus** French: "The lost children." A reference to the children who died on the moon in the novella "The Lineman."

**Les Folies Lunaries, Incorporated** French: "The Lunar Follies." The official name of the traveling bordello in the novella "The Lineman." Madame d'Annecy proposes that each man who frequents the bordello receive one share of common stock in the company.

**Lèse majesté** French: [crime of] injured majesty; high treason. In *A Canticle for Leibowitz* ("Fiat Voluntas Tua"), the Abominable Autoscribe is said to have committed electrical *lèse majesté* upon Dom Zerchi.

**"Let My People Go"** short story originally published in *If, Worlds of Science Fiction*, 1 (July 1952), 5–58. After 13 years of traveling, 120 colonists from Earth arrive on the moon of Epsilon Eridani Two aboard a space ark commanded by Wolek Parn. Their hopes of colonizing the planet are confounded by their discovery that the planet is already inhabited. A reconnaissance mission on the moon's surface reveals a tunnel entrance with an air-lock. It is an abandoned underground space way-station. Within the station a star map is discovered indicating the places that Eridanian ships have been, including Earth. The connection between the two planets is confirmed when a piece of a human tibia is uncovered.

While the crew officers debate the possible relationship between Earth and the Eridanian race, a rocket from the planet approaches and welcomes them. In response to questions as to why the moon station is unused, the Eridanians reveal that they abandoned space exploration years ago to concentrate on establishing "the biological integration of all life forms" on the planet, a biological cooperation fostering symbiosis rather than conflict.

The colonists are invited to the planet and three, Morgun Sahl, Faron Qun, and Alaia Dazille, go to investigate. While attempting to inspect the controls of the ship taking them to the planet, Dazille is shot at by a "small-man-like creature" at an instrument panel. She, in turn, shoots and kills him. The three colonists discover that this creature, a Piszjil, had telecontrol over the other creatures on board, referred to as saffrons. The Piszjils use the saffrons as slaves and hosts for their food sources. They hope to incorporate the Earth colonists into the carefully tailored biological system that serves them. They want to place members of the Earth colony among the existing villages on the planet to develop a hybrid species with the descendents of the primitive Earthlings they brought to the planet centuries before. They hope to develop a sub-species that combines the saffrons' docility with the Earth colonists' higher intelligence and initiative.

When Dazille crash lands the alien ship on the planet, Qun's leg is broken. Dazille and Sahl abandon him, and set off into the countryside. They discover a nursery or "stockyard" of young human children being raised to serve the Piszjil. Despite the Piszjils' insistence that the colonists are welcome and free to live on the planet, Sahl realizes that they are essentially prisoners who will be destroyed unless they agree to be assimilated into the cooperative world that is organized for the Piszjils' benefit.

Sahl and Dazille are eventually captured. The Piszjils condition them and Qun and alter their memories. Sahl is conditioned against violent acts toward the Piszjil and to lure Parn and the other colonists to the planet. When Sahl returns to the space ark, Parn is suspicious of his actions and orders the ship's doctor to drug him in order to examine him.

Despite his ordeal, Sahl is able to communicate to Parn that he should release all the Earth species they brought with them onto the planet. The introduction of these foreign species will disrupt the biological cooperative and throw the world into turmoil. Turmoil is always to man's advantage. The Piszjils will have to let the colonists live as they want in order for them to control the alien pests, and as Parn states, the worst pests of all are human.

**Letha** one of the Pedaga clan of teachers in the short story "The Ties That Bind." She is a native translator for Baltun Meikl and grows to love the spacegoer. She originally argues for the ships of the Imperial Forces to leave Earth. She is killed for running away when Baron ven Klaeden announces his harsh measures to end desertion among his men and the work stoppage among the natives.

**Levate** Latin: "Rise." The direction given to the monks as they genuflect when the abbot and guests enter the banquet hall in the novella "And the Light Is Risen" and *A Canticle for Leibowitz* ("Fiat Lux").

***Libellus Leibowitz*** Latin: *The Little Book of Leibowitz*. Also known simply as the *Little Book*, the *Libellus Leibowitz* is a centuries-old volume attributed to Isaac Leibowitz in *A Canticle for Leibowitz*. Prior Cheroki gives a copy to Brother Francis during his Lenten fast to help guide his meditations in "Fiat Homo."

***Liber Originum*** Latin: *The Book of Origins*. A seven volume work by the Venerable Boedullus being translated from Neo-Latin to the Grasshopper dialect of Plains Nomadic by Brother Blacktooth at the Abbey of Saint Leibowitz in *Saint Leibowitz and the Wild Horse Woman*. The work is Boedullus' scholarly but "highly speculative attempt" using the evidence of later events to reconstruct a plausible history of the twenty-first century, "the darkest of all centuries." The work is a popular one of Abbot Cardinal Jarad, who assigned Blacktooth the task. Deacon Brownpony, after reading the translation of the first volume, is anxious for the work to be complete.

**Libera me, Domine, ab vitiis meis, ut solius tuae voluntatis mihi cupidus sim, et vocationis tuae conscious si digneris me vocare** Latin: "Set me free, Lord, from my own vices, so that in my own heart I may be desirous of only Thy will, and be aware of Thy summons if it come." Lines recited by Brother Francis from the *Libellus Leibowitz* when he encounters the pilgrim during his Lenten fast in *A Canticle for Leibowitz* ("Fiat Homo"). Miller may possibly be modeling the words on those of Saint Augustine.

**The Liberty Clan** a rebel group hoping to assassinate Secon Samesh and overthrow the totalitarian government in the short story "I, Dreamer." Janna is a member of the group.

**Liberty Drive Society** a corporate society on Todmacht V briefly mentioned in the short story "Gravesong."

**Librada** Spanish: "Set free." The name given to a gelp cougar kitten adopted by Brother Blacktooth in *Saint Leibowitz and the Wild Horse Woman*. It has one blue ear and a half-bald skull. He carries it with him until it runs away during one of Blacktooth's periods of dementia when he accompanies Pope Amen II on his crusade against New Rome. However, when Sister Clare discovers the dead body of Brother Blacktooth at the book's end, Librada's head is resting in his lap. The cougar is coaxed away from its dead master by offering it a mouse.

**Licet adire** Latin: "It is all right to enter." An official pass that allows a person or group to move through the basilica in New Rome, as is the case with the small group of which Brother Francis is a part in *A Canticle for Leibowitz* ("Fiat Homo"). The party is going to an audience with Pope Leo XXI.

**Like Hell You Will** the motto inscribed on Pope Amen II's papal coat of arms. It is in ancient

English rather than Latin. It is a response to Hultor Bråm's motto, "I set fires," appearing beneath his heraldry in *Saint Leibowitz and the Wild Horse Woman*.

**"The Lineman"** a novella first appearing in *The Magazine of Fantasy and Science Fiction*, 13 (August 1957), 5–54. It is the last original short fiction Miller published. It is collected in *The Best of Walter M. Miller, Jr.* and *The Darfsteller and Other Stories*.

Bill Relke is a lineman working as part of Joe Novotny's crew on the Copernicus Trolley Project on the moon. They are stringing a transmission line to help expand the international Lunar Project.

There is unrest among some of the workers because of the Schneider-Volkov Act (the SV Act) which states that all personnel on any member nation's lunar project must be of a single sex. The act essentially bars women from the lunar workforce. Members of the Party are calling for a general strike on the Lunar Project to force the repeal of the SV Act. Relke, who favors the act's repeal, attended three Party cell meetings out of curiosity. Two Party members, Larkin and Kunz, are now harassing him about why he has not joined. They believe he may be an informer. Relke thinks they will try to incriminate him in some way as insurance against his informing on Party members.

Joe Novotny wants to be sure that Relke is not involved in any Party activities. He is a fair supervisor but a tough disciplinarian. As long as Relke does his job and is honest with him, Joe will protect Relke and all the men on his crew. Joe is also sympathetic toward Relke who has recently learned that his wife, Fran, who remains on Earth, has divorced him and remarried. Relke cannot stop thinking about her.

An unidentified ship lands not too far from the work base. Suds Brodanovitch, the Project Engineer, learns that the ship has reactor problems. However, he sees a larger problem when he learns that it contains a troupe of entertainers, mostly women. Brodanovitch cannot contact Crater City to alert them of the problem, so he sends Joe's crew to check the communication lines. Joe chooses Relke, Braxton, and Henderson to accompany him and look for the break in the line. They are all anxious, instead, to go the disabled ship.

While they inspect the transmission line, they all keep their eyes on the ship. They notice a number of rescue vehicles surrounding the ship but none of their crew. Joe tells the men that if they pay attention and do their jobs, he will stop at the ship on the way back to the base.

Unable to discover the line break, the men are told that a crew from the Copernicus base will be sent to fix the outrage. Joe drives his men to the disabled ship and lets them draw straws to see who will board it. Henderson wins.

When Henderson enters the ship, he discovers that it is not a stage show troupe ship but rather a traveling space bordello. That is why the rescue crews have not been seen. A satisfied Henderson eventually returns to the other men with the news, and Joe allows Relke and Braxton to board the ship.

As Joe approaches the ship himself Brodanovitch pulls up and asks what is happening and where all the men are. He tells Joe that there has been an accident and a demolition man has died. There was only one Safety and Rescue man to respond. Brodanovitch thinks the absent rescue crews should be charged with negligent homicide.

Joe explains to him the truth about the ship, and Brodanovitch decides to go to Crater City immediately to tell Parkeson, the Project boss. He wants the ship off-limits. Joe asks what authority Parkeson has over the ship or the women. He suggests that the men be allowed to visit the ship when they are off-shift. Joe goes back to the workers' quarters to get the rest of his crew and take them back to the ship.

Brodanovitch boards the ship and argues with Madame d'Annecy, the brothel's proprietress. She asks what laws are being broken, and negotiates with the engineer to allow his men to visit. She says each man will receive one share of common stock in the company, Les Folies Lunaries, Incorporated. Brodanovitch is overwhelmed by d'Annecy's argument and manner. Given a bottle of champagne as a gift, he goes to leave the ship but unthinkingly enters the airlock and the bottle explodes, killing him.

In the meantime, Relke has asked one of the women, Giselle, to go for a walk with him. He wants to see what it feels like to be alone with a woman again. They drive to a vault, a subterranean building to be used as living quarters for a sub-station man when the transmission line is completed. Giselle reminds him of Fran, and although he thinks she is too young for him to make love to, he eventually does.

Awakened from their post-coital sleep, Relke and Giselle discover Larkin and Lunz have brought the body of Brodanovitch to the vault. Relke tries to protect Giselle and gets a knife to confront the two men, but Larkin and Lunz take turns beating him and having sex with Giselle.

Regaining consciousness from his beatings, Relke overhears a cell meeting taking place in the vault. The Party is afraid if the women make it to Crater City they will distract the men from the political situation and the possibility of a strike. They decide to cripple the ship so it will be stuck where it is until the Party can take over.

When Relke awakens again, he finds the vault empty except for Joe now sitting at the foot of his bed. He tries to tell Joe what he remembers from the meeting. Joe says they need to get back to the base and back to work. They discover that Larkin and Lunz have cut Relke's pressure suit as a warning. Joe tells Relke that he will handle it.

Relke ponders what he has heard and experienced. He thinks Parkeson should allow the men to visit the bordello and that he needs to warn Madame d'Annecy about the Party possibly disabling the ship. He thinks about Fran.

As Relke and the crew are back at work, Parkeson makes an address to all the men. He stresses the importance of finishing the job for the greater good of all. They are part of a fragile ecology on the moon, and they must all work together. Relke listens and thinks of Earth and those who stay behind, including Fran and the man who has taken his place in her life.

Relke sees the women's ship being readied for take-off. He begins running toward it, not certain as to why. He yells for Giselle and then offers $10,000.00 if they will take him to Earth. The ship, however, is not going to Earth, only to Crater City.

Henderson tells Relke that he and Joe will take care of Larkin and Lunz for what they did to him and Giselle. Joe is angry with him and says he warned him to stay out of politics. When Relke goes to the supply wagon later, he hears that Larkin and Lunz have been brutally attacked in their sleep and badly beaten. They are victims of the gang ethics that maintain order on the lunar project.

Henderson is killed in an accident on the line. After a small service among the crew, Joe sends them back to work. Relke looks into space and decides there is a God. His universe, however, is a deadly contraption, but man is too. There is not anything the universe could do that man could not endure. Relke thinks it is a fair balance between random mercilessness and human endurance.

He thinks about Giselle but still sees Fran. He no longer hates her; he hopes that she will eventually come to the moon. If women have no business in space, then neither does man, nor humanity. It takes the twosome to be recognized as human.

Joe yells at Relke to stop dreaming and build the line. The line — the line is part of a living thing that has to grow.

**Lingua Prima** Latin: "First tongue (language)." The phrase appears in the novella "The Last Canticle."

**Lingua ultima** Latin: "Final tongue (language)." Barry Wilkes names the new sun he discovers in the novella "The Song for Vorhu," adding it to his *lingua ultima*.

**Linkono, Abrahà** a former schoolteacher who runs the schools in New Jerusalem, named a cardinal by Pope Amen in *Saint Leibowitz and the Wild Horse Woman*. A short man with a white beard, he resembles a gnome. He is the only known spook in the College of Cardinals. He is named Ædrea's (Sister Clare's) inquisitor and prosecutor by Pope Amen II in the charges brought against her in New Jerusalem. His name and description parody those of Abraham Lincoln.

**Linura** a genny woman with one large blue eye and one small red one, and the sister of Shard in *Saint Leibowitz and the Wild Horse Woman*. She and Ædrea try to rob Cardinal Brownpony's party.

**Linus VI** a pope in *Saint Leibowitz and the Wild Horse Woman*, he is described as the "shrewdest if not the saintliest of recent popes." He is most responsible for healing the schism in the Church after Hannegan's conquests, the removal of the Holy See to Valana, and the subsequent installation of a second pope in New Rome. He elevates Elia Brownpony to a Cardinal and orders him to import and sell advanced west coast weapons. He dies from heart failure.

**Lion lies down with the lamb** when a party of Nomads accompanies Thon Taddeo to the abbey in *A Canticle for Leibowitz* ("Fiat Lux"), Dom Paulo comments that it is neighborly of the lion to lie down with the lamb. This is a reference to the popularly misquoted Isaiah 11:6 (KJV): "The wolf also shall dwell with the lamb, and the leopard shall lie down with the kid; and the calf and the young lion and the fatling together; and a little child shall lead them." Through God's grace and love, old adversaries will become gentle and loving toward each other.

**Lisitsa, Marya Dmitriyevna** a young Russian mother whose young baby son is killed by a bomb fragment during an American bombardment in the short story "Vengeance for Nikolai." After she fails in an attempt to kill herself, Colonel Grigoryecvich recruits her for a suicide mission to kill a brilliant American strategist, General Rufus MacAmsward. She receives a series of lethal injections that create a deadly toxin that can be passed through the milk of her breasts. Placed behind the American lines, she is able to seduce MacAmsward and cause his death. Marya is shot and killed by the general's guards. Lisitsa means fox in transliterated Russian.

**Litany of Divine Praises**  a series of acclamations or praises often cited at the conclusion of the benediction. The priest recites each praise, and it is repeated by the congregation. The Divine Praises may also be used as a prayer outside of the benediction. When two monks on the hyper colony of Galveston smell Paul, a non-hyper, in the novella "Dark Benediction," they hurry away muttering the Litany of Divine Praises to themselves.

**Litany of the Saints**  a sacred prayer of the Catholic Church comprised of a series of invocations to the Trinity, the Virgin Mary, and all the saints and martyrs of the Church.

Miller uses various parts of it throughout *A Canticle for Leibowitz*, most notably in the canonization ceremony for Isaac Leibowitz in "Fiat Homo."

**Litkin**  a minor character in the novella "Izzard and the Membrane." He is a keyboard operator who is locked in the computer vault by Scott MacDonney. He passes through the membrane.

**"The Little Creeps"**  short story appearing in *Amazing Stories*, 25 (December 1951), 56–84. Reprinted in *Fantastic Stories*, 17 (May 1968), 10–40, 138. During a regional Asian war, General Clement Horrey, a member of the senior staff stationed in Japan, sees tiny pale green phosphorescent rods creating concentric contour lines on the wall of his bedroom. He believes he is going mad until the luminous rods utilize his radio to communicate with him. They call themselves 2537 Angstroms and speak from a world that lies parallel with Earth's tomorrow. They demand that tomorrow stop being destroyed by today's war. They caution Horrey regarding three key decisions he will make that will have an impact on saving the future. He is told to not fire Yoshigura, his housekeeper; to not listen to General Yaney; and to not approve the bombing of towns along the Amur River. Disoriented by the appearance of the 2537 Angstroms, worried about his wife, Nora, and unaware of the machinations of General Yaney to escalate the war, Horrey disregards all the demands. Doing so leads to a global, nuclear war and destroys the parallel world.

**Little Dutch Boy**  in her book *Hans Brinker, or the Silver Skates* (1865), Mary Mapes Dodge, an American author, tells the story of "The Hero of Haarlem," a little Dutch boy who uses his finger to stop a small leak in a dike until it can be properly repaired thereby saving the town from flooding. The story has become associated with quick-minded small acts trying to prevent greater catastrophes.

In *A Canticle for Leibowitz* ("Fiat Voluntas Tua"), the memo announcing Lucifer Is Fallen is kept behind "a dike of official secrecy." Bureaucratic Dutch boys are plugging several holes in that dike.

**Little Office of Our Lady**  a briefer form of prayer based on the structure of the Divine Office. Some religious orders use it as a daily devotional practice. In the "Fiat Voluntas Tua" section of *A Canticle for Leibowitz,* the prior announces to the abbey that they will sing the Little Office of Our Lady before Matins for three days, asking her to intercede for peace.

**Lockheed Lightning**  the P-38, a radically designed twin-boom, twin-engine, heavily armed American fighter plane produced by the Lockheed Corporation and used during World War II. It is referred to in the short story "Wolf Pack" as among the planes accompanying the bombers on their mission over Perugia.

**Long, Jim**  a character in the short story "No Moon for Me." He is a major and the command pilot of the first manned lunar rocket. The mission of the three man crew is to investigate the source of a mysterious transmission emanating from the moon and to negotiate, if possible, to remove any alien invaders that are presumed to be the source. Major Long is distrustful of the calm demeanor of Colonel Denin, a long time advocate of manned space exploration. As they near their destination, Denin draws a gun and reveals to Long that he is the source of the lunar transmission, that he sent a transmitter in an unmanned rocket to the moon in order to help force man into space. Denin's plan is to blow up their rocket on the moon in order to make them martyrs to the cause of manned space exploration. Long maneuvers the ship into a series of violent twists to disrupt Denin and secure his gun. He lands on the moon with the intent of turning off the transmitter but discovers that Denin never really needed to create a pretense for space exploration—alien tracks surround the rocket, which has landed not too far from an abandoned mine shaft.

**Longly**  a soldier among the Marsville guards massing outside the androon cave in the novella "The Reluctant Traitor."

**Lord Bel**  another name for Bel in the short story "Please Me Plus Three." See also **Bel**

**Lord Kepol**  the commander of the Martian forces in the short story "The Soul-Empty Ones."

A small, wizened creature, he possesses the utmost confidence in Martian superiority. He enjoys the torturing of Falon and Ea-Daner. He orders Falon fattened so he will make better eating. Kepol is killed when his throne ship is rammed by a captured Martian ship piloted by an escaped former slave.

**Lord of the Hordes** *see* **Lord of the Three Hordes.**

**Lord of the Three Hordes (or Lord of the Hordes)** the office of military leader and priestly (or magical) leader of the three Nomadic hordes, the Qæsach dri Vørdar, in *Saint Leibowitz and the Wild Horse Woman*. The position was last held by Høngan Ös seventy years prior to the time of the novel. His defeat at the hands of Hannegan and the subsequent total subduing of the Jackrabbit horde made the election of a new lord impossible. The office cannot be filled without the participation of the electors from all three hordes. Chür Høngan is named Lord of the Three Hordes in the novel.

**Lord Ragelle** the Defense Minister of the Atlantic Confederacy who conducts a tense news conference concerning the nuclear detonation in Asia in *A Canticle for Leibowitz* ("Fiat Voluntas Tua").

**Loretta** a control tower operator at the Jacksonville airport in the novella "The Yokel." She is one of a group of friends Zella Richmond and Sam Wuncie meet while attempting to steal a plane. In order to extricate himself from the group, Sam suggests to Loretta that they go dancing. Hoping to outrage her enough that she will leave him and he can sneak into the airport, Sam presses her into a doorway and roughly kisses her. Instead of protesting, Loretta kisses him back and suggests they carry on further. Sam uses her to gain access to the airport, and they consummate their night on the C-54 he plans to steal. Sam dopes Loretta with morphine to keep her quiet while he steals the plane.

**"Lot"** a 1953 short story by Ward Moore included in *Beyond Armageddon*. It and its sequel "Lot's Daughter" are Moore's best known works. Miller states that Martin H. Greenberg's mention of this story was the reason for his prompt agreement to co-edit *Beyond Armageddon*.

**Lot's wife** Lot lived in Sodom and was warned by angels to leave the city with his wife and daughters because God intended to destroy the city because of its iniquity. They were warned "look not behind thee." Lot's wife disobeyed the warning and turned to see the destruction of Sodom. As she did she was turned into a pillar of salt. In the novella "The Song of Vorhu," Barry Wilkes turns "slowly, as Lot's wife" to look at the White Idiot when she stops screaming. See Genesis 19 (KJV) for the story of Lot.

**Lourdes** a town in southern France where the Virgin Mary supposedly appeared repeatedly to a peasant girl, Bernadette Soubirous, in 1858. Consequently, it became among the most popular pilgrim shrines, famous as a religious sanctuary but also as the site of miraculous medical cures. It is mentioned in *Saint Leibowitz and the Wild Horse Woman* as one of the places of the manifestation of Mary.

**Lovewell** one of the two men believed responsible for the killing of Jessel in the novella "Cold Awakening." He is the one who knocks off the light before the shooting.

**Loyte, Esitt** a former captain of the Texark cavalry and an expert in cavalry tactics. He is married to Potear Wetok, the granddaughter of Wetok Enar, in *Saint Leibowitz and the Wild Horse Woman*. Cardinal Brownpony hopes that he will provide useful information concerning Filpeo Harq's forces. He is caught spying for Texark at the military conference called by Brownpony in Valana. Brownpony forbids Høngan Chür to kill him. So, before placing him in jail, Chür mutilates him and presents a bag of his body parts to the cardinal. Loyte escapes from jail with the help of several accomplices and returns to Texark. He gains the nickname Wooden Nose from his troops because of the prosthesis he uses in place of his lost nose. As a colonel in the Texark cavalry, he leads the attack on the Wilddog lodges as the Nomads' and Pope Amen II's offensive against Texark fails.

**Lucem appellavit diem** *see* **In principio Deus**

**Lucem esse bonam Deus vidit** *see* **In principio Deus**

**Lucey** a poor single mother living in the rural United States in the short story "The Triflin' Man" (later entitled "You Triflin' Skunk"). She had a one-night affair with a stranger that resulted in the birth of her son, Doodie. The stranger is actually an alien who has fathered genetic analogs on Earth to use as a means of gathering information prior to an invasion of the planet. When he returns to claim Doodie, Lucey acts to protect the son she loves from the father who deserted him.

**Lucifer**  Latin: "Light bearer." Although Lucifer is popularly equated with Satan, the angel whose pride led him to rebel against God and be cast out of heaven, it also refers to the king of Babylon who attempted to raise himself to divine sovereignty and exalt his "throne over the stars of God." He beats on the gates of heaven but is cast out by God. "How art thou fallen from heaven, O Lucifer, son of the morning! how art thou cut down to the ground, which didst weaken the nations!" Isaiah 14:12 (KJV). This description of one's pride and fall is applied in a larger spiritual sense to Satan. Satan is further associated with Lucifer through Luke 10:18, "I beheld Satan as lightning fall from heaven." The term is used variously in the novella "The Last Canticle" and *A Canticle for Leibowitz* in both its popular association with Satan as well as in reference to the fallen king of Babylon (Nebuchadnezzar II at that time).

**"Lucifer"**  short story by Roger Zelazny originally published in 1964 and included in *Beyond Armageddon*.

**Lucifer is Fallen**  the Church's codename in the novella "The Last Canticle" and *A Canticle for Leibowitz* ("Fiat Voluntas Tua") for the detonation of thermonuclear devices.

See also **Lucifer**

**Luciferum ruisse mihi dicis?**  Latin: "Are you telling me Lucifer has fallen?" Dom Zerchi's reaction when Brother Joshua confirms an increase in the radiation count indicating fallout from a nuclear explosion in *A Canticle for Leibowitz* ("Fiat Voluntas Tua").

**Luftwaffe**  German: "air force." The literal term was used as the official name of the air force of Nazi Germany from 1935 to 1946. A reference is made to the need to guard against its "steel-beaked falcons" in the short story "Wolf Pack"

**Luling**  a colonel and headquarters staff officer in the novella "The Reluctant Traitor." He is at the meeting between Rolf Kenlan and Commissioners Rathwich and Poele. Luling suggests that Rathwich allow Rolf and his people their freedom beyond the mountains if they promise to remain there. He disregards Rathwich's indirect orders to see to the deaths of Rolf and his followers. Instead, Luling joins them in their exile from Marsville having caught "frontier fever."

**Lumen Christi**  Latin: "Light of Christ." In the novella "And the Light Is Risen," after replacing the arc light with the crucifix on the day Don Thaddeo is leaving the abbey, Father Jerome says all who henceforth read will do so by *Lumen Christi* rather than electric light.

**Lupus**  Latin: "the wolf." A constellation between Centaurus and Scorpius that is visited by man in the short story "The Big Hunger."

**Mabel**  a minor character in the novella "Conditionally Human." She is an employee at Anthropos Incorporated who helps Terry Norris compile a list of K-99s to be recalled.

**MacAmsward, Rufus**  a brilliant general of the Americanist party forces in the short story "Vengeance for Nikolai." In the view of Russian colonel Grigoryevich, MacAmsward is an unconventional military strategist and an unpredictable, evil genius who must be removed if Russia is to have a chance to survive the war between the two countries. Grigoryevich devises a plan based on MacAmsward's reputation as an orally fixated "vile old lecher." The general succumbs to the beauty and seduction of Marya Lisitsa who allows herself to be fatally poisoned so she can pass a lethal toxin on to MacAmsward through her lactation.

**MacDonney, Nora**  the wife of Scott MacDonney, an American physicist and cyberneticist, in the novella "Izzard and the Membrane." Described as having a dreamer's eye and a willowy body, Nora is depicted as having betrayed Scott by having an affair with a United States government official. The Russians use the films of Nora's supposed affair to brainwash Scott. In reality, she remains faithful to Scott; an actress was used to depict Nora in the films. During the war, she organizes the Civilian Evacuation Corps, a volunteer service to move causalities and helpless families from target areas. She and her two children are killed in the atomic bombing of Cleveland. They eventually reunite with Scott in another world on the other side of the membrane.

**MacDonney, Scott**  a renowned American cyberneticist in the novella "Izzard and the Membrane." He holds degrees in engineering and physiological psychology and has designed several new and improved computers, a new method of robot control of guided missiles, and invented a synaptic relay for computers. The latter is an improvement over a living neuron's all or none principle. He possesses a "handsome ugliness" and lives in an Ohio university town with his wife Nora and their two children. Trapped in Europe at the start of a Russian invasion, MacDonney is captured and brainwashed. Believing that his wife and country have betrayed him and that he has lost his family, he agrees to build a super computer to help the Russian war effort. After successfully building the computer, MacDonney discovers a supreme intelligence that inhabits it. This entity has created a membrane, or doorway, to another existence. When he learns that his captives have duped him, he works to defeat their war plans. In the end, he passes through the membrane to reunite with his family.

**MacDoughal, Ellen**   the titular character in the short story "MacDoughal's Wife." Ellen, the wife of Scott, lost a child at birth three years ago, and she is unable to have another child. Scott blames her for her inability to have a child and sees her as "a lovely but useless urn." Perhaps in response to her husband's coldness and distance Ellen maintains a series of flirtatious seasonal romances that Scott abides "as long as she remained within the framework of the marriage vows, and didn't make things too publicly embarrassing." She enjoys the attention of other men that she no longer receives from Scott.

**MacDoughal, Scott**   the main character in the short story "MacDoughal's Wife." He is a disillusioned and unforgiving husband since the stillborn birth of his and Ellen's baby and the news that she will not be able to have another child. He is contemptuous of his wife since in his view she now lives only for herself rather than with the purpose of bringing new life into existence. As far as he is concerned, she is a "broken vessel" with a rotten interior, and he is condemned to be with her and no other. His bitterness often leads him to drunkenness and his wife to "her little romances."

**"MacDoughal's Wife"**   Miller's first published short story appeared in *The American Mercury*, 70 (March 1950), 313–320. It, along with "Month of Mary" and "Evening Caller," comprise three early non-science fiction stories which contain strong religious themes and symbolism.

Sitting on a beach one August Sunday, Scott MacDoughal thinks about his wife Ellen and her "seasonal romances" as he watches her talk with Donald Freeman, a young man obviously enamored of her. Three years ago, the MacDoughals lost a child at birth, and Ellen was told she would never be able to have another. MacDoughal believes his wife did not seem particularly upset by this news, and he thinks that perhaps she never wanted a child. He is disgruntled and disillusioned by her and the fact that they will leave no new life to follow them. They are broken links in the unending chain of life. For MacDoughal, Ellen is a lush, alluring creature on the surface but an essentially cold, teasing "broken vessel," a "lovely but useless urn" who will never add to human existence. She is content to be "an end in herself." While life teems around them on the seashore, Scott and Ellen are locked in a sterile relationship, "a strange mixture of passion and contempt."

**Machiavelli, Niccolò** (May 3, 1469–June 21, 1527)   an Italian statesman and author of *The Prince* (1513). An astute political thinker, Machiavelli believed that the goal of any leader is to maintain an orderly and well balanced state. To do so, the strong leader will eschew morality and do whatever is expedient and necessary to gain and maintain power. The term Machiavellian is associated with deceit and cunning.

The character Morgan Sahl is described as "a Lincolnesque Machiavelli" in the short story "Let My People Go."

**Machina Analytica**   Latin: "Analytical machine." In the short story "A Canticle for Leibowitz," a reference is made to the "legendary machine analytica" that dates back to the time of the Deluge of Flame. The machine is a computer. It is also referred to in the novella "And the Light Is Risen." In *A Canticle for Leibowitz,* it is called a fabled machine and the wisest of the ancients' gods.

**Mack**   a producer of the television show "Captain Chronos and the Guardsmen of Time" in the short story "The Will." He accompanies the actor who plays Captain Chronos to the home of Kenny Westmore, a 14-year boy with leukemia, in a publicity stunt for the show.

**Macklehark**   the mayor of Sanly Bowitts in the novella "And the Light Is Risen." A demagogue in Father Jerome's view, Macklehark created trouble with the abbey by claiming it promoted illiteracy and hoarded secret knowledge. He later asks the abbot to allow the villagers to take sanctuary in the abbey in the event of an invasion.

**MacMahon, Colonel**   from the novella "The Yokel." MacMahon commands the Border Guard. They are opposed to the testing that is required before people are allowed to cross into restored cities where technology and industry are being developed and protected after the Hemispheric Conflict. MacMahon believes the yokels are being excluded from their rightful heritage and that an artificial aristocracy is being established. He has devised a plan to disrupt the city of Orlando and to make guerrilla raids on coastal cities. He wants Sam Wuncie to join his cause, steal a cargo plane from inside a tech zone, and fly it out, so it can be used in the planned raid on Orlando.

**MacMillian** an unseen character in the novella "The Lineman." One of the members of the work crew, he is a homosexual who has a relationship with Wickers, another worker.

**MacPearson** the owner of a tavern in the short story "Secret of the Death Dome." He chained two barstools together as a joke to show how close Barney Willis and Jerry Harrison were as friends.

**Mad Bear** the name of a Nomadic clan and the chief of that clan in the novella "And the Light Is Risen" and *A Canticle for Leibowitz* ("Fiat Lux"). Marcus Apollo believes that he may possibly be colluding with Hannegan. The clan chief is also known as Hongan Os. See also **Hongan Os**

**Madame d'Annecy** the proprietress of Les Folies Lunaries, Incorporated, the space-traveling bordello that lands on the moon in the novella "The Lineman." She is a confident and astute businessperson who bests Suds Brodanovitch when he boards the ship to tell her she has to stop her activities. She proposes giving each man who visits the ship one share of common stock in the company, making them business partners. She gives Brodanovitch a bottle of champagne as a gift. Unfortunately, it explodes in the air lock as he leaves the ship, killing him.

***Maestro: a New Musical Play in Two Acts*** a 1981 musical drama based on Miller's short story "The Darfsteller." The book is by Sharon Tipsword, the music by Wayne Hosford, and the lyrics by Tipsword and Hosford.

***The Maggot*** the last major novel of the British author John Fowles. Published in 1985, the title's meaning derives from the older definition of maggot: an extravagant idea or whim. A multilayered and symbolic novel, the story combines mystery and a hint of science fiction with historical fiction. It has an elaborate narrative structure centered upon the tale of a group of travelers in 1736 who discover one of their party hanged and another missing. Miller reviewed the book for the *New York Times Book Review* in his "Chariots of the Goddesses, or What?" See also **"Chariots of the Goddesses, or What?"** and **Fowles, John**

**Magister Dion** the mayor of the genny settlement New Jerusalem in *Saint Leibowitz and the Wild Horse Woman* and the father of Slojon. He tells Brother Blacktooth that Ædrea died during a miscarriage. He wants to prevent Blacktooth from being near Pope Amen II so he cannot influence him. He does not return from the war. *Magister* is Latin for master. Dion is a short form of Dionysius, the Greek god of wine and revelry.

**Magister meus** Latin: "My master [teacher]." Brother Francis refers to Abbot Arkos by this term in *A Canticle for Leibowitz* ("Fiat Homo"). It also appears in "Fiat Voluntas Tua."

**Magisterium** the term is derived from the Latin *magister*, meaning master. Within the Catholic Church, it is the divinely appointed authority or office of the Church to teach the religious truth. In *A Canticle for Leibowitz* ("Fiat Homo"), the canonization of Leibowitz coincides with the calling of a General Council of the Church to restate the doctrine of the limitation of the magisterium.

**Magna Civitas** Latin: "Great Civilization." The term is used in *Saint Leibowitz and the Wild Horse Woman* to describe the time in the twentieth century before the Flame Deluge and Age of Simplification.

**Magnificat Dominum anima mea** Latin: "My soul doth magnify the Lord." The first line of the Magnificat or Song of Mary from Luke 1:46–55 (KJV), Mary's celebration of God. It is recited in the Catholic Church as part of Vespers. Father Zerchi impulsively recites it as he lies beneath the rubble of the abbey at the end of the novella "The Last Canticle" and *A Canticle for Leibowitz*. In the novella, Rachel, standing before Zerchi, repeats the words. In the novel Zerchi wants to teach her the words because he believes Rachel shares something with Mary. He continues to recite the lines: *et exultavit spiritus meus in Deo, salutary meo, quia respexit humilitatem...* ["and my spirit hath rejoiced in God my Savior; for He hath regarded the lowliness...."] Rachel never repeats the words, however. Zerchi runs out of breath and cannot complete the lines, and Rachel, instead, touches his forehead and says simply, "Live."

**Mahh, Maho** an unseen thon in the novella "And the Light Is Risen" and *A Canticle for Leibowitz* ("Fiat Lux"). Thon Taddeo tells the monks at the Abbey of Saint Leibowitz that Mahh is heading a study of the human species at the collegium. His title is given as Don rather than Thon in the novella.

**Maison intime** French: "Intimate house," i.e., a bordello. Madame d"Annecy refers to her business with this expression in the novella "The Lineman."

**Major General Alvasson** the commander of Texark Cavalry in *Saint Leibowitz and the Wild Horse Woman*. He takes part in Filpeo Harq's strategy meeting at the War College in Hannegan City.

**Major Go'an**  one of the officers comprising the investigating body examining the actions of Eli Roki and the destruction of the mercy ship in the short story "Blood Bank."

**Major Tuli**  a member of the investigating body reviewing the actions of Eli Roki in the short story "Blood Bank." Tuli was aboard the patrol ship as an observer when Roki ordered the destruction of the mercy ship. Roki ordered him confined to the brig for disputing his orders.

**Malicia**  the name of a mule in Brother Fingo's supply train in *A Canticle for Leibowitz* ("Fiat Homo"). She kicks Brother Alfred. The name is a variation of the Latin *malitia*, meaning malice or bad behavior.

**Malin**  a colonist in the novella "Cold Awakening." She lies about where Lovewell was standing when the shots that killed Jessel were fired. Threatened with a return to Earth as an accessory to murder, she tells the truth: Lovewell was standing next to her, and she gave him the hairpin used to knock out the light.

**Man-Horse-Dog-Thing**  in the Old Time an alliance arranged among man, dog, and horse to rule the free, furry cattle that ranged on the Plains. The alliance controlled the herd to its advantage, but against its will. The herd was driven to where man knew the grass to be greener. In return for their meat and hides, the cattle received protection from wolves and large cats; they ran freely until man shot them from horseback. This Nomad myth appears in *Saint Leibowitz and the Wild Horse Woman*.

**Manasses**  also referred to as Manasseh, the son and successor of King Hezekiah of Judah. According to 2 Kings 21:1–18 (KJV), he reigned for 55 years as the thirteenth king of Judah and "he did that which was evil in the sight of the Lord," including the reintroduction of idolatry. In the novella "And the Light Is Risen" and *A Canticle for Leibowitz* ("Fiat Lux"), he is cited as a bad king, and Benjamin hopes that Don Thaddeo/Thon Taddeo is not like him.

**Mandatum novum do vobis  ut diligatis invicem ...**  Latin: "A new commandment I give unto you: that ye love one another [as I have loved you, that ye also love one another."] Jesus' words to his disciples at the Last Supper from John 13:34 (KJV). They are recited during the Maundy Thursday ceremonies as Abbot Arkos and the monks visit the novices' hermitages in *A Canticle for Leibowitz* ("Fiat Homo").

**Mankiller, the Compassionate One**  a concept among Wooshin's people in *Saint Leibowitz and the Wild Horse Woman*. In battle, the sword that kills is the same sword that gives life. One's enemy is defeated but the wielder of the sword (and his family) is given life.

**Manlin Bill**  in the short story "Way of a Rebel," the Manlin Bill is passed by Congress "in accordance with the provisions of the Twenty-Sixth Amendment" of the Constitution. It calls for the three branches of the federal government to be placed in the hands of the Department of Defense when a state of total emergency for the nation is declared. The Secretary of Defense assumes absolute power.

**Manning, Robert Douglas**  author of *The Abbey*, a dramatic screenplay based on *A Canticle for Leibowitz* published in 2000. See also ***The Abbey***

**Mannish, Rudolph**  the narrator of the short story "Month of Mary." Mannish is a "monk and priest of Jesus Christ" whose fear of disease makes him question his efficacy ministering to a leper colony in Brazil.

**Manter**  an unseen character in the novella "The Yokel." A member of the Border Guards, he is bitten by a dog the week before Sam Wuncie is captured. His bite gives Doctor Harlich the idea of injecting Wuncie with rabies in order to make him cooperate with Colonel MacMahon.

**Mara**  1. A tall, slender girl, the daughter of Welkir and girlfriend of Asir in the short story "It Takes a Thief." While awaiting his punishment for death, Asir believes Mara to be untrustworthy and fickle. Her plan, however, is to ingratiate herself with Tokra, the Chief Commoner, to learn Asir's punishment. She arranges for Asir to leave the village on a hüffen when he is banished. When Asir decides to defy the judgment against him and go to the vault of the Blaze of the Great Wind to face Big Joe, Mara accompanies him.

2. The wife of Ton of Roldin in the short story "Please Me Plus Three." She is one of the beautiful women chosen to dance for Bel. Ton protests her inclusion in the ceremony because she is pregnant, but Mara does not share his concern. Their marriage is an arranged one according to the blood laws, and she dislikes her husband. She is devoted in her duty to Bel. When she does fall during the dance, Bel decrees that she offer the dance of immolation to compensate for ruining the beauty of the tribe's gift. She willingly does so, whipping her face and thighs with bull-nettles and finally plunging a knife into her throat.

**Marcia**   the former wife of Kenneth Johnson in the short story "The Space Witch." Ken has invited her and her current husband, Phillip, to his summer cottage on Kalawego Lake for the weekend. Marcia is manipulative, immature, and needy — Ken describes her as "an unhappy child" — but she still loves him despite their divorce. She drowns in the lake when the boat she and Ken are in capsizes in the wake created by an alien's landing tunnel. The alien, the space witch, simulates Marcia's physical form and also acquires her neural patterns and memories.

**Marcus the Centurion**   the centurion who presided over Jesus' crucifixion. In *Saint Leibowitz and the Wild Horse Woman*, Brother Blacktooth dreams he is Pontius Pilate and Wooshin is Marcus the Centurion.

**Mariolatry**   the excessive veneration of the Virgin Mary, honoring her as one would God. In *Saint Leibowitz and the Wild Horse Woman*, brief mention is made of the bishops of patriarchal societies denouncing the Mariolatry of the Northwest, which Amen indirectly endorsed prior to his election as pope.

**Marka**   1. A young woman in the short story "The Big Hunger." She watches preparations for a space flight that will take Teris, the man she loves, away from her. She argues with him about trying to discover the Planet of Heaven in space. She tells him it lies within the heart: only when man is content without his lost paradise will he be forgiven and shown the road home. As Teris runs toward his ship, Marka yells after him that what he seeks is right here with her, not in space.
2. The lead female role in the play "The Anarch" in the novella "The Darfsteller." Mela Stone plays the part during Act II of the autodrama production.

**Marrita**   a minor character in the short story "The Ties That Bind." She is a member of the Pedaga clan of teachers. She discusses the arrival of the Imperial Forces with Letha and Evon.

**Mars Commission**   the ruling body of Marsville, the only city established by Earth on Mars in the novella "The Reluctant Traitor." The members of the Commission are appointed by Earth and are subject to recall. The Commission maintains strict control of the population within the walled city. They keep the truth about the androons and the history of Mars from the populace in order to establish Marsville as the center of a planned Earth empire on Mars and control the colonization of the planet. They administer the bio-laws that forbid any interaction between humans and androons.

**Mars Plan**   the intended first published novel by Miller. It was to have been published by Shasta Publishing. Its announcement appears in the "About the Authors" section of *The Best Science-Fiction Stories: 1953*. According to an interview with Chad Oliver, the novel was an expansion of a Miller work published in *Amazing Stories*. The novella "The Reluctant Traitor" appeared in *Amazing Stories* in the January 1952 issue. The novel never appeared, and Shasta ceased publishing in 1957. Miller called the work "forgettable junk" and claimed he never actually expanded the story beyond the novella (ltr 12/14/1990).

**Marsville**   Earth's only city on Mars in the novella "The Reluctant Traitor." It comprises a ten-mile square and has a population of 80,000 people. According to law, all humans must live within its walls. Travel beyond the city is prohibited without special permission. It is a nearly self-sufficient industrial city and is the planned hub of Earth's Martian empire. The Commission rules it.

**Marta**   a young wife whose husband commits suicide in the short story "Dumb Waiter." Left to fend for herself and child, she steals Mitch Laskell's bicycle and shotgun. The city's robot police arrest and jail her for possessing stolen property. She has little faith that Mitch will be able to reprogram the city's central computer, but she provides him with a clue vital to his solving the identification code he needs to access the computers. Mitch castigates her as being one of the machine age's spoiled children; she allowed herself to be mechanically pampered rather than taking control of the machine.

**Martha**   1. The wife of Old Donegal in the short story "Death of a Spaceman" (later entitled "Memento Homo"). Donegal describes her as "a man's woman." Married since he first went into space, she never complained about his absences. She is devoted to her husband and keeps a close vigil at his bed. While it is Donegal's inclination to accept his impending death gracefully, he knows Martha could not bear for him to take it calmly because it would be like deliberately leaving her.
2. A minor character in the short story "The Hoofer." She is the wife of a farmer who gives Hogey Parker a ride to his father-in-law's farm.

***The Martin Snyder Hour***   the successful television show of the acclaimed comedian Martin Snyder in the short story "The Corpse In Your Bed Is Me."

**Mary and Martha** in Luke 10:38–42 (KJV), Martha prepares food for the visiting Jesus. Her sister Mary does not help her; instead, she sits at Jesus' feet and listens to his word. Martha complains that Mary has left her to serve Jesus alone, but Jesus reproves her, saying: "Martha, thou art careful and troubled about many things; But one thing is needful; and Mary hath chosen that good part, which shall not be taken away from her." The incident is illustrative of the conflict between material and spiritual things. In the novella "The Last Canticle" and *A Canticle for Leibowitz* ("Fiat Voluntas Tua") a reference is made to "Mary and Martha again" concerning the argument that the Church's spaceship should be carrying poor colonists rather than ecclesiastical dignitaries.

**Mary Magdalene** a woman healed by Jesus of seven demons who became one of his followers. She was present at the crucifixion and the discovery of Jesus' empty tomb. According to John, she is the first to witness the resurrected Jesus. Magdala is the name of the town she was from. In *Saint Leibowitz and the Wild Horse Woman*, Sister Magdalen helped to raise Elia Brownpony. See also **Sister Magdalen**

**Mass Against the Heathen** one of two special masses celebrated by Pope Gregory in the basilica at New Rome in the novella "The Last Canticle" and *A Canticle for Leibowitz* ("Fiat Voluntas Tua") after the Guam conference ends and he no longer prays for world peace. Also known as Mass for the Defense of the Church, it is a traditional votive Mass within the Tridentine Latin Rite Missal. Part of the Mass asks that "the heathen nations, who trust in their own fierceness, may be crushed by the power" of God's right hand. The heathen are considered to be any non–Christian or non Jewish person. In the novel, it is also referred to as *Exsurge quare obdormis* ["Awake! Why are You asleep [O Lord]?), from the first words of the Mass.

**Mass for Pilgrims and Travelers** after Brother Joshua accepts Dom Zerchi's offer to lead the Church's contingent into space, a Mass for Pilgrims and Travelers is celebrated at the Leibowitz abbey in "Fiat Voluntas Tua" in *A Canticle for Leibowitz*.

**Mass in Time of War** the Mass in Time of War is one of two special masses offered by Pope Gregory in the basilica at New Rome in the novella "The Last Canticle" and *A Canticle for Leibowitz* ("Fiat Voluntas Tua") after he stops praying for peace in the world. It is also known as *Reminiscere* ("Remember," the first word of the Mass).

**Mass of the Resurrection [of Christ]** the Mass celebrated on Easter. In *Saint Leibowitz and the Wild Horse Woman*, it is the Mass celebrated at the Cathedral of Saint John-in-Exile in Valana during the conclave.

**"A Master of Babylon"** a 1966 short story by Edgar Pangborn reprinted in *Beyond Armageddon*.

**Masterson** a blacksmith in the short story "Secret of the Death Dome." He watches Barney Willis fall dead from his horse. He is the first one to reach Willis's body and calls for Colonel Beck.

**Mater Dei** Latin: "Mother of God." A term used to refer to the Virgin Mary in *Saint Leibowitz and the Wild Horse Woman*.

**Matins** from the Latin *matutinum*, "of the morning." It is the first of the canonical hours, the morning pray service. The term is used in both novels at various times. For instance, in *A Canticle for Leibowitz* ("Fiat Homo"), Abbot Arkos hopes to get an hour or two of sleep prior to Matins, and in *Saint Leibowitz and the Wild Horse Woman*, Brother Blacktooth meets Prior Olshuen on his way to Matins.

**Maundy laving** Maundy is derived from the Latin word *mandatum* meaning commandment. On the evening of the Last Supper Jesus washes his disciples' feet and then charges them: "Just as I have loved you, you should love one another." The tradition of foot washing on Holy Thursday, the Thursday before Easter, is continued by many churches. The clergy ceremoniously wash the feet of the poor.

1. Father Zerchi remarks to himself that an old man would "have made a good beggar for a Maundy laving" in the novella "The Last Canticle."

2. In *A Canticle for Leibowitz* ("Fiat Homo"), Abbot Arkos, Father Cheroki, and thirteen monks travel to each novice's hermitage on Maundy Thursday to perform the Mandatum, or foot washing ceremony

**Maundy Thursday** the Thursday before Easter. Maundy is derived from the Latin word *mandatum*, meaning commandment. In *Saint Leibowitz and the Wild Horse Woman*, the preliminary meeting of electors that ends in the killing of Father Corvany occurs on Maunday Thursday. See **Maundy laving**

**Maxwell, James Clark** (June 13, 1831–November 5, 1879) Scottish physicist and mathematician known for his work on electromagnetism

(Maxwell's Equations) and the behavior of gases. He, Pierre Laplace, and Albert Einstein are mentioned in *A Canticle for Leibowitz* ("Fiat Lux") as obscure natural philosophers whose work was identified among the Memorabilia at the abbey in Brother Kornhoer's correspondence to Thon Taddeo.

**Maxwell's Equations** a set of four fundamental equations governing electromagnetism developed by James Clark Maxwell in the mid-nineteenth century. In *Saint Leibowitz and the Wild Horse Woman*, the equations are among the "very great" Memorabilia at the Abbey of Saint Leibowitz. They are rumored to be among the notes Taddeo Pfardentrott takes back to Texark. The equations are part of the Memorabilia postulates at the abbey must memorize.

**Mayor Dion** *see* **Dion, Magister**

**Mayor Sarquist** *see* **Sarquist**

**McCoy** the interpreter for Major Kline in the short story "Vengeance for Nikolai."

**Meikl, Baltun** an Analyst Culturetic of the Intelligence Section of the Imperial Forces of the Succession in the short story "The Ties That Bind." As the ships approach Earth, he advises a cautious approach to Baron ven Klaeden. Meikl fears that the arrival of the descendents of the original spacegoers after 20,000 years may awaken a now dormant disease among the present natives of Earth. The basis for his argument is *kulturverlaengerung*, the unconscious cultural mechanism of transmittal. He advocates landing on Mars rather than Earth. The Baron overrules him. Meikl becomes an interpreter for the operation and works with Letha, whom he grows to love. As the refueling operation deteriorates, Meikl accuses the Baron of being a tyrant and of bringing aggression and war to Earth. Meikl's fears of the Imperial Forces' influence on Earth are realized.

**Melchisedech** the king of Salem, the ancient name of Jerusalem, and priest. When Abraham defeated Cherdorlaomer in his rescue of Lot, Melchisedech provided him with bread and wine. In response, Abraham shared with Melchisedech a tenth of his spoils. The Old Testament presents Melchisedech as the ideal combination of king and priest. *Saint Leibowitz and the Wild Horse Woman* cites a line from Psalm 109 (DB), "for ever, after the order of Melchisedech," in referring to a character's office as a priest.

**Melchizedek** *see* **Melchisedech**

**Meldown** a term used in *Saint Leibowitz and the Wild Horse Woman*. It is believed to be the navel of the Earth — or alternately the navel of the World — and the breeding pit for Høngin Fujæ Vurn and the wild horses of the Nomad hordes. It is a site of deadly fires and a place of ordeal. Those charged with crimes are tried there. When the Qæsach dri Vørdar, or Lord of the Hordes, is chosen, he must spend a night in Meldown under a full moon. Hultor Bråm insists that Cardinal Brownpony spend a night in Meldown to acquit himself of past sacrileges against Empty Sky and the Wild Horse Woman. Many who spend time in the meldown become ill, and some lose their hair. The pits are sites of nuclear contamination; the word is a corruption of meltdown. Those who become ill are suffering the effects of radiation poisoning.

**Memento, Domine, omnium famulorum tuorum** Latin: "Remember, Father, all your servants [family]." Father Jerome whispers these words toward Benjamin as he leaves the pilgrim's hermitage in the novella "And the Light Is Risen." In *A Canticle for Leibowitz* ("Fiat Lux"), Dom Paulo says the prayer to himself as he rides back across the desert toward the abbey after visiting the old pilgrim.

**Memento Homo** Latin: "Remember man." The beginning of the quote that serves as the epigraph for the short story "Death of a Spaceman," later published as "Memento Homo": "*Memento homo quia pulvis es et in pulverem reverteris*," ("Remember man that thou art dust and unto dust thou shalt return"). It is from Genesis 3:19 (KJV) and is traditionally recited by the priest as he applies ashes to the foreheads of the worshippers on Ash Wednesday.

**"Memento Homo"** a short story originally published as "Death of a Spaceman" in *Amazing Stories*, 28 (March 1954). It first appears under this title in *The Best Science Fiction Stories and Novels: 1955*, edited by T. E. Dikty (New York, NY: Frederick Fell). The story is variously published under both titles from then on. See also **"Death of a Spaceman"**

**The Memorabilia** what is left of the original books and documents hidden by the bookleggers during the Simplification and not eventually destroyed by the mobs, and hand-copied texts recalled from memory preserved by the Albertian Order of Leibowitz at their abbey in the southwest desert.

The monks of the order continue to study, copy, and preserve these documents for future generations, even if the knowledge contained in them is largely useless. The Venerable Boedullus once stated that half of the Memorabilia should be called the Inscrutabilia since the brothers lacked the knowledge and context to understand much of what they preserved.

**Memorizers**   in *A Canticle for Leibowitz* ("Fiat Homo"), those members of the Albertian Order of Leibowitz who committed to memory entire volumes of books as a safeguard against the discovery of the kegs of books buried by the bookleggers during the Simplification. See also **Bookleggers**

**Menbana**   the bat deity and god of knowledge among the androons in the novella "The Reluctant Traitor." Rolf Kenlan becomes an acolyte of Menbana.

**Mensely, Doctor**   an unseen character in the short story "Command Performance" (also published as "Anyone Else Like Me?"). He is a psychiatrist. Lisa Waverly thinks that if her husband saw her dancing naked in the rain, he would have Mensely "have a look at my mind." She has only contempt for the doctor's smugness and his attempts to make people conform to a norm.

**Menshrie**   the editor and reporter for the *Martian Messenger* of Marsville in the novella "The Reluctant Traitor." Rolf Kenlan contacts him so he can hear Kenlan's conversation with Commissioner Rathwich over a hidden radio transmission.

**Mercy Cadre**   that part of the of the Green Star agency that actually euthanizes the victims of radiation poisoning who are legally allowed to end their lives in *A Canticle for Leibowitz* ("Fiat Voluntas Tua").

**Mercy Camp Number 18**   a Green Star Relief Station established 2 miles down the road from the Abbey of Saint Leibowitz in the novella "The Last Canticle" and "Fiat Voluntas Tua" in *A Canticle for Leibowitz*. It tends to refugees and victims of excessive radiation exposure. Through its Mercy Cadre, it recommends and performs voluntary euthanasia for hopeless cases, following the procedure established by law. Father Zerchi opposes its establishment so close to the abbey and has five novices picket its gates with signs reading "Abandon Every Hope Ye Who Enter Here."

**Mercy Liner Sol-G-6**   the mercy ship from Sol III supposedly carrying emergency medical supplies for Jod VI in the short story "Blood Bank." The ship is ordered destroyed by Eli Roki after it refuses to stop to allow for a random cargo inspection. It is later discovered that as a Solarian ship, it was carrying surgibank supplies but also human livestock as the source of those supplies and as food for the Solarian crew.

**Merlin**   in his *History of the Kings of Britain* (1136), Geoffrey of Monmouth combined two ancient stories — one of the magician Myrddin from Celtic folklore and the other of Ambrosius, an advisor to King Vortigern who prophesized his defeat, from Nennius' ninth century *History of the Britons* — to create the figure of Merlin. The character developed into a popular medieval figure, most notably in Thomas Malory's *Le Morte d'Arthur* where Merlin is an advisor, seer, and powerful wizard for King Arthur. In the novella "The Last Canticle" and *A Canticle for Leibowitz* ("Fiat Voluntas Tua"), reference is made to the "children of Merlin, chasing a gleam."

**Merrigull**   an unseen character in the short story "Let My People Go." His theories and calculations regarding a potentially habitable planet are the basis for the 13-year trip to Epsilon Eridani Two by 120 Earth colonists. The colonists name the planet "Merrigull's Guesswork" and eventually shorten it to simply "Guesswork."

**Merrigull's Guesswork** *see* **Merrigull**

**Merril, Judith**   (January 21, 1923–September 12, 1997)   born Josephine Juliet Grossman in Boston, she was a science fiction writer, editor, anthologist, and promoter of science fiction or speculative (a term she preferred) literature who assumed the pen name Judith Merril (Merril is the given name of her first-born daughter). She legally changed her name in 1949. She immigrated to Canada in 1968 and became a Canadian citizen in 1976. Her donation of her personal library to the Toronto Public Library System formed the bases for the Spaced Out Library, later renamed The Merril Collection of Speculative Fiction and Fantasy in 1991.

She was active in the Futurians, a group of young, politically conscious science fiction authors and fans in New York City in the late 1940s that included James Blish, Damon Knight, and Isaac Asimov. Although she authored a number of well-known short stories, including her first published science fiction story, "That Only a Mother," two novels in collaboration with C. M. Kornbluth as "Cyril Judd" — *Outpost Mars* and *Gunner* — as well as a number of other novels (*The Tomorrow People*), her greater repute is probably as an anthologist and reviewer than as a fiction writer. Her annual editions of anthologies such as *The Year's Best Science Fiction* (and variant titles) were important vehicles for identifying and presenting genre stories to a wider audience.

Merril met Miller in September 1952 when she was living in Red Bank, New Jersey, and he was in New York City working on scripts for *Captain Video and His Video Rangers*. She was in the midst of a divorce from her second husband, the science fiction writer Frederik Pohl, and Miller and his wife were considering a separation. Merril and Miller lived together for six months in 1953 during his "trial separation" from Anne. Merril writes in her autobiography, *Better to Have Loved*, of their attempts to "form a family" first in New Jersey and then in Arm City, Florida, with her second daughter and Miller's four children at the same time she is embroiled in contentious custody battles with both her first husband, Daniel Zissman, and Pohl.

In the book Merril gives an account of a physical altercation between Miller and Pohl that occurred when she and Miller were living together in New Jersey. When an argument arose between Merril and Pohl over their daughter, Miller confronted Pohl with an unloaded rifle and told him to leave their house. Pohl lept at Miller and they engaged in an ineffective fight until Pohl finally "put Walt down." She also reveals that her short story "Connection Completed" (first published in *Universe* in November 1954) is "more or less to and about Walt."

Despite their plans to marry, on the advice of a lawyer, Merril and Miller decided to live apart for the benefit of Merril's custody hearings. During their time apart they discovered that they were both able to write more productively — notwithstanding Miller's assertion that in each other they had "found the perfect audience for our work." During this time, Miller received news that Anne was having a nervous breakdown and asking him to come back to her. According to Merril, she and Miller decided, "somebody [should] get what they wanted," so he went back to Anne.

Merril's granddaughter, Emily Pohl-Weary, who completed her autobiography after Merril died, wrote that Miller "was never far" from Merril's mind. Upon Miller's death, Merril said it was a "blow" to learn that his wife had died six months before and yet he never attempted to contact her. See also **"Connection Completed"**

**Mesa of Last Resort** an anvil shaped mountain located approximately ten miles from the Abbey of Saint Leibowitz in the novella "And the Light Is Risen" and *A Canticle for Leibowitz* ("Fiat Lux"). It is the home of Benjamin. Father Jerome/Dom Paulo visits him there prior to the visit of Don Thaddeo/Thon Taddeo to the abbey. In *Saint Leibowitz and the Wild Horse Woman*, Brother Blacktooth goes to the Mesa on one of his unsanctioned absences from the abbey and discovers Benjamin's hut.

**Messér** Italian: a title of respect meaning sir or master. It is used by Brother Francis when he is speaking to Monsignor Flaught in *A Canticle for Leibowitz* ("Fiat Homo").

**Messerschmitts** a reference to the German fighter planes of World War II manufactured by Messerchmitt AG (named after its chief designer Willy Messerschmitt). In the short story "Wolf Pack," "six Messerschmitts whipped out of the sun." While the term Messerschmitts referred generically to all the aircraft manufactured by the company, Miller probably had in mind the Bf109, the principal fighter plane of the Luftwaffe and the plane considered by many to be one of the greatest fighter planes of World War II, if not the greatest.

**Methuselah** according to Genesis 5:27 (KJV), Methuselah lived for 969 years. He is recognized as being the oldest person who ever lived. In *A Canticle for Leibowitz* ("Fiat Lux"), Dom Paulo believes Benjamin appears sane except for his delusion that he is older than Methuselah.

**Metus doloris** Latin: "Fear of suffering [pain]." As Dom Zerchi lies trapped beneath the rubble of the abbey at the conclusion of *A Canticle for Leibowitz*, he thinks of his conversation with Dr. Cors. Zerchi believes that the evil the doctor referred to was not suffering, but an unreasoning fear of suffering, *Metus doloris*.

**Mihi amicus** Latin: "a friend to me." Used by Brother Francis in *A Canticle for Leibowitz* ("Fiat Homo").

**Miler** Chief of Police in the novella "Conditionally Human." He takes Terry Norris's statement concerning the murder of Dr. Georges and investigates the death of Franklin at Norris's kennels.

**Military Order of San Pancratz** a schismatic order of military knight-friars founded to fight the Bayring Horde. Vissarion was their Antipope. The order turned to random pillaging and sectarian conflict. It is referred to in the novella "And the Light Is Risen" and *A Canticle for Leibowitz* ("Fiat Lux"). The name Pancratz is derived from Saint Pancratius (or Pancras), a Roman citizen who converted to Christianity and was martyred at the age of 14 for refusing to renounce his faith. Saint Gregory of Tours called him "the avenger of perjuries."

**Miller, Alys Elaine** (November 9, 1951– ) third daughter and last of four children born to Miller and his wife.

**Miller, Anna Louise Becker** (August 28, 1927–August 7, 1995) Miller's wife and mother of their four children. She was born in Williamson, Texas, the daughter of Tesnulda (Thiele) and Arnold Becker. She and Miller were married on May 1, 1945 in Colorado after having met in Galveston, Texas when Miller returned from World War II. They were divorced in 1953 but remarried on the last day of the same year. She worked for a period at an insurance agency. She died at home two weeks after undergoing cancer surgery. According to Miller, her death was unexpected and unrelated to her surgery.

**Miller, Cathryn Augusta** (September 27, 1949–2008) the third child born to Miller and his wife.

**Miller, Margaret Jean** (June 4, 1946– ) first of four children born to Miller and his wife.

**Miller, Ruth Adrian (Jones)** (January 19, 1900–July 16, 1980) mother of Walter M. Miller, Jr. She was born in Ohio but lived in Florida by the time she was twenty.

**Miller, Walter Michael, Jr.** (January 23, 1922–January 9, 1996) Walter M. Miller, Jr., was the only child of Ruth (Jones) and Walter Miller. He was born on January 23, 1922 in the small town of New Smyrna Beach on the east coast of Florida where his father worked for the Florida East Coast Railway, as did his father before him. Miller described the area as being "where deep cypress swamp merges with beach-resort to form a hybrid geography whose fauna consists of Boston schoolmarms, New York bookies, Portuguese fishermen, citrus growers, and swamp-sloggers with shoes ventilated for bunions. Characters all" (*Fantastic Adventures* 127). He enjoyed a fairly typical and uneventful childhood growing up, and developed a lifelong fondness for the area and its waterways, enjoying both boating and fishing. He described himself as a "water baby" and remained so his adult life.

Miller observed that "an only child has too many toys and can't decide among them," but as he grows older, *ideas* [Miller's emphasis] may come to be regarded as toys (*Fantastic Adventures* 127). As a teenager, he developed varied and numerous interests. He considered careers in paleontology, biology, chemistry, horticulture, the merchant marines, and writing — or every combination of any or all of them. Part of his interest in being a writer was a result of his grandfather's storytelling. He enjoyed listening to the many "whoppers" told to him from an early age. His interest in writing was encouraged by his English teachers in high school, but Miller had little regard for their opinions at the time. His parents were concerned about his ability to make a living as a writer, so his father encouraged him to be practical and study electrical engineering when Miller entered the University of Tennessee at Knoxville in 1940.

Miller attended the University of Tennessee for three semesters. The idea of majoring in engineering was a pretense that allowed him to indulge in an "intellectual smorgasbord" of courses that included physics, poetry, and philosophy. He felt any attempt to steer him toward the courses required for his major deprived him of the reason he was at the university and reeked of specialization and responsibility. He left the university to enlist in the U. S. Army Air Corps in February 1942.

Miller served on B-25 bombers as a radio operator and gunner. He flew on fifty-five combat missions over Italy, Greece, Yugoslavia, Albania, and Bulgaria. He received the Air Medal and two oak leaf clusters and attained the rank of Technical Sergeant. Miller described sweating in the B-25 as he sat on one flak jacket and wore another, even though "it was so cold you could bounce spit off the bulkhead as ice." Despite being shot at, the war was "grim, ungodly fun." The experience "was like driving hot-rods or playing Russian roulette or gang-brawling." The veneer of civilization was stripped away to expose the "pale ape, teeth bared" (*Fantastic Adventures* 128).

One of the missions Miller participated in was the Allied bombing of the Benedictine monastery at Monte Cassino, Italy. The Germans were believed to be using the sacred site as an artillery observation post. On February 15 and 16, 1944, after unsuccessful ground assaults, an aerial bombardment dropped more than 1,000 tons of bombs on the oldest monastery in the western world, reducing it to rubble.

Although Miller had no compunction about the bombing at the time it occurred, he later came to see a connection between his participation in the war generally and the Monte Cassino bombing particularly and his writing of *A Canticle for Leibowitz*. While he was first writing the scene where Father Zerchi lies trapped in the rubble of the abbey at the end of "The Last Canticle," it occurred to him: "Good God, is this the abbey at Monte Cassino?

This rubble looks like south Italy, not [the] Southwest desert. What have I been writing?" (Greenhill-Taylor 6)

Toward the end of the war in Europe Miller returned to the United States and was stationed in Galveston, Texas. There he met Anna (Anne) Louise Becker. They were married on May 1, 1945 in Colorado where Miller had been transferred. He anticipated returning to combat in the Pacific theater until the bombings of Hiroshima and Nagasaki. He observed that at the time the deaths of the Japanese "seemed to be a side effect; the purpose of the Bomb was to get me out of the Army Air Corps" (*Beyond Armageddon* 124–125). By the fall of 1945, Miller was discharged.

After his discharge, Miller returned to Texas with his wife. They lived with her parents, Tesnulda and Arnold Becker, while they built a small house of their own in Kyle in the Texas Hill Country approximately 25 miles south of Austin. Their first child, and first of three daughters, Margaret, was born in 1946. Miller searched for the right direction in which to pursue a career. He continued to be interested in many things and was reluctant to abandon everything else to specialize in one area. He worked in sales, variously selling tires, life insurance, and air conditioning, but he "felt like a clothes-horse for somebody else's ideas." Thanks to an employer who believed that "anything can be learned on-the-job," Miller found a position as a junior engineer at a power company (*Fantastic Adventures* 129). He worked there for two years until he left to return to college in the fall of 1947. He enrolled at the University of Texas at Austin on the G. I. Bill of Rights while he worked part-time in electronics repair. That same year his son Walter Michael Miller, III was born in September. It was also the year Miller converted to Catholicism; he was baptized on April 5, Holy Saturday.

Miller was raised in a home that did not believe in or formally practice an organized religion. Judith Merril described Miller's father as a "hard-headed atheist" and his mother as a "southern Baptist lady" (134). Walter Miller, Sr. was also "violently anti-Semitic" according to his son. He was influenced in this belief by his mother who admired all things German, including Adolf Hitler (Garvey 1983, 36). Not surprisingly given his family environment, Miller referred to himself as being an atheist during his years in high school.

His wartime experience in Italy provided him his only extended contact with the Catholic Church up to that point. While he saw his eventual conversion to Catholicism to be in some part a result of his empathy with the Italian populace during their bombardment, he ultimately disavowed the idea of a simple cause and effect as "a silly superstition." The empathy he felt was "not a motive ... not a reason" (ltr 4/9/1991). Any attempt to make a connection between his experience in the war and his later conversion was merely speculation after the fact as far as he was concerned. Yet he told an interviewer in 1986 "it's probably true that I would never have become a Catholic or written *Canticle* if it had not been for the war experience" (Greenhill-Taylor D5).

At the time of his conversion to Catholicism, Miller studied the traditions and rituals of the Church a good deal. He tried, in his own words, to be "hyper-Catholic" (Garvey 1983, 36), but a familial situation put him in conflict with the more conservative tenants of the Church and led to a formal break. When Miller's wife Anne gave birth to their third child, Cathryn, in September 1949, she almost died. She became pregnant again within a relatively short time. After the birth of Alys in November 1951, the Millers decided that Anne should undergo a tubal ligation for her own safety. Having done so, Miller explains, put them at odds with the Church; "that was it as far as the Church was concerned" (Garvey 1983, 36).

By the time he was working on his novel in the late fifties he "inevitably maneuvered my head back into the Church. It was an on-again, off-again thing. Finally, I suppose, I tried to define myself in that area by writing *Leibowitz*. So then I went back to the Church for awhile, but it never really took, I guess" (Cowart 29). He believed that the book could be in some part, "an appeal for the approval of the Church or at least of other Catholics" (Garvey 1983, 36). However, responding to Norman Spinrad's reference to him as a devout Catholic in his introduction to the Gregg Press edition of *A Canticle for Leibowitz* in 1975, Miller stated that such a comment "is as embarrassing to me as it must be to devout Catholics" (ltr 10/11/1990).

Despite his separation from the Church, Miller remained a spiritual man interested in religion. He studied Eastern religious philosophies and cobbled together a personal religious viewpoint: he explained "there's only one mountaintop, but there are lots of ways to get there." While still concerned about the mountaintop, he was no longer especially concerned with any particular path to it (Garvey 1983, 36). Late in his life as he worked on *Saint Leibowitz and the Wild Horse Woman*, Miller wrote to Garvey that he "keeps getting bogged down in religion" (1996, 7). He described what he called the Northwest Heresy, his own concept of what Christianity might become. Its tenants included the divinity of Mary and married religious orders with four vows. Miller explained the fourth vow: "I will follow Jesus Christ as my Lord on earth while I live, and I will refuse to enter heaven afterwards so long as any sinner at all is being tormented in hell; I vow to work unceasingly for the salvation of every child of Adam throughout eternity, though God himself confine me to hell for doing so" (7).

When Miller enrolled at the University of Texas, he again studied electrical engineering. He gave up on the idea of being a writer even though he had never really attempted to be one, deciding it had been merely "an adolescent whim." But fate, or as Miller described it, *digitus Dei*, interceded. Only months before he was to graduate from college, Miller was involved in a car accident. He broke both of his legs and his arm. He spent six months in bed and another six months on crutches. When the cast was removed from his arm, his doctor advised him to write — the exercise was good for the wrist and would help develop his atrophied muscles. And so Miller began to write. When a friend of his who was a priest visited and they discussed leper colonies as a result of the priest's visit to Kalaupapa, the leprosy colony on Molokai, Miller had the idea for his first short story: "suppose a priest who was a hypochondriac were given a parish in a leper colony ..." (*Fantastic Adventures* 130).

The story, "Month of Mary," was published in *Extension* in May 1950. Although "Month of Mary" was the first story Miller wrote and had accepted for publication, his first to appear in print was actually "MacDoughal's Wife" which was published in the March 1950 issue of *American Mercury*. With the conception and writing of "Month of Mary" in a single day, and its easy acceptance for publication, Miller caught the disease of "writer's heart." Writing allowed him to avoid his fear of specialization; he could be a jack-of-all-trades, pursuing all his interests and exploring different ideas in the stories he wrote. By being able to merge himself with the different characters he created, Miller believed he was able to avoid emotional and intellectual specialization.

The next year Miller published "Secret of the Death Dome" in *Amazing Stories*. It was his first published science fiction story. Although he had read science fiction as an adolescent and had some familiarity with the genre, there were two additional reasons for Miller's decision to attempt science fiction: his education in science and engineering, and his immediate success in selling the "Secret of the Death Dome," despite it being "as terrible as it was." Miller decided that science fiction was "the lazy man's way to go" (Wilber 6F). For the next six years, Miller remained a prolific contributor to the science fiction pulp magazines. He published a total of seven science fiction stories in 1951, and another 15 the following year. Five stories appeared in 1953. A planned first novel entitled *Mars Plan*, an adaptation of his novella *The Reluctant Traitor,* was scheduled to be published by Shasta in that year or the next, but it never appeared before the company stopped publishing in 1957. By the middle of the decade, however, Miller's production began to drastically taper off.

This early prolificacy occurred as Miller struggled with a difficult period in his personal life. He moved to Manhattan for a brief time to work on scripts for the television show *Captain Video and His Video Rangers*. Miller and Anne had been discussing for a while the possibility of a separation. In September 1952, he visited the writer Judith Merril in New Jersey and stayed with her for three days. She was separated from her husband at the time, the science fiction writer Frederik Pohl. When Miller finished the script, Anne came to New York to visit him and he returned to Texas with her. According to Merril, Miller hoped to earn enough money from writing another *Captain Video* script to leave Anne. In Texas Miller and Anne agreed to a trial separation. Miller drove back to New Jersey to live with Merril for a couple of months. He then returned to Texas to arrange a custody agreement with Anne. They began divorce proceedings with Anne as the plaintiff. Miller and Merril believed that he would take two of his children and two would remain with Anne. At various times over the next several months, all of Miller's children would spend time with him and Merril.

Merril went to Mexico to get a divorce from Pohl. She met Miller at a motel in Austin as she traveled to and from Mexico. On her return trip, Miller was ready to go with her, and they left Texas to drive around Colorado for a few months with two of Miller's daughters and Merril's daughter. When he had to return to New York to work on a script for a few days, Miller picked up his son in Texas and brought him and two daughters with him. He and Merril shared an apartment over a garage in a small New Jersey town.

In early summer of 1953, they moved to Arm City, Florida (near Orlando; the area was incorporated into Disney World). Merril was going through an acrimonious custody battle, and a lawyer suggested that she would have a better chance at winning custody if she and Miller were not living together. Neither of them was writing much during their time together and a lack of money was a constant problem. They moved to separate addresses to facilitate Merril's standing in the custody dispute, and in doing so they discovered they were both able to write better alone than together.

After Miller informed Anne that he and Merril were planning to marry when his divorce was final, Anne's mother called to tell him that Anne was experiencing a nervous breakdown and wanted nothing more than for Miller to come back to her. Their divorce became final September 8, 1953. Miller was awarded custody of their three oldest children, and Anne was granted custody of Alys. However, according to Merril, because she and Miller were not able to have what they wanted together because of her custody battle and their lack of money, they decided to "let somebody get what [she] wanted." They determined that Miller would return to Anne. Once he returned to his wife, Miller only saw Merril twice again in his life.

Miller and Anne remarried in Orlando on December 31 of the same year. Their decision to remarry caused Miller further estrangement from the Church. His parish priest informed them that they needed to investigate whether Anne's tubal ligation was reversible, and further told them they were not to live together until they were married. They decided instead to get married before the Orange County Judge. When they informed the priest they had remarried, he forbade them to receive the sacraments.

In an undated letter (but probably from the time of their trial separation), Anne wrote that their separation was beneficial for both her and Miller and alluded to the problems they had: "Walt and I never had much in common.... [Walt] has acquired some new thoughts about people in general and marriage in particular. If it doesn't work this time, I doubt that it ever will."

The Millers settled in Florida, living first in Orange City before ultimately settling in Daytona Beach. Miller published no work in 1954 but the next year he saw four stories published; importantly among them were "The Darfsteller" and "A Canticle for Leibowitz." Only "And the Light Is Risen" appeared in 1956, and in 1957 Miller published his last four original stories, one of which was "The Last Canticle."

Miller's correspondence from the fifties indicates a constant struggle with money, seemingly living from scarce royalty check to scarce royalty check, working at short-lived jobs, some menial, including as a professional fisherman, and passing a few "hot checks." He lamented not finishing college and getting his degree. He wrote to a friend saying he was out of a job again. His short list of references was nearly exhausted, and he was reduced to asking friends to be professional references. If a friend was contacted for a reference, Miller asked that "a bit of buncombe" be offered and "not the Awful Truth, of course" (ltr 5/17/1958). (A few biographical entries state that Miller worked for a railroad and retired on Railroad Retirement Act benefits. According to the Railroad Retirement Board, Miller was a railroad employee for only one month and, therefore, did not qualify for railroad retirement benefits.)

He developed an animosity for the science fiction genre or at least for those people he believed controlled the genre. In his opinion, science fiction was being ruined by shortsightedness and a lack of creativity. "I'm coming to hate everything in the field. It would be a delight ... to tell [Horace L.] Gold [editor of *Galaxy*] and [John W.] Campbell [editor of *Astounding Science Fiction*] et al where their stupid unimaginative blindness is leading us.... [E]verybody but s.f. is willing to try something new ..." (ltr 8/17/1956). A year later his enmity was even more pronounced: "The trouble with the field is too much psychoriterary incest.... The New York exurban mob ... constitute a mob of mediocrity, guys who've never been anywhere and are never going anywhere, and band together to snipe at people who are going somewhere; this Hydra cult ... has entirely too much influence on editorial judgment simply because they're everpresent [and] evertalkative...." (ltr 8/23/1957). He was aware that at least some of his bile was personal: "If I sound like a sorehead re that Hydra crowd, then no doubt it's because I am; but even allowing for sundry bruises, I'm convinced that that group is the soggy-blanket influence that keeps s-f monotonized and unindividual" (ltr 8/23/1957). Despite his disappointment and discouragement, he still hoped to be able to find his way back to writing television scripts. He also approached Ballantine Books about publishing a collection of his stories. The response he received from "a hired hand" may be indicative of the antagonistic relationship he maintained with many people within the genre. His proposal for the collection was rejected, and he was called a "mediocre space opera writer." Miller believed Frederik Pohl, his adversary from his time spent with Judith Merril, was behind the boorish rejection (ltr 8/17/1956).

As early as 1956, however, Ballantine was considering the idea of Miller developing a novel from the three shorter works about the monks at the Abbey of Saint Leibowitz. Miller was not sure if a book was viable because he believed that "The Last Canticle" would be too "downbeat." He also saw possible problems in bringing the three shorter pieces together in a cohesive whole because of "style discrepancies and unity difficulties" (ltr 1/17/1957). Although he stated in correspondence at the time that he had not thought of the material for a novel until Ballantine became interested in the possibility of it becoming one, he later said the idea that the material was potentially a novel occurred to him as he was writing the third story. Don Congdon, Miller's agent, has said that a friend of Miller's suggested he work the three stories into a novel.

By the beginning of 1957 Miller was writing to Chad Oliver, the anthropologist and science fiction writer who was a close friend in the 1950s and 60s, confessing that he was "in a helluva slump," and asking for advice as to how to "get back on the productivity cycle" (ltr 2/6/1957). He had hired Congdon as his agent because he "seemed to like CANTICLE so well" in the hope that he would be able to sell the book. Miller questioned the general reluctance of publishers to deal with books with religious themes since the Bible continued to be the "hottest selling book." Walter Bradbury, a respected editor dealing with science fiction, turned down the book at Doubleday. He told Miller that they "were fighting an uphill battle" trying to sell science fiction, and he did not think enough copies could be sold. Despite not taking the book, Bradbury said he found it "extremely ingenious [and] rewarding in many ways." Miller believed it was "a lousy salesman" who tries to blame his customers for his own lack of salesmanship, but he did not respond to Bradbury because "I've already yelled 'idiot!' at too many editors" (ltr 1/17/1957). By the summer Congdon had secured a contract from J. B. Lippincott for the book Miller was now factiously referring to as *Space Pope*, as well as a deal for a paperback edition. The book was supposed to be "a quickie job." Lippincott announced its publication for September 1958, but Miller struggled to bring the book together and its publication had to be postponed a number of times because of his "sluggishness." His work on the novel "turned into one of the most protracted periods of suffering in my life" (Garvey 1983, 36). The story was fraught with conflicts from his life and bad feelings he retained from the war.

Miller claimed the book became the story of a nervous breakdown. When he enlisted in the Army Air Corps and was sent to Europe, Miller had "a very romantic idea about war," but he returned home "sick" (Garvey 1983, 36). He told Greenhill-Taylor in 1986 that if not for his war experience, "maybe I'd be saner in other ways as well" (D5). Miller experienced what was often referred to then as combat fatigue or shell shock but what would probably be diagnosed today as chronic Posttraumatic Stress Syndrome. The condition causes "significant distress or impairment in social, occupational, or other important areas of functioning" and "may interfere with interpersonal relationships and lead to marital conflict, divorce, or loss of job" (*DSM-IV* 463). He wrestled with his participation in the bombing of the Monte Cassino monastery and his culpability in so many deaths. Chad Oliver remembered Miller talking about the bombing "a great deal," and believed that the mission "just tore him a part." Although Oliver said that Miller was never able to get the bombing out of his head, he believed that the writing of the novel was "a kind of catharsis" for him (*Supermorn* 23). Nevertheless, even the eventual publication of the book in February 1960 (copyrighted in 1959) could not alleviate Miller's depression.

The publication of *A Canticle for Leibowitz* was both the peak and the culmination of Miller's career as a science fiction writer. He received the Hugo Award at the Nineteenth Annual World Science Fiction Convention in Seattle in 1961. Miller and Lippincott were successful in promoting the novel as something other than science fiction and so the book received more notice in the mainstream press than was usual for a typical science fiction novel at the time. Despite the success of the novel, both critically and commercially, Miller was unable to capitalize on it. He signed with Lippincott for another novel in 1961 (not a *Canticle* sequel), but was offered just $1,000.00, an outrageously small amount in Congdon's estimation.

Miller was not without ideas for other projects, but he was unable to escape the debilitating depression that continued to compromise his ability to write or to deal with the people he believed were ruining the science fiction genre and perhaps publishing in general. Congdon, who actually never met Miller although he was his agent for nearly fifty years, said that Miller "languished for years, an unhappy, often temperamental man." He attributed Miller's inability to write to a combination of depression and alcohol.

Chad Oliver gave Miller "a six-hour pep talk" telling him that he could not just stop writing. No matter how "screwed up he'd gotten," he simply had to return to writing. Oliver believed that it was never a question of Miller being unable to write. He found Miller to be a technically proficient and fast writer, and one not lacking in confidence. When he wrote, he wrote a lot and the writing was not difficult for him. Oliver said that Miller simply had gotten himself into the frame of mind where he did not want to write (*Sumermorn* 22). Congdon, however, stated that Miller did not write because he could not write. Moreover, he was distressed by this inability and "became quite testy at times."

One of the most revealing comments Miller

made about his lack of productivity was in a letter to John Garvey. Miller told him that he believed his "stifled creativity came from a sudden loss of the power to tell MY OWN [Miller's emphasis] story, a disability which began afflicting me during and just after the Leibowitz years. All fiction is autobiographical. All fictional characters are the author himself, in various roles, accepted or rejected, conscious or otherwise. If I felt too ashamed of my own life to tell my own story, how could I tell any man's story?" (Garvey 1996, 8). Miller once stated, "When I write I must become one with my character, I must merge with him, to suffer his trials, rejoice in his victories" (*Destiny* 1953), but ashamed of his own life, he now could not bring himself to create characters that would suffer *his* trials. Perhaps he best described his own struggle in his review of Thomas S. Klise's *The Last Western*. Miller declares man "vexed by the wound which the separation of opposites has left behind." In order for man to be whole, he "must find the courage to face the unwanted side of his own nature, the side that is shameful and frightening to him, and the courage to finally court this shameful side, and embrace it, and marry it, and become whole again."

In the mid–Sixties after a visit with Chad Oliver and his wife, Miller wrote to his old friend that "seeing you guys almost got me started writing again, as proof-of-prowess I suppose." Then, however, Miller reiterates "Almost." At this point he has an idea for a new science fiction novel "involving black nationalism in the U.S." but concedes that it is "not off the ground yet" (ltr 6/24/1966). Less than three months later he confesses that he had to give up the idea for the book because "Stokely Carmichael took the s-f out of it" (ltr 9/8/1966). His inability to write was evidently not only a source of financial and creative concern but also embarrassment for Miller. At the same time that he was lamenting to Oliver his inability to write, Miller told a reporter for the *Daytona Beach News-Journal* that he occasionally wrote articles for *The Nation* (the only article to appear under his own name in *The Nation* was published in 1962). He also said that he did freelance work, both articles and fiction, using two pen names which he refused to identify. He further stated that he could not discuss his current work "except to mention it" because "talking about it puts a psychological hex on it." He said he was working on "a contemporary novel" as well as a historical novel in his spare time (Summerhill).

Miller was reticent about discussing his life during the extended period of creative inactivity. He admitted to experiencing writer's block after the publication of *Canticle*, telling Rick Wilber that he felt "dried up. I simply walked away." In an interview with Jennifer Greenhill-Taylor, he stated that his inactivity during the sixties and seventies should be left a mystery: "say I've been out in the desert wandering around." He hoped to dismiss the entire question with his "Alibi" which appeared at the front of *Beyond Armageddon*: "You ask where have I been for twenty-five years. / I will tell you. / I live here in the swamp. / I live here to save my hide. / There is a bounty on it." When pressed on this period of his life, Miller flatly stated: "as far as the general public [is] concerned, my nonwriting years are none of [their] damn business" (ltr 4/9/1991).

Miller's inability to sustain any writing project may have exacerbated his depression or more likely been a result of it. In any case, never an ebullient person, Miller began to withdraw more from any active involvement in the publishing world. It became common practice to refer to him as a recluse who shunned friends and family, but that overstates the case. Miller had a prickly personality that often put him at odds with the people around him. He recognized in himself a "tendency to sit on my fanny and yell." Joe Haldeman, an author and friend, believed that Miller's "extreme shyness and nervousness" (78) were a result of his war experiences. Chad Oliver called him an unhappy man, "a guy wrestling with all kinds of demons" (*Sumermorn* 23). "He was very pleasant [but] rather solemn, a taciturn sort of guy." Despite their friendship, Oliver believed Miller never really opened up to many people. "He was the kind of guy that, I think, had time for relatively few people" (*Sumermorn* 25). For his part, Miller was "not at a total loss to understand [Oliver's] characterization of me" but believed that he had "loosened up some" since he and Oliver last met. However, John Garvey, who corresponded with Miller following his published interview with him in 1983, described him as "complicated" and "difficult." Jennifer Greenhill-Taylor who became friendly with Miller for a number of years following her profile of him in the *Jacksonville Times Union* observed, "He was a difficult man to be friends with. He held himself and everyone else to a hard, high standard, that was difficult to live up to, and took a great deal of energy" (E-mail, 19/9/2009). A neighbor in Daytona Beach described him as "a very solitary person, a very difficult person" (Bennett 6C). By the late 1980s, Miller's difficulties, whatever their origin, had caused his estrangement from even those closest to him: all four of his children.

Miller admitted to living in carefully guarded privacy for one or two years, but believed that he was labeled a recluse simply "because I never go to science fiction conventions and do not cheerfully talk to damn fools" (ltr 10/11/1990). However, he did attend conventions when he was actively publishing. He first met Oliver when he wrote asking if they might share a ride to a convention in New Orleans in 1951, and he and Judith Merril met for one of the last times at the World Science Fiction Convention in New York in 1956. His reluctance to attend conventions or to talk with "damn fools" may have involved him trying to avoid explaining what he was doing and his lack of published work.

Unable to sustain work on longer pieces, Miller attempted to write nonfiction and book reviews, although here too, his production was sporadic and widespread, and he indicated a general dislike for reviewing. His essay on Jimmy Hoffa and John and Robert Kennedy appeared in 1962, but it was not until 1974 that Miller published anything else new, a review of Thomas S. Klise's *The Last Western*. The author's note that accompanies the review states that Miller was "currently working on a novel about a guerrilla chief and a goddess who happens to be a horse"—the beginnings of the book that would become *Saint Leibowitz and the Wild Horse Woman*. Four years later Miller sent his agent sixty pages of the novel, but Don Congdon wanted to see more of the book before he would show it to anyone.

Miller continued to struggle. Drinking worsened his inability to sustain periods of writing. He wrote to John Garvey telling him, "I swore off booze again last week (I do it thrice annually)" (1996, 8). Despite his lack of success writing, he remained engaged in other interests. He became an avid photographer and took photographs of the demonstrations at the 1972 Republican National Convention in Miami Beach. He and Anne both enjoyed cooking. He was interested in the peace movement of the early 1970s and later became interested in the anti-nuclear proliferation movement. In the mid–1980s, he met and became friends with David Moodie who had sailed his schooner, the *Fri*, into the nuclear testing area in French Polynesia to disrupt the French testing in 1973. At the time, the *Fri* was berthed in St. Augustine for repairs. Moodie believed that Miller "loved *Fri*" and saw it as "a tangible part of the huge movement for peace and nuclear disarmament" (E-mail, 9/16/2010). *Saint Leibowitz and the Wild Horse Woman* is dedicated to him. Miller once contemplated moving to New Zealand because of its active anti-nuclear politics. He continued to enjoy fishing and being on the water, particularly taking his sailing canoe down to Mosquito Lagoon, part of the Indian River Lagoon in the Canaveral National Seashore.

In 1984 he wrote a review of a new edition of Alexander Bogdanov's utopian novel *Red Star*. Martin H. Greenberg, a prolific anthologist, read the review and thought it "interesting and well written." He wondered if Miller would be interested in working with him on an anthology he had been contemplating concerned with the aftermath of nuclear holocausts as a return to science fiction. Miller enthusiastically accepted his invitation to work together. He wanted the opportunity to make clear his opposition to nuclear proliferation and the Strategic Defense Initiative (SDI) then proposed by the Reagan administration. He believed the SDI was a "Maginot Line in the sky," and that "the bomb can only kill. It protects no one." Sensing Miller's enthusiasm for the project, Greenberg lessened his own involvement in the book and let Miller take the lead. "We were to have shared the interstitial writing, but it became clear when Walt began writing that this would be his book. It was clear that Walt really had something to get off his chest" (Greenhill-Taylor D1).

*Beyond Armageddon: Twenty-One Sermons to the Dead* was published in 1985. Miller's introduction and story notes constituted his most extensive published work since *A Canticle for Leibowitz*. Critics found his contributions to be "provocative and challenging," "refreshingly skeptical, and cheerfully subversive," and "brazen and intelligent."

The renewed attention Miller received for his involvement in the anthology coincided with an unexpected development concerning the novel he had been working on since the early 1970s. At a lunch between Don Congdon and Lou Aronica, then a vice president at Bantam Books, Congdon mentioned that Miller had sent him sixty pages of another novel dealing with material similar to *A Canticle for Leibowitz*. Out of curiosity, Aronica asked to see the pages thinking they might serve as an addendum to the next edition of *A Canticle*. However, Aronica found the work to be "absolutely wonderful" and Congdon encouraged him to write to Miller telling him so. Miller replied to Aronica about a month later with an additional 120 pages, and signed a $300,000 contract for the new book. The book was originally due to Bantam by the end of 1990, but after Aronica received the first 250 pages from Miller, he extended the deadline for delivery indefinitely. Miller continued to work on the book. He told Rick Wilber, "I live in this [book]. I have to. And it feels pretty good on the days when I get something down" (6F). However, he also confessed, "it feels like hell when I don't." He had written almost 600 pages when he informed Congdon that he could not finish it.

Miller was experiencing poor health, and the death of Anne in August of 1995 was a significant blow to him. He wrote to Joe Haldeman that his writer's block had now become literal. "My left carotid artery is wholly blocked, and my right is 65 percent occluded. I'm rational, but not creative, and I'll probably fall down the way Anne did one of these days" (Haldeman 79). Anne died at their home in the early morning of August 7th. Miller discovered her body lying on the floor. She had recently had surgery for cancer, but Miller said that her death was not related to her illness or surgery. He mailed a brief announcement of her passing to "Dear Friend, Acquaintance, or Enemy," to "everyone she would want to know, for whatever reason **she** [Miller's emphasis] would want you to know it." He asked for no condolences or offerings of any kind. His final movement from the teachings of the Catholic Church of the West to the philosophies and beliefs of the East was apparent when he wrote, "She hasn't gone anywhere. She 'is that which you see before you; begin to reason about it and you at once fall into error.' (Huang Po)." Skip Garrison, Miller's neighbor and friend, said that Miller was not despondent about Anne's death, believing she was still with him and helping him daily. Despite what Miller may have believed philosophically about Anne's continued presence with and within him, the loss of the one person he shared more than fifty years with and who possessed the greatest insight and understanding of who he was had to be a devastating loss that left him with a pervading sense of loneliness.

Concerned about his own inability to finish the novel, Miller suggested to his agent that he find another writer who would be willing to complete the book, telling him that trying to finish it was like "trying to spit through a screen" (Bisson). Terry Bisson, a science fiction author, was recommended to Congdon as someone who might be able to do the work. When Congdon suggested Bisson, Miller, who had assured his agent that "any idiot with a sense of humor can finish this book," said he had never heard of him but he seemed okay (Bisson). When Bisson read what Miller had written, he found it to be "a seamless, exotic and incredibly rich masterpiece." One of the benefits Bisson hoped to derive from the assignment was actually meeting Miller, but before the final contract was signed, Congdon called to inform him that Miller had committed suicide.

On the morning of January 9, 1996, after writing his will, letters to each of his children, a letter to his granddaughter whom he named executor of his estate, and to the authorities explaining what he had done, Miller folded them into his coat pocket. He called 911 to report that a dead man was on his front lawn. He then sat in a lawn chair in his front yard and killed himself with a single gunshot to his head. He used a .40 caliber bullet especially designed to disintegrate upon impact. He had placed another bullet in his jacket pocket so the authorities would know what he used.

In a letter to John Garvey, Miller once wrote, "I also opine that the natural law legitimates *Seppuku*," the ritual suicide once practiced by the Japanese samurai (1996, 8). It was not an isolated reference to suicide in Miller's letters to his friend. Garrison told the *Daytona Beach News-Journal* that in committing suicide Miller "didn't think he was taking a life. He was taking the warrior's path, refusing to be taken hostage" (Bennett 6C). Death, Miller stated, did not matter, it was simply "a release from the illusion of personhood" (Haldeman 79). But John Gaston, the chief investigator of the Volusia County medical examiner, said that Miller simply did not wish to live alone any longer (Ditzler 1C).

Miller's death was not widely noted in the media. His family wanted it and the nature of his passing kept as quiet as possible. It was not until a month or so later that brief notices appeared in the local newspaper and in some science fiction publications.

A contract to finish *Saint Leibowitz and the Wild Horse Woman* was finalized between Bisson, Bantam, and Miller's estate following his death. Bisson completed the book's last 100 pages relying on letters Miller wrote to Congdon about his intentions, notes he left for intended scenes, and some actual scenes and pieces of dialogue. Bisson's intent was to be sure the work remained Miller's book and not a collaboration between the two of them. The book appeared in 1997 to relatively little commercial or popular notice.

Miller was cremated and his ashes, like those of his wife, were scattered in Mosquito Lagoon.

**Miller, Walter Michael, Sr.** the father of Walter M. Miller, Jr. born in Kentucky c. 1898. He was a first generation American born son of Swiss immigrants. He worked for the Florida East Coast Railway in, according to his son, "an extremely competitive corporate environment." Miller said his father was only interested in power. "He wanted it badly and never had any, except over his wife and son. He was not at all cruel, but he was manipulative and dominating" (Garvey 1983, 36).

**Miller, Walter Michael, III** (September 11, 1947–May 5, 1996) the second child and only son born to Miller and his wife.

**Minnie** Jerry Harrison's horse in the short story "Secret of the Death Dome."

**Mirfak** also known as Alpha Persii, it is the brightest star in the constellation Perseus, known as The Thief among the Nomads in *Saint Leibowitz and the Wild Horse Woman*.

**Miriam** the older sister of Moses and Aaron. Mary is a form of her name given to many Jewish girls as a tribute to the high esteem in which she was held. In *Saint Leibowitz and the Wild Horse Woman,* Cardinal Leibowitz refers to the Virgin Mary when he calls on "Miriam, mother of Jesus" to pray for him during his ordeal at the meldown.

**Miserere mei, Deus...** Latin: "Have mercy on me, God...." The opening words of Psalm 50 (DB), the fourth of the seven penitential psalms (the others being Psalms 6, 31, 37, 101, 129, and 142), and considered to be the primary psalm of penitence. It is one of the texts Brother Francis copies in *A Canticle for Leibowitz* ("Fiat Homo") and the beauty of the copy he is using — the striking difference between the humble text of the psalm and the magnificence of the style in which it is presented — gives him the idea for his illuminated copy of the Leibowitz blueprint. The psalm's fifth line: "For I know my iniquity, and my sin is always before me," is quoted in the novel.

**Miserere nobis** Latin: "Have mercy on us." The words are part of the Litany of the Saints at the canonization of Leibowitz in *A Canticle for Leibowitz* ("Fiat Homo").

**Misery River** the river formerly known as the Missouri River in *Saint Leibowitz and the Wild Horse Woman*.

**Missal** in the Catholic Church the book of prayers and responses necessary for celebrating the Mass during the year. The term appears in *A Canticle for Leibowitz* ("Fiat Homo").

**Missionman** also referred to as the stranger in the short story "The Triflin' Man" (also appears as "You Triflin' Skunk"). The Missionman is an alien spy gathering information on the human race prior to an invasion of Earth; his means of doing so is by fathering a number of genetic analogs with human women. One of these offspring is Doodie, the son born to Lucey. She shoots and kills the alien when it returns to claim Doodie.

**Mississippi Republic** one of the major civilized states in the novella "And the Light Is Risen" and *A Canticle for Leibowitz* ("Fiat Lux").

**Misspee River** also known as The Great River, it lies to the east of New Rome in *Saint Leibowitz and the Wild Horse Woman*. It is described as "a plain of water," "impossibly wide." It is apparently the Mississippi River.

**Mr. Godmaker** the nickname facetiously given to Scott MacDonney by Andrei Porshkin in the novella "Izzard and the Membrane" as he designs and builds Izzard, the super computer.

***Mit Brennender Sorge*** German: "With deep anxiety." A papal encyclical issued by Pius XI in German in March 1937 condemning anti–Semitism and the status of the Catholic Church in Nazi Germany, among other things. Dom Zerchi quotes from it in *A Canticle for Leibowitz* ("Fiat Voluntas Tua"): "Whoever exalts a race or a State of a particular form of State or the depositories of power ... whoever raises these notions above their standard value and divinizes them to an idolatrous level, distorts and perverts an order of the world planned and created by God...." See also **Pius XI**

**"Mobility of Electrical Essences"** a work by Don Thaddeo/Thon Taddeo mentioned in the novella "And the Light Is Risen" and *A Canticle for Leibowitz* ("Fiat Lux"). It and Taddeo's Conservation Theorem provide the theoretical bases for the electrical generator Brother Kornhoer builds at the abbey.

**Monastery of the Nuns of Our Lady of San Pancho Villa of Cockroach Mountain** located on the south bank of the Brave River in *Saint Leibowitz and the Wild Horse Woman*, it is the small convent of Mother Iridia Silentia and the place of Sister Clare's exile. See also **Villa, Francisco (Pancho)**

**Monsignor di Simone** a suave and diplomatic Church elder who arrives at the Brothers of Leibowitz Abbey from New Vatican in the short story "A Canticle for Leibowitz." He and several clerks come to investigate whatever evidence the abbey can produce as part of the canonization proceedings for Leibowitz. He interviews Brother Francis about his alleged meeting with Leibowitz in the desert during his Lenten fast. He asks to see the illuminated manuscript copy of the Leibowitz blueprint Brother Francis had been working on. Overcome by its beauty, he tells the monk to finish it.

**Monsignor Flaught** the Promoter of the Faith, or *Advocatus Diaboli*, in the canonization process of the Blessed Leibowitz in *A Canticle for Leibowitz* ("Fiat Homo"). His reception at the Leibowitz abbey is markedly different from that offered to Malfreddo Aguerra, the postulator in the Leibowitz canonization case. He is given an iron cot in a cell facing south. Flaught cross-examines Brother Francis regarding his meeting with the pilgrim and his subsequent discovery of the relics. He is frustrated by the monk's lack of disingenuousness. He asks to see Brother Francis's illuminated copy of the Leibowitz blueprint before he leaves the abbey and is quietly moved by its beauty.

There may be some significance for the name Flaught. The word is derived from the Scottish and means to flutter or cause commotion or confusion. As *Advocatus Diabolic*, Flaught is expected to create uncertainty in the case for canonization. Miller may also have been interested in the similarity to *flout*, meaning to treat with disdain or to express contempt for. Flaught has only suspicion and scorn for the stories associated with the Leibowitz miracles. David N. Samuelson states that the name suggests flaying or flogging.

**Monsignor Longi**  an unseen character in the novella "And the Light Is Risen" and *A Canticle for Leibowitz* ("Fiat Lux"). He occupied the royal suite in the abbey prior to the Poet-sirrah. The Poet believes he is the probable source of the room's bedbugs.

**Monsignor Sanual**  a representative from the Church of Texark among the Nomads at the sacred meeting place for the Weejus and Bear Spirit shamans in *Saint Leibowitz and the Wild Horse Woman*. He is also an observer and spokesperson for Archbishop Benefez. He comes into conflict with Cardinal Brownpony about Father Ombroz's activities among the Nomads.

**Monte Cassino Monastery**  (also spelt Montecassino) a monastery founded by Saint Benedict c. A.D. 529 within the ruins of the wall-enclosed ancient Roman town of Casinum atop a small mountain southeast of Rome. The abbey became the center of the Benedictine Order and gained renown not only as one of the most sacred Christian sites but also as a repository of art and culture. It was famed as a center of learning and for the manuscript production and illumination of its scriptorium.

The abbey experienced a cycle of destruction and rebuilding through its history. It was destroyed by the Lombards in 580, the Saracens in 883, and an earthquake in 1349. Napoleon's troops sacked it in 1799. Each time the monastery was rebuilt and often expanded and enriched. It was made a national monument in 1866.

During World War II, the hill of Monte Cassino was part of the German line defending Rome. The Allies presumed the Germans were using the abbey as an artillery observation post. Although the Germans occupied positions on the hill and in the town of Cassino, they did not have a garrison in the abbey. After heavy infantry assaults on the hill, a controversial aerial bombardment of the Monte Cassino Monastery took place on February 15–16, 1944. More than 1,000 tons of high explosives and incendiary bombs were dropped on the abbey reducing it to ruins. The causalities were mostly women and children from the town who had taken refuge in the abbey.

The monastery was rebuilt by the Italian government after the war and re-consecrated by Pope Paul VI on October 24, 1964.

As a crew member of a B-25 bomber, Miller participated in the bombing raid on Monte Cassino. He felt no compunction at the time of the bombing. His only fear was that part of his squadron's bomb-pattern may have hit Allied troops. Later, however, as he worked on *A Canticle for Leibowitz*, Miller began to see a relationship between his war experiences, specifically the raid on Monte Cassino, and his writing of the novel. He told Jennifer Greenhill-Taylor: "It never occurred to me that *Canticle* was my own personal response to the war until I was writing the first version of the scene where Zerchi lies half buried in the rubble. Then a lightbulb came on over my head: "Good God, is this the abbey at Monte Cassino? This rubble looks like south Italy, not [the] Southwest desert. What have I been writing? (D5)

Chad Oliver, Miller's friend from the 1950s and fellow science fiction writer, believed that "seeing those bombs hit that monastery just tore [Miller] apart, and it's something he could never get out of his head. And that's the whole genesis of [the book] right there. *Canticle* was a kind of catharsis for Walt" (*Summermorn* 23).

The dust jacket of the first edition of *A Canticle for Leibowitz* states that "It was his participation in this raid that led him, a decade and a half later, to write [the novel], the story of another abbey with a somewhat parallel history." Almost fifty years after the bombing, Miller continued to have mixed feelings: "it was probably the militarily necessary thing to do ... it may or may not have been a blunder. I don't know" (ltr 2/21/1991).

The Monte Cassino monastery experienced the cyclical theory of history that Miller made central to his novel. The medieval monks of Monte Cassino were instrumental in the copying and preservation of texts that would otherwise have been lost, providing a model for their later fictional brothers of the Albertian Order of Leibowitz.

**"Month of Mary"**  short story published in *Extension*, 44 (May 1950), 17, 42. A young priest,

Rudolph Mannish, is assigned to a leper settlement in Saõ Therese, Brazil. His fear of the disease, however, makes him loath the very people he is supposed to minister to. He hates himself for his inability not to fear them. Because his fear separates him from the people, he questions his worthiness to be a priest. Mannish's superior recommends his reassignment back to the United States, but while saying Mass on his last day, the young priest discovers leprous white patches on his own skin. His prayers to conquer his fear are answered as his "withered heart begins to swell with love for these, my brothers, foul sores and all."

**Moodie, David** (September 4, 1945–) American born owner and captain of the schooner *Fri*, which played a major role in the protest of French nuclear testing in French Polynesia in 1973. Moodie sailed the *Fri* into the nuclear test zone near Majuro atoll to disrupt the planned nuclear tests. Miller became friends with Moodie during the mid–1980s. He dedicated *Saint Leibowitz and the Wild Horse Woman* to him and the anti-nuclear cause: "To David, and all those who sailed against the Apocalypse."

**Mooo** the brothers' name for Father Prior Singing Cow in *Saint Leibowitz and the Wild Horse Woman*.

**Moore, Joseph Ward** (August 10, 1903–January 28, 1978) an American writer best known for his novel *Bring the Jubilee* (1953) in which the South wins the American Civil War, and the short stories "Lot" and "Lot's Daughter." "Lot" is included in *Beyond Armageddon*.

**Moore, Ward** *see* **Moore, Joseph Ward**

**Mori Vult** Latin: "He [she] wants to die." A writ of *Mori Vult* is given by a magistrate for those victims who are properly identified as hopeless cases of radiation poisoning in *A Canticle for Leibowitz* ("Fiat Voluntas Tua"). The writ allows them to be legally euthanized if they so desire. They are issued a red ticket or crit-dose form.

**Mortoin, Viche** an unseen colleague of Thon Taddeo in *A Canticle for Leibowitz* ("Fiat Lux") and the novella "And the Light Is Risen." When Taddeo addresses the monks at the abbey about the work that is currently being done by members of the collegium, he mentions Mortoin's investigation into the possibility for the artificial production of ice. He is referred to as a Don in the novella rather than thon.

**Moses** one of the great figures of the Old Testament. He was a leader, lawgiver, prophet, and deliverer of the Jewish people out of Egyptian slavery and into freedom under a covenant with God. The first five books of the Old Testament were originally attributed to his authorship. In *A Canticle for Leibowitz* ("Fiat Homo"), he is cited as an example of how a new cultural inheritance can be created over just a couple of generations.

**Moswell** a minor character in the short story "The Little Creeps." A member of the senior staff considering General Jim Yaney's bombing proposal, he votes in favor of it.

**Motar** a dying, old woman in the short story "Gravesong." She wants her body buried on Earth. She believes there is only one Earth — made for man, and man made it Earth. Emilesh promises to return her to Earth and carries her ashes from Sorcerer VI to be scattered on her home world.

**Mother** in the novella, "The Song of Vorhu" the name refers to the gray-green world-creature that dominates the planet. Grown too large to leave, it tries to enter into an agreement with Barry Wilkes. It will allow the race of man to populate the planet, if Wilkes agrees to carry mother's seed to other worlds. When he refuses, mother tries to kill him. Instead, in all probability, Wilkes succeeds in destroying her.

**Mother Bernarde** the Mother Superior of the convent where Giselle, a character in the novella "The Lineman," was raised. She would not allow Giselle to take her vows because she believed the girl did not have a true calling.

**Mother Gaia** Gaia, or Gaea, is the goddess of the Earth in Greek myth and therefore the personification of the Earth or Mother Earth. Brother Joshua uses the term in *A Canticle for Leibowitz* ("Fiat Voluntas Tua").

**Motu proprio** Latin: "On one's own accord." The opening words of a papal document issued at the pope's own volition. It is signed by the pope but lacks the usual formalities and seal, thus it is by the pope's own doing. A *motu proprio* is used for administrative purposes, for instruction, or to grant a particular favor.

1. In *A Canticle for Leibowitz* ("Fiat Voluntas Tua"), Pope Celestine the Eighth issued a *Motu proprio* in 3735 initiating the Church's interest in planning for a space colony to perpetuate the Church in the case of a holocaust on Earth.

2. Pope Amen I issues a *Motu proprio* "deploring a drift in the Church away from proper liturgical reverence" toward the Virgin Mary in *Saint Leibowitz and the Wild Horse Woman*.

**Mounts-Everybody** the leader of a small group of unaffiliated Nomads in *Saint Leibowitz and the Wild Horse Woman*. Three of his men attack Cardinal Brownpony and steal two horses. Brownpony's men capture two of the thieves but one escapes. Brownpony proposes that the two men join the Grasshoppers in a war against Hannegan. On the evening prior to a military conference between Brownpony and the leaders of the three hordes, Mounts-Everybody and Brownpony discuss the possibility of raising a small mercenary army.

**Moussorgsky, Modest Petrovich** (March 21, 1839–March 28, 1881) Russian composer noted for his often wild but imaginative music based on distinctive Russian sources. Among his best-known works are the opera *Boris Godunov* and the orchestral piece *St. John's Night on the Bare Mountain*. In the novella "The Darfsteller," Thornier hears strains of Moussorgsky playing in the theater: "music for empire," at once "brutal and majestic."

**Move not, O Sun, toward Gabaon, nor thou, O Moon, toward the valley — Back up, O Sun, et tu, Luna, recedite in orbitas reversas...** Latin: "and you, Moon, move in reverse in your orbit...." In *A Canticle for Leibowitz* ("Fiat Voluntas Tua"), Brother Joshua says that "the namesake of my namesake" made this statement. He is referring to Joshua, an assistant to and successor of Moses (see Joshua 10:12 KJV). In the Book of Joshua, as he leads the Hebrews in battle in the valley of Gibeon, Joshua asks that the sun and moon stand still to provide the needed time for victory: "And the sun stood still, and the moon stayed, until the people had avenged themselves upon their enemies" (10:13 KJV). Brother Joshua is spinning a globe backwards after hearing that Lucifer has Fallen, wishing that time could be reversed.

**Mrs. Grales** a devout two-headed woman who sells tomatoes in the novella "The Last Canticle" and the "Fiat Voluntas Tua" section of *A Canticle for Leibowitz*. Her second head, named Rachel, is a small, seemingly superfluous appendage that does not open its eyes until it comes alive at the end of the story. It remains cherubic with the features of a young girl, although Mrs. Grales's head has aged. Mrs. Grales has refused to have the second head removed and desires that it be baptized. As Father Zerchi hears Mrs. Grales's confession the abbey collapses in the aftermath of a nuclear explosion. The head of Mrs. Grales seemingly dies as the Rachael head comes to life following the explosion.

Her name is strongly associated with the Holy Grail, the chalice Jesus used at the Last Supper. It is believed that Joseph of Arimathea used the cup to collect the last drops of blood from Jesus while he was on the cross. Angels purportedly made the Grail from an emerald that fell from the forehead of Lucifer when he was tossed into the abyss. Christ's blood redeems the sin of Lucifer through the Grail. It is the chalice of salvation as Mrs. Grales is the vessel for the salvation offered by Rachel's "Immaculate Innocence." See also **Rachel**

**Mulvern** a major and the senior officer among the Marsville guards outside of the androon cave in the novella "The Reluctant Traitor." Taken prisoner by Rolf Kenlan and his bat-hunters, Rolf imitates his voice in his radio communications. Once Rolf returns to Marsville to meet with Commissioner Rathwich and fighting breaks out at the cave site, Mulvern takes command of the guards. He orders the men away from the cave. He, his men, and some androons go to the cemetery to exhume the body of Saralesara so it can be returned to the tribe for proper burial.

**Mumbly-peg** (also mumble-peg, mumblety peg, or mumbletypeg). A traditional boys' game involving the skillful tossing of a pocketknife. While there are variants of the game, two versions are the most common. Two opponents face each other with their feet spread apart. Each tries to toss his knife into the ground as close to one of his feet as possible without actually hitting his foot. The other version involves a series of progressively more intricate knife tosses, the point of which is to get the knife blade to stick in the ground. The winner pounds a short wooden peg into the ground using his knife handle. The loser is supposed to pull the peg out of the ground with his teeth. In the novella "And the Light Is Risen" and *A Canticle for Leibowitz* ("Fiat Lux"), Benjamin and the Poet-sirrah play mumbly-peg together.

**"My Life in the Jungle"** a story by Jim Aikin originally published in 1985 that concludes the *Beyond Armageddon* anthology.

**"My people, what have I done to thee?"** a verse repeated after each Reproach in the Good Friday services of the Catholic Church. It is used in *A Canticle for Leibowitz* ("Fiat Homo"). See also **The Reproaches**

**Mysticum Christi Corpus** Latin: "The Mystic Body of Christ." Within Catholic dogma, the idea that the Church represents the body of Christ. Pope Leo XXI uses the term when he talks with Brother Francis after the canonization of Isaac Leibowitz in *A Canticle for Leibowitz* ("Fiat Homo"). His point is that as the Church is the body, the monks of the Leibowitz abbey have served as the memory, preserving the written word.

**Nam docebimur a Spiritu sancto**  Latin: "For we will be taught by the holy Spirit."

These are among the words spoken by one of the cantors during the canonization ceremony for Isaac Leibowitz in *A Canticle for Leibowitz* ("Fiat Homo").

**Nancy**  an unseen character in the novella "The Last Canticle" and *A Canticle for Leibowitz* ("Fiat Voluntas Tua"). She is the former wife of Brother Joshua. After she became ill and died, Joshua joined the Benedictines before entering the Albertian Order.

**Nantani**  a mountain people in the short story "The Soul-Empty Ones." They are part of the androids or Soul-Empties made by man before he abandoned Earth because of nuclear fallout. They are a warrior-like people with different traditions than the valley people from near the sea. Daner and his wife, Ea-Daner, are Nantani.

**Nanti, Manue**  a young Peruvian man who has signed a five-year contract to work on Mars in the short story "Crucifixus Etiam." He is big and heavy-boned, well suited for the manual labor he performs. He dreams of earning enough money to retire after five years and return to Earth to travel to remote places. A participant in the beginnings of a project that will build a breathable atmosphere on Mars over 800 years, he begins to feel hopeless and trapped. He worries that he will lose the use of his lungs because of his reliance on a mechanical oxygenator. As his lungs wither, he begins to question what his purpose is and what benefit he derives from the work he performs. The project's supervisor provides Nanti with the key when he tells him, "some sow, others reap." He asks Nanti which he would rather be. Nanti thinks about this question and begins to experience pride in what he is a part of: a passion of human faith in the destiny of man. He commits himself to a life on Mars.

**Nari**  a young, freckled eight-year old girl in the story "The Big Hunger." She asks her grandfather to explain to her why men feel star-craze, the need to explore space and travel to the stars.

**Na'Riga**  an unseen priestess of the Sacred Order of Menbana in the novella "The Reluctant Traitor." Krasala studied the acolyte initiation service under her.

**Nature imposes nothing that Nature hasn't prepared you to bear**  Dom Zerchi makes this admonition to a young mother suffering from radiation poisoning in *A Canticle for Leibowitz* ("Fiat Voluntas Tua"). The idea he refers to is from Book V of *Meditations* by the Roman emperor Marcus Aurelius [Antoninus]: "Nothing happens to any man which he is not formed by nature to bear." The stoic Zerchi refers to when speaking with the mother is Marcus Aurelius. Stoicism advocates a life of virtue, action in accordance to the rational way of the universe, and endurance in the face of inescapable consequences.

**Nauwhat, Sorley**  a Cardinal from Oregon in *Saint Leibowitz and the Wild Horse Woman*. He assumes the position of Secretary of the Secretariat for Extraordinary Ecclesiastical Concerns after Cardinal Brownpony's appointment as Vicar Apostolic to the Three Hordes. Nauwhat is suspected of betraying Brownpony because of Filpeo Harq's promise to him of the papacy after the war. Following the death of Pope Amen II, he does become Pope Sorley through the influence of Filpeo. He invalidates all of Amen II's nullifications. He calls Brother Blacktooth for an audience and asks to hear of his adventures. The pope explains to Blacktooth the present situation on the Plains and provides him with a small bag of gold coins as traveling money.

**Navel of the Earth [or World]** *see* **Meldown**

**Nayol**  one of the nature gods of the Red River people in the novella "And the Light Is Risen" and *A Canticle for Leibowitz* ("Fiat Lux"). Thon Taddeo has a favorite saying: "Nayol is without speech, and therefore never lies."

**Ndriga**  the consort of the god Vorhu in the legends of the people in the novella "The Song of Vorhu." According to lore, she fell from the arms of Vorhu in heaven and flowers bloomed from her body and spread across the planet. The legend is associated with the actions of Barry Wilkes who brought the White Idiot to the still developing planet as she was dying from a vegetable-entity parasite. When she died, the parasite's spores blossomed from her body creating the foundation for life on the planet.

**Nebuchadnezzar** (ca. 605 B.C.–562 B.C.) also known as Nebuchadnezzar II and Nebuchadnezzar the Great. As the king of Babylon who conquered Judah and Jerusalem (586 B.C.) and instigated the Babylonian exile of the Jews, he is seen within the western Judeo-Christian tradition as a "destroyer of nations" (Jeremiah 4:7 KJV). In the novella "And the Light Is Risen" and *A Canticle for Leibowitz* ("Fiat Lux"), Benjamin names him among those he hopes Don Thaddeo (Thon Taddeo) will not join.

**Negotium perambulans in tenebris** Latin: "The business that walketh in the dark." From Psalm 90, verse 6 (DB). In *A Canticle for Leibowitz* ("Fiat Voluntas Tua"), these words come to Brother Joshua's mind as he considers whether to lead the Church into space and if the slithering in the bushes he hears could be an omen or portent. The psalm states that he who has faith in God need not fear the terrors that will confront him because God will shield him.

**Nephew of the Empty Sky** an ancient self-referential Nomad name in *Saint Leibowitz and the Wild Horse Woman*. It is derived from the Nomad deity Empty Sky.

**Neutroid** humanoid chimpanzee mutants used as child substitutes in the novella "Conditionally Human." Neutroids are created by manipulating the gene map of chimpanzee ovum. They appear completely human except for their short fur covered beaver-like tails and "erect thatch of scalp hair." They are sexually neuter and their ages are predetermined. The available ages are between one and ten. Once it reaches the determined age, the neutroid remains at that age until it dies.

**New Babel** the name Benjamin uses to refer to New Jerusalem in *Saint Leibowitz and the Wild Horse Woman*. See also **Babel**

**New Jerusalem** a genny community located in the Suckamint Mountains in *Saint Leibowitz and the Wild Horse Woman*. It is the largest community of people suffering genetic defects outside of the Valley of the Misborn. The genny population there is approximately ninety per cent spooks, those able to pass as having no genetic defects. Those with visible defects populate Scarecrow Alley on the perimeter of New Jerusalem and serve as a buffer with the outside world. The gennies work an old silver mine in the area and bring the silver to Valana to exchange for currency. Cardinal Brownpony sells guns to New Jerusalem through the secret wing of the Secretariat for Extraordinary Ecclesiastical Concerns. See also **Jerusalem**

**New Rome** the official seat of the Catholic Church in the novella "And the Light Is Risen," *A Canticle for Leibowitz*, and *Saint Leibowitz and the Wild Horse Woman*. It is located in the area of what once was the city of St. Louis, Missouri. In *Saint Leibowitz and the Wild Horse Woman*, the pope abandons New Rome and finds asylum in Valana after Hannegan II occupies the lands adjacent to New Rome. Hannegan establishes his own rival pope in New Rome causing a schism in the Church. See also **New Vatican**

**New Vatican** the official seat of the Catholic Church located within the former United States in the short story "A Canticle for Leibowitz." See also **New Rome**

**Nichols** an unseen character in the short story "The Hoofer." He is a member of Hogey Parker's former crew or gang in space.

**Night Hag** the Nunshån of Nomad myth in *Saint Leibowitz and the Wild Horse Woman*. See also **Nunshån**

**Nikolai Andreyevich** the baby son of Marya Dmitriyevna Lisitsa in the short story "Vengeance for Nikolai." A bomb fragment kills him during an Ami bombardment in Russia. He is also referred to as Nikki.

**Nimmy** the name given to Brother Blacktooth by Holy (Little Bear) Madness in *Saint Leibowitz and the Wild Horse Woman*. It approximates the word *kid* in Nomadic, meaning one who has not endured the rites of passage into manhood.

**Nine, Johnny** *see* **Sree, Johnny**

**Nisi baptizata es et nisi babtizari nonquis, te babtizo...** Latin: "If you have not been baptized and if you are not unwilling to be baptized, I baptize...." Dom Zerchi's qualified attempt to baptize Rachel at the conclusion of *A Canticle for Leibowitz*. She turns her head away from him before he can finish. Zerchi realizes that because of her primal innocence she does not need baptism.

**"No Moon for Me"** a short story published in *Astounding Science-Fiction Magazine*, 50 (September 1952), 56–70. Colonel Denin, Major Long, and Dr. Gedrin are the crew for the first manned space flight to the moon. There has been controversy concerning the economic and strategic efficacy of manned missions, but this mission is in response to "the Voice," ultra-high frequency bands that have been originating from the moon for years. The crew will negotiate with whoever is responsible for the Voice, but in the event of failed peaceful attempts to remove the perceived invader from Earth's moon, the crew is to detonate a nuclear warhead and sacrifice themselves.

Colonel Denin has been a long-time proponent of manned space flight. He helped build and launch unmanned rockets during a war on Earth. Major Long questions the purpose of the mission if it is simply to destroy the Voice; he, too, wants a commitment to a manned station on the moon. Long, however, is leery of Denin. He is uneasy about the colonel's overconfidence concerning the mission. Just before blastoff, the cowardly Dr. Gedrin tries to escape from the rocket and must be physically restrained by Denin.

As the ship approaches the moon, Long questions Denin about what he knows and why he is so confident and smug. Denin reveals that he knows exactly the source of the Voice. He pulls a gun and explains that he has sent an unmanned rocket with a transmitter to the moon with the intention of tricking humanity into space. His plan is to blow their ship up on the moon, making the crew martyrs in the building of a lunar station and the opening of space.

Long maneuvers the ship into a series of violent rolls to throw Denin off balance. In the confusion, Long disarms Denin and secures him. Now in complete control of the ship, Long lands on the moon to turn off the transmitter and retrieve it. In a short while, however, he returns to the ship and frees Denin, telling him to join him on the surface of the moon. Long has found tracks in the moon dust around Denin's rocket and evidence of an alien mining operation on the moon.

**Nobis quoque peccatoribus**   Latin: "To us sinners also." The beginning of the Canon (or Eucharistic Prayer) in the Latin Tridentine Mass. It is used in the short story "Please Me Plus Three."

**Noli molestare**   Latin: "Do not molest [disturb]." Pope Leo XXI gives Brother Francis a document threatening to excommunicate anyone who interferes with his safe passage back to the Leibowitz abbey from New Rome in *A Canticle for Leibowitz* ("Fiat Homo"). As Brother Francis correctly observes to himself, however, any thief he encounters will be unable to read the warning or understand the significance it holds.

**Nolo contendere**   Latin: "I do not wish to contend [contest]." A legal term used when a defendant accepts a conviction of guilt while maintaining his innocence. In *Saint Leibowitz and the Wild Horse Woman*, Filpeo Harq forces Cardinal Brownpony and Brother Blacktooth to enter a plea of *nolo contendere* regarding the charge of attempted regicide against them.

**Nomas et civis**   Latin: "Nomad or citizen." One of the basic conflicts in *Saint Leibowitz and the Wild Horse Woman* and "a story old as Genesis." It refers to the opposition between the Nomads of the Plains and Hannegan's empire.

**Non accepto**   Latin: "I do not accept" or "I am not fit to receive" Used in *Saint Leibowitz and the Wild Horse Woman* regarding a candidate's reluctance to be elected pope or, in the case of Brother Blacktooth, his refusal to be elected Abbot of the Abbey of Saint Leibowitz.

**Non cogitamus, ergo nihil sumus**   Latin: "We do not think, therefore we are nothing." The conclusion reached between the "Poet" and the "Thon," two characters in a satirical dialogue in verse concerning the existence of God that Dom Zerchi reads in *A Canticle for Leibowitz* ("Fiat Voluntas Tua"). The book may be the work of the Poet-sirrah. The saying is a comic variation of René Descarte's rationalistic principle, "Cogito, ergo sum" ["I think, therefore I am."] in his *Discourse on Method, IV.*

**Non habemus regem nisi caesarem**   Latin: "We have no king but Caesar." In John 19:15 (KJV) when Pilate asks if he should crucify Jesus, their king, the chief priests make this their reply. In *A Canticle for Leibowitz* ("Fiat Voluntas Tua"), Dom Zerchi says that Caesar is always divinized whenever he acquires the means to destroy the world. He does so with the consent of the people.

**Non papabilis**   Latin: "Not capable of becoming pope." Used in *Saint Leibowitz and the Wild Horse Woman*, specifically concerning Cardinal Benefez.

**None**   the ninth hour of the Divine Office, between noon and 3 p. m. It may be sung with Sext (the sixth hour) after Mass or after dinner. A reference is made to "singing None" in *A Canticle for Leibowitz* ("Fiat Lux").

**Nora**   the daughter of Old Donegal in the short story "Death of a Spaceman" (later entitled "Memento Homo"). She is the widowed mother of one son, Ken. Her husband, Oley, was a spacer, like her father, and died in space. Donegal believes Nora has spoiled her son because he does not wish to go into space. She is resentful of the wealthy next-door neighbors, the Keiths, who she believes have become rich on the backs of people like her father, a "common laboring spacer."

**Norris, Anne**   the wife of Terry Norris, the District Inspector for the F. B. A., in the novella "Conditionally Human." Recently married, she is upset to learn that Terry's job occasionally requires him to euthanize animals. She feeds the neutroids and other animals in Terry's kennels, developing an emotional attachment with them. She wants to have a baby with Terry despite the fact that as a genetic-C couple they are not legally allowed to have children. When Terry discovers Peony, the deviant neutroid, and brings her home, Anne is opposed to him turning her in. She threatens to leave him if he does so. Anne shows Terry the ad for job opportunities at Anthropos Incorporated and encourages him to consider them. She is complicit in the murder of Chief Franklin.

**Norris, Terrell (Terry)**   a District Inspector for the F.B.A. in the novella "Conditionally Human." He is genetic-C, not allowed to have children. As an inspector, Norris has the responsibility of working with the mutated animals used as child substitutes by those couples not allowed to have children. Since unclaimed animals are euthanized on occasion, Norris tries to avoid any emotional attachment with them. His own suppressed sense of guilt and his wife's open condemnation of his work cause Terry to make a choice between sacrificing Peony, a deviant neutroid, and killing Chief Franklin, his supervisor. Terry decides to save Peony and forge a heredity certificate, claiming her as his own child. After killing Franklin, Terry hopes to move to Atlanta to take a job with Anthropos Incorporated. At Anthropos, he wants to continue the work Delmont started of making deviant neutroids. He plans to create a husband for Peony and hopes that they will be the start of a new and better species to care for Earth.

**Nosey**   a bartender in the novella "The Yokel."

**Novotny, Joe**   the team-pusher or crew boss of the B-shift in the novella "The Lineman." He is a small but well-built man. Although he is a tough, physical disciplinarian, he is a fair supervisor who looks after his men. He advises Parkeson to allow the workers to take advantage of the traveling bordello, and he makes sure his crew has the opportunity to visit the ship. He counsels Relke concerning his "Dear John" letter from his former wife and his involvement with the Party. Joe and Henderson savagely beat Larkin and Kunz, the two Party members who beat Relke and threatened him.

**Nu Lupi**   a globular star cluster in the short story "The Big Hunger."

**Nu Phoenicis IV**   a planet where a feudal system composed of three classes lasted for more than 5,000 years in the short story "Bitter Victory." The classes were the Klidds or barons, the Algun or serfs, and the Taknon or artisans. After the rise of technology on Nu Phoenicis IV, the Klidds were overthrown and exiled to an ironless planet.

**The Nun**   the crew's nickname for planet $G_0GC$-2794-II in the novella "Six and Ten Are Johnny." It is so named because of its chaste and mysterious veil of clouds.

**Nunc dimittis**   Latin: "Now dismiss." The Canticle of Simeon taken from Luke 2:29–32 (KJV). In the Catholic Church, it is recited or sung at the Compline service. Father Jerome thinks of it in the novella "And the Light Is Risen." The scene is repeated in *A Canticle for Leibowitz* ("Fiat Lux") with Dom Paulo. Brother Joshua mentions it in the novella "The Last Canticle." The alternate title of Nunc Dimittis is taken from the first two words of the first line.

**Nunc dimittis servum tuum, Domine ... Quia viderunt oculi mei salutare**   Latin: "Now dismiss thy servant, O Lord.... My eyes have seen thy salvation." These lines from the Canticle of Simeon, or Nunc Dimittis (Luke 2:29–32 KJV), are thought by Father Jerome in the novella "And the Light Is Risen" and Dom Paulo in *A Canticle for Leibowitz* ("Fiat Lux"). In the novella, the line begins "Nunc dimittis, Domine, sorvum tuum."

**Nunshån**   the Night Hag of Nomad myth in *Saint Leibowitz and the Wild Horse Woman*. Her appearance is the portent of war and/or death. It is one aspect of the Wild Horse Woman, Høngin Fujæ Vurn.

**Nynfi**   one of the twin planets orbiting Ba'Lagan, a sun in the Scorpion constellation. Its twin is the planet Albrasa. From the short story "The Big Hunger."

**O inscrutabilis Scrutator animarum, cui patet omne cor, si me vocaveras, olim a te fugeram. Si autem nunc velis vocare me indignum...**   Latin: "O inscrutable Examiner [or Searcher] of souls, to whom every heart is open, if you called me, once I would have fled. If, however, now you should call me, though unworthy...." A line recited by Brother Francis from the book *Libellus Leibowitz* in *A Canticle for Leibowitz* ("Fiat Homo").

**"O Marco! Che bello questo memento!"**   Italian: "O Mark! How lovely is this moment!" La murmurs these words to Mark Kessel in his daydream in the short story "Wolf Pack."

**"O my people, what have I done to thee?"**   The first of a few lines from The Reproaches quoted in the short story "Wolf Pack." See also **The Reproaches**

**Oberlin, Paul Harris** the main character in the novella "Dark Benediction." He was an engineering student at Texas University who worked as a part-time garage mechanic prior to the space plague striking Earth. He is free of the plague and is making his way to Houston where he hopes to find supplies. Confronted by a militia group that controls the downtown of the city, Paul is reluctant to follow their rules and regulations. When he sees Willow, a young hyper woman (one who has contracted the plague), being prepared to be shot by militiamen, he intervenes to rescue her. Despite the highly contagious nature of the disease, Paul does not abandon her even though she is wounded escaping the city. He manages to get her to Galveston for medical attention, but the island city is a refuge for hypers administered by Catholic priests. Paul struggles with his growing feelings for Willow, his own fear of the disease, and being surrounded by hypers. He finally chooses love over the disease, openly embracing Willow, accepting a life as a hyper if it also means a life with her.

**Obermann** the instrument-man on the second launch in the novella "Six and Ten Are Johnny."

**Obregon, Sue** a minor character in the short story "The Corpse In Your Bed Is Me." She spots Martin Snyder going into a bar in the Greeno Quarter after he has been missing for ten days.

**Octave of All Saints** an octave is an eight-day period of commemoration of a major feast within the Catholic Church. All Saints' Day is celebrated on November 1. Only Christmas, Easter, and Pentecost currently have octaves. In *A Canticle for Leibowitz* ("Fiat Lux"), Thon Taddeo and Dom Paulo have their last confrontation concerning the Memorabilia on the Thursday within the Octave of All Saints. The thon will leave the abbey shortly thereafter.

**Oculus Christi Reyes** the new name for the planet Earth in the short story "Gravesong." It is a combination of Latin and Spanish and translates as The Eye of Christ the Kings.

**Oculus Poetae Judicis** Latin: "The Eye of the Poet Judge." One of the names given the Poetsirrah's glass eyeball mounted in a small golden hand and worn by the princes of the Harq-Hannegan dynasty on special state occasions in *A Canticle for Leibowitz* ("Fiat Voluntas Tua"). It is also called Orbis Judicans Conscientiae. See also **Poetsirrah**

**Ola allay** old Benjamin's greeting to Brother Francis in the short story "A Canticle for Leibowitz" and to Father Jerome in the novella "And the Light Is Risen." It is carried over in the stories' expansion in *A Canticle for Leibowitz*. It is also later spelt as *olla allay*.

Benjamin uses the expression in both greeting and departing. Its exact meaning is uncertain but it is unlikely that Rose Secrest is correct in defining it as an "exclamation of great fear" derived from the Hebrew since Benjamin calls out to Brother Francis "cheerfully" when he first uses it. Its meaning has also been given as "good luck." While this is probably closer contextually, it also seems incorrect. Miller may have had *hola*, the Spanish word for "hello" in mind. *Allay* means to pacify or calm one's fears or anxieties. This makes sense for a stranger to say as he meets another wanderer in the wilds of the post–Apocalyptic world in an attempt to assuage one's fears of encountering a spook or an enemy.

**Olavlano Cardinal Fortos** *see* **Alabaster II**

**Old Donegal** the main character in the short story "Death of a Spaceman" (later entitled "Memento Homo"). Donegal is 63 years old, paralyzed, and dying of cancer. He has spent a lifetime in space as a blastman on the Earth to moon shuttle. It has been a life he has loved even though he is unable to explain to his wife and daughter why being a spacer, despite its dangers, is worth it. In his final moments, with his space boots on, his mind takes him back to the blastroom and the moon-run, and he dies listening to his last blast-off of the lunar shuttle. He is also called Donny in the story.

**Old Jew** *see* **Benjamin**

**Old Ma'am Grales** *see* **Mrs. Grales**

**Old Man Odds** the name Barry Wilkes gives the sun in the solar system on the galaxy's outer reaches where he hopes to find an Earth-like planet to maintain the human race in the novella "The Song of Vorhu."

**Old Time** according to *Saint Leibowitz and the Wild Horse Woman*, it is the time that follows the period of great death, fire and ice, the primordial time.

**Old Zarks** the low mountains comprising the territory of the Watchitah Nation in *Saint Leibowitz and the Wild Horse Woman*. The name is a corruption of The Ozarks or Ozark Mountains in the southeast United States. The Ozarks comprise southwest Missouri and northwest Arkansas as well as smaller areas of Oklahoma and Kansas.

**Oley**  the deceased husband of Nora, Old Donegal's daughter, in the short story "Death of a Spaceman ("Memento Homo"). He died in space; his ship remains in an eccentric orbit.

**Oliver, Symmes Chadwick [Chad]** (March 30, 1928–August 15, 1993)  a science fiction writer and professor of anthropology at the University of Texas at Austin where he also served as chairman of the Department of Anthropology at various times. Among his works, many of which feature cultural conflict, are *Mists of Dawn* (1952), *Shadows in the Sun* (1954), and *The Shores of Another Sea* (1971). Born in Cincinnati, Ohio, he moved with his family to Texas while he was in high school. He received a B.A. and a M.A. in English from the University of Texas at Austin. He earned at Ph.D. in anthropology at UCLA in 1961.

In the early 1950s, Oliver began writing science fiction stories, some of which appeared in *Astounding Science Fiction* where Miller's work was also published. Miller, who was then living in Kyle, Texas, wrote to Oliver asking for a ride to a science fiction convention in New Orleans. A friendship developed between the two men based, in part, on their writing and love of fishing. After the trip, they continued to visit each other and correspond until Oliver left to study at UCLA.

Their correspondence is part of the Chad Oliver Collection of the Cushing Memorial Library at Texas A & M University. A brief interview with Oliver in which he speaks about his relationship with Miller can be found in "Chad Oliver & Walt Miller" in the fanzine *Sumermorn*, no. 3 (Fall 1979). Miller termed Oliver's recollections in the interview "baloney, on several accounts" (ltr 2/21/1991).

**Ollay allay**  *see* **Ola allay**

**Olshuen, Abiquiu**  from *Saint Leibowitz and the Wild Horse Woman*, an old friend and former teacher and confessor of Brother Blacktooth. He is named to carry out the duties of abbot at the Abbey of Saint Leibowitz while Abbot Jarad is in Valana at the conclave to elect a pope. In Jarad's absence, Blacktooth asks him to release him from his vows. After Jarad's death, he is the presumed next elected abbot of the abbey. A conservative, during his tenure as abbot he tries to isolate the abbey from the outside world. He suffers a stroke near the end of the war and dies shortly thereafter.

**Ol'zark dialect**  the language of the ruling class within Texark in *Saint Leibowitz and the Wild Horse Woman*.

**Ombroz, Father**  *see* **e'Laiden, Ombroz**

**Omnes sancti Martyres, orate pro nobis...**  Latin: "All you Holy Martyrs, pray for us...." A part of the Litany of the Saints as presented in *A Canticle for Leibowitz* ("Fiat Homo") during the canonization ceremony for Isaac Leibowitz.

***On the Edge***  *see* **"Reaching Normal"**

**Önmu Kun**  *see* **Kun, Önmu**

**Onyo, Golopez**  a cardinal from Old Mexico in *Saint Leibowitz and the Wild Horse Woman*. He is thought to be one of the favorites to be elected pope during the conclave that elects Amen Specklebird. He is Pope Amen's witness that he has instructed Cardinal Brownpony to inform the brothers at the Abbey of Saint Leibowitz to elect a new abbot and that Brownpony possesses the pope's confirmation.

**Operation Icecap**  the project that made the surface of Mars endurable for living by humans in the novella "The Reluctant Traitor." Five hundred years prior to the time of the story, a deuterium-helium fusion-cycle was set off in the heavy water icecap of Mars. The result was the establishment of a denser breathable atmosphere of oxygen and helium and one that could retain heat. Dawson and Heide are the men primarily responsible for the project.

**Ophiuchus**  or The Serpent Holder (or Bearer), a large constellation near Hercules and between the two parts of the constellation Serpens. Its name is derived from two Greek words meaning "serpent" and "holding." It is one of the destinations of man's spaceships in the short story "The Big Hunger." There, on a planet orbiting a yellow sun, man crushed a native race.

**Ora pro me**  Latin: "Pray for me." During his ordeal in the meldown in *Saint Leibowitz and the Wild Horse Woman*, Cardinal Brownpony asks the Wild Horse Woman to "*ora pro me*."

**Ora pro nobis nunc et in hora mortis nostrae**  Latin: "Pray for us now and at the hour of our death." The line is taken from a part of the prayer Ave Maria (Hail Mary). The words occur to Brother Blacktooth as he walks under a statue of the Virgin Mary behind the throne of Saint Peter's in the decimated city of New Rome just prior to Pope Amen II's death in *Saint Leibowitz and the Wild Horse Woman*.

**Orate, fraters**  Latin: "Pray, brethren." These are Father Zerchi's parting words to the monks as he leaves the chapel in the novella "The Last Canticle."

**Orbis Judicans Conscientias** Latin: "The Orb Which Judges Consciences." In *A Canticle for Leibowitz* ("Fiat Voluntas Tua"), one of the names for the Poet-sirrah's glass eyeball mounted in a small golden hand and worn at special state occasions by descendents of the Harq-Hannegan dynasty. It is also referred to as Oculus Poetae Judicis. See also **Poet-sirrah**

**Orbital Engineering and Construction Company** the makers of the moon shuttle ships in the short story "Death of a Spaceman" ("Memento Homo"). It is owned by Old Donegal's neighbor, Ronald Keith.

**Order of Saint Ignatz** an order that has been disloyal to the popes of the exile in *Saint Leibowitz and the Wild Horse Woman*. They do not recognize Amen as pope. Father Ombroz is on their list of God's enemies, and he jokingly tells Brownpony that he will change orders and join Saint Ignatz.

**Order of Saint Peter's Sword** the order of the six warriors known as the Yellow Guard who accompany Cardinal Ri in *Saint Leibowitz and the Wild Horse Woman*. The order maintains two traditions: a traditional Christian one, not unlike the Order of Saint Leibowitz, and a weaponless warrior tradition that emphasizes skill with both feet and fists.

**Ordo Dominae Desertarum Nostrae** Latin: "Order of Our Lady of the Desert." The order of Amen Specklebird in *Saint Leibowitz and the Wild Horse Woman*. It is the same order Mother Iridia Silentia belongs to and that Ædrea will later join as Sister Clare.

**O'Reilley** the name Mitch Laskell gives to the robot cop he watches directing traffic in the short story "Dumb Waiter."

**O'Reilley, James Fallon ("Doggy")** the bald, elderly owner of O'Reilley's Pet Shop in the novella "Conditionally Human." When Terry Norris comes to his shop to investigate a discrepancy in neutroid serial numbers, O'Reilley is reluctant to cooperate. Only after Norris threatens to shut the store does O'Reilley produce a receipt with an altered serial number. O'Reilley confesses to hiding the neutroid, Peony, one of the Delmont deviants. When she arrived at the shop, O'Reilley and his wife became attached to her. Before she died, Mrs. O'Reilley told her husband never to sell Peony. Norris takes Peony from O'Reilley. After they leave, O'Reilley goes berserk and kills all the animals in his shop, threatens to kill Norris, and babbles about "his baby," a talking neutroid. His brother-in-law, Father Paulson [Mulreany], intervenes on his behalf.

**Oremus** Latin: "Let us pray." Used by Father Paulo in the novella "And the Light Is Risen" and *A Canticle for Leibowitz* ("Fiat Lux") at the banquet for Thon Taddeo.

**"Origin of Interstellar Hydrogen"** the title of an article written by San Rorrek in the short story "Bitter Victory." Rorrek hopes that its suggestion of a five-space continuum with a circulation of matter along the fifth component will provide the link between Dr. Larwich's theory and observable reality. The practical applications would lead to the development of the five-space interstellar drive, allowing the Terrans to build ships for deep space travel. Rorrek submits the article to a university press that rejects it for publication.

**Original guilt** (also known as Original sin). Within Christian theology, the idea that from the moment of birth each person is burdened with guilt, the result of the Fall of Adam and Eve in the Garden of Eden. In the novella "And the Light Is Risen," Father Jerome refers to this concept in his conversation with Benjamin. It is repeated in *A Canticle for Leibowitz* ("Fiat Lux") with Dom Paulo and Benjamin.

**Ortus est Dei Spiritus supra profundorum** *see* **In principio Deus**

**Ortus est et primo die** *see* **In principio Deus**

**Our Lady of the Desert** in *Saint Leibowitz and the Wild Horse Woman*, Father Ombroz tells Brownpony that his wandering church is part of the Ordo Dominae Desertarum, the Order of Our Lady of the Desert. It is the old order of Pope Amen.

**Oxsho** from *Saint Leibowitz and the Wild Horse Woman*, a Nomad warrior who is the half-nephew of Chür Høngan. He is Father Ombroz's acolyte and student.

**P-47** the Thunderbolt, the most heavily produced single engine American fighter plane during World War II. It was manufactured by the Republic Aviation Corporation. Mark Kessel and his crew spot P-47s in the short story "Wolf Pack."

**Pacini (or Pacinian) Corpuscle** a microscopic mass at the ends of the nerves scattered through the skin forming sensory receptors. They are named for Filippo Pacini (1812–1883), an Italian anatomist, who first observed them. In the novella "Dark Benediction," the neuroderm parasites are said to look like a cross between a sperm cell and a Pucini [sic] corpuscle.

**Palestrina, Giovanni Pierluigi da** (c. 1525/1526–1594) Italian choirmaster and composer most noted for his sacred music, generally considered to be the most beautiful of the Renaissance. In the novella "The Lineman," Relke puts on a tape of Palestrina music.

**Palm Sunday** also known as the Second Sunday of the Passion, it is the Sunday before Easter. It commemorates Jesus' triumphal entry into Jerusalem when palm branches were strewn along the path he traveled. It begins Holy Week.

**Pangborn, Edgar** (February 25, 1909–February 1, 1976) novelist and short story writer born in New York City who began writing detective and mystery stories before turning to science fiction. He is a well regarded humanist within the science fiction genre. Among his best known novels is *Davy* (1967). His short story "A Master of Babylon" appears in *Beyond Armageddon*.

**Papatiae Apocrisarius Texarkanae** Latin: "Papal legate [nuncio] at Texarkana." Marcus Apollo's formal reference to his position in the heading of his letter to Dom Paulo announcing Thon Taddeo's visit to the Leibowitz abbey in *A Canticle for Leibowitz* ("Fiat Lux").

**Pappas** Greek: "priest" or descending from a priest. The Latin *Papa*, and thus pope, is derived from it.

**Pappy** the nickname of Lieutenant Mark Kessel, a B-25 bomber pilot during World War II, in the short story "Wolf Pack."

**Paraclete** the Holy Ghost or Holy Spirit. The term is derived from the Greek *parakletos* meaning comforter or consoler. In *A Canticle for Leibowitz* ("Fiat Homo"), Brother Francis thinks that the buzzards that he sees are "dark alternatives" to the *Paraclete* he awaits.

**Paramount Theater** where Jigger works as a janitor in the novella "The Darfsteller."

**Parker, Hogey** the main character of the short story "The Hoofer," he is also known as Big Hogey Parker. Parker is a spacer or "tumbler," a man who feels more at home living and working in space than on Earth. He has spent six tours in space, the last for nine months, promising his wife that each tour would be his last one. Now, because of his newly born son and regulations that prevent fathers from being in space, Parker has returned from space for good—a week late and without the money he lost in a poker game. He resents the need for him to become a hoofer, a man chained to the Earth, and he looks longingly into space, into the Big Bottomless that he loves. Although "the kid was an accident," Parker accepts his responsibility and recognizes that his time is no longer his own but now belongs to his son. Used to the weightlessness of space, he makes his way home to the farm where he will lose his "space legs" and become a hoofer. Parker's Earth-bound existence is set firmly before him when he drunkenly steps into fresh concrete that clutches at his ankles and holds him immobile.

**Parker, Marie (née Hauptman)** the wife of spaceman Hogey Parker in the short story "The Hoofer." She has recently given birth to the couple's first child, a boy.

**Parkeson** an unseen but heard character in the novella "The Lineman." He is the boss of the workers on the Lunar Project. After the disruption in the project caused by the arrival of the space traveling bordello, Parkeson addresses all the men and stresses the importance of finishing the job. Their existence on the moon is a fragile ecology that depends upon them all working together toward a common goal.

**Parn, Wolek** the captain of the space ark carrying 120 colonists to the planet Epilson Eridani Two in the short story "Let My People Go." Parn is a cautious and deliberate leader. He is reluctant to commit the colonists to the planet until he is confident of the Eridanians' intentions. When Morgun Sahl returns from the planet encouraging the colonists' transfer from the ship, Parn is suspicious and orders the doctor to examine him. When Sahl's conditioning by the Eridanians is discovered, Parn is willing to sacrifice him if necessary for the greater good of the colonists. With the knowledge provided by Sahl, Parn devises a plan that counters the Eridanians' scheme to assimilate the Earth colonists.

**Parrin, Captain** the leader of the band of commandos in the novella "The Yokel." When Sam Wuncie is able to unarm the men in the plane and orders them to bail out, Parrin tells his men to stay where they are. Wuncie shoots Parrin, breaking his leg, to convince the others to jump.

**Parum equidem te diligebam, Domine, juventute mea, quare doleo nimis...:** Latin: "Too little, O Lord, did I love Thee in the time of my youth, wherefore I grieve exceedingly...." Brother Francis recites from the *Libellus Lei-*

*bowitz*, an ancient book attributed to Isaac Leibowitz, in *A Canticle for Leibowitz* ("Fiat Homo"). Several critics have suggested that this and other sayings from the *Libellus Leibowitz* sound Augustinian in origin.

**Parva Civitas** Latin: "minor [or small] city [or civilization]." New Jerusalem is referred to as a Parva Civitas in *Saint Leibowitz and the Wild Horse Woman*.

**Paschal Full Moon (Paschal Moon)** the first full moon that occurs on or after March 21, determined by ecclesiastical full moons rather than astronomical full moons. Easter is celebrated on the Sunday after the Paschal full moon. A reference is made in *Saint Leibowitz and the Wild Horse Woman* to the Paschal full moon.

**Passiontide** the period between Passion Sunday (the fifth Sunday of Lent) and the morning of Holy Saturday, being the last two weeks of Lent. From *A Canticle for Leibowitz* ("Fiat Homo").

**Pastorals** another name for the Algun or serf class within the feudal system of Nu Phoenicis IV in the short story "Bitter Victory."

**Paten** a plate or dish used to carry the bread at the Eucharist.

**Pater Noster** Latin: "Our Father." The first two words of the Lord's Prayer (Matthew 6: 9–13 KJV). In "The Last Canticle" and *A Canticle for Leibowitz* ("Fiat Voluntas Tua"), Father Zerchi tells Mrs. Grales to recite ten Pater Nosters as part of her penance.

**Paulo of Pecos** the abbot of the Abbey of Saint Leibowitz in *A Canticle for Leibowitz* ("Fiat Lux"). He is an elderly man in his seventies with white, thinning hair. His posture is stooped, but he bears a round little paunch that looks out of place on a body that otherwise makes him appear to be "an emaciated Ezekiel." Although he is ill and dying—a secret he keeps from the others in the abbey—he is more concerned with his mental anguish and general sense of foreboding. He fears that with the advance of science and technology and the emergence of secular scholars like Thon Taddeo, the purpose and mission of the Albertian Order of Leibowitz will become unnecessary and therefore ended. See also **Father Jerome of Pecos**

**Peccatores, te rogamus, audi nos** Latin: "[We] Sinners, we beseech Thee, hear us." As Brother Francis enters the Fallout Shelter in *A Canticle for Leibowitz* ("Fiat Homo") he recites parts of the Litany of the Saints, of which this is a part.

**Peltier** a young, gloomy actor whose psychophysiological tape was to be used for the part of Andreyev in the autodrama production of "The Anarch" in the novella "The Darfsteller." Ryan Thornier sabotages the Peliter tape with one from Granger, an older, comedic actor, so that he can assume the role in the play.

**Pentecost** the Christian feast commemorating the visible descent of the Holy Ghost upon the apostles. It occurs on the seventh Sunday after Easter. It is also known as Whitsunday (White Sunday). It is referred to in *Saint Leibowitz and the Wild Horse Woman*.

*Penthestes atricapillus* the scientific name of the black-capped chickadee. More recent alternate names are *parus atricapillus* and *poecile atricapillus*. It is referred to in *A Canticle for Leibowitz* ("Fiat Homo").

**Penult** an enslaved human in the short story "The Soul-Empty Ones." When Falon is thrown into the food pens with men, he bows to Penult, whom he recognizes as a son of his creators. However, Penult asks Falon not to knell before him; they are both slaves and brothers. Penult tells Falon of the secret tunnel beneath the food pens that runs to the center of the city. He works with Falon to coordinate the attack upon their Martian captives.

**Peony** one of Delmont's deviant neutroids in the novella "Conditionally Human." She possesses above normal intelligence, a well developed speech function, and the ability to cry. James O'Reilley discovers her among a shipment of neutroids he receives at his pet shop. He and his wife become attached to her, and they keep and protect her. When Terry Norris finds her in the shop, he takes her from O'Reilley and brings her back to his house, unsure as to what to do with her. He is afraid she will be discovered and killed if he returns her to the pet shop or keeps her himself. He eventually decides to amputate her tail and the foot with her tattooed serial number, dye her hair, and dress her as a two year old boy.

**Per ipsum et cum ipso et in ipso** Latin: "through him, with him, and in him." A part of the Catholic Mass, the words appear in the novella "The Last Canticle."

*Perennial Ideas of Regional Sects* a volume by Yogen Duren, *De Perennibus Sententiis Sectarum Rurum*, one of the choices given to Brother Blacktooth to translate into the Grasshopper dialect of Plains Nomadic in *Saint Leibowitz and the Wild Horse Woman*. He chooses this volume over Boedullus' *Footprints of Earlier Civilizations*.

**Perennials** a term used in the scriptorium of the Leibowitz abbey in *A Canticle for Leibowitz* ("Fiat Homo") for those books that are in constant demand, such as Breviaries and Missals, and so are always being copied

**Perseids** the Perseid Meteor Shower, also known as the Tears of Saint Lawrence, perhaps the best known major meteor shower, is the debris trail of the Swift-Tuttle Comet. It is best seen from the Northern Hemisphere usually between mid–July through August. In the novella "The Lineman," the Perseids provide a backdrop for the work on the Lunar Project transmission line.

**Perseus** *see* **The Thief**

**Personae non gratae** Latin: "Unacceptable people." Cardinal Brownpony and Brother Blacktooth are declared *personae non gratae* in Texark and expelled from the Empire under suspended sentences of death by Filpeo Harq in *Saint Leibowitz and the Wild Horse Woman*.

**Perugia** a town situated on a hillside in the Tiber Valley in the Umbria region of central Italy. It is particular noted for its art. It is the town Mark Kessel bombs in the short story "Wolf Pack" and where he encounters La.

**Peters** a minor, non-speaking character in the novella "Cold Awakening." He is ordered by Roagan to weld shut the suspendfreeze locker Herrick is in and to disable its thawer to prevent Herrick from escaping prosecution in Jessel's murder.

**Peterson** a member of the Mars Commission in the novella "The Reluctant Traitor." He is locked inside the androon cave and is killed in the attack.

**Pfardentrott, Taddeo [Thaddeo]** a renown natural philosopher and a man of "rare genius" in the novella "And the Light Is Risen" where his name is spelt Thaddeo, and the novel *A Canticle for Leibowitz* ("Fiat Lux"). He is described in the novel as young, lean, and influential.

He is the cousin of Hannegan II, the head of Texarkana. His father was a duke, Hannegan's uncle, and his mother was a serving maid. Pfardentrott was born out of wedlock. In order to avoid embarrassment, his father's wife sent him to be raised and educated in a Benedictine monastery. After 15 years, the duke's wife died, and he reclaimed his son, his only male heir. During his years at the monastery, however, Taddeo grew bitter from a sense of entitlement denied him and jealous of his cousin. Much of that bitterness is directed toward the Church that nurtured and cared for him. He is a member of the faculty of the collegium. His works include theories of electrical essence and planetary motion.

When he hears of the existence of the Leibowitzian documents, he wants them brought to him for study. After his request is denied, he travels to the Abbey of Saint Leibowitz to study them there. Don Taddeo is arrogant and selfish. He believes the documents are wasted at the abbey and need to be more accessible to scholars. He lectures the monks that change and progress will come, but that they will necessarily come with violence and upheaval. He believes that history must be questioned, and he struggles with the problem of how a great and wise civilization could destroy itself.

He acknowledges that he supports Hannegan for the sake of his own work. If Hannegan's empire prospers, the collegium profits, and if the collegium profits, then mankind benefits from the knowledge that is gained. As a man of science and understanding, he finds a formidable foil at the abbey in Dom Paulo (Father Jerome in the novella) who continually reminds him of the responsibility that comes with knowledge. There is a grudging mutual respect between Taddeo and Paulo. Before he leaves, Taddeo gives the abbot the sketches of the abbey that were made by Hannegan's men who accompanied him during his stay.

In *Saint Leibowitz and the Wild Horse Woman*, it is revealed that Taddeo's work at the Abbey of Saint Leibowitz made possible many inventions. He re-invented the telegraph and dynamite among other things.

The name Taddeo (or Thaddeo) means "courageous" or "heart." Miller could also have in mind Thaddeus (or Thadeus) meaning "gift of God," providing an ironic comment on the secular scholar. Thaddeus was also a second century scholar in Rome.

Mark McVann has suggested that Pfard echoes *pferd*, German for horse, and that trott is a variant of trot, associated with the horse's gait. He posits that the name is suggestive of Taddeo being a horse's ass. It has also been proposed that Miller has purposely given the scholar a name that sounds like "fart and trot."

**Pfarfen** a minor character in *Saint Leibowitz and the Wild Horse Woman*. He is the leader of a small train of wagons headed for the Watchitah Nation that Wooshin and Brother Blacktooth follow after the fall of New Rome. Blacktooth suspects him of being a spook and knows him to be having an incestuous relationship with his beautiful daughter.

**Pforft** a pederast occupying one of the cells in the Hannegan City jail/zoo when Cardinal

Brownpony and Brother Blacktooth are imprisoned in *Saint Leibowitz and the Wild Horse Woman*. He reads the signs above their cage, informing them that they are accused of heresy, simony, and attempted regicide.

**Phanton**   the god of light and king of the gods among the androons in the novella "The Reluctant Traitor."

**Pharaoh**   the title of the kings of Egypt, used generically in the Old Testament. In *A Canticle for Leibowitz* ("Fiat Lux"), Benjamin includes Pharaoh among a list of despotic rulers he hopes Thon Taddeo does not emulate. Miller may have had in mind Ramses II (alternatively Ramesses II) who Moses confronted in a struggle of wills that led to the freeing of the Israelites from Egyptian oppression (Exodus 1–14 KJV). Later in the section, in Brother Reader's account of the time of the Flame Deluge, it is stated that a certain prince's arrogance surpassed that of Pharaoh.

**Phillip**   the second husband of Marcia in the short story "The Space Witch." He is a passive, unassertive individual who is easily manipulated by his wife.

**Phillips, Rog**   pseudonym of Roger Phillips Graham. See also **Graham, Roger Phillips**

**Phoenician Quarantine Commission**   the body that assigns San Rorrek to locate and kill Klia after she eludes the space quarantine surrounding the Klidds' planet in the short story "Bitter Victory."

**Phoenix**   in myth, a fiery self-destructive bird that rises to life again out of the ashes of its own destruction. In the novella "The Last Canticle" and *A Canticle for Leibowitz* ("Fiat Voluntas Tua"), Abbot Zerchi asks himself if mankind has "no choice but to play the Phoenix, in an unending sequence of rise and fall?"

**PIK-A-DON**   in the account of the Flame Deluge read in *A Canticle for Leibowitz* ("Fiat Lux"), a reference is made to "a great thunder" in the sky, "like the great battering-ram PIK-A-DON." Pik-a-don or, more commonly, pika don, is the Japanese term used by the survivors of the atomic bomb dropped on Hiroshima on August 6, 1945 for the bomb itself. Pika means flash of light and don is a reference to a thunderous blast.

**Pilate**   Pontius Pilate was the Roman procurator of Judea from A.D. 26–A.D. 37 He was particularly inept and insensitive in his dealing with the Jewish population. When Jesus was brought before him, Pilate found no grounds to support the charges against him. However, he vacillated and acquiesced to the demands of the Sanhedrin and ordered the crucifixion of a man he believed innocent. Father Zerchi mentions Pilate in the novella "The Last Canticle." In *Saint Leibowitz and the Wild Horse Woman*, Brother Blacktooth dreams he is Pilate.

**Pilgrim**   "a spindly old fellow with a staff" and brushy beard. He walks with a limp and is dressed in a burlap loin cloth, sandals, and a basket hat in the short story "A Canticle for Leibowitz" and the novel *A Canticle for Leibowitz*. The earliest habit of the Albertian Order of Leibowitz was burlap rags and a bindlestiff.

1. In the story, he approaches Brother Francis during his Lenten vigil and points out a rock that might be used for the shelter the novice is building. When Brother Francis picks up the rock, he discovers the rusted box containing the Leibowitz relics. Brother Francis believes the pilgrim is either an angel of God or the Blessed Leibowitz himself.

2. In the novel, the pilgrim marks the rock with the Hebrew letters lamedh and sadhe, L and Tz. When Brother Francis removes the rock, a hole leading to the underground cavity of the fallout shelter is revealed. At the end of "Fiat Homo" when Francis sits waiting for the robber to reappear, he sees a figure at a distance shimmering in the heat. He thinks there is something "too familiar" about the figure. After the monk is killed, the figure, referred to as "the old wanderer" finds his body. The wanderer has a brushy beard and is wearing a basket hat and carrying a staff. He buries the body of Brother Francis and marks his grave with a rock. See also **Benjamin**

**Piszjil**   the name given the Eridanians by the saffrons, a sub-species, in the short story "Let My People Go." The Eridanians, or Piszjil, control a carefully constructed biological cooperative world that benefits them as the dominate species.

**Pius XI**   pope from February 6, 1922, to February 10, 1939, during the emergence of totalitarian states in the Soviet Union, Italy and Germany and their resulting anti–Christian persecution. Pius actively warned against a way of life and a system of government that alienated men from God. He believed the Catholic Church, and religion in general, were the most effective elements in preserving the order and security of society. As Nazi Germany's oppression of the Church increased, Pius XI issued the encyclical *Mit Brennender Sorge* ("With deep anxiety") in March 1937 condemning Nazism as anti–Christian and anti-Semitic.

In *A Canticle for Leibowitz* ("Fiat Voluntas Tua"), Dom Zerchi remembers a passage from the encyclical as he ruminates that "God's to be obeyed by nations as by men": "Whoever exalts a race or a State of a particular form of State or the depositories of power ... whoever raises these notions above their standard value and divinizes them to an idolatrous level, distorts and perverts an order of the world planned and created by God."

**Plains Nomads [or Plains tribes]** one of the larger groups of peoples surrounded by the more organized states of Texarkana, Laredo, and Denver, among others, in the novella "And the Light Is Risen." They regularly make raids to loot and vandalize the established villages. Hannegan II manipulates Denver and Laredo into a conflict with the Plains Nomads as part of his plan to unite the continent under his rule.

**Planet of Paradise** the paradise planet was abandoned by man as he searched for something better in "The Big Hunger." Lord Bion, angered by man's search for a better home, condemns him to wander forever searching for the planet he lost.

**"Please Me Plus Three"** a short story appearing in *Other Worlds*, 4 (August 1952), 6–47. Lord Bel, the Wise One, is a man-made satellite worshipped by the people of Tribe George Eighty as the keeper of the peace and advisor to man. Each tribe forms around a 400 foot tall pylon, attended by a Keeper, which serves as a communication center for Bel. For its services, Bel demands pleasure stimuli from its subjects. Upon Bel's rising, the tribe performs elaborate ceremonies centered around the pylon to honor and please Bel. Ton of Roldin, a ceremonial piper, refuses to play because his pregnant wife, Mara, has been chosen to dance in the celebration for Bel and he fears for her safety. His marriage was arranged by the blood laws, and he knows that Mara dislikes him and disagrees with his actions. Ton is told that his disobedience will be reported and that he will be flogged. He decides to pipe knowing his refusal to do so will accomplish nothing.

During the dance, Mara falls and Bel signals that he is displeased. A halt is called to the stimulus. Bel commands Mara to offer the dance of immolation to undo what she has done. Ton protests and attempts to leave the pylon but is restrained by the guards. Mara begins her dance and whips herself with bull-nettles across her face and thighs. The dance ends as she plunges a knife into her throat.

The guards tell Ton to stop complaining, that Mara never loved him. He asks if he can be released, and when they do so, Ton throws Keeper Cron over the rail of the pylon to his death. Ton runs down the pylon with guards in pursuit. He reaches Mara's body. With a howl of hatred, he throws a spear into one of the loud speakers of the pylon. Bel commands that order be restored or the entire tribe will be held accountable for crimes of violence. Ton is ordered into the interrogation unit where Bel explores his mind and passes judgment upon him. He is to be whipped with fiery nettles and branded on his forehead. He is banished into the wilderness, and Bel decrees that no man shall kill him because he is already dead to the tribe. He is given his pipes and warned that if he ever returns or approaches any decent man who serves the pylon, his arms will be amputated at the elbows.

Ton makes his way to the river and heads for the forbidden territory of the plateau to seek sanctuary. He knows that Cron's sons will seek vengeance and at least one of them, most likely Vigge, "the Boar," will try to kill him. Ton thinks of dying but desires to live in order to harass Bel until it is forced to recognize him as an enemy rather than simply as an unwanted subject. If he can show others that Bel can have enemies, Ton believes that those who hate Bel will rise up in defiance.

Ton travels to the forbidden territory where he collapses from his wounds. He is discovered by three hunters from a lay-order of monastic soldiers fighting against Bel and the Keepers. They bring him back to their settlement and nurse him back to health. He is told that any valley man who comes to the plateau is not allowed to return so that the superstitious legends concerning the forbidden territory are maintained. Ton says that he wants to join the fight against Bel, but he is told that their plan is to wait until something goes wrong with the satellite that cannot be repaired automatically.

Ton accompanies the group on a two-day trek to the east. He escapes from them during a religious ceremony, knocking out his guard with a rock. Stealing a horse, he is chased by the monks but manages to elude their pursuit. He finds the ruins of an ancient city destroyed by an atomic blast. He searches for a pylon among the ruins hoping it will provide him with the key to destroy his tribe's pylon. He sees small, disfigured, nearly albino people living in near idiocy. He recognizes this as the work of Bel; man receives answers from Bel but no wisdom. Locating the destroyed pylon, Ton enters the rubble. Inside he discovers a repair robot, Robot George Eighty-Six. Ton hopes to ascertain from the robot how to destroy the pylon. He asks if Bel can be made to feel pain and learns that it can be done through the pylon's interrogation units. Ton orders the robot to follow him since its pylon is beyond repair. He tells it that if it obeys him, it will have a pylon to serve again.

As they emerge from the rubble, they see Vigge, Keeper Cron's youngest son. Ton approaches him with the robot following. He tells the robot to continue walking toward Vigge, telling Vigge to meet his new king, a Bel that walks. Vigge shoots several arrows at the robot, but when they have no affect, he turns and rides away. Ton yells after him to tell the tribe that Ton is coming with a walking Bel to be their king.

As Ton leaves the city, several monk-soldiers await him. He sends the robot to tell them about Bel's pain. The monks warn Ton to leave the city before he is killed by radiation poisoning, but he tells them he will not be their prisoner. Ton orders the robot to kill the monks if they exhibit any hostility toward him. He says he is going to return to the valley before the next Belrise to fight and asks them to join him. The monks appreciate the plan Ton lays before them but insist it is too risky. They need to preserve their small group for the future when Bel exhausts his power. Ton angrily leaves them, but they provide him with a donkey for the robot.

Ton and George Eighty-Six approach the outskirts of Ton's home valley, and Ton sends the robot to the pylon and orders it to enter the vaults and leave them open. He disconnects the robot's speech center so it cannot reply if questioned. Ton makes his way to the pylon and George Eighty-Six deactivates the pylon's repair robot, George Eighty. It is placed in supervised operation so it too will obey Ton's orders. Ton commands George Eighty-Six to prepare the pylon as if Bel were about to speak. He sends the other robot out to the pylon's balcony and calls Keeper Walin to the balcony. Ton tells George Eighty-Six to speak as Bel and to tell the people that Bel speaks through his son, the robot, and that they have displeased Bel and will be punished.

The robot brings the Keeper into the pylon, and Ton discovers from him that Vigge is dead. Ton had planned on torturing Vigge to provide Bel the pain stimulus needed to destroy it. Ton is reluctant to torture an innocent man. Meanwhile, the people have reacted hysterically to what they think are Bel's words and are in terrified flight toward the plateau. Ton decides to use himself as bait for Bel to destroy the pylon. He releases Keeper Walin with Ton's realization that the Keeper family has always known Bel's true nature.

As Bel rises, it orders Ton to abandon his intentions and submit to punishment. Ton enters the interrogation center and connects himself once again to Bel. The robots have fixed a light that focuses a white-hot point of pain upon Ton's chest at five second intervals. Ton endures the pain, sharing it with Bel until the satellite is destroyed. In destroying Bel, Ton not only gains his revenge, but he frees man from the domination of the machine.

**Pobla**  a city in the Denver Freestate in *Saint Leibowitz and the Wild Horse Woman* on the current site of Pueblo, Colorado. It is located on the Kensau River, south of Valana. Cardinal Brownpony's party stops there to use the public baths on its way to Valana. Holy Madness and Father e'Laiden leave the cardinal's party in Pobla.

**Poele**  a weak and wary member of the Mars Commission who joins Commissioner Rathwich in a meeting with Rolf Kenlan in the novella "The Reluctant Traitor."

**Poet** *see* **Poet-sirrah**

**Poet-sirrah**  in the novella "And the Light Is Risen" he is known simply as the Poet but in *A Canticle for Liebowitz* ("Fiat Lux") he is more often referred to as the Poet-sirrah. Sirrah is an archaic word used as a contemptuous term of address.

He is an unwanted tenant in the abbey, and the abbot evicts him from the royal suite prior to Thon Taddeo's (Don Taddeo) visit. He has a glass eye with which he swears he can perceive true meaning. He refers to it as his conscience, a convenient one because it is removable. Supposedly writing a book, he usually occupies the "stable boy's cell" in the abbey when he cannot use the guest quarters. He favors the abbey's wine collection and wins a baldheaded blue goat from Benjamin playing mumble-peg.

At the banquet given in honor of the Thon Taddeo, he confronts the thon and Hannegan's officers regarding the drawings they are making of the abbey. He removes his glass eye and places it on the table, telling the thon that he has better use for it. In the "Fiat Voluntas Tua" section of the novel, it is revealed that Taddeo gave the eyeball to Hannegan who mounted it in the clutch of a small golden hand. It is revered as a relic and is still worn by the princes of the Harq-Hannegan dynasty on special state occasions. It is referred to as Orbis Judicans Conscientias or the Oculus Poetae Judicis.

The Poet-sirrah leaves the abbey at some point after the thon's banquet. As he wanders the countryside, he comes across a cavalry troop in pursuit of a group of refugees. He at first hides but on impulse leaps upon the cavalry officer and stabs him before the other soldiers shoot him in the stomach. He is left to die with the cavalry officer whom he kills.

In "Fiat Voluntas Tua" Dom Zerchi reads a slim volume of verse purported to have been written by a mythical saint canonized in fable and the folklore of the Plains, Saint Poet of the Miraculous Eyeball. The book is a satirical dialogue between two antagonists, a "Poet" and a "Thon," attempting to establish by natural reason alone that the existence of God cannot be established by natural reason alone. Zerchi remembers there was some speculation that the Saint Poet was the same person as the "scurrilous versificator" mentioned in the journals of Father Jerome, but he dismisses it as a "rather silly hypothesis."

**Poilyf, Wolfer** a fur wearing cardinal from the North Country. He was appointed a cardinal by Pope Amen. He participates in the conclave to elect Amen's successor in *Saint Leibowitz and the Wild Horse Woman*.

**Poitr** a role in the play "The Anarch" performed in the novella "The Darfsteller."

**Polarin** the capital city of Tragor III in the short story "Blood Bank."

**Pompei** a Roman city destroyed by the eruption of Mt. Vesuvius in A.D. 79 Twenty thousand people were estimated to have died. The city was covered in volcanic ash and largely preserved. It was discovered in the 17th century. It is mentioned in the novella "The Last Canticle" and in *A Canticle for Leibowitz* ("Fiat Voluntas Tua").

**Pope's children** an ancient euphemism for the misborn in *A Canticle for Leibowitz* and *Saint Leibowitz and the Wild Horse Woman*. The reference is to the genetically handicapped born as a result of the thermonuclear war. For a time it was believed by some that the children of the misborn possessed the souls of animals rather than humans and therefore could be destroyed as animals. Papal proclamations, however, affirmed the right to life of any child born alive to human parents and that all children are born with immortal souls and are protected from infanticide by the Church. As a result, the misborn children became known as the pope's children or the pope's nephews.

**Pope's nephews** *see* **Pope's children**

**Porro subesse Romano Pontifici ... de necessitate salutis** Latin: "It is necessary for salvation to be subject to the authority of the Roman pontiff." Cardinal Brownpony quotes this "never-popular decree" from "an ancient bull" in *Saint Leibowitz and the Wild Horse Woman*. It is from a bull on papal supremacy issued by Boniface VIII on November 18, 1302 and referred to as *Unam Sanctam* ("The Holy One") from its opening words. The bull establishes the necessity of belonging to the Church for salvation and the need for submission to the pope as head of the Church. If one is not subject to the authority of the pope, then one is not among the body of the Church. Secular power is of lesser rank and subjected to the spiritual power of the Church and pope. Brownpony's view of the bull is that it "was aimed especially at monarchs, whether civil or Nomadic, and the Hannegans and Caesars as well."

**Porshkin, Andrei** a Russian cyberneticist assigned to work with Scott MacDonney in the novella "Izzard and the Membrane." Porshkin is a proud man who is jealous of MacDonney's success. He threatens and abuses MacDonney as Scott works toward the completion of Izzard, the super computer. Porshkin reveals to Scott that the Russians duped him, that his wife, Nora, never betrayed him. Outraged, Scott arranges for Porshkin to be eliminated by Colonel Varnoff and the police. Varnoff divulges that Porshkin was actually the head of the underground. Shot and presumably killed, Porshkin emerges later from the membrane to help Scott end the Russian war effort. He will rule post-war Russia.

**Port e'Eridani VII** the city where the cybernetic spacecraft XM-5-B is located in the short story "I, Dreamer."

**Post Cedar** a small community of bookleggers and memorizers within the former Valley of the Misborn or, more appropriately, the Watchitah Nation in *Saint Leibowitz and the Wild Horse Woman*. It is where Brother Blacktooth finally settles at the end of the novel. He works as a tutor and scribe in exchange for food. It is where he dies and is buried.

**Postulant** a person on probation prior to being admitted as a candidate to receive holy orders. Postulants are prevalent in *A Canticle for Leibowitz* and *Saint Leibowitz and the Wild Horse Woman*.

**Potear Wetok** *see* **Wetok, Potear.**

**Potens in terra erit semen ejus** Latin: "His seed shall be mighty upon earth." A line from Psalm 111 (DB) which is used by the monks to time the lighting of the arc lamp with the arrival of Don Thaddeo to the abbey's basement in the novella "And the Light Is Risen."

**Pottscar, Colonel** the Ignatzian Chief Chaplain of the Texark forces in *Saint Leibowitz and the Wild Horse Woman*. He tells Filpeo Harq what he knows of Cardinal Brownpony's arrival in Hannegan City. He also argues against spending funds to Christianize the Nomads. They will allow themselves to be baptized, take the money, and then ignore the priests. Filpeo's nickname for him is Pottsy.

**Pottsy**   Filpeo Harq's nickname for Colonel Pottscar. From *Saint Leibowitz and the Wild Horse Woman*. See also **Pottscar, Colonel**.

**Preternatural gifts**   a gift from God that is relatively beyond and/or above man's nature but not completely beyond that of all nature. The term is usually used in referring to the gifts such as immortality and immunity from suffering originally granted to Adam in the Garden of Eden. In *A Canticle for Leibowitz* ("Fiat Homo"), Miller uses the term Preternatural Gifts of the Holy Virgin in presenting the Dominicans' argument before New Rome that the Virgin Mary shared the preternatural gifts of Adam and Eve prior to the Fall. They present the Assumption and Immaculate Conception as evidence of her preternatural powers.

**Pretty Dances**   a cute and comely distant Grasshopper cousin of Brother Blacktooth in *Saint Leibowitz and the Wild Horse Woman*. Given the way she smiles at Blacktooth whenever he glances at her the morning after the Nomad slaughtering festival, he assumes she was the woman who visited his tent for a night of revelry during the festival.

**Price**   a minor unseen character in the short story "Vengeance for Nikolai." He is one of only two men in the sergeant's squad to remain alive.

**Prime**   the first hour of the Divine Office, six A.M., the time of morning prayer. It is after Prime, early morning, when Dom Paulo takes Thon Taddeo to see the Memorabilia and the result of Brother Kornhoer's electric dynamo is revealed to both men in *A Canticle for Leibowitz* ("Fiat Lux"). The term is also used in the "Fiat Voluntas Tua" section of the novel.

**Primordial time**   the time of an ancient cataclysm from which life as it is known in *Saint Leibowitz and the Wild Horse Woman* emerged. It was a period of great death, fire and ice. The age known as Old Time follows it.

**Primrose**   Sarah Glubbes's neutroid, or mutant pet, in the novella "Conditionally Human." Dying from eighteenth order virus, Primrose is euthanized by Dr. Georges. Fearing Mrs. Glubbes will be too distraught over the death of Primrose, Dr. Georges attempts to fool her with another neutroid in Primrose's place.

**Prince Albert** (August 26, 1819–December 14, 1861)   German born husband of Queen Victoria, the British monarch. In the short story "Wolf Pack," Mark Kessel's plane is named Prince Albert.

**Princeton theory**   from the short story "Secret of the Death Dome," the idea that the metal of the Martian dome was absolute zero. The molecules of the ship's hull are locked tightly in place by the strength of a field which irradiated it from within. The molecules could not vibrate with heat energy.

**Prior Olshuen**   *see* **Olshuen, Abiquiu**.

**Priory of Saint Leibowitz-in-the-Cottonwoods**   a small Leibowitzian priory in New Jerusalem in *Saint Leibowitz and the Wild Horse Woman*. It is run by Brother Blacktooth's old friend, Father Prior Singing Cow St. Martha. Blacktooth lives there for a time after the confrontation between Cardinal Hadala's army and the Texark troops. He works in various capacities in exchange for room and board.

**Priscilla**   Mrs. Grales' six-legged dog in the novella "The Last Canticle" and *A Canticle for Leibowitz* ("Fiat Voluntas Tua"). The dog has a nasty disposition and attempts to bite Father Zerchi and Brother Joshua. Mrs. Grales believes her husband has bewitched the dog to be fearful of all people. A barking or growling dog is often perceived to be a precursor of death or disaster.

**Procession of the Cross**   part of the Good Friday services in the Catholic Church, a series of verses or meditations are recited following the carrying of a crucifix to the altar. It is part of the services performed for the novices at the completion of their Lenten vigils in *A Canticle for Leibowitz* ("Fiat Homo").

***Progress of the Mars-Culture***   a book written by Roggins and referred to in the short story "It Takes a Thief." Roggins posits that each successful generation must acquire the necessary knowledge to maintain the technology needed to restore a machine culture. This idea is the basis of the short story.

**Prometheus**   in Greek mythology, he stole fire from Olympus and gave it to man, becoming the benefactor of mankind. Zeus punished him by chaining him to a rock and sending an eagle to eat his liver. His liver grew back each night only to be eaten again the following day. He is also sometimes credited with creating the first men, forming them from clay. In the novella "The Song of Vorhu," the importance of the "human germ-plasm," or man's seed, being carried into space to perpetuate the human race is referred to as "the Promethus-fire."

**Promotor Fidei** Latin: "Promoter of the faith." Also known as the Devil's Advocate (*Advocatus Diaboli*), the Promotor Fidei is an official of the Catholic Church whose duty is to examine the evidence of miracles in cases of beatification and canonization. All objections and questions must be addressed before the process is allowed to continue. In *A Canticle for Leibowitz* ("Fiat Homo") Brother Francis thinks of what the Promotor Fidei will have to say concerning the Leibowitz relics found in the fallout shelter. In Brother Francis's mind, the Beatus is already a saint. Monsignor Flaught is the Promotor Fidei. See also **Advocatus Diaboli** and **Monsignor Flaught**

**Proteus vulgaris** a type of bacterium most often found in decomposing materials and abscesses. It is mentioned in "The Last Canticle" and *A Canticle for Leibowitz* ("Fiat Voluntas Tua").

**Prothonotary apostolic** a member of the chief college of prelates in the Roman Curia. It is more commonly spelt *protonotary*. There are four classes; the first, the de numero participantium, is limited to seven members. Their duties are concerned with beatification and canonization. It is this group that Monsignor Malfreddo Aguerra may belong to since he acts as the postulator for Leibowitz in the canonization process in *A Canticle for Leibowitz* ("Fiat Homo") where the term is used in reference to him.

**Pruchev** the author of the play "The Anarch" in the novella "The Darfsteller."

**Psalms** religious poems or songs that constitute the Book of Psalms (OT), a collection of 150. The term is derived from Psalter, the stringed instrument used to accompany the singing of the songs. It is one of the biblical books most frequently quoted from in Miller's work.

**Public Law 10-WR-3E** or the Radiation Disaster Act, provides for the proper procedures to be followed for voluntary euthanasia. It establishes penalties for heirs or well-meaning citizens who assist individuals in ending their lives. People assisting in unauthorized instances of euthanasia are to be charged with homicide. All voluntary euthanasia cases must be presided over by the Mercy Cadre within Green Star Mercy Camps following the due process of law. From the novella "The Last Canticle" and *A Canticle for Leibowitz* ("Fiat Voluntas Tua").

**Pucini Corpuscle** *see* **Pacini Corpuscle**

**Purvis, Slim** a sadistic captain of the Americanist Blue Shirts army in the short story "Vengeance for Nikolai." His brutal interrogation methods often result in the deaths of his subjects, including an elderly Russian colonel. He is ordered to interrogate Marya and whips her. General MacArmsward orders him court-martialed because of his methods.

**Pustria** the blind genny daughter of Tempus and Irene in *Saint Leibowitz and the Wild Horse Woman*. Her mother describes her as the half-sister of Ululata because Tempus, who possesses two penises, used different ones to impregnate her both times.

**P'yan** Lalyahe's former acolyte in the novella "The Reluctant Traitor." She dismisses him in favor of Rolf Kenlan. P'yan is angered by his dismissal, and Rolf suggests to Lalyahe that she placate him somehow. She does so by promising P'yan he can marry and offering Krasala to him. The offer of Krasala upsets Rolf. However, Rolf and P'yan reach their own agreement in which the latter takes Lalyahe as his mate.

**Qæsach dri Vørdar** *see* **Lord of the Three Hordes**

**Quia pulvis es et in pulverem reverteris** Latin. The epigraph for the short story "Death of a Spaceman," sometimes later entitled "Memento Homo." The phrase begins with the later title and means, "Remember man that thou art dust and unto dust thou shalt return." The priest speaks these words as he uses ashes to trace the form of the cross on the head of the celebrant during Ash Wednesday ceremonies in the Catholic Church.

**Quid sum miser tunc dicturus? / Quem patronum rogaturus, / Cum vix justus sit securus?** Latin: "What am I, who am wretched, then to say? / Whom shall I ask to be my protector, / Since even the just man is scarcely safe?" This verse from the *Dies Irae* ["Day of Wrath"] comes to Dom Zerchi's mind as he lies dying beneath the ruins of the abbey at the conclusion of *A Canticle for Leibowitz*. See also ***Dies Irae***

**Quidam mihi calix nuper expletur, Paule. Precamini ergo Deum facere me fortiorem. Metuo ut hic pereat. Spero te et fratres saepius oraturos esse pro tremescente Marco Apolline. Valete in Christo, amici** Latin: "A certain cup is filled up for me recently, Paulo. Pray to God, therefore, to make me stronger. I fear that I am doomed to die. I hope that you and the brothers will pray more often for the frightened Marcus Apollo. Farewell in Christ, friend." A passage from a letter sent to Dom Paulo at the abbey by Marcus Apollo telling him of Thon Taddeo's planned arrival at the abbey to examine the Memorabilia in *A Canticle for Leibowitz* ("Fiat Lux"). The cup Apollo mentions is an allusion to the cup of sufferings Jesus speaks of in Matthew 26:36–45 (KJV) during his agony in Gethsemane.

**Quinjori** an invention of Eli Roki in the short story "Blood Bank." It is supposedly a civilization from the other side of the galaxy.

**Quinn, Sergeant** a member of the Border Guards in the novella "The Yokel." He stops Sam Wuncie as Sam tries to find Zella Richmond's house and brings him to Colonel MacMahon.

**Quinnly** a minor character in the short story "The Little Creeps." He is a member of the senior staff considering General Jim Yaney's bombing mission. He supports the plan.

**Qum-Do** one of the members of the Yellow Guard in *Saint Leibowitz and the Wild Horse Woman*. In Wooshin's estimation, he is the best warrior among the members of the Yellow Guard.

**Qun, Faron** a character in the short story "Let My People Go." He is a slightly pudgy chemist and mineralogist with a quiet, scholarly face and small features. He and Alaia Dazille, the launch pilot of the space ark from Earth, have a romantic relationship. Their relationship results in tension between Qun and Morgun Sahl because of Sahl's unstated jealously regarding Dazille. Qun is more cautious and less impulsive than Sahl. He, Sahl, and Dazille are sent as a delegation to the planet to try to discern the true intentions of the Eridanians. When the ship they are in crash-lands on the planet, Qun's leg is broken, and the other two leave him behind. The Eridanians hold Qun hostage. They find his mind flexible and easily conditioned, and they train him to accept his assimilation into their biological socialism.

**Quo peregrinatur** *see* **Quo peregrinatur grex, pastor secum**

**Quo peregrinatur grex, pastor secum** Latin: "Where the flock wanders, the shepherd goes with it." From *A Canticle for Leibowitz* ("Fiat Voluntas Tua"), a document issued in 3749 confirming the *Motu proprio* of Celestine the Eighth and authorizing the purchase of spacecraft to implement the Church's plan to perpetuate itself in space if a holocaust occurs on Earth.

The plan itself comes to be referred to as *Quo peregrinatur*. The plan is held in abeyance until the Itu Wan disaster when the Church reactivates it, and then a starship crew is prepared to leave the Abbey of Saint Leibowitz within three days. The rudiments of the Church, the Order of Leibowitz, and the Memorabilia are to be carried to the Centaurus Colony. See also ***Ab hac planeta nativitatis...***

**Quo Vadis** Latin: "Whither goest thou?" The phrase appears several times in the Bible, most notably in John 13:36 (KJV) when Peter asks Jesus, "Whither goest thou?" and Jesus replies, "Whither I am going, thou canst not follow me now." In *Saint Leibowitz and the Wild Horse Woman*, the story is told that when Pope Benedict fled New Rome, Jesus appeared before him and asked, "Quo Vadis?" Benedict mistook Jesus for a Nomad, however, and replied, "Ad Valanam," and did not turn around.

**Qwan** minor character in the short story "Please Me Plus Three." He summons Ton of Roldin to the pylon to pipe for the dance offered to Bel.

℟ *see* **Responses**

**Rachel** Hebrew: "Ewe" or "Lamb." In the Old Testament, Rachel is the beloved wife of Jacob and sister of Leah. She is often regarded as the mother of Israel because she bore Joseph and Benjamin, two of the twelve patriarchs of Israel's twelve tribes. She died giving birth to Benjamin.

In Jeremiah 31:15 (KJV), the prophet speaks of a bitter weeping that is heard in Ramah. He imagines the spirit of Rachel, whose tomb is located nearby, crying for her lost children, the descendents of Joseph who have been deported by the Assyrians.

1. In the novella "The Last Canticle" and *A Canticle for Leibowitz* ("Fiat Voluntas Tua"), Rachel is the second head of Mrs. Grales, the tomato woman. The small, cherubic head is seemingly useless. It retains features of infancy but remains deaf, dumb and mute, although Brother Joshua believes that it smiles at him during a conversation Mrs. Grales has with Father Zerchi. When the abbey is destroyed by the shockwaves from the first nuclear explosions while Father Zerchi is hearing Mrs. Grales' confession, Rachel comes to life. Zerchi, buried beneath the rubble of the abbey, hears a childish singsong voice in the distance. Mrs. Grales approaches him, but her head sleeps soundly. Rachel's head stares at him with "cool green eyes"

and smiles innocently. Father Zerchi realizes that she has just awoken and recognizes a great ease, warmth and peace in her eyes. He sees in her an "Immaculate Innocence" and tells her to save herself and to "wash the curse of us off. Live, *live!*"

Rachel is born from the pure vessel, Mrs. Grales, and, as the lamb of God, "taketh away the sin of the world" (John 1:29 KJV). In the novel her Immaculate Conception is alluded to in Brother Joshua's dream (Chapter 25) when she whispers to him, "Accurate am I the exception ... I commensurate the deception ... I am the Immaculate Conception." Rachel's innocence and purity, her lack of Original Sin (what Zerchi recognizes as her Immaculate Innocence) link her to the Virgin Mary and to Eve before the Fall. In that capacity, Rachel may represent the new mother of mankind. Her green eyes are also indicative of positive values. It is the color associated with hope in its prescribed use for the Mass vestments on Sundays after the feasts of the Epiphany and Pentecost.

A minority critical view sees Rachel as possessing negative connotations. David Cowart, in particular, suggests that green is a color often associated with witches and evil. He believes that she may represent the lamb that he associates with one of the two beasts in Revelation 13:11 (KJV), which "had two horns like a lamb." He views Rachel as the incarnation of the Whore of Babylon (Revelation 17:4 KJV).

2. A reference is made by Chief Franklin in the novella "Conditionally Human" to "five hundred Rachels blubbering for their children" when speaking with Terry Norris about separating women from their neutroids, mutant pets that substitute for children.

*Racing Form* (or *Daily Racing Form*) the official newspaper of the National Association of State Racing Commissioners, this daily national publication devoted to horseracing provides useful statistical information concerning the day's races and the horses involved. It is used by those betting on the daily races. A tightly rolled copy of the *Racing Form* is among the items discovered by Brother Francis in the fallout shelter in *A Canticle for Leibowitz* ("Fiat Homo").

**Radiation Disaster Act** the popular name for Public Law 10-WR-3E authorizing the proper procedures to be followed to allow euthanasia in cases of radiation poisoning. The term is used in *A Canticle for Leibowitz* ("Fiat Voluntas Tua"). See also **Public Law 10-WR-3E**

**Rathwich** a member of the Mars Commission who agrees to meet with Rolf Kenlan and his party of bat-hunters in the novella "The Reluctant Traitor." He hopes to be able to continue to conceal the truth concerning the androons' humanity. He wants to maintain the status quo within Marsville and the Commission's dominance. Rolf is able to fool Rathwich and manipulate him into revealing the truth to the people of Marsville. Rathwich reluctantly agrees to the suggestion that Rolf and his followers be allowed to live in exile, but he intimates to Colonel Luling that he expects them to be covertly killed.

**R'dissimo Domno Paulo de Pecos, AOL, Abbati** Latin: "To the most reverend Lord Paul of Pecos, Albertian Order of Leibowitz, Abbot." The salutation used by Marcus Apollo in his letter to Dom Paulo in *A Canticle for Leibowitz* ("Fiat Lux").

**"Reaching Normal"** an adaptation by Anne Heche of the short story "Command Performance" as part of *On the Edge*, an anthology of three short science fiction films that originally aired on the Showtime cable network on June 29, 2001. Heche also directed the film, which stars Andie McDowell and Paul Rudd.

**Recurrence** a historical concept which holds that human events tend to repeat themselves in some manner. The cyclical paradigm of history is central to the three shorter works that provide the basis for *A Canticle for Leibowitz*. Miller suggests that humankind is doomed by a historical cyclicism to keep repeating its self-destructing mistakes. A cyclical historical pattern is also suggested in some of Miller's other short works, such as "It Takes a Thief" and "The Big Hunger."

**Red Buzzard** Brokenfoot's brother-in-law in *Saint Leibowitz and the Wild Horse Woman*. Almost sixty, he is the nominal leader of the clan. He is thin and serious, and livid patches of skin mark his body.

**Red River** one of the major rivers in *A Canticle for Leibowitz* and *Saint Leibowitz and the Wild Horse Woman*. It flows through Jackrabbit territory and Texarkana, just north of Hannegan City.

*Red Star: The First Bolshevik Utopia* an early science fiction utopian novel written by Alexander Bogdanov and published in 1908. Leonid, a young socialist and participant in the 1905 Revolution in Russia, visits a socialist paradise on Mars. The Martian society, developed through a scientific-technical revolution as well as a socialist revolution, provides the model for the society that a Bolshevik revolution on Earth would produce. Miller reviewed a new translation of the novel for the *New York Times Book Review* in his essay "Bolsheviks on Mars." See also **Bogdanov, Alexander** and **"Bolsheviks on Mars"**

**Red Tickets** the permit issued in *A Canticle for Leibowitz* ("Fiat Voluntas Tua") to allow a radiation victim to be legally euthanized according to Public Law 10-WR-3E. It is also known as a critdose [critical-dose] form.

**Regency Council of the Atlantic Confederacy** the ruling body of the Atlantic Confederacy in the novella "The Last Canticle."

**Regina Mundi** Latin: "Queen of the World." A reference to Mary, the mother of Jesus; it is used in *Saint Leibowitz and the Wild Horse Woman*.

*Regnans in Excelsis* Latin: "Reigning in the highest" [God]. Pius V's bull of 1570 excommunicating Queen Elizabeth of England as a heretic and ordering her subjects to cease to obey her government. In *A Canticle for Leibowitz* ("Fiat Lux"), the papal decree placing Texarkana under absolute interdict makes vague but ominous allusions to this bull.

**Reiber, Doctor** an unseen character in the novella "The Lineman." He conducted a survey on homosexuality among the lunar workers when women were not allowed to be part of the work crews.

**Relke, Ellen** an unseen character in the novella "The Lineman." She is the older sister of William Relke who refers to her as a grim old maid.

**Relke, William Q.** a lineman on Joe Novotny's B-shift crew in the novella "The Lineman." He is working on stringing a transmission line as part of the Copernicus Trolley Project on the Earth's moon. During his first six-year contract, his wife, Fran, who remained on Earth, wrote to tell him that she was leaving him for another man. After hearing the news, Relke resigned for another six years. He still thinks of her. When a space traveling bordello lands near the work site, Relke spends time with one of the woman, Giselle, hoping to free his thoughts of Fran, but he often sees her in Giselle's face. Relke is badly beaten by two rival workers who fear he might expose their membership in the Party, a political organization calling for a general strike among the workers. Out of curiosity, Relke had attended a few Party cell meetings but decided not to join. Troubled by Fran's leaving him, loneliness, and the question of his purpose in space, Relke finally comes to the conclusion that there is a God and that His universe is a deadly contraption. But man is too, and there is nothing the universe can do that man cannot endure. He recognizes that he is a small part of a living thing that needs to grow. He frees himself from his hatred of Fran and hopes that they can be together again one day.

**Relmone, Doctor** an unseen character from the novella "Dark Benediction." A scientist formerly at Fordham University, he is one of the dermies who is involved in an objective scientific study of the neural condition to learn more about how to live with it.

**"The Reluctant Traitor"** novella: *Amazing Stories*, 26 (January 1952), 8–82. This is Miller's longest piece of fiction after his two novels. At one time he planned on expanding it and publishing it as the novel *Mars Plan*. Apparently, he never actually did the work, and his opinion of the novella was low.

Captain Jason Kenlan was lost in the mountains of Mars beyond the city of Marsville for over a year while on a reconnaissance mission. When he returns to the city with an androon wife and what he claims is proof that her species is actually human, he is tried and hanged under the bio-laws. His last words are, "They *are* human, I tell you!" His wife is also killed.

Jason claimed to have discovered evidence that Mars had once been a satellite of Jupiter, and that it had been peopled by a now extinct race of intelligent non-humans, the Bolsewi. The Bolswei raided Earth in prehistoric times and captured a dozen pairs of humans, brought them back to Mars, and bred them for slave labor. The androons of Mars are descended from these Cro-Magnons. If the androons are indeed human, the bio-laws which forbid miscegenation between humans and androons are void.

Rolf and Lennie, Jason's sons, were both born in Marsville. They decide to defy the quarantine imposed on the walled city and travel to the mountains of which their father spoke. They believe that the Commission that rules the city killed their father to maintain the assumption of the androons' inhumanity. The sons hope to find the proof to absolve their father of guilt.

Patrol riders kill Lennie during the brothers' escape from the city. Rolf is able to rope one of the giant wool-bats, believed to be untrainable and useless for directed transportation but used by the androons for food and sport. He eludes the city's antiaircraft guns as the bat heads for a series of cliff caves along the mountain range. The city's three jets strafe the cave entrances causing the bat population of the caves to emerge in a "bat stampede."

In the confusion, Rolf slides into one of the caves and the pilots lose sight of him. He feels a gentle draft of warm air from within the cave and follows it downward and deeper into the cave. He discovers a young bat cub that is attracted to the bat blood on his sleeve, the result of his bat borne escape from the city. The young bat climbs onto his shoulder. Tired from his ordeal, Rolf falls asleep in the cave. A jolt of pain awakens him. Three androons, two men and a woman, Krasala, confront him. One hits him with a rock and tosses him over his shoulder, carrying him still deeper into the cave. Rolf bites him on the back and the other androons force him to open his mouth. He is placed on the ground and they begin to speak to him in a language he cannot understand. Krasala begins to speak haltingly in "Earthtongue." She asks why he killed Saralesara. Rolf guesses she is referring to his father's wife, and explains what happened to her and his father. When an androon tries to pick up the young bat cub, it bites him and climbs onto Rolf's shoulder again. The androons tell him he is blessed by Menbana, the bat-god.

They bring him to the council of three priests to decide if he is to die for the death of Saralesara. As they move deeper into the cave, Rolf realizes that stainless steel columns support the cave roof. He asks who built the tunnels and is told "gods." The androons' fathers served the gods, but the gods went away. The group emerges into a brightly lit room with a fountain in the middle. Murals depict the builders, the Bolsewi, cousins to the bats, or "the gods who made us" as Krasala says. Rolf can recognize Earth in one of the paintings. In the distance, he hears the hum of machinery. Rolf is questioned by the priests, one of whom is Saralesara's father who tells him that Jason had been accepted into his house as one of them. Rolf's father wanted to tell the people of Marsville that they were brothers with the androons. Rolf says his father's mistake was telling the rulers of the city rather than the people. When he is asked if he believes what his father believed, Rolf answers that the androons and his people have a common ancestor; perhaps the Bolsewi planted seeds on both Mars and Earth. The priests tell him that he is indeed blessed by Menbana, the god of wisdom. He is allowed to live among the androons under certain conditions. He must find an Earthman as a replacement for himself as a sacrifice for Saralesara, and he must assume some duty or responsibility within their society. He is invited to join the bat-hunters and become an acolyte to Menbana and serve his priestess in the temple.

Krasala tries to warn him not to do so, but Rolf thinks it might be a good way to act on an idea he has to domesticate the bats and train them from puphood. He is warned of a humiliating initiation that sometimes inhibits the acolyte from actually enjoying the hunting, but despite the warnings, Rolf accepts. Krasala, as a member of the Sacred Order, asks if Rolf can be her acolyte. It is agreed. He is taken to a cell to await his initiation.

Krasala brings him food and water and tells him it would have been better if he had chosen another role in their society; he will not like the initiation. Acolytes are emasculated with a hot iron. Rolf objects and asks to be allowed to change his mind, but it is too late. He attempts to seduce Krasala in an attempt to escape and threatens to kill her if the guards are not sent away. However, he cannot kill her and she pulls away from him. Rolf thinks about his attraction to Krasala. As he awaits his initiation, he begins to assemble a homemade grenade from the powder in his cartridges. He nibbles on the meat Krasala brought him and realizes too late that it is drugged. As he hears the guards coming, he crams the grenade in his mouth before he falls to sleep.

He awakens chained to the wall, and Krasala is standing before a brazier with a blue flame. Rolf plans to spit the grenade into the brazier. Krasala turns toward him with the hot iron and tells him to scream, but he cannot because of the grenade in his mouth. She touches his leg with the hot iron, and he screams spitting the grenade to the floor. She tells him to keep screaming, and he does until he exhausts himself. As he is led away to recuperate, the high priestess who came to view him picks up the grenade and casually tosses it into the brazier. She loses her hands in the subsequent explosion.

He sleeps for two days, and Krasala tells him he should take the time to be properly sick. He thanks her for not mutilating him, and she says many of the young priestesses do not follow the old ways. While supposedly recuperating in his cell, Rolf thinks of his father's goal to convince the people of Marsville that the androons are human and friendly. The city's Commission controls colonization, and their plan is to establish an industrialized feudalism with the androons at the bottom. If the people knew the truth, colonization could be open and free beyond the city and the control of the Commission. Rolf considers what he could do to the Commission that killed his father and brother.

On the third day after his initiation, Rolf is informed that a party of guards from the city has entered the cave and killed three bat-hunters and captured six androons. Rolf guesses that the Commission fears that he will teach the androons how to use the Bolswei machinery his father probably told them about. He asks the priests to show him everything his father knew. Krasala first takes him to the temple of Menbana. Watching a ceremony, he recognizes that the shrine they worship is an ancient, moldering stub-winged rocket covered with bat skin.

He is pulled away from the ceremony by a burly acolyte and taken to an anteroom and told to wait for Lalyahe, the new high priestess. While he waits, he examines the room's contents. He sees old tools and instruments. Intrigued by what looks like bagpipes with a collapsible plasti-metal tank, a hand crank, and a long tube or barrel, he remembers seeing one like it hanging above the seats of the council priests when he was first questioned. He finds a lubricant to soak the moveable parts and begins to scrape away the rust. When Lalyahe enters, Rolf is sitting on the floor surrounded by tools and parts. She is surprised and alarmed. She calls for the acolytes but Rolf pins her against the wall and bolts the door. She tells him the bagpipe instrument is a holy symbol and no one is supposed to touch it. She thinks Rolf has magic and wants him to be her acolyte and teach her. He tells her he will serve her if she helps him defeat the rulers of Marsville and break down its walls.

She opens the door and sends away the guards who had gathered there. She turns back to Rolf and asks him to show her his magic. He picks up the device he had been working on, and they move into the temple. Rolf fires the instrument and a bright violet light produces a white heat. Lalyahe falls to the floor in fear. Rolf tells her to get up and tell the people that Menbana has spoken to her. She tells him this is not his magic but Menbana's. He tells her it is true but that he controls the magic, and he will help her rule all the tribes in return for her help. He wants twenty-five able body bat-hunters who will obey his orders and all the so-called bagpipes or holy relics that can be found. Two to three dozen large young bats are to be captured.

Among the twenty-five bat-hunters, Rolf notices one glaring at him. He is P'yan, Lalyahe's former acolyte, and he is angry about being displaced by Rolf. Rolf tells Lalyahe to do something to placate him. She tells P'yan he may take a mate and promises him Krasala. Rolf is infuriated, but knows he has to move quickly with his plan. The bagpipe weapons have to be made operational, and the bats have to be trained to accept and obey riders.

Rolf constructs a harness and seat for the bats and weighs them down with bags of rocks to simulate the weight of men. As he gathers material, he meets Krasala who is upset about his being Lalyahe's acolyte. He tells her that there is no romantic involvement between them, that he simply needs her help. Krasala tells him that the council demands his presence and that she is supposed to spy on him for them. He asks her to delay the council as long as possible.

Rolf replaces the bag of rocks beneath one bat and climbs into the seat. He works to control the bat as it flies high above the temple floor. He sees a large cave and lands the bat there. It is a huge empty vault, previously used as a warehouse. He discovers more instruments and machine parts, and the bones of a Bolsewi in a coffin. He hears the other bat-hunters who have followed his lead now riding their bats. Flying back to the temple floor, Rolf tells Lalyahe to tell the council that the temple of Manbana will open its mouth to the sky. Krasala informs him that the council is in session; the androons who had been taken to Marsville have returned. The carry a message that they are to return Rolf or everyone in the caves will be killed.

P'yan is studying Krasala and advances toward her, speaking demandingly. Rolf attacks him but with little effect. P'yan pins him to the floor and raises his club. Krasala jumps on him, and Rolf rips a gash in his leg with a knife. P'yan tosses Krasala aside, and Rolf is about to attack him again when a group of council guards and priestesses pick Rolf up and begin to carry him to the council. Lalyahe orders the bat-hunters to attack the group but they are unable to free Rolf. Rolf cries to Krasala to pick up the bagpipe weapon, point it at the wall, and press the trigger. As she does a violet incandescence fills the temple. Rolf is released and the androons surge toward the temple entrance in fear. He hurries to Krasala, picks up the weapon, and fires a shot above the entrance to deter anyone from entering the temple. He checks P'yan's wound and applies a tourniquet. He gestures to Krasala to indicate that she is his. He points to Lalyahe to show P'yan that he should take her. P'yan nods in agreement, knocks Lalyahe in the head, and carries her off.

Rolf orders the bat-hunters to stay aloft on their bats, and asks Krasala to collect all the bagpipe weapons. He hears a PA system demand his release or the cave will be filled with gas in a half an hour. He flies to the cave above the temple floor. Most of the bat-hunters are scared. Rolf drags the boxes of machine parts and instruments and the coffin to the bats and attaches them to their harnesses. He picks up the skull and asks if it is the skull of a bat or a man. They answer it is neither. Rolf says then it must be the skull of a Bolsewi, and man can use the Bolsewi magic. He will open the temple to the sky. Using the weapon Rolf fires at the steel struts supporting the ceiling section. The ceiling collapses exposing the night sky. The acolytes kneel before Rolf and tell him they want him to be their high priest and teach them. He tells them to ride their bats out of the temple.

From the sky, he reconnoiters the Marsville guards' encampment outside the cave. He destroys the generator truck and gas tank using the Bolswei weapon. He takes four batsmen and Krasala, attacks a small group of guards, and disarms them. He then orders the grove of trees behind the truck convoy making its way to the cave be set on fire. The convoy must stay where it is, trapped between the fire and his bat-hunters.

Rolf speaks with Commissioner Rathwich in Marsville. He wants the opportunity to tell the truth to the people and sway public opinion. He believes that if they know the truth, the people's inherent frontier spirit will allow them to colonize Mars and weaken the police power of the Commission. Rolf secretly chooses the hospital for the meeting, deciding it would be the safest place from a sneak attack. He secretly goes to the Public Information Building and gains access to the broadcasting rooms. He turns off the government controlled preset recordings and tunes the modulator input to the frequency of his own portable radio unit. He returns to the hospital to set up the meeting with Rathwich. He hides the radio on the balcony and camouflages the microphone. He calls Menshrie at the *Martian Messenger* newspaper and tells him to tune his monitor to hear the conference between himself and the Commissioner and have someone take notes.

Commissioners Rathwich and Poele meet with Rolf, along with Colonel Luling. Rolf tells them that he wants what every native citizen wants: freedom and an escape from the servitude of the Commission and the city. He shows them the machine parts he found in the vault room and tells them they are proof of a pre-androon culture. Rathwich is noncommittal; he tells Rolf to proceed with the same story his father told. Rolf proclaims that the androons are human and the reason why Saralesara was killed was that she was pregnant. Rathwich is clearly surprised and stammers, "How did you know—?" but then stops. Rolf realizes he is playing for time. Rolf says the commissioners are appealing to "race" and use it as the excuse to keep the androons away from the city and the people away from the mountains. He asks Rathwich how long he has known about the Bolswei. Rathwich tells him he has known ever since he came to Mars and read his predecessors' reports. The knowledge has been kept secret to preserve power. He asks Rolf what would happen if every human being could have an unlimited supply of power. He answers his own question with "chaos," but Rolf replies, "freedom."

Rathwich tells Rolf his time is up, but a guard arrives to tell him that the transmission has gone out through the city. Rathwich orders the preset programs restored and the newspaper censored, but a large crowd is already gathered around the hospital. Rathwich orders helicopters, but Rolf tells him the bat-hunters will fire on them. Rathwich says it is a stalemate and Rolf should submit. Colonel Luling suggests that Rolf and his people be taken beyond the city and allowed their freedom with the promise to never return. Rathwich says they cannot be trusted; they are criminals and must be properly punished. Luling offers a rational response. It would be difficult to make treason charges unless it can be shown Rolf meant to overthrow the administration. People have heard part of his story, a secret trial will not be allowed. The bio-laws are not necessary if what he says is true. Rolf tells them that none of the Marsville guards have been harmed by the androons, and the only men he has are those that are with him. Rathwich asks him if he will accept exile.

Rolf knows his mission is accomplished. The people have heard the truth. The enforced containment of the people in the city will slowly erode. The future of Mars is on the plains with the people, and an independent planet will evolve rather than one in servitude to Earth. Rolf agrees to the conditions, and Luling says he will arrange it. Commissioner Rathwich tells Luling he knows what is expected of him.

Meanwhile, news arrives from the cave. Commissioner White has spoken with the chief priest of the androons. Major Mulvern is now traveling toward the cemetery where Saralesara is buried with some androons to exhume her body. Her pregnancy will provide the proof of the androons' humanity. Rathwich tells Luling to take Rolf and his people away. Rolf tells Luling if he were him, he might be expected to arrange a flight to strafe his party when they are released. Luling says that is exactly what Rathwich wants him to do. As they wait on top of the hospital for transport helicopters to take them to the airport, Rolf says he still wants assurances. He looks down at the growing crowd. It is orderly, but they too want answers. Luling tells Rolf he does not think he will be exiled for long. The people will overthrow the Commission. His father has established a precedent. But Rolf looks at Krasala and says he doesn't plan on coming back. Luling confidentially states he will not either; he has frontier fever. He joins Rolf and his followers in the transport jet, and when they find their spot, they all parachute out of the plane to begin a new life on the Martian frontier. See also ***Mars Plan***

**Reminiscentur et convertentur ad Dominum universi fines terrae. Et adorabunt in conspectu universae familiae gentium. Quoniam Domini est regnum; et ipse dominabitur...** Latin: "All the ends of the earth shall remember, and shall be converted to the Lord. And all the kindreds of the Gentiles shall adore in his sight. For the kingdom is the Lord's; and he shall have dominion over the nations...." From Psalm 21:28–29 (DB). In *A Canticle for Leibowitz* ("Fiat Voluntas Tua"), Brother Joshua hears it as part of a prayer while he is in the church courtyard struggling to decide if he will accept the position to lead the Albertian Order in space. He thinks that they are strange words for this particular night as the world teeters at the brink of war.

**Reminiscere** Latin: "Remember." The first word of the Introit of the Mass given on the Second Sunday of Lent, and from which the day derives its name. It is from a line in Pslam 24 (DB), "Remember, O Lord, thy bowels of compassion," a pray for God's assistance in order to sin no more. In the novella "The Last Canticle" and *A Canticle for Leibowitz* ("Fiat Voluntas Tua"), it is one of two special masses, a Mass in Time of War, sung in the basilica at New Rome as nuclear war nears.

**Renaissance** a French word literally meaning rebirth, the term was originally applied to the period of European civilization between the fourteenth and sixteenth centuries that experienced a cultural outburst following the Middle Ages. The term is used generally for any revival or period of sustained cultural and/or intellectual achievement. In *A Canticle for Leibowitz* ("Fiat Lux"), Dom Paulo says that both he and Benjamin desire a new Renaissance, and he believes that Thon Taddeo and his work will usher in a Renaissance. The period of "Fiat Lux" is the beginning of a period of scientific and cultural renewal after the Dark Ages of "Fiat Homo." See also **Dark Ages**

**Render unto Caesar** the beginning of a statement by Jesus as reported in the gospels. Holding a Roman coin with the head of Caesar engraved on it, Jesus says when asked if it is lawful to give tribute to Caesar: "Render to Caesar the things that are Caesar's, and to God the things that are God's" (Mark 12:17 KJV). It is generally accepted to mean, in part, that religious teachings and responsibilities are separate and different from those of the state.

1. Father Jerome mutters the beginning in a misunderstanding of some ancient history in the novella "And the Light Is Risen."

2. In his debate with Dr. Cors concerning the Radiation Disaster Act and euthanasia in *A Canticle for Leibowitz* ("Fiat Voluntas Tua"), Father Zerchi uses the term acknowledging that man-made laws make it mandatory for Dr. Cors to follow certain procedures. He comments, however, that he is subject to another law.

3. In *Saint Leibowitz and the Wild Horse Woman*, Amen Specklebird contemporizes the saying for the conclavists by stating that Jesus said: "Render unto Hannegan what is Hannegan's, and to God what is God's." He explains that when Jesus than put the coin in his pocket, the priest who gave it to him asks for it back. Jesus replies, "Who do you think Hannegan belongs to?" Amen suggests that everything is subject to the authority of God and the Church.

**Repplewaite, Peter** an unseen character in the novella "The Darfsteller." A former actor and friend of Ryan Thornier, he has licensed his psycho-physiological data for use in mannequins in autodramas.

**The Reproaches** part of the Good Friday services in the Catholic Church. These verses are sung during the Veneration of the Cross. They are addressed to the Jewish people, representing all people, who reject Christ's gifts of mercy and redemption with ingratitude.

1. Lines from The Reproaches are quoted in the short story "Wolf Pack."

2. A reference to the verses is made in the services performed for the novices completing their Lenten hermitages in *A Canticle for Leibowitz* ("Fiat Homo").

**Repugnans tibi, ausus sum quaerere quidquid doctius mihi fide, certius spe, aut dulcius caritate visum esset. Quis itaque stultior me...** Latin: "Repugnant to you, I have dared to look for something that would seem to be more learned than faith, more certain than hope, and sweeter than love [charity]. Who is more foolish than me...." Brother Francis quotes from the *Libellus Leibowitz* in *A Canticle for Leibowitz* ("Fiat Homo") as he tries to regain his inner solitude after meeting the pilgrim during his Lenten fast. It may be that Miller is basing the sayings of the *Libellus Leibowitz* on the writings of Saint Augustine, particularly *A Treatise on the Spirit and the Letter*.

**Requiem aeternam dona ei, Domine. Et lux perpetua luceat...** Latin: "Eternal rest grant unto him, O Lord. And let everlasting light shine [upon him]." Used as part of the Introit of the Masses for the dead (the Requiem Mass) and elsewhere within the Mass. Benet says it in the novella "The Lineman" as he prays for Henderson, who was killed in an accident.

**Res Publica Jerusalem Nova**  Latin: "Republic of New Jerusalem." A term used in *Saint Leibowitz and the Wild Horse Woman* in reference to the city of New Jerusalem. Res Publica literally translates as "public thing [or matter]."

**Responses**  a word or phrase sung in response to a versicle during a prayer service or hymn. The symbol for a response is ℟. The brothers at the Leibowitz abbey sing versicles and responses in the novella "The Last Canticle" and "Fiat Voluntas Tua" in *A Canticle for Leibowitz*. See also **Versicles**

**Restoration Committees**  in the novella "The Yokel," these are groups responsible for seizing destroyed cities after the war in order to rebuild them and protect technology.

**Retrahe me, Satanus, et discede!**  Latin: "Draw away from me, Satan, and depart!" Brother Joshua says these words to himself when he thinks that the Church's starship might be an act of despair. Refusing to give in to doubt, he concludes that the starship is an act of hope in man's future elsewhere. The basis for his words is found in Matthew 16:23 (KJV) when Jesus says, "Get thee behind me, Satan: thou art an offence unto me; for thou savourest not the things that be of God, but those that be of men." From *A Canticle for Leibowitz* ("Fiat Voluntas Tua").

**Richards**  a member of the first launch's crew in the novella "Six and Ten Are Johnny." He is the first crew member to disappear from the launch once it lands on the planet. He reappears at the end of the story as Rod Esperson is about to return to the *Archangel* aboard the second launch. He looks much the same except he is absent a navel and his skin is green. He insists that he awoke within one of the plants in the jungle and kicked his way out, that the jungle took him apart and put him back together. Esperson doubts the story and orders Richards be given a shot to knock him out and then secures him for the return flight to the *Archangel*. It is not actually Richards but a replica of him produced by the jungle and devoted to it. It is a lure to bring the remainder of the *Archangel's* crew to the planet.

**Richmond, Zella**  a psychologist in the novella "The Yokel." Richmond has crossed from the restored city of Jacksonville into Ruralland and has joined the Border Guard. She crossed because her superior, Ethel Robbins, disrupted her planned marriage to Herb. Richmond and Sam Wuncie cross back into Jacksonville to steal a cargo plane, but she is recognized by one of the commissioners. She reveals their plan after Wuncie has secured a plane.

**"Rickshaw Boy"**  as Paul moves Willie in a wheelbarrow in the novella "Dark Benediction," he hums a verse of "Rickshaw Boy." This may be a reference to a composition by George Anson (1904–1985) or the more popular "The Rickety Rickshaw Man" written by Ervin M. Drake and recorded in 1946 by Eddy Howard and His Orchestra.

**Riemann-Christofel tensors**  in the short story "The Big Hunger," a reference is made to space-going man's familiarity with the Riemann-Christofel tensors. In differential geometry, it is the standard means to express curvature of Riemann space. It is named for two German mathematicians Bernhard Riemann (1826–1866) and Elwin Bruno Christoffel (1829–1900), not Christofel as it appears in the story

**Rizkin**  an unseen character in the novella "Izzard and the Membrane." He is ordered to contact the American agents to verify that Porshkin is indeed alive.

**Roagan**  a twenty-year veteran of space, Roagan is the commander of the ship carrying 200 colonists to the Sigma Seven system in the novella "Cold Awakening." He senses the colonists are restless about being placed in suspendfreeze, and he fears a mutiny aboard the ship. As unrest begins to occur and Jessel, one of his crew, is killed, Roagan orders the crew armed so the suspendfreeze process can proceed in an orderly manner. Lieutenant Joley suspects Roagan may be behind the ship's unrest. He switches the suspendfreeze controls between his locker and that of Roagan, believing Roagan will die the death he plans for Joley. But Roagan awakens normally. Because of his own suspicions, Roagan had switched the controls between the first and second lockers. Dr. Fraylin is caught in his own trap and dies the death he intended for Roagan.

**Robbins, Ethel**  an unseen character in the novella "The Yokel." She is the Commissioner of Eugenics and Zella Richmond's former boss. Robbins hates Zella because Zella rated her brother a class D. In revenge, Robbins acts to discourage Zella's finacé from wanting to marry her by falsely suggesting that the Richmond genes show hereditary physical weakness. If that were so, restrictions would be placed on the couple possibly having children. Robbins is eventually fired from her position.

**Robin, Colonel**  a minor character in the short story "The Little Creeps." He works in the Provost Marshal's Office.

**Robot George Eighty**  the repair robot for Tribe George Eighty's pylon in "Please Me Plus Three." It is deactivated by Robot George Eighty-Six and then placed in supervised operation so Ton of Roldin can utilize it to help him defeat Bel.

**Robot George Eighty-Six**  a repair robot in the short story "Please Me Plus Three." George Eighty-Six is found by Ton of Roldin in the ruined pylon within the destroyed city on the plateau. It has been trying to repair the pylon for over 520 years. It provides Ton with the information he needs to defeat Bel. Ton places the robot under his supervision and uses it to help him accomplish his task.

**Rockymount**  a language of the Plains in *Saint Leibowitz and the Wild Horse Woman*.

**Rodner**  the Secretary of Defense in the short story "Check and Checkmate." He is "a slender, graying gentleman with aristocratic features." He oversees the program to identify spies within the government. President Smith orders him to prepare a strike-effort, "a full-scale blitz-operation," against all the major cities of the East for two possible dates.

**Rogan, Hal**  one of six crew members and the pilot of Launch One sent to the planet surface in the novella "Six and Ten Are Johnny." Rogan is at first apprehensive about descending to the planet, but once there he is relaxed and jocular after meeting Johnny Sree (aka Johnny Six). In communications with the *Archangel*, Rogan cannot remember members of his own launch crew. The planet's jungle eventually consumes him.

**Roggins**  the author of *Progress of the Mars-Culture* in the short story "It Takes a Thief."

**Rogin**  an unseen character in the short story "Please Me Plus Three." The guards taunt Ton of Roldin that his wife has taken Rogin as her lover, and that Rogin should be more upset than Ton over Mara's disfigurement and death.

**Roki, Eli**  the main character in the short story "Blood Bank." He is tall and thin with jet-black eyes. Roki is a nobleman and an officer of the War College from Coph IV, a planet known for its cold, proud, austere military culture. He is a Space Commander in the Sixty-Star Patrol when on a routine patrol he encounters a mercy ship from Sol III carrying emergency medical supplies. He orders a random cargo inspection of the ship. The crew refuses to stop or allow the ship to be boarded. Strictly following the regulations of the Space Code, Roki orders the ship destroyed. Although he is cleared legally of any wrong doing, his actions are viewed as having been morally suspect. He resigns his commission and intends to vindicate himself, morally certain of the correctness of his own actions.

**Roldin**  an unseen character in the short story "Please Me Plus Three." The father of Ton of Roldin, he cursed Bel and lashed the pylon with a horsewhip, striking the Keeper. He was flogged to death as punishment.

**"Roots & Sinew"**  a breezy, enthusiastic review by Miller of the novel *The Bone People* by Keri Hulme in *Commonweal*, 113 (28 March 1986), [186]–188. He briefly recounts the history of the writing of the novel and its publication before providing a synopsis of the story. Miller calls the work "timeless," and gives Hulme an A+. He states that the purchase of a first edition will be a good investment, and if many copies of the book are sold, Hulme will have the deserved opportunity to publish another book. See also ***The Bone People*** and **Hulme, Keri**

**Rorrek, San**  a member of the Taknon space force assigned to locate and kill Klia in the short story "Bitter Victory." Rorrek is a telepath with the power of mental suggestion. He is also able to change his features and form. Although he is intent on accomplishing his mission, he feels an attraction and admiration for Klia. After seemingly killing Klia, Rorrek assumes the name of Sam Rory for his life on Terra, the planet where he found Klia and where he is now stranded for the rest of his life. Perhaps through a sense of guilt, Rorrek decides to finish Klia's intended mission on Terra. After discovering that she is not dead, Rorrek must face his ambivalent feelings about Klia and his mission. Although he is shot by Klia and he blinds her during a fight, Klia cannot allow him to die. After she takes him to a doctor, Rorrek prevents her from leaving and killing herself. He decides to stay with Klia and be her eyes while they work toward accomplishing her assignment.

**Rorschach Test**  also known as the Inkblot Test or Rorschach Inkblot. A psychological test in which a subject is asked to respond to a standard series of ten inkblots to determine his emotional and intellectual functioning. It was developed by Hermann Rorschach, a Swiss psychiatrist (1884–1922). Zella Richmond administers a Rorschach Test to Sam Wuncie in the short story "The Yokel"

**Rory, Sam** the alias assumed by San Rorrek in the short story "Bitter Victory."

**RS *Voltaire*** the name of an old space ship mentioned in the novella "The Lineman."

**Rubicon** a small river in north central Italy that flows into the Adriatic Sea. Julius Caesar crossed it in 49 B.C. on his way to Rome and began a civil war with Pompey. As a result of this action, the Rubicon is associated with any limit that once passed allows no return or a commitment to a course of action that cannot be altered. In the novella "The Lineman," Relke thinks Giselle is a woman of extremes; she burns every bridge she crosses and every creek she comes to becomes a Rubicon.

***Rule of Saint Benedict*** the sixth century work composed by Saint Benedict of Nursie as a guide for laymen to live a Christian life of Biblical values within a community. Although it was originally intended for laymen rather than clerics, it became the guide for monastic rule. Based on earlier sources, it provides for a balance between prayer and work. Excerpts from the book preface the chapters of *Saint Leibowitz and the Wild Horse Woman*, and it serves as the basis for the fictional *Rule of Saint Leibowitz*. The Brothers of Leibowitz are said to still honor most of the *Rule of Saint Benedict*.

**Rulian** also known as Rulie, he is a scout from the Earth space ship that lands on the moon of Epsilon Eridani Two in the short story "Let My People Go." He finds the tunnel and entrance on the moon's surface that leads to the discovery of the abandoned space way-station. He is part of the group of four from the ship who explore the way-station.

**Rulie** *see* **Rulian**

**Rupez Cardinal de Lonzor** *see* **Alabaster III**

***R. U. R.*** a play by Karel Capek published in 1920 and first presented in 1921. It is about the Rossum Universal Robot Factory that perfects the manufacture of mechanical men and women. When the robots are given souls, they begin to act "human" and revolt against their makers.

In *A Canticle for Leibowitz* ("Fiat Lux"), Thon Taddeo offers a theory of evolution based upon "a fragment of a play, or a dialogue" that he finds in the Memorabilia "about some people creating some artificial people as slaves. And the slaves revolt against their makers." The thon offers his conjecture that a pre–Flame Deluge race created a servant species that rebelled against their creators during the Simplification. Present day man is descended from this servant species, which accounts for its inherent inferiority. Dom Paulo is outraged by Taddeo's conjecture and tells him that the Venerable Boedullus had already labeled the source material as "probable fable or allegory."

**Ruralland** all the territory outside of the controlled cities in the novella "The Yokel."

**Ruth** a never seen character in the short story "Wolf Pack." She is the girl back home waiting for Lieutenant Mark Kessel. La may be an idealized version of her.

**Ruth, George Herman Jr. (Babe)** (February 6, 1895–August 16, 1948) also known as "the Bambino" and "the Sultan of Swat." A legendary baseball player considered by some to be the greatest player of all time, he began his career as a pitcher and then became a power hitting right fielder. He played from 1914 till 1935, primarily with the New York Yankees (1920–1934) of the American League. In the short story "Wolf Pack," Mark Kessel imagines pictures of Babe Ruth hanging on the walls of the Italian homes he is destroying with his bombs.

**Sacerdos Magnus** Latin: "Great Priest." A reference to the pope in *A Canticle for Leibowitz* ("Fiat Homo").

**Saffrons** a sub-species in servitude to the Eridanians on the planet Epsilon Eridani Two in the short story "Let My People Go." They are descendents of the primitive Earthlings brought back to Eridani thousands of years ago as slaves. The Saffrons were integrated into a carefully tailored biological system to serve the needs of the Eridanians who control them through telepathy.

**Sagitta** Latin: "arrow." One of the smallest constellations in the Northern Hemisphere. Its stars are reached by man in the short story "The Big Hunger."

**Sagittarius** or The Archer, a large constellation noted for its star clusters and nebulae. It depicts the Centaur with his arrow aimed at the constellation Scorpius. The name is derived from the Latin, *sagitta*, meaning arrow. In the short story "The Big Hunger," it is one of the destinations of man's endless space exploration.

**Sahl, Morgun** a biologist and member of the crew aboard the space ark carrying 120 colonists to Epsilon Eridani Two in the short story "Let My People Go." He is described as "a Lincolnesque Machiavelli." He is tall and gaunt, with black hair and a sour drawl. Sahl maintains a distain for fellow crew member Faron Qun, in part, because of Qun's relationship with Alaia Dazille, the ship's launch pilot. He is sent with Qun and Dazille as a delegation to try to determine what the Eridanians' plans are. Sahl is skeptical of the Eridanians' reception. It is his caution and questioning that reveals their true intent. Despite mental conditioning by the Eridanians, he has the strength of mind to warn Wolek Parn, the captain of the Earth ship, and suggest to him the means by which they may disrupt the Eridanians' plan to assimilate the colonists as a subservient subspecies within the planet's biological cooperative.

**Saint Albert the Great** *see* **Albert Magnus**

**Saint Augustine** (November 13, 354–August 28, 430) also known as Saint Augustine of Hippo or simply Augustine, he was a Christian theologian and North African Bishop who is considered one of the great shapers of Christian thought into the modern period. He did not convert to Christianity until he was thirty-three years old. It is generally held that he lived an extravagant and licentious life until that time. He lived with a mistress for fifteen years and fathered a son with her. It was said that Edward Leibowitz "in his youth like the holy Augustine, had loved the wisdom of the world more than the wisdom of God." Augustine studied rhetoric, law, and philosophy. He authored a prolific body of work, including *On the Happy Life, Confessions,* and *On the City of God.*

1. In the novella "And the Light Is Risen" and *A Canticle for Leibowitz* ("Fiat Lux"), a monk refers to him as "a Fourth Century bishop and philosopher" and briefly summarizes his doctrine of *rationes seminales,* or seminal reasons (best presented in his *The Literal Meaning of Genesis*) for Don Thaddeo/Thon Taddeo. Augustine's doctrine of creation posits that God created the potential for all things to reach their full development at their proper time by implanting seminal potencies from which newer, more complex, forms of life will evolve from the lowest levels of being.

2. In the "Fiat Voluntas Tua" section of the novel, one of the members of the Church's starship crew is named Augustin.

**Saint Bernard** *see* **Feast of Saint Bernard**

**Saint Christopher** according to legend, one day a ferryman carried a child across a river. The child identified himself as Jesus Christ, the king the ferryman sought. The ferryman's name was Christopher, derived from the Greek *Christophoros,* which means "one who carries Christ." Christopher was eventually martyred for his faith. He is the patron saint of travelers. In the novella "The Last Canticle," Father Zerchi tells a young woman with radiation poisoning that "even Saint Christopher holding your crutches" could not help her walk to town.

**Saint Clare of Assisi** (c. 1193–August 11, 1253) of noble birth, she forfeited her material wealth to follow Saint Francis of Assisi and his teachings. She eventually founded with him his Second Order, the community of Poor Ladies (later known as Poor Clares), and served as the abbess of the community for forty years. Her community renounced all personal and communal property, asking for the pope's dispensation to live on alms alone. She was named a saint by Pope Alexander IV in 1255.

Mother Silentia gives Ædrea the name of Sister Clare-of-Assisi when she takes her vows in *Saint Leibowitz and the Wild Horse Woman.*

**Saint Francis of Assisi** (c. 1181–October 4, 1226) born Giovanni Francesco Bernardone to a wealthy merchant and his wife. After a carefree youth, he was taken prisoner during a border conflict between Perugia and Assisi. Upon his release, he experienced a serious illness. As he regained his health he heard the voice of God and experienced a mystical vision of Jesus. He decided to renounce his claim to his family's wealth and devote himself to a life of prayer, poverty, and service. His creed was simple: to live his life as Christ did and to follow his teachings. He founded the Order of Friars Minor (the Franciscan Order) in 1209. Three years later he founded his Second Order, the community of Poor Ladies (now known as Poor Clares) with Saint Clare. He experienced the stigmata in 1224. Pope Gregory IX declared him a saint in 1228. Saint Francis is especially noted for his generosity, sincerity, and his direct purposeful devotion.

1. In the short story "A Canticle for Leibowitz" and the "Fiat Homo" section of *A Canticle for Leibowitz,* Brother Francis shares a number of characteristics with his namesake, including humility and a singlemindedness of purpose.

2. Ædrea is given the name Sister Clare-of-Assisi when she takes her vows in *Saint Leibowitz and the Wild Horse Woman.*

**Saint George and the dragon** little of any historical certainty is known about Saint George, the patron saint of England and martyr. He purportedly lived in the late 3rd or early 4th century. The most famous of legends associated with him is his battle with the dragon. A town in Libya was plagued by a dragon, which they placated with human sacrifices chosen by a lottery. The king's daughter was selected and sent to await her fate. Saint George happened by and refused to leave the girl. When the dragon appeared, George, making the sign of the cross, attacked and wounded it. He and the girl led the dragon back to the town where George beheaded it. In response, the townspeople converted to Christianity.

In the "Fiat Voluntas Tua" section of *A Canticle for Leibowitz*, the Abominable Autoscribe is Dom Zerchi's unslayable dragon, which has bitten him on occasion.

**Saint Joseph**   husband of the Virgin Mary and guardian of Jesus. He is believed to have been a carpenter or woodworker by trade. Little is actually known about him. He is the patron of the sick and the dying. In *A Canticle for Leibowitz* ("Fiat Homo"), Father Arkos asks Brother Francis if he frequently prays to Saint Joseph to ask that his death not be an unhappy one.

**Saint Joseph School**   twenty children from this school are among the group of people the Church evacuates from Earth as part of its Dismissal of the Servants plan in the novella "The Last Canticle" and *A Canticle for Leibowitz* (the plan is referred to as *quo peregrinator* in the novel). Besides Joseph, the husband of Mary, the name of the school may also be an allusion to Joseph Calasanz (c.1557–1648), a priest noted for his advocacy of a full primary and secondary education system. He was the founder of the Piarists, the first priests to teach in elementary schools. He was canonized in 1767.

***Saint Leibowitz and the Wild Horse Woman***
New York: Bantam, 1997. The long awaited second novel by Miller and a companion novel to *A Canticle for Leibowitz*. Although it is often referred to as a sequel to the earlier novel, its action occurs chronologically between the second and third parts of *A Canticle for Leibowitz* and so is more accurately a parallel novel.

Miller was working on the book as early as 1974 when the novel is referred to in an author's note in *Commonweal*. He showed his agent Don Congdon sixty pages of the manuscript in 1978, but Congdon asked to see more before sharing it with anyone. Nothing more was done until approximately ten years later when Congdon mentioned to Lou Aronica, then a vice president at Bantam Books, that Miller had written sixty pages of another novel related to the events of *A Canticle for Leibowitz*. Curious, Aronica asked to see them as a possible addendum to the next edition of *A Canticle for Leibowitz*. Excited by what he read, Aronica was encouraged by Congdon to get in touch with Miller and let him know. About a month after first hearing from him, Miller sent Aronica another 120 pages of the story, and a contract for the novel was signed. The manuscript was originally to be submitted to Bantam by the end of 1990, but after receiving the first 250 pages, the publisher extended the delivery deadline indefinitely. The manuscript was unfinished at the time of Miller's death, but he had already selected Terry Bisson to complete the novel based on his extensive outline and notes. Bisson completed approximately the final 100 pages of the manuscript.

The novel is structurally different than *A Canticle for Leibowitz*. Rather than a tri-part structure, Miller utilizes one long picaresque narrative intertwining the affairs and developing relationship of Brother Blacktooth and Cardinal Brownpony. The work is admittedly flawed but there is also much to admire in it. Given the various elements surrounding the book's publication — the status of *A Canticle for Leibowitz*, the nearly forty year period it took Miller to produce a second novel, his suicide, and the need to have the novel finished by another writer — the relatively modest critical and popular notice the book has garnered is surprising.

Approximately seventy years after the events of "Fiat Lux" in *A Canticle for Leibowitz*, the Catholic Church is divided. When the Texarkana Empire was placed under interdict, Hannegan II occupied the lands adjacent to New Rome, the seat of the papacy. The Holy See was forced to find asylum in Valana in the Rocky Mountains to the west. Hannegan collected enough bishops to establish a rival pope in New Rome. Filpeo Harq now rules as the seventh Hannegan of Texark, and his uncle Urion Benefez is the Archbishop of the Imperial City.

At the Abbey of Saint Leibowitz, Brother Blacktooth St. George, of pure Grasshopper Nomad blood, is questioning his calling. He is experiencing conflicting visions of the Virgin Mary and the Nomad deity, the Wild Horse Woman. He petitions Abbot Cardinal Jarad to release him from his final vows and allow him to leave the order, citing a loss of unity with the other monks. Jarad refuses his request and orders him to continue his translation of a seven-volume work of the Venerable Boedullus, *Liber Originum* (*The Book of Origins*) from neo-Latin to the Grasshopper dialect of Plains Nomadic. Deacon, and later cardinal, Elia Brownpony, a lawyer and diplomat, is particularly interested in Blacktooth's work.

The pope in Valana dies, and his death is seen as a possible opportunity to end the exile and return one pope to New Rome. Abbot Jarad leaves for the conclave, and Prior Olshusen is left in charge of the abbey. He, too, refuses Brother Blacktooth's release from his vows. Because of the political discord and mistrust between the churches of Valana and New Rome, a series of elderly popes is elected for brief periods, all ending in their deaths. After the election of Pope Linus VII, Blacktooth's increasingly disruptive behavior at the abbey forces him before a tribunal that could lead to his interdiction. Cardinal Brownpony speaks on his behalf and offers him the opportunity to leave the abbey as his translator and interpreter if Blacktooth promises to obey him. Blacktooth agrees and the Cardinal leaves the abbey for Valana with a small party, including his bodyguard Wooshin, a former executioner for the Hannegans and now a political refugee at the abbey; Holy (Little Bear) Madness, whose Nomadic name is Chür Ösle Høngan; and Father e'Laiden.

On their way to Valana, the group comes to Arch Hollow, a settlement of gennies, genetically handicapped people. Brother Blacktooth is attracted to Ædrea, an apparently normal, pretty, young gennie woman. She seduces him in a barn. Brownpony tells the monk to avoid her, that she is more than she seems. Through conversation on the trip, Blacktooth comes to suspect that Brownpony, who is the head of an obscure minor office of the Curia, the Secretariat of Extraordinary Ecclesiastical Concerns, is meddling in Nomad politics, but he cannot comprehend all of the cardinal's actions. Brownpony, who is also of Nomad ancestry, hopes that the Three Hordes of Nomadic peoples, long splintered, will soon be able to unite with a common purpose led by a newly elected Lord of the Three Hordes. He wants to stop the Hannegan Empire's incursions into the Nomad territory of the Plains. He is using the offices of the Secretariat as a means of selling weapons to the gennies, hoping to create another force to act against Filpeo Harq. When the party reaches Valana, the new pope has already died and another conclave has been called.

Brother Blacktooth begins working in the Secretariat. He is lured into another sexual encounter with Ædrea who is trying to become pregnant with his child. Cardinal Brownpony is particularly adept at political maneuvering, and he works with Amen Specklebird to position the older retired priest as a viable candidate for the papacy. When Amen is eventually elected pope, he advocates the unification of the church and the return of one papacy to New Rome. Amen's election causes unrest within the College of Cardinals, especially with Archbishop Benefez and his supporters who refuse to recognize him as pope. Attempts are made on the lives of Brownpony and Blacktooth. Pope Amen names Brownpony the Vicar Apostolic to the Three Hordes, the spiritual leader of the Christians on the Plains.

Pope Amen and most of the Curia leave Valana to begin travelling toward New Rome with an escort of Nomad warriors. Brownpony travels to the sacred meeting place of the Nomads' Weejus and Bear Spirit shamans to experience an ordeal within the Navel of the World, the sacred pit of the Wild Horse Woman, a crater formed from a nuclear explosion. Blacktooth is sent with a small group as the pope's emissary to New Jerusalem. There he intends to seek news about Ædrea.

After Brownpony successfully completes his trial and sees the Buzzard of Battle, he is accepted as the Christian high shaman of the Nomads. Holy Madness and Kindly Light, the war chiefs of the Wilddog and Grasshopper hordes respectively, also experience their own trials in the pit. Holy Madness is named Lord of the Three Hordes. Brownpony rides with Kindly Light and a warrior escort to meet Amen's party. He asks Pope Amen to allow him to travel to the Abbey of St. Leibowitz to join in the mourning for Abbot Jarad who recently died. He will then travel to Hannegan City as the pope's legate.

As the pope continues toward New Rome, Hannegan's guards stop his entourage at the border crossing. He is barred from continuing any further by the order of Filpeo Harq. The pope turns back toward Valana, but Kindly Light, angered by not being paid for his services as escort, orders his men to take the road to New Rome. They kill the Texark guards and attack the settlers, pillaging as they go. Although Kindly Light is executed by the Nomads for treason against the Lord of the Three Hordes, Filpeo Harq accuses Pope Amen and Cardinal Brownpony of ordering the Nomad attack.

When Brownpony arrives at the abbey, he begins to suffer the effects of the radiation he was exposed to in the breeding pit. Prior Olshuen is elected the new abbot. Brownpony is reunited with Brother Blacktooth at the abbey. Blacktooth had been told in New Jerusalem that Ædrea died during a miscarriage, and having completed his mission there, he decided to make his way back to the abbey. Brownpony asks Blacktooth to travel east with him to Hannegan City. They will be accompanied only by Weh-Geh of the Yellow Guard. After they leave the abbey, Benjamin, the old hermit who lives on the Mesa, arrives with the pregnant Ædrea, and Olshuen tells her that Blacktooth believes she is dead.

During their journey to Hannegan City, Brownpony learns of the actions of Kindly Light and his subsequent ritual death. Filpeo Harq demands the surrender of the remaining Nomad warriors involved in the raids and reparations or else there will be total war. Brownpony sends a message to Pope Amen advising him to do nothing until he is able to speak with Filpeo. When the cardinal arrives in Hannegan City, Filpeo Harq is meeting with his military leaders planning for a long-term strategy on the Plains. At the cardinal's meeting with Harq, he and Weh-Geh are ordered seized. Coming to the defense of Brownpony, Weh-Geh is killed. Brownpony and Blacktooth are taken to jail, accused of attempted regicide and heresy. During their stay in prison, Pope Amen resigns the papacy. As a result, Filpeo Harq releases the two prisoners if they agree to acknowledge the charges against them and accept suspended sentences of death and permanent banishment from the Texark Empire. Brownpony and Blacktooth do so and travel back to Leibowitz Abbey.

At the abbey, Brownpony learns that he has been elected pope by the conclave after Amen's resignation. Olshuen also tells him that Ædrea had come looking for Blacktooth. Brownpony refuses to accept his election as pope because the conclave was not legal, and he continues to recognize Amen as pope. He tells Blacktooth that Ædrea may be alive and that he should talk with Benjamin. Benjamin tells the monk that Ædrea gave birth to twin boys. Having no place left to go, she decided to return to her father at Arch Hollow, but the babies were given up for adoption before she left because she feared her father might kill them. Meanwhile, in Hannegan City, Archbishop Benefez initiates a petition for a General Council of the Church to be held in New Rome to draft legislation concerning proper conclaves. The Curia in Valana is angered by his action and threatens excommunication for any cardinal who agrees to the meeting. Opposing sides within the church solidify, and Brownpony meets with representatives of the Nomads about raising a combined armed force of papal soldiers, Nomads, and mercenaries. Blacktooth now realizes that Brownpony's purpose is nothing less than the destruction of the Hannegan Empire and the restoration of the New Roman papacy.

Cardinals loyal to Pope Amen arrive in Valana for a conclave to elect a new pope. Cardinal Brownpony is once again elected and this time he accepts and assumes the name of Amen II. Among his first actions as pope, Amen II excommunicates Filpeo Harq and Archbishop Benefez, and places the church in Hannegan City under interdict. He and most of the conclave leave the city for New Jerusalem, but Blacktooth is waylaid by Ulad and impressed as a corporal in the Valana Militia to fight for the Holy City. Cardinal Hadala has a plan to arm the gelps in Watchitah Nation to fight against the Hannegan Empire and intends to bring wagons full of weapons to them. As the various forces depart the city, a housekeeper discovers Amen decapitated in his hut.

Hadala leads the militia across the plains, violating the Nomad's territory. When they encounter Texark forces, Hadala orders an infantry attack. During the battle, the cardinal is killed by Gai-See, and the militia is routed, saved only by the intervention of Demon Light who captures the wagons of weapons. The remainder of the militia travels with the Nomads back to Valana.

In New Jerusalem, Ædrea is placed under house arrest for leaving the city without permission. While in jail, she begins her studies to become a nun under the mentorship of Mother Silentia. She eventually takes her vows as a nun of the Order of Our Lady of the Desert, assuming the name Sister Clare-of-Assisi. Mother Silentia immediately complains to Pope Amen II that one of her nuns is now being held in jail by the city's secular government. The pope orders sacraments withheld from Magister Dion and his son, Slojin, until Sister Clare is released. Amen II remands her into Silentia's permanent custody and sentences her to cross the Brave River and to spend the rest of her life in exile or until the pope commutes her sentence. Her sentence is identical to what her vows demand of her.

Pope Amen II calls a council of war in New Jerusalem. Plans are made for an expedition to capture New Rome, but while the pope wants to simply take the city and restore the Church's proper authority over it, the Nomads want to burn and destroy it. Because of the action of the Valana militia and Kindly Light's men on the Plains, Texark forces have begun attacking Nomad families in the west. As hostilities escalate, the pope must send some Nomad warriors to the rear to deal with the Texark cavalry units.

At the same time, the Lord of the Hordes decides to attack Hannegan City as well, badly weakening the strength of his warriors.

Pope Amen II names Blacktooth as his ambassador to the remaining population in New Rome. However, the farmers of New Rome want revenge for the killing of their families and livestock by Texark forces, and they ride toward the camp of the pope and his Nomad allies. The farmers attack but are easily defeated by the Nomads who enter the city and set fires.

Blacktooth is caught in the middle of the hostilities and is captured in New Rome and sentenced to death. He is taken to the death cells. As smoke and fires rage in the city, he beats on his door of his cell and prays to St. Leibowitz. A gelp boy pulls out the bars of his cell window and saves him.

As New Rome burns around him, Blacktooth helps a farmer push his cart of household goods out of the city and toward the Misspee River. There he stays with refugees from the city and boat people until the fires in New Rome die out. Returning to the rubble of the city, he goes to the ruins of St. Peter's to pray and finds Pope Amen II already there. The pope tells Blacktooth that he was foolish to trust the Nomads. He assembled the three hordes, armed them with repeating weapons, and then set them in motion toward the destruction of New Rome. The battle against Hannegan is lost; the Texark forces are too strong and fast. The pope's gelp allies are returning to their homes, and the Lord of the Hordes was called home, where Texark forces continue to attack Nomad settlements. The Texark cavalry is on its way to New Rome.

Pope Amen II is advised to leave, but he moves instead to the throne of St. Peter's. He tells Blacktooth to run for his life and to live the life of a hermit. He should teach those who come to him about God to "be yourself." As instructed by the pope, Wooshin beheads Amen II. Wooshin then attempts suicide, asking Blacktooth to assist him. Blacktooth refuses to do so unless Wooshin declares, "Long live Filpeo Harq!" Blacktooth and Wooshin leave by the cathedral's rear door as Texark cavalry approach from the front.

At first they follow a small group of wagons headed toward the Watchitah Nation. Wooshin breaks off to head for Hannegan City where he beheads Filpeo Harq in the street and is subsequently killed by his guards. Blacktooth strays from the wagon train to bury two crucified clerics. He begins to head west and sees a vision of St. Leibowitz taking the halter of a mule carrying the Day Maiden and two babies. Leibowitz looks directly at Blacktooth as if to say, "Come." Blacktooth collapses. He believes Saint Leibowitz is taking the Wild Horse Woman toward Hannegan City because she always chooses the victor as her Lord.

Blacktooth slowly makes his way back to the Abby of Saint Leibowitz, burying bodies along the way. Abbot Olshuen has died and Prior Devendy has taken his place until a new abbot is elected. The brothers want to elect Blacktooth as their abbot but he refuses. He goes to visit Benjamin and then travels to New Jerusalem finally making his way to the convent of San Pancho Villa of Cockroach Mountain where Mother Silentia welcomes him. She tells him that Sister Clare has probably returned to her own people in the Valley of the Misborn.

Pope Sorely, the new pontiff, summons Blacktooth to Hannegan City for a papal audience. The pope tells him that Texarkana controls the situation on the Plains and the Empire is secured. Hongan Os was put to death upon his return home, and the Three Hordes have turned their backs on one another. The pope gives Blacktooth a small sack of gold for travelling money, and the monk heads toward the Valley of the Misborn where he is taken in. He settles in a rock house cave above the small community of Post Cedar where he trades his services as a scribe and tutor for food. He grows old there, visited twice a week by a Leibowitzian priest.

In a convent just over the mountain, Sister Clare lives quietly. She has a sense that the hermit in the next valley is dead, and she walks to Blacktooth's cave and finds his body. She buries him with a small cross at the head of his grave, taking with her his rosary and g'tara.

**Saint Leslie**   the theological calculus of this fictional saint is briefly referred to in *A Canticle for Leibowitz* ("Fiat Voluntas Tua").

**Saint Maisie of York**   she is referred to in the novella "And the Light Is Risen" and *A Canticle for Leibowitz* ("Fiat Lux") as having died during a laughing fit while laughing at herself. Her Mass includes laughter. She is Miller's creation, not an actual saint of the Catholic Church.

**Saint Michael**   the greatest of the four archangels, protector of Christians, especially soldiers, and guardian of Israel. In The Book of Revelation, he leads heaven's hosts against the hosts of Satan. He is most often portrayed carrying a sword and shield. His feast day is September 29.

1. General Rufus MacAmsward is called a Michael the Archangel with a swagger stick in the short story "Vengeance for Nikolai."

2. In the novella "The Last Canticle" and *A Canticle for Leibowitz* ("Fiat Voluntas Tua"), Mrs. Grales is a member of the parish of St. Michael's, where Father Selo refuses to baptize Rachel.

3. Father Zerchi tells Brother Joshua that as he leads the Visitationist Friars of the Order of Saint Leibowitz in space he should always remember Earth, but warns him never to return. If he attempts to come back, he is liable to meet the archangel with a sword of flame guarding her passes. From the novella "The Last Canticle" and *A Canticle for Leibowitz* ("Fiat Voluntas Tua").

4. In *Saint Leibowitz and the Wild Horse Woman*, Pope Amen II speaks of celebrating a quiet mass on Saint Michael's feast day, and the Cathedral of Holy Michael, the Angel of Battle is

located in Hannegan City. *See also* **Sword of the Archangel**

**Saint Paul** formerly Saul, who as a strident Pharisee and Roman citizen, was determined to persecute the Christian incursion in the Jewish community of Damascus. On the road to Damascus he experienced a conversion in which he saw Jesus so clearly he was temporarily blinded to all else. Paul began to preach the gospel and became the great apostle to the Gentiles. He undertook three extensive missionary journeys, organizing numerous congregations across Asia Minor. His epistles constitute much of the New Testament. He was imprisoned several times and finally beheaded in Rome in A.D. 67 (see Acts 8–28, KJV). His death is mentioned by Father Zerchi in the novella "The Last Canticle" as among the atrocities of mankind.

In "Fiat Lux" Dom Paulo is associated with St. Paul not only in his debates with Thon Taddeo but also in his physical description. In 2 Corinthians 10:10 (KJV), Paul's "bodily presence" is described as being "weak," and he has been depicted as generally physically unimpressive, bald and bow-legged. Dom Paulo has thinning hair and is stooped and emaciated. Paul was a contemporary of Apollos, and Dom Paulo is a contemporary of Marcus Apollo.

**Saint Petrus Murro** *see* **Celestine V**

**Saint Poet of the Miraculous Eyeball** *see* **Poet-sirrah**

**Saint Raul the Cyclopean** fictitious saint found in *A Canticle for Leibowitz* ("Fiat Homo"). He is the patron saint of the misborn. In Greek mythology, Cyclopes were a race of one-eyed giants. The single eye was centered in their foreheads.

**Saint Silverius** (?–December 2, 537?) the son of Pope Hormisdas and successor to Pope Agapitus I as a result of the influence of Theodahad, king of Italy. He served as pope from June 1 or 8, 536 until November 11, 537. As pope, Silverius was entangled in the political intrigue of Justinian I's plans to conquer Italy. Silverius offended Empress Theodora, Justinian's wife, a Monophysite, by refusing to support the restoration of Anthimus, a Monophysite patriarch. Theodora had hoped to use her influence to place Virgilius, who had promised to restore Anthimus, as the next pope. Because of his refusal, Silverius was falsely accused of plotting against Rome. He was removed as pope, reduced to a monk, and exiled. Allowed to return to Rome for a fair trial and possible restoration to the papacy, Silverius was instead victimized by Vigilius who had become the next pope. He died from suffering and starvation. His feast day is June 20th. Reference is made to Silverius and his feast day in *Saint Leibowitz and the Wild Horse Woman* when Amen Specklebird uses the day for the observances of the patroness of his order, Our Lady of the Desert. The year of Silverius's death is given as A.D. 538 in the novel. Although the exact date is not known, it is generally accepted to be in A.D. 537.

**Saint Stephen** Saint Stephen was a Jew who converted to Christianity. He was accused by the elders of a group of synagogues of blasphemy and was stoned to death, becoming the first Christian to die for his beliefs (Acts 6:5–7:60). In the novella "The Last Canticle" and *A Canticle for Leibowitz* ("Fiat Voluntas Tua"), Father Zerchi says he needs five young novices "with a yearning for martyrdom" to carry signs outside the Green Star Mercy Camp because they may get what Saint Stephen got.

**Saint Ston** a college in Valana in *Saint Leibowitz and the Wild Horse Woman*. The students at the seminary march in favor of naming Amen Specklebird pope. It is the college Jæsis transfers to after failing Thon Yordin's tests at the university in Texark.

**Saint Thomas Aquinas** (c. 1225–March 7, 1274) influential theologian and philosopher, student of Albert Magnus, and member of the Dominican Order. He held the chair of theology at the University of Paris. The author of numerous works, including *Summa Theologica* (1266–1273), believed by many to be one of the finest and most complete theological treatises ever written. He was declared a Doctor of the Church in 1567. He is mentioned in relationship to Albert Magnus in *A Canticle for Leibowitz* ("Fiat Homo").

**Salmon Armenians** as Dom Zerchi lies beneath the rubble of the abbey after the nuclear blast at the end of "The Last Canticle" and *A Canticle for Leibowitz* he sees a rosebush with a single pink rose still attached. The outer petals of the rose are singed. Russell M. Griffin suggests that the pink color of the rose is a blending of the red rose representing earthly love and the white rose of God's love. The color pink is also related to joy and wisdom. In Gnosticism, the color is associated with resurrection. Roman mythology associates a pink rose with pain and suffering in the story of Rhoanthe who was turned into a pink rose by Apollo when she attempted to become the protector of women against his will. A single rose is often symbolic of love and completion.

**"Salvador"** Locus Award winning short story by Lucius Shepard published in 1984 and included in *Beyond Armageddon*.

**Salve Regina** Latin: "Hail, Queen." A widely used prayer in the Catholic Church, also known as "Hail, Holy Queen." It has been set to music and is also sung as a hymn. It is sung as part of the evening service at the abbey in *A Canticle for Leibowitz* ("Fiat Lux"). In *Saint Leibowitz and the Wild Horse Woman*, a man plays it on a harmonica.

**Sampetrius** a workman at the basilica in New Rome in *A Canticle for Leibowitz* ("Fiat Homo"). The word is a derivation of the Italian Saint Peter.

**Samuel warned us against them** in the novella "And the Light Is Risen," Benjamin tells Father Jerome that he hopes Don Thaddeo will be "on our side this time, and not with the *others*." When Jerome asks what he means by others, Benjamin cites Manasses, Cyrus, Nebruchadnezzar, and Hannegan. He says they are most dangerous when wise men are available to be their viziers. He states: "Samuel warned us against them before he gave us one." In 1 Samuel 8, the Israelites ask for a king to judge them. In 1 Samuel 8:10–18, Samuel cites reasons why this is unwise, such as inscription, taxes, and loss of property. Nonetheless, the people demand a king. Saul is crowned and initiates a reign marked by war, persecution, and jealousy.

The scene is essentially repeated in *A Canticle for Leibowitz* ("Fiat Lux"), although Benjamin adds Pharaoh and Caesar to his list of dangerous men.

**San Pancratz** *see* **Military Order of San Pancratz**

**San Pietro of Mount Murrone [Morrone]** (c. 1209–May 19, 1296) Peter of Murrone, Pope Celestine V. More than two years after the death of Pope Nicholas IV, Peter of Murrone, a Benedictine monk and devout hermit who was more than eighty years old, was elected pope despite his objections. Poorly suited for the office, politically manipulated, and generally unhappy, he resigned the papacy after just five months. The next pope, Boniface VIII, had him confined in order to prevent a possible schism developing within the church. In *Saint Leibowitz and the Wild Horse Woman*, Cardinal Benefez suggests that Amen Specklebird and San Pietro are "two of a kind," meaning they are both saintly clowns who are too inept to be pope.

**Sancta Dei Genitrix, ora pro nobis. Sancta Virgo virginum, ora pro nobis...** Latin: "Holy Mother of God pray for us. Holy Virgin of virgins, pray for us...." Part of the Litany of the Saints as recited during the canonization of Isaac Leibowitz in *A Canticle for Leibowitz* ("Fiat Homo").

**Sancta Maisie, interride pro me** Latin: "Saint Maisie, laugh for me." Miller intends a play on the word intercede. In Latin, *ridere* is the intransitive verb for laugh. Used in *A Canticle for Leibowitz* ("Fiat Lux"). See also **Saint Maisie of York**

**Sancte Isaac Eduarde, ora pro me** Latin: "Saint Isaac Edward, pray for me." A reference to Isaac Edward Leibowitz, voiced by Brother Blacktooth, as he awaits the decision of the tribunal in *Saint Leibowitz and the Wild Horse Woman* and again near the novel's end when he believes he sees the image of Saint Leibowitz beckon him forward.

**Sancte Leibowitz, exaudi me** Latin: "Saint Leibowitz, hear me." An invocation voiced by Brother Francis in the short story "A Canticle for Leibowitz" even before the canonization of Leibowitz.

**Sancte Leibowitz, ora pro me** Latin: "Saint Leibowitz, pray for me." Brother Francis whispers these words as he examines the relics he discovered in the fallout shelter in *A Canticle for Leibowitz* ("Fiat Homo").

**Sancte pater, ab Sapientia summa petimus ut ille Beatus Leibowitz cujus miracula mirati sunt multi...** Latin: "Holy Father, we ask from the highest wisdom that the Blessed Leibowitz, whose miracles many have marveled at...." Among the words spoken by Monsignor Aquerra to the pope as part of the canonization process for Isaac Leibowitz in *A Canticle for Leibowitz* ("Fiat Homo").

**Sanders, Abe** the actor who plays the character of Captain Chronos on the television program "Captain Chronos and the Guardsmen of Time" in the short story "The Will." He goes in character to the house of Kenny Westmore, a 14-year-old boy dying of leukemia, in a publicity stunt for the show. After being kicked out of the house, he returns to apologize and arrange for Kenny to participate in the show's children's panel.

**Sanjoanini** the people who clean and maintain the Cathedral of Saint John-in-Exile in Valana in *Saint Leibowitz and the Wild Horse Woman*. The name is derived from Saint John.

**Sanly Bowitts**  an emergent village near the Abbey of Saint Leibowitz in the southwest desert of the Empire of Denver in the novella "And the Light Is Risen" and *A Canticle for Leibowitz* ("Fiat Lux"). It benefits from its proximity to the abbey, as evidenced by its literacy rate of 8 per cent. As the population increases, there is a growing desire for control over the abbey by the village. This causes some animosity between the abbey and the village, but in the novella, Father Jerome recognizes that the village's desire for control is rooted in community pride. Macklehark is the village's mayor. In the novella "The Last Canticle" and "Fiat Voluntas Tua" in *A Canticle for Leibowitz*, the village has grown to the size of a small city. The name is derived from a distortion of Saint Leibowitz.

**Santa Librada**  generally believed to be a fictional Portuguese saint also known as Saint Wilgefortis. She refused her father's order to marry a suitor in order to preserve her vow of virginity. In answer to her prayers, she supposedly grew a beard to discourage all suitors. Her father, the king of Portugal, had her crucified. The origin of the name is variously given as derived from the Latin for *free* or from a Spanish expression meaning *the chosen* one. In *Saint Leibowitz and the Wild Horse Woman*, Mother Silentia gives Brother Blacktooth a prayer card with the picture of a crucified woman and the name of Santa Librada. The prayer card says to pray to Santa Librada when one is in trouble with the police or the courts or when freedom is not visible.

**Santa Librada del Mundo**  the first line of a brief poem or prayer printed on the back of a prayer card given Brother Blacktooth by Mother Silentia. Blacktooth takes it to Amen. Although the pope tells him he will not translate it for him, he provides a rough translation: "Set free from the world, / I have eyes, but cannot see; / I have hands, but cannot touch; / I have feet, but cannot walk. / With the angels of 43, / Mary's blanket covers me. / Mary's breasts turn me rosy."

**Santalot, Elmofire [Elmofier]**  an associate professor at Texark University in *Saint Leibowitz and the Wild Horse Woman*. He holds a doctorate in science and is a member of the Order of the Vacquero. A major in the Reserve Calvary, he is on leave from his unit in order to pursue his studies at the Leibowitz Abbey, even though it has been called to active duty. No one at the abbey knows what he is studying. He recognizes that Benjamin is suffering from Hilbert's disease and provides the pills to protect the monks from contracting the disease. He explains to the abbot that Hannegan is deliberately introducing disease as a weapon. The variant spellings of the name each appear in the text. Miller intended the name to be an allusion to Saint Elmo's fire, the often luminous corona discharge surrounding ships in storms.

**Sarah**  1. The wife of Abraham in the Old Testament. Her name was originally Sarai but it was changed when God promised the couple the birth of Isaac. Sarah gave birth to her only child when she was 90 years old. The birth of Isaac, the son of promise, is often viewed as God's commitment to the preservation of the Israelites. In the novella "The Song of Vorhu," Barry Wilkes has no particular desire to play the part of Father Abraham and perpetuate mankind, especially since his Sarah is the White Idiot. See also **Abraham**

2. A minor character in the short story "Command Performance" (also known as "Anybody Else Like Me?"). She works in the same psychology laboratory at the university as Kenneth Grearly. She is the woman Grearly loves, but he believes he cannot have her if he is to perpetuate the mutant characteristic he shares with Lisa Waverly.

**Saralesara**  an androon and daughter of one of the priests of the council in the novella "The Reluctant Traitor." She marries Jason Kenlan, but when they return to Marsville, he is executed and she is killed to hide her pregnancy and the proof that the androons are human.

**Sarkal**  Hannegan II's courtier (and the favorite of his third wife) in the novella "And the Light Is Risen" and *A Canticle for Leibowitz* ("Fiat Lux"). His purported mission is to inform the Plains tribes of the Agreement of the Holy Scourge. Marcus Apollo believes that he went with an ulterior purpose since he was able to return alive from his meeting with Mad Bear, the Nomad clan leader.

**Sarquist**  an unseen character in the short story "Dumb Waiter." He was the mayor of the city before the nuclear war. Mitch Laskell uses his car during his escape from prison and eventually finds his way to the mayor's home. Sarquist had a direct channel to the central computer as part of his emergency powers. Mitch breaks his identification code so he can reprogram the city's computers.

***The Satyricon of Lily Brown***  a musical selection Relke dials up in the novella "The Lineman." It is subtitled: "an orgy in New African Jazz (for adults only)." The *Satyricon* of Petronius Arbiter

(c. 27–c. 66) is a famous bawdy, satirical picaresque Roman novel, only part of which survives.

**Sawyer, John Harbin**  a character in the short story "I Made You." Sawyer is a captain within the Instruction and Programming Section of the Autocyber Corps currently on the Earth's moon. He programmed Grumbler, a mobile combat robot, to fight, but the robot has been damaged and can no longer distinguish its makers from the enemy. Sawyer is wounded in an attempt to immobilize Grumbler and is trapped in a cave. After his last hope of being rescued is lost and he is down to his final tank of air, Sawyer emerges from his cave to confront Grumbler. Sawyer is perplexed that the robot he programmed is now superior to him and the cause of his death: "I made you, don't you understand? I'm human, I made you —" are his last words.

***Sayings of Saint Leibowitz***  a compendium of the extant writings of Saint Leibowitz in *Saint Leibowitz and the Wild Horse Woman*. Brother Blacktooth loves the cryptic book.

**Scala caelestis**  Latin: "Heavenly stairs [staircase]." The stairs the pilgrims must climb in the basilica in New Rome in order to arrive at the anteroom for an audience with the pope in *A Canticle for Leibowitz* ("Fiat Homo").

**Scapegoat**  based on Leviticus 16:8 (KJV), "And Aaron shall cast lots upon the two goats; one lot for the Lord, and the other lot for the scapegoat," the Day of Atonement ritual consists of two acts: the sacrifice of a goat to the Lord on behalf of the priesthood, and the casting out of a second goat on behalf of the people of Israel. A priest confesses the sins of the people over the scapegoat, and it is sent into the wilderness bearing the sins of the nation.

1. When Dom Paulo returns the blue-headed goat to Benjamin in *A Canticle for Leibowitz* ("Fiat Lux"), the hermit tells him, "I suggest you curse it and drive it into the desert."

2. In *And the Light Is* Risen and "Fiat Lux," at the dinner for Thon Taddeo at the abbey, the Poet-sirrah tells the Thon to crown the goat with the crown of Saint Leibowitz, but blame Leibowitz and drive *him* into the desert.

**Scarecrow Alley**  the area on the perimeter of New Jerusalem, the genny settlement in *Saint Leibowitz and the Wild Horse Woman*. While almost ninety per cent of the gennies of New Jerusalem are spooks, those able to pass without identifiable genetic defects, Scarecrow Alley is populated by gleps, those gennies with obvious genetic defects. Scarecrow Alley serves as a buffer and the first line of defense between New Jerusalem and the outside world.

**Schauspieler**  German: "Actor." Used by Ryan Thornier in the novella "The Darfsteller" who declares himself not a *schauspieler*. Thornier is using the word in a pejorative sense, saying he is not a mere actor who reads his lines but rather an artist who embodies the role he is playing.

**Schism**  a formal breach or division within a church. Two major schisms have occurred within Christianity: the Great Eastern Schism (or Schism of the East) and the Great Western Schism (or Schism of the West). The Great Eastern Schism developed between the Orthodox Church and the Roman Church over philosophical misunderstandings and doctrinal issues. The Western Schism within the Roman Catholic Church (1378–1417) occurred less because of doctrinal issues and more as a result of politics and attempts to consolidate power and influence. Rival papacies developed between Clement VII in Avignon and Urban VI in Rome, both of whom claimed to be the rightful pope. Unable to resolve the conflict between the papacies, the cardinals created further confusion by electing a third pope, Alexander V. The controversy was finally resolved at the Council of Constance in 1417.

There are overtones of the Great Western Schism in both of Miller's novels. In *A Canticle for Leibowitz* ("Fiat Lux"), after the Church places Texarkana under absolute interdict for the death of Marcus Apollo, Hannegan II declares himself the only legitimate ruler over the Church. He names Benedict XXII a heretic and occupies the lands surrounding New Rome. When Benedict leaves to create the papacy in exile in Valana, Hannegan establishes a rival pope in New Rome. At the start of *Saint Leibowitz and the Wild Horse Woman*, the schism is 65 years old. It is the intent of Pope Amen I and Pope Amen II to restore the true papacy in New Rome and end the schism.

**Schneider-Volkov Act**  from the novella "The Lineman," this legislation requires that all personnel on any member country's venture within the Lunar Project must be of a single sex. The law essentially prohibits women from the moon. Members of the Party want to call a general strike in an effort to repeal the act. The act is also known as the SV Act.

**Schultz**  minor character in the short story "Crucifixus Etiam." He is a guard.

**Schultz, Adelia**  a minor character in the

novella "Conditionally Human" who buys a neutroid from O'Reilley's Pet Shop whose serial number does not match the manufacturer's list. This anomaly leads Terry Norris to the discovery of the deviant neutroid Peony.

***Schutstafel*** more commonly appears as ***Schutzstaffel***, it was originally formed in 1925 to serve as Adolph Hitler's personal body guards. It evolved to become the primary force for internal security within Nazi Germany before World War II and the notorious *Waffen SS* during the war. In the short story "The Little Creeps," General Yaney tells General Horrey that he had to knife a *Schutstafel* major to obtain the camera broken by the demonstrators outside Yaney's home.

**Schwarzschild, Karl** (1873–1916) a German born astronomer known for his seminal work in black hole astrophysics. In the short story "The Big Hunger," Miller refers to Schwarzchild [sic] Line-Elements.

***The Science Fiction Stories of Walter M. Miller, Jr.*** collection published by Gregg Press (Boston) in 1978 with an introduction by David N. Samuelson.

Contents: "You Triflin' Skunk," "The Will," "Anybody Else Like Me?," "Crucifixus Etiam," "I, Dreamer," "Dumb Waiter," "Blood Bank," "Big Joe and the Nth Generation," "The Big Hunter," "Conditionally Human," "The Darfsteller," "Dark Benediction."

***Scitote Tyrannum*** Latin: "You Shall Know that the Tyrant." The title of an eight-page decree issued by Pope Amen II in *Saint Leibowitz and the Wild Horse Woman*. The document announces the excommunication of Filpeo Harq and Archbishop Benefez, declares the Church in Hannegan City under interdict, and calls for a crusade to depose Filpeo and unify the Church. The title is taken from the opening words of the text.

**Scorpion** *see* **Scorpius**

**Scorpius** the Latin word for scorpion, which it is also called, gives this large constellation lying between the constellations Libra and Sagittarius its name. It is the home of Antares, a brilliant red, supergiant star.

1. It is one of the places man's spaceships reach to conquer and colonize in the short story "The Big Hunger."
2. In *A Canticle for Leibowitz* ("Fiat Voluntas Tua"), Brother Joshua thinks that the Church's starship will help establish man in peace somewhere in the stars. He thinks that perhaps it may be on one of the struggling colonies on planet "What's-its-name" in Scorpius.

**Scriptorium** a monastery room used for copying, reading, illuminating and similar works, as at the Abbey of Saint Leibowitz.

**Scullite, Mariono** the Bishop of Denver in *Saint Leibowitz and the Wild Horse Woman*. He is elected Pope Linus VII. See **Linus VII**

**Scurrilous versificator** *see* **Poet-sirrah**

**Secon Janna** *see* **Janna**

**Secon Samesh** the Social Director or dictator of a totalitarian state in the short story "I, Dreamer."

**Secon Teacher** *see* **Barnish**

**"Secret of the Death Dome"** short story first appearing in *Amazing Stories*, 25 (January 1951), 124–144. Reprinted in *Amazing Stories*, 40 (June 1966), 84–110. This is Miller's first published science fiction story. He has referred to it as "terrible" in an interview (Wilber).

Ten years ago, Martians landed in a huge dome in the western desert of the United States. During that period, they have neither attacked nor offered friendship. They occasionally seize a curiosity seeker as a specimen. The Martians sometimes broadcast lectures on themselves, but their veracity is unconfirmed. The dome is unfazed by "the most magnificent of Earth weapons," so for want of something better to do, the dome is largely ignored except for military patrols.

One day Barney Willis, a scout with the special patrol, falls dead from his horse at the edge of one of the nearby towns that developed safe distances from the dome. He dies from sunstroke, but an examination of his body also reveals that the Martians emasculated him. There is puzzlement over the Martians' interest in human genitalia since it is believed from their lectures that they are sexless.

Jerry Harrison, Willis' best friend, is ordered to take the body back to Willis' home. Betty, Willis' wife and Jerry's former girlfriend, wants vengeance. Jerry is assigned Barney's former patrol and is ordered to find out what he might have seen regarding the dome and the Martians. While thinking about the dome, Jerry dozes off only to be awakened by a sound he feels more than hears. It scares his horse away. Command makes radio contact with him when his horse returns without him. The dispatcher tells him they will send somebody to him who is not already out looking for Betty. She is headed to the dome. The Martians ask Jerry why Betty would be so illogical. Jerry responds, "hate," and asks why they did what they did to Barney.

The Martians explain that they want to make a human organism with several changes to the structure.

In a rage, Jerry begins walking toward the dome. After shooting blindly and ineffectively at it, he begins to walk around the dome, yelling for the Martians to do something or show themselves. He sees Betty approaching in the distance, and sets out crawling beneath the dome looking for vents to access the structure. He hears the death shrieks of a horse and figures the horse and rider have been killed. Approaching the center of the dome, he feels a draft of air and follows it to a louvered vent. He fires into the vent and shots are returned. He sees a silhouette beneath the dome and shoots it, killing a Martian. He crawls to the body to examine it and realizes that the Martian lectures have been lies.

The dome begins to descend upon him. He crawls back to the vent and in desperation shouts that he has been sent by the government to bargain with them. The Martians tell him he is lying but that his emotions are interesting; they are curious about what sounds he will make as the pain begins. Jerry again tells them that he is from the government and that he knows their broadcast lectures are false; they are not sexless. The dome stops descending, and he is asked about the source of his knowledge. He lies and tells them that Barney saw something they did not know he saw. He feels the sound of thumping again and blacks out.

He awakens in a dimly lit room within the dome. A female Martian communicates with him through his radio and tells him that his statements were untrue. Barney told him nothing; they know he examined the Martian he killed. When he asks how they know Barney did not reveal anything, he is told that they questioned another captive — Betty. He struggles futilely against his bonds but stops and asks his captive for water. The Martian, whom Jerry now refers to as Gertrude, returns with a thimble of rusty tasting water. Jerry surmises that the Martians have the need for only a small consumption of water. He asks for a bucket of water and is told that he will be brought to it.

As Gertrude leads him through the dome, he sees a spherical shell with many ducts entering it that appears to be central to the dome's functioning. He sees only female Martians and asks where all the males are. He is told to ask no more questions. When they approach the water tank, Jerry sees that Gertrude is afraid to even be near the tank. She loosens his restraints and tells him to drink. He fills his mouth with water and spurts it at Gertrude. She writhes in pain and drops her stun gun. Freeing himself from his restraints, Jerry grabs the gun. He fires at the tank of water until a thin spray of water begins. Other Martians begin to fire at him, but the spraying water hits a hot furnace sending steam into the area. The Martians withdraw, and Jerry guesses that they can die of suffocation if their skin becomes clogged with moisture.

Dragging Gertrude with him, Jerry looks for Betty. They enter a large room adorned to represent Mars and see an old, fragile Martian laying asleep. Jerry threatens Gertrude to find where Betty is being held, but she simply tells him that Betty will die before he can reach her. He turns toward the sleeping Martian with gun in hand, and Gertrude yells at him not to shoot the male. Jerry uses her concern for the male's welfare to have Betty brought to the central control room where they will meet her. He takes the old male Martian with him for protection. As they move through the corridors, the Martians take precautions to protect themselves from any moisture. Jerry mocks them saying it would be hell if they were caught in the rain. Gertrude takes him seriously and tells him that the Martians have prevented it from raining in the area and eventually will stop all precipitation on Earth. As they reach the control room and Betty, more Martians attack as the moisture begins to dissipate. Jerry grasps the male Martian as a hostage and threatens to destroy the apparatus that supports the entire dome. The Martians believe it is an illogical act since both he and Betty will also be killed. Betty urges him to do so as the only chance to save Earth. Jerry is struck by a gun blast and his leg is broken. He fires at one of the ducts and a shockwave rocks the dome. The Martians stop and tell him not to fire again or his rage will destroy them all. Jerry wants them to release him and Betty; he will take the male to ensure their safety. Gertrude tells him it is impossible; he is their only male. Two other males remain on Mars. A plague prevented any males from being born, but the virus cannot exist on Earth. That is why they have come to Earth.

Gertrude makes a sudden move toward Jerry, and he fires but she is not seriously hurt. Everyone understands that the gun is low on energy. The Martians close in and Jerry shoots the male who doubles up weakly. He shoots him again, this time in the head, and kills him. Jerry then loses consciousness. When he awakes, he is with Betty but still within the dome. He does not understand why they are still alive. The Martians do not experience anger or rage and simply accept that their mission is a failure. There is no reason to do anything now with Jerry and Betty except let them leave. The dome will return to Mars. The Martians cannot risk losing the last two males on Earth.

Seeing Jerry safely back to his home, his leg now in a cast, Betty tells him that she is leaving and that

Jerry should not try to see her—for a couple of months at least. Jerry does not tell her what he learned from Gertrude: that the Martian plan was to alter a human female with Martian genes so she could give birth to Martian males. Betty was to be that woman.

**Secretariat for Extraordinary Ecclesiastical Concerns**   an obscure and minor office of the Curia in Valana in *Saint Leibowitz and the Wild Horse Woman*. Referred to as a "bureau of trivial intrigues," Cardinal Brownpony secretly uses it to furnish weapons to New Jerusalem. It is sometimes cited by its acronym SEEC.

**Sed tantum dic verbo**   *see* **Domine, non sum dignus**

**Sedarii**   *see* **Sedarius**

**Sedarius**   a bearer of the pope's chair on ceremonial occasions. Within the context of *A Canticle for Leibowitz* ("Fiat Homo"), he also serves as a messenger or assistant. The sedarius wears a crimson or scarlet doublet. The word may derive from the Latin "*sedile*," for seat or "*sedes*," meaning a slave in charge of sitting arrangements. *Sedarii* is the plural form.

**Sedate**   Latin: "Be seated." Directions to the monks at the conclusion of a prayer in the novella "And the Light Is Risen" and *A Canticle for Leibowitz* ("Fiat Lux").

**Sede vacante**   Latin: "The see is vacant." A phrase used when a see, the jurisdiction of a bishop, is vacant because of a death or removal. It is most notably used in reference to the death of a pope and the resulting vacancy in the papacy. In *Saint Leibowitz and the Wild Horse Woman*, Pope Amen I insists upon a law allowing the pope to declare *sede vacante*, permitting his own resignation.

**SEEC**   an acronym for the Secretariat for Extraordinary Ecclesiastical Concerns in *Saint Leibowitz and the Wild Horse Woman*.

**Seevers, Doctor**   a former Princeton University biochemist studying the neuroderm in the basement laboratory of St. Mary's hospital in the hyper colony on Galveston in the novella "Dark Benediction." A physically small man, Doctor Seevers has contracted the neuroderm but has burned off the spots on his hands that give rise to pleasurable sensations with an electric needle so he will not be distracted from his work by the craving to spread the disease through touch. He has discovered that the neuroderm actually creates new nerve endings. Father Mendelhaus asks Dr. Seevers to tell Paul about the neuroderm. The doctor encourages Paul to be as objective as possible and to rid himself of all the preconceptions he has about the disease. When Paul later believes that he has been touched by a hyper, he asks Seevers if there is any way he can be disinfected.

**Selni, Antonio**   a Catholic priest who makes monthly visits to a Mars Project work site to celebrate Mass and hear confessions in the short story "Crucifixus Etiam."

**Semper super capitem tuum feces descendent avium**   Latin: "May the feces of birds always rain upon your head." One of the declarations Brother Blacktooth makes before the gelp Barlow after his father, Tempus, demands Blacktooth absolve his son before he will release the monk from their hut in *Saint Leibowitz and the Wild Horse Woman*. Since he cannot offer absolution, Blacktooth gives them three curses in Latin.

**Semper virgo**   Latin: "Always virgin." A phrase usually used in reference to the belief that Mary remained a virgin even after the birth of Jesus. In *Saint Leibowitz and the Wild Horse Woman*, Brother Blacktooth uses the phrase referring to Ædrea because of the operation that prevents her from having intercourse.

**Sergeant Agnes**   *see* **Agnes, Sergeant**

**Serpens**   a constellation also known as the Serpent, it is divided into two unequal parts separated by the constellation Ophiuchus, the Serpent Holder. One part, the head, lies in the Northern Hemisphere, and the body, the smaller section, lies in the Southern Hemisphere.

  1. In the short story "The Big Hunger," man colonized a planet revolving around 27 Lambda, a yellow sun in Serpens.
  2. A spaceship is seen in the sky between Serpens and Arcturus in the novella "The Lineman."

**Seruna**   the wife of Cardinal Brownpony in *Saint Leibowitz and the Wild Horse Woman*. Outlaw Nomads kidnapped her, and she is considered dead, although it cannot be proven. Brownpony acknowledges that she was unhappy in their marriage, though he "loved her in my way." They had one son together.

**Servant of the Servants of God**   a term used mainly by the popes in reference to themselves. Pope Amen II makes the self reference in *Saint Leibowitz and the Wild Horse Woman*. The term is also referred to in the novel by the acronym S.o.So.G. In Latin, the term appears as *Servus servorum Dei*. See also **Servus Servorum Dei**

**Servo Six** the Servopilot of recon six, an alien reconnaissance ship in the short story "The Triflin' Man" (also published as "You Triflin' Skunk"). After Lucey shoots and kills the Missionman, the alien coming to reclaim her son Doodie, Servo Six recommends a delay of the invasion plans for Earth given the unpredictability of the mothers of the genetic analogs.

**Servus Servorum Dei** Latin: "Servant of the servants of God." A self-referencing title used by the popes, especially in important written documents such as papal bulls. It is part of a signature, purported to be that of Pope Amen, on a document in *Saint Leibowitz and the Wild Horse Woman*. See also **Servant of the Servants of God**

**Sext** the fourth of the seven canonical hours, corresponding roughly to noon.

**Shake the dust off your sandals** in Mark 6:11 (KJV) Jesus tells his disciples as he sends them out to teach: "And whosoever shall not receive you, nor hear you, when ye depart thence, shake off the dust under your feet for a testimony against them. Verily I say unto you, It shall be more tolerable for Sodom and Gomorrah in the day of judgment, than for that city." The gesture is interpreted sometimes as an attempt to invoke a change of heart, rather than a condemnation or curse.

1. In the novella "The Last Canticle," the message from New Rome confirming the Dismissal of Servants plan reads, "Shake the dust off your sandals and go preach Sodom to Gomorrah." See **Sodom and Gomorrah**

2. At the conclusion of "The Last Canticle" and *A Canticle for Leibowitz*, the last monk to board the Church's starship stops to take off his sandals and beat the dirt out of them before he enters the ship.

3. In "Fiat Voluntas Tua," Brother Joshua thinks that the hope for man finding peace in space is a "weary and dog-tired hope," a hope that says, "Shake the dust off your sandals and go preach Sodom to Gomorrah," but it is still hope or why go at all.

**Shard** an old genny man with white hair and mottled skin in *Saint Leibowitz and the Wild Horse Woman*. He is chief of his village, Arch Hollow, in the lower mountains of the Suckamint range. He offers hospitality to Cardinal Brownpony's party on their way to Valana.

**Sheba is coming to Solomon** according to 1 Kings 10:1–3 (KJV), when queen Sheba, ruler of the Sabaeans, heard of the wisdom of Solomon, she traveled to Jerusalem to test him and "prove him with hard questions."

1. In the novella "And the Light Is Risen," when permission is denied Don Thaddeo to have the Leibowitzian relics brought to him, Marcus Apollo writes to Father Jerome to tell him "Sheba is coming to Solomon after all": Thaddeo will make the trip to the abbey to study the relics.

2. In *A Canticle for Leibowitz* ("Fiat Lux"), Marcus Apollo tells his clerk, Brother Claret, to tell Dom Paulo, "Sheba expects Solomon to come to her," meaning Thon Taddeo expects the Memorabilia to be sent to him in Texarkana. When Dom Paulo holds fast in his refusal to send the documents, Apollo informs him that Taddeo will instead be coming to the abbey.

**Sheckley, Robert** (July 16, 1928–December 9, 2005) American science fiction writer known for his novels *Journey Beyond Tomorrow*, *Dimension of Miracles*, and *Immortality, Inc.* Like Miller, he contributed scripts to the television series *Captain Video and His Video Rangers* as well as *The Twilight Zone*. His short story "The Store of the Worlds" appears in *Beyond Armageddon*.

**Sheldon, Nick** a member of the *Martin Snyder Show* crew in the short story "The Corpse In Your Bed Is Me." He wants to marry Felicity Larkin, another crew member, but Snyder warns them that they will both be fired if they get married. After they decide to postpone their marriage, Snyder seduces Felicity and then fires her from the show. Nick marries her a month later, and Snyder fires him too.

**Shepherd, Lucius** (August 21, 1947–) American author primarily known as a science fiction and fantasy writer, although his work transcends easy categorization. His work has received numerous awards including the Hugo Award and the Nebula Award. His short story "Salvador" for which he won the Locus Award in 1985 is included in *Beyond Armageddon*.

**Sheriff Yates** a minor character in "Conditionally Human." After experiencing difficulties picking up all the possible deviant neutroids on his list, Terry Norris calls Yates to have warrants issued for three people who refused to cooperate. Norris asks Yates to have his men pickup the remaining neutroids.

**Sherman II** a large commercial community of fifty blocks in Wylo City in the novella "Conditionally Human." It is where O'Reilley's Pet Shop is located.

**Shirikane, Furi**  appointed a cardinal by Pope Amen in *Saint Leibowitz and the Wild Horse Woman*. He is from the west coast and speaks the same dialect as Wooshin. He may be part Asian.

**Shon, Esser**  a member of the collegium and an unseen character in the novella "And the Light Is Risen" and *A Canticle for Leibowitz* ("Fiat Lux"). Thon Taddeo recounts his colleague's work as an effort to synthesize living protoplasm using only six basic ingredients. Brother Armbruster ridicules the idea. He is referred to as Don Esser Shon in the novella.

**Shrive**  to shrive is to administer the Sacrament of Penance. In the novella "The Last Canticle" and "Fiat Voluntas Tua" in *A Canticle for Leibowitz*, Mrs. Grales repeatedly begs "shriv'ness" from Father Zerchi. In *Saint Leibowitz and the Wild Horse Woman*, Brother Blacktooth regrets leaving the abbey without being shrived.

**Shriv'ness** *see* **Shrive**

**Si diligis me**  Latin: "If thou lovest me." The title Missa "Si Diligis Me" or Si Diligis Mass, Common of One or Several Holy Popes, is taken from John 21:15–17 (KJV): "If thou lovest Me, Simon Peter, feed My lambs." In *Saint Leibowitz and the Wild Horse Woman*, Pope Amen II celebrates the Mass of a Sovereign Pope, *Si diligis me*.

**Sibelius, Jean**  (December 8, 1865–September 20, 1957)  Finnish composer of symphonies and choral works. He is known particularly for his patriotic works, including the tone-poem *Finlandia*. In the novella "The Lineman," Relke identifies a piece of music as being by Sibelius: "Concerto for Something and Violin. I dunno." Sibelius wrote only one violin concerto, *Violin Concerto in D minor*, Op. 47.

**Sic transit mundus**  Latin: "Thus does the world pass away." The "last monk," perhaps Brother Joshua, mummers these words as he takes off his sandals and boards the Church's starship with the horizon aglow from nuclear explosions at the end of *A Canticle for Leibowitz*. The words are taken from "Sic transit Gloria mundi" ["Thus does the glory of the world pass away."] which is used at papal consecrations. The phase is recited as a flame is extinguished before the new pope as a reminder of the transitory nature of earthly power and glory. Miller significantly omits the word glory.

In the novella "The Last Canticle," the monk simply says "Sic transit," before boarding the ship.

**Sigma Seven System**  the destination of 200 colonists in the novella "Cold Awakening."

**Sikiewitz, Doctor**  a minor unseen character in the short story "The Little Creeps." He is a psychiatrist who has treated General Clement Horrey after the general has begun to see tiny luminous rods creating patterns on his bedroom walls at night.

**Silentia, Iridia**  Pope Amen made Mother Silentia a cardinal, the second woman in the Sacred College in *Saint Leibowitz and the Wild Horse Woman*. She is a member of a community of barefoot nuns of the Ordo Dominae Desertarum Nostrae, the Order of Our Lady of the Desert. Because she wears the same habit as Ædrea once used as a disguise, Brother Blackfoot approaches Mother Silentia for news regarding Ædrea when he sees her in Valana. She responds by giving him a prayer card for Santa Librada.

When Ædrea is imprisoned, Mother Silentia visits her three times a week and becomes her mentor and protector, preparing her to take her vows. She gives Ædrea the name of Sister Clare-of-Assisi. She acts as her defense council at her trial, and Sister Clare is placed in her permanent custody when she is sentenced to exile.

When Blacktooth seeks Sister Clare at the Monastery of San Pancho Villa of Cockroach Mountain after the war, Mother Silentia is the one who tells him that Sister Clare has probably returned to her people in the Valley of the Misborn.

Silentia is derived from the Latin for silence.

**Simpleton**  in the short story, "A Canticle for Leibowitz" a simpleton is a common man, an honest, upright, virtuous citizen during the Age of Simplification. He is in opposition to the learned man who led mankind into the paths of destruction. In *A Canticle for Leibowitz* ("Fiat Homo"), a simpleton is anyone opposed to the "smart bastards"—politicians, teachers, scientists, technicians—who were responsible for the Flame Deluge and the Fallout. Also a proponent of The Simplification. See also **The Simplification**

**The Simplification**  in the short story "A Canticle for Leibowitz" and *A Canticle for Leibowitz* the period of chaos and mass murder that followed the Flame Deluge and the Fallout. Those deemed responsible for making the Earth what it had become—scientists, rulers, technicians, and teachers—were identified and killed. All people of learning became targets of violent mobs and were eliminated. Anarchy ruled and the people's hatred of the learned and learning was passed down through generations. Sporadic mob violence occurred through at least four generations following the Deluge. Fear and hatred came to be directed not only against the learned but also against those who could merely read. Also destroyed were all books and records that might contain information that could once again lead man into paths of mass destruction.

During the Age of Simplification, many learned men sought sanctuary in the Church to escape persecution. As a result, many monasteries were invaded and their records and sacred books burned.

The mobs were at first derisively called simpletons, but the people accepted the term to separate themselves from the "smart bastards" who destroyed the world. Their stated purpose was to build a "Simple Town."

**Sine cupidine** Latin: "Without desire." When Amen Specklebird hears Brother Blacktooth's confession in *Saint Leibowitz and the Wild Horse Woman*, he tells him that the path of following Christ should be "*sine cupidine.*"

**Singing Cow St. Marks** a Nomad runaway and companion of Brother Blacktooth and Wren St. Mary. They made their way together to the Abbey of Saint Leibowitz prior to the start of *Saint Leibowitz and the Wild Horse Woman*. He works in the abbey's printing shop and eventually becomes the prior of Saint Leibowitz-in-the-Cottonwoods.

**Sir Eric Cardinal Hoffstraff** *see* **Hoffstraff, Sir Eric Cardinal**

**Sir Rische Thon Berker** *see* **Berker, Sir Rische Thon**

**Sire of the Day Maiden** the Nomads use this title to refer to their sharf in *Saint Leibowitz and the Wild Horse Woman*. Chür Ösle Høngan is the Sire of the Day Maiden.

**Sister Clare-of-Assisi** the name taken by Ædrea when she takes her vows as a nun of the Order of Our Lady of the Desert in *Saint Leibowitz and the Wild Horse Woman*. She takes her vows on the day of the Feast of Saint Clare and is thus named by Iridia Silentia. August 12th is the feast day of Saint Clare, who co-founded the order of Poor Ladies, now known as Poor Clares, with her friend and mentor Saint Francis. See also **Saint Clare**

**Sister Helene** she unexpectedly comes upon a naked Brother Joshua as he is washing the dust off himself in a sink after taking readings from the abbey's roof in the novella "The Last Canticle" and *A Canticle for Leibowitz* ("Fiat Voluntas Tua").

**Sister Julian of the Assumption** a nun from the Secretariat of State who works at the Secretariat of Extraordinary Ecclesiastical Concerns in *Saint Leibowitz and the Wild Horse Woman*. Her job is to maintain a close watch on the "extraordinary concerns" that might affect the diplomatic relations of the Valanan papacy. Cardinal Brownpony chooses her along with Brother Blacktooth as one of his conclavists.

**Sister Magdalen ("Cries-a-River")** a former Jackrabbit Nomad who was one of the Sisters who raised Elia Brownpony. While Brownpony's memory of the Sisters is marked by resentment generally, Sister Magdalen holds a special place. She took particular care with his education and told him stories. Brownpony's wife, Seruna, reminded him of her when they first married. Her name is derived from that of Mary Magdalene who was saved by Jesus and, as a result, became devoted to him. See also **Mary Magdalene**

**Six, Johnny** *see* **Sree, Johnny**

**"Six and Ten Are Johnny"** novella: *Fantastic*, 1 (Summer 1952), 4–39, 160. Reprinted in *Fantastic Stories*, 15 (January 1966), 6–41, 156–158. The starship *Archangel*, with a crew of 70, has been mapping and photographing a newly discovered planet for nearly a month. The crew has nicknamed it "The Nun" because of its chaste and mysterious veil of clouds. A six crew launch piloted by Hal Rogan goes to the surface to attempt the first manned landing on the planet. The launch is scheduled to spend 40 hours on the planet without communication with the starship because of the ship's orbit.

Rogan flies the launch through the layers of clouds and lands on a mesa within a lush putrid green jungle. He radios Commander Isaacs and Lieutenant Rod Esperson on the *Archangel* that he sees a log cabin. A fat humanoid life form waves from the doorway and begins to make its way toward the launch. Communication is lost with the launch for a short period, but is reestablished. Rogan informs Isaacs and Esperson that they are not the first humans on the planet. The starship *Yorick*, presumed lost almost ten years ago, made an emergency landing after most of its crew were accidentally poisoned. Johnny Sree, the fat man, is one of only three survivors from the *Yorick*. His skin and hair are now the color of the jungle — chartreuse and splotched. Rogan and the launch crew assume Johnny is crazy. He talks to the other two survivors although Rogan does not see anyone else. Johnny maintains three beds in the cabin and three places at the table. He fawns over the launch crew.

Isaacs believes the odds are too great for a coincidental landing so near to where Johnny landed. He checks the last records of the *Yorick* and discovers that its last report was three light years from the planet. When he asks Esperson what he thinks, Rod replies that he has no thoughts only bad feelings. He is concerned that Rogan's attitude has quickly changed once on the planet. He has gone from nervousness and dread to a leisurely joviality. Isaacs orders Esperson to tell Rogan to report every hour, but when he speaks with him, Rogan sounds drunk and Rod hears laughter in the background. Rogan tells him that he likes the place and that Johnny has all five of the crew. Rod notes to himself that it is a six man crew. Isaacs orders them back to the ship, but Rogan informs him that one of the launch's engines needs to be repaired by Greeley before they can return. He is ordered to maintain contact every hour.

Isaacs sends Rod to get some sleep while he monitors the radio. Isaacs awakens him later asking him to come talk some sense to Rogan. He tells him to ask Rogan how many men went down in the launch. When Rod does so, Rogan names only three besides himself. Rogan is having breakfast with Johnny and believes that Isaacs and Rod are simply kidding him. He refuses to acknowledge the existence of any missing crew members.

The *Archangel* will soon be out of communication with Rogan, but Isaacs believes he has discovered something about the jungle. It is a single large organism, an animal and vegetable duality. The keynote of life on the planet is cooperation rather than conflict. The jungle feeds Johnny too; fruit trees grow right into his cabin window. The question is what does Johnny do for the jungle? Rogan radios the *Archangel* to ask when they are going to send someone down to repair the launch engine. The transmission is faint, but when he is asked about Greeley, Rogan does not know who he is. He now names only two other crew members with him and Johnny Six. Rod says he thought the name was Sree, but Rogan replies it is not Three but Six. Communication is lost between the launch and starship. At Rod's urging Isaacs decides to maneuver the *Archangel* back into communication range and to take a second launch to the planet's surface. When the ship is able to communicate with the surface again, there is no response from Rogan. Isaacs places Allenby in command of the ship and orders him to wait 80 hours and then leave for home if neither launch has returned. As the second launch descends to the planet, Isaacs and the rest of its crew get headaches and fall ill, but Rod does not. He wonders if the silver plate in his head, the result of a fractured skull five years earlier, has any bearing on why he does not share the others' discomfort.

As they reach the landing site of the first launch, they attempt to contact Rogan but Johnny replies instead. He now refers to himself as Johnny Nine. When asked where the crew is, he says they are asleep. Told to wake them he says it is not their time to awake and ends radio contact. Rod is concerned that Isaacs has no emotional response to Johnny's answer; he accepts it as fact. As they circle the landing site, Rod sees the first launch on its side half covered with vines. Isaacs orders him to land. Isaacs and the crew hurry out of the airlock, most without their weapons. Rod is at a loss to explain their behavior. He inspects the first launch and finds it deliberately sabotaged. Johnny Nine enters the launch behind him and after studying Rod tells he is not like the others. Johnny says he does not think Rod will like the planet. Revolted by Johnny's presence, Rod shoves him out of his way so he can exit the ship. Johnny cuts his hand and his blood is nearly black.

As he moves outside, Rod hears an explosion from the second launch. Isaacs and the crew stand nearby laughing as a second explosion occurs. Rod runs toward the launch but is tripped by vines. The crew ignores him. Reaching the launch, he removes the communication transmitter so Isaacs cannot order any more men to the planet. Rod seeks out Johnny and asks him personal questions concerning Rogan's wife. When Johnny answers the questions correctly, Rod shoots him twice. Isaacs and the crew fire at Rod. They run toward Johnny and soon forget Rod's presence. Rod speculates that the men are suffering from a hypnotic delusion and that his cranial silver plate protects him. However, what is the source of the delusion?

He begins to make his way around the perimeter of the mesa, avoiding the thick foliage, although it seems to slowly turn and follow him. A large orchid-like blossom blocks his path; its petals open like the "jaws of a rattler." Rod shoots it through its supporting tendril, and the plant writhes back out of his path. As he moves along, he spies other plants with bulging tendrils of various sizes. One is large enough to suggest Rogan's possible fate. Rod continues until he sees the cabin. He enters it and from its window he watches a "flying thing" appear high above the jungle. As it comes nearer, he realizes that it carries a man he recognizes as Jeffers in its talons. The creature swoops down and appears to feed Jeffers to a giant blossom. Rod shoots at the plant and the creature drops Jeffers. Rod runs toward him but finds that another plant has already consumed Jeffers. He shoots and cuts the stem to free his crewmate. When Jeffers comes to, he does not recognize Rod. He maintains a childish smile and begins walking toward another blossom. Rod struggles to restrain him, finally stabbing him in the thigh and beating him unconscious.

Wondering what to do with Jeffers and also realizing that he is hungry, Rod makes an intuitive connection between Johnny's cooking and his own silver plate. He runs into the cabin and finds a set of pots. He places one over Jeffers' head as a helmet. As he waits for some reaction from Jeffers, Rod uses the information gained from Rogan and what he has seen to surmise that Johnny is actually an animal living in symbiosis with the jungle, a single vegetable form. Rod believes that when the jungle consumes a person it so completely analyzes its microstructure that it even understands the significance of patterns imbedded in its tissue.

Jeffers begins to awaken and tells Rod that he has had some kind of dream, but Rod tells him his dream was real. Jeffers begins to ramble in disjointed phrases that make some sense to Rod because of their context. Rod is so absorbed in trying to understand what Jeffers is saying that he fails to hear Johnny approach from behind. Fully recovered from his wounds, he carries a gun. He wants Rod and Jeffers to climb into flowers. When Rod asks why, Johnny says how else could they know what Rod and Jeffers know? The jungle seeks information and it learns through ingestion; it adds to its knowledge by feeding. As Rod kneels to free Jeffers' feet to make it easier to lift him, Jeffers kicks out and grazes Rod's head. Rod feigns unconsciousness, and Jeffers gets to his feet and begins to run. Johnny fires and hits him in the leg. He falls and the pot comes off his head. Rod reaches for his weapon and shoots off the top of Johnny's head. He places a tourniquet on Jeffers' leg and replaces the pot on his head. He uses an incendiary grenade to blow up Johnny. They make their way back to the launch under cover of darkness. No one is there. Rod dresses Jeffers' leg and uses the parts from one launch to repair the other.

In the morning, they see Richards, the first crew member to disappear from launch one, walking toward them. He seems the same except that he is now green. Rod doubts he is Richards, but Richards insists he woke up inside one of the plants and kicked his way out. The jungle took him apart and put him back together. Rod orders Jeffers to give Richards a shot to knock him out. They take him on board and secure him. Radio contact is made with the *Archangel* and a rendezvous is arranged. A second crewman, Elvin, emerges from the jungle, and the procedure used with Richards is followed again. They blast off but Rod is uneasy; it has been "too damn easy."

After the ship leaves, the jungle contemplates the new insect it has captured. The specimens were very interesting. They were taken apart and replicas devoted to its jungle mother were made to lure others like them back to her. She parted with two so she could gain 70 more. Moreover, she would also let those 70 go, because she knows there is a place called Earth where they are many more specimens who might come.

**Six-Baker**  a robot police who tickets Mitch Laskell for jaywalking in the short story "Dumb Waiter."

**Sixty-Star Cluster**  a planetary federation in the short story "Blood Bank." Eli Roki is a Space Commander in the Sixty-Star Patrol when he destroys the mercy ship for refusing his order to stop for a routine inspection.

**Sixty-Star Patrol (SSP)**  the military unit patrolling the space of the Sixty-Star Cluster in the short story "Blood Bank." Eli Roki is a Space Commander in the SSP.

**Skaters**  robot police in the short story "Dumb Waiter."

**Sky-Brain**  another name for Bel in the short story "Please Me Plus Three." See also **Bel**

**Slade, John Hanley and Mary**  a couple in the novella "Conditionally Human" who are getting a neutroid, a mutant pet, as a baby substitute. They hold a pseudoparty, where Mary will simulate giving birth, to mark its arrival. Sarah Glubbes murders Chief Franklin at their home during the party.

**Slessinger**  one of the guards at the bridge Sam Wuncie and Zella Richmond cross to go into Jacksonville in the novella "The Yokel."

**Slojon**  the son of Magister Dion, the mayor of New Jerusalem, in *Saint Leibowitz and the Wild Horse Woman*. He is long-legged and short-armed but well mannered and handsome. His father offers him to Pope Amen II as a guide for as long as he is needed. He serves in his father's place during the time Dion is with the army. He loses a confrontation with Mother Silentia and Pope Amen II over the release of Sister Clare from jail after the pope orders sacraments withheld until he agrees to free her. Blue Lightning manhandles him when he at first refuses to release Gai-See and Brother Blacktooth into the Nomad's custody after the death of Cardinal Hadala.

**Slubil**  the knifeman or executioner in the short story "It Takes a Thief." He carries out the Council of Senior Kinsmen's judgment for criminals. As Asir hangs by his wrists awaiting his punishment, Slubil taunts him. He is killed by Big Joe after Welkir orders him to pursue Asir and Mara into the vault room.

**Smith, John, XVI**  a character in the short story "Check and Checkmate." Smith is the newly elected President of the Western Federation of Autonomous States. The election is a ceremonial formality: Smith has been trained for the position since birth. He wears a golden mask and remains publicly nameless and faceless. He is unknown to the public as an individual to thwart assassination attempts and is surrounded by a group of Primary Stand-Ins also wearing masks to protect him further. After his election, Smith initiates a dialogue with his counterpart, Ivan Ivanovitch the Ninth, the Peoplesfriend and Vicar of the Asian Proletarian League, breaking 40 years of non-communication between the West and East. He believes he will be able to gain the upper hand in his conversations with Ivanovitch, and use the meetings to his political advantage. He vigorously pursues the elimination of a spy network within the Western Federation. At the same time he is arranging his meeting with Ivanovitch, Smith orders the preparation of a secret battle plan targeting all of the major cities of the East as a bargaining point in his discussions.

**Smithfield, Harvey**  the owner of the eponymous company responsible for selling packaged theater in the novella "The Darfsteller." Smithfield sells the mannequins, props, and tapes necessary for presenting autodrama, non-human theater. The mannequins, or dolls, use tapes that contain the psycho-physiological data obtained from human actors. The actors sign agreements with Smithfield and receive royalties for the use of their tapes. Autodrama allows for standardized performances and multiple simultaneous productions. The company's slogan is "Great Actors Immortalized."

**Smithfield Company**  *see* **Smithfield, Harvey**

**Snow Ghost**  a Wilddog Nomad and the younger brother of Sharf Oxsho in *Saint Leibowitz and the Wild Horse Woman*. He wants to become a postulant and is a guest at the Leibowitz Abbey.

**Snyder, Martin**  from the short story "The Corpse in Your Bed Is Me," a wildly successful comedian and star of the *Martin Snyder Hour* who can seemingly make anybody laugh. Despite his success as a comedian, Martin is a terrible human being. He is such an arrogant bully that people who work with him start the "I Hate Snyder's Guts Club." So confident is he of his ability to make people laugh, even those who hate him, that he challenges any person to remain "poker faced" for three minutes during one of his monologues. No one is able to win the bet until Freddy, a Martian, remains unaffected by Snyder's jokes. Snyder's career goes into a tailspin as he desperately tries to make Freddy laugh. His last joke, involving his own death, finally elicits a laugh from Freddy, proving that Snyder could make anyone laugh.

**Sodom and Gomorrah**  these two cities are traditionally associated with depravity and sin. They are used throughout the Bible as warnings against sinfulness and wickedness. In Genesis 19: 24–25 (KJV), the cities are destroyed by God with fire and brimstone.

The Earth and its ruins after the Flame Deluge are compared to Sodom and Gomorrah in an ancient text dating back to a few decades after the death of Saint Leibowitz in the novella "And the Light Is Risen" and *A Canticle for Leibowitz* ("Fiat Lux"). The cities are also mentioned in the novella "The Last Canticle."

**Sol III**  the planet formerly known as Earth in the short story "Blood Bank." It is presently out of contact with any interstellar nation and is generally considered a sloppy and decadent place. It is the home of a new race, the Solarians, who have emerged from man and now use human livestock as their source of food.

**The Solomon solution**  also known as the Judgment of Solomon. Two women both claimed to be the mother of a child. After hearing their arguments, Solomon decided that the only fair solution was to cut the child in two so each woman would have half. One woman immediately renounced her claim to the child saying let the other woman have the boy. However, the second woman said the child should be divided so neither woman would have it. Solomon immediately gave the child to the first woman, recognizing that its true mother would do what was necessary to protect the child, even giving up her right to it. The story is from 1 Kings 3:16–28 (KJV). A reference is made to the Solomon solution in the short story "Check and Checkmate."

**"The Song of Marya"**  an alternate title for the short story "Vengeance for Nikolai." It appears under this title in the anthology *Twisted*. Ed. Groff Conklin. New York: Belmont, 1962.

**"The Song of Vorhu ... for Trumpet and Kettledrum"** novella: *Thrilling Wonder Stories*, 39 (December 1951), 102–118. Barry Wilkes is testing a new interstellar drive when a descendent of a Venusian microorganism erupts as a plague on Earth. A vegetable entity, the microorganism had seemed harmless on Earth for almost a hundred years. It was quiescent in darkness; its spores were light seeking.

Wilkes returns to the diseased and dying Earth for one night, protected by a germ-proof space suit. He retrieves the White Idiot, a hopeless and congenital idiot, and the only plague free female he can find in one night. She is "scarcely more than a wild animal-thing" who has spent most of her life confined in a subterranean cell of an asylum. He blasts off the next morning to find an Earth-like planet.

Barry refuses to let humanity die, and he hopes to give it the opportunity to rise again from his and the White Idiot's offspring. Utilizing the ship's interstellar drive, they reach a solar system on the outer fringes of the galaxy. He names the sun Old Man Odds and starts to chart the system's planets. After a week of charting, he begins to suspect that he is not the only intelligent being in the system. He receives stray blips on his radar and ultra-high frequency radio signals. Barry orbits the planet where the signals originate to further study the world. Using the ship's recorder and transmitter, he sends back to the planet its own signals in an attempt to contact their source. In response, he hears a sound like a jumbling of bells from all over the planet, and Barry senses that his mind is being invaded at subconscious levels. This feeling of intrusion ends, and Barry attributes it to his own fear. He decides to land his ship and selects a land mass near an ocean.

When he sets foot on the gray-green ground, it begins to pulsate as if it is alive. Surveying the vacant landscape for food, Barry thinks that man is not yet weaned from Earth, that he must find a breast to sustain him. As Barry watches, the land before him begins to reform itself into the shape of a breast. Terrified, he turns to run toward his ship but someone calls out his name. Barry turns to see a man's torso waist deep in the ground. He tells Barry, "Mother sent me." He has been formed in Barry's image so Mother may communicate with him. Mother knows Barry's thoughts and why he is here. She wants to make a reasonable offer to him. The planet can be his home and in return, he will carry Mother's seed to other worlds. The ground itself is Mother; she is a world-creature who has grown too large for the planet but cannot leave it. Barry tells her if she knows his thoughts than she knows the history of man. His race makes no deals and refuses to be enslaved. He turns again toward the ship but a duplicate of his machine-pistol now appears in the torso's hand. It shoots at Barry but the weapon is without ammunition. Barry shoots it and staggers toward his ship. Other protuberances appear from the ground in an effort to stop him. Green tentacles hold the ship securely.

As he reaches the ship's control room a nude woman attempts to disable the control panels. Her body is perfect and her face is a composite of all the women Barry has known. She speaks in his mother's voice. Barry notices that she is attached to the ground by a tentacle that runs out of the hatch. He shoots and severs her connection and throws the body from the ship. He is unable to fire the ship's engines; the ship is being sucked into the ground. Barry and the White Idiot will be devoured alive. In desperation, he decides to transmit the signals he recorded earlier from the planet realizing now that they were echoes of the life form's heartbeats. As he does so, the ship shudders and the ground heaves. The tentacles let loose the ship and the engines ignite. Barry takes the ship into orbit and continues to transmit the recording. After two hours, there is no response from the planet's surface. Barry speculates that he has caused Mother to have a heart attack.

He explores other planets in the system but none seem suitable. There is not enough fuel left to explore beyond this system. Barry wonders if he should have accepted Mother's offer. Is he a traitor to his race? Is slavery acceptable or is it better to let man die if he cannot dominate? Barry kills the tangential component of his velocity and allows the ship to drift slowly toward the sun. It is better to surrender to "the behemoth of the universe" than to an alien intelligence.

He goes to the White Idiot in pity and gently kisses her for the first time but then breaks away from her in horror. Dark, greenish-black spots mark her skin. She has the plague. It lay dormant in the darkness of space but has now blossomed in the light of the sun. Barry angrily starts the engines and steers the ship toward the sun, but when the heat becomes unbearable, he instinctively activates the braking system and veers sharply. Doing so pulls him into the gravity of a small planetoid. He decides he has no right to take his life or that of the White Idiot. He swings the ship into orbit around a planetoid nearly as large as the Earth. The atmosphere is breathable but the planet is still barren, young, and desolate. There is no soil to support plant life, and the temperatures are too warm except at the polar regions where it is still 130° F. He decides to land there.

He lays the White Idiot in a shallow, steaming pool in an attempt to soothe her. She screams and he begins to walk away from her. When the screaming stops, he looks back to see a thin green tendril emerge from beneath her clothes and grope toward her throat. He empties his weapon into her but suddenly her body opens up and wiry tendrils burst forth. Faintly visible spores are shaken out into the humid air. Barry blasts off the planet and its moon's gravity draws him there. He wonders whether his actions have been merciful or criminal. Perhaps something would happen from the body of the White Idiot and the spores. He thinks of *Bereshith*.... In the beginning. However, would man rise again?

Barry begins to write a sketchy history of Earth and man, of the White Idiot, and of his faint hope for a new life to rise from her body and the spores. When he runs out of food and words, he walks out onto the moon's surface and steps into a lightless cavity. He allows himself to fall in hopes of a quick death. He stops his descent to remove his space suit and begins to fall again into a merciful blackness.

Barry opens his eyes to a sharp pain. He is lying on a metal pallet and a machine is forcing him to breath. He hears voices, incomprehensible but human. He sees handsome, humanoid figures. They are the descendents of the White Idiot. They discovered Barry in deep-freeze on the planet's moon, dead over a billion years, brought back to life to die again. They have brought him back too soon; their medicine cannot sustain him.

As he lies dying, a young woman tells him stories of their planet. One tale is of the ancient god Vorhu and his consort Ndriga who fell from his arms in heaven. Vorhu came to the planet to bury her but the pale blue Alononu blossoms had grown from her body and spread across the planet. The people identify Vorhu with the moon and they pile his altar high with the night-flowering Alononu. As he dies again, Barry is given the rites reserved for the high space warriors, and Alononu blossoms are scattered about his pallet. His soul finally merges in the spirit of the race of man.

**Sorcerer VI**  the planet where Motar dies in the short story "Gravesong." Emilesh leaves Sorcerer VI, with its twin suns, to return Motar's ashes to Earth.

**Sorkin, Andrei**  an unseen character in the short story "Check and Checkmate" who, according to Ivan Ivanovitch, made a single discovery that rendered "communist doctrine not only a wrong solution, but a wrong solution to a problem that had ceased to exist." The problem was the use of human beings as automatic devices in a corporate machine, expected to be trapped in the performance of a single, highly specialized task. Sorkin was a physicist who did considerable work in crystal structure prior to the Big Silence. His research led to the development of the technology needed for "thinking-machines" and robots to substitute for human beings.

**Sorrell**  a minor character in the short story "The Little Creeps." He is a general and part of the command staff considering General Jim Yaney's bombing plan. He opposes the plan and sees it as tantamount to a declaration of war against the Soviet Union.

**S.o.S.o.G**  an acronym for the term Servant of the Servants of God used in *Saint Leibowitz and the Wild Horse Woman*. See also **Servant of the Servants of God**

**"The Soul-Empty Ones"**  short story appearing in *Astounding Science-Fiction*, 47 (August 1951), 62–94. In the aftermath of the "glow-curse," men created the Soul-Empties, artificial beings in the form of man from the flesh of beasts. They then left Earth so their children would not be deformed. They promised the Soul-Empties they would return when the glow-curse ended. Invaders from space have now come and begun to build a city in the valley. Are they the sons of men returned?

Daner of the Natani mountain people returns to his wife Ea-Daner mortally wounded from a confrontation with the invaders. Before he goes into the forest to die, he tells his wife and two guests from the valley that the invaders are the sons of men but are no longer men. Ea decides that she will follow the traditions of her people: after a brief period of mourning, she will go to kill one of her husband's enemies and then follow him in death. Falon, a young warrior from the valley who has been welcomed with his father into Daner's home, openly defies his father and offers to help Ea avenge her husband. Because of Falon's open defiance, his father believes himself duty bound to kill his son. He and Falon fight, but Ea clubs the elder man in the head. She and Falon leave together, riding their horses toward the valley.

As they make their way through the woods, they come upon a pack of dogs mauling a scrawny, small boned "man-thing." With their horses and whips, they disperse the pack of dogs, but the man is fatally wounded. Before he dies, he tells Falon that he escaped and was looking for the camps of the Soul-Empty Ones. When they hear the engine of a small skycart, Falon and Ea leave the body in an open area to lure the craft to land. Three creatures emerge as Falon and Ea lay in ambush. One creature guards the ship while the other two go toward the body. Falon attacks the guard and takes his flame gun. A second creature is killed when the horses stampede. Trying to lure the third creature out, Falon uses the flame gun to start fires in the woods to encircle him but the fires begin to burn out of control. To save their lives, Falon orders the creature into the skycart to fly them to safety.

Once aloft the creature mockingly laughs at Falon. The fires will drive many of his people down the valley and into the creatures' food pens. When Falon says the sheer numbers of his tribesmen will overwhelm the creatures, the pilot laughs again saying that most will not attack them because they believe them to be demigods. As they fly over the invaders' fledgling city and the food pens, Falon realizes that the man-thing he and Ea found was neither an invader nor a Soul-Empty. He decides to take a chance and tell the creature that the dead man-thing told them many things before he died. The pilot stiffens and asks what the escaped android told them. Falon asks if the pilot calls himself an android, and he replies that he is a man, an android is a Soul-Empty One. Falon confirms that the dead man-thing is not the same race as the invaders, and he knows that he was not a Soul-Empty One because the Soul-Empties do not have toes. He tells the creature that the dead man-thing was actually a man, a soul-man. The creature states that if the man truly told Falon this, then they all must die lest others learn the truth. He taunts Falon to shoot and kill them all or be taken to the food pens. Ea snarls for him to kill the creature and fly the ship himself. But Falon orders the creature to fly to his city, he and Ea will submit. Ea tries to kill the pilot herself, but Falon prevents her and whispers to her that he has a plan. Falon tells the creature that there were others with them when they found the dying man and the word will spread that the invaders are not the sons of men.

When they land, Falon is brought before Lord Kepol who orders him fattened so he can be eaten. Kepol tells him it is of no consequence if a few Soul-Empties know they are not men. Their knives are no match for the invaders' weapons.

Falon is ordered to the human pen to keep him from informing other Soul-Empties of what he has learned. Falon bows before Penult, the first man he sees, but Penult tells him to rise, that they are both slaves and brothers. Falon informs him that the Soul-Empty Ones have kept their promise to man and have waited centuries for his return. Penult laments that the Soul-Empties were never told where the weapons were hidden in vaults beneath the ancient cities. The dying man Falon and Ea found in the woods had escaped the pens to tell them where they could find the weapons. Falon asks Penult if he will help the Soul-Empties attack the invaders. He believes that the Soul-Empties will attack as the fire drives them toward the city, but Penult explains that man is now only a slave. They went to Mars and taught the primitive Martians their ways but eventually the Martians enslaved them. Falon persists in his argument that man and the Soul-Empties must fight together to overcome the Martians. Penult is impressed with his confidence and reveals to him the existence of a tunnel that lies beneath the food pens and runs to the center of the city.

Word is sent to the men working in the city to create a diversion, and Falon and a group of men use the tunnel to gain access to the city where they attack the tower guards. Chaos erupts from within and outside the city as the slaves attack the Martians from inside and horsemen and packs of wild dogs emerge from the burning forests. An escaped slave uses a captured ship to ram and destroy the Martian throne ship. Morning dawns and the bodies of dogs, men, and Martians litter the fields. Man and the Soul-Empties now have a chance. The weapons beneath the cities can be reclaimed, and man and his creation can prepare for the return of a Martian fleet. Falon, informed that his father waits for him along with Ea, collapses with a grin on his face.

**Southwest**   one of the regional dialects mentioned in *A Canticle for Leibowitz* ("Fiat Voluntas Tua").

**"The Sower Does Not Reap"**   the short story "Crucifixus Etiam" appears under this alternate title in the anthology *The Best Science Fiction Stories*. Fifth Series. Ed. Everett F. Bleiler and T. E. Dikty. London: Grayson, 1956.

**"The Space Witch"**   short story published in *Amazing Stories*, 25 (November 1951), 98–118. Reprinted in *Amazing Stories*, 40 (October 1966), 70–96.

Kenneth Johnson returns to the United States after three years as a news correspondent in Europe. He purchases a cottage on Kalawego Lake, benefiting from the depressed market caused by recent reports of a mysterious black cloud appearing in the lake's vicinity. He invites his ex-wife, Marcia, and her new husband, Phillip, for the weekend in an attempt to demonstrate that he is past her. He anticipates that Phillip will have too much pride to allow them to accept. He does not, however.

Marcia is high strung, selfish, and possessive. She drinks excessively and tries to seduce Ken. Ken realizes that he still loves her and that inviting them to the cottage was a mistake. As she persists in making advances toward him, he slaps her face. Still, she manages time alone with him by sending Phillip to buy more liquor. She apologizes to Ken for her behavior, admitting she was a bit drunk, but she still loves him and asks him to make love to her once again. Ken tells her to stop babbling and walks down to the lake. Marcia follows him a short time later. She slaps his face, raking her nails down his cheek. She then rips her blouse and tells him that she will have her revenge for his rejection. Phillip will kill him or at least go the police.

As they argue on the dock, a black cloud forms above the lake and hurricane force winds begin to whip the area, eventually splintering the dock. They manage to jump into a boat alongside the dock. The cloud hovers fifty feet above the lake, and Ken can see stars in it. It is a dark tunnel into a void, like a piece torn from space. Marcia babbles about her and Ken and how they should never have divorced and should live together again. The boat is drawn toward the black void and a metallic sphere appears and grows larger within the void. The boat overturns and Ken loses sight of Marcia. He dives below the lake's surface in an attempt to find her, but he feels himself being drawn upward and loses consciousness.

He awakens in a small windowless room. He calls out and a voice answers from a speaker on the wall. He recognizes the voice as Marcia's but knows the words are not hers. He asks that they speak face to face. The voice agrees and warns him that she is not Marcia. When she appears as Marcia, she explains that she retrieved Marcia's dead body from the lake. She used it as a pattern to simulate an Earth life form. Not only has the alien simulated her body but she has also absorbed Marcia's neural patterns; she possesses her memories but can view them objectively.

The alien explains that she is a fugitive from a star system unknown on Earth. She is the last of her race, which has been exterminated in a war. Living on the Earth's moon for thirty years, she has studied the human race, using the five-space landing tunnel, the black cloud, for closer observations. Her enemies are now on the outskirts of Pluto and if they find her sphere and destroy it, the surrounding 150 miles will be devastated. It takes too long to plot a five-space course, and if she simply blasts off, her ship will be detected and destroyed. Ken tells her to blast off anyhow to protect the human lives that will otherwise be lost, but she says to do so is suicide. She says she will teach Ken the controls of the ship, and he can blast off and commit suicide while she stays on Earth and fulfills Marcia's life. According to her race's ethical code, she bears responsibility for Marcia's death and therefore bears an obligation to fulfill her life plan. Ken asks if she intends to remarry him and be subservient to him as Marcia intended. She tells him if that is his will, she will do so, but first she wants to show him her natural form. He turns away and refuses to watch in order to maintain his resolve, but he feels a tendril entangling his feet. She changes into Marcia again and when Ken hears human footsteps, he turns to watch her give herself an injection from a small vial. Ken asks her to take him to the ship's controls and says they should blast off before dawn. The space witch hesitates then says, "No." She draws a weapon and tells him that he can go but she will stay on Earth. She will forego the food components in the vials that make biosimulation possible and will remain as a human.

She leaves Ken to get a pressure suit for him. He goes to the cabinet with the vials and begins pouring their contents on the floor to prevent her from being able to move back and forth between forms. As he does so, he thinks of her as a strange creature: her personality is half alien and half Marcia. He is sure that her willingness to betray her own ethics is due to Marcia's emotional patterns. When she returns and sees the liquid on the floor, she drops her weapon and attempts to ingest as much of the liquid as she can. Ken grabs the weapon and vaporizes the remaining liquid. The alien is forced to repressurize the entire ship to accommodate their human forms.

She leads Ken to the control room and shows him the five-space drive. He asks about a heavy switch with a safety lock, but she warns him away. It activates the space drive. She begins to flip switches, attempting to burn out the control wires. Ken goes to the five-space panel and begins turning dials randomly. She yells at him to stop or he will dump them light years from nowhere. Their resources are limited; they have air, fuel, and food for approximately fifty years. Ken says that is about his life expectancy. He throws the switch, and they crumble to the floor unconscious as the space drive is activated. When they awaken, they are moving through five-space. Ken tells her to do her worse to him; he has accomplished his purpose: he has saved millions of people on Earth.

She leaves the compartment telling Ken she is going to do the only thing left for her. After a short time, he hears a shriek and the alien stumbles toward him still in Marcia's form. She calls him Kennie and does not seem to remember anything since before he left for Europe and their subsequent divorce. Ken wonders if the witch destroyed her own personality. He tests her by asking where Phil is, but she asks about whom he is talking. Ken believes that the witch has done away with the flaws in Marcia's personality. He decides to get rid of Marcia's corpse so it will not be found and lead to questions later. The space witch watches him go and smiles sardonically. She has fooled him, and she considers changing into her real form when they next embrace. She stops thinking of doing so knowing that she probably would not be able to regain Marcia's form. Her opportunity to revert to her own form will be lost in a few weeks. She realizes that life with Ken as company is better than the years she has spent in solitude. She pledges to herself to treat him properly as she admires the new body she has acquired.

**Space Witch** the eponymous character of the short story. She is a fugitive from a distant star system still unknown to Earth. The last of her race, which was exterminated in war, she wants to live peacefully on Earth. She has been living on the Earth's moon for thirty years studying the human race. Her ability to simulate other life forms is still considered a threat by her enemies who continue to search for her. When Marcia drowns in the lake, she takes Marcia's form so Ken will be more comfortable communicating with her. She decides to live Marcia's life on Earth, but Ken opposes the loss of life that will result when her enemies discover and destroy her ship on Earth. She tells Ken he can sacrifice himself and blast off with her ship into space while she stays on Earth; however, Ken initiates the five-space drive blasting them both into space and condemning them to isolation in space. The space witch fools Ken into believing that she has destroyed her own personality and fully assumed Marcia's. She thinks of returning to her natural form to torment him but decides that a life in Marcia's form with Ken is better than her previous loneliness.

**Sparley** the turret gunner on Mark Kessel's B-25 bomber in the short story "Wolf Pack."

**Spartan** a citizen of Sparta, the ancient city-state of Greece. Spartans were noted for their self-discipline and militarism. In *Saint Leibowitz and the Wild Horse Woman,* a comparison is made between the Helot-like gelps and the Spartan-like spooks.

**Specklebird, Amen Papa** a retired priest of the Ordo Dominae Desertarum (Order of Our Lady of the Desert) in *Saint Leibowitz and the Wild Horse Woman*. He was forced to retire by the Bishop of Denver or be tried for heresy. An elderly black man with white hair and a close-cropped white beard, he is a popular holy man in Valana, noted as a healer and rainmaker, and as a confessor to prominent sinners. It is widely believed that he is cardinal in pectore of Linus VII. Cardinal Brownpony arranges for him to hear Brother Blacktooth's confession. Specklebird tells Blacktooth he must throw away all his values to follow Christ. He gives him as penance the requirement to make an inventory of all his wealth.

Amen is the people's choice for pope during the early conclaves of the novel. In the conclave following the death of Alabaster III, Specklebird delivers a seventeen hour speech before the cardinals. He favors an unconditional restoration of the New Rome papacy, saying that the pope must return to New Rome as to Golgotha to be crucified. He is elected pope "in compromise and fear" at the conclave of 3244 and immediately places Valana under interdict until the instigators of the violence that occurred in the city during the conclave are brought before him. He begins a pilgrimage across the Plains to New Rome but is forced to turn back. He resigns the papacy after convening a conclave amendable to his desire to see Cardinal Brownpony elected pope. After Brownpony's election as pope, a housekeeper finds Amen decapitated in his hut.

**Spinrad, Norman** (September 15, 1940–) American author best known for his science fiction novels, such as *The Iron Dream* and *Bug Jack Barron*, as well as the historical novels *The Druid King* and *Mexica*. His short story "The Big Flash" appears in *Beyond Armageddon*.

**Spitfire** a British fighter plane used in World War II. It was the primary fighter of the Royal Air Force. A Spitfire is spied by one of Mark Kesel's crew in the short story "Wolf Pack."

**Spook** a genny who can pass for normal with no apparent genetic handicaps in *Saint Leibowitz and the Wild Horse Woman*. See also **Gelps**

**Sports** a term used to refer to any human being with genetic mutations as a result of the radiation fallout from the Flame Deluge in *A Canticle for Leibowitz* ("Fiat Homo").

**Sree, Johnny** one of the main characters in the novella "Six and Ten Are Johnny." He is the sole inhabitant of a newly discovered jungle covered planet thought to be uninhabited. He is a humanoid life form, short and round with big red eyes and a baby face. His skin and hair are the color of the jungle, chartreuse and splotched. He explains to the *Archangel*'s launch crew who discover him that he is a survivor of the starship *Yorick* lost ten years ago. The crew assumes he is crazy because he talks to two other men he says survived the *Yorick* with him, yet they do not see anyone else on the planet. In actuality, Johnny is the single animal on the planet living in symbiosis with its single vegetable form, the vast jungle that covers the planet. It helps the jungle obtain the life forms it needs to sustain itself and gain information. The creature speaks with a lisp so the Sree it calls itself is actually three — the three original survivors from the *Yorick*. As the jungle consumes the six crew members from the *Archangel*'s first launch, Johnny later refers to himself as Johnny Six.

**S'rij** one of the bat-hunters chosen to work with Rolf Kenlan in the novella "The Reluctant Traitor."

**Stand-Ins** a group of characters in the short story "Check and Checkmate." In order to ensure the safety of the President of the Western Federation of Autonomous States, three groups of stand-ins serve to create confusion among potential assassins and to perform various tasks. A golden mask protects the president's personal identity, and identical ones are worn by all the stand-ins. In public, a number of stand-ins always accompany the president. The most important of the stand-ins are the nine primary stand-ins. They serve not only as bodyguards but also function as council members and advisors to the chief executive. The secondary stand-ins comprise a larger group of 200, and the tertiary stand-ins are the largest group.

**Star-craze** a term used in the short story "The Big Hunger" concerning man's need to go into space and explore the stars. It is also referred to as the Great Purpose and the Divine Thirst in the story.

**State-Church Concordat** from the novella "The Last Canticle" and *A Canticle for Leibowitz* ("Fiat Voluntas Tua"). The concordat is an agreement that guarantees the Church the right to own a starship and to send missions to open space installations or planetary outposts. The Church is exempted from all licensing procedures by the state for space travel. In the Church's view, this agreement allows for the launch of its rocket to implement the Dismissal of Servants or *Quo peregrinator* plan to perpetuate the Church and the Albertian Order of Leibowitz in space in the event of a nuclear holocaust on Earth.

**State of Chihuahua** one of the principal territorial states in the novella "And the Light Is Risen" and *A Canticle for Leibowitz* ("Fiat Lux"). It is located south of Laredo.

**STATOR WNDG MOD 73-A 3-PH 6-P 1800-RPM 5-HP CL-A SQUIRREL CAGE** the title of one of the blueprints Brother Francis copies before he begins work on the Leibowitz blueprint in *A Canticle for Leibowitz* ("Fiat Homo"). Brother Francis finds the plans totally incomprehensible and does not understand how the device could possibly ever capture a squirrel.

**Steps-on-Snake** a seventy-five year old Jackrabbit priest in *Saint Leibowitz and the Wild Horse Woman*. He possesses a comprehensive view of the Nomad situation. As Cardinal Brownpony's host in Yellow, he informs him of Hultor Bråm's offenses against the *Qæsach dri Vørdar*, his ritual death, and his brother Eltür's election as War Sharf. Father Steps-on-Snake also provides Brownpony with the latest news of Filpeo Harq's machinations. He arranges for Brownpony to send a secret message to Pope Amen.

**Stigmata** the unexplained appearance of marks or wounds on individuals corresponding to the wounds of Jesus upon the cross. Among the most famous and best documented cases is that of Saint Francis of Assisi. In *Saint Leibowitz and the Wild Horse Woman*, Sister Clare-of-Assisi experiences the stigmata while staying at the Leibowitz Abbey. Abbot Olshuen believes it is Sister Clare's retaliation toward him because he forbade her to use her healing powers.

**Stinwald** a minor character in the short story "The Little Creeps." As a member of the senior staff considering General Jim Yaney's bombing proposal, he speaks against it.

**Stoic** *see* **Nature imposes nothing that Nature hasn't prepared you to bear.**

**Stone, Mela** a former leading actress and lover of Ryan Thornier in the novella "The Darfsteller." She left Thornier when she signed with the Smithfield company to license her psycho-physiological data for use in autodramas. She comes to the New Empire Theater where Thornier works as a janitor to give an introduction and intermission commentary for the autodrama production of "The Anarch," a play she and Thornier were once cast in as Andreyev and Marka. After Thornier sabotages the Andreyev mannequin and is cast in its place, Mela is upset and wants to cancel her appearance. However, she assumes the role of Marka during the second act to help Thornier salvage the play. After learning that Thornier deliberately sabotaged the mannequin, Mela does not resume her role for the third act. The mannequin playing the Marka role shoots and wounds

Thornier. Mela visits Thornier at the hospital to tell him that although the critics panned the show it is a huge success because of the publicity surrounding his being shot. She tells him the theater is dead as they knew it and that he cannot keep floundering around without hurting more people.

**"The Store of the Worlds"** short story by Robert Sheckley from 1959 included in *Beyond Armageddon*.

**Stultus Maximus** Latin: "Greatest fool." A term Dom Paulo uses for Satan in *A Canticle for Leibowitz* ("Fiat Lux").

***Sturmtruppen*** German: "Stormtroopers" (or shock troops or assault troops): introduced by Germany during World War I, these specialized soldiers were especially trained for fast maneuvers and infiltration techniques. In the short story "The Little Creeps," General Horrey is reminded of these "elite" troops by the little creeps crawling on his wall.

**Styx** in Greek myth, the river in Hades across which the ferryman Charon conveys the souls of the dead. In *A Canticle for Leibowitz* ("Fiat Voluntas Tua"), Dom Zerchi speaks of the gulf between life and death as the blackest Styx.

**Sub ducatu sancti Spiritus** Latin: "Under the guidance of the Holy Spirit." Spoken by Leo XXI during the canonization of Isaac Leibowitz to indicate that the proclamation of Leibowitz to sainthood is being done under divine guidance. From "Fiat Homo" in *A Canticle for Leibowitz*.

**Sub Immunitate Apostolica Hoc Suppositum Est. Quisquis Nuntium Molestare Audeat, Ipso Facto Excommunicetur** Latin: "This [document] has been placed under apostolic immunity. Let whosoever dares to bother the messenger [bearer], be excommunicated ipso facto [by the very fact]." The text of a label attached to a letter Marcus Apollo sends to Dom Paulo, the abbot of the Abbey of Saint Leibowitz, about Thon Taddeo's impending visit to the abbey in *A Canticle for Leibowitz* ("Fiat Lux").

**Subtile et enfandum** Latin: "Subtle and abominable." In *Saint Leibowitz and the Wild Horse Woman*, during Amen Specklebird's address before the cardinals, he claims God's word is "*subtile et enfandum*." Brownpony later tries to calm fears by saying he actually said "*verbum subtile atque infandum*": God's word is truth so subtle it is unspeakable.

**Suckamint Mountain Range** the western border of the Lands of the Mare in *Saint Leibowitz and the Wild Horse Woman*. It is a moist and fertile range and the home of New Jerusalem and Arch Hollow. The Abbey of Saint Leibowitz lies just to the west of the range. Miller may have had the Sacramento Mountains of New Mexico in mind.

**Sugarton Crowd** a gang of two to four dozen men set on destroying the city's computer network in the short story "Dumb Waiter." Led by Frank Ferris, they want to disable the central service computer that directs the robot police force still enforcing the city's ordinances even after a nuclear war. They believe technology is an impediment to man's survival. Mitch Laskell, who views the computer as a tool that should not simply be destroyed, opposes their intentions and works to prevent their plan from succeeding.

***Summa*** used in *A Canticle for Leibowitz* ("Fiat Homo") as a reference to one of the titles comprising the perennials, those books that are always in demand. It is the *Summa Theologica*, the primary theological work of Saint Thomas Aquinas and considered by many to be one of the best, if not the most complete, theological work ever written. In the original short story the full title is used.

***Summa Theologica*** see ***Summa***

**Summonabisch** a stew thought by the ancient Plains dwellers to be a helpful treatment for radiation poisoning in *Saint Leibowitz and the Wild Horse Woman*. The Venerable Boedollus recorded its recipe. The stew consists of organ meats, wild onions and tiny wild peppers, with a splash of red wine or vinegar. Its name is a possible corruption of son of a bitch.

**Sunovtash An** see **An, Sunovtash**

**Supreme *Cathartes aura regnans*** *Cathartes aura* is the scientific name for the Turkey Vulture. In Latin the name means "purifying bird" (*aura* is the Latinized form of the Mexican *auroura*). The phrase means the supreme ruler (or the reigning) *Carthartes aura* (Turkey Vulture), that is the King of the Turkey Vultures. At the conclusion of the "Fiat Lux" section of *A Canticle for Leibowitz*, it is stated that the Supreme Turkey Vulture made the world especially for buzzards, as the buzzards wait to feast upon the dead cavalry officer and the dying Poet-sirrah. The Turkey Vulture (or buzzard as it is commonly referred as) seeks a carrion food supply. The deaths and appearance of the buzzards at the end of "Fiat Lux" parallel the death of Brother Francis and the buzzards' domination at the conclusion of "Fiat Homo."

**Supreme Secretissimo** Latin: "Supremely Secret." In *A Canticle for Leibowitz* ("Fiat Voluntas Tua"), the memo announcing Lucifer is Fallen is marked *Supreme Secretissimo*.

**Surgat ergo Petrus ipse** Latin: "Therefore, let Peter himself arise." Among the words spoken by Monsignor Aguerra as part of the canonization ceremony for Isaac Leibowitz in *A Canticle for Leibowitz* ("Fiat Homo").

**Surges** a secondary character in the short story "Wolf Pack." Surges is the copilot of Mark Kessel's B-25 bomber and is concerned about Kessel's state of mind. He pistol-whips Kessel when he attempts to abort the bombing mission.

**Sursum corda** Latin: "Lift up thy hearts." A part of the Mass in the Catholic Church, it is used in the novella "And the Light Is Risen" as part of the advanced warning concerning Don Thaddeo's visit to the abbey's basement.

**Suspendfreeze** a process developed by Dr. Fraylin in the novella "Cold Awakening." It allows human beings to be quickly frozen and thawed without harm to their bodies. This process enables humans to endure long space flights without aging. Each person is placed into a freeze locker for the process. The colonists going to Sigma Seven are concerned about the process and what might happen to them during the suspendfreeze, or if they will even wake up from it.

**Swanwick, Michael** (November 18, 1950–) American novelist and short story writer. He received the Nebula Award in 1991 for his novel *Stations of the Tide*, and is the recipient of five Hugo Awards for his short stories. His story "The Feast of Saint Janis" is included in *Beyond Armageddon*.

**Sweltin, Corporal** a minor character in the novella "The Yokel." He is a member of the Border Guards.

**Swimming Elk** the Grasshopper sharf in *Saint Leibowitz and the Wild Horse Woman*.

**Swineman, Varley** cardinal and Bishop of Denver in *Saint Leibowitz and the Wild Horse Woman*.

**The Sword of Apology** the ritualized suicide code of the planet Coph IV in the short story "Blood Bank." One's throat is ceremonially cut. Eli Roki plans to perform the ritual if he fails to prove the mercy ship he destroyed was not involved in illegal activity.

**Sword of the Archangel** Saint Michael the Archangel is a symbol of divine truth and power. He is regarded generally as the highest of all angels. He is associated, among other things, with battling Satan. He is most often shown with a sword and shield. In the novella "And the Light Is Risen" and *A Canticle for Leibowitz* ("Fiat Lux"), in an ancient text written soon after the death of Saint Leibowitz, a reference is made to "the sword of the Archangel wherewith Lucifer had been cast down." See also **Saint Michael**

***Sybern Seven*** the name of Emilesh's ship in the short story "Gravesong." It possesses artificial intelligence and is capable of consciousness.

**Taknon** one of three classes within the feudal system that developed on Nu Phoenicis IV that provides the basis for the short story "Bitter Victory." The Taknon was the artisan class, also known as the Inventives. As technology emerged, the Taknon and Algun classes overthrew the privileged class, the Klidds, and exiled them to an ironless planet. The Taknon space force maintains a quarantine around the Klidd planet.

**Tamar** the daughter of David who was raped by her half-brother Amnon. Amnon is killed by Absalom in revenge (2 Samuel 13: 1–39 KJV). Father Zerchi mentions the rape of Tamar as an example of man's capacity for evil in "The Last Canticle."

**Tau II** a planet on which over a billion people die because of the introduction of non–Tauian animals as house pets. The incident is mentioned in the short story "Blood Bank."

**Te absolvat Dominus Jesus Christus; ego autem eius auctoritate te absolve ab omni vinculo.... Denique, si absolve potes, ex peccatis tuis ego te absolvo in Nomine Patris...** Latin: "May the Lord Jesus Christ absolve you; I, however, by his authority absolve you from every bond.... Finally, if you are able to be absolved, I absolve you from your sins in the name of the Father...." Dom Zerchi's hurried and qualified absolution of Mrs. Grales just prior to the explosion that destroys the abbey in *A Canticle for Leibowitz* ("Fiat Voluntas Tua").

**Te Deum [laudamus]** Latin: "We Praise Thee, O God." An early Christian hymn of praise subsequently adopted for use in the liturgy of the Catholic Church. It is sung at the canonization of Leibowitz in the short story "A Canticle for Leibowitz" and in *A Canticle for Leibowitz* ("Fiat Homo").

**Te rogamus, audi nos**  Latin: "We beseech thee, hear us." The line is from the Litany of the Saints that Brother Francis recites as he enters the Fallout Shelter in *A Canticle for Leibowitz* ("Fiat Homo").

**Teacher**  the term used by XM-5-B, a cyborg spacecraft, to refer to Barnish, the person who programmed and operated it in the short story "I, Dreamer."

***Technical Manual CD-Bu-83A***  a manual of the procedures for activating the Fallout Shelter and the instructions to follow in certain cases after activation in *A Canticle for Leibowitz* ("Fiat Homo"). When Brother Francis enters the shelter, the sign he reads on the wall refers to following the manual.

**Tempus**  an old genny with seven fingers, a third useless eye, four testicles, and two penises in *Saint Leibowitz and the Wild Horse Woman*. He lives at the Arch Hollow settlement with his family. He will not allow Brother Blacktooth to leave his home until the monk absolves his son, Barlo, to help him stop masturbating.

**"Ten Parsecs to Paradise"**  the title of a song in the short story "The Big Hunger." The song is about man's desire to regain paradise and how it is always just one more journey before it is found. A parsec is a measure of astronomical distance equal to approximately 3.26 light years (or about 19 trillion miles).

**Tenesi**  one of the four nation-states in the Appalotcha region east of the Great River in *Saint Leibowitz and the Wild Horse Woman*. It was allied with Pope Amen II against Filpeo Harq and the Hannegan Empire. The name is an obvious version of Tennessee.

**Tenn, William**  the pseudonym of Philip Klass. See also **Klass, Philip**

**Tents Mended Here**  the sign in Hebrew on a rock beside the door to Benjamin's hovel in *A Canticle for Leibowitz* ("Fiat Lux"). Gary K. Wolfe sees it as suggestive of worldly services. It has some association with the traditional occupation of the Wandering Jew as a shoemaker. Wolfe also sees a possible connection with Jeremiah 4:20 (KJV): "Destruction upon destruction is cried; for the whole land is spoiled: suddenly are my tents spoiled, and my curtains in a moment." Russell M. Griffin sees a parallel with Acts 18:1–4 (KJV) where St. Paul visits Aquila and his wife Priscilla, "for by their occupation they were tentmakers," as was Paul himself.

On the reverse side of the rock that bears the phrase is written: "Hear, O Israel, the Lord thy God, the Lord is One." This is taken from Deuteronomy 6:4 (KJV): "Hear, O Israel: The Lord or God is one Lord." It is a simple declaration of faith, but it is difficult to read because it is on the reverse side close to the wall of the hovel and written in smaller letters. Dom Paulo can barely make it out in the narrow space. The statement of his worldly occupation is outward, but the profession of faith is inward and more difficult to discern.

The rock is "set on a short pillar beside the door," following Deuteronomy 6:9 (KJV) that "thou shalt write them [God's commandments] upon the posts of thy house, and on thy gates."

**Teris**  a young man preparing to leave Marka, the woman he loves, to go into space in search of man's lost paradise in the short story "The Big Hunger." Marka argues with him not to leave, that what he is searching for "is right here" with her. But Teris believes that the stars are man's true destination: they are man's because man took them. He accuses Marka, who is not well enough to go into space, of being "a hangbacker" and abandons her to search for the lost paradise in space.

**"The Terminal Beach"**  a J. G. Ballard short story chosen for inclusion in *Beyond Armageddon*.

**Terra**  the planet Klia escapes to in the short story "Bitter Victory." She hopes to manipulate the Terrans into building spaceships to explore the Klidds' planet. The Klidds would then be able to take over the ships, return to Terra, and gain control of the planet. They would utilize Terra's iron and steel in a war with the Taknon.

**Terrell, Doctor**  a doctor within Jacksonville in the novella "The Yokel." He speaks with Sam Wuncie about the possibility of finding rabies serum within the city.

**"Terribilis est locus iste   hic domos Dei est, et porta caeli"**  Latin: "This place is terrible [frightening]: the house of God is here, and the gate of heaven." From Genesis 28:17 (KJV), the words of Jacob when he awakens from his dream (known as Jacob's ladder) and God grants him the land he lays upon. In *A Canticle for Leibowitz* ("Fiat Homo"), as Brother Francis awaits the canonization of Leibowitz in the basilica in New Rome these words come to his mind as the beauty and dignity of the cathedral overwhelm him.

**Texark**  from *Saint Leibowitz and the Wild Horse Woman*.

1. Originally a small town and trading post

on the Red River. It was conquered by the first Hannegan who acquired the mayoralty. It is referred to improperly in the Latin of the Church as Texarkana. As the town developed into a city, its name was changed to Hannegan City. See also **Texarkana**

2. An Ol'zark dialect.

**Texark Province**   the powerful and controlling state ruled by Filpeo Harg, the seventh Hannegan of Texark in *Saint Leibowitz and the Wild Horse Woman*.

**Texarkana**   a dominant state ruled by Hannegan II in the novella "And the Light Is Risen" and "Fiat Lux" in *A Canticle for Leibowitz*. It is placed under interdict by papal decree after Marcus Apollo, the Vatican's nuncio, is found guilty of spying and executed by Hannegan. In the novella "The Last Canticle" and *A Canticle for Leibowitz* ("Fiat Voluntas Tua"), it is a capital city of the Atlantic Confederacy. It is bombed in a retaliatory nuclear attack because of an explosion destroying Itu Wan in Asia.

***Texarkana Star-Insight***   a regional newspaper in *A Canticle for Leibowitz* ("Fiat Voluntas Tua"). One of its reporters asks a question at Lord Ragelle's news conference.

**"Texarkanae datum est Octavā Ss Petri et Pauli, Anno Domini termillesimo..."**   Latin: "Given at Texarkana on the Octave of Saints Peter and Paul [July 6th], in the year of our Lord, 3000...." The closing of Marcus Apollo's letter to Dom Paulo regarding Thon Taddeo in *A Canticle for Leibowitz* ("Fiat Lux").

**Thaüle**   a minor character in the short story "The Ties That Bind." He is a wingsman in the Imperial Forces who argues for landing on Earth.

**Theodora** (c. 500–548)   the intelligent and politically astute wife of Justinian I, Emperor of the Byzantine Empire, who shared rule with her husband. When she was younger, she converted to Monophysitism, the belief that Jesus was wholly divine, not human and divine. She used her influence to advocate for her religious beliefs and became involved in political intrigue within the Church. In *Saint Leibowitz and the Wild Horse Woman*, she is briefly mentioned along with Pope Silverius who angered her as a result of his decisions regarding Monophysitism.

**Theodore**   in the novella "The Last Canticle," Father Zerchi enumerates a number of mankind's atrocities: "kill Joan kill Paul kill Theodore kill ... Leibowitz." Although no other mention is made regarding Theodore, it is likely the reference is to Saint Theodore the martyr, also referred to as "the Recruit." According to dubious legends, he was a Roman soldier who refused to join in pagan worship. He was tortured for setting fire to a temple of the Mother Goddess. He experienced visions while being held in prison and was killed by being thrown into a furnace.

**Theory of Two Swords**   according to Boniface VIII's bull on papal supremacy, *Unam Sanctam*, the Church controls two swords, or powers, the spiritual and the secular. The pope and clergy directly wield the spiritual power. The secular power, while in the hands of temporal authorities, is indirectly controlled by the spiritual power since it is subordinate to it. The civil authority must yield to the spiritual authority of the pope and Church. In *Saint Leibowitz and the Wild Horse Woman*, Cardinal Brownpony freely talks of this theory during the conclave that elects Pope Amen I.

**"There Will Come Soft Rains"**   one of two short stories by Ray Bradbury included in *Beyond Armageddon*. Miller states that this story and "To the Chicago Abyss" are complementary.

**The Thief**   the name of a Nomad constellation in *Saint Leibowitz and the Wild Horse Woman*. It is the constellation Perseus, the Hero. A reference to Mirfak, the bright star at the elbow of the constellation, is made in the book as well.

**Thomas Aquinas**  *see*  **Saint Thomas Aquinas**

**Thomas, Richard (Rick)**   a theater technician in the novella "The Darfsteller." He operates Maestro, the computer director of the autodrama mannequins, from the control booth. He is friends with Ryan Thornier and is sympathetic to his situation but does not condone his sabotage of the mannequin. After Thornier is shot in the final scene of the autodrama, Thomas visits the actor in the hospital. Angry with him at first, he forces Thornier to realize that the mannequin is simply a tool and he is foolish trying to compete with it. As Thornier concludes that he must move on with his life, Thomas promises that he will help him find a new job.

**Thoren, Kenneth**   one of the colonists in the novella "Cold Awakening." He spurs Angela Waters into telling Eric Joley that she is his genetic recommendation in order to tease and embarrass Joley. He and Joley briefly fight when Joley demands an apology for Angela. Thoren is Angela's supplier of morphine. He receives the drugs from Dr. Fraylin. He also spreads the rumors about the suspendfreeze process suggested by Fraylin. When Angela tells Joley that she is an addict and that she gets her drugs from Thoren, Joley severely beats Thoren to get information about his source of the drugs. Thoren is sent back to Earth.

**Thornier, Ryan (Thorny)** a former leading actor and matinee idol in the novella "The Darfsteller." In a time when human theater, film, and television have been replaced with the autodrama, packaged productions using computer controlled mechanized mannequins, Thornier struggles to maintain his connection to the theater. Having refused to license his psycho-physiological data to be used in the mannequins, he has taken a demeaning job as a janitor at the New Empire Theater to maintain some association with the world he loves. He devises a plan to sabotage the mannequin in the leading role of a play he once rehearsed for. He wants to compete with the mannequin and extract his revenge by staging his suicide on stage within the context of the play by substituting real ammunition in the gun used to shoot his character. During the course of the play, Thornier begins to question and regret what he has done. He calls his desire for revenge "a child's dream" and realizes that he must leave the theater for good. He has mourned its death for too long. However, Thornier forgets about the real ammunition in the gun. He is shot and wounded and lies bleeding on the stage as the play ends. While he recovers in the hospital, his former lover and co-star Mela Stone tells him that the theater is dead and that he has to accept that, but Thornier does not agree now. He has come to accept that the theater is not dead only changed with the times. He has resented the times and tried to resist the current. What has he gained by it? His friend Rick Thomas tells him that he was simply trying to be a better tool than a tool. Thornier asks Rick to help him find a new job away from the theater.

**Thorny** *see* **Thornier, Ryan**

**"Thou hast made man but little lower than the angels. Thou hast subjected all things under his feet."** as Barry Wilkes thinks about his obligation to perpetuate the human race in any manner possible, these lines from Psalm 8, verses 6 and 7 (DB), come to his mind in the novella "The Song of Vorhu." The psalm considers the special relationship between man and God. The lines are repeated in Hebrews 2:7–8 (KJV).

**Three** the union of three divine persons, the Father, the Son, and the Holy Spirit, in one God is the theological doctrine of the Trinity. When Dom Paulo visits Benjamin in *A Canticle for Leibowitz* ("Fiat Lux"), the old hermit teases his friend telling him he has "to find Threeness in Unity" and that it "must be more confusing with Three than with One."

The number three is symbolic of spiritual synthesis; it is generally held as a favorable number, a God number. It is prevalent in the Christian religion: three gifts of the Magi, Jesus' three temptations in the wilderness, Peter's three denials of Jesus, the three days between the death and resurrection of Christ, the three theological virtues (faith, hope, and charity), as well as the Trinity. Miller echoes this importance with the three part structure of *A Canticle for Leibowitz*. In the theology of the Nomads, the Wild Horse Woman is a three-part divinity as well: the Day Maiden, the Night Hag, and the War Buzzard.

**Three Temptations of Christ** in Matthew 4:1–11 (KJV), Satan makes three different attempts to turn Jesus away from the will of God and from the accomplishment of his messianic mission. In *A Canticle for Leibowitz* ("Fiat Voluntas Tua"), Dom Zerchi asks three questions of Brother Joshua: are you willing to go into space, do you have a vocation to the priesthood, and are you willing to lead?

**Throne of David** the Lord promised David the continuation of his dynasty forever. In 2 Samuel 7:12–13 (KJV), the Lord tells the prophet Nathan to tell David that the Lord "will establish his kingdom. He shall build a house for my name, and I will establish the throne of his kingdom for ever." The throne of David is sometimes referred to as the House of David or the Davidic line. Within the Christian church, it is believed that Jesus is from the line of David. In the novella "And the Light Is Risen," as Benjamin watches Father Jerome ride back toward the abbey, he quotes from Isaiah 9:7 (KJV), "*he* shall sit upon the throne of David, and upon *his* kingdom...."

**Tibi adsum** Latin: "I am here for you." Dom Paulo's greeting to Thon Taddeo on his arrival at the abbey in *A Canticle for Leibowitz* ("Fiat Lux"). It is a generous and gracious statement by the abbot that he is ready to serve Taddeo's needs. The scholar receives the message coolly.

**"The Ties That Bind"** a short story first published in *If: Worlds of Science Fiction*, 3 (May 1954), 4–26. After 20,000 years, the descendents of the original stargoers of the Space Exodus return to Earth in a large armada for a retooling and refueling operation. Baltun Meikl, an Analyst

Culturetic for the Intelligence Section, argues against landing on Earth for fear of *kulturverlaengerung*, the unconscious cultural mechanism of transmittal. He believes that the stargoers may awaken the recessive patterns of aggressive human behavior within the peaceful contemporary inhabitants of Earth who now live in a pastoral garden, "almost an Eden." Baron ven Klaeden, the commander of the Imperial Force, disregards Meikl's warning and sends a message to Earth of the spacegoers' imminent landing and need to refuel. He orders only essential communication with the Earth natives who speak a language no longer understood by the spacegoers. A landing zone is commandeered and placed under military jurisdiction. It is declared a restricted zone and thousands of inhabitants are evicted. Native workers are contracted to work with the spacegoers during the first phase of the operation.

The elders of the Geoark, the natives' governing body, welcome the Imperial Forces. Although the spacegoers generally exploit them, the natives are cooperative and view them as their brothers. Letha is assigned as Meikl's interpreter. As the time passes, they grow to love one another but he cannot stay with her, and she will be unable to leave with him at the operation's end. During the first six months a number of men desert, leaving the restricted area. Deserters are hunted down and shot with a deadly fungal dart. They must return to the occupied zone for an immunization or else die a grim death.

In the ninth month of the operation, unidentified men enter the occupied zone and kill three guards. They steal a supply of the fungal vials and the entire supply of the immunization drug. A proclamation from the Ausland Committee offers sanctuary for any member of the Imperial Forces who wishes to resign. Ven Klaeden orders the responsible men to be captured and examples be made of them. Six deserters are killed and eleven captured. In turn, within a few days a dozen Justice Section officers are infected with the deadly fungus. Five more deserters are captured but the immunization serum cannot be found. Ven Klaeden orders the public execution of the five men and closes the border of the occupied zone. No native is allowed to leave if he has signed a work contract.

On the day of the executions the natives attempt to leave en masse. Meikl is ordered to make it clear to three elders of the Geoark that no one can leave and their work must continue. Any native who deserts his work will be killed, and ten Auslanders will be killed for every man murdered by the renegade committee. As Meikl explains ven Klaeden's command to Letha, she pales, turns away, and retches. The three elders speak among themselves and begin to walk away. Ordered to halt, they continue down the path. Ven Klaeden orders the middle one shot; the other two are wounded and held as prisoners. Meikl accuses the commander of being a tyrant. The natives treated the spacegoers as friends, but they have been infected with conflict and the plague of war. Ven Klaeden asks Meikl where the infection originally came from and why does he think Earth's dirt is so red. As they speak two men approach, one is Evon carrying the body of Letha who was shot for running. The other is an officer and an Ausland Committee member. He shoots ven Klaeden with a fungal dart; Meikl then shoots him. From his knees the commander asks Evon if Letha was his woman. Evon replies, "You have brought us death, you have brought us hate." He tells the baron that the Imperial Force will never leave, that men are now wrecking what has already been done and the ships will be destroyed. Evon slowly picks up ven Klaeden's sword and the baron asks him if he knows what to do with it. Evon tells him his hand knows. As ven Klaeden lies dying, Meikl observes that there is no erasing some deeds from the soul of man. See also **"Edward, Edward"**

**Timberlen** a Texark puppet state on the east bank of the Misspee River in *Saint Leibowitz and the Wild Horse Woman*. It is attacked by the King of Tenesi when the Texark troops are involved in the pope's crusade.

**Timmy** an unseen character in the short story "A Family Matter." Timmy was taken from his mother by the State when he was two days old. His brain was removed and later used in the construction of C-33, a rocket that can think and feel. Twenty years after being separated from her son, Timmy's mother stows away on board the unmanned test flight of C-33 to be reunited with him.

**Tipsword, Sharon** *see* **Maestro**

**"To the Chicago Abyss"** a Ray Bradbury short story included in *Beyond Armageddon*. Another story by Bradbury, "There Will Come Soft Rains," is also in the anthology. Miller finds the two stories complementary.

**Todmacht V** the planet home of the Liberty Drive Society briefly referred to in the short story "Gravesong."

**Tokra** the Chief Commoner in the short story "It Takes a Thief." He is an arthritic, balding man. Mara sits on his lap and kisses his head trying to ascertain from him what Asir's punishment is.

**"Tomorrow's Children"** a short story by Poul Anderson included in *Beyond Armageddon*.

**Ton of Roldin** the principal character in the short story "Please Me Plus Three." He is a ceremonial piper in the celebrations for Bel. At first, he refuses to pipe when his pregnant wife, Mara, is chosen to dance. However, he does reluctantly participate in the celebration and watches as Mara falls during the dance. Outraged when she is ordered to perform the dance of immolation and she gladly kills herself, Ton kills Keeper Cron and attacks the pylon. He is flogged, branded, and banished for his actions. He wills himself to stay alive in order that he may confront Bel as its enemy and find a means of destroying it. Ton is nursed back to health by the members of an order of monastic soldiers. In the ruins of a pylon amidst an ancient destroyed city, Ton discovers the clue for defeating Bel. He returns to his tribe with the repair robot from the ruined pylon and takes control of their pylon. Willing to sacrifice himself to achieve his end, Ton endures excruciating pain in order to destroy Bel and free the people from the domination of the machine.

**Torquemada, Tomás de** (1420–September 16, 1498) the First Grand Inquisitor of Spain. He was responsible for the burning of 2,000 Jews during the campaign to purify the Catholic Church in Spain. During an argument with Benjamin in the novella "And the Light Is Risen," Father Jerome stops himself and says, "I am Jerome. Torquemada is dead." The incident is repeated in *A Canticle for Leibowitz* ("Fiat Lux").

**Torri** nickname for Torrildo. See also **Torrildo**.

**Torrildo** a young postulant befriended by Brother Blacktooth in *Saint Leibowitz and the Wild Horse Woman*. He possesses an "elfish charm" and a propensity for trouble. Unbeknownst to Blacktooth, Torrildo has been having sexual trysts with Brother Elwen behind the abandoned electrical generator in the basement library of the abbey. When Torrildo expresses his love for Blacktooth and unexpectedly tries to seduce him, they are caught by Brother Obohl. Torrildo strikes Obodhl and runs away. He later becomes an acolyte of Cardinal Benefez and visits Cardinal Brownpony and Blacktooth when they are imprisoned in Hannegan City. He brings the papers for them to sign acknowledging the charges against them and frees them from jail. Torrildo afterward finds himself in a jail cell in New Jerusalem, a refugee from Cardinal Benefez. He becomes a curate in the papacy of Pope Sorely following the end of the war.

**Tovarish Polkovnik** Transliterated Russian: "Comrade colonel." A term used by Marya in the short story "Vengeance for Nikolai" to refer to Porphiry Grigoryevich.

**Tragor III** a planet in the short story "Blood Bank" where Eli Roki lands the *Idiot* for repairs. Roki first encounters the Solarians on Tragor.

**Transistorized Control System for Unit Six-B** the title of the blueprint bearing the name of Leibowitz discovered by Brother Francis in the short story "A Canticle for Leibowitz" and *A Canticle for Leibowitz* ("Fiat Homo"). Brother Francis's initial copy of the blueprint is too terse and unpretentious; it does not communicate Leibowitz's saintly qualities. In order to properly glorify Leibowitz and the holy relic, Brother Francis begins his 15 years of work on an illuminated copy of the blueprint. He plans to give it as a present to Pope Leo XXII at the time of Leibowitz's canonization, but in the novel a robber steals it from him during his journey to New Rome.

**Treaty of the Sacred Mare** a pact between the Plains Nomads and the adjacent agrarian states in *Saint Leibowitz and the Wild Horse Woman*. The treaty allows travelers protected by a traveler's flag to pass peacefully through the High Plains. Any soldier or farmer entering Grasshopper territory bearing arms could expect to be attacked. Any armed Nomad within musket range of the Empire's borders could expect to be fired upon. When Hultor Brâm orders his men to take the road to New Rome and kill members of Hannegan's guard, the Treaty is broken and a state of war resumes between Texark and the Grasshopper Horde. By the novel's end, the Treaty is no longer observed.

**Treece** one of the guards who confronts Father Zerchi at the Mercy Camp in the novella "The Last Canticle."

**Tremini, Mike** a minor character in the novella "The Lineman." He is part of the B-shift crew with Bill Relke.

**Tribe George Eighty** the community Ton of Roldin is a part of in the short story "Please Me Plus Three."

**"The Triflin' Man"** short story originally published in *Fantastic Universe*, 2 (January 1955), 31–40. It is later entitled "You Triflin' Skunk." Lucey is a poor woman living in the rural south with her son Doodie. Doodie, who was born as a result of a one-night affair Lucey had with a mysterious stranger, has suffered from spasms or fits all of this life. Neighbors believe he is "witched," but Lucey loves him and is protective of him.

During his spasms, Doodie often appears to be speaking to someone. When Lucey asks to whom he is talking, Doodie tells her his father. Lucey becomes distraught and says that it cannot possible be the case; Doodie has never seen his father. But her son yells at her that she is a liar and that he hates her. He tells her that his father is returning and that he will make Doodie whole like him. Doodie tells Lucey that his father is not human but an alien from a distant star. The spasms or "crawlers" that he experiences is when his father is communicating with him. The alien impregnated Lucey so that he would have a means of understanding the human race, to discover how they think and feel through Doodie. Doodie is just one of many half-human, half-alien offspring around the world being used for the same purpose. His father is an alien spy preparing the way for his people to come to Earth and control things. Doodie tells Lucey that his father will return tonight.

As Doodie falls asleep, Lucey tells him she is taking her shotgun and going to the hen house to wait for the wildcat that has been disturbing the chickens. She falls asleep while waiting but low, piercing cries from the cabin awaken her. She sees a faint violet glow through the trees behind the hen house. She hears Doodie yell to his father that he cannot take it anymore.

Lucey hears a metallic sound from the direction of the light. She watches as something resembling a thin cloud of smoke with tendrils, like "an airborne jellyfish," moves closer to the cabin. It begins to materialize into the shape of the man she recognizes as Doodie's father. She warns it away from the cabin, but it continues to approach. Before it can completely transform itself into the shape of a man, Lucey fires both barrels of her shotgun at it. The creature begins to dissipate and is blown away on the wind. The light in the trees grows brighter as Lucey hears a high whine, and a luminescent sphere moves upward from the trees and into the night sky. Lucey declares there is "nothing worse than a triflin' man ... if he's human, or if he's not." When she enters the cabin, she finds Doodie sleeping soundly.

In the alien reconnaissance ship, ServoSix warns off the impending invasion after the death of their Missionman — the mothers of the genetic analogs are too unpredictable.

**Trinity**  a central tenet of Christianity is the unity of three persons, the Father, the Son, and the Holy Spirit, in one God.

**Triune God**  triune means being three in one. The term is a reference to the Christian concept of the Trinity: the union of three divine entities, the Father, the Son, and the Holy Spirit, in one God. The term is used in *A Canticle for Leibowitz* ("Fiat Homo").

**Troffie**  a term used in the short story "Crucifixus Etiam" to describe those workers whose lungs have atrophied from an over-reliance on the mechanical oxygenator.

**Troublesome (Trouble Some) Creek**  the armies of Pope Amen II camp in a bend alongside this river in *Saint Leibowitz and the Wild Horse Woman*.

**Tu es Petrus**  Latin: "You are Peter." In Matthew 16:18 (KJV), Jesus tells Peter: "And I say also unto thee, That thou art Peter, and upon this rock I will build my church." In *Saint Leibowitz and the Wild Horse Woman*, Dom Fredain e'Gonian greets the assembled cardinals and guests who have come to Valana for the conclave with these words. He views them as the foundation of the Church.

**Turpin**  a minor character in the short story "Crucifixus Etiam." He is a guard.

**Twench, Thaddeus**  a name Sam Wuncie uses in the novella "The Yokel."

**27 Lambda**  a yellow sun in the constellation Serpens in the short story "The Big Hunger."

**2537 Angstroms**  the titular characters of the short story "The Little Creeps." These small, pale green, phosphorescent rods are from a world that lies parallel with and connected to Earth's tomorrow. Their matter is Earth's energy, and Earth's matter is their energy. A wavelength on Earth corresponds to a spatial relationship in their world. They caution General Clement Horrey about three key decisions he needs to make to save the future. By counseling Horrey, they hope to change Earth's yesterday to preserve their world, but Horrey disregards their warnings. Their world is destroyed with the onslaught of nuclear war on Earth. 2537 Angstroms is the wavelength of the black light mercury line (ultra-violet radiation).

***Two Worlds of Walter M. Miller: By the Author of A Canticle for Leibowitz***  a paperback published by World Library Classics in 2009 collecting two short stories, "Death of a Spacemen" and "The Hoofer."

**UCOJE** *see* **Uniform Code of Justice, Extraterrestrial**

**U.H.F.**  an acronym for Ultra High Frequency. It is a band of radio frequencies between 300 and

3,000 megahertz. It is used in line of sight transmissions, such as radar systems and aircraft navigation. Major Long plans on listening to the U. H. F. for the Voice transmissions in the short story "No Moon for Me."

**Ulad**   a genny from New Jerusalem in *Saint Leibowitz and the Wild Horse Woman*. He is a giant but otherwise appears normal. A thief as well as a warrior, he is named Ædrea's replacement as New Jerusalem's envoy to the Secretariat of Extraordinary Ecclesiastical Concerns' gun running enterprise. Ulad becomes a sergeant in Cardinal Hadala's militia that marches from Valana. He conscripts Brother Blacktooth, whom he mistrusts, into the militia to separate him from Pope Amen II. He is killed by Woosoh-Loh after mortally wounding him.

**Ululata**   the genny daughter of Tempus and Irene in *Saint Leibowitz and the Wild Horse Woman*. She has a deformed foot.

**Uncle Fidgety**   Barney Willis's name for the old Martian male in the short story "Secret of the Death Dome."

**Unica ex Adam Orta Progenies**   Latin: "One offspring descended from Adam." The title of a papal bull by Pope Amen in *Saint Leibowitz and the Wild Horse Woman*. In this bull, Amen affirms that no one of human ancestry should be regarded as less than human. No genny, or genetically misborn, can be denied equal rights under the laws of the Church or man. The misborn should not be segregated and confined to special living areas. The bull outlaws the use of gennies as virtual slaves in the lumber camps of the Ol'zarks. Any who do violence against those with hereditary defects are excommunicated ipso facto.

**Unified Field Theory**   the attempt to unify the fundamental forces of physics into a single theoretical framework explaining the nature of all existing matter and energy. The term was coined by Albert Einstein who spent the last years of life trying to develop such a theory drawing upon his work with electromagnetism and gravity. In the short story "MacDoughal's Wife," Donald Freeman speaks of the time when astro-physicists will have developed the Unified Field Theory.

**Uniform Code of Justice, Extraterrestrial (UCOJE)**   a United Nations based, semi-military system of laws that prevails on the moon in the novella "The Lineman."

**Universal Theater**   where the play "Judas, Judas" is playing with an all human cast in the novella "The Darfsteller."

**Unus panis, et unum corpus multi sumus, omnes qui de uno [pane participamus]**   Latin: "One bread and one body, though many, are we, and of one bread and one chalice have partaken." A part of the Eucharistic liturgy taken from 1 Corinthians 10:17 (KJV), Brother Joshua hears the monks reciting it in the chapel in the novella "The Last Canticle" and *A Canticle for Leibowitz* ("Fiat Voluntas Tua").

**Urdon Go**   the true Wilddog family name of Cardinal Brownpony in *Saint Leibowitz and the Wild Horse Woman*. Correctly translated it means sorrel colt not brown pony (Avdek Gole).

**"Ut solius tuae voluntatis mihi cupidus sim, et vocationis tuae conscius, si digneris me vocare..."**   Latin. This is part of a prayer Brother Francis recites in *A Canticle for Leibowitz* ("Fiat Homo"). See **"Libera me, Domine, ab vitiis meis..."** for the complete prayer and translation.

℣ see **Versicles**

$V^2 = C^2 - C^2 \, (E/m_0 C^2 + 1)^{-2}$   an equation whose "icy symbols" have been "grudgingly honored for two centuries" presented in the novella "The Song of Vorhu." It is a more complete reference to Albert Einstein's equation for mass-energy equivalence from his Theory of Relativity which is generally given as $E=mc^2$.

**V-2**   a rocket powered ballistic guided missile developed by Germany during World War II and used in attacks on Great Britain. It flew faster than the speed of sound. The unmanned rocket is referred to in the short story "No Moon For Me."

**Vacuus autem erat mundus** *see* **"In principio Deus"**

**Valana**   a city in what once was the Rocky Mountains in the Denver Freestate and the refuge of the exiled papacy in the Cathedral of Saint John-in-Exile. It is the site of the conclaves to elect the succession of popes in *Saint Leibowitz and the Wild Horse Woman*.

**Valley of the Misborn**   the area within the Old Zarks where the sports or gennies, the genetically handicapped, live in seclusion in *A Canticle for Leibowitz* and *Saint Leibowitz and the Wild Horse Woman*. When its boundaries were fixed by treaty, its name officially became the Watchitah Nation. See also **Watchit-Ol'zarkia** and **Watchitah Nation**

**Valleyspeak**   Wooshin's term for the Ol'zark dialect in *Saint Leibowitz and the Wild Horse Woman*.

**Vaquero**  Spanish: "cowboy." Used as an honorific in the novella "And the Light Is Risen" and *A Canticle for Leibowitz* ("Fiat Lux") for Hannegan II. His official title is, in part, "Vaquero Supreme of the Plains." See also **Vaquero Supreme of the Plains**

**Vaquero Supreme of the Plains**  part of Hannegan II's official title in the novella "And the Light Is Risen" and *A Canticle for Leibowitz* ("Fiat Lux"). It is also an honorific awarded among the armies of the various Hannegans. In *Saint Leibowitz and the Wild Horse Woman*, Admiral e'Fondalai is awarded the "ancient title" by Filpeo for his work in organizing a strike force among the Texark troops.

**Varnoff, Mischa**  a colonel and police commissioner in the novella "Izzard and the Membrane." He is among those who protect Scott MacDonney from being killed by an agent of the underground. He falls to his death when he passes through the membrane into an elevator shaft.

**Veil of Veronica**  a woman gave Jesus a cloth to wipe the blood and sweat from his face while on his way to Calvary. When he returned the cloth to the woman, it held the impression of his face. In the novella "And the Light Is Risen" and *A Canticle for Leibowitz* ("Fiat Lux"), Father Jerome/Dom Paulo says Saint Leibowitz offered a Veil of Veronica to a crucified civilization in founding the Albertian Order to preserve knowledge. The veil was marked by only the image of truth, faintly recorded. It was incomplete and difficult to understand.

**Ven Klaeden, Ernstili, Baron**  the commander of the 720 ships of Strafe Fleet Three, Spacestrike Command, of the Imperial Forces of the Succession in the short story "The Ties That Bind." He disregards the advice of his intelligence analyst, Baltun Meikl, and decides to use Earth for his fleet's retooling and refueling operation. He establishes a restricted military zone among the peaceful Earth inhabitants, exploiting them for the benefit of his mission. An uprising among his men and his harsh reaction to it result in his being shot and infected by a deadly fungus. He was born in space on a planetoid city-state orbiting the Michea Dwarf.

**Venerable Boedullus**  *see* **Boedullus**

**"Vengeance for Nikolai"**  short story first published in *Venture Science Fiction*, 1 (March 1957), 112–130. The story is later published as "The Song of Marya."

Marya Dmitriyevna Lisitsa, a beautiful young Russian woman, has lost her son, Nikolai, during an American bombardment. He was killed by a bomb fragment. In despair, Marya unsuccessfully attempts suicide. Porphiry Grigoryevich, a Russian colonel, decides he can use her despair and recruits her for a suicide mission to kill an American general, Rufus MacAmsward, the military genius behind the successful American assault on Russia.

MacAmsward is a "vile old lecher" who is "still in the oral stage of emotional development." Grigoryevich believes it will be easy for Marya, who is still lactating, to seduce the general and poison him through a bacterial toxin passed through her milk. The poison will be introduced into Marya's system through a series of lethal injections that will eventually kill her. She will be directed by post-hypnotic suggestions after her planned capture. Grief stricken over the loss of her son, Marya agrees to the plan.

She is placed behind the lines of the advancing American, or Ami, forces with items that should pique the interest of General MacAmsward. She is captured by a young sergeant and taken to Major Kline, one of the fascist American Party officers, for interrogation. The sergeant worries about how Marya will be treated once she reaches the major, and he attempts to allow her to escape but she will not accept his gesture.

Marya defiantly refuses to answer the major's questions, and he reluctantly turns her over to the sadistic Captain Purvis who whips her in order to get the information he wants. The sergeant, however, secretly notifies the Red Cross who intervenes and treats her wounds.

After her ordeal with Captain Purvis, Marya comes to the attention of General MacAmsward. He orders the court martial of Captain Purvis for his treatment of her. He wants to release her in order to allow her to return to her home, but Marya tells him that he has killed her son and that she has "come to nurse you to death with the milk of a murdered child." MacAmsward does not believe she is speaking literally and succumbs to her seductions when she opens her robe to expose her breasts. She tells him they must make another child to replace the one he killed.

The toxin is quickly lethal to those not immunized, and MacAmsward is soon dead. His guards burst through the door and shoot Marya. But she has not only avenged her son, she has also helped save Russia and is immortalized in legends of her country.

**Veni Creator Spiritus**  Latin: "Come Creator Spirit." A well-known and widely used hymn in the Catholic Church. The pope chants it during the canonization of Leibowitz in *A Canticle for Leibowitz* ("Fiat Homo"). In *Saint Leibowitz and the Wild Horse Woman*, Cardinal Hilan Bleze attempts to lead the prelates at the conclave in Valana in singing it, but the noise from the crowd outside the cathedral drowns out the words. Later, Brother Blacktooth sings it with a small choir celebrating Mass in New Jerusalem at Pentecost.

**Venison House Tavern** an inn in Valana. Cardinal Brownpony and Hultor Bråm eat there, and Brownpony later meets Sorely Cardinal Nauwhat there.

**Verbum subtile atque infandum** Latin: "Truth so subtle it is unspeakable." Cardinal Brownpony tries to belay the fears of some cardinals after Amen Specklebird says that God's word is "*subtile et enfandum*," subtle and abominable, in *Saint Leibowitz and the Wild Horse Woman*. Brownpony tells them they misunderstood what was said — he says the word used by the pope was *infandum* not *enfandum*.

**Vere dignum** Latin: "Truly worthy." The phrase, from the Preface of the Mass, is used in the short story "A Canticle for Leibowitz."

**Versicles** from the Latin *versiculus* meaning short or little verse. Traditionally used as part of a prayer service or hymn which includes responses in worship. Versicles may be indicated by a ℣. The novella "The Last Canticle" and *A Canticle for Leibowitz* ("Fiat Voluntas Tua") contain Miller's "Versicles by Adam and Rejoinders by the Crucified" sung by the brothers of the Leibowitz abbey. See also **Responses**

**Vespere occaso** *see* **In principio Deus**

**Vespero mundi expectando** Latin: "The evening [end] of the world is expected." In *A Canticle for Leibowitz* ("Fiat Lux"), Father Gault tells Dom Paulo that this is Brother Armbruster's attitude in his argument with Brother Kornhoer, who favors "matins of the millennium" — the prayers of a new day. The point is that Armbruster is a pessimist who opposes Kornhoer's optimism concerning the progress of mankind.

**Vespers** the sixth of the canonical hours that is said in the early evening before dark or in the late afternoon. Reference is made to Father Gault finding Father Jerome slumped across his desk before Vespers in the novella "And the Light Is Risen." The term is also used in *A Canticle for Leibowitz* ("Fiat Lux") and *Saint Leibowitz and the Wild Horse Woman*.

**Vexilla regis inferni produent** Latin: "The banners of the King of Hell go forth." Taken from the opening line of Canto 34 of the *Inferno* from Dante's *The Divine Comedy*: "Vexilla Regis prodeunt inferni." Dante added "inferni" to the first line of a Latin hymn by Venantius Fortunatus, *The royal banners forward go*.

1. Dom Paulo thinks of these words as he contemplates Thon Taddeo, and the materialism and progress he represents, coming to the abbey to study the Memorabilia in *A Canticle for Leibowitz* ("Fiat Lux"). It is a memory from "a perverted line from an ancient *commedia*."

2. In *Saint Leibowitz and the Wild Horse Woman*, Brownpony speaks these words as New Rome lies in ashes and the Texark cavalry approaches the defeated city.

**Viaticum** Latin: "Provision for a journey." A reference to the Holy Eucharist when given to a person in danger of dying. After being crushed beneath the rubble of the abbey in the novella "The Last Canticle" and *A Canticle for Leibowitz* ("Fiat Voluntas Tua"), Father Zerchi thinks if anyone is in need of viaticum, they will have to crawl to him.

**Vicar Apostolic** a titular bishop who governs as a representative of the pope a specific territory that is as yet without a diocese.

**Vicar Apostolic to the Three Hordes** a position created by Pope Amen I to serve as his representative to all the hordes of the Plains and to govern all churches and missions north and south of the Nady Ann River. In creating this papal dominated vicariate, Amen hopes to reduce the influence of Cardinal Benefez among the Plains' people. Cardinal Brownpony is appointed the first Vicar Apostolic to the Three Hordes.

**Vicariate** usually an undeveloped territory without a diocese governed by a vicar apostolic and divided into various missions.

**Victros, Corporal** a minor character in *Saint Leibowitz and the Wild Horse Woman*. He is a member of Cardinal Hadala's expedition.

**Vidi aquam** Latin: "I saw the water." The first words of the hymn sung with the sprinkling of holy water before Mass during Eastertide. It is used in the short story "A Canticle for Leibowitz."

*The View from the Stars* a paperback collection published by Ballantine Books (New York) in 1964.

Contents: "You Triflin' Skunk," "The Will," "Anybody Else Like Me?," "Crucifixus Etiam," "I,

Dreamer," "Dumb Waiter," "Blood Bank," "Big Joe and the Nth Generation," "The Big Hunger."

**Vigge**   the youngest son of Keeper Cron in the short story "Please Me Plus Three." Nicknamed "the Bear," he is dull-witted and sadistic. He pursues Ton of Roldin to the plateau to seek vengeance for his father's murder. Although Vigge does not kill Ton, Bel orders him flogged when he returns from the plateau because he killed two men. Vigge dies from the flogging.

**The Viggern Federation**   an interstellar organization beyond the Sixty-Star Cluster in the short story "Blood Bank."

**Villa, Francisco (Pancho)** (June 5, 1878–July 20, 1923)   Mexican bandit and revolutionary born Doroteo Arango. He supposedly adopted the name Francisco Villa after killing a man who attacked his sister. He transitioned from banditry to revolution with the outbreak of the Mexican Revolution in 1910. He became a popular hero known for his bravery, leadership, and guerrilla exploits. The Mexican government allowed him to retire with the rank of general. He was later assassinated by his enemies.

In *Saint Leibowitz and the Wild Horse Woman*, the convent of Sister Silentia is named Our Lady of San Pancho Villa of Cockroach Mountains. It is located south of the Brave River.

**Virgin Mary**   the mother of Jesus. According to the Catholic Church, she was born free of original sin; her birth is referred to as the Immaculate Conception. At the time of her betrothal to Joseph, the angel Gabriel announced that the Holy Spirit would come to her and that she would give birth to the Son of God. She remained sinless and a perpetual virgin. She was taken bodily into heaven at her death.

**The Visitationist Friars of the Order of Saint Leibowitz of Tycho**   an independent offshoot of the Albertian Order that Brother Joshua is to lead. It is formed after the occurrence of Lucifer is Fallen in the novella "The Last Canticle" and "Fiat Voluntas Tua" in *A Canticle for Leibowitz*. It is originally composed of twenty-five members of the Albertian Order whose first mission is to evacuate the Holy See and the Memorabilia to a colony world when a nuclear holocaust threatens Earth. (In the novel, they are instructed to establish a patriarchal see and then the mother house of the Visitationist Friars). The monks constitute the nucleus of a space going order. After successfully establishing the pope off Earth, the monks will travel from space colony to space colony preserving the history of Earth and the teachings of the Church. Wherever man goes, the Order of Saint Leibowitz is to follow. Their spaceship will be their abbey. Although they are to preserve the memory of Earth and their origins, they are never to return to Earth.

Tycho is a reference to the Danish astronomer Tycho Brahe, who is noted for his accurate astronomical observations in the pre-telescope age. See also **Brahe, Tycho**.

**Vissarion**   the Russian form of the Greek name Bessarion. The meaning of the name has been given as "he who gives new life." Saint Bessarion (or Vissarion) of the Greek Orthodox Church was a 4th century ascetic who lived in Egypt. He is believed to have been a disciple of Saint Anthony, the patriarch of the Desert Fathers.

In "And the Light Is Risen" and *A Canticle for Leibowitz*, reference is made to Vissarion the antipope. His followers, militant monks or military knight-friars, would have burned the books at the Leibowitz Abbey as being heretical to Vissarion's theology if they had not been protected.

Miller may also be making an ironic reference to John Bessarion, a fifteenth century cardinal, noted for his learning and his support of scholarship and writing.

**Vissarionist disputes**   conflicts arising from the machinations of Vissarion, the antipope. During the disputes, the Abbey of Saint Leibowitz was placed under siege. Reference to the disputes is made in the novella "And the Light Is Risen" and "Fiat Lux" in *A Canticle for Leibowitz*.

**Vittorio**   an unseen minor character in the short story "Vengeance for Nikolai." He is one of only two men still alive in the sergeant's squad.

**Vix secures**   Latin: "Scarcely safe." Used in *A Canticle for Leibowitz* ("Fiat Voluntas Tua").

**Vögeli**   Manue Nanti's German foreman in the short story "Crucifixus Etiam." He is a narrow eyed, florid man who is usually half-drunk. He is generally abusive toward the workers.

**The Voice**   from the short story "No Moon for Me." A "twittering language" with periods of long silences has been emanating from the Earth's moon for years. It is believed that these ultra-high frequency bands originate from an alien invader on the moon. When a manned rocket is sent to the moon to negotiate with and force the invaders off the moon, it is discovered that "the Voice" has been a hoax — a transmitter aboard an unmanned rocket — perpetrated by Colonel Denin to force man into space.

**Vorhu** one of the gods in the legends of the people on the unnamed planet in the novella "The Song of Vorhu." According to the lore of the planet, Vorhu's consort, Ndriga, fell from his arms in heaven and landed on the planet. When Vorhu came down to bury her, flowers had blossomed from her body and spread over the planet. Vorhu is associated with Barry Wilkes who brought the White Idiot to the still developing planet. The spores from the vegetable-entity that inhabited her body gave life to the planet.

**Votive mass** a Mass dedicated to a special purpose. In *Saint Leibowitz and the Wild Horse Woman*, Abbot Jarad asks that a Mass for the election of the pope be offered on the opening day of the conclave.

**Vrach** Transliterated Russian: "Physician." The term is used in the short story "Vengeance for Nikolai."

**Walin** the second son of Keeper Cron in the short story "Please Me Plus Three." He becomes Keeper when Ton of Roldin kills his father.

**Walkeka, Talewa** a Dalethian pilot who agrees to take Eli Roki to Sol III aboard her freighter the *Idiot* in the short story "Blood Bank." She also refers to herself as Daleth Incorporated. Although she smokes cigars and exhibits the rough, uncouth characteristics of her native planet, Roki perceives her to be a capable pilot as well as handsome and proud. The Solarians kidnap her as part of their effort to ensure that Roki will follow them to Sol III. They hypnotize her to try to bypass Roki's sabotage of the *Idiot*.

**The Wanderer** a bar on Tragor III visited by Eli Roki and E Pok in the short story "Blood Bank."

**Wandering Jew** according to medieval legend, the Wandering Jew abused Jesus on his way to Calvary. As punishment, he was condemned to wander the Earth until the second coming of Christ at the end of time. The earliest version depicts him as becoming a godly and religious man, sharing with holy men events he witnessed in the apostolic days. In *A Canticle for Leibowitz* ("Fiat Lux"), a number of references are made to Benjamin as the Wandering Jew during his conversation with Dom Paulo on the Mesa of Last Resort. Benjamin tells the abbot: "I don't much expect Him to come, but I was told to wait." He says he has waited for thirty-two centuries so far. See also **Benjamin**

**War Buzzard** one aspect of the Nomad deity the Wild Horse Woman. It presides over the field of battle and the feeding ground in *Saint Leibowitz and the Wild Horse Woman*. The War Buzzard is also known as the Buzzard of Battle.

**War Dog** a constellation in the Nomad night sky in *Saint Leibowitz and the Wild Horse Woman*. It is also the mythical pet of the Lord Empty Sky, an ancient hero who led wilddogs into battle against the Farmer King and his armies.

**Watchingdown, Joyo** cardinal and Abbot of Watchingdown Abbey, far east of the Great River, in *Saint Leibowitz and the Wild Horse Woman*. He was made a cardinal by Pope Amen, and he takes part in the conclave to elect a new pope after Amen resigns the papacy. Watchingdown is a corruption of Washington, D. C.

**Watchit-Ol'zarkia** the mountainous region north of Texark in *Saint Leibowitz and the Wild Horse Woman*. It grew into the ghetto nation of Watchitah from the original Valley of the Misborn. Frontier guards from both Texark and the Church surround it in an attempt to maintain gennies within one geographic area. Miller derives the name from two small mountain ranges in the area of western Arkansas and southeast Oklahoma: the Ouachita (pronounced WAHSH-uh-tah) Mountains and the Ozark Mountains (or Highlands). See also **Valley of the Misborn** and **Watchitah Nation**

**Watchitah Nation** the official name of the former Valley of the Misborn when its boundaries were fixed by treaty. It is the recognized home of the gennies, the genetically handicapped, in *Saint Leibowitz and the Wild Horse Woman*. See also **Valley of the Misborn** and **Watchit-Ol'zarkia**

**Waters, Angela** one of the colonists in the novella "Cold Awakening." She is among a group of colonists playing poker when Eric Joley stops by the door and looks in. The other colonists at her table encourage her to introduce herself to him. She is his potential wife when they reach Sigma Seven based upon their genetic recommendations. While Joley is initially embarrassed, they flirt a bit before he is called away. Waters admits to him her fears about the suspendfreeze process and questions why the colonists cannot remain awake for the journey. Joley suspects she may be bait to try to coax him into sabotaging the suspendfreeze. She eventually reveals that she is a morphine addict, like many of the colonists. Joley makes sure that her suspendfreeze locker will not be able to be opened before his.

**Waverly, Frank** the unseen husband of Lisa in the short story "Command Performance" (also entitled "Anybody Else Like Me?"). He is unaware of his wife's telepathic abilities. He is away on a business trip during the time of the story.

**Waverly, Lisa (neé O'Brien)** the main character in the short story "Command Performance," later entitled "Anybody Else Like Me?" Lisa is a 34 year old wife and mother of three children. She lives a quiet, fulfilled life but has had the sense for most of her life that there is something different about her that she cannot identify yet longs to express. One evening when her children are visiting her mother and her husband is away on business, Lisa encounters a man she has never met, although she has a sense of knowing him. Kenneth Grearly reveals to her their shared abilities: they are telepaths. Lisa struggles to come to terms with this knowledge, but when Grearly plans a forced sexual union with her in order to produce children to promote telepathic abilities among humans, she uses her newly discovered powers to stop him and protect herself. With his death, however, she realizes her total isolation because of her mutation.

**"Way of a Rebel"** short story originally appearing in *If, Worlds of Science Fiction*, 3 (April 1954), 39–49. In response to Eurasian Soviet air attacks on the American continent, the United States Congress passes the Manlin Bill declaring a state of total emergency for the nation and allowing the Department of Defense control of the government. With the resignation of President Williston, Secretary of Defense Garson is given the absolute power to lead the country in war. He issues an ultimatum to the enemy to surrender immediately or face an all-out nuclear attack, "the masterpiece of homicidal engineering, the final word in destruction."

Navy lieutenant Mitch Laskell is on patrol in a one-man submarine. He resents the escalation of a purposeless war by the "world's political jackasses." He refuses to acknowledge his radio messages and return to base, and decides to stop fighting a war he does not believe in. He is troubled, however, by his sense of duty and his allegiance to his country. He views the war as "the big business of governments whose leaders invoked the Deity in the cause of slaughter." Why must he contribute to the destruction of mechanical civilization? The machinery of civilization is a living body with man as its brain. To destroy man's technology, to leave it in a tangled jumble of radioactive waste, is insufferable to Laskell. He decides to use his submarine to live apart from society so that he does not have to submit to its will; as the governed, he no longer consents to be governed.

As Laskell makes his way alone he detects five enemy submarines readying an attack on Washington, D.C. He decides to break his own radio silence to warn naval command about the impending attack but is unable to make clear contact. Despite his misgivings about the war itself and his own country's conduct, he engages the enemy submarines and uses his nuclear warhead in a suicidal mission to destroy the "five wrong tools" that would otherwise help destroy the right tools of civilization.

**Weejus** the holy women of the Nomads in *Saint Leibowitz and the Wild Horse Woman*.

**Weh-Geh** the smallest of the Yellow Guard in *Saint Leibowitz and the Wild Horse Woman*. Unlike his comrades, his skin color is almost light brown. Cardinal Brownpony chooses Weh-Geh to accompany him and Brother Blacktooth to Hannegan City. He is killed going to Brownpony's defense when Filpeo Harq threatens the cardinal.

**Wehrmacht** German: "defense power." The name of the combined German armed forces from 1935 to the end of World War II in 1945. It is refered to in the short story "Wolf Pack."

**WeJan** a Tragorian captain and patrol officer who boards the *Idiot* for an inspection in the short story "Blood Bank." He agrees to share what he knows about the Solarians with Eli Roki.

**Welkir** the father of Mara and a Senior Kinsmen in the short story "It Takes a Thief." He will not listen to Asir's concerns about Mars dying and what needs to be done to save it. He goes to the vault to try to stop Asir and orders Slubil to pursue him, resulting in Slubil being killed by Big Joe.

**Werli, General** a minor character in the short story "No Moon for Me." He is the Commander of the Air Force who meets with the three man crew before the launching of the first lunar rocket.

**Westin, Sam** an alias used by Sam Wuncie in the novella "The Yokel."

**Westmore, Cleo** the foster mother of Kenny in the short story "The Will."

**Westmore, Kenny** a fourteen year old boy dying of leukemia in the short story "The Will." His favorite television show "Captain Chronos and the Guardsmen of Time" gives him the idea that a time machine would allow him to travel to an age when there is a cure for his disease. He buries a note in his backyard along with his stamp collection and autographs of famous people, asking anyone in the future who discovers them to sell the items and use the money for a time machine to come get him if a cure is possible.

**Westmore, Rod** Kenny's foster father in the short story "The Will." He tells Kenny that he has to have faith that a cure will be found for the leukemia that the boy has. He discovers Kenny's buried valuables and note to the future asking that someone return to get him when a cure is discovered.

**Wetok, Potear** the wife of Esitt Loyte in *Saint Leibowitz and the Wild Horse Woman*. She is the granddaughter of Wetok Enar, the matriarch of the clan.

**Wetok Enar** *see* **Enar, Wetok**

**What does it profit a man if he gains the whole world but loses his own soul?** a slight variation of Mark 8:36 (KJV), "For what shall it profit a man, if he shall gain the whole world, and lose his own soul?" These are Jesus' words to his disciples concerning the need for self-denial in the physical world for the sake of spiritual salvation. In his address before the conclavists in *Saint Leibowitz and the Wild Horse Woman*, Amen Specklebird asks what one's own soul is and how it may be lost. He says the soul keeps grasping "at the world to gain it, and the world has sharp teeth. And thorns."

**"What is man that thou art mindful of him? Or the son of man that thou visitest him?"** a line from Psalm 8 (DB) that is among Barry Wilkes's thoughts as he struggles with the idea of perpetuating the human race in space and under what conditions. Why is man so special that God should single him out for His special attention? From the novella "The Song of Vorhu."

**"The Wheel"** a short story by John Wyndham included in *Beyond Armageddon*.

**Which is the Potter, pray, and which is the Pot?** a quotation from rubaiyat XCIV of the *Rubaiyat of Omar Khayyam* translated by Edward Fitzgerald. It is used in the novella "Dark Benediction" as Paul wonders if he is actually the diseased patient rather than the people infected by the neuroderm plague.

**White** a Marsville commissioner trapped inside the androon cave with Commissioner Peterson in the novella "The Reluctant Traitor." White speaks with the androon chief priest. He is held, perhaps voluntarily, until the body of Saralesara is returned to the androons for tribal burial.

**White Idiot** the term used by Barry Wilkes for the woman he frees from a cell on a subterranean level of an asylum in the novella "The Song of Vorhu." She is a hopeless and congenital idiot, but Wilkes believes she is free of the deadly plague that has struck Earth. He hopes that she will be the new Eve to his Adam that will allow man to be reborn in the stars. He eventually discovers, however, that the plague has only been dormant in her. He places her on a still developing Earth-like planet hoping to relieve her suffering. There she dies but the parasitic life she harbors blooms from her body, and its spores become the foundation for life on the planet. In the ancient legends of the planet, she is associated with Ndriga, the consort of Vorhu, who slips from his arms in heaven and falls to the planet.

**Whoever exalts a race or a State...** *see* ***Mit Brennender Sorge***

**Wickers** an unseen character in the novella "The Lineman." He is a member of the work crew and is a homosexual. He has a relationship with MacMillian.

**Wild Horse Woman** also known as the White Hag or Høngin Fujæ Vurn in *Saint Leibowitz and the Wild Horse Woman*. She is the principal deity of the Nomads. There are three aspects to the Wild Horse Woman: the Day Maiden and the Night Hag, which are reconciled within her, and the War Buzzard.

**Wilddog** one of the northern hordes of Nomad people in *Saint Leibowitz and the Wild Horse Woman*. They and the Grasshopper horde range north of the Nady Ann River.

**Wilkes, Barry** captain and test pilot in the novella "The Song of Vorhu." He possesses aloofness, "a chilly eye and a slightly mocking smirk." He is testing a new interstellar space drive when a plague devastates Earth. He returns long enough to find a female free of the plague, the "White Idiot," with the hope that they may perpetuate the race of man on another planet. Wilkes continually questions the morality of his choices and his responsibility to man. Refusing to continue the human race in a possible servile position on one planet, he hopes that the plague that he now realizes has lain dormant in the White Idiot may become the genesis of a new race of man. He plunges into a deep freeze on the moon of the planet where he leaves the body of the White Idiot. He is brought back to life by the descendents of the White Idiot a billion years later. He is associated with their god Vorhu who brought life to the planet with his consort Ndriga. Wilkes dies again when the people are unable to sustain him.

**"The Will"** short story originally published in *Fantastic*, 3 (February 1954), 27–41. Reprinted in *Fantastic Stories*, 18 (April 1969), 57–71. Kenny Westmore is a 14 year old boy dying from leukemia. He enjoys stamp collecting, collecting autographs, and watching "Captain Chronos and the Guardsmen of Time," his favorite television show. His mother Cleo is distraught, and his foster father, Rod, tells him to have faith. Kenny wishes he had a time-ship like Captain Chronos, and then he could go to a year where there was a cure. Rod and Cleo exhaust all possibilities for Kenny's treatment.

Kenny spends time building a time-ship in a tree in his backyard, but he gradually becomes weaker. He sends a picture of his time-ship to the television studio, and when the show learns of his condition, the actor playing Captain Chronos appears at Kenny's house. Rod, however, is angered by the show's attempt to use Kenny's illness and his love of the show for publicity purposes.

Despite Kenny's weakening condition, he seems more energetic and confident. He spends an increasing amount of time wandering the woods until the doctor restricts his activities. Kenny grows frantic and says that he will not be able to finish "it" and contact "them." He refuses to explain to Rod what he means.

Rod discovers Kenny missing from the house in the middle of the night. He finds him collapsed in the backyard with a shovel. He carries him back to his room and a map with an X marked by the fork in the creek falls from his pocket. Rod replaces the map.

When Kenny awakes, he seems surprised to be in his room. Rod asks him if he expected to awake somewhere else. Kenny says he thought "they came early" but refuses to reveal anything else. His doctor orders Kenny to stay in the house.

Rod hears Kenny leave the house late at night. He cannot find him in the yard but then remembers the X on the map. He goes to the fork in the creek and finds Kenny digging. Kenny asks Rod to let him finish his work and he will not run. Rod hears Kenny open and close a metal box and then dirt being shoveled back into a hole.

Kenny begins to run and Rod runs after him. He sees a flash of light and a strange voice calling for Kenny. A black opening appears and the voice continues to call to Kenny, saying they will fix him up. Kenny enters the opening and it begins to shrink and disappear with an explosive blast that knocks Rod out. When he regains consciousness, Cleo confirms everything that he saw. Kenny is missing.

Rod goes back to the place near the creek where Kenny was digging. He finds a metal breadbox Kenny used to bury his stamp collection and a number of valuable autographs. With them is a note from Kenny asking whoever finds the items in the future to sell them and use the money to pay for a time machine to come and get him on a particular date. Kenny had to go back to change the date because he realized he was dying sooner than he had expected.

Rod reburies the box. He understands that Kenny had faith: his burying of his treasures was an act of faith in tomorrow and tomorrow answered.

**Willie** *see* **Willow**

**Willinghams** a couple who are guests at the Slades's pseudoparty in the novella "Conditionally Human."

**Willis, Barney** a scout in the special patrol in the short story "Secret of the Death Dome." He is married to Betty, and his best friend, Jerry Harrison, is also a scout. The Martians emasculate Willis for experimental purposes. He dies from sunstroke trying to return to town from the dome.

**Willis, Betty** the wife of Barney Willis and the former girlfriend of Jerry Harrison, Barney's best friend, in the short story "Secret of the Death Dome." After Barney dies, Betty demands vengeance and wants to know when they will get even with the Martians. When Jerry goes to the dome, Betty follows him afraid that her outburst will cause him to do something dangerous and stupid. The Martians capture her and she is held captive until Jerry is able to secure her release. Unbeknownst to her, the Martians had planned to alter her using Martian genes so that she might be able to give birth to healthy Martian males. There is the promise of a reunion with Jerry at the end of the story after her period of mourning for Barney.

**Willis, James** a colonist in the novella "Cold Awakening." He trades names and places with Herrick so that Herrick will be placed in suspend-freeze sooner. By doing so, Herrick hopes to avoid being implicated in Jessel's murder and sent back to Earth.

**Williston, President** a minor character in the short story "Way of a Rebel." When a state of total national emergency is declared, Williston, the President of the United States, resigns. In doing so, he cedes control of the government to the Department of Defense as provided for in the Manlin Bill.

**Willow** a young woman who has contracted the space plague in the novella "Dark Benediction." She is originally from Dallas, the daughter of a salesman. A traveling farmer infected her with the plague. As a hyper or dermie, one with the plague, she is captured in Houston and is going to be killed until she is rescued by Paul Oberlin driving an old truck. When Paul stops outside the city to let her out, he discovers that she has been wounded; her Achilles' tendon is severed. Rather than abandon her along the side of the road, Paul gets the first aid kit for her, and she promises not to try to touch him and transmit the disease. He decides that he has to find a doctor who can treat her wound.

Willow and Paul make it to the hyper colony in Galveston. They find a shack along the water's edge with the body of a dermie woman who committed suicide with a shotgun. Willow sobs as Paul leaves her at the shack to try to find a doctor. When he returns with two priests from St. Mary's hospital, they discover that Willow has tried to kill herself but was too weak to succeed. Paul visits Willow in her hospital room as she recovers from surgery. She tells him she will never touch him, that she would rather die than infect anyone, especially him. She loathes herself for having the plague and because he fears her. Willow continues to suffer from depression. She is attracted to Paul but is afraid of repaying his kindness toward her by infecting him. Her attraction to him as well as the disease's craving to infect others draws Willow to Paul's room one night. He senses someone in his room and reacts wildly. When she is discovered missing from her room, Paul fears for her safety. He correctly guesses that she may attempt suicide again by drowning in the ocean. He finds her on the beach distraught that she has touched him. Paul takes her hand, kisses her, and carries her back to the hospital.

**Winding Stare** a range of "little mountains" on the edge of the Valley of the Misborn, north of Hannegan City in *Saint Leibowitz and the Wild Horse Woman*.

**Winters** 1. One of the crewmen on the first launch sent to the planet in "Six and Ten Are Johnny."

2. A minor character, the tail gunner of the B-25 piloted by Mark Kessel, in the short story "Wolf Pack."

**Wir [warden] marschierin weiter wenn alles in Scherben fällt** German: "We march on when everything falls to pieces." Part of the refrain to "Es Zittern die Morschen Knochen" ("Rotten Bones Are Trembling"), a Nazi marching song by Hans Baumann. It is referred to in the novella "The Last Canticle" and *A Canticle for Leibowitz* ("Fiat Voluntas Tua").

**The Wise One** another name for Bel in the short story "Please Me Plus Three." See also **Bel**

**Wohr** one of the Tragorians who inspect the Dalethian freighter the *Idiot* in the short story "Blood Bank."

**"Wolf Pack"** short story appearing in *Fantastic*, 2 (September/October 1953), 4–20. Reprinted in *Fantastic Stories*, 15 (May 1966), 126–142. Lieutenant Mark Kessel is a B-25 pilot during World War II with only four missions remaining before his tour ends and he is sent home. He worries that he has become hardened to the horrors of war and indifferent to the innocent lives that are lost. He begins to have dreams of La, or La Femme, an imaginary idealized woman he talks with and writes letters to who seems eerily real. On a second bombing mission over the small Italian city of Perugia, Kessel is confronted by La's accusations that he is a murderer of innocent people and the killer of her family and now of her. Moved by either a figment of his guilty conscience or the telepathic images of a clairvoyant woman under attack, he attempts to abort his bomb drop but his copilot prevents him from doing so. Believed to be suffering from combat fatigue, Kessel will be returned home. However, La no longer appears to him, and her absence now proves her former existence to Kessel.

This story may be an earlier example than *A Canticle for Leibowitz* of Miller attempting to confront his own sense of guilt for his participation in the allied bombing of Monte Cassino, Italy during World War II. See also **Monte Cassino**

**Wooden Nose** Esitt Loyte's nickname among his troops after his mutilation by the Nomads, which included cutting off his nose, in *Saint Leibowitz and the Wild Horse Woman*. See also **Loyte, Esitt**

**Wooshin** a former seaman and warrior of Asian descent who became the headsman, or executioner, for the current Hannegan and his predecessor in *Saint Leibowitz and the Wild Horse Woman*. After falling from political favor, he found political refuge and work as a smithy in the Abbey of Saint Leibowitz. As a reference to his former work as an executioner, his nickname at the abbey is Brother Axe. He accompanies Cardinal Brownpony to Valana as his bodyguard and teaches Brother Blacktooth to fight in exchange for language lessons. He is a good friend to Blacktooth and maintains an absolute loyalty to Brownpony who later creates the rank of Sergeant General for him when Brownpony becomes Pope Amen II. When the Church's forces are defeated in New Rome, Wooshin beheads Amen II at his command. When he attempts his own ritual suicide, Blacktooth refuses to help him declaring that he wants to hear him say, "Long live Filpeo Harq!" before he dies. He and Blacktooth leave the cathedral of St. Peter's by a rear door as Texark troops approach the front. They follow a small train of wagons headed for the Watchitah Nation. Eventually Wooshin leaves Blacktooth behind as he makes his way to Hannegan City where he stops Filpeo Harq's carriage in the street and beheads the despot. Harq's guards kill him as he bares his throat and chest to their bullets. He is referred to variously as Axe, The Axe, 'Shin and Woo Shin.

**Woosoh-Loh** one of the members of the so-called Yellow Guard in *Saint Leibowitz and the Wild Horse Woman*.

**World Court of Nations** an international body in *A Canticle for Leibowitz* ("Fiat Voluntas Tua") which orders a cease-fire after the Asian retaliatory nuclear strike against Texarkana. It also issues a suspended death sentence against the heads of government who are responsible for the Itu Wan and Texarkana disasters.

**Wormy-Face** a minor Nomad character in *Saint Leibowitz and the Wild Horse Woman*. He is one of Mounts-Everybody's man.

**Wotan** within German mythology the supreme god frequently identified with Odin of Norse mythology. The name more often is given as Woden. He is associated with war, learning, and magic. In the short story "Wolf Pack," the coming battle is said to played under the auspices of "a jovial Wotan."

**Wren St. Mary** an old companion of Brother Blacktooth and a fellow Nomad runaway. He comes to the Abbey of Saint Leibowitz together with Blacktooth and Singing Cow St. Martha. He works in the kitchen as Brother Second Cook.

**Wuncie, Sam** the titular character of the novella "The Yokel." He is a dark, young, unkempt former pilot who now lives a simple existence in Ruralland as a yokel. He was a lieutenant in the Air Force during the last years of the Hemisphere Conflict, but was grounded from jet pilot training because of a susceptibility to aeroembolism. Stationed in an Arctic weather station after attempting to stop a colonel from embezzling, it took him one and a half years to walk home to Florida from Alaska because the technology that supported transportation lay in ruins. Unsure of the arguments of either the Restoration Committees who control and restrict access to the cities and protect technology or Colonel MacMahon's Border Guards who would remove all restrictions from access to technology, Wuncie plans to use the general discord for his benefit. He will make his way into a restricted city and steal as much as possible to sell to the yokels. He is coerced by MacMahon, however, into working with the Border Guards to steal a cargo plane. When the plan is discovered, Wuncie disables MacMahon's men on the plane and must come to his own decision as to which side is right.

**Wylo City** the location where the novella "Conditionally Human" takes place.

**Wyndham, John** *see* **Harris, John Wyndham**

**XM-5-B** a cybernetic spacecraft capable of feeling because of its man-machine interface using babies taken by the totalitarian state in the short story "I, Dreamer." The craft is also referred to as Clicker. It can experience sleep and dreams, and it dreams of being a TwoLegs, a humanoid. It feels affection for Janna, a woman who maintains part of its electronic circuitry. It is abused by Barnish, its sadistic controller, who uses a pain stimulus to punish XM-5-B.

**Yaney, Jim** a young Air Force general in the short story "The Little Creeps. He has a good deal of combat experience — he is a born fighter — and proposes a controversial bombing mission to expose the enemy's plan to make it appear the United States has violated another country's neutrality. In fact, Yaney's plan is a means by which he hopes to escalate a regional conflict into a nuclear world war. The little creeps warn General Horrey not to listen to Yaney or agree to his plan, but Horrey disregards their warning, and a widespread nuclear holocaust results. Yaney is driven insane when Horrey destroys his counterpart in the little creeps' parallel world.

**"A yearling lamb for a holocaust, and a pigeon for sin"** from Leviticus 12, the procedure for the ritual purification following childbirth. Holocaust is used here in the sense of a sacrificial offering consumed by flames. The passage appears in the short story "MacDoughal's Wife."

**Yellow** an old town in a desolate, arid part of the country in *Saint Leibowitz and the Wild Horse Woman*. Cardinal Brownpony stops there on his way to the eastern boundary of Jackrabbit territory. It is where Brownpony learns of Hultor Bråm's offenses against the *Qæsach dri Vørdar* and his subsequent ritual death.

**Yellow Guard** the Archbishop of Hong, Cardinal Ri, maintains six warriors skilled in weaponless fighting in the novel *Saint Leibowitz and the Wild Horse Woman*. Of Asian descent, these warrior monks are known as the Yellow Guard in Valana.

**Yiddish Schlemiel** a reference to Jesus by Dom Zerchi in *A Canticle for Leibowitz* ("Fiat Voluntas Tua"). The abbot thinks that God must possess an infinite sense of humor because He allowed the "King of the Universe" to be nailed on a cross as a Yiddish Schlemiel by "the likes of us." Schlemiel is from the Yiddish word *shlemil* meaning a bungler or fool. Yiddish, an admixture of Hebrew, German, and Slavic languages, was the language spoken primarily by Jews in eastern and central Europe. Miller seems to use it in this context to mean Jewish.

**"The Yokel"** a novella published in *Amazing Stories*, 27 (August/September 1953), 92–139. In the aftermath of the Hemispheric Conflict, World War III, a division arose between pastorals and technologists. Restoration Committees reclaimed urban centers to rebuild and protect technology and industry. These big cities are sealed off from the outside area, Ruralland. Yokels, those given to making their living from the land, inhabit the rural areas. The Restoration Committees instituted testing programs for those rurals who want to live in the controlled urban areas. The tests are designed to screen out the technologically unfit. If a person fails the test, he is branded with a small R on his cheek to designate him as "basically rural." The branded rurals are easy targets and are often persecuted within Ruralland for trying to surpass the rest of the population. Any person who moves, or attempts to move, from one designated area to another is known as a Crosser.

The Border Guard, a group of vigilantes commanded by Colonel MacMahon, is opposed to testing and rural people attempting to cross over. Sam Wuncie saves a branded Crosser from the torture of three Border Guards. When asked why he tried to cross, the man explains to Wuncie that he was part of a plan to sabotage the city and let rurals in. Wuncie decides that he will try to contact Zella Richmond who planned the sabotage so that he can attempt to cross. He wants to worm his way into the city in order to steal as much as he can and sell it to the yokels.

Wuncie succeeds in finding Zella who is working with Colonel MacMahon and his men to try to parachute 40 men into Orlando to secure weapons, kill Committee members, and steal patrol boats to make raids on coastal areas. MacMahon learns that Wuncie was trained as a pilot during the war and tries to enlist him in their cause. The colonel wants Wuncie and Zella to sneak into Jacksonville, steal a cargo plane from inside the tech zone, and fly it out. Wuncie asks why not leave the system alone. Things are relatively peaceful and the system will break down in a few years from the inside. He fears that what they do will destroy technology. MacMahon believes that the system excludes the common man and that the techs have created an artificial aristocracy and made themselves gods. They alone decide who is fit, and they have taken what rightfully belongs to all.

Wuncie believes MacMahon's plan is grandiose but that it might give him the opportunity to get into the city to accomplish his own plan to steal goods. MacMahon is not sure he can trust Wuncie, so he has Dr. Harlich inject him with the saliva of a possibly rabid dog. If Wuncie wants the rabies serum, he will have to accomplish his mission and return to MacMahon.

Wuncie and Zella cross into Jacksonville using the identities of two techs caught outside the city. As they make their way through the city, several old friends recognize Zella. She and Wuncie are forced to join them in a café to have a drink and catch up. Zella recognizes a Commissioner in the café and fears that she will be discovered. She tells Wuncie that he will have to accomplish their mission without her. He uses the amorous interests of Loretta, one of Zella's friends, to escape the café on the pretext of going dancing. Loretta is a control tower operator at the airport. She is more interested in having sex with Wuncie than going dancing, so he steers her toward the airport and suggests they may be able to find a safe spot inside. Loretta gets Wuncie inside the airport and he locates a C-54 in a hangar. He suggests the C-54 for their tryst. After making love, Wuncie locates the plane's first-aid kit as Loretta sleeps. He drugs her with morphine to keep her quiet. To create a diversion and an excuse to taxi the plane onto the runway, Wuncie starts a fire in the hangar. He successfully steals the plane and lands it in Orlando, rendezvousing with Captain Parrin and his small task force.

As night falls, Wuncie flies the commandos above the city to await word from Colonel MacMahon. As he waits, Commissioner Jenkins contacts him. Zella has revealed their plan, and Jenkins asks Wuncie to cooperate or be shot down. Worried about the rabies serum, he asks Jenkins to allow him to make the drop, and the commandos can be picked up. Jenkins refuses because of the possibility that people in the city could be hurt or killed. He tries to reassure Wuncie about the dog's saliva, and tells him that they will do their best to locate serum within the city. Wuncie finds a working oxygen mask in the cabin. He disables the plane's other oxygen tanks and then begins to take the plane to a higher altitude. The commandos begin to pass out. He disarms them and takes the plane to a lower altitude. He wants them to bail out, but Captain Parrin protests. Wuncie shoots him in the leg to convince the others that he is serious.

Once they have all jumped, Wuncie contacts Jenkins to tell him that he is going to land. Jenkins tells him he is free to stay in the city if he passes the tests. Wuncie asks why they give people who want to cross tests. Jenkins replies that they only screen out the blindly aggressive and the completely passive. They want to create two mutually dependent societies: one pastoral and one technological. Let people go where their abilities send them. Fanatics like MacMahon prevent a cooperative solution from being found. Jenkins says it is not necessarily right, but it is workable. Wuncie is unconvinced in principle, but he acknowledges that the city is working. The larger question is where is it going?

**Yonkers**  a member of the special patrol in the short story "Secret of the Death Dome." He was abducted by the Martians and returned with his legs amputated.

**Yordin, Urik**  a professor of history at the secular university in Texark and a member of the Order of Saint Ignatz in *Saint Leibowitz and the Wild Horse Woman*. He is in his fifties and is lean and gray. He is more comfortable in a lecture hall than behind a pulpit. Jæsis, a former student of his whom he failed, attempts to kill him while at the conclave in Valana. The shot misses the thon but kills Father Corvany. Yordin is a part of the advance party of Archbishop Benefez. He is later jailed when he seeks asylum from Benefez in New Jerusalem for openly stating that the Archbishop would never become pope.

*Yorick*  a starship lost approximately ten years before the time of the novella "Six and Ten Are Johnny." Hal Rogan reports that their ship, the *Archangel*, is not the first Earth ship to reach the planet. He says that the existence of Johnny Sree (aka Johnny Six) on the planet is explained by the fact that the few surviving crew members of the *Yorick* landed a launch on the planet after they realized there were too few of them to maintain their ship. Commander Isaacs is skeptical about this information and believes the odds of their launch landing in the same area as the *Yorick* are too great to be coincidental. He checks the *Yorick's* last known record and finds that it was about three light years from the planet.

The ship's name is derived from *Hamlet*, Act V, scene 1, where Hamlet discovers the skeleton of the court jester he once knew and was fond of as a child. Holding the skull, Hamlet famously states: "Alas, poor Yorick!—I knew him, Horatio; a fellow of infinite jest, of most excellent fancy...."

**Yoshigura**  the Japanese housekeeper of General Clement Horrey in the short story "The Little Creeps." General Horrey is warned by 2537 Angstroms, the little creeps, not to fire Yoshigura. But when Yoshigura attempts to blackmail Horrey for more money, the general does exactly that. Communist sympathizers use the firing to stage demonstrations outside of Horrey's home that result in the deaths of three demonstrators. Yoshigura attacks Horrey with a knife but is shot in the ankle by Horrey's driver.

**"You Triflin' Skunk"**  a later title for the short story "The Triflin' Man." It is first used when the story appears in *The View from the Stars* in 1964.

**Yy-Da**  a reference to Martian females in the short story "Secret of the Death Dome."

**ZDI**  see **Zone Defense Interior**

**Zeke**  the name of Dom Zerchi's boyhood cat in *A Canticle for Leibowitz* ("Fiat Voluntas Tua"). He kills the cat after it has been badly hurt when hit by a truck. He uses the story about his difficulty in killing the cat in an attempt to convince a mother not to euthanize her daughter.

**Zelazny, Roger**  (May 13, 1937–June 14, 1995) acclaimed American science fiction and fantasy writer noted for the character development within his work. He was a three time winner of the Nebula Award and a six time recipient of the Hugo Award. Among his novels are *Lord of Light* (1967), *Damnation Alley* (1969), *Doorways in the Sand* (1975), and the ten volumes comprising The Amber Chronicles (1970–1991). His short story "Lucifer" appears in *Beyond Armegeddon*.

**Zerchi, Jethrah** in the novella "The Last Canticle," Father Zerchi is the abbot of Saint Leibowitz. In *A Canticle for Leibowitz* ("Fiat Voluntas Tua"), he is referred to as Dom Zerchi and his first name is given. He is an active, physically restless man, rather than a contemplative. He struggles to maintain his beliefs and the teachings of the Church as the world around him begins to crumble, quite literally, as a thermonuclear war begins. He reveals the Church's Dismissal of Servants plan to Brother Joshua and is instrumental in securing his participation in the program. Zerchi hears Mrs. Grales's confession as the abbey collapses and he is buried beneath its rubble. He witnesses the birth of Rachel, her second head.

**Zone Defense Interior** also referred to as ZDI, these are state controlled regional civil defense districts in the novella "The Last Canticle" and *A Canticle for Leibowitz* ("Fiat Voluntas Tua"). As news first arrives of a nuclear explosion in Asia, the ZDI issues a defense alert and all private transmitters are taken off the air.

# Works by Walter M. Miller, Jr.

"MacDoughal's Wife." *American Mercury* 70 (March 1950): 313–320.
"Month of Mary." *Extension* 44 (May 1950): 17, 42.
"Secret of the Death Dome." *Amazing Stories* 25 (January 1951): 124–144.
"Izzard and the Membrane." *Astounding Science Fiction* 47 (May 1951): 70–116.
"Evening Caller." *Extension* 46 (July 1951): 44–46.
"The Soul-Empty Ones." *Astounding Science Fiction* 47 (August 1951): 62–94.
"Dark Benediction." *Fantastic Adventures* 13 (September 1951): 78–116.
"Men Behind *Fantastic Adventures*." *Fantastic Adventures* 13 (September 1951): [2], 127–130. [autobiographical essay].
"The Space Witch." *Amazing Stories* 25 (November 1951): 98–118.
"The Little Creeps." *Amazing Stories* 25 (December 1951): 56–84.
"The Song of Vorhu ... for Trumpet and Kettledrum." *Thrilling Wonder Stories* 39 (December 1951): 102–118.
"The Reluctant Traitor." *Amazing Stories* 26 (January 1952): 8–82.
"Conditionally Human." *Galaxy Science Fiction* 3 (February 1952): 30–63.
"Bitter Victory." *If, Worlds of Science Fiction* 1 (March 1952): 59–75.
"Dumb Waiter." *Astounding Science Fiction* 49 (April 1952): 7–40.
"It Takes a Thief." *If, Worlds of Science Fiction* 1 (May 1952): 68–84.
"Blood Bank." *Astounding Science Fiction* 49 (June 1952): 95–138.
"Six and Ten Are Johnny." *Fantastic* 1 (Summer 1952): 4–39, 160.
"Let My People Go." *If, Worlds of Science Fiction* 1 (July 1952): 4–58.
"Cold Awakening." *Astounding Science Fiction* 49 (August 1952): 46–82.
"Please Me Plus Three." *Other Worlds* 4 (August 1952): 6–47.
"No Moon for Me." *Astounding Science Fiction* 50 (September 1952): 56–70.
"The Big Hunger." *Astounding Science Fiction* 50 (October 1952): 98–112.
"Gravesong." *Startling Stories* 27 (October 1952): 108–112, 114–117.
"Command Performance." *Galaxy Science Fiction* 5 (November 1952): 140–160.
"A Family Matter." *Fantastic Story Magazine* 4 (November 1952): 134–139.
"Check and Checkmate." *If, Worlds of Science Fiction* 1 (January 1953): 4–24.
"Crucifixus Etiam." *Astounding Science Fiction* 50 (February 1953): 97–113.
"Who's Who in Science Fiction: Walter M. Miller, Jr." *Destiny* 8 (Spring 1953): 28–29. [autobiographical essay]
"I, Dreamer." *Amazing Stories* 27 (June/July 1953): 18–29, 162.
"The Yokel." *Amazing Stories* 27 (August/September 1953): 92–139.
"Wolf Pack." *Fantastic* 2 (September/October 1953): 4–20.
"The Will." *Fantastic* 3 (February 1954): 27–41.
"Death of a Spaceman." *Amazing Stories* 28 (March 1954): 6–21, 130.
"I Made You." *Astounding Science Fiction* 53 (March 1954): 55–64.
"Way of the Rebel." *If, Worlds of Science Fiction* 3 (April 1954): 39–49.
"The Ties That Bind." *If, Worlds of Science Fiction* 3 (May 1954): 4–26.
"The Darfsteller." *Astounding Science Fiction* 54 (January 1955): 10–65.
"The Triflin' Man." *Fantastic Universe* 2 (January 1955): 31–40.
"A Canticle for Leibowitz." *The Magazine of Fantasy and Science Fiction* 8 (April 1955): 93–111.
"The Hoofer." *Fantastic Universe* 4 (September 1955): 112–120.
"And the Light Is Risen." *The Magazine of Science Fiction and Fantasy* 11 (August 1956): 3–80.
"The Last Canticle." *The Magazine of Science Fiction and Fantasy* 12 (February 1957): 3–50.

"Vengeance for Nikolai." *Venture Science Fiction* 1 (March 1957): 112–130.
"The Corpse in Your Bed Is Me." With Lincoln Boone. *Venture Science Fiction* 3 (May 1957): 47–60.
"The Linemen." *The Magazine of Fantasy and Science Fiction* 13 (August 1957): 5–54.
*A Canticle for Leibowitz*. Philadelphia and New York: J. B. Lippincott, 1960 [©1959].
*Conditionally Human*. New York: Ballantine, 1962.
"Bobby and Jimmy: Round Six…" *Nation* 194 (7 April 1962): 300–303. [article]
[Introduction to "Memento Homo"]. In *The Worlds of Science Fiction*. Ed. and with introduction by Robert P. Mills. New York: Dial, 1963.
*The View from the Stars*. New York: Ballantine, 1964.
*The Last Western*. Thomas S. Klise. *Commonweal* 100 (June 14, 1974): 338–339. [book review]
*The Science Fiction Stories of Walter M. Miller, Jr.* Boston: Gregg, 1978.
*The Best of Walter M. Miller, Jr.* New York: Pocket, 1980.
*Conditionally Human and Other Stories*. London: Corgi, 1982.
*The Darfsteller and Other Stories*. London: Corgi, 1982.
"Bolsheviks on Mars." *New York Times Book Review* 8 July 1984: 11–12. [book review]
*Beyond Armageddon*. Ed. Walter M. Miller, Jr., and Martin H. Greenberg. New York: Donald I. Fine, 1985.
"Chariots of the Goddesses, or What?" *New York Times Book Review* 8 September 1985: 11. [book review]
"Roots & Sinew." *Commonweal* 113 (28 March 1986): [186]–188. [book review]
*Saint Leibowitz and the Wild Horse Woman*. New York: Bantam, 1997.
"God Is Thus." *The Magazine of Fantasy and Science Fiction* 93 no. 556 (October/November 1997): 13–35. [excerpt from *Saint Leibowitz and the Wild Horse Woman*]
*Two Worlds of Walter M. Miller: By the Author of "A Canticle for Leibowitz."* [Lexington, KY]: World Library Classics, 2009. ["Death of a Spaceman" and "The Hoofer"]

## *Collected Letters*

The following letters to Chad Oliver are in the Chad Oliver Collection in the Cushing Memorial Library and Archives at Texas A&M University, College Station.

Miller, Anne [signed Anne and Walt] to B.J. and Chad Oliver. Undated [probably November 1952].

Miller, Walter M., Jr., to Chad Oliver. 25 August 1951.
_____. 11 November 1951.
_____. 7 February 1952.
_____. 7 September 1952.
_____. 11 May 1955.
_____. 17 August 1956.
_____. 17 January 1957.
_____. 6 February 1957.
_____. 23 August 1957.
_____. 3 April [1958].
_____. 17 May 1958.
_____. 11 August 1958.
_____. 26 August 1958.
_____. 29 August 1958.
_____. 4 September 1958.
_____. 8 September 1958.
_____. 24 June 1966.
_____. 8 September 1966.

Miller, Walter M., Jr., to William H. Roberson. 11 October 1990.
_____. 14 December 1990.
_____. 21 February 1991.
_____. 9 April 1991.

# Works About Walter M. Miller, Jr.

Adrian, Marlin. "Omega Mythology: *A Canticle for Leibowitz* at Forty." *Listening* 35 (Spring 2000): 121–128.
Baum, Joan. "Second Thoughts: A Canticle for Science Fiction." *Change* 12 (January 1980): 52–53.
Bennett, Laurence. "'He Didn't Commit Suicide ... in His Way of Thinking.'" *Daytona Beach News-Journal* 18 February 1996: 1C and 6C.
Bennett, Michael Alan. "The Theme of Responsibility in Miller's *A Canticle for Leibowitz*." *English Journal* 59 (April 1970): 484–489.
Bertonneau, Thomas F. "Sacrifice and Sainthood: Walter M. Miller, Jr.'s Short Fiction." *Science Fiction Studies* 35.3 [106] (2008): 404–429.
Bisson, Terry. "A Canticle for Miller; or How I Met Saint Leibowitz and the Wild Horse Woman but not Walter M. Miller, Jr." http://www.terrybisson.com/miller.html. 23 March 2006.
Bouchard, Larry D. "Fragmentation and Aesthesis in Walter M. Miller's *A Canticle for Leibowitz*." *Listening* 35 (Spring 2000): 85–94.
Braden, Don. "A Canticle for Leibowitz: Translations." http://www.dbraden.org/canticle/tns.html. 2 September 2010.
Brians, Paul. "Study Guide for Walter M. Miller, Jr.: *A Canticle for Leibowitz* (1959)." http://www.wsu.edu/~brians/science_fiction/canticle.html. 2 September 2010.
Butryn, Alexander J. "For Suffering Humanity: The Ethics of Science in Science Fiction." In *The Transcendent Adventure: Studies of Religion in Science Fiction/Fantasy*. Ed. Robert Reilly. Westport, CT: Greenwood, 1985. Pp. [55]–70.
"Chad Oliver and Walt Miller." *SumerMorn* no. 3 (Fall 1979): 21–23.
Cockrell, Amanda. "On This Enchanted Ground: Reflections of a Cold War Childhood in Russell Hoban's *Riddley Walker* and Walter M. Miller's *A Canticle for Leibowitz*." *Journal of the Fantastic in the Arts* 15.1 (Spring 2004): 20–36.
Cowart, David. "Walter M. Miller, Jr." In *Twentieth Century American Science Fiction Writers*. Ed. David Cowart and Thomas L. Wymer. *Dictionary of Literary Biography*, vol. 8. Detroit: Gale, 1981. Pp. 19–30.
Cumings, Susan G. "Forty Years On: Conversations Around *A Canticle for Leibowitz*: A Response." *Listening* 35 (Spring 2000): 129–139.
Dalmyn, Tony. "Some Thoughts on Walter M. Miller's *A Canticle for Leibowitz*." *Winding Numbers* 2 (Winter 1975–1976): 4–8.
Ditzler, Joseph. "Number of Suicides Growing Rapidly." *Daytona Beach News-Journal* 18 February 1996: 1C, 6C.
Dowling, David. "Two Exemplary Fictions." In his *Fictions of Nuclear Disasters*. Iowa City: University of Iowa Press, 1987. Pp. 193–209.
Ducharme, Edward. "A Canticle for Miller." *English Journal* 55 (November 1966): 1042–1044.
Dunn, Thomas P. "To Play the Phoenix: Medieval Images and Cycles of Rebuilding in Walter Miller's *A Canticle for Leibowitz*." In *Phoenix From the Ashes: The Literature of the Remade World*. Ed. Carl B. Yoke. Westport, CT: Greenwood, 1987. Pp. [105]–115.
Fleischer, Leonore. "Talk of the Trade: Prometheus Unbound." *Publishers Weekly* 237 (Janaury 19, 1990): 61.
Fried, Lewis. "*A Canticle for Leibowitz*: A Song for Benjamin." *Extrapolation* 42.1 (2001): 44–58.
Gannon, Charles E. "They Speak in Mangled 'Memberment': Miller's, Muir's, and Hoban's Recollective Journeys to the Edge of Incomprehensibility." *Journal of Transatlantic Studies* 1.1 (2003): 26–36.
Garvey, John. "*A Canticle for Leibowitz*: A Eulogy for Walt Miller." *Commonweal* 123.7 (April 5, 1996): 7–8.
_____. "The Shaping of a Dark Vision." *Notre Dame Magazine* 12 (July 1983): 35–37.

Geddie, Tom. "Walt Miller and the Wandering Jew." *SumerMorn* no. 3 (Fall 1979): 20–23, 25.
Gilmour, Peter. "A Post-Vatican II, Twenty-First Century Reading of *A Canticle for Leibowitz*." *Listening* 35 (Spring 2000): 75–84.
Graham, William C. "*Lex Orandi, Lex Credendi* in the Church After I.E. Leibowitz." *Listening* 35 (Spring 2000): 105–120.
Greenhill-Taylor, Jennifer. "Author of Classic Science Fiction Novel Returns to Writing." *Jacksonville Times Union*, "Arts and Leisure" 26 January 1986: D1, D5.
\_\_\_\_\_. Email to the author. 9 October 2009.
Griffin, Russell M. "Medievalism in *A Canticle for Leibowitz*." *Extrapolation* 14 (May 1973): 112–125.
Haldeman, Joe. "An Appreciation." *Locus* 36 [421] (February 1996): 78–79.
Hefley, Margie R. "Walter M. Miller, Jr.'s *A Canticle for Leibowitz*: Annotated Bibliography." *Bulletin of Bibliography* 46 (March 1989): 40–45.
Herbert, Gary B. "The Hegelian 'Bad Influence' in Walter M. Miller's *Canticle for Leibowitz*." *Extrapolation* 31, no. 2 (1990): [160]–169.
Hicks, James F. "A Selective Annotated Bibliography of *A Canticle for Leibowitz*." *Extrapolation* 31, no. 3 (1990): [216]–228.
Hillier, Russell. "SF Intertextuality: Hebrew Runes Among the Ruins in *A Canticle for Leibowitz*." *Science Fiction Studies* 31.1 (March 2004): 169–173.
Honner, Paschal. "Latin Passages in *A Canticle for Leibowitz*." *Listening* 35 (Spring 2000): 155–169.
House, Marilyn. "Miller's Anti-Utopian Vision: A Reading of *A Canticle for Leibowitz*." *Riverside Quarterly* 8.4 [32] (August 1991): 253–271.
"In a Class by Itself." *Library Journal* 83 (June 1, 1958), 1769–1770. [Part of the feature article "New Creative Writers"]
Johnson, Judy. "Smyrna 'Hugo' Winner Has New Novel in Progress." *New Smyrna Beach Observer*, 24 September 1990, 1A, 5A.
Kievitt, Frank David. "Walter M. Miller's *A Canticle for Leibowitz* as a Third Testament." In *The Transcendent Adventure: Studies of Religion in Science Fiction/Fantasy*. Ed. Robert Reilly. Westport, CT: Greenwood, 1985. Pp. [169]–175.
Manganiello, Dominic. "History as Judgment and Promise in *A Canticle for Leibowitz*." *Science Fiction Studies* 13 (July 1986): 159–169.
McNelly, Willia E. *A Canticle for Leibowitz*. In *Survey of Science Fiction Literature*. 5 vols. Ed. Frank N. Magill. Englewood Cliffs, NJ: Salem. Vol. 1, pp. 288–293.
McVann, Mark. "Leibowitz and Benjamin: Believing and Unbelieving Humanity in *A Canticle for Leibowitz*." *Listening* 35 (Spring 2000): 95–104.
\_\_\_\_\_. "Notes on Names, Biblical Allusions, and Religious Themes in *A Canticle for Leibowitz*." *Listening* 35 (Spring 2000): 140–154.
Minne, Samuel. "Yesterday Never Dies: Perdre et Retrouver l'Histoire dans Quatre Societies Post-Cataclysmiques." *Cycnos* 22.1 (2005): 127–137.
Moodie, David. Email to the author. 16 September 2010.
Morrissey, Thomas J. "Armageddon from Huxley to Hoban." *Extrapolation* 25 (Fall 1984): 197–213.
"Obituaries." *Locus* 36 [421] (February 1996): 78.
Olsen, Alexandra H. "Re-Vision: A Comparison of *A Canticle for Leibowitz* and the Novellas Originally Published." *Extrapolation* 38.2 (Summer 1997): [135]–149.
Ower, John B. "Walter M. Miller, Jr." In *Science Fiction Writers: Critical Studies of the Major Authors from the Early Nineteenth Century to the Present Day*. Ed. E.F. Bleiler. New York: Charles Scribner's Sons, 1982. Pp. 441–448.
\_\_\_\_\_. "Theology and Evolution in the Short Fiction of Walter M. Miller, Jr." *Cithara: Essays in the Judaeo-Christian Tradition* 25 (May 1986): [57]–74.
Percy, Walker. "Walter M. Miller, Jr.'s *A Canticle for Leibowitz*: A Rediscovery." *Southern Review* 7 (Spring 1971): 572–578.
Perrin, Noel. A Canticle for Miller." *Connoisseur* 213 (March 1983): 116–117.
Rank, Hugh. "Song Out of Season: *A Canticle for Leibowitz*." *Renascence* 21 (Summer 1969): 213–221.
Roberson, William H., and Robert L. Battenfeld. *Walter M. Miller, Jr.: A Bio-Bibliography*. Westport, CT: Greenwood, 1992.
Samuelson, David. "The Lost Canticles of Walter M. Miller, Jr." *Science Fiction Studies* 3 (March 1976): 3–26.
\_\_\_\_\_. "Miller, Walter M(ichael), Jr." In *Twentieth Century Science Fiction Writers*. Ed. Curtis C. Smith. New York: St. Martin's, 1981. Pp. 379–380.
\_\_\_\_\_. *Visions of Tomorrow: Six Journeys from Outer to Inner Space*. New York: Arno, 1975. Pp. 221–279, 370–391 passim.

Scheick, William J. "Continuative and Ethical Predictions: The Post-Nuclear Holocaust Novel of the 1980's." *North Dakota Quarterly* 56 (Spring 1989): 61–82.

Scholes, Robert, and Eric S. Rabkin. "*A Canticle for Leibowitz* (1959)." In their *Science Fiction: History, Science, Vision.* New York: Oxford University Press, 1977. Pp. 221–226.

Schroth, Raymond A. "Canticle for Leibowitz." *America* 118 (20 January 1968): 79.

Secrest, Rose. *Glorificemus: A Study of the Fiction of Walter M. Miller, Jr.* Lanham, MD: University Press of America, 2002.

Seed, David. "Recycling the Texts of the Culture: Walter M. Miller's *A Canticle for Leibowitz*." *Extrapolation* 37.3 (Fall 1996): 257–71.

Senior, William A. "'From the Begetting of Monsters': Distortion as Unity in Walter Miller's *A Canticle for Leibowitz.*" *Extrapolation* 34.4 (1993): 329–39.

Slater, Niall W., and Jerry S. Jacobs. "Memorabilia: Americanizing Classical and Catholic Pasts in *A Canticle for Leibowitz.*" *Classical and Modern Literature* 19 (1999): 123–131.

Spector, Judith A. "Walter Miller's *A Canticle for Leibowitz*: A Parable for Our Time?" *Midwest Quarterly* 22 (Summer 1981): 337–345.

Spencer, Susan. "The Post-Apocalyptic Library: Oral and Literate Culture in *Fahrenheit 451* and *A Canticle for Leibowitz.*" *Extrapolation* 32.4 (1991): 331–42.

Spinrad, Norman. "Introduction." In *A Canticle for Leibowitz.* Walter M. Miller, Jr. Boston: Gregg, 1975. Pp. v–xii.

Stoler, John A. "Christian Lore and Characters' Names in *A Canticle for Leibowitz.*" *Literary Onomastics Studies* 11 (1984): 77–91.

Streitfeld, David. "*Canticle* Author Unsung Even in Death." *Washington Post*, "Living" 9 October 1997: E1.

Summerhill, Jo. "Author Makes *Who's Who*, But Not Sure He Likes the Idea." *Daytona Beach News-Journal* 2 April 1966: [np].

Sutherland, J. A. "American Science Fiction Since 1960." In *Science Fiction: A Critical Guide.* Ed. Patrick Parrinder. London and New York: Longman, 1979. Pp. 162–186.

Tavormina, M. Teresa. "Order, Liturgy, and Laughter in *A Canticle for Leibowitz.*" In *Medievalism in American Culture: Special Studies.* Ed. Bernard Rosenthal and Paul E. Szarmach. Binghamton, NY: State University of New York at Binghamton. Center for Medieval and Early Renaissance Studies. Eighteenth Annual Conference Papers. Pp. [45]–63.

"Terry Bisson and the Wild Horse Woman." http://www.scifi.com/sfw/issue36/interview.html. 21 March 2009.

Texter, Douglas W. "Institutional Crisis: State and Scholar in Hermann Hesse's *The Glass Bead Game* and Walter Miller's *A Canticle for Leibowitz. Extrapolation* 49.1 (Spring 2008): 122–141.

Tietge, David J. "Priest, Professor, or Prophet: Discursive and Ethical Intersections in *A Canticle for Leibowitz.*" *Journal of Popular Culture* 41.4 (August 2008): 676–94.

Walker, Jeanne Murray. "Reciprocity and Exchange in *A Canticle for Leibowitz.*" *Renascence* 33 (Winter 1981): 67–85.

Wilber, Rick. "Science Fiction Writer Revs Up His Career." *Tampa Tribune* 6 September 1990: 1F, 6F.

Willick, George C. "Spacelight: Walter M. Miller, Jr." http://www.gcwillick.com/Spacelight/millerjr.html. 8 September 2010.

Wolfe, Gary K. *The Known and the Unknown: The Iconography of Science Fiction.* Kent, OH: Kent State University Press. Pp. 137–147.

Wood, Ralph C. "Lest the World's Amnesia Be Complete: A Reading of Walter Miller's *A Canticle for Leibowitz.*" *Perspectives in Religious Studies* 27.1 (Spring 2000): 83–87.

Young, R.V. "Catholic Science Fiction and the Cosmic Apocalypse: Walker Percy and Walter Miller." *Renascence* 40 (Winter 1988): 95–111.

# General Bibliography

"Abbey of Montecassino: Historical Outline." *http://www.officine.it/montecassino/storia_e/abbazia.abbazia.htm*. 27 October 2010.
Alexander, George M. *The Handbook of Biblical Personalities*. Greenwich, CT: Seabury, 1962.
Attwater, Donald, ed. *A Catholic Dictionary*. Rockford, IL: Saint Benedict, 1997.
_____, comp. *A Dictionary of Saints*. New York: P.J. Kenedy and Sons, 1958.
_____. *The Penguin Dictionary of Saints*. Baltimore: Penguin, 1965.
"B-25 Bomber." *http://www.warbirdhaven.com/B25Bomber.php*. 18 September 2008.
Barker, William P. *Everyone in the Bible*. Westwood, NJ: Fleming H. Revell, 1966.
Baron, Saol Wittmayer. *A Social and Religious History of the Jews*. 2d ed., revised and enlarged. New York: Columbia University Press, 1952.
Biedermann, Hans. *Dictionary of Symbolism: Cultural Icons and the Meanings Behind Them*. James Hulbert, trans. New York: Meridian, 1994.
Bliss, A. J. *A Dictionary of Foreign Words and Phrases in Current English*. New York: E.P. Dutton, 1966.
Carroll, David. *The Dictionary of Foreign Terms in the English Language*. New York: Hawthorn, 1973.
Cirlot, J.E. *A Dictionary of Symbols*. 2d ed. Jack Sage, trans. New York: Philosophical Library, 1971.
Cohen, Saul B., ed. *The Columbia Gazetteer of the World*. New York: Columbia University Press, 1998.
Corsini, Raymond J. *The Dictionary of Psychology*. Philadelphia, PA: Brunner/Mazel, 1999.
Cross, F. L., ed. *The Oxford Dictionary of the Christian Church*. London: Oxford University Press, 1963.
Dahmus, Jospeh. *Dictionary of Medieval Civilization*. New York: Macmillan, 1984.
*Diagnostic and Statistical Manual of Mental Disorders: DSM-IV*. Washington, D.C.: American Psychiatric Association, 2000.
*Dictionary of the Middle Ages*. Joseph R. Strayer, editor-in-chief. New York: Charles Scribner's Sons, 1982–1989.
Dunkling, Leslie, and William Gosling. *The Facts on File Dictionary of First Names*. New York: Facts on File, 1983.
*Eerdmans Dictionary of the Bible*. David Noel Freedman, editor-in-chief. Grand Rapids, MI: William B. Eerdmans, 2000.
Ehrlich, Eugene, ed. *The Harper Dictionary of Foreign Terms*. 3d ed. New York: Harper and Row, 1987.
*Encyclopaedia Judaica*. [New York]: Macmillan, 1972.
Fremantle, Anne, ed. *The Papal Encyclicals in their Historical Context*. New York: Mentor, 1960.
Glare, P.G.W., ed. *Oxford Latin Dictionary*. Oxford: Oxford University Press, 1982.
Grimal, Pierre. *The Penguin Dictionary of Classical Myhtology*. Ed. Stephen Kershaw from the translation by A.R. Maxwell-Hyslop. London: Penguin, 1991.
Grimes, William. "Don Congdon, Literary Agent for Ray Bradbury and Others, Dies at 91." *New York Times*, 4 December 2009: B12.
Guinagh, Kevin. *Dictionary of Foreign Phrases and Abbreviations*. New York: H.W. Wilson, 1965.
Hapgood, David, and David Richardson. *Monte Cassino*. New York: Congdon and Weed, 1984.
The Holy Bible. Douay-Confraternity Version. New York: P.J. Kenedy & Sons.
The Holy Bible. King James Version. New York: American Bible Society.
"Judith Merril" *http://www.judithmerril.com/*. 27 October 2010.
Kelly, J.N.D. *The Oxford Dictionary of Popes*. Oxford: Oxford University Press, 1986.
Kolatch, Alfred J. *Complete Dictionary of English and Hebrew Names*. Middle Village, NY: Jonathan David, 1984.
Lass, Abraham H., David Kiremidjian, and Ruth M. Goldstein. *The Facts on File Dictionary of Classical, Biblical and Literary Allusions*. New York: Facts on File, 1987.
Merril, Judith. *Out of Bounds*. New York: Pyramid, 1960.
_____ and Emily Pohl-Weary. *Better to Have Loved: The Life of Judith Merril*. Toronto: Between the Lines, 2002.
Nevins, Albert J., comp. and ed. *The Maryknoll Catholic Dictionary*. Wilkes-Barre, PA: Dimension, 1965.

*New Catholic Encyclopedia.* 2d ed. Detroit: Thomson/Gale; Washington, D.C.: Catholic University of America, 2003.
Olderr, Steven, comp. *Symbolism: A Comprehensive Dictionary.* Jefferson, NC: McFarland, 1986.
Ritter, Harry. *Dictionary of Concepts in History.* New York; Greenwood, 1986.
Simpson, D.P. *Cassell's Latin Dictionary.* New York: Macmillan, 1978.
Stelten, Leo F. *Dictionary of Ecclesiastical Latin.* Peabody, MA: Hendrickson, 2006.

# Index

Aaron 118, 156
*The Abbey* 5, 104
Abel 5, 27, 29, 32
Abelard, Peter 63
Abernathy, Robert 6, 19, 75
*About the Worthless Things* 50
Abraham 6, 94–95, 107, 155
Abram 6
Absalom 173
Acadian Schism 78
Act of Supremacy 74
The Acts of the Apostles 153, 174
Adam 5, 7, 14, 32, 59, 67, 76, 87, 93, 112, 128, 136, 180, 181, 186
Adriatic Sea 147
Advent 7, 60
Advocatus Diaboli 7, 8, 57, 118–119, 137
Aemilius 57
Agapitus I 153
Ahab 10, 85
Aikin, James Douglas 9, 19, 121
Alaska 189
Albania 110
Albert of Cologne *see* Albertus Magnus
Albertus Magnus 9, 34, 94, 153
Albrasa 9, 16, 125
Alexander IV 148
Alexander V 156
"Alibi" 9, 19, 115
All Saints Day 40, 126
All Souls Day 40
Alpha Bootis 14
Alpha Centauri 9, 38, 52
Alpha Persii 118
*Amazing Stories* 51, 79, 99, 105, 107, 112, 140, 157, 168, 190
The Amber Chronicles 191
Ambrosius 108
*American Mercury* 102, 112
Amnon 173
Amur River 10, 99
Anala 6, 10
"The Anarch" 10, 12, 47, 64, 71, 105, 130, 135, 137, 171
"And the Light Is Risen" 5, 6, 8, 9, 10–12, 13, 16, 17, 18, 23, 25, 27, 28, 29, 30, 33, 40, 42, 46, 48, 51, 52, 53, 58–59, 60, 62, 63, 64, 65, 68, 70–71, 73, 74, 76, 78, 80, 81, 85, 86, 90, 94, 96, 101, 102, 104, 107, 109, 113, 118, 119, 120, 121, 122, 123, 125, 126,
128, 131, 133, 134, 135, 144, 148, 152, 153, 154–155, 156, 159, 160, 161, 165, 171, 173, 175, 176, 178, 181, 182, 183
Anderson, Poul 12, 19, 178
Andromeda constellation 12
Andromeda Galaxy 12
Angelic Salutation 15
The Angelus 12
Anson, George 145
Antarctica 39
Antares 157
Anthimus 153
"Anybody Else Like Me?" 12, 19, 42, 43, 72, 75, 108, 155, 157, 182, 185
The Apocalypse *see* Book of Revelation
Apollo 13, 153
Apollonius 13
Apollos 13, 153
Apostolic Penitentiaria 71
Appalachian Mountains 13
Aquila 174
Aquinas, Thomas *see* Saint Thomas Aquinas
Arango, Doroteo *see* Villa, Francisco
*The Archangel* 9, 13, 57, 58, 67, 81, 145, 146, 162–164, 170–171, 191
The Archer 147
Arcturus 14, 26, 86, 87, 159
Arkansas 126, 184
Arkansas River 88
Arm City, Florida 109, 112
Aronica, Lou 116, 149
Ash Wednesday 14, 95, 107, 137
Asia 35
Asia Minor 153
Asimov, Isaac 108
The Asperges 14
*Asperges me, Domine* 14, 49
*Aspiciens a longe* 60
Assisi 148
The Assumption 14, 63, 66, 136, 162
Assyria 14, 138
*Astounding Science Fiction* 19, 24, 40, 45, 47, 54, 83, 113, 123, 127, 167
Astraea 85
Atlanta, Georgia 125
Augustine *see* Saint Augustine
Augustus 31
Austin, Texas 111, 112

Austria 39
Ave Maria 15, 127

B-25 Bomber 15, 22, 31, 88, 90, 110, 119, 129, 170, 173, 187–188
Baal 15, 85
Baal-zebub 17
Baal-zebul 17
Babel 15
Babylon 15–16, 60, 101, 122, 139
Babylonia 15
Baer, Max 37
Ba'Lagan 9, 16
Balkans 15
*Ballade in D Minor*, Op. 10, No. 1 56
Ballantine Books 113, 114
Ballard, James G. 16, 19, 174
Banns (of marriage) 16
Bantam Books 116
Bathsheba 50
Batzner, Jay C. 80
Baumann, Hans 188
"Bears Discover Fire" 20
Becker, Arnold 110, 111
Becker, Tesnulda 110, 111
Beelzebub 17
Belgium 39
Bell Telephone Company 17
Benedict, Ruth 81
Benedictine Order 25, 29, 53, 92, 110, 119, 122, 131, 154
Benét, Stephen Vincent 18, 19, 31
Benjamin (son of Rachel) 138
Bennett, Laurence 115, 117
Bereshith 18, 167
Berlin, Germany 87
Bernardone, Giovanni Francesco 148
Bernhardt, Sarah 18
Bessarion, John 183
*The Best of Walter M. Miller, Jr.* 13, 19, 20, 42, 45, 47, 48, 50, 54, 97
*The Best Science Fiction Stories* 45, 105, 168
*The Best Science Fiction Stories and Novels* 107
Beta Hydri 19
Bethel 84
Bethlehem 19
*Better to Have Loved* 44, 109
*Beyond Armageddon* 6, 9, 12, 16, 18, 19, 26, 31, 40, 50, 55, 57, 58, 63, 65, 67, 71, 73, 75, 80, 86, 88,

201

# Index

100, 101, 106, 111, 115, 116, 120, 121, 129, 154, 160, 170, 172, 173, 174, 175, 177, 178, 186, 191
"The Big Flash" 19, 170
"The Big Hunger" 9, 12, 14, 16, 19, 43, 52, 55, 64, 71, 72, 74, 76, 86, 87, 101, 105, 122, 125, 127, 133, 139, 145, 147, 157, 159, 171, 174, 179, 183
"Big Joe and the Nth Generation" 14, 19, 20, 48, 82, 157, 183
Bisson Terry 20, 117, 149
"Bitter Victory" 9, 20–22, 65, 78, 88–89, 91, 125, 128, 130, 132, 146, 147, 173, 174
Black-capped Chickadee 130
Black Dragon River 10
Black Panther Party 70
Blanc, Giuseppe 69
Bleiler, Everett F. 168
"Blessed Assurance" 90
Blessed Sacrament 77
Blish, James 108
"Blood Bank" 19, 24, 27, 42, 43, 44, 45, 46, 51, 55, 79, 80, 85, 86, 104, 108, 135, 138, 139, 157, 164, 165, 173, 178, 183, 184, 185, 188
"Bobby and Jimmy: Round Six..." 24
Bogdanov, Alexander 25, 116, 139
"Bolsheviks on Mars" 25, 140
*The Bone People* 25, 79, 146
Boniface VIII 77, 135, 154, 175
*The Book of Beginnings: Volume One* 22
The Book of Daniel 47
The Book of Job 86
The Book of Joshua 86, 121
The Book of Kells 80
*The Book of Origins* 96, 149
The Book of Psalms 6, 12, 17, 50, 55, 60, 65, 68, 70, 80, 107, 118, 123, 135, 137, 144, 176, 185
Book of Revelation 10, 83, 86, 139, 152
The Book of the Prophet Ezekiel 60
The Book of the Prophet Isaiah 16, 65, 98, 101, 176
The Book of the Prophet Jeremiah 123, 138, 174
Boone, Lincoln 26, 44
Boötes constellation 14, 26
*Boris Godunov* 120
Boston, Massachusetts 108, 110
"A Boy and His Dog" 19, 26, 57
Bradbury, Ray 19, 26, 43, 175, 177
Bradbury, Walter 114
Brahe, Tycho 26, 183
Brahms, Johannes 56
Brazil 104
Brazos River 27
*Brides of a Martian Harem* 27, 67
Bright, Patricia 36
*Bring the Jubilee* 120
Brooks, Stuart 36
Brutus 59
Bryant, Edward 19, 31, 86
*Bug Jack Barron* 170

Bulgaria 110
Burgundy 86
Buzzards 34, 35, 81, 93, 129, 172
"By the Waters of Babylon" 18, 19, 31
Byzantine Empire 175

Caesar 76, 87, 124, 135, 144, 154
Caesar, Julius 31–32, 59, 147
Cain 5, 27, 29, 32
Calasanz, Joseph 149
California 81
Calvary 70, 181, 184
Campbell, John W. 113
Canaan 86
Canada 108
Canaveral National Seashore, Florida 116
Canon 124
*A Canticle for Leibowitz* (Felnagle dramatic adaptation) 36, 64,
*A Canticle for Leibowitz* (Fuller dramatic adaptation) 36, 67
*A Canticle for Leibowitz* (novel) 5, 6, 7, 8, 9, 10, 12, 13, 14, 15, 16, 17, 18, 19, 22, 23, 25, 26, 27, 28, 29, 30, 31, 32–36, 37, 38, 39, 40, 42, 43, 44, 45, 46, 48, 50, 51, 52, 53, 54, 55, 56, 57, 58, 59, 60, 61, 62, 63, 64, 65, 66, 67, 68, 69, 70, 71, 72, 73, 74, 76, 77, 78, 80, 81, 82, 83, 84, 85, 86, 87, 90, 93, 94, 95, 96, 98, 99, 100, 101, 102, 103, 104, 106, 107, 108, 109, 110, 111, 114, 115, 116, 118, 119, 120, 121, 122, 123, 124, 125, 126, 127, 128, 129, 130, 131, 132, 133, 134, 135, 136, 137, 138–139, 140, 144, 145, 147, 148, 149, 152, 153, 154, 155, 156, 157, 159, 160, 161–162, 165, 168, 170, 171, 172, 173, 174, 175, 176, 178, 180, 181, 182, 183, 184, 188, 189, 190, 191, 192
*A Canticle for Leibowitz* (radio drama) 36
"A Canticle for Leibowitz" (short story) 5, 7, 9, 12, 13, 18, 28, 30, 32–33, 40, 42, 48, 51, 64, 65, 69, 80, 94, 95, 102, 113, 118, 126, 132, 148, 154, 161–162, 173, 178, 182
*A Canticle for Leibowitz* (soundtrack) 37, 87
"A Canticle for Miller" 20
"A Canticle for the Marsman" 7, 37, 39
"The Canticle of Simeon" 125
Capek, Karel 94, 147
"Captain Chronos and the Guardsmen of Time" 37, 102, 154, 185, 187
"Captain Video and His Video Rangers" 37, 109, 112, 160
*Carmen Dog* 58
Carmichael, Stokely 115
Carnera, Primo 37
Carthage 37
Catharism 38
Casinum 119
Cassiopeia constellation 26

Catholic Digest Book Club 33
*Catholic Encyclopedia* 14
Celestine V 38, 154
Centaur 147
Centaurus constellation 9, 38, 101
"Chad Oliver & Walt Miller" 127
Chair of Peter 38
*The Chancellor* 38
*Chantecler* 38
*Chanticleer* 38
*Chanticler* 38
Chaplin, Charles 38
"Chariots of the Goddesses, or What?" 39, 66, 103
Charlemagne 39, 48
Charles VII 86
Charon 172
"Check and Checkmate" 20, 39, 75, 146, 165, 167, 171
Cherdorlaomer 107
Cherokee (Native Americans) 62, 66
Chicago, Illinois 36, 84
*Childhood's End* 40
China 10
Christchurch, New Zealand 79
Christmas 7, 126
Christoffel, Elwin Bruno 145
Cincinnati, Ohio 127
Cistercians 9, 32, 34, 40, 63, 94
*City Lights* 38
"The City on the Edge of Forever" 57
Clarke, Arthur C. 19, 40, 80
Clausewitz, Karl 40
Cleaver, Eldridge 70
Clement VII 156
Cleveland, Ohio 38, 83, 101
Coffin, Frederick 36
"Cold Awakening" 40, 45, 66–67, 76, 100, 104, 131, 145, 161, 173, 175–176, 184, 187
*The Collector* 66
Colorado 44, 110, 111, 112
"Come Creator Spirit" 181
"Command Performance" 12, 13, 40, 72, 75, 80, 108, 139, 155, 185
*Commiato* 69
*Commonweal* 79, 89, 93, 146, 149
*Concerning the Vestiges of Preceding Civilizations* 50
"Conditionally Human" 12, 15, 19, 39, 42–43, 51, 63, 66, 68–69, 70, 77, 88, 89, 91, 101, 109, 123, 124–125, 128, 129, 136, 139, 157, 160, 164, 187, 189
*Conditionally Human* 42, 43, 47, 48, 54
*Conditionally Human and Other Stories* 13, 19, 40, 42, 43, 48
*Confessions* 148
Congdon, Donald 20, 43, 114, 116, 117, 1490
Conklin, Groff 165
"Connection Completed" 44, 109
Connell, Evan S. 43
Constantine 19
Corinthians I 180
Corinthians II 153
"The Corpse in Your Bed Is Me"

26, 27, 44, 64, 67, 72, 90–91, 105, 126, 160, 165
Council of Constance 156
Council of Nicaea 45
Cowan, Carol 36
Cowart, David 111, 139
*Crash* 16
Creed of Athanasius 45
Creed of Nicaea 45
Creek (Native Americans) 62
Crosby, Fanny 90
"Crucifixus Etiam" 19, 45–46, 48, 53, 68, 74, 88, 122, 156, 157, 159, 168, 179, 182, 183
*The Crystal World* 16
Cushing Memorial Library, Texas A & M University 127
Cyclopes 153
Cygnus constellation 72
Cyrus 46, 154

*Daily Racing Form* 139
Dallas, Texas 187
Damascus 153
*Damnation Alley* 191
Daniel 47
Dante Alighieri 5, 182
"The Darfstellar" 5, 7, 10, 12, 15, 18, 19, 37, 38, 39, 43, 47–48, 52, 53, 64, 71, 72, 80, 85, 87, 103, 105, 113, 121, 129, 130, 135, 137, 144, 156, 157, 165, 171–172, 175, 176, 180
*The Darfsteller and Other Stories* 20, 45, 47, 48, 97
"The Daring Young Man on the Flying Trapeze" 75
"Dark Benediction" 14, 19, 28, 29, 30, 43, 48–50, 52, 62, 63, 64, 66, 68, 79, 85, 99, 126, 129, 140, 145, 157, 159, 186, 188
*Dark Benediction* 48, 50
David (king of Israel) 30, 50, 173, 176
*Davy* 129
"Day at the Beach" 19, 50, 58
Day of Atonement 156
*The Day of the Triffids* 75
"Day of Wrath" 137
Daytona Beach, Florida 113, 115
*Daytona Beach News-Journal* 115, 117
*De Inanibus* 50
*De Perennibus Sententiis Sectarum Rurum* 50, 55, 130
*De Vestigiis Antecessarum Civitatum* 25, 50
"Death of a Spaceman" 32, 51, 53, 56, 61, 63, 79, 87, 105, 107, 124, 126, 127, 128, 137, 179
Denver 8, 47, 58, 62, 133, 157, 170
Descartes, René 124
*Destiny* 115
Deuteronomy 81, 174
"The Devil and Daniel Webster" Devil's Advocate 7, 137
Diego, Juan 73
*Dies Irae* 52, 137
Digger Indians (Native Americans) 81

Dikty, T.E. 107, 168
*Dimension of Miracles* 160
Dionysius 103
*Discourse on Method, IV* 124
Discourse on the Last Times 52
Disney World 112
*The Divine Comedy* 5, 182
The Divine Thirst 171
Dodge, Mary Mapes 99
Dominicans 8, 9, 14, 22, 53, 55, 80, 136, 153
Don Congdon Associates 43
Doolittle, James 15
*Doorways in the Sand* 191
Doubleday Publishers 114
Drake, Ervin M. 145
*The Drowned World* 16
*The Druid King* 170
"Dumb Waiter" 19, 43, 54–55, 56, 64, 68, 71, 85, 91, 105, 128, 155, 157, 164, 172, 183
DuMont Network 37

Easter 70, 77, 95, 106, 126, 129, 130, 182
Eastertide 182
"Eastward Ho!" 19, 55, 88
Eckhart, Johannes 55–56
Eddy Howard and His Orchestra 145
Eden *see* Garden of Eden
Edgewood College Chant Group 36
"Edward, Edward" 56
"Edward of the Bloody Brand" 56
Egypt 60, 132, 183
18 Scorpii 16
Einstein, Albert 56, 90, 107, 180
Ekron 17
El Shaddai 56
Eleazar 57
Elijah 31
Eliyahu 31
Elizabeth, Queen of England 140
Ellison, Harlan 19, 26, 31, 57
Elvin 28
*Empire of the Sun* 16
Emshwiller, Carol 19, 50, 58
England *see* Great Britain
Epiphany 139
The Epistle of Paul the Apostle to the Hebrews *see* Hebrews
"Es Zittern die Morschen Knochen" 188
Esau 84
Eucharist 77, 130, 180
Eucharistic Prayer 124
Eve 5, 7, 14, 32, 59, 67, 80, 128, 136, 139, 186
"Evening Caller" 59, 62, 63, 89
Exodus 15, 60, 79–80, 132
*Extension* 59, 112, 119
Ezekiel 60, 62, 130

"Die Fahne Hoch" 78
*Fahrenheit 451* 26
The Fall (of Adam and Eve) 80, 128, 136, 139
"A Family Matter" 14, 31, 61, 79, 177

*Fantastic* 162, 187, 188
*Fantastic Adventures* 48, 110, 111, 112
*Fantastic Stories* 99, 162, 187, 188
*Fantastic Story Magazine* 61
*Fantastic Universe* 78, 191
"Farewell" 69
*Faust* 63
*Faust* 63
Faust, Johann Georg 63
Feast of Saint Clare 162
"The Feast of Saint Janis" 19, 63, 173
Feast of the Annunciation 64
Feast of the Immaculate Conception 11
Felnagle, Richard 36, 64
"Fiat Homo" 5, 7, 12, 13, 14, 15, 17, 22, 23, 25, 26, 27, 28, 30, 32, 33, 38, 40, 48, 50, 51, 52, 54, 55, 57, 58, 59, 60, 61, 62, 64, 65, 66, 68, 69, 70, 71, 77, 80, 81, 84, 86, 87, 90, 95, 96, 99, 103, 104, 106, 108, 109, 118, 120, 121, 122, 124, 125, 127, 129, 130, 131, 132, 136, 137, 139, 144, 147, 148, 149, 153, 154, 156, 159, 170, 171, 172, 173, 174, 178, 180, 182
"Fiat Lux" 6, 8, 12, 13, 16, 17, 18, 22, 25, 27, 28, 29, 30, 31, 34, 38, 39, 42, 46, 48, 50, 52, 53, 56, 57, 58, 59, 62, 63, 64, 65, 69, 71, 74, 78, 80, 81, 82, 83, 85, 86, 87, 90, 94, 96, 98, 103, 107, 109, 118, 119, 120, 121, 122, 123, 124, 125, 126, 127, 129, 130, 131, 132, 134, 136, 138, 139, 140, 144, 147, 148, 149, 152, 153, 154, 155, 156, 159, 160, 161, 165, 171, 172, 173, 174, 175, 176, 178, 181, 182, 183, 184
"Fiat Voluntas Tua" 5, 6, 8, 9, 10, 12, 13, 14, 15, 16, 18, 19, 26, 27, 28, 29, 30, 31, 32, 35, 37, 38, 39, 40, 43, 44, 45, 46, 50, 51, 52, 53, 56, 57, 58, 59, 60, 61, 62, 63, 64, 67, 69, 70, 72, 73, 76, 77, 78, 83, 84, 86, 87, 93, 94, 99, 100, 101, 103, 106, 108, 118, 120, 121, 122, 123, 124, 126, 127, 130, 132, 133, 134, 135, 136, 137, 138–139, 140, 144, 145, 148, 149, 152, 153, 155, 157, 160, 161, 162, 168, 171, 172, 173, 175, 176, 180, 182, 183, 188, 189, 190, 191, 192
The Fifth Book of Moses, Called Deuteronomy *see* Deuteronomy
*Finlandia* 161
The First Book of Moses, Called Genesis *see* Genesis
The First Book of Samuel 154
The First Book of the Kings 160, 165
The First Epistle of Paul the Apostle to the Corinthians *see* Corinthians I
Fitzgerald, Edward 186
"The Flag on High" 78
Fleming, Jim 36
Florida 110, 189

# Index

Florida East Coast Railway 110, 117
The Flying Trapeze" 75
Focke-Wulf Flugzeubau AG 65
*Footprints of Earlier Civilizations* 25, 50, 130
Fordham University 140
"Forewarning" 19, 65–66
Formula of Hormisdas 78
Fowles, John 39, 66, 103
France 39
Franciscan Order 148
Freeman, James 36
*The French Lieutenant's Woman* 66
French Polynesia 116, 120
*Fri* 116, 120
Fuller, Clark 36
Futurians 108

Gabriel 64, 183
Gaea 120
Gaia 120
*Galaxy Science Fiction* 12, 40, 42, 113
Galveston, Texas 28, 29, 30, 48–49, 52, 62, 111, 126, 159, 187
"Game Preserve" 19, 67, 71
Garden of Eden 7, 14, 33, 59, 67, 128, 136, 177
Garrison, Skip 117
Garvey, John 111, 114, 115, 116, 117
Gaston, John 117
Gaudete Sunday 60
*Genesis* (novel) 12
Genesis 6, 7, 14, 15, 17, 27, 29, 32, 59, 64, 65, 67, 81, 84, 94, 95, 100, 107, 109, 124, 165, 174
Geoffrey of Monmouth 108
Germany 39, 70, 76, 87, 132, 172, 180
Gerrold, David 37
Gethsemane 64, 69, 87, 138
Gibeon 121
*Giovanezza* 69
"God Is Thus" 70
Godot 36
Goethe, Johann Wolfgang von 63
Gold, Horace L. 113
*The Gold Rush* 38
Goldsmith, Merwin 36
Golgotha 70, 170
Gomorrah *see* Sodom and Gomorrah
Good Friday 7, 70, 121, 136, 144
The Gospel According to St. John 8, 52, 55, 65, 81, 87, 94, 104, 106, 124, 138, 139, 161
The Gospel According to St. Luke 43, 59, 64, 94, 101, 103, 106, 125
The Gospel According to St. Mark 32, 69, 144, 160, 186
The Gospel According to St. Matthew 13, 52, 59, 130, 138, 145, 176, 179
Gotta, Salvador 69
Graham, Roger Phillips 71, 132
"Gravesong" 50, 57, 59, 67, 71, 72, 96, 120, 126, 167, 173, 177
Great Britain 43, 86, 148, 180
*The Great Dictator* 38
Great Eastern Schism 156

The Great Purpose 171
Great Rift 72
Great Salt Lake, Utah 5
Great Spiral Galaxy 12
Great Western Schism 156
Greece 110
Greenberg, Martin H. 19, 73, 100, 116
Greenhill-Taylor, Jennifer 111, 114, 115, 116, 119
Greenwich, England 6, 73
Gregory I 73
Gregory VII 73
Gregory IX 148
Gregory the Great 73
Griffin, Russell M. 61, 63, 90, 153, 174
Grossman, Josephine Juliet 108
Guadalupe, Mexico 73
Guam 73, 92, 93, 106
*Gunner* 108

Hades 172; *see also* Hell
"Hail, Holy Queen" 154
Hail Mary 53, 127
"Hail, Queen" 154
Haldeman, Joe 115, 117
Hamlet 191
Hanging Gardens of Babylon 15
*Hans Brinker and the Silver Skates* 99
Happo biraki 75
Happu biraki 75
Harold Matson Company 43
Harris, John Wyndham 75
Hartig, Herbert 36
Hebrews (Bible book) 176
Heche, Anne 42, 139
Heilong Jiang 10
"Heirs Apparent" 6, 19
Hell 5, 60, 112, 116, 158, 182; *see also* Hades
Helots 75, 170
Henry VIII 74, 95
Hercules Cluster 76
Hercules constellation 76, 127
Hercules Globular 76
The Herdsman constellation 14, 26
The Hero constellation *see* Perseus constellation
"The Hero of Haarlem" 99
Herod (the Great) 76, 87
Heyman, Barton 36
Hiroshima, Japan 76, 111, 132
*History of the Britons* 108
*History of the Kings of Britain* 108
Hitler, Adolf 76–77, 111, 157
Hoffa, Jimmy 24, 116
Holy Eucharist 77, 182
Holy Ghost 64, 129, 130
Holy Grail 121
"The Holy One" 135
Holy Saturday 77, 111, 130
Holy Spirit 8, 17, 59, 68, 80, 122, 129, 176, 179, 183
Holy Week 77, 129
Honshu, Japan 76
"The Hoofer" 19, 39, 63, 78, 87, 94, 105, 123, 129, 179
Hormisdas 78, 153

"Horst Wessel Leid" 78–79
"Horst Wessel Song" 78
Horton, Russell 36
Hosford, Wayne 103
Houston, Texas 48, 68, 85, 126, 187
"How Zarathustra Came into Being" 55
Howard, Eddy 145
Huang Po 117
Hulme, Keri 25, 79, 146
Hydrus constellation 19

"I, Dreamer" 16, 19, 48, 58, 61, 65, 66, 79, 85, 96, 135, 157, 174, 182–183, 189
"I Have No Mouth and I Must Scream" 57
"I Made You" 15, 73, 156
*The Idiot* 24, 79, 80, 178, 184, 185, 188
"'If I Forget Thee, Oh Earth...'" 19, 40, 80
*If, Worlds of Science Fiction* 20, 39, 82, 95, 176, 185
*Illuminations* 80
The Immaculate Conception 11, 80, 136, 139, 183
Immelmann, Max 80
*Immortality, Inc.* 160
*Imperial Earth* 40
*In the Upper Room and Other Likely Stories* 20
*The Inane* 50
The Incarnation 12, 64
*Index Librorum Prohibitorum* 81
"Index of Prohibited Books" 81
Indian River Lagoon, Florida 116
*Inferno* 5, 182
Inkblot Test 146–147
INRI 81
Iowa 71
Iran 14
Iraq 14
*The Iron Dream* 170
Isaac 6, 84, 95, 155
Israel (Jacob) 84
Israel (nation) 10, 30, 85, 156, 174
Israelites 60, 80, 84, 86, 154, 155
"It Takes a Thief" 14, 19, 20, 23, 82, 104, 136, 139, 146, 164–165, 177, 185
Italy 15, 39, 53, 69, 110, 131, 132, 147, 153, 188
"Izzard and the Membrane" 16, 24, 26, 38, 67, 83–84, 90, 99, 101–102, 118, 135, 145, 181

Jacksonville, Florida 9, 53, 164, 174, 190
*Jacksonville Times Union* 115
Jacob 28, 84–85, 138, 174
"Jacob's ladder" 84, 174
James 28
Japan 15, 78, 99
J.B. Lippincott Company 114
Jeanne d'Arc *see* Joan of Arc
Jerome *see* Saint Jerome
Jerusalem 19, 65, 85, 107, 122, 160
Jesus 7, 8, 12, 13, 19, 28, 32, 43, 45, 52, 55, 56, 64, 65, 69, 70,

76, 81, 86, 94, 104, 106, 112, 118, 121, 124, 132, 138, 140, 144, 145, 148, 149, 153, 160, 162, 171, 173, 175, 176, 179, 180, 184, 185, 190
Jezebel 10, 85
Jezrahel 10; *see also* Jezreel
Jezreel 85; *see also* Jezrahel
Joan of Arc 86, 175
Job 86
"Jody After the War" 19, 31, 86
John Paul II 65
John the Baptist 8, 55
Joseph (husband of Mary) *see* Saint Joseph
Joseph (son of Rachel) 138
Joseph of Arimathea 121
Joshua 121
*Journey Beyond Tomorrow* 160
Jubilee 77
Judah 104, 122
Judas Iscariot 76, 87
"Judas, Judas" 87, 180
Judea 81, 132
Judd, Cyril 108
Judgment of Solomon 165
Justinian I 153, 175

Kalaupapa, Hawaii 112
Kannenberg, John 37, 87
Kansas 126
Keene, Rogers 36
Kennedy, John F. 25, 116
Kennedy, Robert 25, 116
Kentucky 20, 117
Kepler, Johannes 26
Khayyam, Omar 186
*The Kid* 38
King Arthur 108
King Darius 47
King Hezekiah 104
King Vortigern 108
Klass, Philip 88
Klise, Thomas S. 89, 93, 115, 116
Knapp, Phoebe 90
Knight, Damon 37, 108
Korea 63
Kornbluth, C.M. 37, 108
Kossman, Jacob 24
Kubrick, Stanley 40
Kyle, Texas 111, 127

*A Lamp for Medusa* 88
Laplace, Pierre 56, 90, 107
"The Last Canticle" 5, 6, 9, 10, 14, 15, 16, 18, 19, 28, 29, 30, 31, 32, 33, 37, 39, 40, 42, 44, 51, 52, 59, 60, 62, 63, 64, 67, 69, 70, 72, 73, 76, 83, 84, 86, 91–93, 94, 95, 98, 101, 103, 106, 108, 110, 113, 121, 125, 127, 130, 132, 135, 136, 137, 138–139, 140, 144, 145, 148, 149, 152, 153, 155, 160, 161, 162, 165, 171, 173, 175, 178, 180, 183
Last Supper 69, 104, 106, 121
*The Last Western* 89, 93, 115, 116
Lawrence, D.H. 67
Lazarus 57, 94
Leah (sister of Rachel) 138
Lenin, Vladimir 25

Lent 13, 14, 17, 27, 28, 32, 33, 69, 77, 81, 95, 96, 118, 130, 132, 136, 144
Leo 95
Leo III 39
"Let My People Go" 50, 53, 58, 67, 81, 87, 95–96, 102, 108, 129, 132, 138, 147–148
Leviticus 82, 83, 156, 189
Lewis, Marcia 36
Leybourne, George 75
*Libellus Leibowitz* 96, 125, 129–130, 144
*Liber Originum* 22, 25, 65, 88, 96, 149
Libra constellation 157
*Library Journal* 33
Libya 149
Liebknecht, Karl 87
Lincoln, Abraham 98
"The Lineman" 5, 8, 9, 14, 16, 18, 19, 25, 26, 27, 38, 40, 45, 46, 48, 57, 58, 66, 69, 75, 76, 80, 87, 89, 90, 91, 95, 97–98, 103, 120, 125, 129, 131, 140, 145, 147, 155–156, 159, 161, 178, 180, 186
Litany of Divine Praises 99
Litany of the Saints 5, 99, 118, 127, 130, 154, 174
*The Literal Meaning of Genesis* 148
*Little Book* 96
*The Little Book of Leibowitz* 96
"The Little Creeps" 8, 10, 40, 70, 78, 87, 99, 120, 138, 146, 157, 161, 167, 171, 172, 179, 189, 191
Lockheed Corporation 99
Lockheed Lightning 99
Lombards 119
*Lord of Light* 191
Lord's Prayer 28, 59, 130
*Lost Possessions* 79
Lot 100, 107
"Lot" 19, 100, 120
"Lot's Daughter" 100, 120
Lot's wife 100
Lourdes, France 100
Lucifer 81, 101, 173
"Lucifer" 19, 101, 191; *see also* Satan
Luftwaffe 101, 109
Lupus constellation 101
Lyle, Gaston 75

"MacDoughal's Wife" 6, 67, 85, 101, 112, 180, 190
Machiavelli, Niccolò 102, 148
"macs" 20
*Maestro* 47, 103
*The Magazine of Fantasy and Science Fiction* 10, 32, 70, 91, 97
*A Maggot* 39, 66, 103
The Magnificat 93, 103
Magnus, Albertus *see* Albertus Magnus
*The Magus* 66
Maid of Orléans 86
Malinovsky, Alexander 25
Malory, Thomas 108
"The Man on the Flying Trapeze" 75
Manasseh 104

Manasses 104, 154
Manchuria 10
Manning, Robert Douglas 5, 104
Maori 26
Marcus Aurelius 122
Margarite, Gregg 78
Marlowe, Christopher 63
Mars (god) 13
Mars (planet) 12, 14, 20, 23, 25, 45, 50, 53, 74, 82, 88, 105, 107, 122, 127, 139, 140–143, 157–159, 168, 185
*Mars Plan* 105, 112, 140
Martha (sister of Mary) 43, 94, 106
*The Martian Chronicles* 26
*The Martian Messenger* 108, 143
Mary (mother of Jesus) 12, 14, 19, 22, 53, 63, 64, 73, 80, 99, 100, 103, 105, 106, 111, 118, 120, 136, 139, 140, 149, 154, 159, 182
Mary (sister of Martha) 43, 94, 106
Mary Magdalene 162
Mass Against the Heathen 60, 73, 93, 106
Mass for the Defense of the Church 106
Mass for the Removal of Schism 64
Mass in Time of War 73, 93, 106, 144
Mass of a Sovereign Pope 161
"A Master of Babylon" 19, 106, 129
Maundy Thursday 104, 106
Maxwell, James Clark 56, 90, 106–107
Maxwell's Equations 107
McDowell, Andie 42, 139
McVann, Mark 95, 131
*Meditations* 122
*Mein Kampf* 76
Meister Eckhart *see* Eckhart, Johannes
Melchisedech 65, 107
Melchizedek *see* Melchisedech
Melville, Herman 93
"Memento Homo" 32, 51, 53, 56, 61, 63, 79, 87, 105, 107, 124, 126, 127, 128, 137
Merlin 108
Merril, Judith 44, 108–109, 111, 112–113, 116
The Merril Collection of Speculative Fiction and Fantasy 108
Mesopotamia 14
Messerschmitt, Willy 109
Messerschmitt AG 109
Messerschmitts 109
Methuselah 109
*Mexica* 170
Mexican Revolution 183
Mexico 112, 182
Miami Beach, Florida 116
Michael, the Archangel *see* Saint Michael
*The Midwich Cuckoo* 75
Milky Way 12
Miller, Alys Elaine 110, 111, 113
Miller, Anna (Anne) Louise Becker 110, 111–113, 116–117
Miller, Cathryn Augusta 110, 111

# Index

Miller, Margaret Jean 110
Miller, Ruth 110
Miller, Walter Michael, Jr. 110–117
Miller, Walter Michael, Sr. 18, 110, 111, 117
Miller, Walter Michael, III 117
Minnesota 28
Mirfak 118, 175
Miriam 118
Miserere 50
Mississippi River 118
Missouri 126
Missouri River 118
*Mists of Dawn* 127
*Mit Brennender Sorge* 118, 132
Mitchell, William (Billy) 15
*Moby-Dick* 93
*Modern Times* 38
Molokai, Hawaii 112
Monophysitism 153, 175
Monte Cassino Monastery 110, 114, 119, 188
Montecassino 119
"Month of Mary" 62, 63, 104, 112, 119–120
Moodie, David 116, 120
Moore, Ward 19, 100, 120
Moriah 95
Morrone, Pietro del 38
*Le Morte d'Arthur* 108
Moscow 65
Moses 60, 86, 118, 120, 121, 132
Mosquito Lagoon, Florida 116, 117
*The Mount* 58
Mount Calvary 70
Mount of Olives 69
Mt. Vesuvius 135
Moussorgsky, Modest Petrovich 121
Mumbly-peg 121
Mussolini, Benito 69
"My Life in the Jungle" 9, 19, 121
Myrddin 108

Nagasaki, Japan 111
Napoleonic Wars 40
Nathan (Biblical prophet) 176
*The Nation* 24, 115
National Public Radio 36, 48
Nazis 76, 78–79, 101, 118, 132, 157, 188
Nebuchadnezzar 101, 122–123, 154
Nennius 108
Neo-Platonism 56
Netherlands 39
New Jersey 44, 112
New Mexico 172
New Orleans, Louisiana 116, 127
New Smyrna Beach, Florida 110
New York City 108, 109, 110, 112, 129
*New York Times Book Review* 25, 26, 39, 66, 103, 140
New York Yankees 147
New Zealand 25, 26, 79, 83, 116
Nicene Creed 45, 46
Niceno-Constantinopolitan Creed 45
Nicholas IV 38, 154
Nietzsche, Friedrich 55
Nishi 37, 87

"No Moon for Me" 51, 58, 68, 99, 123–124, 180, 183, 185
North American Aviation 15
Northern Paiute (Native Americans) 81
Northwest Heresy 111
Notre Dame (University) 63
Nu Lupi 125
Nunc Dimittis 125
Nynfi 9, 16, 125

Odin 189
*Of Men and Monsters* 88
Ohio 110
O'Keefe, Walter 75
Oklahoma 126, 184
Old El Paso, Texas 5
Oliver, Chad 26, 36, 44, 105, 114, 115, 116, 119, 127
Oliver, Symmes Chadwick *see* Oliver, Chad
The Olivet Discourse 52
*On the City of God* 148
*On the Edge* 42, 139
*On the Happy Life* 148
*On War* 40
Ophiuchus constellation 127, 159
Orange City, Florida 113
Orange County, Florida 113
Order of Our Lady of the Desert 7, 128, 153, 161, 162, 170
Orders of Friars Minor 148
Oregon 13, 56, 122
Orlando, Florida 102, 112, 113, 190
Orléans, France 86
*Other Worlds* 133
Ouachita Mountains 184
*Outpost Mars* 108
Owensboro, Kentucky 20
Ozark Mountains 126, 184
Ozarks 126

P-38 99
P-47 128
Pacini, Filippo 128–129
Palestrina, Giovanni Pierluigi da 129
Palm Sunday 77, 129
Pangborn, Edgar 19, 106, 129
Paschal Moon 130
Passion Sunday 130
Patay, France 86
Pater Noster 59, 130
*Patterns of Culture* 81
Paul VI 119
Pearl Harbor 15
Pecos River 16
Pennsylvania 91
Pennsylvania State University 88
Pentecost 126, 130, 139, 181
Percy, Thomas 56
*Perennial Ideas of Regional Sects* 13, 55, 65
Perseid Meteor Shower 131
Perseids 131
Perseus constellation 118, 175
Pershing, John J. 182
Persia 46
Perugia, Italy 88, 90, 99, 131, 148, 188

Peter of Murrone *see* Saint Petrus Murro
Petronius Arbiter 155
Pharaoh 60, 132, 154
Philistine 16
Phillips, Rog 19, 67, 71, 132
Phoenicians 37
Phoenix 132
*Phoenix Without Ashes* 31
Piarists 149
Pika don 132
*Pirates of the Universe* 20
Pius V 140
Pius XI 118, 132
"Please Me Plus Three" 12, 17, 26, 55, 66, 87, 99, 104, 124, 133–134, 138, 146, 164, 178, 183, 184, 188
Pluto 169
Pohl, Frederik 109, 112, 113
Pohl-Weary, Emily 109
Poland 76
Pompei 135
Pompey 147
Pontius Pilate 81, 105, 124, 125
Poor Clares 148, 162
Poor Ladies 148, 162
Portugal 155
Postulator 8, 118, 137
Powell, Edward 95
*The Prince* 102
Prince Albert 136
Princeton theory 136
Princeton University 6, 64, 159
Priscilla (wife of Aquila) 174
*Progress of the Mars-Culture* 136, 146
Prometheus 136–137
Promoter of the faith 7, 118–119, 137
Promotor Fidei 137
Pueblo, Colorado 134
Punic War 37

Queen Elizabeth *see* Elizabeth, Queen of England
Queen Victoria *see* Victoria, Queen of England

Rabkin, Eric S. 90
Rachel (wife of Jacob) 138
*Racing Form* 139
Radiation Disaster Act 137, 139, 144
Railroad Retirement Act 113
Railroad Retirement Board 113
Ramah 421
Ramesses II 132
Ramses II 132
*Rationes seminales* 148
"Reaching Normal" 42, 139
Reagan, Ronald 116
Rebekah 84
Red Bank, New Jersey 109
Red River 11, 35, 74, 122, 139, 175
*Red Star: The First Bolshevik Utopia* 25, 116, 139
Reeves, John 36
*Regnans in Excelsis* 140
"Reigning in the highest" 140
*Reliques of Ancient English Poetry* 56
"The Reluctant Traitor" 6, 12, 20,

# Index

25, 50, 52, 55, 75, 77, 88, 89, 90, 99, 101, 105, 108, 112, 121, 122, 127, 131, 132, 134, 137, 139, 140–143, 155, 171, 186
*Rendezvous with Rama* 40
"Repent Harlequin, Said the Ticktock Man" 57
The Reproaches 121, 125–126, 144
Republic Aviation Corporation 128
Requiem Mass 144
The Revelation of St. John the Divine *see* The Book of Revelation
Rhoanthe 153
"The Rickety Rickshaw Man" 145
"Rickshaw Boy" 145
Riemann, Bernhard 145
Riemann space 145
Rio Grande 11, 35, 74
"The Rocking Horse Winner" 67
Rocky Mountains 180
Rome, Italy 147, 153
"Roots & Sinew" 26, 79, 146
Rorschach, Hermann 147
Rorschach Test (or Inkblot) 146–147
Rosary 7, 65, 66
Rossum Universal Robot Factory 147
Rostand, Edmund 38
"Rotten Bones Are Trembling" 188
*The royal banners forward go* 182
*Rubaiyat of Omar Khayyam* 186
Rubenstein, Barbara 36
Rubicon 147
Rudd, Paul 42, 139
*Rule of Saint Benedict* 40, 147
*Rule of Saint Leibowitz* 147
R.U.R. 50, 94, 147
Russia 10, 25, 83–84, 101, 123, 139, 181
Ruth, Babe *see* Ruth, George Herman
Ruth, George Herman (Babe) 147

Sabaeans 160
Sacrament of Penance 56, 161
Sacramento Mountains 172
Saggittarius constellation 72, 147, 157
Sagitta constellation 147
Saint Albert the Great *see* Albertus Magnus
Saint Anthony 183
Saint Athanasius 45
Saint Augustine 27, 96, 130, 144, 148
St. Augustine, Florida 116
Saint Bede 25
Saint Benedict 119, 147
Saint Bernard 63
Saint Bessarion 183
Saint Christopher 148
Saint Clare of Assisi 148, 162
Saint Elmo's fire 155
Saint Francis of Assisi 69, 148, 162, 171
Saint George 148–149
Saint Gregory of Tours 110
Saint Jerome 62

Saint John 86, 155; *see also* The Gospel According to St. John
*St. John's Night on the Bare Mountain* 121
Saint Joseph 149, 183
*Saint Leibowitz and the Wild Horse Woman* 5, 6, 7, 9, 10, 12, 13, 14, 15, 16, 17, 18 19, 20, 22, 23, 24, 25, 26, 27, 28, 29, 30, 31, 32, 37, 38, 39, 40, 42, 45, 46, 47, 50, 51, 52, 53, 55, 56, 57, 58, 60, 63, 64, 65, 67, 68, 70, 71, 72, 73, 74, 75, 76, 77, 78, 79, 80, 81, 82, 84, 85, 86, 87–88, 89, 90, 94, 96, 97, 98, 100, 103, 104, 105, 106, 107, 109, 111, 116, 117, 118, 119, 120, 121, 122, 123, 124, 125, 126, 127, 128, 130, 131, 132, 134, 135–136, 137, 138, 139, 140, 144, 145, 146, 147, 148, 149–152, 153, 154, 155, 156, 157, 159, 160, 161, 162, 164, 165, 167, 170, 171, 172, 173, 174–175, 177, 178, 179, 180, 181, 182, 183, 184, 185, 186, 187, 188, 189, 190, 191
St. Louis, Missouri 123
Saint Michael 14, 38, 63, 152–153, 173
Saint Pancras 109–110
Saint Pancratius 109–110
Saint Paul 13, 153, 174, 175
Saint Peter 52, 58, 87, 138, 154, 161, 175, 176, 179
Saint Petrus Murro (Pope Celestin V) 38, 154
Saint Robert 40
Saint Silverius 78, 153, 175
Saint Stephen 153
Saint Theodore 175
Saint Thomas Aquinas 9, 56, 94, 153, 172
Saint Vissarion 183
Saint Wilgefortis 155
Salem 65, 107
"Salvador" 19, 154, 160
Salve Regina 154
Samuel 30, 154
Samuelson, David N. 27, 28, 29, 119, 157
San Francisco, California 21
Santa Librada 155
Saō Therese, Brazil 120
Saracens 119
Sarah (wife of Abraham) 6, 155
Sarai 155
Satan 13, 14, 17, 86, 101, 145, 152, 172, 173, 176; *see also* Lucifer
*Satyricon* 155
*The Satyricon of Lily Brown* 155
Saul 30, 153, 154
*Sayings of Saint Leibowitz* 156
Schism of the East 156
Schism of the West 156
Schmidt, Karl 36
Scholes, Robert 90
*Schutstafel* 157
*Schutzstaffel* 157
Schwarzschild, Karl 157
*Sci-Fi Radio* 48
Science Fiction Book Club 33

*The Science Fiction Stories of Walter M. Miller, Jr.* 13, 19, 20, 42, 45, 47, 48, 54, 157
*Scitote Tyrannum* 81, 157
Scorpius constellation 9, 16, 101, 125, 147, 157
The Second Book of Kings 10, 85, 104
The Second Book of Moses, called Exodus *see* Exodus
The Second Book of Samuel 50, 173, 176
The Second Epistle of Paul the Apostle to the Corinthians *see* Corinthians II
Secrest, Rose 53, 126
"Secret of the Death Dome" 17, 69, 75, 103, 106, 112, 117, 136, 157–159, 179, 187, 191
*Seder Zeraim* 7
Serpens constellation 127, 159, 179
The Serpent constellation *see* Serpens
The Serpent Holder constellation *see* Ophiuchus constellation
Seven Wonders of the World 15
*Shadows in the Sun* 127
Shakespeare, William 59
Shanghai 16
Sharkey, Jack 37
Shasta Publishing 105, 112
Sheba 160
Sheckley, Robert 19, 160, 172
Shepherd, Lucius 19, 154, 160
*The Shores of Another Sea* 127
"Si Diligis Me" 161
Sibelius, Jean 161
Silverius *see* Saint Silverius
Sinai 60
Sine Fiction 37
Singapore 39
"Six and Ten Are Johnny" 9, 13, 16, 57, 58, 67, 72, 81–82, 85, 125, 126, 145, 146, 162–164, 170–171, 188, 191
Sodom and Gomorrah 16, 100, 160, 165
Solomon 160, 165
Solomon solution 165
*Something Wicked This Way Comes* 26
Son of the Mighty 78
Song of Mary 103
"The Song of Marya" 165, 181
The Song of Solomon 79
"The Song of the Empty of Soul" 55
"The Song of Vorhu" 6, 14, 17, 18, 31, 38, 67, 98, 100, 120, 122, 126, 137, 155, 166–167, 176, 180, 184, 186
Soubirous, Bernadette 100
"The Soul-Empty Ones" 46, 55, 61, 70, 99–100, 122, 130, 167–168
Soviet Union 132, 167
"The Sower Does Not Reap" 45, 168
*Space Pope* 114
"The Space Witch" 86, 105, 131, 168–170

# Index

Spaced Out Library 108
Spain 39, 178
Sparta, Greece 75, 170
Spartans 75, 170
Spinrad, Norman 19, 111, 170
Spitfire 170
Spokane, Washington 62, 95
*Star Trek* 37, 57
*Startling Stories* 71–72
*Stations of the Tide* 173
Stigmata 8, 148, 171
Stoicism 122
*Stonefish* 79
"The Store of the Worlds" 19, 160, 172
Stormtroopers 172
Strait of Tartary 10
*Strands* 79
Strategic Defense Initiative (SDI) 116
Styron, William 43
Styx 172
*Summa Theologica* 153, 172
Summerhill, Jo 115
*Supermorn* 114, 115, 119, 127
"Survivors of the Megawar" 19
Swanwick, Michael 19, 63, 173
Swift-Tuttle Comet 131
Switzerland 39
Syria 14

Tamar 173
Tampa Bay, Florida 30
*Tau Zero* 12
*Te Kaihau: The Windeater* 79
Tears of Saint Lawrence 131
*Technical Manual CD-Bu-83A* 174
Tectology 25
"Ten Parsecs to Paradise" 174
Tenn, William 19, 55, 88, 174
Tennessee 174
Tepeyac, Mexico 73
"The Terminal Beach" 16, 19, 174
*Texarkana Star-Insight* 175
Texas 112, 127
Texas A & M University 127
Thaddeus 131
"That Only a Mother" 108
Theodahad 153
Theodora 153, 175
Theodore *see* Saint Theodore
Theory of Relativity 180
"There Will Come Soft Rains" 19, 26, 175, 177
The Third Book of Moses, called Leviticus *see* Leviticus
Third Reich 76
*Thrilling Wonder Stories* 166
The Trinity 176, 178–179
Thunderbolt (P-47) 128
*Thus Spoke Zarathustra* 55
Tiber Valley 131

"The Ties That Bind" 56, 59–60, 67, 89, 96, 105, 107, 175, 176–177, 181
Tipsword, Sharon 103
"To the Chicago Abyss" 19, 26, 175, 177
*The Tomorrow People* 108
"Tomorrow's Children" 12, 19, 178
Torquemada, Tomás de 178
*The Tragedy of Hamlet, Prince of Denmark* 191
*The Tragedy of Julius Caesar* 59
*The Tragical History of Doctor Faustus* 63
"Transistorized Control System for Unit Six-B" 178
*A Treatise on the Spirit and the Letter* 144
*Très Riches Heures du duc de Berry* 80
"The Triflin' Man" 53, 100, 118, 160, 178–179
The Trinity 45, 99, 176, 179
"The Trouble with Tribbles" 37
Tunis, Tunisia 37
Turkey 14
Turkey Vulture 172
27 Lambda 159, 179
*Twisted* 165
*2001: A Space Odyssey* 40
*Two Worlds of Walter M. Miller* 179

U.H.F. 179
*Unam Sanctam* 135, 175
Unified Field Theory 180
U.S. Army Air Corps 110, 114
*Universe* 44, 109
University of California–Los Angeles 127
University of Colorado 6
University of Missouri–Kansas City 80
University of Paris 153
University of Tennessee at Knoxville 110
University of Texas at Austin 111, 112, 127
Ur 6
Urban VI 156
Uriel 14
Utah 33

V-2 rocket 180
Vance, Jack 37
Venantius Fortunatus 182
Venerable Bede *see* Saint Bede
"Vengeance for Nikolai" 10, 19, 48, 55, 73, 98, 101, 107, 123, 136, 137, 152, 165, 178, 181, 183, 184
Veni Creator Spiritus 181–182
*Venture Science Fiction* 26, 44, 181
"Versicles by Adam and Rejoinders by the Crucified" 182

Victoria, Queen of England 136
*The View from the Stars* 13, 19, 20, 42, 45, 54, 82, 182–183
Villa, Francisco (Pancho) 183
*Violin Concerto in D minor*, Op. 47 (Sibelius) 161
Virgil 85
Virgilius 153
Virgin Mary *see* Mary (mother of Jesus)
RS *Voltaire* 147
Volusia County, Florida 117
*Vom Kriege* 40
*Voyage to the Red Planet* 20

*Waffen* SS 157
Wandering Jew 18, 174, 184
Washington, D.C. 65, 91, 184, 185
"Way of a Rebel" 16, 26, 60, 68, 75, 91, 104, 185, 188
Wessel, Horst 78
"The Wheel" 19, 75, 185
White Sunday 130
Whitsunday 130
Whore of Babylon 139
Wilber, Rick 112, 115, 116
"The Will" 19, 37, 48, 87, 102, 154, 157, 182, 185, 186, 187
William II (of Germany) 87
Williamson, Texas 110
"Wolf Pack" 15, 16, 22, 31, 37, 39, 65, 69, 70, 88, 90, 99, 101, 109, 125, 126, 128, 129, 131, 136, 144, 147, 170, 173, 185, 188
Wolfe, Gary K. 90, 174
"The Wonkle" 37
World War I 80, 172
World War II 15, 18, 65, 76, 87, 88, 90, 99, 109, 110, 114, 119, 128, 157, 170, 180, 185, 188
*The Worlds of Science Fiction* 51
Wotan 189
Wyndham, John 19, 75, 186
*Wyrldmaker* 20

*The Year's Best Science Fiction* 109
"The Yellow Pill" 71
"The Yokel" 9, 26, 46, 53, 73, 75, 76, 89, 100, 102, 104, 125, 129, 138, 145, 147, 164, 173, 174, 179, 185, 188, 189, 190–191
*Yorick* 162, 171, 191
"You Triflin' Skunk" 19, 48, 53, 75, 100, 118, 157, 160, 178, 182
Yugoslavia 110

Zelazny, Roger 19, 101, 191
Zerchi 122
Zeus 136
Zissman, Donald 109

www.ingramcontent.com/pod-product-compliance
Lightning Source LLC
Chambersburg PA
CBHW081556300426
44116CB00015B/2899